The Red and the Green

The Red and the Green

THE RISE AND FALL
OF COLLECTIVIZED AGRICULTURE
IN MARXIST REGIMES

Frederic L. Pryor

PRINCETON UNIVERSITY PRESS

PRINCETON, NEW JERSEY

Copyright © 1992 by Frederic L. Pryor
Published by Princeton University Press, 41 William Street,
Princeton, New Jersey 08540
In the United Kingdom: Princeton University Press, Oxford

All Rights Reserved

Library of Congress Cataloging-in-Publication Data

Pryor, Frederic L.
The red and the green : the rise and fall of
collectivized agriculture in Marxist regimes /
Frederic L. Pryor.
p. cm.
Includes bibliographical references (p.) and index.
ISBN 0-691-04299-3
1. Communism and agriculture. 2. Collectivization of
agriculture—Communist countries. 3. Agriculture and
state—Communist countries. I. Title.
HX550.A37P79 1992 306.3'45—dc20 91-32459 CIP

This book has been composed in Linotron Caledonia

Princeton University Press books are printed on acid-free paper
and meet the guidelines for permanence and durability of the
Committee on Production Guidelines for Book Longevity
of the Council on Library Resources

Printed in the United States of America

1 3 5 7 9 10 8 6 4 2

For Zora

————————————

CONTENTS

Appendixes

MAPS, TABLES, AND DIAGRAMS

DIAGRAMS

ACKNOWLEDGMENTS

RESEARCH for this book was financed in part by grants from the Hoover Institution in Stanford, California; the National Council for Soviet and East European Research; the Swarthmore College Faculty Research Fund; and the U.S. National Science Foundation. I am grateful for this financial support but must add the caveat that these institutions are not responsible for my errors, nor do they necessarily agree with my conclusions.

A major part of the library work for this project was carried out at the Hoover Institution during the academic year 1989–90, where I greatly benefited from its research facilities and conversations with the staff. I spent a useful fortnight carrying out research at the Zentrum für kontinentale Agrar- und Wirtschaftsforschung at the Justus-Liebig University in Giessen, Germany. I am also grateful for help received in the many other libraries whose collections I consulted. Traveling and interviewing farm directors, government officials, and experts in various Marxist regimes was an important part of the research for this book, and, over the past five years I have been fortunate to visit a number of the countries discussed in this study.

For reading the entire manuscript and making useful comments I would like to thank Josef Brada, Karen Brooks, Mary Capouya, Peter Elek, Zora Pryor, and Jack Repcheck. I am also grateful to Thomas Bernstein, Hans Binswanger, Josef Brada, John Caskey, Paul David, Steven O'Connell, F. M. Scherer, David Smith, Robert Weinberg, Larry Westphal, Tyrene White, Christine Wong, and Susan Woodward for their comments on preliminary drafts of individual chapters of this study. In addition, I presented early drafts of several of the chapters at the American Economic Association annual meeting, the Hoover Institution, Swarthmore College, the University of Pennsylvania, Wesleyan University, and the University of California at both Berkeley and Santa Cruz. The comments received on these occasions were especially beneficial.

The manuscript was closed on 10 January 1991, and only the most important changes in the next few months following that date could be taken into account.

ABBREVIATIONS

CMEA	Council of Mutual Economic Assistance, an organization whose members included Cuba, Mongolia, Vietnam, and all East European nations except Albania and Yugoslavia
E	Estimated
EC	(European) Economic Community
FAO	Food and Agricultural Organization of the United Nations
GATT	General Agreement on Tariffs and Trade
GDP	Gross domestic product
ILO	International Labour Office of the United Nations
LCW	V. I. Lenin, *Collected Works* (1960–71)
MEW	Karl Marx and Friedrich Engels, *Marx-Engels Werke* (1961–67)
MTS	Machine-tractor station
N.A.	Not available
NCC	Not completely comparable
NEP	New Economic Policy (of the Soviet Union)
NMP	Net material product (roughly equal to the net national product minus services)
OECD	Organization for Economic Cooperation and Development, an organization whose members included Australia, Canada, Japan, New Zealand, and the United States, as well as most nations in Western Europe
SEV	The Soviet abbreviation for CMEA
SITC	Standard Industrial Trade Classification
SPD	Social Democratic Party of Germany
SW	J. V. Stalin, *Works* (1953–55)
SWMT	Mao Tse-tung, *Selected Works of Mao Tse-tung* (1975–77)
TFP	Total factor productivity

PART I

Introduction

Chapter 1

AN OVERVIEW OF THE MAJOR PROBLEMS
AND THEMES

THE REORGANIZATION of agricultural production units into large-scale state and collective farms has been the most radical change of economic institutions implemented by Marxist governments. In contrast to the nationalization of industry and the replacement of the market by central planning and administration, this institutional change has transformed not only ownership and the way in which production units have functioned, but also the way in which laborers have gone about their work and have related to each other. The forced collectivization of agriculture has also been a searing historical experience in Marxist regimes, during which tens of millions died from starvation and mistreatment, while countless others suffered greatly as a result of the coercion.[1]

History has not unfolded as nineteenth-century Marxists expected. Socialist revolutions arising from domestic political forces have not occurred first in industrialized nations, but rather, for the most part, in predominantly agricultural countries with relatively low levels of economic development. Furthermore, despite commonplace notions about "peasant conservatism" and the difficulty in reorganizing and reforming agricultural production, Marxist regimes have paid particular attention to transforming the institutions of the rural sector, even while agriculture was the largest sector in the economy and when such changes were most difficult to implement. Furthermore, this institutional change occurred in many countries without extensive agricultural mechanization or high lev-

---

[1] Estimates of deaths in the Soviet Union resulting directly or indirectly from collectivization range from 11 million upward. For instance, according to the careful estimations of Robert Conquest (1986), elimination of the rich farmers (*kulaks*) was a crucial part of the collectivization drive in the Soviet Union and resulted in the deaths of 6.5 million. Another 8 million died in famines in the Ukraine and Kazakhstan that were an integral part of the program. In China, estimates of deaths from land reform and collectivization from 1946 through 1957 range from 250,000 to 5 million or more; Moise (1983, p. 142) estimates between 1 and 1.5 million for the land reform, although later evidence suggests this may be high. The real violence came in the period 1958–61 when the government attempted to consolidate the collective farms into communes and precipitated a famine, when, according to the estimates of Banister (1987, p. 85), 30 million died. In most other Marxist regimes land reforms and collectivization were not so violent, although as discussed in chapter 4, the governments employed considerable coercion.

Marxist Regimes in the 1980s in the Western Hemisphere

MOLLWEIDE EQUAL AREA PROJECTION

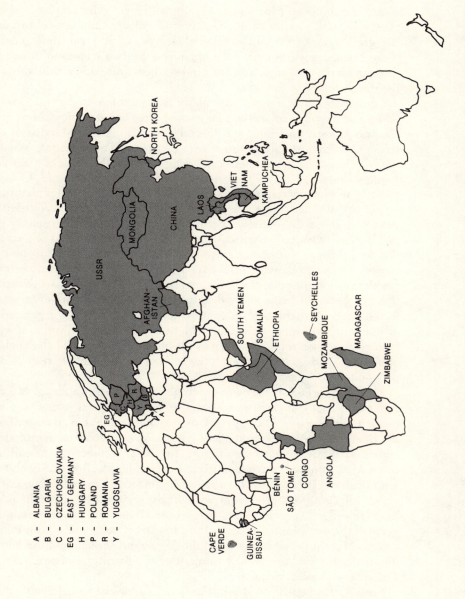

Marxist Regimes in the 1980s in the Eastern Hemisphere

A – ALBANIA
B – BULGARIA
C – CZECHOSLOVAKIA
EG – EAST GERMANY
H – HUNGARY
P – POLAND
R – ROMANIA
Y – YUGOSLAVIA

NORTH KOREA

VIET NAM
KAMPUCHEA

MONGOLIA

CHINA

LAOS

USSR

AFGHAN-
ISTAN

SOUTH YEMEN

SOMALIA

ETHIOPIA

SEYCHELLES

MOZAMBIQUE

MADAGASCAR

ZIMBABWE

EG
P
C
H
R
Y
B
A

CAPE
VERDE

GUINEA-
BISSAU

BÉNIN

SÃO TOMÉ

CONGO

ANGOLA

els of rural education and where administration of large-scale agriculture was probably neither cost effective nor necessary. In Marxist terminology, the relations of production were probably too advanced in comparison to the forces of production. Finally, although Marx emphasized the relatively similar paths of development of industry and agriculture and laid great moral stress on the value of all types of physical labor, most of these Marxist governments have organized the two sectors in dissimilar ways and have treated urban and rural workers quite differently, often to the disadvantage of the latter.

Contemporary Marxists, particularly those influenced by the ideas of Stalin, have ready explanations for each of these apparent deviations from classical Marxist doctrines. But in analyzing such issues, Marxists of any stripe have greater difficulty in answering a more basic question: What is the best way for a government professing to follow the ideas of Marx and Lenin to organize agriculture so as to enhance the economic development of an entire nation? Although Marxist-Leninist doctrines about the organization of agriculture may leave much to be desired, discussion in the West about the optimal organization of agriculture is certainly not much more advanced. Enormous attention has been focused on "saving the family farm," but many more organizational issues need to be discussed. Indeed, relatively little data are available to study many critical problems—for example, the horizontal linkages between farms or vertical linkages between farms and either upstream or downstream enterprises in the chain of production. In contrast to the analysis of the organization of industry, no formal academic field studying the organization of agriculture exists; no scholarly journals devoted to the topic fill the shelves of libraries; and no standard analytic methods are available to resolve disputes on policy questions.

First and foremost, this is a study about the organization of Marxist economies, both in theory and practice. I have chosen agriculture because it allows a series of analytic issues to be examined in an easier fashion than other sectors would allow. This book is an examination of ideas and their influence, and how, given the heterogeneity of agriculture, these ideas can be stretched to their furthest limits. But this is also an empirical investigation of the origins, organization, and development of agriculture in thirty-three identified Marxist regimes shown on the maps here. In order to provide some perspective, I also investigate certain aspects of the organization of agriculture in market economies, both to test various Marxist propositions about the development of agriculture and to illuminate the differences and similarities of agricultural organization in various economic systems.

Finally, this book is an attempt to synthesize a vast and straggly scholarly literature in both East and West on a number of theoretical and empirical issues about agricultural organization. In order to keep the discussion manageable, many issues cannot be discussed in depth and the reader is referred to the appropriate references for further analysis. I must also leave to others the task of carrying out detailed case studies to advance our knowledge of agriculture in individual countries. Nevertheless, I hope that the analytical framework and the comparative perspective provided herein enriches the case-study approach by allowing a separation of key causal factors. For instance, which aspects of agricultural organization and policy can be attributed to Marxist-Leninist doctrines? Or to the type of agriculture practiced in various countries? Or to the particular historical circumstances of the different nations? Or to the decisions arising from the unique political mechanisms of particular nations? I also try to show why, despite the deficiencies in performance of collectivized agriculture, it is highly doubtful that state and collective farms will disappear quickly, even in some nations where Marxist parties have been voted out of power.

But first it is necessary to delimit the topic, especially by defining two crucial terms, *socialist agriculture* and *Marxist regimes*, so that the subject matter and the sample can be specified. Then I briefly summarize the role of agriculture in the sample countries in order to provide an overview of the economic context within which agriculture is organized. Finally, I indicate briefly the major questions investigated and the path along which they are approached.

SOCIALIST AGRICULTURE

For purposes of this study I define *socialist agriculture* in terms of institutions of production rather than particular types of governmental intervention. *Collectivization* is the process including nationalization or expropriation of private farms and the creation of large-scale cooperative and state farms. For most of recorded history, governments have interceded in the agricultural sector in order to reinforce or suppress market forces and channels of distribution, to encourage production, or to influence rural incomes. For this reason governmental intervention per se provides little indication about the economic system of agriculture. The definition of socialist agriculture as represented by institutions of production gives rise, however, to a number of complications.

General Considerations

Marx and Engels told us little about institutions of agricultural production functioning in socialist economies. They made only scattered comments from which emerges a murky picture of what agriculture would be like when full communism arrives.[2] They foresaw an economy of high productivity and disciplined workers, but with no markets or money, so that exchange of products between urban and rural areas would, in some manner, be "direct." Such an arrangement would be facilitated by the fact that the ideas and outlooks of those living in the two areas would be similar.

Up to now, Kampuchea between 1975 and 1978 has been the only Marxist nation to attempt to realize such a communist agricultural system. The Pol Pot regime expropriated all land, formed relatively large-scale, self-sufficient production units, and effectively eliminated both trade and money. Party or government cadre—often soldiers in their teens—directed the labor force, providing workers with agricultural inputs received from the central government, and distributing food rations, housing, and clothing according to norms unrelated to an individual's work. Food was also communally consumed. The farms, in turn, supplied the central government with deliveries of particular goods.[3] The scholarly community has focused little attention on this unique attempt to realize Marx's vision, in part because the mass murders accompanying this Kampuchean transformation have been more important to study, and in part because high productivity, a crucial aspect of full communism, was not achieved in this nation.

More usual production institutions of socialist agriculture are state farms, collective farms, and communes, all of which are forms of large-scale agriculture. It is, of course, possible to have a socialized urban sector without a socialist agricultural sector, a situation arising in Poland and Yugoslavia from the mid-1950s to the present, as well as in a number of Marxist African nations. It is also possible to conceive of a socialist agricultural sector that produces a plantation crop exhibiting economies of scale, combined with a predominantly private urban sector that provides complementary products and services. This latter system does not appear to be stable in the long run and is not exemplified in any of the nations of the sample.[4] Socialist agricultural institutions are usually accompanied

---

[2] This discussion is based on Pryor (1985b), which provides all of the relevant quotations.

[3] A highly detailed eyewitness account of life on one of these units is provided by May (1986), and other interesting views are presented in Kiernan and Boua (1982 chap. 10). Most journalists and scholars have focused their attention on such notable aspects of this system as the extreme cruelty of the government and the division of the population into different classes so that each received different amounts of food and other rations, rather than on more mundane aspects of how the economy worked. By far the most systematic examination of the economic system is by Twining (1989), although many gaps in his study remain due to lack of reliable information.

[4] It has been most closely approximated in São Tomé and Seychelles. Before independence, both were predominantly plantation economies in which the plantations were primarily owned by foreigners (especially in the former). São Tomé immediately nationalized

by certain other features that are neither necessary nor sufficient for the system to function, for instance, rules against firing workers on state farms or removing members from collective farms.

It is important to emphasize that *communal agricultural systems* found in some developing nations, especially in sub-Saharan Africa, have little in common with *socialist agriculture*. In the former systems, the community can place restrictions on what a farmer can do with the land, on the date when certain agricultural activities can begin or end, and even on the farming techniques that are employed. In some cases land is also distributed by traditional political leaders, but nevertheless, families farm the land individually and individual wealth is not merged. Of course, cooperative work efforts occur and may be of considerable significance, but they are both informal and voluntary; these arrangements include trading labor or participating in work gangs that spend a certain amount of time on the farms of each member (Pryor 1977). In contrast to the beliefs of African political leaders such as Julius Nyerere of Tanzania or Leopold Senghor of Senegal, experience in Africa has shown that communal agriculture has little in common with collectivized farming and, indeed, these systems do not lead easily to socialist agriculture.

State Farms

A state farm is simply a factory-in-the-field that is owned by the government. In most cases the government or a government board appoints a director, who hires workers and manages the farm in the same manner as the hired manager of a capitalist plantation. Although the workers may receive bonuses based on production, their primary source of income is a wage, and the government thus absorbs most risks of production.

Some cases are, however, hard to classify. For instance, in Yugoslavia the public sector has certain residual rights in the nonprivate farms (for example, the members cannot sell the assets and pocket the receipts), so that these enterprises might be considered state farms. Nevertheless, these "socially owned" farms operate essentially as producer cooperatives and are run by worker councils, which set the basic policy guidelines and hire the farm managers. Thus these farms combine features of both systems. In other East European nations, as I will indicate, the difference between state and collective farms has eroded.

State farms can be formal production units ultimately administered by a central authority such as a ministry of agriculture. Other types of state farms, sometimes called "institutional farms," include those farms at-

these estates and Seychelles began a slow but relentless nationalization drive. Both nations, however, also began to create government-owned enterprises in the urban sector.

tached to state-owned industrial plants such as the *podkhozi* in the
USSR, farms operated by special development agencies (for instance, in
Seychelles), farms operated by the army, local governments, primary
schools, or universities (for example, experimental stations) or farms operated by the Marxist party (for instance, in the Congo). In most of the
countries these institutional farms hold only a small percentage of the
land in the state farm sector; a notable exception is Bénin, however,
where they constitute 95 percent of the state farm sector.[5] In other countries, these institutional farms, although relatively small in total area, increased in importance. Most notably, during the 1980s the government of the Soviet Union encouraged factories to administer farms in
order to supply food for factory canteens. As Hedlund has emphasized
(1989), these attempts to increase total farm output often divert specialized managerial resources in industry from where they can best be employed.

According to Stalinist dogma, the state farm is a "higher form of socialism" than the collective farm, and until the late 1980s some Marxist regimes such as Albania, Mongolia, Romania, and the USSR were slowly
converting their collective farms to state farms. By no means is this
dogma universally accepted: during the mid- and late-1980s Nicaragua
converted a number of its original state farms into cooperatives (or even
divided them up into private farms). The government of Seychelles has
also announced its intention to transform its state farms into cooperatives
once the state farms are operating on a profitable basis; this does not,
however, seem likely to occur in the near future.

State farms are, of course, not unique to socialism, and they also exist
in almost all capitalist nations, serving either as experimental farms or in
some cases a source of revenue when they are leased out to private farmers. These farms represent either remnants of the original "crown land,"
or of past land reforms, or of deliberate attempts by the government to
set up a limited number of government farms. Indeed, some instances
can also be cited in which nominally capitalist nations such as Malaŵi
have more extensive and more successful state farm systems than nominally Marxist regimes such as Madagascar (Pryor 1990c).

Collective Farms

I use the term *collective farm* to designate a farm where production is
carried out jointly (a group of people work together under a single man-

---

[5] According to the data from SEV (annual, 1988), in the mid-1980s such institutional
farms amounted to about 16 percent of total farm land in Romania, 9 percent in Czechoslovakia, and less than 6 percent in the other Council of Mutual Economic Assistance
(CMEA) nations. Hedlund (1989) has an illuminating analysis of the *podhozy* in the USSR,
while Després and Khischuk (1990) explore those operated by the military. The Bénin

agement) and where the net receipts or income of the farm (receipts after taxes have been paid and agricultural inputs have been purchased) are divided among the members according to a formula that takes into partial account the amount of work the members contributed to the common effort. The government contract with the farm usually has two parts: a fixed rent (that is, compulsory deliveries of certain crops at a specified price) and an agreement to buy all produce above this limit, usually at a higher price. The collective farm members bear all risks of production shortfalls. In some cases the government has modified this residual-income principle by providing a floor income for members of the cooperative; in these cases the farms receive a government subsidy or loan if net receipts are not sufficient to cover expenses and payments to members. In some countries (e.g., Cuba, Hungary, and Bulgaria until 1959) these farms paid rent to the farmers who brought land into the collective; in other countries no compensation was paid. In some countries the land belonged to the collective as a whole; in other countries, to the government (a matter discussed in greater detail in chapter 3); and in still other countries (e.g., most of the nations of East Europe) to the people who brought the land into the collective, or their heirs. In some countries (e.g., Yugoslavia and, to a lesser degree, Bulgaria and Cuba in the late 1980s) the farms had certain elements of self-management with elected representatives on the administrative council of the farm; in other countries, the farm was administered in a highly centralized fashion.

As Adam Fforde (1989, p. xii) warns us: "Knowledge of formal, or legally constituted, social structures does not necessarily tell us much about underlying 'reality.'" For purposes of discussion in the following chapters, it is useful to keep in mind that collective farms can operate in quite different ways, even with the same formal rules:

1. In a *cooperative farm* the members appoint their own managers and make their own decisions. They are voluntary organizations, and, in their occasional appearance in several Marxist regimes, they have often had quite different members from year to year (e.g., in Laos, as shown by Evans 1990, chap. 4). Such a *producer cooperative* must be distinguished from a *service cooperative*, in which a group of people band together to market their crop, buy agricultural inputs, rent a combine, hire a technician, or participate together in some project perhaps related to farming but not directly involved in all phases of the productive process. Both of

---

case, discussed briefly by Godin (1986, pp. 201–3), has arisen because foreign plantations were minuscule (less than three thousand hectares in the 1930s) so that the government did not find much land to nationalize easily. Most of the institutional farms in Bénin (64 percent of the area) were plots of towns and schools which, relying on unpaid labor, produced a crop whose sales yielded funds to finance investment in infrastructure. Such farms, of course, acted to convert a tax-in-kind to money revenues. The other farms were usually vertically integrated agricultural processing enterprises owned by the state.

these, of course, are also different from a *consumer cooperative*, in which consumers unite to purchase in bulk in order to reduce the retail margin they otherwise would pay. Although simple, these distinctions are often blurred and, as a result, have given rise to enormous confusion; for instance, the varied interpretations of Lenin's last pronouncement on cooperatives (see chapter 2). A producer cooperative must also be distinguished from various forms of mutual aid or cooperative arrangements among farmers who, however, farm their lands individually.

2. In a *pseudo-cooperative farm* the unit has few cooperative elements and is really managed as a state farm. One type of pseudo-cooperative farm existed in the USSR for many decades: the state and party appointed the farm directors and expected them to meet production and other goals determined by the government. The directors, in turn, managed the farm in an hierarchical fashion; members had almost no influence over who led them, how they were led, or what work they carried out. These pseudo-cooperative farms had for several decades a second-class status: they received no state subsidies; they always had a lower priority in obtaining scarce agricultural inputs; they could not own their own machines but had to rent machine services from the Machine Tractor Station (MTS); their older members received no social insurance payments from the government; and the members had to absorb the agricultural risks by receiving a share of the net income, rather than a fixed wage. A strange type of pseudo-cooperative farm occurred in Bénin in the 1970s and 1980s where farmers in a particular area were forced to combine their land and rent it to a cooperative (a *périmètre* or *coopérative d'aménagement rural*) which, in turn, was managed by a team from a state company. Both the landlords and the landless in the area also had the option of working for the cooperative and receiving a wage.[6] Still other variants of pseudo-cooperatives could be found in other countries. Pseudo-cooperatives were most often found in nations where the party and/or government was highly organized in rural areas; for example, many East European nations and China.

3. In a *nominal-cooperative farm* the collective unit can serve either as a mask of the operations for a private company or of agriculturalists actually farming their land individually. One interesting example of the former has occurred in Guyana (Standing and Szal 1979, pp. 72–73; Thomas 1983) where groups of private individuals, such as urban civil servants, organized cooperatives. They obtained free land, low-interest credit, and tax privileges and then farmed the land individually, hiring outside labor for the actual farm work. Other Guyanese cooperatives had "dormant

[6] This type of pseudocooperative began under a previous non-Marxist government. Mondjannagni (1977) and Godin (1986) provide further details.

members" with formal voting rights that allow a private firm to call itself a cooperative. A different type of nominal-cooperative farm existed in Viet Nam during the 1970s where the collective farm often served as a mask for individuals or hamlets to carry out their individual agricultural activities with a minimum of outside interference.[7] In the highlands of Georgia in the Soviet Union, the collective farms also appeared to play a strategic role in the private economy of its members and, as such, were different from collectives in the Russian Republic.[8] In different forms nominal-collectives also arose in still other countries such as Cape Verde (or the "pre-cooperatives" in the Congo), where the size of the collective fields has been relatively small in comparison to the private fields on the same farm. In Laos, collective farms were so loosely organized that for many years farmers could pull their land out of the cooperative relatively easily (Evans 1990). The Somali "range cooperatives" represented a nominal-cooperative in a herding context: cattle were held privately and pieces of range land were assigned to individual families who, in some manner, were supposed to cooperate with each other and to obey the grazing rules set forth by the government. Sometimes political authorities foster nominal-cooperatives as the first step toward full cooperativization; in other cases nominal-cooperatives arise where party discipline is weak in the rural areas, a situation occurring in most Third World Marxist regimes. Nominal cooperatives are most likely to be found where the state and party are weakly organized in the rural areas; for instance, Africa, Yemen, and southeast Asian nations such as Laos and Viet Nam.

Collective farms are not the exclusive property of Marxist regimes and they have been sponsored in some form by non-Marxist governments as well. For instance, in the 1980s they existed on a large scale in Algeria, Israel, and Tanzania and, on a lesser scale, in other nations such as Ghana. Still other non-Marxist regimes feature small-scale cooperative farms, either in the form of small groups of people voluntarily banding together to farm jointly or in the form of small-scale experiments under

[7] According to Fforde (1989, pp. 6, 80), up to 75 percent of the collective farms in North Viet Nam were nominal in the late 1970s. His definition of *nominal* is somewhat looser than mine, since he includes farms in which the key decision-making unit is the brigade or hamlet and, although some production is collective, some important economic activities such as pig raising were carried out privately.

[8] Dragadze's village study (1988) suggests that a major function of the collective farm has been to supply foodstuffs to members that they could not obtain in stores and that the farm was organized in a sufficiently loose fashion so that one family member often substituted for the formal member in order to accumulate family work points for the distribution of agricultural products not delivered to the state. Moskoff (1984, p. 159) presents data showing that collective farm workers in Georgia worked on the farm many fewer days than those in the Russian Republic.

governmental aegis; an example of this occurred in the United States in the late 1930s.[9]

Communes

The term *commune* has widely different meanings, but in this study I use the word to describe a large-scale farm unit that has governmental powers as well; that is, the same authorities carry out both economic and political functions.[10] These units of production could be found in China from the late 1950s to the early 1980s, Mongolia from the late 1950s through the late 1980s, Kampuchea under Pol Pot, or to a much lesser extent, Ethiopia in the late 1970s (in those cases where some Peasant Associations formed cooperatives). I omit from consideration those situations where economic and political power structures are fused in an informal manner. Most often these large-scale communes operate according to the cooperative principle in the division of the income, although in some cases the salary system appears to be used.

In many cases it is difficult to decide whether a particular production unit is a cooperative or part of a commune in which government authorities at a local level play a critical role in the management of the unit. For instance, in North Korea after 1961, the County (Kun) Agricultural Management Committee received extensive powers to participate in farm decision-making, although the cooperatives still retained their formal identity.[11] If this means that the county governments are the predominant unit in farm decision-making, then North Korean collectives must be classified as communes, with the smaller units acting as profit centers; the exact manner in which decision-making powers are distributed between the county and the farm are difficult for an outsider to determine. Similarly, by the late 1960s in China, the teams (in this case, villages) were profit centers with considerable autonomy. If the central communal administration had relatively little power, then the Chinese communes

[9] Infield (1945) tells the bizarre story of the 262 cooperative and state farms established in the late 1930s in the United States. Zablocki (1980) describes voluntary efforts to establish cooperative farms in the United States thorough the mid-1970s.

[10] My use of the term *commune* should not be confused with other meanings of the word; e.g., the cooperative farms (found in the USSR in the 1920s and discussed by Wesson [1963]) where the members eat or live together, or the village communities of nineteenth-century Russia, or the small governmental units (without any agricultural functions) in some countries such as France or Yugoslavia. These units are not discussed in this study.

[11] I refer to East Germany, North Korea, South Yemen, and the Congo, rather than the German Democratic Republic, the Democratic People's Republic of Korea, the People's Democratic Republic of Yemen, and the People's Republic of the Congo so as to avoid confusion with their capitalist counterparts, which might also be considered democratic, albeit in a different sense.

should be considered as a network of cooperative farms operating within a governmental unit called a commune. Although these kinds of definitional problems raise difficulties of classification, they do not impede other aspects of this analysis.

A Case Study: The USSR

We can understand these different forms of agriculture organization more concretely and, at the same time, gain a clearer idea about some of the major themes of this study by examining briefly the experience of the Soviet Union. I must stress, however, that the Soviet experience is not typical of other Marxist regimes and that the purpose of the many mini-case studies of countries in this book is to provide flesh for the barebone definitions and generalizations.

Before the major Soviet collectivization drive began in the last two months of 1929, individual peasants farmed over 95 percent of the land; moreover, the overwhelming majority of these peasants belonged to village communities, which controlled economic life of the village (Nove 1969, p. 106). The government's role in agriculture was primarily as a purchaser of grain; and in the mid-1920s it bought roughly three-quarters of the marketed grain. As noted in chapter 3, unlike most Marxist regimes, collectivization had not been preceded by a government-directed land reform, although considerable ownership changes had occurred through peasant land takeovers after the revolution.

Although in chapter 2 I discuss in detail the many reasons for collectivization, three economic reasons appeared most important in the USSR: the need to achieve greater production and marketed sales through the alleged economies of large-scale farming; the necessity to modernize agriculture; and the desire to force farmers to sell their crops to the government at low prices so that the profits could be used to finance industrialization. The degrees to which these and other goals of collectivization were achieved are analyzed for many Marxist regimes in chapters 7 and 8.

The government consolidated private farms into collectivized farms with the aid of specially recruited urban workers and party officials. Within several months more than half of the peasant population had joined the collectives. The administrative excesses committed to achieve these results were so extreme that in March 1930 Stalin, who initiated this "voluntary" drive, attempted to deflect criticism by placing most of the blame on the zeal of local officials. Other Marxist regimes that collectivized later learned a great deal from these policy lessons (see chapter 4). Subsequently, more than half of the collective farms disbanded, but the offensive resumed and in 1934 more than three-quarters of all peasant households and crop areas were collectivized and organized into farms averaging roughly seventy households and four hundred hectares. Few of these collective farms were genuine producer cooperatives— many were pseudo-cooperatives directed by cadre selected by the party or government and most of the remainder were nominal-cooperatives formed by farmers wishing to avoid outside interference in their activities. Over time, however, most of the nominal cooperatives were transformed into pseudo-cooperatives. Autonomous and genuine producer cooperatives were not a feature of Soviet agriculture.

In the mid-1920s Stalin had stressed the formation of large state farms, but the difficulties inherent in this policy rapidly became apparent. As a result, in the collectivization drive, the government placed most stress on the formation of collective farms. In 1934, for instance, state farms covered less than 10 percent of total crop area. They were somewhat larger than the collective farms and averaged about 430 workers and 2,400 hectares (USSR, Central Statistical Board 1969, p. 127).

The state farms received detailed output, input, and investment plans; furthermore, if costs could not be met, they received subsidies or loans. They were less autonomous than collective farms, which received delivery and input quotas of a less detailed nature, but which could not rely on subsidies. In the early years farm officials carried out considerable experimentation on organizing and administering these collective and state farms, a topic receiving greater attention in chapter 5.

After the Second World War the government began to consolidate collective farms into much larger units and, in addition, to transform many into state farms. After the death of Stalin in 1953, these trends accelerated so that by the late 1980s state farms comprised more than twice the land of the collective farms (see table 5.1). Furthermore, the government dissolved the MTSs and partly sold, partly gave away their equipment to the collective farms. Collective farmers, moreover, began to receive a minimum wage and, although producer prices paid to these farms were increased several-fold, subsidies to these farms increased dramatically, as did their unpaid debts, which were periodically cancelled. In brief, the differences between the collective and state farms began to disappear, a trend apparent in other Marxist regimes as well.

In the late 1980s the Gorbachev government took the first tentative moves toward decollectivization; that is, the conversion of state and collective farms into either private (corporate or individual) farms, or tenant farms with long-term leases, or genuine producer cooperatives. In the USSR these policy steps were taken mainly in the form of leasehold contracts to households and, in certain republics such as Georgia, the breaking up of highly unprofitable collective and state farms into individual farms. As indicated in chapters 10 and 11, by the end of 1990 this decollectivization movement was still in its initial stages, in contrast with a number of other nations under discussion in this book.

The aims of collectivization and the organization of agriculture that resulted had a considerable impact both on the functioning of the farms (see chapters 5 and 6) and on the policies pursued by the government to encourage production (see chapter 7). These elements, in turn, greatly influenced the performance of the agricultural sector (see chapter 8). Further consideration of these implications of the organizational forms, however, would put us far ahead of our story.

The Institutional Mix

As I discuss in greater detail in chapters 3 and 4, the institutions of socialist agriculture are by no means uniform among Marxist regimes. Only a few Marxist regimes have communes, and the mix between private, cooperative, and state farms varies considerably. To provide an overview, four clusters of countries can be distinguished in the 1980s: (1) Some Marxist regimes did not have a very large socialist agricultural sector. In some cases, for example, the majority of African Marxist regimes, as well as Grenada, Poland, and Yugoslavia, this was because not much collectivization was carried out. In other cases such as China, Kampuchea, Laos, or Viet Nam in the late 1980s, this was because these nations carried out some type of decollectivization; (2) In other Marxist regimes, mostly in East Europe, the agricultural sector was dominated by collective farms; (3) In still other Marxist nations, most notably Bulgaria (in the mid-1980s), Cuba, Guyana, São Tomé, and the USSR, state farms predominated; and (4) In a final group including China (in the 1970s) and Mongolia (in the 1970s and 1980s) the agricultural sector was dominated by communes with the subunits run as pseudo-cooperatives. An important question explored in chapter 3 is why particular nations have adopted one or another form of socialist agriculture.

MARXIST REGIMES

The purpose of this brief discussion is to select the sample for analysis, not to condemn or praise certain nations. I choose my particular definition for analytical convenience to examine particular questions; for other types of comparative studies, a much different definition of "Marxist regime" may be more suitable. In particular, I am interested in the impact and implementation of Marxist ideas and have shaped my definition accordingly.

Since Marx wrote little about the operation of socialist economies or agriculture, some readers may be uncomfortable with my terminology and wish to label the countries in my sample as "Marxist-Leninist" or "socialist" or "communist." Each of these labels also raises problems, especially for developing nations whose governments have embraced Marxist ideas and ideals, but which have neither a Leninist-type political party nor the resources to implement the type of welfare and other programs associated with socialism.

The Approach of This Study

The classical definition of *socialism* refers to ownership of the means of production. Table 1.1 provides a rough measure of the importance of governmental ownership. A brief glance at the table reveals that this share varies enormously among the countries, in part because some nations have started along this path at an earlier date and in part because various governments have forced the pace of nationalization at different speeds. The pattern of nationalization is quite distinct (a matter discussed for East Europe in Pryor 1973, chapter 2). For our purposes it is necessary to note only that the degree of nationalization in agriculture is generally much lower in most other sectors; the exceptions, such as São Tomé and Seychelles, have arisen from very particular historical circumstances. It should also be mentioned that certain non-Marxist socialist countries have a much higher percentage of workers in the state and cooperative sector (59.8 percent in Algeria in the early 1980s, according to Algeria 1981, p. 59) than most of the countries in this table.

As I have argued at length elsewhere (Pryor 1986, chap. 8), distinguishing Marxist regimes by ownership or by other economic criteria such as the relative share of governmental expenditures in the gross domestic product (GDP), or replacement of market mechanisms of allocation by governmental central planning and economic administration, is not very useful since most Third World nations calling themselves Marxist and attempting to achieve a socialist economy would be excluded from this list. For the same reason distinguishing Marxist regimes by the degree to which they are pursuing general socialist development policies such as increasing social equality and participation in national decision-making, development of idealistic individuals unfettered by acquisitive motives, or reduction of alienation also does not seem helpful.

A more fruitful approach in selecting a sample of Marxist regimes employs both ideological and implementation criteria. A necessary but not sufficient *ideological condition* is whether the leading officials in the government have been strongly influenced by Marxist ideas; that is, if a communist party controls the government or if the elite in power has been strongly influenced by some version of Marxism. In some Third World countries such as Guinea-Bissau or São Tomé, an official declaration of

TABLE 1.1
The Share of the Labor Force in the Public and Cooperative Sectors

		State sector			Cooperative sector		
	Date	AFF	Other Sectors	Total	AFF	Other Sectors	Total
Africa							
Angola	1984	2.2%	30–50%	9–14%			
Bénin	1980	0.4	11.7	3.5			
Cape Verde	1985	n.a.	n.a.	51.2			
Congo	1982	n.a.	n.a.	14.7			
Ethiopia	n.a.	n.a.	n.a.	n.a.			
Guinea-Bissau	1984	n.a.	n.a.	13.4			
Madagascar	1980	0.8	41.3	5.3			
Mozambique	1980	2.9	70.4	12.9	0.6%	0.4%	0.5%
São Tomé	1981	86.0	60.0	74.5			
Seychelles	1985	57.5	58.3	58.2			
Somalia	1981	0.6	47.8	4.8	1.7	8.4	2.2
Zimbabwe	1983	4.0	28.4	25.5			
Americas							
Cuba	1981	75.6	98.5	93.3	3.8	0.0	0.9
Grenada	1981	15.7	38.1	31.9			
Guyana	1980	42.3	23.4	25.6			
Nicaragua	1982	11.0	33.0	22.8	2.2	0.0	1.0
Asia							
Afghanistan	1981	0.6	26.1	10.6	8.7	0.0	5.3
China	1986	3.3	64.4	27.1	0.2	16.9	6.7
Kampuchea	n.a.	n.a.	n.a.	n.a.			
Korea, North	1965	8.0	100.0	43.2	92.0	0.0	56.8
Laos	n.a.	n.a.	n.a.	n.a.			
Mongolia	1979	n.a.	n.a.	63.1	n.a.	n.a.	36.6
Viet Nam	1984	10.9	21.1	13.8	70.0	n.a.	50.3
Yemen, South	1982	10.7	47.5	42.8	30.7	5.3	5.5
Europe							
Albania	1979	n.a.	n.a.	49.8			
Bulgaria	1965	16.1	90.1	57.3	82.7	8.4	41.3
Czechoslovakia	1985	99.1	98.8	98.9 (combined public and cooperative)			
Germany, East	1987	19.8	87.6	80.2	78.7	7.0	14.8
Hungary	1987	50.4	11.6	86.8	47.0	11.6	7.4
Poland	1978	14.1	96.4	71.6	6.8	n.a.	2.0
Romania	1977	11.9	92.5	62.8	72.2	5.9	30.3
USSR	1970	39.4	99.2	84.1	59.5	0.9	15.5
Yugoslavia	1981	11.6	94.0	68.5	0.4	n.a.	n.a.

Source: See Statistical Note A. For Zimbabwe and South Yemen, the percentage of production is used; for Poland, the state sector outside agriculture includes the small number of cooperatives. For several other countries the calculations are very approximate, so "other sectors" cannot be easily estimated.

Notes: AFF = agriculture, forestry, and fishing.

The percentages represent the share of the economically active population who are working in enterprises owned either by some level of government or cooperatively. In cases of mixed ownership, the practices of the statistical agencies of each nation are used, since sufficient data to adjust for complete comparability are not available.

this adherence has not been made, but it is clear from other evidence that Marxist ideas have played a crucial and open role in intellectual life of the ruling party. The strength of the commitment is important, because some political leaders such as Jean-Bedel Bokassa of the Central African Republic have, at one time or another, proclaimed their country to be Marxist or to be "following" scientific socialism primarily to obtain foreign aid from the Soviet Union.

Ideally we should supplement self-identification with a checklist of specific beliefs; for example, in the existence of a vanguard party serving as the leading political/economic force in the nation, in the importance of the class struggle in forging a socialist nation, in scientific socialism transcending all local characteristics of the society, and so forth. But in many cases it is difficult to determine the official party line on these matters or, when these phrases are used, to ascertain what they really mean or the strength of belief in these doctrines. Thus these more sophisticated ideological criteria cannot easily be employed.

Self-identification, of course, has its own difficulties and its use raises the problem of the audience and purpose for such symbolic declarations. For tactical purposes, the party or governing elites in some countries have not openly announced the influence of Marxist ideas on their policies. The self-identification criterion must be modified to include three other cases: (a) Particular governments such as the People's Revolutionary Government (PRG) of Grenada, which readily acknowledged the influence of Marxism in its closed councils (Pryor 1986), but for political reasons did not make this announcement publicly; (b) Other governments such as Cape Verde were dominated by parties founded by those who were Marxist, but they did not choose to identify themselves in this manner in public and we have no information about their self identification behind closed doors. Without evidence to the contrary, we must infer that they are Marxist parties; (c) Some other governments, whose self-identification and founding ideologies are vague, must be included because they have adopted as principal policy measures a set of economic, political, and social policies similar to those followed in openly declared Marxist regimes; for instance, the Seychelles government has announced its intention to eliminate the private ownership of the means of production in order to eliminate exploitation (René 1982, p. 30).

An important *implementation condition* is that the government must have sufficient political power to effect crucial structural changes in the economy in a socialist direction. In some cases such as the Comoro Islands (the Soilih government), the government did not last long enough to effect these changes. In other countries such as San Marino, the self-proclaimed Communist Party dominated the ruling coalition for some years, but was unable to carry out significant structural reforms. Similarly, in countries such as Surinam (under Desi Bouterse), Ghana (under Jerry Rawlings), or Chile (under Salvadore Allende), the leading political leaders may have had Marxist sympathies or have been allied politically with Marxists, but they were also unable to institute key structural changes in the economy.

This implementation criterion does not mean that the Marxist party has achieved a "revolutionary breakthrough"—that is, a decisive change in the society—but that it has at least been able to implement a sufficient number of Marxist policies to reveal the orientation of the government. This is because I wish to include in the sample those regimes that have attempted but failed to put major Marxist agricultural organizational ideas into practice in order to be better able to isolate those factors permitting these structural changes to be realized.

My criteria, of course, are difficult to apply because of problems in deciding whether the political beliefs of the dominant party should be considered as Marxist or as some other brand of socialism; for example, African socialism. In addition, the difference between populism and Marxism is often difficult to distinguish (Keller 1987). In two cases (Guyana and Madagascar), the government has proclaimed the strong influence of Marxism on its program, but the Communist Party recognized by the Soviet and other communist parties is not the ruling party. I follow my own criteria and consider these countries as Marxist regimes.

Difficulties of classification also appear concerning countries in which a significant Thermidorean reaction has occurred; that is, where the government or Marxist party has lost its ideological fervor but nevertheless maintains many of the institutions and policies arising when Marxist ideology played a more active role. I have, for instance, included Somalia but excluded Mali since the latter country has maintained fewer of the "socialist institutions." A final problem of classification arises because Marxist-Leninist ideas may no longer be determinant in implementing (in contrast to making) policy. For instance, Mathieu Kérékou, the President of Bénin, had a useful insight when he complained in 1981 that "the government and revolutionary structures no longer exist in reality, for the bureaucrats have virtually seized power on the government's back" (Decalo 1987, p. 11). Although this may have been merely an excuse for his own failures of leadership, there may have been an important element of truth to the statement as well.

Others have treated such borderline cases differently from me because they have examined different issues from those associated with the organization of agriculture, which serves as the focus of this book. Research Note A includes a further discussion of these issues and, in addition, presents three other lists of Marxist nations. My own list has thirty-three countries, of which twenty-six are found in all of the other three lists. At least one authority disputes my inclusion of Cape Verde, Guinea-Bissau, Guyana, São Tomé, Seychelles, Somalia, and Zimbabwe, and another disputes my exclusion of Algeria, Burkina Faso, Burma, Burundi, Ghana, Guinea, Mali, Surinam, Syria, Tanzania, and Zambia. These eighteen nations of contention must be considered borderline cases.

To digress for a moment, the difficulties in identifying Marxist regimes impede the development of a theory explaining why certain governments, but not others, have become Marxist regimes. Although this question is best left to political scientists and historians, we can answer a simpler but related question of how the process proceeded.[12] Nine of the nations became Marxist regimes as a result of decisive military interference by another Marxist nation; eleven, as a consequence of an extensive civil war, either against the existing government or an occupying power; an additional eleven, as the result of a coup or a revolution from above; and two, as the outcome of an election. Of the twenty-four countries that became Marxist without decisive outside interference only one can be considered industrialized (Czechoslovakia) and only one other (Czarist Russia), as semi-industrialized. Fifteen of these nations were also colonies within the last two decades of becoming Marxist regimes, and another five had experienced wars against foreign invaders. Thus the question of why one political-economic system was chosen can be narrowed to the problem of determining the distinguishing characteristics of those poor nations, often recently decolonized or ravaged by war, that are discussed in this study with a similar group of nations that did not become Marxist regimes.

This exercise of determining the path to power provides some interesting clues to how the various governments have functioned. As I show in later chapters, however, it tells us little about how agriculture has been organized or, for that matter, which nations have decollectivized.

Finally, this study focuses primarily on the forty-year period from 1950 to 1990. Any study dealing with Marxist regimes only in the 1990s would undoubtedly omit a number of countries in my list. For instance, from 1989 through January 1991, the citizens of some of the countries of my sample voted out Marxist governments (Cape Verde, Czechoslovakia, East Germany, Hungary, Nicaragua, and Poland). In others the Marxist regimes disappeared, either as a result of a coup or invasion (Grenada,

[12] Nations with decisive interference by another Marxist regime include: Bulgaria, East Germany, Hungary, Laos, Kampuchea, Mongolia, North Korea, Poland, and Romania. Nations with extensive civil war include: Albania, Angola, China, Cuba, Guinea-Bissau, Mozambique, Nicaragua, South Yemen, Viet Nam, Yugoslavia, and Zimbabwe. Nations with coups or revolutions from above include: Afghanistan, Bénin, Congo, Czechoslovakia, Ethiopia, Grenada, Guyana, Madagascar, Seychelles, Somalia, and the Soviet Union. Nations with elected Marxist parties include Cape Verde and São Tomé. Among the 24

Somalia) or merger with a non-Marxist regime (South Yemen). In still other nations the top government leaders have either renounced Marxism-Leninism (e.g., Bénin), distanced themselves from these doctrines (e.g., Angola, Mozambique), declared that for their economy Marxism-Leninism has failed (e.g., Ethiopia), or reached a state of ideological exhaustion (Guinea-Bissau, Guyana, Madagascar, São Tomé, and parts of Yugoslavia). In a final group of nations the Thermidor will perhaps have proceeded sufficiently far by the mid-1990s so that the label "Marxist regime" would no longer aid analysis. Although prediction is risky, these countries might include Afghanistan, Angola, Bulgaria, Congo, Kampuchea, Laos, and Mongolia. Under certain conditions, as I discuss briefly in chapter 11, it is also possible that some other countries not on my list may become Marxist regimes or that certain countries such as Nicaragua might vote back into power revitalized Marxist parties, especially if the non-Marxist governments prove incapable of dealing successfully with the nation's economic problems. Marxism-Leninism may be ill in the early 1990s, but it is far from dead.

Since this book is a study of the impact of Marxist ideas on the organization of agriculture, it is not vitally important to determine whether I have included all Marxist regimes in the analysis or whether my sample includes some regimes that others consider as non-Marxist. What is critical is that the sample includes a wide enough range of governments in which Marxism has had a crucial influence on agricultural policy so that many national experiences are taken into account.

It is not my intention in this book to march the reader through thirty-three case studies, but rather to use these cases to illuminate a series of general propositions about agricultural organization in Marxist regimes. I present much of the important information about specific countries in tabular form for reference purposes. Thus sufficient data are available for readers who wish to omit some countries from the analysis and to recalculate my statistical results.

FORCES UNDERLYING THE ROLE OF AGRICULTURE

In various Marxist regimes agriculture has played different economic roles—as a source of food for the urban areas, as a source of exports, as a source of labor for urban industrial growth, and as a source of finance for urban investment. These roles have differed according to the level of eco-

nations that had become Marxist regimes without decisive outside interference, the following were recent colonies: Angola, Bénin, Cape Verde, Congo, Grenada, Guinea-Bissau, Guyana, Madagascar, Mozambique, São Tomé, Seychelles, Somalia, Viet Nam, South Yemen, and Zimbabwe. The following had also experienced recent wars against foreign aggressors: Albania, China, Czechoslovakia, the USSR, and Yugoslavia.

nomic development and the available land area, the share of the labor force in agriculture, what foodstuffs are produced, the importance of exports, and other key economic factors. The level of economic development also influences the government's ability to administer a collectivized agricultural sector in a centralized fashion and, as I indicate in chapters 10 and 11, to carry out a successful decollectivization. The economic size of the nation is important because of the relatively greater economic role of foreign trade in small countries and, I should add with regard to Third World nations, the particularly strategic nature of agricultural exports. Because several of the countries discussed in this study may be unfamiliar to some readers, it is useful to present several tables that summarize these causal factors in a systematic fashion.

Population, Level of Development, and Land Area

The nations discussed in this study cover a wide range of economic conditions. Table 1.2 shows some key economic variables and table 1.3 summarizes these data from a worldwide perspective. For this exercise it is instructive to divide the Marxist regimes into three groups—core countries of the Socialist Commonwealth, other core countries, and periphery, depending upon their political and economic closeness to the Soviet Union. This type of division provides insight since the three groups have very different economic characteristics and illustrates the heterogeneity of the sample under analysis.

Those core countries classified as belonging to the Socialist Commonwealth have a relatively high per capita income and also a much lower population density (more arable land per capita) than the world average. The other core countries (the numbers are dominated by China) have relatively lower per capita incomes, a much smaller share of the gross world product, and considerably higher population density than the world average. The peripheral nations have a still lower per capita income and a smaller share of the gross world product, but have a population density roughly equal to the world average.

The Importance of Agriculture

Table 1.4 presents several key indicators of the relative importance of agriculture in the economies of the sample nations. Again, the major message is the heterogeneity of the sample. In later chapters I refer to specific aspects of the data.

The share of the labor force in agriculture gives the simplest picture of its relative weight in the economy: this sector employs three-fifths or more of the labor force in most of the African and Asian Marxist regimes in the economy, but in the Marxist regimes in the Americas and Europe this share is much lower.[13]

The value added in agriculture as a percentage of factor price GDP gives another type of measure of the relative importance of agriculture. Dividing this series with data on the share of the labor force in agriculture allows us to compute the relative GDP per economically active in the two sectors which, in turn, provides a comparison of the relative productivities and/or compensation of labor of agricultural and nonagricultural sectors. In the third data column, I designate as "relatively backward" (RB) those agricultural sectors whose relative GDP per worker is less than one-fourth that of the nonagricultural sectors in the same nation. This measure not only indicates those countries where some type of agricultural reorganization is most necessary, but also where such reorganization is most difficult. It is noteworthy that these relatively backward agricultural sectors occur primarily in countries in Africa and Asia. Although Cuba appears an exception, problems with the data in this country may appear because of some anomalies in the pricing of agricultural and nonagricultural products.

The last four columns present some indicators of the role of agriculture in foreign trade. This is important for a later discussion of how, in these countries, an overvalued exchange rate has worked to the particular detriment of agriculture, and an examination of a useful proposition by Colburn (1986) that the private sector in agriculture has a particularly strong bargaining position in those countries where agricultural exports or imports are important. Of the twenty-four countries for which data are available, trade in agricultural goods is relatively unimportant in only five nations (this class is designated as O in the table), most of which are in East Europe. At the other extreme, agricultural exports play an extremely important role in total exports of nine nations (Bénin, Cuba, Ethiopia, Grenada, Guinea-Bissau, Madagascar, Nicaragua, São Tomé, and Somalia; this class is designated XX in the table). It is noteworthy that in six of these nine countries, agricultural products play a key role in imports (Cuba, Ethiopia, and Nicaragua are the exceptions), which means not only that their agricultural sectors are relatively specialized

---

[13] For Cape Verde, Mongolia, Seychelles, and South Yemen natural conditions are not very suitable for agriculture, and this may also be the case for North Korea, which is mountainous. I am puzzled, however, by the inclusion of São Tomé in this list, since it is a very poor nation specializing in agricultural exports. Moreover, this nation has a relatively low degree of urbanization (only 15.6 percent of the population lived in urban areas larger than two thousand people). The census data for 1981 do not suggest that agricultural workers are classified in related industries: the share of the economically active engaged in forestry and fishing is 4.8 percent and in agro-industries, 1.2 percent. The degree to which the São Tomé data are comparable to those of the other nations is unknown.

TABLE 1.2
Some Key Economic Variables of Marxist Regimes, 1980

	Population (1000s)	Population per arable hectares	Per capita GDP (% of U.S.)	Notes on GDP
Core Countries: Socialist Commonwealth				
Bulgaria	8,862	2.1	43.0%	
Cuba	9,724	3.0	30.9	Very rough estimate.
Czechoslovakia	15,225	2.9	61.4	
Germany, East	16,737	3.3	69.2	
Hungary	10,771	2.0	48.3	
Kampuchea	6,400	2.1	4.2	Very rough estimate.
Laos	3,683	4.2	4.2	Very rough estimate.
Mongolia	1,663	1.4	4.2	Very rough estimate.
Poland	35,578	2.4	43.9	
Romania	22,201	2.1	34.6	
Viet Nam	54,175	8.2	2.8	Very rough estimate.
USSR	265,542	1.1	49.3	
Total	450,501			
Weighted average		1.5	42.2	
Core Countries: Other				
Albania	2,671	3.8	20.7	Very rough estimate.
China	1,017,561	10.2	10.3	See note below.
Korea, North	18,025	8.0	10.4	Very rough estimate.
Yugoslavia	22,295	2.8	41.5	
Total	1,060,552	9.6		
Weighted average		1.1	11.0	
Countries of the Periphery				
Afghanistan	15,950	2.0	5.2	
Angola	7,581	2.2	6.1	
Bénin	3,464	1.9	4.7	
Cape Verde	296	7.4	8.3	
Congo	1,605	2.4	8.6	
Ethiopia	37,717	2.7	2.8	
Grenada	89	6.4	13.2	
Guinea-Bissau	809	2.8	3.4	
Guyana	792	1.6	14.2	
Madagascar	8,714	2.9	5.2	
Mozambique	12,094	3.9	5.6	
Nicaragua	2,672	2.1	17.6	
São Tomé	94	2.6	6.0	
Seychelles	63	12.6	18.4	
Somalia	4,674	4.4	3.6	
Yemen, South	1,969	12.6	4.7	

TABLE 1.2 (cont.)

	Population (1000s)	Population per arable hectares	Per capita GDP (% of U.S.)	Notes on GDP
Zimbabwe	6,976	2.7	8.2	
Total	105,559			
Weighted average		2.7	5.0	
Grand total	1,616,612			
Grand weighted average		3.7	19.3	

Source: The population data come from United Nations (1988a, table 3), the land data come from Food and Agricultural Organization (data files), and most GDP data come from Robert Summers and Alan Heston (1988).

Notes: Summers and Heston (1988) estimate the per capita GDP of China as 264 percent that of India; the World Bank (annual, 1982, p. 110) estimates the same statistic as 121 percent that of India. I have taken an unweighted average as my estimate. The estimates designated as "very rough" represent little more than educated guesses on my part.

TABLE 1.3
Summary of Key Economic Parameters of Marxist Regimes

Groups of Nations	Percent of World		
	Population	Arable Land	GDP
Classified by Political Criteria			
Core Countries			
Socialist Commonwealth	10.0%	20.1%	15.8%
Other	23.6	7.6	9.7
Countries of Periphery	2.4	2.7	0.4
Total	36.0	30.4	26.0
Classified by Continents			
Africa	1.9	2.1	0.3
America	0.3	0.3	0.3
Asia	25.0	8.3	9.2
Europe	8.9	19.6	16.2
Total	36.0	30.4	26.0

Source: See Table 1.2.

Notes: To calculate these percentages for the GDP, I had to make rough estimates for nations not included in the calculations by Summers and Heston (1988).

TABLE 1.4

The Economic Role of Agriculture, 1980

	Percent of Economically Active Population in Agriculture: 1980	Value Added in Agriculture as Percent of Factor Price GDP, 1979–81	Rel. Agr. Sec. Dev.	1979–1981 Agricultural Trade as Percent of:		Class	Major Agricultural Exports for Countries where Agricultural Exports are Important
				Exports	Imports		
Africa							
Angola	73.8	—	—	12.0	17.5	O	Oils, cocoa, cotton
Bénin	70.2	46.7	G	92.4	26.5	XXM	Bananas
Cape Verde	33.1	20.5	—	37.8	45.9	XM	
Congo	62.4	13.3	RB	2.3	16.7	O	Coffee, hides
Ethiopia	79.8	50.9	G	92.9	13.8	XX	Oil seeds
Guinea-Bissau	82.3	38.4	RB	57.1	30.7	XXM	Coffee, spices
Madagascar	80.9	48.0	RB	82.8	20.3	XXM	Nuts, cotton, sugar
Mozambique	84.5	—	—	41.5	13.6	X	
São Tomé	56.1	c. 23.6	RB	c. 99.3	c. 24.5	XXM	Cocoa
Seychelles	14.0	7.2	—	16.6	20.4	M	
Somalia	75.5	48.2	G	97.7	39.7	XXM	Animals
Zimbabwe	72.8	14.1	RB	37.9	3.4	X	tobacco, cotton, sugar
Americas							
Cuba	23.8	c. 6.8	RB	86.6	17.6	XX	Sugar
Grenada	c. 28.5	c. 20.8	G	90.6	30.7	XXM	Spices, bananas, cocoa
Guyana	26.8	22.6	G	45.5	15.7	X	Sugar, rice
Nicaragua	46.6	c. 24.9	G	87.6	14.6	XX	Coffee, cotton, meat, maize

Asia							
Afghanistan	61.0	c. 54.6	49.9	15.4	G	X	Fruits, cotton
China	74.2	c. 34.5	22.3	38.7	RB	XM	Vegetables, fruits, tea
Kampuchea	74.4	—	—	—	—	—	
Korea, North	42.8	—	—	—	—	—	
Laos	75.7	—	—	—	RB	—	
Mongolia	39.8	c. 13.2	—	—	—	—	
Viet Nam	67.5	—	—	—	RB	—	
Yemen, South	41.1	c. 12.1	1.9	15.0	RB	O	
Europe							
Albania	55.9	—	—	—	—	—	
Bulgaria	22.7	22.6	—	—	G	—	
Czechoslovakia	12.9	13.4	4.4	13.5	G	O	
Germany, East	10.0	11.8	—	—	G	—	
Hungary	19.9	24.9	23.4	11.4	G	X	Meat, cereals, vegetables
Poland	29.8	26.6	6.3	16.8	G	O	
Romania	28.3	26.4	—	—	G	—	
USSR	20.0	c. 12.4	3.9	26.5	G	M	
Yugoslavia	32.3	12.4	11.8	10.4	G	O	

Source: See Statistical Note A.

Notes: Dashes (—) indicate no data are available. The *c.* before the factor price ratios indicates that some type of estimate was made. For countries where only the market price GDP data were available, the calculated ratio was increased by 5 percent; for countries where only a net material product data were available, the calculated ratio was decreased by 20 percent (to take into account the omitted depreciation and service sectors, as well as the fact that the data are calculated in market prices). For several other countries, I made smaller adjustments. For Cape Verde, Grenada, São Tomé, and Seychelles the data cover more sectors than agriculture since they include fishing and forestry; and for these particular nations the data refer respectively to 1980, 1981, 1981, and 1985.

Rel. ag. sec. dev. = relative agricultural sector development. If the value added per economically active in agriculture is less than one-fourth the value added per economically active in the nonagricultural sphere, the agricultural sector is considered "relatively backward" (RB). The G designates a situation where the value added per person in agriculture is greater than one-fourth of non-agricultural sectors.

Trade in agricultural goods includes all trade in SITC categories 0, 1, 21, 22, 232, 29, 4 and certain categories within 26. It proved impossible to use exclusively "general" or "special" imports and exports for this calculation. The trade "class" is defined in terms of total exports or imports and is designated as O if agricultural exports and imports comprise less than 20 percent of the totals; X or M if agricultural exports or imports comprise 20 to 49.9 percent of the totals; and XX or MM if agricultural exports or imports comprise 50 or more percent of the totals. For the major exports, "oils" refers to vegetable oils. The important exports are only listed for countries with a trade "class" of X or XX.

but also that they face more risks on the world market because of their lack of self-sufficiency in food. Later chapters discuss the role of these factors in a more rigorous and thorough fashion.

For the most part I have based this study on the primary and secondary literature of the thirty-three nations under review, supplemented by unpublished reports of international organizations. For some chapters, particularly those dealing with the most recent agricultural reforms, I have also used materials gathered from interviews of experts and government officials both inside and outside of the nations, as well as from discussions with farm directors and workers in eight of the nations under review.

Any broad study of the economic organization of agriculture in Marxist regimes must deal with five major topics: the important ideological views about the sector; the origin and development of the major forms of productive units; the internal organization of the farms and their external links with related sectors; major governmental agricultural policies and their results; and the changes in the organizational structure in recent years. These topics guide the analysis in the following chapters.

The next chapter, which forms the second segment of this introduction, focuses on both the general Marxist doctrines on agriculture and the policy issues leading to collectivization. Although classical Marxist writers wrote extensively about agriculture, they included little discussion about collectivization or the organization of agriculture in the transition to communism. This raises a number of questions: To what extent are the parallels drawn by Marx between the paths of economic development in agriculture and industry persuasive? To what degree have Marxian predictions about developments in agriculture been validated in leading capitalist nations over the last century? If, as I argue, only partial responsibility for agricultural collectivization can be laid at the doorstep of Marx, what were the other crucial elements in this decision in the Soviet Union? If many of the specific policy problems leading to Soviet collectivization were specific to that country, why did most other Marxist regimes also collectivize? To answer these and similar questions, it is essential to separate Marxist propositions, attitudes, and examples and to provide some notion of the range of policies receiving justification from the same doctrinal source.

Land Reforms and Collectivization

This part deals with the painful processes of creating a socialist agricultural sector. Most, but not all Marxist regimes have carried out land reforms, but the specific measures of these reforms have been quite different. The most important causal mechanisms for these differences receive considerable attention and give rise to a number of questions: How can the different types of land reform measures be explained? Why have certain Marxist nations collectivized and others not? What are the key relationships between the land reform and collectivization processes? Why have different countries focused either on state farms or collective farms? And why have various Marxist regimes taken very different strategies to achieve full collectivization? The comparative analyses in chapters 3 and 4 provide useful clues for the answers to these questions.

Structural Elements

Chapters 5 and 6 focus attention on both external and internal organizational issues. The former refers to horizontal and vertical integration of the farms; that is, the size of the farms and the manner in which they obtain inputs and sell their outputs. The latter refers to the way in which the state and collective farms organize their productive activities and compensate their labor force. From the descriptive materials a number of questions arise: Why have collective and state farms continued to grow in size over the years? How do the various ways for resolving problems of external organization influence the performance of the agricultural sector or the ease with which decollectivization can occur? What are the competitive and complementary elements between the socialist agricultural sector and the individual plots that are allowed farmers on collective farms? What are the options facing collective and state farm managers in organizing production and how does this choice effect performance or the speed of organizational change? The analysis yields insights into these questions and is supplemented by a research note presenting a model of decision-making by collective and state farm directors in a centrally planned economy in order to show in a rigorous fashion why it is likely that the dynamic efficiency of these farms is lower than in market economies.

Policy and Performance

The performance of agriculture is influenced not just by the organizational structure, but also by governmental policies. Chapter 7 deals with policies issues and three critical questions about them: Although policies vary a great deal from one country to another, depending upon the specific agricultural conditions, what are the elements common to all? To what extent are these policies distinctly influenced by Marxist doctrines? And to what extent are such policies tied to the organizational structure of agriculture? In chapter 8 I examine what the major differences are in agricultural performance between Marxist and non-Marxist nations. This quantitative exercise requires a separation of the respective influences of Marxist ideology in general, central economic planning of agriculture, and collectivization. I place particular emphasis on dynamic, rather than static, criteria of evaluation and show that the lower growth of total factor productivity is the major distinguishing characteristic of Marxist agriculture. This conclusion parallels Murrell's (1989) empirical analysis of Marxist foreign trade showing that these nations have a lower generation and adoption of technological and organizational innovation than comparable nations in the West.

Reforms and the Future

In chapter 9 I examine the question of decollectivization from the viewpoint of the farmer and try to review those factors that increase the difficulty of the process. For instance, decollectivization is more likely to occur in Marxist regimes with agricultural sectors employing a relatively simple technology than in those nations which have a relatively mechanized agriculture and in those countries where property rights can be enforced. In the next two chapters I analyze problems of the reform of the organization of agriculture from the viewpoint of the government. In chapter 10 I investigate the different types of agricultural reforms taking place in the various Marxist regimes at the beginning of the 1990s and explore the major problems arising in changing the property relations, of marketizing the agricultural sector, and of changing farm management practices. A research note covers in greater detail the agricultural reforms in China, Guyana, Hungary, and the USSR. Chapter 11 provides an analysis of some macroeconomic issues, including the phasing of economic and political reforms and the timing of particular economic changes that play a major role in the success of agricultural reforms. The book ends with some reflections on the rise and possible fall of collectivized agriculture.

The furrow plowed in this book is long and difficult, and at this point the fruitfulness of the harvest is far from certain. Much more can be said about what should be done and how it should be accomplished, but since the major goals of the analysis should be clear, this prologue should end. Now it is time to roll up our sleeves and begin.

Chapter 2

THE MARXIST THEORY OF AGRICULTURAL
DEVELOPMENT AND COLLECTIVIZATION

AGRICULTURAL COLLECTIVIZATION is a difficult task, even in the eyes of its most fervent supporters. Stalin once confided to Winston Churchill that the political stresses during collectivization were greater than those of World War II (Churchill 1950, p. 498). Why then should any Marxist regime attempt to collectivize agriculture, especially when its organizational resources might be used for other purposes with a more immediate economic payoff?

Most of this chapter deals with Marxist theories about agriculture and the arguments derived from Marx's ideas and attitudes that have led to collectivization, rather than to the motives of those making the actual decision to collectivize. That is, I focus primarily on the cognitive aspects of the ideology of collectivization, rather than the more political or emotional aspects. I place particular emphasis on the parallels Marx drew between economic development in the agricultural and manufacturing sectors.

When analyzing the purely economic aspects of agriculture, Marx, Engels, Lenin, and others writing before the Bolshevik revolution (hereafter the "classical phase") developed a set of propositions about long-run sectoral trends, which they tried to apply to various situations. The first step is to review these doctrines about the development of the agricultural sector in order to demonstrate that although they say little *directly* about state and collective farms, they provide a set of ideas that have been used as the intellectual basis for collectivization.[1] I also pay attention to certain

---

[1] For the moment I do not concern myself with the correctness of these doctrines. This is the focus of Research Note B, in which I show that in a descriptive sense several of these propositions turn out to be useful (although Marx's proposed mechanism is wrong). Thus my argument differs from that of David Mitrany (1961) in two important respects: I do not believe that all of Marx's doctrines on the development of agriculture are wrong, and I believe that these doctrines were *indirectly*, rather than *directly* related to the collectivization campaign.

In any discussion of Marxist doctrine, the references provide a problem since so many editions of the basic writings are available. In the notes the following abbreviations are used: MEW = Marx and Engels (1961–67); LCW = Lenin (1960–71); SWMT = Mao (1975–77); and SW = Stalin (1953–55). Since the opinions of these men on many questions of agricultural policy were in considerable flux over the years, I have also put in square brackets the original date when the cited materials were written.

of Marx's attitudes toward farmers and agriculture, because these may have had greater influence than his carefully specified doctrines. Other aspects of Marx's purely economic analysis of agriculture, for instance, his doctrines of agricultural rents, are irrelevant for this discussion.

The next phase of doctrinal development (hereafter the "implementation phase") arose when Marxists attempted to specify the policies a Marxist government should take toward agriculture. This was a problem not just for those Marxist parties attempting to gain electoral success, but also, of course, for the young Marxist governments in the USSR, China, and elsewhere. Certainly the leading figures in the debate attempted to link their proposed policies with Marxist developmental doctrines on agriculture; for instance, the subtitle of Karl Kautsky's classic study (1902) of the "agrarian question" was A View of the Trends in Modern Agriculture and the Agricultural Policies of Social Democracy, which consciously linked these two aspects of the argument.[2] Nevertheless, the discussion on collectivization in Marxist regimes was greatly influenced by a series of additional political and social considerations, so that the analysis has a much different flavor from that of the classical phase. In this second step of my analysis, I focus particular attention on some of the most important theoretical arguments used to justify the collectivization of agriculture pursued by Stalin, Mao, and other Marxist leaders. I label these ideas "Marxoid," because, although they were allegedly derived from Marx, they required additional assumptions; indeed, such Marxoid arguments might also be refuted with other arguments drawn from Marx.

The subsequent phase (hereafter the "reassessment phase") has lasted from the late 1960s to the present. The last part of this chapter examines how the various Marxoid arguments for collectivization have been received in the last half century and how important Marxists have begun to consider agricultural collectivization as a final goal, rather than as a means to achieve socialism. This reassessment has been associated with some dramatic reversals of agricultural policy such as decollectivization.

Many of the arguments in all three phases of the debate were based on the contrasts between socialist and individual agriculture, which originates in Marx's attitudes toward the peasantry. Although many of his ideas changed over the years, a leitmotif underlying his views, namely that smallholders are individualistic, can be understood in three different ways.[3] First, their intellectual horizons are limited to their own small

[2] Lenin called this book "the most noteworthy contribution to recent economic literature" since the publication of the third volume of Das Kapital.

[3] Marx's views on the peasantry are scattered among a number of his writings. In his young years his most striking formulation is in Der achtzehnte Brumaire des Louis Bonaparte [1852] (MEW, vol. VIII, chap. 7). I draw primarily from his more mature views represented in Das Kapital, vol. I [1867] and III [1894] (MEW, vols. XXIII and XXV). A brief

piece of land, the income derived from it, and their families. Second, they are not socialized by modern production methods; that is, within the smallholder sector there is little division of labor and cooperative specialization. Third, their production is primarily for themselves or for a limited market, rather than a worldwide market. Collectivized agriculture signifies that the key decision-making units do not have the individualistic orientation of the smallholder or the capitalist owner of the farm. More specifically, productive decisions are made by those with a socially larger horizon, there is a division of labor among the workers, and production is linked with the national and international economy.

This set of distinctions between socialist and individual agriculture reinforces the natural bias of urban intellectuals leading various Marxist parties against the peasantry. From such considerations it can be understood more clearly, for instance, why Jaime Wheelock, the Nicaraguan (Sandinista) minister of agriculture, opposed handing over the land seized from Somoza and his allies to the peasants on the grounds that "this type of land reform destroys the process of proletarianization in the countryside and constitutes a historical regression" (Collins 1986, p. 80).

THE CLASSICAL PHASE: HISTORICAL EVOLUTION OF AGRICULTURE

Marx and Engels laid down several clear doctrines about the evolution of agriculture that were far from uncritically accepted by their followers. They argued that two critical causal factors drive the evolution of the farm sector. First, economies of scale and size are extremely important in agriculture: large farms have greater productivity than small farm units because they permit a greater division of labor and more extensive mechanization.[4] Second, large-scale farms are in a better position to take advantage of new advances in agricultural technology, especially new chemical (for instance, fertilizers) and mechanical inventions.

In his discussion in *Capital* of "the so-called primitive accumulation," Marx traced the evolution of agriculture in England from the serf to the rural wage worker and the emergence of the capitalist farmer, who rented land from the landlord and hired the workers.[5] In the competitive

but useful summary of Marx's general views about the peasantry is provided by Duggett (1975).

[4] "Economies of scale" refers to additional productivity (or lower costs) occurring when all factors of production (land, labor, capital) are increased by a certain multiple; "economies of size" refers to the additional productivity (or lower costs) when some production factors are increased. For my purpose the distinction is not important; in the econometric studies discussed in Research Note B, the distinction is important in determining how the equations are specified and interpreted.

[5] Karl Marx, *Das Kapital*, vol. I (MEW, vol. XXIII). This brief discussion draws especially on part 7, chap. 24.

processes of emergent capitalism in the rural sector, the independent landowning smallholders disappear as a social group. Thus he viewed the long-term evolution of the agricultural sector in the same manner as the industrial sector and events in the agricultural development of England as prototypical of capitalist agricultural development in general.[6]

With the growth of production for the market (commodity production) and the spread of capitalism in agriculture, Marx and Engels foresaw agricultural labor productivity rising with increasing mechanization so that fewer farmers would be needed to feed a given number of urban people. Without going through the steps of their logic, which in most cases was quite simple, it is necessary to note only that they made the following five predictions: (1) the average land area of farms would become larger; (2) the farm sector would become increasingly differentiated, and, in essence, the inequality of the size distribution of farms would become greater, with the land being held by ever fewer people (a concentration and centralization of capital); (3) the smallholder could not compete against the large farms and would lose his land ("become annihilated"); (4) these small farmers would be transformed into proletarians, either staying on the land to work for others or emigrating to the city; the average number of hired workers per farm would increase; and (5) the form of payments to the landlord would change from a system of labor rents to sharecropping to fixed rents in money (a proposition which is not closely integrated with the others).

It is not necessary here to examine whether these propositions are true, a statistical exercise that is carried out in Research Note B using data for fifteen industrial nations for fifty or one hundred-year periods. I show that except for the increasing acreage of average farms, none of the other propositions receives much support. Of particular importance, the percentage of hired farm workers as a share of the agricultural labor force is not increasing but declining in most countries, suggesting that static economies of scale are not important. I also cite supporting evidence taken from various studies on a microlevel.

In sum, Marx argued that in the long term, capitalism condemns small-scale peasant farming to "gradual extinction, without appeal and without mercy." He did note, however, that the particularities of the process would differ according to historical circumstances and pointed to variations on this theme in England, France, and Russia. Nevertheless, the five propositions previously outlined appear as part of ideological rosary of orthodox Marxism, so obvious that they do not require demonstration or justification but merely need to be recited whenever agricultural pol-

---

[6] Much of this discussion occurs in the context of his remarks on ground-rents; e.g., in part VI of *Das Kapital*, vol. III (MEW, vol. XXV).

icy questions with regard to the organization of the agricultural sector are under examination.

Marx's economic ideas about the evolution of agriculture were also colored by some of his attitudes toward the farmer and his views about the "idiocy of rural life." For instance, he wrote that "small landed property creates a class of barbarians standing halfway outside of society, a class combining all the crudeness of primitive forms of society with the anguish and misery of civilized countries."[7] His contempt for farmers was that of a fastidious urban intellectual with little experience or understanding of rural life. It is an attitude that has led Marxist policymakers to view farmers as an object of their policies, rather than a subject and to interpret rural resistance to collectivization solely as the result of the ignorance of the peasants, who can be corrected only by force since they are incapable of understanding their own best interests.

But Marx held out the hope of salvation. With the spread of market relations into the countryside, the increase in rural mechanization, and the diffusion of modern communications networks into rural areas, the cultural and economic level of the workers in the rural and urban sectors would converge. Although such a process does not necessarily require collectivization, it encouraged Marxist policymakers to change the psyche of the farmers by means of a hyperindustrialization of agriculture, which featured huge tractors (leading to problems of compacting of the earth) and stables (leading to some difficult ecological problems). Such attitudes also played an important role in promulgating policies to proletarianize the farmers so that they became rural wage earners, rather than agriculturalists with ties of responsibility to specific pieces of land.

Reception of the Theses by Followers of Marx

Marx's theses about the development of the agricultural sector aroused enormous controversy among his followers (Hussain and Tribe 1984). Three main lines of attack can be distinguished:

OBJECTION 1: EMPIRICAL

The early discussion of these Marxist propositions focused particularly on the results from the German censuses of 1881 and 1895 (Germany, Kaiserliches statististches Amt 1898). Opponents of the Marxist propositions pointed out that the number of small farms increased between the two census years in Germany and that the average size of a farm (measured

---

[7] The first citation comes from the *Manifesto*, part I (*Manifest der Kommunistichen Partei* (MEW, vol. IV); the second, from *Das Kapital*, vol. III, chap. 47, last paragraph (MEW, vol. XXV).

in "used agricultural area") declined. As I show in Research Note B, such results were an artifact of the census definitions; in fact, these census results prove very little. Kautsky (1902) used agricultural census results for a much longer period and for more countries to examine these Marxist propositions; in this respect his approach had more statistical validity.

OBJECTION 2: MICROECONOMIC

The microeconomic mechanisms underlying Marx's propositions came under strong attack. Many German social democrats argued that economies of scale in agriculture were not so great as Marx implied and, moreover, depended both upon the particular crop and the intensity of agriculture. For instance, although wheat production may exhibit economies of scale, tomato growing does not. Such economies of scale may also occur in extensive agriculture such as animal husbandry in the American West, but not in intensive horticulture as found in the Netherlands or many parts of Germany.[8] Furthermore, diseconomies of scale or size arise for many reasons; for instance, agricultural activities are heterogeneous and a labor force is difficult to control, especially when spread over a large area and carrying out tasks in a sequential manner so that it is difficult to pin responsibility of the final results for a given piece of land on any one worker. Moreover, many of the economic advantages of large machines such as threshers could also be gained by smallholders, either by renting the machines or by combining into a cooperative and owning them jointly. Much evidence was available that smallholders as well as those with large farms were to take advantage of new agricultural technologies. These objections and others were aimed at the assumption that developments in industry and agriculture are parallel.

OBJECTION 3: STRUCTURAL AND MACROECONOMIC

Some followers of Marx such as Kautsky (1902) argued that although the large farms are more productive in general, some strong counteracting tendencies operate against their formation in the short- to medium-run in many countries. Both Kautsky and Lenin pointed out that in some

---

[8] Arising from this Marxist discussion, the most exhaustive (and exhausting) refutation of the various reasons offered for economies of scale in agriculture was a seven hundred–page book by the social democrat Eduard David (1903). David examined every phase of agriculture to determine the economies of scale, concluding that in European conditions the economic conditions for the small farm are more favorable than those for a large farm. A shorter version of his argument is presented in a translated article in Hussain and Tribe (1984). With his typical courtesy, Lenin called this book a collection of "bourgeois prejudices and bourgeois lies under the cover of quasi-socialist catchwords." In later decades, economies of scale have been examined by the calculation of production functions; however, seldom have these statistical results been tied to changes in the organizational structure of the farm sector.

cases smallholder production is so self-contained that it is not strongly affected by market forces; that is, since smallholders often do not sell much on the market, the competition of the large producers, who have lower costs, is not important and that any competitive effect can be offset by longer work hours and a lower standard of living ("self exploitation").[9] Furthermore, many smallholder families can maintain their parcels, either from the results of supplementary handicraft production or by family members working in rural or urban industries, aided in later decades of the century by dramatic improvements in transportation that have lowered costs of commuting.

Kautsky also pointed out that the growth of the large farm is impeded because it is often less a question of the accumulation of machinery and the hiring of additional labor than of buying up other farms, a process that occurs only very slowly. More important trends, he argued, were the increasing importance of rented land and the financial centralization of farm mortgages held by a relatively small group of financiers.

Lenin stressed particularly that the increasing social and economic differentiation of the rural sector occurring with the growth of market production had an important impact on farm size. Such forces of differentiation are manifested by, for example, the type of agriculture carried out, the degree to which labor and equipment is hired in or out, or the development of a rural proletariat. In addition, he described two quite different paths the market transformation of agriculture could take: the gradual transformation of large feudal latifundia into large capitalist estates (the Junker route), and the emergence of small capitalist farms that gradually consolidate, as large farms drive out smaller farms (the American route). As I show in chapter 4, these have important parallels in the development of socialist agriculture.

Debate among early Marxists on these issues became so intense and lasted so long that at the German Social Democratic (SPD) Congress in Kassel in 1920 a resolution read: "At present it is not possible to reach agreement in the economic importance of various sizes of agricultural undertakings" (Mitrany 1961, p. 40). Among Marxists, at least in the West, debate still rages on the relative economic advantages of small and large farms, the relative importance of economies of scale, and the ability of

[9] Lenin's major discussions are contained in *The Development of Capitalism in Russia* [1899] (LCW, vol. III); and "The Agrarian Program of Social-Democracy in the First Russian Revolution" [1907] (LCW, vol. XIII). The distinction between the Junker and American routes is contained in his preface to the second edition (pp. 31–34); his analyses focusing more specifically on German and American agriculture can be found in "The Capitalist System in Modern Agriculture" [1910] (LCW, vol. XVI, pp. 423–46); and "New Data on the Laws Governing the Development of Capitalism in Agriculture" [1915] (LCW, vol. XXII, pp. 13–102).

smallholders to take advantage of new agricultural technologies.[10] Such disagreements have erupted in a variety of contexts; for instance, in the disputes among historians over how English agriculture developed over the centuries (Aston and Philpin 1987).

Implications of the Doctrines for Collectivization

For the moment, I will assume that these propositions are correct. What then is their relevance for policy-making for Marxist parties either in or out of power?

Clearly any policy conclusions drawn depend in part on the importance given to specific propositions. If greatest attention is placed on the relative decline of the agricultural labor force with increasing productivity, then a Marxist regime can afford to wait until the size of the agricultural labor force becomes quite small before attempting collectivization. If primary attention is placed on the growth of labor productivity, then such a government might stress the hyperindustrialization of agriculture, rather than selecting appropriate technologies by means of more traditional economic criteria. If, on the contrary, primary attention is placed on the disappearance of small farms, then Marxist regimes might place considerable emphasis on farm amalgamation and the development of a rural proletariat. Furthermore, none of these Marxist propositions specifies the rate at which these trends are occurring, and relevant assumptions could have a considerable effect on the short-run policies that are advocated. Finally, the types of policies advocated in agriculture depend upon what is believed to be happening in the rest of the economy. For instance, Kautsky (1902) rejected nationalization of the land (a measure urged by Marx and Engels in the *Communist Manifesto* when they thought the revolution imminent) because this measure would be counterproductive if the revolution did not occur for several decades.

The link between policy prescriptions and basic trends is further obscured by political and social forces of the day. In a parliamentary system a Marxist party out of power must avoid alienating the peasantry, which is often an important voting group. Even if the party believes that perpetuation of the smallholders decrees "universal mediocrity," it may feel it necessary to advocate certain measures to ameliorate the plight of the peasant. Similarly, a Marxist party in power must take account of certain objective conditions in the agricultural sector before collectivizing agriculture (for instance, the stage of mechanization, the availability of modern techniques, the literacy of the rural population), even though it be-

[10] An extremely interesting debate on this matter was occasioned by a controversial essay by Djurfeldt (1981) and was carried on in the next two years in the same journal.

lieves that ultimately the agricultural sector must consist primarily of large mechanized farms.

In sum, Marx's theoretical and empirical analyses tell us little about when or how, or even why, collectivization should take place in a country aspiring to become socialist. In trying to translate theory into policy, it is the underlying assumptions, especially with regard to short-run issues, that appear sufficiently crucial as to obscure key ideas about the long-term trends that occasioned the original policy reflections. It is to these shorter-run issues concerning collectivization that I now turn.

THE IMPLEMENTATION PHASE: ARGUMENTS FOR AGRICULTURAL COLLECTIVIZATION

This discussion focuses on several canonical Marxists—Marx, Engels, Kautsky, and Lenin—and three later Marxist writers—Stalin, Mao, and Cabral. My intent is to outline briefly the major intellectual and ideological arguments for collectivization. Many of these justifications were based on propositions only loosely derived from Marx on matters about which he never wrote. Quite opposite arguments can be based on other parts of Marx's writings. These Marxoid ideas have had, nevertheless, considerable intellectual force.

Several limits must be given to this discussion: First, I am more interested in the distinct ideas offered in the debate, rather than the fascinating history of discussion surrounding them. Second, since most major participants changed their minds on many issues connected with collectivization, I have also elected to focus on their ideas in their last metamorphoses in order to simplify discussion. Finally, I wish also to concentrate primary attention on the arguments offered to the public or to party activists for collectivization, rather than on the specific political considerations that led to the actual policy decisions. In sum, I wish to examine those strands of argument most closely tied to the original issues raised by Marx and Engels about agriculture so as to allow for the separation of ideological from other considerations and to show how intellectual currents in Central and Eastern Europe have influenced the Third World.

Before beginning this part of the survey it is important to make one additional distinction. Arguments about the possible success of collectivized agriculture often isolate one key factor of agricultural production on which to peg the major arguments: for Stalin it was *land*, and the most important institutional change was to combine the small farms into much larger units; for Mao it was *labor*, and the most important policy step was to combine the labor efforts of previously isolated farmers; and for a disparate group of theorists (including Nikolai Bukharin, some members of the Left Opposition, and, a generation later, Edvard Kardelj in Yugoslavia) it was *capital*, and the most important institutional change was to create a capital intensive agriculture before collectivization could be successful.[11] The empirical analysis in the following chapters provides evidence that the Bukharin-Kardelj approach makes the most sense.

Some Canonical Writers

In the late nineteenth and early twentieth centuries, Marxists devoted relatively little intellectual energy to the question of collectivization. Rather they focused their attention on more immediate questions: Should woods and waters be nationalized? What state support should be given to agricultural service cooperatives? What measures should be taken to eliminate such feudal relics as hunting privileges, the strip system, village commons, or the village government that might periodically redistribute land among families? Should tariffs be placed on agricultural imports?

In the *Communist Manifesto*, Marx and Engels foresaw that in the transition to socialism, one early step would be the "abolition of property in land and application of all rents of land to public purposes." Neither Marx nor Engels discussed in very concrete terms what the final organizational form of the inevitable collectivized agriculture would be, alluding in later writings only to large-scale and highly mechanized units of production.[12] Although Marx had nothing to say about the process of col-

[11] This notion can also be found in the canonical texts, for instance, in an argument by Marx and Engels from *Die deutsche Ideologie* [1846] (MEW, vol. III, p. 29):

"The setting up of a collective economy presupposed the development of machinery, the use of natural resources, . . . [and] the supersession (Aufhebung) of the contradiction between town and country. Without these conditions the collective economy would not in itself be a new productive force, lacking all material basis and resting on a purely theoretical foundation; in other words it would be a mere freak."

Some Marxists have argued that the Bukharin-Kardelj position basically reflects the ideas of Lenin. They note that Lenin believed only large-scale agriculture could be collectivized and they point to his writings as "The Agrarian Question and the 'Critics of Marx'," [1901] (LCW, vol. V, esp. pp. 161–62) or his essay "New Data on the Laws Governing the Development of Capitalism in Agriculture," [1915] (LCW, vol. XXII), where he argued that "large scale" refers to capital-intensity and not the area of the farm per se. Since Lenin's position about what should be collectivized and how it should proceed shifted considerably over time and depended upon political circumstances, it does not seem useful to associate him with this particular position.

During the NEP, as Cox (1986, p. 27) has shown, others argued along this line. In putting Bukharin's name to this notion, I refer to his ideas as of the mid-1920s when he was at the apex of his power and could write what he really believed. Horvat (1976, chap. 3) has a useful discussion of the somewhat inconsistent ideas of Kardelj about collectivization and the role that service cooperatives could play in modernizing and preparing the private sector for collective farming.

[12] For instance, in "Brief an V.I. Sassulitsch, Erster Entwurf" [1881] (MEW, vol. XIX, p.

lectivization, Engels made some extensive observations on the problem shortly before his death:

> When we are in possession of state power, we shall not think of forcibly expropriating the smallholder (with or without compensation), as we shall have to do with big landowners. Our task in relation to the smallholder consists above all in effecting a transition of his private property and possessions into cooperative property, not forcibly but by example and the offer of social assistance for this purpose.
>
> As soon as our party is in possession of state power, it has only to expropriate the large estate owners, just like the manufacturers in industry. Whether this expropriation occurs with or without compensation will not depend primarily on us but on the circumstances in which we come to power and from the behavior of the Mr. Estate Owner himself. . . . The large estates so obtained will be turned over to the rural workers who are cultivating them who will be organized into cooperatives to exercise the totality of control. Under what conditions this will occur we can not exactly say.[13]

German social democracy was split on the advisability of collectivization or nationalization of land, either now or in the future when the party should gain power. Kautsky's views were roughly similar to Engels, but he was less certain about particular aspects.[14] At one time August Bebel argued that since the peasant was doomed, his land should be the first to be expropriated, but he later moved away from this position. Certain

---

389), Marx notes the future transformation of Russian agriculture from a strip system and communal control to a system of collective, mechanized enterprises with undivided fields. He does not describe either the process by which this is accomplished or the final organizational form. Some internal evidence suggests that the Soviet editors publishing this draft tampered with the text. My attempts to get a photocopy of the original draft in Marx's handwriting from the Marxism-Leninism Institute in Moscow proved fruitless.

[13] Friedrich Engels, "Die Bauernfrage in Frankreich und Deutschland" [1894] (MEW, vol. XXII, p. 499, my translation). Hussain and Tribe (1981b, p. 71) point out that some of the founding fathers of Marxism in Russia such as G. Plekhanov took seriously Marx's ideas about economies of scale in agriculture and opposed the confiscation and parcelization of estates, believing that these farms would be more productive than the resulting reorganized agriculture would be.

[14] Kautsky (1902, p. 440) noted that expropriation, especially of small farmers, was not necessary (leaving open the possibility that large farms would be nationalized). He argued that small farmers would combine their parcels voluntarily when they saw how much more productive cooperative farms could be, a position taken later by some Soviet writers during the NEP period. Nevertheless, he also argued (p. 129) that farmers would never voluntarily become members of a productive cooperative without becoming proletarianized first (i.e., losing their land); and still at another point in the same book (p. 299), he noted that socialist agriculture cannot really come about without a "socialization" (*Vergesellschaftlichung*) of the farmer through close economic relations with large agricultural enterprises so that they can learn another mode of life. This ambivalence about the process of creating a socialist agriculture is seen in many other writers on the topic.

agricultural specialists in the German Social Democratic party such as Eduard David rejected Marx's ideas about the superiority of large over small farms and argued that collectivization was a bad idea at any time.

Kautsky raised an interesting argument about service cooperatives, namely that group ownership of agricultural machinery or group purchases of fertilizer can freeze existing property relations on the land.[15] He claimed that service cooperatives can be manipulated by the large landowners and that such cooperatives permit small landowners to gain some of the benefits of large-scale production without combining their properties into production cooperatives.

In Russia, Lenin thought highly of Engels's analysis and repeated his words on several occasions, even while voicing his foreboding about the development of the peasantry in Soviet conditions; for instance, that they would be the "last capitalist class," a phrase often cited by Stalin.[16] In November 1917 when the new Soviet government nationalized the land, Lenin did not address the question of cooperatives, but he believed that some of the large expropriated estates should remain as state farms, a position rapidly overtaken by events.

Lenin's own ideas on agricultural organization showed a strange evolution.[17] In 1903 he advocated expropriating large estates and turning them into producer cooperatives, although he did not specify how such cooperatives would be organized. In 1907 he took a more radical stance and urged the nationalization of all land, although he also did not bother to describe how the state farms should be organized. His attempts to form state farms from the expropriated estates after the Bolshevik revolution failed, primarily because the peasants simply seized the land first and began to farm it privately before the government could seize control. Lenin's last contributions on agricultural organization came in two vague essays written early in 1923. The first focused primarily on service and consumer cooperatives in the agricultural sector, which he advocated should be the major thrust of the cooperative movement in the immediate future and which would give rise to "civilized cooperators." Ironi-

[15] Kautsky (1902, pp. 117). Solomon (1977, pp. 68) has noted that A. V. Chayanov, a noted Russian agricultural economist, provided empirical evidence that different farming activities have different optimal scales and urged the creation of service cooperatives so that these could be captured. As I point out in chapter 11, in the 1990s some of the East European nations appear to be following the institutional implications of Chayanov's approach.

[16] The quotation comes from V. I. Lenin, "Speech to the Third Congress of the Communist International" [1921] (LCW, vol. XXXII, p. 484).

[17] The two writings to which I refer are: "To the Rural Poor: An Explanation for the Peasants of What the Social Democrats Want" [1903] (LCW, vol. VI); and "The Agrarian Programme of Social-Democracy in the First Russian Revolution, 1905–1907" [1907] (LCW, vol. XIII). His 1917 ideas are found in "Report on Land" [November 1917] (LCW, vol. XXVI, pp. 257–61).

cally, after passing through a phase of collectivized agriculture, this is the model of agricultural organization toward which certain Marxist regimes such as Laos and Viet Nam seem to be heading.

The second essay deals in a few sentences with the ideas of Robert Owen and others on agricultural production cooperatives and then speaks equally hastily about some type of unspecified cooperative societies, without providing any programmatic thrust other than emphasizing the importance of leading the smallholder into cooperatives not by force but by education—a "cultural revolution would be necessary"—and economic incentives. He also observed that this voluntary process would take considerable time, at least a decade or two. In a previous essay, moreover, he had stressed that "under no circumstances . . . should we immediately propagate purely and strictly communist ideas in the countryside. As long as our countryside lacks the material basis for communism, it will be . . . fatal for communism to do so."[18]

Clearly these remarks from 1923 are banal and do not rise beyond the ideas of Engels over a quarter-century before. Lenin's declaration of various types of cooperatives as socialist institutions because the proletariat had control of the state was a metaphysical idea of little importance. By no means can these random thoughts be viewed as a coherent set of ideas about the future of Soviet agriculture since they do not address such serious problems as the relations of agricultural cooperatives to the rural differentiation occurring with market production, or Kautsky's problem about service cooperatives acting to freeze property relations, or a dozen other difficulties connected with different types of cooperatives that Lenin did not carefully distinguish. Although these incoherent ruminations of a dying man were used in the late 1920s by most major participants in the debate about agricultural policy to support their ideas—Stalin even claimed them as support for his forced collectivization of the

---

[18] The two essays "On Cooperation" (LCW, vol. XXXIII, pp. 467–79) were written in early January 1923 when Lenin was limited by his doctors to dictating only five to ten minutes a day. These essays directly contradict the contempt for agricultural service cooperatives he showed in his 1903 essay "To the Rural Poor" (LCW, vol. VI, p. 392). Lewin (1968) tells the story of the circumstances in which the 1923 essays were written: despite his efforts to place them as part of Lenin's dying attempt to correct the political deformations occurring in the USSR at that time (and a gradual acceptance of many of Trotsky's ideas), he must admit (p. 114) that the passages in these remarks are "confused" and that the new doctrine "creates as many problems as it solves."

The bizarre story of the manner in which participants in later Soviet debates transmuted these two essays plus earlier random articles (e.g., Lenin's "Consumers' and Producers' Cooperatives" [1921] (LCW, vol. XXXII, p. 370) into Lenin's grand "cooperative plan" told by Carr and Davies (1969, pp. 920–24). The quotation comes from "Pages from a Diary" [January 1923] (LCW, vol. XXXIII, p. 465).

peasantry—they appeared to represent little more than mainstream Soviet thought in the early years of the New Economic Policy (NEP).

Stalin on Collectivization: The Trumpet Sounds

Stalin originally opposed collectivization and, in 1925, even toyed with the idea of deeding each peasant a parcel of land.[19] In his later writings after he changed his mind, he offered several basic ideas to justify collectivization of the peasantry.

ECONOMIES OF SCALE OR SIZE

On a number of occasions in the late 1920s Stalin argued that simply combining farms would lead to increases in total production. For instance, he cited the Khoper district, where crop area (and, by implication, production) allegedly increased 30 to 50 percent by this simple change.[20] He also emphasized on numerous occasions that small peasant farming produces the smallest marketable surplus, a claim that has a vague economies-of-scale argument underlying it. Khrushchev used a similar argument to bring about a doubling of the average size of collective farms. Stalin did not use an argument advanced by some later Marxist leaders that collectivization would allow a more efficient short-term use of agricultural labor, especially during the slack agricultural season, or that collectivization would reduce the farming risks facing any individual farmer since highly local production risks (for instance, damage by hail or flooding of particular fields) would be shared by a larger group of people.

DYNAMIC EFFICIENCIES AND GROWTH

These refer particularly to the ability to incorporate new agricultural technologies; it was often combined with an economies-of-scale argument. According to Stalin, "small peasant farming is unable to accept and master new technical equipment, it is unable to raise productivity of labor to a sufficient degree, it is unable to increase the marketable output of agriculture to a sufficient degree. . . . The strength of large-scale farming, irrespective of whether it is landlord, kulak, or collective farming, lies in the fact that large farms are able to employ machinery, scientific knowledge, fertilizers to increase the productivity of labour."[21] This idea

[19] Although these remarks may have been the deliberate attempt to deceive, Trotsky (1971, pp. 27) believed Stalin was serious and scornfully discusses the idea. The debates about collectivization in the Soviet Union are intricate and difficult to follow; I found Moshe Lewin (1975) an especially useful guide.

[20] J. V. Stalin, "Concerning Questions of Agrarian Policy in the U.S.S.R." [December 1929] (SW, vol. XII, p. 160).

[21] The first quotation comes from Stalin, "Political Report to the C.C. to XVI Congress

has been subsequently extended. For instance, H. Machunga, the Mozambique minister of agriculture proclaimed in 1981: "Some people think it is not possible to organize cooperatives because most people are illiterate and have a low technical level. Our response is simple. 'The organization of peasants into cooperatives is the quickest way to resolve these problems' " (Marleyn and others 1982). A reverse twist to this argument appeared in an official document of the Somalia government (Ministry of Planning and Coordination 1971, p. 9), which stated that the government was not able or willing to extend any effective aid to smallholders and that it would only deal with cooperatives.

The argument that peasants are incapable of absorbing technological changes is often countered in the West with equal dogmatism: with the right incentives, smallholders are highly open to technological innovation. A more balanced view is that everything depends upon the manner in which such innovations are introduced, either in a cooperative or a smallholding system, and that the problem is not resolved by beautiful speeches.

EXTRACTION OF SURPLUS

In its weakest form this argument states merely that collectivization leads to greater rural savings and investment. In the mid-1920s, however, Evgeny Preobrazhensky put forward the notion of "primitive socialist accumulation" and argued that the resources necessary for industrialization of the urban sector would have to come from agriculture.[22] As late as October 1926 Stalin denied this proposition in his fight against Trotsky and the "left." Three years later in his battle against Bukharin and the "right," he discussed an alleged "grain strike" by the *kulaks* and admitted that it would be necessary to levy a "tribute" upon the peasants, albeit for a short time, in order to finance industrialization.[23] Stalin also advanced the strange argument that raising the price of grain paid by state agencies would hurt, not help, poor peasants because the difference between the official and free market prices would be greater in the spring when poor peasants purchase grain to tide them over until the fall harvest.

---

of C.P.S.U. (B)" [June 1930] (SW, vol. XII, p. 286). The second quotation comes from "On the Grain Front" [May 1928] (SW, vol. XI, p. 88).

[22] See especially Preobrazhensky (1965, pp. 88). These ideas were originally published in journal form in 1924 and in book form in 1926.

[23] Stalin's explicit or implicit arguments in 1926 against turning the terms of trade against the rural sector included: "The Economic Situation of the Soviet Union and the Policy of the Party" [April 1928] (SW, vol. VIII, pp. 123–56); and "The Opposition Bloc in the C.P.S.U.(B)" [October 1926] (SW, vol. VIII, pp. 235). His turnabout is signaled in his essay "The Right Deviation in the C.P.S.U. (B)" [April 1929] (SW, vol. XII, esp. pp. 52–59). Alec Nove (1971) notes that the forced requisitions to obtain grain in the Ural-Siberian area in 1927–28 were an implicit acceptance of this notion.

Although I have found no explicit statements by Stalin on the matter, it seems likely that he also saw an assured supply of grain from the countryside as a key to political power and stability. It seems unlikely that such considerations would have received much public discussion, even if they may have played a critical role in the collectivization decision.

EQUALITY

Stalin noted that collectivization would halt the increasing income inequality allegedly occurring in the countryside (that is, class differentiation), and he appeared to suggest that it would improve the quality of rural life by allowing the government to provide basic services to the poor peasants more easily. He also emphasized that collectivization would end the exploitation of the peasantry by the *kulaks* through such measures as usury, low wages, and other baneful practices.

Unlike later Marxist leaders, however, Stalin did not stress that collectivization would allow more equal access to the land by the peasants or, by narrowing the urban-rural income gap, that it would stem the flow of peasants to the city. He also did not stress that collectivization would enable the basic economic and social needs of poor villagers to be met, a line of argumentation given prominence in speeches of some Marxists outside the top leadership in the USSR.

INDIVISIBILITY OF THE PLANNING SYSTEM

Closely tied with the extraction-of-surplus argument was the notion that serious economic planning cannot exist unless all major sectors come under the planning system and that agricultural planning is impossible if production is carried out by private farmers. That is, collectivization would permit the government the necessary direct control to carry out a consistent policy of economic development. Since the ideological statements about collectivization did not attempt to analyze different kinds of planning, this is more an argument by metaphor than a serious analytic statement.

This type of argument has been often repeated since that time, finding a colorful expression a half century later in a speech by Fidel Castro: "There are still a few tens of thousands of [private] farmers left. Working with them is much more difficult [than with cooperatives]; it is terrible, virtually insolvable because one must discuss and make plans with tens of thousands of them" (Mesa-Lago 1988, p. 63).

ACCELERATING HISTORY

In the nineteenth century the Narodniki, a group of agrarian populists, argued that it was possible to move directly from the communal agriculture of the traditional Russian peasant to socialism without going through capitalist farming, proletarianization, or, for that matter, collectivization.[24] Marx had noted that under certain conditions, for instance, a socialist revolution in the West and the prevention of capitalist destruction of these traditional peasant relations, such a skipping of a capitalist stage might be possible. Lenin and some of his colleagues had argued that capitalist penetration had proceeded too far for this to occur. On a number of occasions before collectivization Stalin suggested that such a transition was possible under the Soviet conditions, due to the capture of power by the proletariat, but he was rather vague on how agriculture would be organized and what elements of communalism would be retained.[25]

POLITICAL ARGUMENTS

Lenin distinguished four strata of the rural population: the poor peasants, who were a potential political support for the Communist Party and its socialization of the countryside; the middle peasantry, whose political allegiances were ambiguous; a rich peasantry (*kulaks*); and the former landlords, who were opposed to the party and its program. The landlords had been eliminated after the revolution, but a number of Marxist analysts also claimed that the *kulaks* served as a serious political threat.

In their published writings neither Lenin nor Stalin went so far as some Soviet historians in claiming that the *kulaks* were fomenting civil war.[26] Nevertheless, in 1918 Lenin stated that the rich farmers were deliberately withholding grain for speculative purposes. From that time to the period of collectivization, Soviet leaders made this argument whenever grain deliveries seemed to be falling short. They held this social group up as the embodiment of evil; for instance, Stalin's characterization of the *kulaks* as bloodsuckers, spiders, and exploiting vampires who have "taken advantage of these difficulties [of the state obtaining grain] in or-

---

[24] These discussions are conveniently summarized by Hussain and Tribe (1981b). The populists considered communal agriculture of the Russian variety as "socialistic." Marx's theoretical hesitation on the problem is shown clearly in the three drafts of a letter he finally sent to Vera Zasulich that are contained in MEW, vol. XIX, pp. 384–406. A much briefer observation by Marx on this matter is contained in his foreword to the second Russian translation (1882) of the *Manifesto* (MEW, vol. XIX, pp. 295–96).

[25] For instance, in his "Foundations of Leninism" [1924] (SW, vol. VI, p. 139); or "Agrarian Policy in the U.S.S.R." (SW, vol. XII, p. 158).

[26] This interpretation is offered, for instance, by some modern Soviet historians such as S. P. Trapeznikov (1981, vol. II, pp. 66–69), who argues these "muck-faced landowners" and "died-in-the-wool reactionaries" "strove to precipitate civil war in the countryside . . . by unbridled campaigns of terror, provocation, sabotage and intimidations of working peasants . . . to clash with the Soviet government on the bread front and force it to abandon the practice of purchasing bread at fixed state prices . . . to abandon its class policy in the countryside. . . . Relying on the support of the Right opportunists the *kulaks* stepped up their anti-Soviet activities, continued to sabotage state grain purchases, and to terrorize the local Party and Soviet executives. . . . In a number of land societies the *kulaks* succeeded in depriving farmhands and poor peasants of their voting rights as members of the societies and declared the law on agricultural as null and void."

der to disrupt Soviet economic policy."[27] Modern research has shown, however, that grain shortages in the Soviet Union at that time can, in good measure, be attributed to incorrect agricultural pricing policies by Soviet authorities.[28]

In the late 1920s the Soviet government put down a number of *jacqueries* in which peasants of all income groups took part. At this time Stalin began to talk about class warfare in the countryside. In urging collectivization Stalin also demanded the elimination of the *kulaks* as a class in order to eradicate what he claimed was a major source of resistance to and sabotage of the government, thus taking Lenin's thesis about differentiation in agriculture occurring in production for the market to its furthest extreme. This message was combined with the call for a renewal of the alliances between the remaining strata of the peasantry and the urban proletariat. If economic differentiation in the countryside were allowed to continue, according to this view, many middle peasants would join the *kulaks* and turn against the workers' state, and the alliance between the poorest stratum and the workers would be weakened because the former would be disappointed at the lack of socialism in the countryside and their own low standard of living. In sum, collectivization would remove all institutions intervening between the peasants and the Soviet state, eliminating all major sources of rural opposition to bolshevism at the same time. As Conquest (1987, pp. 120, 219) has also noted, by destroying the old elite in the non-Russian areas, collectivization also destroyed the transmitters of nationalist ideas that might threaten the integrity of the multinational Soviet state.

Other types of political arguments were secondary. For instance, unlike some later Marxist leaders such as Mengistu of Ethiopia, Stalin never argued that collectivization would permit a wider sharing of political power among the peasants. Stalin sometimes hinted that collectivization should proceed so that the Soviet Union could serve as an example of socialism to others. This, however, was merely a rhetorical attempt to make collectivization an end in itself, rather than as a one-among-several competing means toward socialism.

SOCIAL ARGUMENTS

Some unstated social arguments for collectivization need to be made explicit, because radical urban intellectuals have often adopted Marx's con-

---

[27] Lenin's claim was made in "On the Famine" [May 1918] (LCW, vol. XXVII, pp. 391–92). During the NEP period these views were toned down. The quotation from Stalin comes from his "On the Grain Front" (SW, vol. XI, p. 87).

[28] This is shown in Jerzy Karcz (1967b). In a later article (1970), Karcz stressed a major problem: major Soviet agricultural policies such as prices were made on the basis of very unsatisfactory statistical information.

temptuous attitudes toward the peasantry. Lenin appeared no exception;[29] and Stalin continued the tradition, viewing the peasantry as a mass upon which to exercise his reforming instincts and political will. The peasant has a "slavish attachment to his little plot of land . . . and prefers to sink into barbarism rather than part with [it]. . . . A great deal of work has still to be done to remold the peasant collective farmer, to set right his individualistic mentality and to transform him into a real working member of a socialist society."[30]

Stalin, as well as Lenin (on occasion), also saw the peasantry as a source of spiritual pollution for the rest of society: "The peasantry, as long as it remains an individual peasantry, carrying on small commodity production, produces capitalists from its midst, and can not help producing them, constantly and continuously."[31] Thus the mere presence of a non-collectivized peasantry was such a social menace that it was necessary to place at the top of the political agenda both institutional changes in agriculture and a remolding of peasant consciousness.

Stalin's class warfare arguments also encouraged a class-based excuse for the excesses of collectivization and the elimination of resistance. As expressed in a novel published in 1934 in Moscow about the *kulaks*, "Not one of them was guilty of anything; but they belonged to a class that was guilty of everything" (Conquest 1987, p. 143). From this argument it was concluded that they had to be severely treated; millions died.

POWER OF EXAMPLE

In the post-World War II era when direct Soviet military and political influence was strong in East Europe, political leaders in the latter nations had little choice about following the Soviet example. After the Stalin-Tito split in 1948, most East European nations seriously started collectivizing.

[29] Lenin's suspicion of the peasantry is revealed in a vivid manner in his 1920 interview with H. G. Wells (Wells 1921, p. 160). Lenin spoke of the difficulty in "defeating the Russian peasant *en masse*" but that "in detail there would be no difficulty at all." During this conversation Wells noted: "At the mention of the peasants, Lenin's head came nearer to mine; his manner became confidential. As if after all the peasants *might* overhear."

[30] Both citations come from Stalin, "Agrarian Policy in the U.S.S.R." (SW, vol. xii, p. 171).

[31] "The Right Deviation" (SW, vol. xii, p. 48). This is, of course, a paraphrase of Lenin's remark that "small-scale production *engenders* capitalism and the bourgeoisie continuously, daily, hourly, spontaneously, and on a mass scale" ("Left-Wing Communism" [April–May 1920], LCW, vol. xxxi, p. 24). Curiously this argument is also taken up by the Hungarian economist, János Kornai (1990, p. 185), who as an economic and political liberal (in the European sense) applauds this development of agricultural institutions. It seems to me that both Lenin and Kornai miss a major point: small-scale production engenders only small-scale capitalism and a petty bourgeoisie more inclined toward populism than political liberalism. In any case, there is little evidence that in recent centuries urban capitalism has had rural roots or that rural petty capitalism is "infectious."

During the political thaw after Stalin's death, these drives slowed down or reversed, and when Khrushchev gained power, the collectivization drives were stepped up again in most nations. None of these policy changes was accompanied by public debate.

Stalin's collectivization program also provided an important example for younger generations of Marxists in Third World nations in which direct Soviet political influence was much weaker. More specifically, these young Marxists saw that the Soviet Union had collectivized, embarked on a rapid investment program, and become one of the world's two superpowers in less than a generation. This argument, really a non sequitur, was more powerful than all of the intellectual rationales previously discussed. The new socialist institutions seemed to be cut from a single cloth and all were necessary for the USSR's success to be replicated elsewhere. Although the causal linkages in this argument were tenuous, the Soviets' economic success was plain for all to see and, therefore, many believed a collectivized agriculture should be an integral part of the economy of any nation wishing to become industrialized with a socialist economic system. In sum, arguments for collectivization based on positive theories about the development of agriculture or immediate policy needs of the government gave way to a more emotional type of argument, a transformation of a cognitive to an integrative ideology.

Of course, some countries such as Czechoslovakia already had an industrial base and did not need the surplus extraction from agriculture to finance further investment. Other countries such as Laos did not have the government or party apparatus either to carry out collectivization or to operate such a system once it was created. In still other nations many of the other arguments were irrelevant.

Nevertheless, the importance of this power of example set by the Soviet Union, the world's first socialist nation, cannot be overemphasized. It meant that the solution adopted for a very specific set of circumstances was copied in nations where these circumstances did not hold. It also meant that the pattern of extreme centralization both in the polity as well as the economy was given an importance out of proportion to original Marxist doctrines on the subject and, furthermore, that such centralization led to same tyranny in other countries that Stalin intended for the Soviet Union.

Mao on Collectivization: The Echo is Muted

Mao's arguments for collectivization were much less forceful than Stalin's. Indeed, in reading his speeches on the subject, it is hard to find a sustained economic argument.[32] At different times he drew from arguments used by Stalin. With the experience of the Soviet Union as an example, collectivization seemed less problematical and less in need of sustained justification; it was clear that "Marxism is fierce . . . and aims to eradicate . . . small-scale production" and that little economic argumentation was necessary.[33] As a result, he presented his case less on the basis of theoretical arguments that were applied to current conditions and more in the form either of exhortations based on examples of successful collectivization or on political arguments. A distinctive strain of his ideas was his voluntarism: "the more backward the economy, the easier, not the harder, a transition from capitalism to socialism" (Zweig 1989, p. 21).

ECONOMIC ARGUMENTS

Mao spoke relatively little about technical economies of scale, although in some of his early writings he seemed to believe that they were important.[34] His theoretical innovations focused more on the impact of collectivization on the labor process. He argued forcefully that working together would generate enthusiasm, so that a group could produce more than the sum of the individuals composing it—a sort of "X efficiency" argument. Socialist consciousness could be raised through participation in such groups and is manifested by increased work effort. Sometimes Mao even claimed that higher productivity on cooperatives could be achieved merely by an exercise of will; for instance, "On no account should the production [of the cooperatives] remain at the same level as that of 'going-it-alone' households or mutual aid teams. Otherwise it would mean failure, and then what's the point of having cooperation at

[32] As in the case of the USSR, I focus only on the ideological arguments presented by the leaders; more developed cases for collectivization were presented by others and are discussed in such sources as Shue (1980) or Nolan (1988, chap. 2). Although Mao wrote considerably on agricultural problems before he gained political power, much of this concerned land reform and relatively little dealt with the agricultural collectivization that he foresaw following such reforms. From the late 1920s onward, Mao seemed to have a cautious approach toward collectivization, an approach reinforced by some disastrous experiments in liberated areas in the foothills of Jiangxi Province in the early 1930s; therefore, he could focus almost all of his discussions on land reform, which was a critical first step in gaining peasant support. Much of the debate in the 1950s about collectivization occurred behind closed doors; by the time Mao was speaking publicly about collectivization, he had already won the political debates and really didn't need to give a set of coherent economic arguments.

[33] Mao, "The Debate over Agricultural Cooperativization and the Present Class Struggle" [October 1955] (1986, p. 632).

[34] This argument is made loosely, but most explicitly, in his essay "Get Organized!" [November 1943] (SWMT, vol. III, pp. 153–61). He repeated the vague arguments for collectivization in this essay for the next decade.

all?"[35] Consciousness is raised at each step of cooperation which is why it is necessary to maintain a steady stream of institutional changes until full collectivization is achieved.

With such an emphasis on the change in attitudes and beliefs induced by cooperative farming, it does not seem surprising that Mao also claimed that machinery was not necessary for such large-scale units and, indeed, cooperatives could occur in farms "without funds, without carts, without oxen, and without the participation of well-to-do or middle peasants."[36] In more sober moments he did recognize that mechanization and the application of improved management, farming techniques, and technology would be necessary in the future to close the gap between the demand for agricultural products and their supply. At times he even contended that the revolutions in ownership and technology were related and that in the future everything would come together. But such cautious utterances were never at the heart of his message.

It is important to stress that Mao did not argue for collectivization in order to squeeze resources recklessly out of the peasantry; indeed, he criticized the Soviet Union for taking such a policy step.[37] Years before the collectivization campaign he saw the dangers of "draining the pond to catch the fish"; nevertheless he seemed to accept the argument, at least implicitly, that the rural sector had to provide the bulk of the resources to finance industrialization. His critique of Soviet policies really concerned the degree to which the government tried to transfer resources from the rural to the urban areas.

POLITICAL AND SOCIAL ARGUMENTS

In a manner similar to Stalin, Mao placed considerable emphasis on the rural class struggle and the different roles of various strata of the peasantry. Unlike many of the intellectuals leading the Soviet revolution,

[35] Mao, "On the Collectivization of Agriculture" [July 1955] (1986, p. 597).

Until the early 1950s, Mao appeared to lean heavily on the ideas in Lenin's essays "On Cooperatives," arguing that the agricultural economy would develop "step by step from individual to collective" in a gradual and voluntary fashion, starting with land reform and service cooperatives (mutual aid teams). Mao repeated these simple ideas many times; for instance, "The Present Situation and our Tasks" [December 1947] (CWMT, vol. iv, pp. 157–76); or "Report to the Secondary Plenary Session" [March 1949] (CWMT, vol. iv, pp. 361–75); or "Mutual Aid and Cooperativization in Agriculture" [October 1953] (1986, pp. 412–19). As growth of agricultural production began to fall short of plan projections, Mao suddenly began to claim that it was possible to move directly to agricultural cooperatives without going through the stage of service cooperatives. Soon the collectivization of agriculture—originally foreseen to require more than 15 years—was implemented in just a few years.

[36] Mao, "Agricultural Collectivization and the Present Class Struggle" (1986, p. 634).

[37] Mao, "On the Ten Major Relationships" [1956] (SWMT, vol. v, p. 291).

Mao came from a peasant background. During the civil war in the late 1920s and 1930s, he began to believe that the poorest segments of the peasantry provided the strongest support for his revolution.

This meant that Mao continually stressed the need to raise the living standards of the poor and lower-middle peasantry and argued that this could come about only through the formation of cooperatives. Any such improvements would also cement the allegiance of this group to the party, which he believed to be particularly important politically since most of the middle peasantry and the few remaining rich peasants would give the regime little support. Although Mao did not exhibit the open contempt for the peasant that is found in the writings of many urban European Marxists, this does not mean that he had much respect for them or that he felt any less hesitation about remolding all of the peasantry to create a socialist consciousness.[38] He was also much more concerned than Stalin over widening class and income differentials in the villages. Such closeness to the peasantry did not prevent him, of course, from instituting the Great Leap Forward and forcing millions of peasants, many of whom did not even belong yet to collective farms, onto communes.

Amílcar Cabral on Collectivization: The Reverberations are Faint

In reading Marxist literature from Third World nations, one finds little repetition of the justifications for collectivization offered by Stalin. In contrast, the most powerful arguments emphasize the link between collectivization and nationalism, especially that occurring with the expropriation of the foreign-owned estates in their countries and transforming them into state or cooperative farms. One obvious alternative of nationalizing estates—dividing them up, and then distributing the land to the workers—seems seldom considered as a viable policy alternative by the urban intellectuals dominating the various parties.

An interesting illustration of the ideology of collectivization in the Third World is provided by Amílcar Cabral who, along with Franz Fanon, is considered by most specialists to be one of the two most important African Marxist theorists. As leader of the liberation struggle against the Portuguese in Guinea-Bissau and Cape Verde, Cabral played important political and military roles as well. With a rare ability to combine practice and theory, he resembled Lenin, as many of his admirers have

---

[38] For instance, after private farmers complained the collectivization program broke his previous promises about the integrity of their land, Mao replied in "Mutual Aid and Cooperativization in Agriculture" [October 1953] (1986, pp. 412–19) that the law said the state would "protect" private property, not that it would "guarantee" it.

pointed out.[39] Most important for my purpose, he had received a university degree in agronomy and was probably one of the few important Marxist writers who had mastered the most important technical aspects of agriculture.

Cabral had some strong ideas about the operation of the agricultural sector, which he expressed primarily in a number of informal talks and writings. He believed that agriculture should be the leading sector and that it should be organized around producer cooperatives: "As to economic policy after liberation, the priority will be on raising food production. Agriculture will come first. . . . [The] priority on agriculture . . . means more than cultivation. . . . We hope to do a lot with producer cooperatives [in agriculture]. But there again we haven't any illusions. It's difficult. You can do it at the beginning only with the best men you have. . . . The comrades in charge of these [liberated] areas must help our people organize collective farming. This is a great experiment for our future, comrades. Whoever does not yet understand this has not understood anything about our struggle."[40]

Indeed, in his attempt to encourage cooperative farming, Cabral offered a good reason not to carry out such a program: "It is a positive thing that land is owned collectively. But this fact has also a negative aspect: the people do not love the land in the same way as farmers who own the land themselves" (Rudebeck 1974, p. 88). In other words, he saw that productivity in cooperative plots was lower than in private plots, at least in the foreseeable future. Since neither of the two countries he was trying to liberate had many large estates run as single economic units (that is, plantations) he did not talk at all about state farms. He also raised few of the political or social arguments of Stalin or Mao; indeed, given the im-

[39] Amílcar Cabral was destined by his parents to become a great African liberator, since he was named after Hamilcar Barca, the first African (Carthaginian) to win an important military victory over the Europeans (Romans); Hamilcar's son, Hannibal, achieved more victories over the Europeans.

The documents of Cabral's movement, Partido Africano da Independência da Guiné e Cabo Verde (PAIGC), have few abstract references to ideology per se such as Marxism-Leninism or African socialism. Cabral refused to label himself and discouraged others from so doing.

Evaluations of Cabral as a Marxist are, however, found in the writings of his admirers such as the various contributions to Barry Munslow, ed. (1986). One dissenter from the prevailing assessment is Jock McCulloch, (1983) who argues (p. 134) from an orthodox Marxist viewpoint that Cabral, in adapting Marxism to African conditions, tampered too much with traditional doctrines to be considered a Marxist.

Most biographies and assessments of Cabral are hagiographic; the most useful studies are Patrick Chabal (1983) and Lars Rudebeck (1974).

[40] The two quotations come from Davidson (1981, p. 102) and Chabal (1983, p. 112). The party platform presented by Rudebeck (1974, p. 255) speaks about "voluntary cooperative exploitation of the land and agricultural production, of the production of consumer goods, and of handicrafts."

portant tribal influences operating in the agricultural sector in Guinea-Bissau, most of these arguments would have been inappropriate.

Although Cabral had enormous insight into the problems of African agriculture and although he felt strongly about the necessity of cooperative farming, I have been unable to locate any statement of his as to why cooperative farms were somehow superior to private agriculture. By the time Cabral was writing (in the 1960s and early 1970s), collectivization of agriculture had become such an unquestioned article of faith that even Marxist agricultural specialists did not worry about its justification or its relation to the original doctrine.

The Bukharin-Kardelj Approach to Collectivization

If large-scale collectivized agriculture is not possible without the employment of highly capital-intensive techniques, as Bukharin and Kardelj argued, then two conclusions must be drawn: The process of collectivization will take a long time, during which large-scale mechanized farms will coexist with small-scale labor intensive farms. Further, full collectivization will not occur until agricultural workers constitute a relatively small share of the total labor force.

An obvious policy dilemma of such a Fabian approach should be readily apparent. By focusing government investment and energies on a small number of large state or collective farms, the country might end up with slow agricultural growth and dual agricultural sectors: a stagnant peasant sector and a money-losing socialist agricultural sector. If, on the other hand, the government channels considerable aid to the private agricultural sector to raise its productivity, such private farms might develop to the extent that collectivization would not be necessary for purely economic reasons—a socialist United States would gain little additional production by collectivizing the large Kansas wheat farms.

A Brief Evaluation

The arguments for collectivization raised by Stalin were primarily tactical and Marxoid; other than a boundless faith in economies of scale or size in agriculture, they had few direct links with the agrarian doctrines of Marx and Engels. Certainly there is nothing particularly Marxist about turning the terms of trade against the peasant or, for that matter, forcing institutional change by deportations and mass murders. The alleged economies of scale or size in agriculture do not imply collectivization at any particular point in time or at any particular level of mechanization. The political and social arguments, as I will point out, have little relation to Marx's original doctrines, other than the same vocabulary.

Clearly, collectivization is a political judgement. In collectivization debates fierce battles between various factions calling themselves Marxist and the enormous amount of personal abuse accompanying these arguments also testify to the tactical, rather than doctrinal, aspect of the decision to collectivize. The example of the USSR, the first government in the world calling itself socialist, was sufficiently strong, however, that the original arguments for collectivization had to be reassessed before Marxist discussions on agricultural policy could return to their original doctrinal roots.

Stalin's intellectual arguments for collectivization, weak as they might seem, had one important strength. The major force of his words and deeds was to turn collectivization of agriculture from a final goal of socialism into an immediate means to achieve socialism, that is, from an end to a means. This ideological sea change could not be easily challenged by mere argumentation but only by the experiences of life, namely by assessment of the economic performance of a system of collective agriculture. In chapter 8 I attempt such an empirical evaluation.

THE SELECTIVE REASSESSMENT PHASE

The word *selective* is used in two senses. First, such reassessment has occurred in only some countries; in the late 1980s two Marxist regimes, those of Cuba and Seychelles, were still actively collectivizing.[41] Second, in the Marxist literature available to me, the reassessment has generally focused not on analytic issues such as the five basic Marxist propositions about agriculture I listed (as in Research Note B), but rather on the disappointing performance of socialist agriculture—in short, on life, rather than theory.

Some Economic Arguments Revisited

In recent years the governments of most Marxist regimes have expressed dissatisfaction with the economic performance of socialist agriculture. In many cases such complaints have focused more on the high costs of pro-

---

[41] Although Cuba's collectivization drive had been stalled in the late 1980s because of a lack of investment funds to construct the necessary housing and social overhead (Gey 1987), the ideological fervor for collectivization was present. In a 1989 trip to Cuba, Maritza López, a student of mine, encountered strong denunciations of both Chinese and Soviet attempted changes in agriculture, whenever she raised the subject.

In Seychelles the exchange rate is highly overvalued, which has led to low food prices and bankruptcies among private farmers. The government has subsidized its own farms, while such a foreign exchange policy has permitted them to obtain private land at low costs. During my 1988 trip, Seychelles officials gave me two major reasons for this land nationalization: it would eliminate exploitation and the government could administer these farms far more effectively than the private owners.

duction than on output per se. In chapter 8 a quantitative comparison of
the performance of agriculture between a group of comparable Marxist
and non-Marxist economies shows that such complaints have an objective
basis, and that the most important difference is the lower growth of total
factor productivity in the Marxist regimes. Among Third World Marxist
nations total production has also been slower, in major part because of
the reorganization of the agricultural sector and because the reorientation
of agricultural policies were too recent to have been assimilated.

The extraction of the agricultural "surplus" has also not worked out as
originally foreseen. As I demonstrate in chapter 7 and in Research Note
E, Preobrazhensky's theoretical argument that industrialization can be
financed primarily by turning the terms of trade against the rural sector
so that savings are extracted from the farmer is only partly correct; such
an attempt can lead to some severe economic difficulties for the entire
economic system. I also provide evidence in chapter 7 that during the
1930s the Soviet Union did not transfer any appreciable surplus from agriculture to industry and that in recent years, net subsidies to agriculture
have been quite high in a number of industrialized Marxist regimes.

The coercive force underlying collectivization in the USSR or China
implies, among other things, a well-trained administrative apparatus and
considerable ruthlessness. In some Marxist regimes, especially those in
the Third World without such an administrative apparatus or the political
will to apply such draconian methods to the rural population, collectivization has often led to a drop in agricultural production and exports.
These trends, in turn, have jeopardized the entire development program, as in Madagascar (Pryor 1990c).

Other Marxoid arguments for collectivization such as the indivisibility
of planning or the acceleration of history have turned out to be irrelevant
to the agricultural management problems at hand. Random factors such
as weather bedevil any attempt to fix firm production goals, and an overly
rigid planning system often impedes the allocation of agricultural inputs
to where they are most needed in the short run. If producer prices or
income received by collectivized farmers are too low, it is also difficult to
stop the emigration of the youngest and most ambitious rural workers to
the city. And even massive infusions of resources into the agricultural
sector, which occurred in the USSR during the Brezhnev period, may
have little impact on total factor productivity if the administration of agriculture is deficient in other ways.

Some Political and Social Arguments Revisited

The political arguments are complex, and only a few of the most important difficulties can be surveyed. The key question is, of course, in what
way is it reasonable to argue that the middle and rich peasants or the

capitalist farmer pose a political threat to a socialist regime? Three answers can be given: (1) these strata of rural society are always politically ready to battle against a Marxist government, no matter how good their personal economic situation might be, and such conflict can either be economic in the form of grain strikes or political in the form of large-scale rebellions; (2) although these rural strata are not ready for such actions by themselves, they are ripe for undertaking such distabilizing economic or political activities if led by outside leaders; and (3) although these rural strata are not ready for such direct confrontation, they act as a source of "spiritual pollution" by providing a petty bourgeois alternative to the socialist consciousness that is considered so important for the consolidation of socialism.

Marx's and Engels's early views of the revolutionary capacity for independent political action by the peasantry were considerably revised by 1869 when they argued that peasants were essentially passive in a political sense, except for small-scale *jacqueries*. Thereafter their views on the matter did not seem to change greatly.[42] Although peasants have played an important political role in some revolutionary movements, these occurred in special circumstances that were different from the situation in the rural sector of the various socialist nations on the eve of their collectivizations.

For most of their history the governments of most Marxist regimes have had a monopoly on the means of coercion and violence and have been deeply entrenched. The notion of peasant political action posing a threat to these regimes, either by direct military actions or by grain strikes, does not appear very plausible.

Furthermore, as experience began to show the party leaders that communism could not be achieved in one generation but would be the task of many, the danger to their creation of a socialist consciousness in the city by permitting a petty bourgeois mentality in the rural areas became less acute. This idea has been reinforced by new knowledge about the real costs of the remolding of rural mentalities and also by the realization that the threat of spiritual pollution becomes increasingly less as the share of the workforce in agriculture declines with economic development.

Underlying the political arguments for collectivization is a deeper social analyses focusing on the notion that some sort of natural class struggle is occurring in the countryside. This approach implies, however, a high degree of social differentiation within the countryside that seems quite

---

[42] These early views are found, for instance, in Karl Marx, *Die Klassenkämpfe in Frankreich, 1848 bis 1850* [1850] (MEW, vol. vii) or Friedrich Engels, *Der deutsche Bauernkrieg* [1850] (MEW, vol. vii). The later change in views is analyzed by Goodman and Redclift (1982).

unlikely, especially after a land reform has taken place that has dispossessed the largest landowners. In chapter 3, I discuss in much more detail these important and difficult issues.

Lenin's image of the proletariat forging an alliance with particular strata of the peasantry, which was adopted by subsequent Marxists in various countries, is misleading because it structures the discussion so as to turn attention away from political, social, and economic forces influencing the reception of cooperatives in the countryside. It would be a strange alliance in which one partner voluntarily accedes to wholesale disruption of its traditional way of life, deportation, and death of many of its members.

Implications of the Reassessment

Depending how the reassessment proceeds, two rather different responses can occur. One reaction is to heed Lenin's words: "Those who are engaged in the formidable task of overcoming capitalism must be prepared to try method after method until they find the one which answers their purpose best" (Wells 1921, p. 157). Experimentation, however, can be costly and the outcomes are far from certain. Political forces can also limit the type of experiments and the manner in which they are carried out.

A second response is to begin to reassess the relationships of means and ends. More specifically, if political leaders view cooperative farms as an historical necessity or as a unit having inherent ethical values, then often a double confusion between *means* and *ends* arises: They see the agricultural cooperative as the only way to achieve higher productivity without considering other methods and policies to accomplish the same economic goal. And they view the cooperative as the only method of providing the necessary socialist education for achieving communism, rather than as the final result of the process of development of the economy and society.

Once these separate means and ends can be separated, then the argument gains strength that collectivization must occur somewhat later along the path toward socialism rather than earlier since it cannot be successful unless the farm sector is operating with capital-intensive modern methods. In some Marxist regimes, especially in Africa, this approach is not difficult to argue because collectivization never proceeded very far. Yugoslavia and Poland also adopted such a response, respectively in 1952 and 1956, in considerable measure as a result of the strong political pressures facing the government. For quite different reasons, China began to adopt such a response in 1979.

Mikhail Gorbachev's remark "I would support any approach [toward agriculture] that proves itself" (*New York Times*, 14 October 1988), shows clearly his view that collectivization *per se* may be a goal, but is not necessarily a means toward socialism. As such, it is a refutation to all of the Marxoid arguments for collectivization previously discussed. Nevertheless, Gorbachev's view of agriculture in a Marxist regime does not mean, as indicated in a number of statements made in 1990, that he wishes to reinstitute private property in land; rather, he prefers leaseholding arrangements by households and small groups instead.

The doctrinal reassessment in Third World Marxist regimes has also been quite varied. In some nations the curious situation has arisen in which the government has wanted to institute a collectivization drive while Soviet economic advisors were actively discouraging such policies.[43] Without considering the specific features of decollectivization efforts in any particular country and taking into account the intra-party debates (for which little information is available), it is difficult to determine whether the policy reversals about collectivization represent a move away from socialism, a temporary expedient occasioned by the balance of political forces, or a return to the roots of classical Marxism in which collectivization is to be carried out on a voluntary basis as farmers become convinced of the clear technical superiority of collective farms and the higher incomes they can obtain as members.

It does appear clear, however, that the economic justifications, as well as some of the underlying political reasons for collectivization that are subsumed under the label of Stalinism, are coming under increasingly critical scrutiny. Marxist ideology may still be important in specifying the goals of the economy. But most of the Marxist nations that have not voted the Communist Party out of power are now engaged in a fascinating search for more appropriate ways to achieve these economic and social ends, and agricultural collectivization during the current stage of their development may be increasingly viewed as inappropriate. Whether or not collectivization is reversible is quite another problem.

[43] Investigation of the advice given by a team of Soviet experts headed by Nicolai Lebidinskiy to the government of Grenada during its Marxist phase reveals that they studiously avoided giving any encouragement to the Grenadian government, which had made extensive collectivization plans. Pryor (1986) discusses this strange episode. In Ethiopia an eight-man Soviet mission headed by V. V. Sokolov drew up a report (Clapham 1988) urging the Ethiopian government to reduce its emphasis on collective farms, to raise real agricultural prices, and to introduce commercial farming, policies that the Ethiopian government appeared in part to adopt by 1988. The changing Soviet views about the desirability of nationalization in the Third World are analyzed by Valkenier (1983) and Jerry Hough (1986).

PART II

Land Reforms and Collectivization

Chapter 3

AGRARIAN REFORMS

SEVERAL different paths have led to socialist agriculture. The Soviet government carried out no agrarian reform; indeed, the peasant land takeovers after the revolution even pushed back the Stolypin land reforms implemented by the Tsarist government. Some nations such as Guyana, Kampuchea, Laos, or São Tomé followed the Soviet pattern and began collectivizing without attempting an agrarian reform. Others such as Cuba and South Yemen combined the two processes. But most countries carried out an agrarian reform as a preliminary step to collectivization; in some cases many years intervened between the two processes, while in other cases only a few years separated the two steps.

The results of the agrarian reforms were also quite different. In such countries as Ethiopia the reforms resulted in a significant transformation of the organization of agriculture. In such countries as Mozambique, they had little impact. And in Afghanistan (in the late 1970s and early 1980s) or Mongolia (in the late 1920s and early 1930s), these reforms created so much resistance that they led to civil war and had to be severely curtailed.

The causes underlying the differences in the measures taken and the phasing of the agrarian reforms, as well as their outcomes, are complex. In this chapter I survey the initial conditions facing each government, the agrarian reform measures taken, the policy strategies pursued, and some major administrative problems encountered in implementing the agrarian reform measures. In the next chapter I examine agricultural collectivization and its relationship with the agrarian reforms; for instance, what economic or political sense does it make to carry out a land reform and redistribute land to the farmers only to confiscate the same land after a few years to form collectives or state farms? At this point, however, I should note that carrying out a land reform before collectivization makes decollectivization easier since returning to the status quo ante collectivization does not restore the previous landed elite, who were often hated.

SOME BASIC CONCEPTS

Since the term *agrarian reform* is often used to refer to three completely independent kinds of changes, some distinctions are in order.

Institutional reforms include all basic changes in the structure of property rights and comprise three different types:

1. *Land reforms* include changes in property rights to land and measures such as restrictions on the levels and kinds of rents, changes in the usage of land by various groups, limits on the amount of land that an individual or family can hold, or modification in the system for registering land titles.

2. *Changes with regard to other production factors* comprise a large number of different measures. For *capital* these policies include changes in access to credit and financial resources, debt cancellation, or adjustments in mortgage conditions. For *labor* they include laws concerning the hiring and payment of labor, abolishment of serfdom, and safety measures. And for *technology* they include changes in the access to new farming methods, for instance, innovative credit packages to obtain new technologies. Although these changes were important in many countries, I pay relatively little attention to them in order to keep the discussion within manageable proportions.

3. *Marketing reforms* include changes in the manner in which agricultural products are purchased, such as replacement of private traders with state marketing boards and changes in the way in which agricultural inputs (equipment, fertilizer, seeds, and pesticides) are sold.

Land redistribution reforms include those measures expropriating, renting, or buying land from certain groups (foreigners, large land owners or renters, political enemies) and giving, selling, or renting such land to other groups (previous tenants, landless labors, smallholders, political favorites). These measures can be carried out without changing the basic property rights or institutional arrangements; however, in many cases these measures are often accompanied by institutional reforms. Because their political impact is so different, it is useful to distinguish three different types of such redistributions:

1. *Land redistribution to individual farmers* includes changes in the land held by individual farmers of different income or social classes with the aim of changing the distribution of land ownership or holdings. In all Marxist regimes, these distributions have led to greater equality of ownership, while in other countries this has not necessarily been the final result.[1]

---

[1] A complication is that in a number of countries such as Nicaragua, North Korea, and Poland, the land redistributed to the private farmers was not accompanied by an official title so that in the future it would be more easily collectivized than private property with official deeds. In some countries, for instance, East Germany, some of the redistributed land was given to farmers only if they farmed it themselves; they lost ownership if they moved away. (The German situation is complicated to describe because in the north the farmers obtained more property rights in the redistributed land than in the south, at least if the deeds I read in various agricultural museums were a representative sample.)

2. *Other changes in the organization of land* include programs to consolidate farms (e.g., the French *remembrement* program after World War II), villagization programs (to bring farmers scattered on individual holdings together in a village), and land resettlement programs (to move groups of farmers considerable distances to new land). In none of these programs is the total amount of land held by any individual family necessarily changed, even though the specific land held may be different.

3. *Collectivization* includes consolidating private or empty lands to form collective farms, state farms, or communes. Many Marxist analysts, such as Deere (1986), combine redistribution of land to individual farmers and collectivization when discussing agrarian reforms in order to demonstrate how the rural population gained from such changes. Such an approach begs an important question about the actual beneficiaries of collectivization. I believe it useful to separate the two kinds of land redistributions, reserving the analysis of collectivization to the next chapter.

Agricultural policy reforms include radical changes in governmental agricultural policies such as pricing, crop priorities, technology policies, or the volume and direction of government investment in agriculture. To simplify discussion these matters are deferred for analysis until chapter 7.

Several general aspects of this typology deserve note. Neither institutional reform nor land redistribution measures are limited to Marxist polities since they have also been taken by variety of capitalist, feudal, and reformist governments over the last two and a half millennia (Tuma 1965). Furthermore, although many of these measures are complementary, they can be taken separately or in stages. The initial situation in which a government finds itself often plays a crucial role in determining the sequencing of the reforms.

STRUCTURAL CHANGES: INSTITUTIONAL REFORMS AND LAND REDISTRIBUTION

Marxist regimes can have a variety of reasons for carrying out institutional reforms and land redistribution. Some motives are political: to gain support from the mass of peasantry, to create structures from which to recruit cadres for agricultural work, or to destroy the power base of the traditional rural elites and to reward their own followers. Some motives are economic: to redistribute rural income, to increase productivity by reducing the inefficiencies arising from barriers to factor flows, to increase production by reducing the impact of the disincentives arising from the previous land tenure system, to introduce new agricultural techniques more easily, or to mobilize the rural sector in a manner to generate more investment. Some motives are social: to reconstruct a new form of rural society corresponding more to the preferences of party doctrine, to modernize the rural sector, or to replace traditional culture with a new ideology. The specific measures taken to achieve such goals depend very much, of course, on the mix of motives, the state of the situation in the rural areas, and the means at hand to the governmental leaders to accomplish any of these goals.

The type of agrarian reform and the manner in which it is implemented (and the use of violence) play a crucial role in the later collectivization process. As argued in the next chapter, collectivization without land reform generally requires more violence or coercion.

Although the complexities of the different land reforms mean that universals about institutional changes in rural areas of Marxist regimes are difficult to discover, one generalization can be drawn immediately: Despite the notoriety of the Bolshevik government for nationalizing all agricultural land shortly after it seized power in 1917, such a policy is not a typical land reform measure of most Marxist regimes for three reasons:

First, only a third of the various Marxist regimes have actually nationalized the land, and these twelve constitute a very heterogeneous group of nations: Albania, Congo, Ethiopia, Guinea Bissau, Kampuchea, Laos, Mongolia, Mozambique, Somalia, Viet Nam, and the USSR. South Yemen nationalized many of the water resources (wells, irrigation facilities), but not the land; in this arid land such a measure gave the government much more effective control over the land than outright nationalization would have brought. Second, land nationalization has not made much subsequent difference either in the manner the government has organized agriculture or in the other agricultural policies the government has pursued. Indeed, nationalization seems merely an indicator of the occurrence of a hyperleftist phase at some point along the revolutionary path.[2] Third, some non-Marxist regimes have also followed a similar policy of land nationalization; in sub-Saharan Africa, for instance, a majority of nations have declared all or most of their land to be state or national lands (Riddell and Dickerman 1986).

In any case, nationalization of land certainly does not solve any important economic problem. As President Luís Cabral of Guinea-Bissau rue-

---

[2] Some governments, for instance, the Congo or Guinea Bissau, nationalized the land simply as a symbolic gesture to reaffirm their "revolutionary commitment," a measure having the effect primarily of frightening away or raising the perceived risks of potential suppliers of capital to the country. Other governments took that step to simplify the process of expropriating land, to tap the alleged revolutionary spirit of the peasantry and gain their support, or to prevent private individuals from either selling or renting land before the government worked out its land policies. Nationalization generally did not prove as effective as other, less dramatic, measures for accomplishing these various aims.

fully observed (Cabral 1979), it is still necessary to have land tenure laws and regulations, as well as procedures for enforcing them. Another example comes from Somali, where economists have noted that land nationalization has also not solved serious problems such as overgrazing (Somali Institute 1975, p. 32).

Table 3.1 presents an overview of the initial situation facing each government and the most important land reform measures. With such information, I can begin to link political and economic payoffs with their costs.[3] We would expect that tenancy reduction and/or land redistribution would be more likely in situations where tenancy is great and where land is very unequally distributed. Indeed, the more equal the initial distribution of land, the more difficult it is to carry out either a land reform or collectivization. The reduction of landlessness would seem an even more important motivation for land reform—a common-sense hypothesis that is not confirmed by the data.

Of the twenty-two nations in the table carrying out land redistributions or reforms, inequalities of land holdings were high or medium-high in fourteen of them, while landlessness appeared high or medium-high in only nine of them. Of the former group, nine countries carried out land reform in the context of postwar reconstruction (Albania, Bulgaria, Czechoslovakia, East Germany, Hungary, North Korea, Poland, Romania, and Yugoslavia), but they appear little different from the twelve other nations in the table with regard to the land inequality or landlessness. Of the six regimes not carrying out land redistribution but taking measures to begin extensive collectivization soon after gaining power (in Grenada, Guyana, Kampuchea, Laos, São Tomé, and Seychelles), the inequalities of landholding were high or medium-high in four of them and landlessness was high or medium-high in three of them. Finally, in the five countries that did not carry either land redistribution or collectivization, land inequalities were high or medium-high in only

[3] As noted above, a land redistribution has a considerable influence on the ease of decollectivization, and for this reason it is useful to consider South Viet Nam, which was absorbed by North Viet Nam and collectivized. In the 1950s both land inequality and landlessness in South Viet Nam were high (FAO, 1966, 1:217). The non-Marxist government, however, carried out land reforms in 1956–60 and also 1970–73; these consisted primarily of expropriation with compensation and land redistribution and were accompanied with very little violence. The 1970–73 reform, which was especially designed to return land to the tiller, also limited ownership to twenty hectares and had a profound impact on the land distribution (Beresford 1989, p. 99), which meant that the distribution of farm land by the time of the takeover was relatively equal with almost no tenancy. These reforms, however, were not accompanied by government directed changes in marketing or debt cancellation. The Viet Cong also carried out land reforms in the areas that it controlled in South Viet Nam.

TABLE 3.1

Agrarian Reform: Initial Situation and Major Institutional Changes

	Prereform Conditions		Land Reforms and Redistribution			
	Inequality of holdings	Landlessness	Major Programs	Violence	Share Redistributed to Farmers	Marketing Changes
Africa						
Angola	High	Low	None	—	Many peasant takeovers	Extensive natl.
Bénin	Low	Low	None	—	—	Some natl.
Cape Verde	High	High	1975	Little	Roughly 3%	Some natl.
Congo	Low	Low	None	—	—	Extensive natl.
Ethiopia	Medium	Medium/ high	1975	Some	Roughly 36%	Extensive natl.
Guinea-Bissau	Medium/ low	Low	1975, 1979	Little	None	Extensive natl.
Madagascar	Medium	Low	None	—	Some peasant takeovers	Extensive natl.
Mozambique	High	Low	1975, 1979	Little	Roughly 3%; also peasant takeovers	Extensive natl.
São Tomé	High	High	None	—	—	Extensive natl.
Seychelles	High	High	None	—	—	Much natl.
Somalia	Low	Low	1975	Little	None	Extensive natl.
Zimbabwe	High	Medium/ low	None	—	About 7%; also some peasant takeovers	Little change

Americas						
Cuba	High	High	1959, 1963	Little	9%	Extensive natl.
Grenada	Medium	Medium	None	—	—	Some natl.
Guyana	High	High	None	—	—	Extensive natl.
Nicaragua	High	High	1979–86	Little	7%	Extensive natl.
Asia						
Afghanistan	Medium	Medium	1978, 1981	Much	<17%	Little change
China	High	Medium	1945–53	Much	About 43%	Extensive natl.
Kampuchea	High	Low	None	—	—	Abolished markets
Korea, North	Medium	High	1945–46	Little	52%	Extensive natl.
Laos	Low	Low	None	—	—	Extensive natl.
Mongolia	Medium	Low	1921–30	Unknown	Unknown	Some state, coop agencies created.
Viet Nam North, South	High/ medium	Medium	1953–56	Much	About 38%	Extensive natl.
Yemen, South	No info.	High	1970	Some	Almost none	Extensive natl.
Europe						
Albania	High	Medium	1946–48	Some	39%	Extensive natl.
Bulgaria	Medium	Low	1946	Little	3%	Extensive natl.

TABLE 3.1 (cont.)

| | Preform Conditions | | Land Reforms and Redistribution | | | |
	Inequality of holdings	Landlessness	Major Programs	Violence	Share Redistributed to Farmers	Marketing Changes
Czechoslovakia	High	Medium/high	1945–48	Little	16%	Extensive natl.
Germany, East	High	High	1945	Some	26%	Extensive natl.
Hungary	High	High	1945	Little	28%	Extensive natl.
Poland	High	Medium	1944, 1945	Little	29%	Extensive natl.
Romania	High	Low/medium	1945–49	Little	8%	Extensive natl.
USSR	Medium/high	Low	1917–19	Some	Peasant takeovers; roughly 29%	Extensive natl.; requisitions, 1918–21
Yugoslavia	High	Low	1945	Little	11%	Extensive natl.

Source: See Statistical Note B.

Notes: Land inequality: Gini coefficient less than 0.35, low; 0.35 to 0.50, medium; over 0.50, high. Where land distribution data are not available, qualitative estimates, taking into account the share of estates, are made. Landless farmers include renters and farm workers. Landlessness: under 20 percent, low; 20 to 50 percent, medium; 50 percent or over, high.

The rating for violence (in contrast to coercion) is a subjective evaluation: the dashed lines indicate that no land reform was carried out; "little" includes none or only sporadic violence accompanying a land reform; "some" is a step upward; and "much" refers to "rural class warfare" initiated either by the government or by massive resistance of private land owners.

Natl. = nationalization.

two of them and none of them had a high or medium-high degree of landlessness.

Such results suggest that inequalities of land holdings were more salient in the land redistribution or collectivization measures than landlessness. Although this outcome might be explained by a sophisticated sociopolitical theory of peasant radicalism, I suspect that factors specific to each of the nations involved would provide more satisfactory answers. For instance, Laos was a country with a low degree of inequality of landholding and landlessness, and its collectivization attempt (a failure discussed in the next chapter) was more likely attributable to the ideological fervor of the leadership rather than to any objective conditions.

Although land inequality problems appeared considerably less pressing in those countries not carrying out either land redistribution or collectivization, it should be noted that these measures occurred in three countries where land inequality was low or medium-low (Guinea-Bissau, Laos, and Somalia) and in ten countries where landlessness was low or medium-low (Bulgaria, Guinea-Bissau, Kampuchea, Laos, Mongolia, Mozambique, Romania, Somalia, USSR, and Yugoslavia).

Of course, some Marxist governments wanting to carry out either land redistribution or collectivization, were constrained. Some lacked the administrative apparatus to administer such programs, although, as I point out later in a case study of Ethiopia, this factor is often overrated. Another important constraint on land redistribution was the risk of falling production, at least in the short run. For instance, where agricultural products comprised an important share of exports, any fall in marketed production could bring about serious balance of payments difficulties and imperil the economic plans of the new regimes, an argument made with considerable force for Nicaragua by Colburn (1986). Of the six nations without important agrarian reforms or collectivization (at least 30 percent of the land collectivized), half were dependent on agricultural exports (Bénin, Madagascar, and Grenada). Finally, quite particular problems occurred in some countries. For instance, in Zimbabwe, the government was constrained by the Lancaster House Agreement, which gave the country independence, from expropriating land without compensation or implementing certain other measures that would have a similar effect.

The policy dilemmas arising from these risks and the tradeoffs that the government must make between political and economic gains and losses of land redistribution were particularly evident in Nicaragua, a country highly dependent upon agricultural exports. The founder of the Sandinistas, Carlos Fonseca, vowed that "in Nicaragua no *compesino* will be without land" (Collins 1986, p. 242). Using this slogan, the Sandinistas redistributed land in the liberated areas before the fall of Somoza. After taking over the government, however, they attempted to maintain the expropriated estates as single units so that agricultural exports could be used as a financing source for an ambitious development program. They also tried to encourage production of middle-income farmers, promising them they could "keep their land forever" (Booth 1987). Moreover, as noted in chapter 2, the government was also reluctant to give land to peasants since they did not want either to strengthen "private enterprise" or a "backward" segment of the population. Of course, the landless peasants felt betrayed and, over the next seven years, increased their agitation for land. Ironically they mobilized support through the mass organizations established by the Sandinista government for quite other purposes. The government felt politically compelled to reduce the land held by any middle- or high-income farmer in order to obtain land to redistribute (Deere and others 1985; Bulmer-Thomas 1987), a measure reducing political pressure but increasing the balance of payments difficulties. Finally, starting in 1986 when the civil war became severe, the government began to turn over land from the state farms and cooperatives to landless peasants in order to strengthen its political control of the countryside, and agricultural exports fell even more.[4]

Land redistributions to private farmers were, with the exception of Ethiopia, relatively unimportant in Africa or the Americas. In contrast, such measures played an important role in most of the Asian and European Marxist regimes, where landlessness was high and where collectivization was postponed. Several casual factors appeared important. In most of the African nations, landlessness was not a problem. Most of the former colonial countries in Africa and the Americas also featured large plantations, which the governments preferred to nationalize immediately either in order to have a ready source of revenues or to maintain production where the former colonial farmers had simply abandoned their land, for instance, in the former Portuguese colonies of Angola, Mozambique, and São Tomé. These nations had the example of the Soviet Union where, in the immediate aftermath of the Bolshevik revolution, the peasants simply seized estates and divided the land among themselves, de-

---

[4] According to MacEwan (1981), the same problems appeared in Cuba, but to a much lesser degree. To a certain extent, the Cuban government was able to release some of this pressure simply by turning over land title to the tenants who farmed the land, an option that was less available in Nicaragua where tenancy was not so important. Moreover, the Cubans did not need to fight a civil war while they were collectivizing the land. The Cubans also had much stronger armed forces to maintain domestic order and prevent political demonstrations for land; according to Spalding (1987, p. 15), the Sandinistas had only a thousand troops at the time of victory. Finally, with regard to the plantations, the workers on these large farms were apparently less interested in smallholder farming than similar workers in Nicaragua, perhaps because they were more recently recruited than in Cuba. As I point out in chapter 10, the relative indifference to smallhold farming also seemed the case in Guyana.

spite the fact that the government had nationalized the land in order to obtain the alleged economies of scale in operating the estates as a single economic unit.[5] Such a case represents a "land reform from below" and has nothing to do with the economic or political system per se.

As I note in greater detail in chapter 10, in 1990 most countries in East Europe were in the process of returning some collectivized land to its previous owners. A serious problem arose from this process, because it required a decision about which land redistribution should be recognized. For instance, before the June 1990 election in Bulgaria certain political parties advocated the abrogation of the 1945 reform.[6] In early 1991, however, it appeared that in most East European nations, the antifeudal agrarian reform would be recognized, but not the antikulak (or communist) reform. These problems take considerable time to sort out. Contrary to expectations, little relation appears between the brutality of the methods of carrying out these agrarian reforms and the reforms that will probably be accepted to serve as the basis of returning the land in the 1990s. In East Germany the choice between the 1945 and 1949 agrarian reforms appeared to be heading toward the courts for final resolution.

Marketing reforms were much more common than other kinds of agrarian reforms and occurred in all but five Marxist regimes (Afghanistan, Bénin, Grenada, Mongolia during the 1920s, and Zimbabwe). They usually took the form of the nationalization of the companies either buying agricultural products for export or selling agricultural inputs to the farmers. In almost all cases, small-scale farmers' markets selling foodstuffs to the population persisted, a lesson drawn from the experience of the Soviet Union which, during its collectivization drive, tried to eliminate such markets and then had to let them function again. An exception was the Pol Pot government of Kampuchea, which eliminated markets and money completely between 1975 and 1978. Other countries clamped down on farmers' markets at a later time, a phenomenon discussed in chapter 6.

These marketing reforms were especially important because the subsequent malfunctioning of rural markets adversely influenced production in two ways: In many countries they failed to supply agricultural inputs such as fertilizers and pesticides in a timely fashion. In many countries, especially in the Third World, they also failed to supply a sufficient vari-

[5] Lenin and other Soviet leaders were unhappy with this turn of events and accepted them only on the basis of political expediency rather than Marxist principles.

[6] Before the June 1990 election in Bulgaria I pointed out to an official of one of these parties, the Nikola Petkov Peasant Union, that since more people gained land from this 1945 reform than lost land, they would lose votes with such a program (a prediction that appeared to come true). I was assured that there were principles more important than votes involved in this issue.

ety and quantity of consumer goods to provide incentives for farmers to market their production (chapter 8). The remainder of the discussion in this chapter focuses exclusively on other aspects of agrarian reform.

PARTICULAR ASPECTS OF LAND REFORMS

Table 3.2 presents a summary of several major features of land reforms in the nations carrying out such measures before beginning a major drive to collectivize.

Reduction of rents paid by farmers can come about by direct government policies to reduce rents (e.g., in Nicaragua or Viet Nam); or by policies resulting in a redistribution of land to the tenants, which effectively eliminates tenancy (e.g., in Ethiopia or China). At first glance rent reduction appears a straightforward measure that can be easily implemented without ill effects on production (assuming that the additional income to farmers will not result in slackening of their agricultural efforts). This is, of course, because the rent represents a pure surplus and a transfer from the tenant to the landowner. Unfortunately, the rental contract can be more complicated and contain counterpayments, so that in return for a certain amount of rent for the land, the landlord supplies inputs such as seeds, water, fertilizer, and equipment, or services such as credit, transportation of crop or supplies, or protection against the depredations of tax authorities or other agents of the central government. Thus the landlords might reduce their counterpayments if the rent is reduced. Since contractual arrangements for these counterpayments are intricate and vary from location to location within a country, it is difficult to cover all possible complications in legislation. For these reasons tenants might actually resist implementation of the rent reduction laws.

In only two countries, Cape Verde and Mongolia, did the government attempt to *change the type of rent*, following Marx's bias against sharecropping and labor rents (chapter 2). In Cape Verde the government wanted to substitute a fixed rent system for a sharecropping system and consolidate holdings. These goals seem peculiar in light of the extreme risks in agriculture: the country is quite arid (and experienced a drought from 1967 until the late 1980s) and the rainfall pattern varies considerably from one strip of land to the next. The previous system allowed a farmer to spread these climatic risks over different pieces of land and share the risks with the landholder. The monetary gains to the tenant of paying less rent might be more than offset by the costs to him of losing this possibility to spread his production risks. Reforms in Mongolia in the early 1920s were aimed at eliminating the labor service that farmers owed landholders.

Setting *limits to land ownership* is an agrarian reform that has also been carried out by capitalist regimes; the same problems arise wherever such limits are applied in any type of regime. In many cases, such limits are differentiated by the types of land (e.g., irrigated and nonirrigated land or land in different locations) or by social characteristics of the landowner (for instance, marital status, number of children, or membership in particular organizations such as the army). The limits depend, in part, upon the population density and the degree to which the government wants to equalize land holdings. These restrictions often have little real impact, since landlords can divide their property among their heirs or hide their ownership where formal land registers are not maintained.[7]

Some Marxist regimes purchased private land exceeding the designated limits, often in cash. An example is Cape Verde, where, as a result, chronic budgetary problems have constrained the agrarian reform process. Of course, those governments purchasing such land with public bonds (e.g., Cuba) or without any compensation at all (e.g., Afghanistan) did not face such constraints, especially when they could repudiate any bond payments at a later date. Cape Verde, however, was discouraged from following such a course because much of this purchased land was owned by its citizens living overseas, whose remittances helped to reduce the serious balance of payments gap—the government did not want to jeopardize this important source of funds.

Debt cancelation is another agrarian reform measure that appears simple but can have a serious impact on production, as noted later in the case study of Afghanistan. These problems were magnified by the inability of most governments to substitute alternative sources of credit. An exception to this generalization was Nicaragua, which flooded the countryside with government credit, an expensive program leading to many defaults, considerable waste of funds, and a rapid abandonment of the program. In many East European nations after World War II mortgage and other debts were effectively canceled by the high rates of inflation.

Interestingly, few land reforms have featured *land consolidation*; indeed the opposite was true for Viet Nam's land reform, where peasants divided the land and each family obtained "some near land, far land, good land, bad land." An alternative procedure would allot each farmer a consolidated plot of varying size reflecting different degrees of fertility;

---

[7] In some cases the limits have little meaning either because they are set much higher than the size of the usual farm or because they cannot be enforced. For instance, in Mozambique (Davidson 1988b), the government put a ten-hectare limit on all farms in some central and northern regions, provided no hired wage labor was used. If wage labor was employed, the owners would, instead, receive a fifty-year lease. Almost all family farms were smaller than ten hectares; moreover, the government did not have the administrative apparatus to enforce these regulations. Indeed, no other commentator on the Mozambique land reforms ever mentioned this provision, which suggests that it was a dead letter.

Americas					
Cuba	Eliminated tenancy	No	67	No	Most large estates maintained intact, which was a significant share of the land.
Nicaragua	Yes	No	35–70	Some	Land limits progressively reduced and more land redistributed to tenants during middle and late 1980s while greatly reducing tenancy. Important program to give land titles to squatters.
Asia					
Afghanistan	No	No	6–10	Some	Failed and mostly rescinded later. Mortgage debt canceled; other debt remained. Some resettlements during land redistribution.
China	Yes	No	Yes	Some	Considerable reduction of tenancy through expropriation. Experience in land reform in independence campaign. Features of reform differed depending upon the year and the place, e.g., debt reduction at some times.
Korea, North	Eliminated tenancy	No	5	Yes	First rent reduction, then land redistribution; Soviet occupation aided reform design and administration.
Mongolia	Elimination of feudal dues	No	Yes	Some	A series of unrelated measures. In late 1920s limits placed on land and livestock, but continually lowered and often total confiscation.
Viet Nam, North	Yes	No	No	Most	Land reform in North began in some areas in 1945. More land redistributed

TABLE 3.2 (*cont.*)

	Rents		Land owner-ship Limits (hectares)	Debt Cancellation	Notes
	Reductions	Change in Form			
					before than after 1953 when the two-step land reform began officially—first step was rent reduction, second step, land redistribution, which eliminated most tenancy. Considerable land reform in South, primarily land redistribution, in early 1970s.
Yemen, South	Eliminated most tenancy		c. 8–16	Some	Some land reform during independence fight. Collectivization combined with land reform.
Europe					
Albania	Eliminated most tenancy through land redistribution		5	Some	Two land reforms (1945, 1946) and an expropriation of herds in 1948. Land redistribution was the key measure in both 1945 and 1946 reforms.
Bulgaria	No	No	20	Some	Simple reform and quickly implemented. Few large landowners.
Czechoslovakia	Yes	No	50	No	Three different land reforms; first only to expropriate German farmers; second and third, more traditional.
Germany, East	No	No	100	No	Land reform was first step in denazification. As the antikulak campaign stepped up in 1949, the acceptable limit of land holdings was lowered.
Hungary	No	No	115	No	Land reform carried out quickly. Anti-kulak campaign started in 1949. Later land consolidation program very impor-tant.

Country					
Poland	No	No	50–100	No	Land reform carried out simultaneously with vast resettlement program in the newly gained Western provinces, in part with peasants from the lost Eastern provinces. Government explicitly promised no collectivization.
Romania	Expropriated most rented land		10–50	No	Land reform legislation almost yearly; legal land limits increasingly disregarded as expropriation of kulaks began.
USSR					During 1917–18 peasants seized estate and crown land and placed it under the supervision of village community; in some places land previously purchased by peasants was also seized by the villages. As a result, tenancy and farm debts arising from mortgages were eliminated. Attempts by the government to preserve some of the larger estates intact for state farms were generally unsuccessful.
Yugoslavia	Eliminated tenancy		25–35	Some	Land reform carried out quickly. In 1953 the limit lowered to 10–15 ha and more expropriation; by late 1980s limit raised to 50 ha in some republics.

Source: The information in this table is drawn from a wide number of sources for the individual nations.

Notes: "Eliminated tenancy" means large scale forms of tenancy; informal or small-scale renting of land may have continued. Although debt elimination may not have been a formal part of the land reform program, it may still have occurred informally with the expropriation of landlords. Moreover, in some countries such as China, interest payments were reduced, which amounts to a reduction in debt. In many of the East European nations after World War II, inflation and currency reform effectively eliminated all debts.

however, this plan would have undoubtedly given rise to endless wrangling. In Ethiopia, land fragmentation remained roughly the same in areas where few peasant holdings were redistributed, and actually increased where redistribution was important.

For countries such as the Congo, Cuba, Ethiopia, and Mozambique (where peasants often live on scattered homesteads, rather than in clusters), *villagization* had the ostensible goal of permitting the government to provide certain amenities and services (e.g., education, health, electricity, clean water). It also allowed greater political control of the rural population and more oversight of the meeting of production quotas. In Ethiopia and Mozambique the government viewed such measures as a necessary first step toward collectivization.[8] In these two countries the promised amenities and services in the new villages usually did not materialize. In many cases these moves were forced on the peasants by the government, and the villages were sited far from the fields or water supplies. By the early 1980s in Mozambique, this program included roughly 15 percent of the rural population; subsequently, however, many villages witnessed a "disaggregation" as peasants drifted away. In Ethiopia by the end of the 1980s, more than a third of the rural population was living in new villages; the program had some unexpected outcomes, including the depletion of scarce forest resources as houses were rebuilt. In the Congo, villagization occurred in the context of forming four hundred village centers to distribute agricultural inputs, services, and technological knowledge, rather than a measure to force farmers to relocate.

Cuba pursued villagization in the late 1970s and early 1980s, encouraging peasants to join collective farms by first providing them with better houses and utilities. The cost to the government was sufficiently great so as to put a brake on the collectivization drive (Gey 1987). In the mid-1980s Romania also began to bulldoze small villages and move peasants to much larger villages; this so-called *systematization* program, which was to have razed about half Romania's villages by the year 2000, gave rise to an international outcry (Hunya 1989). After the fall of Ceaucescu, the new government quickly repudiated this program.

Settlement programs have not generally been part of agrarian reforms. Sometimes such programs have been used to remove politically suspect populations from one area to another—in Ethiopia this was carried out under the guise of famine relief—or as part of other efforts to develop new farming areas and reduce overpopulation in others. Khrushchev's New Lands Campaign in the mid-1950s in the USSR was an example of

---

[8] For Ethiopia, Cohen and Isaksson (1987b) analyze the program for a particular province. Cohen (1986) and Giorgis (1989) also have some insightful comments on governmental motives. For Mozambique, Hanlon (1984, pp. 128–29) has some extremely useful remarks.

a successful settlement program; Madagascar's much more limited resettlement attempts provide an example of programs with much less success (Pryor 1990c). Such countries as Ethiopia, Somalia, and Zimbabwe tied resettlement programs to the creation of state and collective farms in the new areas.

SOME IMPORTANT STRATEGIC DECISIONS

In any agrarian reform the government must make certain strategic decisions. Some of these concern the intensity of the rural class struggle, that is, the targets of reform, the use of the landlords and rich peasants after the reforms, and the degree of violence to be employed. Other, more mundane, strategic decisions must also be made, for instance, the speed of the reform and the redistributional objects.

Targets of Reform

Traditional Marxist-Leninist theory distinguishes five classes: landlord, rich peasant, middle peasant, poor peasant, and landless worker. Marxist leaders generally have agreed that land should be taken from the first two groups (which are considered politically unreliable) and distributed to the politically more reliable last two groups.

Sometimes the definition of rural classes is approached by examining the amount of labor hired-in or hired-out (or the amount of farm equipment rented-in or rented-out). But this raises many difficulties since for a given peasant family it often depends upon the stage in the life cycle of the family and other factors not intrinsic to the problem at hand.[9] The existence of nonfarm employment further muddies the relation between land and income.

In most cases it appears easiest to look at the problem in terms of land rental. Landlords are defined as those receiving a significant portion of their income from land rents. At any given time, however, many farmers may rent out land, either because they are old or sick, they do not yet have children to help them farm their land, or because they spend most of their time in other economic activities such as handicraft or wage work. None of these farmers may be rich in any sense of the word.

Classification of rich, middle, and poor peasants simply by the amount of land they own leads to some knotty problems. In many countries rural class differentiation was not very great, as in rural Russia.[10] Moreover, in

[9] In the Soviet context, the debates about such problems are conveniently analyzed by Cox (1986).

[10] In the Soviet Union, the seeming lack of a marked class differentiation has an important implication: "The revolution in the countryside during 1917 and 1918 seemed, on the sur-

most countries peasant wealth and land ownership depends a great deal on the composition of the family and the individual's stage in the life cycle: a single man may be in line to receive land, but at the present time is landless; a farmer may hold considerable land, but he may also have an extended family living with him so that, on a per capita basis, each has only a small amount of land. A farmer may have certain rights in a piece of land (e.g., right of usage), but not others (e.g., rights to irrigation water). In these cases land ownership per se may be almost meaningless and, moreover, not closely tied to income.

Although in some countries land ownership is the chief criteria of wealth and the basis of class differentiation in the countryside, the situation is not so clear in other countries. It is not my purpose to explore the intricacies of comparative rural sociology, but it must be added that the concept of rural class structure itself raises many difficulties in particular situations. Not the least of these is that differentiation of wealth may be considerably less important to an individual peasant than kinship ties or ties of mutual dependency to other peasants in the community or even ethnicity, if different from those controlling the government. Indeed, Marx's comparison of French peasants to "potatoes in a sack" implies a homogeneity of lifestyle and outlook transcending any differences in wealth.[11] Furthermore, insofar as peasants in many nations strive to accumulate wealth and become a *kulak*, they may view wealth differentiation more as an incentive toward greater work and production than as a situation to be improved through forced land redistribution, which could, in fact, reduce their own wealth in the future.

For my purpose it is important to note only that the determination of "undeserving" landholders and of "deserving" poor peasants and landless to receive land raises numerous questions of interpretation for any would-be land redistributor. The dilemma is compounded when landlordism is not prevalent and the distribution of land is relatively equal: in such cases the larger the group stigmatized as rich peasants, the greater the political problems in redistributing land and the more violence must be employed to achieve this policy end (Moise 1978). On the other hand, the easier it is for landlords to flee to another country (e.g.,

---

face, to confirm the experience of 1905 that any tendencies toward peasant differentiation had not developed to the point where the political actions and interests of different groups of peasants had diverged significantly." It is not surprising, therefore, that shortly before the collectivization campaign, "those government pronouncements, and the many commentaries on them in the Soviet press of that period, were based on class categorizations of peasant households for which they had no evidence or theoretical justifications at all" (Cox 1986, pp. 20, 216).

[11] This image is found in *Der achtzehnte Brumaire des Louis Bonaparte* [1852] (MEW, vol. VIII, chap. 7).

the case of the North Korean land reform in 1946), the less violence is necessary.

Landlords and Rich Peasants after the Redistribution

Taking land away from landlords and rich peasants, although it robs them of their economic power base, is one matter; crushing them as a social group is quite different. The latter step can occur at the time of the land reform, as in China, at the time of collectivization, as in the Soviet Union, or not at all, as in North Korea. Certainly the landlords and rich peasants have technical skills that could be of considerable use in raising agricultural production, especially if these farmers reconstituted their wealth through greater productivity rather than inheritance.

Of the nations listed in table 3.1, considerable violence (in contrast to coercion, which is not lethal) occurred during the agrarian reforms in Afghanistan, China, and South Yemen. The circumstances were quite different in each. I discuss the Afghan case in considerable detail later. In China, during the Civil War, many landlords and rich peasants were killed, especially because there was a chance that the Guomindang might regroup and restore them to their land.[12] After seizure of power in the entire country, the pattern of violence continued to some extent despite certain attempts by the government to reduce it (Moise 1983). Government and party cadres staged public trials of rich peasants and landlords, encouraged former tenants and employees to "speak bitterness," and meted out beatings and death according to the alleged crimes and perceived attitudes of the culprits. Those landlords who survived, however, ended up with about the same amount of land as the middle peasants, although they were burdened with many social disadvantages.[13] In South Yemen, violence occurred as part of the civil war and the seizure of power since the landlords constituted an opposition force to the Marxist party.

Another problem arises with the treatment of near and distant family members of landlords and rich peasants. In China until the 1980s, direct descendants and widows were stigmatized with such class labels, even

---

[12] Some estimates of these deaths are found in footnote 1 of chapter I.

[13] Moise (1983) presents data on land holdings before and after the land reforms. Vietnam provides a contrast to China in that apparently fewer landlords were killed, but former landlords ended up with much less land than middle peasants. In both countries, however, those classified as rich peasants generally emerged from the land reforms with more land than the middle peasants. In North Korea, the former rich peasants and landlords were offered land holdings roughly equal to the average size holding, but most often in a different village.

though at the time of the agrarian reform they may have been poor themselves (Chan et al. 1984, pp. 21, 165).

It is difficult to generalize about views toward the rural class struggle since they seem to vary, not only from country to country, but also within the ruling elite in particular countries. In Nicaragua, for instance, the minister of the interior, Tomás Borge-Martínez, once noted that "Class struggle can be seen either from the point of view of hate or from the point of view of love. State coercion is an act of love" (Powelson and Stock 1987, p. 239). Despite the ferocity of this statement from an important party leader, violence against landlords and rich peasants was relatively slight, in part because the government was dependent upon the private farmers for producing export crops (Colburn 1986). The government even used bourgeois specialists to run the new state farms.

Speed of Implementation

The faster the implementation of agrarian reforms, the greater the possibility of inequities; hence many of the political benefits of the program may be obviated by the creation of a large group of discontented peasants. The slower the implementation, the more opportunity landlords and rich peasants have to sell their fields to other peasants and to avoid both expropriation and political opprobrium. In well-organized agrarian reform programs, as in China and Viet Nam, land reforms in particular villages were carried out relatively quickly, but cadres then revisited the villages at least once to correct inequities. In other nations, for instance, Afghanistan, reassessment did not occur.

In some countries the speed of implementation was influenced by a deliberate phasing of different aspects of land reform. In China and Viet Nam, for instance, a rent reduction campaign was completed before a redistribution program began. Indeed, in the former nation interest reduction, considerable debt cancellation, and tax reform were also included in the first stage (Shue 1980). By way of contrast, in most of the East and Central European nations, the first phase consisted of expropriation of land from Germans, from German collaborators, and from large landowners (the antifeudal phase), while the second phase was expropriation of land from rich peasants (the anti-kulak phase). Although such sequencing took longer, it did allow the government to focus its administrative energies upon one major task at a time.

Redistribution Objects

For agricultural production, necessary inputs include land, tools, equipment, water, fertilizer, seeds, pesticides, and transportation. In an agrarian reform these inputs are often difficult to distribute, either because of lumpiness (an ox for plowing cannot be easily divided into fractions) or because of contract complexities. For instance, if the owner of a truck has a number of implicit agreements with farmers about when and how the transportation services can be used, and the truck is expropriated by a state agency, then this agency must make a series of contracts with the previous customers for services that may be difficult to specify in sufficient detail to provide certainty to the farmers. Even if only land is the object of redistribution, serious contractual difficulties arise where land tenure and rental arrangements for land are tied to counterpayments by the landlord in the form of needed inputs. In these cases land reform is likely to lead to considerable disruption since such counterpayments cannot easily be taken into account. In Cape Verde land reform, for instance, it proved difficult for some farmers receiving land in the redistribution programs to obtain the water and transportation services necessary for successful farming.

Agrarian Reforms and Administrative Problems

Here I outline a number of administrative factors important in the reform process. For illustration I present short case studies of Ethiopia and Afghanistan, which represent respectively successful and unsuccessful land reform programs when judged by administrative (but not economic) criteria.

General Administrative Considerations

Most of the Marxist parties taking power have had relatively little experience in government administration, especially in carrying out complicated agrarian reform measures. The exceptions to this generalization are China, Guinea-Bissau, Mozambique, and Viet Nam, where the seizure of power involved considerable fighting and the holding of territory for many years before the fighting ended. Although prolonged fighting also occurred in Angola, Cuba, Nicaragua, Yugoslavia, and Zimbabwe, for example, these Marxist parties had relatively little experience in rural administration because the nature of the fighting did not permit land to be held very long by their troops, or because the Marxist insurgents did not want to complicate their problems and compromise their support by administering territory, or because their leading cadre were urban intellectuals who did not focus much attention on problems of rural administration.

The agrarian reforms in North Korea and in all East European nations except Albania and Yugoslavia were guided in part by Soviet officials at-tached to the occupation forces who had experience in such matters. In these countries the new governments were also able to draw upon a civil service with experience in rural administration. In some of the Marxist nations in the Third World such as Angola, Guinea-Bissau, Mozambique, and São Tomé, administrative difficulties in implementing reform arose because these governments were unable to persuade former administrators to retain their jobs. Similar difficulties occurred in countries such as Afghanistan where the different Marxist governments purged experienced government officials either from the previous non-Marxist government or from the wing of the rival Marxist party.

The administration of agrarian reform also raises some strategic problems. If, on the one hand, the reform is implemented from above, or the top down, then local conditions may not be taken into account fully and production is adversely affected. Moreover, if the party is weak in the countryside and if the reform cadres are primarily from the urban areas, these cadres may make decisions in too schematic a fashion, so that both equity and production are adversely affected (Bernstein 1970, 1979). If, on the other hand, the agrarian reform is implemented from below, then the goals of the reform may be subverted because of a divergence between local and national goals (e.g., the peasant land seizures in USSR after the Bolshevik revolution, or attachment to particular people or land by local cadre). The obvious compromise solution is reform carried out by the farmers and local officials, following guidelines and under the direction of cadre from the party and/or government. The correct balance, however, is difficult to achieve.

Simplicity of Agrarian Reform

Clearly land redistribution is administratively simplest when tenants farming particular pieces of land can receive ownership of the land they have tilled, as in North Korea. Redistribution is administratively more complicated when farmers are assigned ownership of confiscated land that they have not previously tilled, as in Cape Verde. Further difficulties arise when this redistribution accompanies a resettlement program, as in Eastern Europe after World War II, or when functioning estates are divided into individual farms and distributed among hired farm workers, as in East Germany and Poland immediately after World War II (Spulber 1957; Wädekin 1982).

Administrative simplicity can vary, depending on the targets of expropriation. Title transfers are easiest to carry out when the landlords are foreign, a situation arising in East Europe and Korea after World War II, or if they are citizens of the former colonial power, a situation occurring after decolonialization in many nations in Africa, or if they are absentee with relatively few functions in the countryside, other than collecting their rent. A variant of the last condition occurs where land ownership is concentrated in either corporations or institutions such as the church.

Administrative simplicity is also related to the structure of the rural economy; for instance, to the degree of interdependence between farmers, or between farmers and landlords, to the degree to which the government attempts to equalize land holdings, to the religion of the peasants and the views of religion toward private property, and to the resistance provided by former rural elites. In redistributing land it is simplest to focus on the extremely large land holders and redistribute their land to the landless, rather than equalizing land holdings among all those who already possess land. And it is, of course, also easier to simply redistribute land than to engage in rural class warfare.

An Administratively Successful Agrarian Reform: Ethiopia

A number of Marxist regimes have been able to carry out successful agrarian reforms; the Chinese case, for instance, has received considerable attention (Bernstein 1970; Shue 1980; Moise 1983). I choose, however, to focus in this case study on Ethiopian reform because it was both highly radical and also carried out quickly without much preparation and with few reliable and trained cadres. Its administrative success was in large part due to its administrative simplicity and to the favorable rural environment.

To contemporary outside observers, the chances for success did not appear great because Ethiopia had one of the most complicated land tenure systems in the world. One province alone was said to have 111 different tenure arrangements and such arrangements varied enormously from province to province. In the north, communal tenure arrangements predominated, where villages or kin groups controlled access to the land. In the south, private ownership and land tenancy were much more prevalent, with about one-third of the landlords absentee and with most of an ethnic group different from the tenants. Grafted onto the land tenure system was a system of fiefs allowing the possessor to extract certain taxes in return for providing certain rural services such as justice. Emperor Haile Selassie had attempted agrarian reform in his early years in power, but it had little effect. Agrarian reform was high on the agenda of many groups opposing him.

The overthrow of the emperor in 1974 occurred quickly, and by the end of the year most of the high-level and many of the middle-level officials of the former regime had been removed, so that local governments began to disintegrate. In March 1975, the political leaders of the country (the Derg) nationalized all farmland, and in late April 1975, they an-

nounced a sweeping set of agrarian reforms which, according to Halliday
and Molyneux (1981), went against all the advice proffered by Chinese,
Yugoslav, and Soviet embassy officials.[14]

Selecting the cadre to implement the reform was difficult because the
Derg had no party apparatus on which to rely. It did not trust the former
governmental officials for such a task, and it preferred to use the armed
forces for other purposes, such as asserting political control. Therefore,
it enlisted sixty thousand urban dwellers (primarily secondary school and
university students) as land reform agents, gave them a short indoctrination course, and sent them into the countryside. About 80 percent of
them were either Amharan or Tigrean, a much different ethnic mix from
the rural population (Zerom 1984, p. 138). It is difficult to imagine a more
unpromising group of land reform cadres.

The major task of the students was to establish Peasant Associations
(PAs), new political/economic units that were supposed to embrace about
two hundred and fifty farms. On the political side, the PAs were to provide certain services, such as justice and security, and to assume the role
of the faltering local governments (Wubneh and Abate 1988). On the economic side, the PAs were to redistribute land titles, help set up service
cooperatives for purchasing farm inputs, buying farm outputs, and, later,
collecting taxes. In many respects the PAs resembled the Russian *mir*
and maintained the social fabric necessary for production.

Implementing land reform through the PAs meant that these changes
in land tenure involved peasant participation and support, a key aspect
in the success of the changes. None of the literature on these reforms
that I have seen has explained exactly why the peasants trusted the student reformers and participated in the PAs. I suspect, however, that
when highly centralized governments fall, the political reverberations
reach even the farthest villages quickly. Since few alternative sources of
authority arose in the rural areas to oppose the new government, and the
students had the visible support of other units of local government and
the armed services, the students were able to gain and retain the trust of
the peasants.

Moreover, the bonds of mutual dependency between landlords and
peasants did not appear strong—most landlords had few functions in the
countryside other than extracting rent and few landlords provided important counterservices in return for the rent. Thus, redistribution of land
titles did not greatly affect the production process, and the service cooperatives set up by the PAs represented an attempt, in part, to replace
the functions previously supplied by some landlords.

[14] For this account I draw freely upon studies by Clapham (1988), Dejene (1987), Rahmato (1984), Göricke (1979), Mengisteab (1984), Ottaway and Ottaway (1978), and Zerom
(1984).

Implementation of the reforms was further aided by the fact that about one third of the farmers were net debtors (Zerom 1984) who benefited from debt cancellation, although complications arose when the creditors were not landlords but other peasants. Although the literature is not very specific about the new sources of credit made available for agricultural production, it seems likely that the credit function was served by the PAs and the state agencies supplying agricultural inputs.

Land redistributions instituted by the PAs with the aid of the students were generally very simple. In the south tenants kept use of the land they were farming or had farmed in the past. Former ownership claims were declared null and void, and relatively few large holdings were broken up. In the north, peasants also kept usage of the land they were farming, and other family claims on the land were nullified. The PAs did not seem to break up many large holdings for redistribution. My own calculations, from somewhat uncertain aggregate data, show a decrease in the gini coefficient in inequality of land holdings (irrespective of ownership) from 0.47 to 0.44, that is, about 3 percent of the land farmed by one peasant was given to another.[15] The PAs made no attempt to consolidate holdings.

In southern Ethiopia where tenancy was high, the land redistribution was carried out in a relatively effective fashion and generally within the year (Göricke 1979; Wubneh and Abate 1988). Although former landlords sometimes resisted, revolts were quelled either by peasants armed by the students or by the army (Mengisteab 1984). In the north, where land was held communally, very different problems arose; but within two years the countryside was also covered by Peasant Associations.

The greatest difficulties occurred because many students were politically to the left of the Derg and had a different political agenda from that of the government's, wanting to make more dramatic changes than they were assigned to implement. With Mao's little red book in their pockets, some attempted to form cooperatives, conduct class warfare, or agitate against the government, which was trying to avoid social strife (Dejune 1987; Ottaway and Ottaway 1978). Within a year, the government sent most of the students back to the cities.

In the years following the agrarian reforms, many of the conceptual and functional weaknesses of the PAs became more evident. The claims

[15] My data for 1974–75 and 1977–78 come from Teka and Nichola (1983). Rahmato's (1984) data before and after the reforms for a number of areas show roughly the same phenomenon. Cohen (1984) cites FAO and World Bank studies, which I have not been able to see, that yield the same results. Ottaway and Ottaway (1978, p. 71) note that the ban on hired labor in the agrarian reforms forced Moslem agricultural workers off the land in the north, but they weren't allowed to receive land in nearby PAs. Thus some members of the landless were not served by the reforms.

of each member of the PA on particular land meant that fewer had reason to emigrate to the cities. This, in turn, meant that the size of average holdings decreased as the population rose (Rahmato 1984). Periodic land redistributions by the PA to the increased membership gave rise to problems. According to one survey by Dejene (1987), more than three-eighths of the peasants polled did not feel secure in their long-term use of the land, and as a result they were reluctant to invest in the land. The jurisdictional boundaries of the PAs were often so hastily drawn that they did not form an effective decision-making unit. The PAs also found it difficult to relieve the shortage of draught power and agricultural inputs—the latter due to inefficiencies of the governmental distribution apparatus—or to encourage production with low prices offered by the government.

Inappropriate government policies also undermined the PAs in the next decade. Furthermore, the cooperative character of the management of the PAs gave way in part over the next decade and a half to a much more centralized management and control exercised by both the party and the government (Clapham 1988, p. 159).

The reforms and subsequent policies of the government can be judged as a failure in an economic sense since agricultural production increased more slowly than the Ethiopian population and, in addition, agricultural exports also did not markedly increase. In an administrative sense, however, the agrarian reforms were a considerable success since the pattern of land ownership was changed so permanently that the old land tenure system can never be reconstituted.

An Administratively Unsuccessful Agrarian Reform: Afghanistan

The Afghanistan agrarian reforms were much less radical than in Ethiopia because they did not attempt to abolish private property in land or to form new administrative units. They were, however, an administrative failure since they were an important contributing factor to the development of armed resistance and civil war lasting almost a decade.

The organization of agriculture in Afghanistan raised many economic problems, and in the two decades preceding the revolution, the government attempted twice to implement agrarian reforms, but with little success.[16] In contrast to Ethiopia, the land tenure situation was complicated

---

[16] Dupree (1980, p. 152) notes that in December 1959 (after Qandahar anti-land-tax riots), the government spread rumors that land reform would shortly follow and that no one could own more than thirty jerib (six ha). "Many large landholders immediately began to sell land to their landless peasants, and land reform by rumor was accomplished." This judgment appears too sanguine; most observers agree that the land reforms of Mohammed Daoud Khan had little effect because they were not implemented seriously.

by many interdependencies between tenants and landlords, who lived in the villages. More specifically, in return for their rent payments landlords provided tenants with rights to irrigation water and credit. Moreover, for centuries in Afghanistan the central government had little direct impact on the villagers; and local notables, who were targets of the land reform, long served as intermediaries between the villagers and the government in order to protect the former from the depredations of the latter. According to Tabibi (1981, p. 64): "For the ruling stratum in the village, as well as the dependent people, the central government was and is a foreign power." For land reform to be successful, the social and political structures of the villages had to be carefully taken into account.

The Afghanistan revolution, which occurred in April 1978, was essentially an army-implemented coup d'état which installed the Marxist government even more quickly than in Ethiopia. After three months in power the government of Nur Mohammed Taraki canceled a large share of farm debts (Decree No. 6), and four months later the government promulgated agrarian reform (Decree No. 8). Implementation of land reform began in January 1979 and, although scheduled to take a year, was officially declared completed in June 1979.

The agrarian reforms had both economic and social goals. According to Hafizollah Amin (who quickly succeeded Taraki to leadership of the party and government), they were "to uproot feudalism in order to move directly from a feudal society to a society where the exploitation of man by his fellow man will be unknown" (Roy 1986, p. 84). Two underlying concepts were that ownership of "abstract land" (i.e., simply a plot of land) was the key element and that the socioeconomic matrix in which that land was situated was unimportant.

Most of the specific features of the reform were unexceptionable and many of the ideas were to be found in the platform of the Khalq (one branch of the Marxist party) of almost a decade before and in the failed land reform of the last prime minister, Mohammed Daoud Khan. The government canceled all mortgage debt that had been held more than five years, placed limits on the amount of land that a family could hold (the amount varying by quality) and purchased the remaining land for redistribution, set aside a small amount of land for cooperatives and state farms, the nucleus of the future socialized agricultural sector, and even established seven MTSs. Those working on the land as renters or laborers had first priority in receiving title.

As in Ethiopia, the government had problems in recruiting cadre to implement agrarian reforms. Afghanistan had about 14,200 villages (Dupree 1978, p. 144), which outnumbered party members, most of whom had remained in the city anyway. The government, moreover, purged many experienced state agricultural officials who might have been able

to administer the land reform because they were tainted by serving under the Daoud regime. The ranks of educated agricultural cadre were
further depleted by savage infighting between the Khalq and Parcham
wings of the Marxist party that led to murder, imprisonment, or banish-
ment of many trained party agricultural cadre. Finally, the government
experienced severe financial problems so that, although it promised compensation for expropriated land, no such payments seem to have materialized; officials later bragged that the entire reform cost less than $10
million (U.S.).

As a result, the government decided to implement the reforms with
relatively fewer cadre than in Ethiopia. These cadre, moreover, spent
only a brief time in each village and, therefore, did not attempt to organize the village in permanent self-governing structures to aid in the implementation of the reform or to sustain the reform after they left. Since
land cadastres designating ownership rights were not available, the cadre
often redistributed the land using highly arbitrary methods.

Almost immediately problems arose because, in both concept and implementation, social and economic interdependencies were neglected.
For instance, peasants who had previously relied on their landlords for
yearly loans for working capital (seeds and fertilizer) found themselves
without credit from this source because the landlords, fearing further expropriation, were unwilling to make additional loans. Governmental attempts to provide substitute credit were highly inadequate and poorly
administered. Water rights, a key element in Afghan agriculture, could
not be obtained by tillers of the redistributed land, not to mention tools,
cattle, and other necessities for production. The reform also disrupted
supplies of agricultural inputs that the new government agencies could
not adequately replace. Finally, although the government took over the
maintenance of irrigation canals and certain other social overhead from
local governments and private parties, it appeared unable to carry out
these functions or to repair the considerable amount of damage that subsequently occurred. A drop in production was inevitable.

The peasants also had many social and political reasons to fear accepting the new land titles. In areas where most farms were smaller than the
maximum allowable limits, landless peasants were often moved to different areas to receive land, in many cases dominated by a different ethnic
group. With the notables of their own villages disaffected and with the
government having little impact on the ordinary affairs of village life,
peasants accepting land had no protection from local retribution after the
reform teams had left, a problem made more severe when groups hostile
to the economic measures of the government began armed resistance and
to cut off the noses of those accepting the new land titles. Given the
strong tradition of land ownership recognized by Islam, expropriation

was anathema to many leading religious figures and peasants also risked religious opprobrium by farming redistributed land.[17]

After the Soviet invasion and their murder of Hafizollah Amin in December 1979, Babrak Karmal, the succeeding prime minister and party leader, began to soften or rescind some aspects of the agrarian reform. In 1981, for instance, he raised the maximum limit of allowable (high quality) land from six to ten hectares a family. In the same year he also began to allow exceptions, for instance, to landlords who increased their marketed output to the state, and to show favoritism in land distribution to families with sons voluntarily serving in the army or police, even though they might already own land (Anwar 1988, p. 215). His government also began to tie water rights to the redistributed land. In the mid-1980s he claimed to have pressed forward with the land reform (Nyrop 1986, p. 188), but no solid evidence is at hand. His successor, Najibullah, raised the maximum limit to eighteen hectares (Economist Intelligence Unite 1987a) and promised returning refugees that they could retrieve all expropriated land.

In a speech in 1984 Karmal noted that the land reform had "lofty and sacred" aims but had been undertaken without "careful and profound study or collection of information" (Nyrop 1986, p. 188). He might also have mentioned that the structure of the rural society and economy were less propitious for land reform than in other countries such as Ethiopia. The result of land reform, combined with other ill-conceived governmental measures, were socially, politically and economically catastrophic, with the country plunged into civil war, in large measure ignited by resistance to land reforms.

SUMMARY AND CONCLUSIONS

Mao (SWMP, vol. IV, p. 374) once noted: "The . . . revolution is great, but the road after the revolution will be longer, the work greater and more arduous." This statement should be memorized by every would-be land reformer, because after the revolution the government must still solve "the agrarian question."

The process of agrarian reform has been influenced by both subjective and objective factors. On the subjective side the degree of ideological fervor of the political leadership and its understanding of Marxism has

---

[17] Many Afghans were well aware of what had happened to the private agricultural sector in the Soviet Union since they had ethnic confreres on the Soviet side of the borders. The propaganda waged by both sides during the land reform was intense, e.g., many mullahs pointed out to the faithful that the Afghan word *kummunist* includes a Pashtu root *kum*, which means "God," and a Dari root *nist*, which means "without" or "denying."

undoubtedly played an important role in the reforms, but too little is known about such matters to be able to generalize.

This chapter has, instead, focused on a series of objective factors influencing the content, speed, and success of land reform. The structure of rural economy and society in most countries varied considerably from country to country. Rather than import land reform recipes from abroad, political leaders handled agrarian reforms in quite different ways, depending in considerable measure on the severity and type of agricultural problems. From the comparative analysis two major conclusions can be drawn: the inequalities of land holdings appeared a more salient factor for land redistribution than landlessness, and, in most countries, nationalization of the agricultural marketing agencies was an important measure of the agrarian reforms. For other measures such as rent reduction or debt cancellation, the Marxist regimes acted in quite different ways. The phasing and speed of agrarian reforms also differed considerably. In some countries agrarian reforms were implemented in careful phases or were a well-planned preliminary step toward collectivization. In others, governmental improvisation was much more apparent.

The administrative success or failure of the reforms has depended in large part upon the complexity of rural society and economy, the specific reform measures selected for implementation, and the manner in which the reforms were executed. In some cases, as illustrated by Ethiopia, the government was able to implement some radical reforms quickly and with untrained personnel because the reforms were relatively simple and tailored to the realities of the land tenure situation. In other cases, as in Afghanistan, the land tenure situation was sufficiently complex that it is doubtful if any but the most carefully prepared and simple agrarian reform measures could have succeeded.

Chapter 4

THE ESTABLISHMENT OF STATE AND COLLECTIVE FARMS

A MARXIST REGIME considering the collectivization of agriculture faces some important policy dilemmas. Should it first institute land reform and collectivize only later when farms are more modern and larger and the farm population is smaller? Or, should it collectivize without land reform in order to avoid any attachments to the land by beneficiaries of the land reform? Instead, should it simply carry out a thorough land reform and then stop without collectivization? If it decides to collectivize should it create state or collective farms? How should it administer the collectivization drive and with what degree of violence or coercion? How fast and how far should it pursue collectivization?

Marxist regimes have answered these questions in quite different ways. In part their answers have depended on such objective factors as the land tenure and ownership patterns when they took power, as well as the means at their disposal to carry out collectivization. Also their answers have depended on subjective factors, such as the farmers' attachment to the land, or the leadership's assessment of the possible results of collectivization on agricultural production, or difficulties in balancing the governmental budget, or exports and imports. Finally, their answers have also depended upon the administrative means available to them, such as the aid or coercion received from other Marxist regimes, especially those with armies stationed in their nation.

This chapter explores the most important conditions before collectivization, the alternative means for collectivizing, and some of the results of the different administrative means. Such a task requires an assessment of the extent of collectivization, the path of collectivization, and the trade-offs among different administrative means.

THE EXTENT AND FORM OF SOCIALIST AGRICULTURE

Since the path to collectivization depends upon the choice of organizational form that a socialist agricultural sector will eventually take, it is useful first to consider the end results of the process. From such data the relationships between the form and the organization of agriculture before collectivization can be most easily seen.

Extent of Collectivization

Table 4.1 presents data on the share of land in the private, cooperative, and state sectors for each Marxist regime in the late 1980s. This period was, for most countries, the beginning of the decline of collectivization; and only two countries, Cuba and Seychelles, continued an active collectivization policy in those years.

These data must, however, be viewed cautiously. In some countries a considerable share of the collective farms were nominal, so that the relative importance of the "real" collective sector is smaller. Another upward bias in the data on collective farms occurs because some countries include certain types of precooperatives in the collective farm sector. Although the data in the table are not completely comparable for these and other reasons, they nevertheless allow us to make some proximate judgments about the extent and form of collectivization.

Very roughly, the relative size of the socialist sector was lowest in Africa, with the sector comprising less than 10 percent of all farm land in all countries except São Tomé, Seychelles, and possibly Angola; in São Tomé and Seychelles, state farms played a particularly important role. The socialist sector was highest in Europe (Poland and Yugoslavia were exceptions) and in all countries except the Soviet Union and Bulgaria, collective farms were the predominant form. In Asia, collectivization was considerably advanced in all countries except Afghanistan and Laos (in Kampuchea the situation was uncertain) and was manifested primarily by collective farms. In North and South America the situation was mixed; the socialist sector was large in Cuba and Guyana and consisted mainly of state farms and it was relatively small in Grenada and Nicaragua. In Grenada, the size of the public sector was mainly due to the actions taken by the previous non-Marxist government of Eric Geary to punish his political enemies among the plantation owners. In Nicaragua, the recorded collectivization represented primarily the expropriation of the estates of Somoza and his closest associates immediately following the Sandinista seizure of power.

In many cases a relatively small socialist sector can be attributed to the cumulative effect of four general causes: (1) the relative unimportance of large plantations, especially those owned by foreigners, that have served in other nations as tempting targets for nationalization; (2) a relatively low level of economic development and a government either lacking the ability to carry out such a program (e.g., in a "soft state") or the political legitimacy to withstand the stresses of the collectivization process; (3) a relatively short period since the assumption of power by a Marxist government, except where the expropriation of previous landholders was a major part of the process of gaining political power; and (4) a reversal of

TABLE 4.1

The Relative Importance of Private and Socialist Agriculture

	Land Reform	Date	Form of Agricultural Organization Percent of Land in:			Definition of Land Concept and Other Notes
			Private Farms	Collective Farms	State Farms	
Africa						
Angola	N	n.a.	n.a.	n.a.	n.a.	
Bénin	N	1981–82	97.2%	1.8%	1.0%	TAL
Cape Verde	Y	1988	96.5	0.4	3.1	Only irrigated land
Congo	N	1973	92.5	0.1	7.4	Cultivated area
Ethiopia	Y	1985–86	92.4	3.9	3.7	Area under crop
Guinea Bissau	Y	1980	95.9	0.3	3.8	Area under crop; estimate very rough
Madagascar	N	1984–85	98.8	0.7	0.5	Cultivated area
Mozambique	Y	1983	94.2	1.3	4.4	Cultivated area
São Tomé	N	1987	3.8	0.0	96.2	TAL
Seychelles	N	1988	44.0	6.0	50.0	Only flat agricultural land; estimate very rough
Somalia	Y	1984	88.6	5.0	6.4	Cultivated area
Zimbabwe	N	1984	98.2	0.3	1.5	TAL

TABLE 4.1 (cont.)

| | | | Form of Agricultural Organization | | | |
| | | | Percent of Land in: | | | Definition of Land Concept and Other Notes |
	Land Reform	Date	Private Farms	Collective Farms	State Farms	
Americas						
Cuba	YS	1987	14.5	12.5	73.0	TAL
Grenada	N	1981	87.0	1.0	12.0	TAL
Nicaragua	N	1986	75.5	11.1	13.4	Total farm land
Guyana	N	1977–88	23.1	—76.9—		Cultivated area
Asia						
Afghanistan	Y	1981–82	94.0	4.1	1.9	Cultivated area
China	Y	1980	—95.6—		4.5	TAL; private farmland is minuscule
Kampuchea	N	1977	0.0	—100.0—		Total farm land
Korea, North	Y	1963	0.0	92.0	8.0	Cultivated area
Laos	N	1986	46.5	53.0	0.5	Cultivated area
Mongolia	Y	1986	0.0	88.6	11.4	TAL
Viet Nam	Y	1975	n.a.	85.2	n.a.	Cultivated area; only North Viet Nam
	Y	1986	18.2	79.8	2.0	Cultivated area: North and South Viet Nam
Yemen, South	YS	1986	29.0	62.4	8.6	Cultivated area

Europe

	Land reform	Year				Measure
Albania	Y	1983	0.5	78.4	21.1	Cultivated land
Bulgaria	Y	1987	10.0	0.0	90.0	TAL
Czechoslovakia	Y	1987	6.1	63.5	30.4	TAL
Germany, East	Y	1987	9.7	82.5	7.7	TAL
Hungary	Y	1987	13.7	71.4	14.9	TAL
Poland	Y	1987	78.0	3.6	18.4	TAL
Romania	Y	1987	15.6	54.7	29.8	TAL
USSR	YI	1987	1.8	30.4	67.8	TAL
Yugoslavia	Y	1981	82.3	0.9	16.8	Total farm holdings

Source: See Statistical Note C.

Notes: For land reform: N = none; Y = yes; YS = yes, but simultaneous with an important collectivization drive; YI = yes, but informal (that is, "from below" and without governmental authorization). n.a. = not available; TAL = total agricultural land.

For many countries the data on the relative importance of state and collective farms are uncertain and indicate only general orders of magnitude. Private plots of cooperative and state farmers are included as part of cooperative for state farms. State farms include "institutional farms," that is, farms managed by factories (*podkhozy*) and social agencies. The farms of communes are classified as cooperatives since they have been managed according to the same principle. I have tried to eliminate "precooperatives," although this was not completely possible in all cases.

a previous collectivization. In Poland and Yugoslavia the initial collectivization never reached a very high level and the two governments postponed a socialist transformation of agriculture until mechanization and
farm productivity rose, the private farm population declined, and greater
political consolidation was achieved. In the late 1980s and 1990s, more
nations have joined this category.

In some cases the relatively small size of the socialist sector was the
result of factors specific to the individual nations. For example, in the
cases of Cape Verde and Zimbabwe, as noted in chapter 3, external constraints proved decisive: in Cape Verde, the constraint was the necessity
to maintain the stream of remittances from immigrants who owned much
of the land, and, in Zimbabwe, it was the provisions of the Lancaster
House agreement establishing the government.

The Form of Socialist Agriculture and Initial Conditions

The form of collectivization depends considerably upon the organization
of agriculture before collectivization occurs. My attempts to link the form
of collectivization to other variables such as population density or level of
economic development were unsuccessful.

The nations with significant socialist agricultural sectors can be roughly
divided into three groups, namely those dominated by state farms, collective farms, and communes. For convenience it is useful to label the
paths to socialist agriculture of the first and second groups as the São
Tomé and the North Korean paths, named after their purest manifestations.[1] Within each of these two groups some variations can be found,
but such intragroup differences are not relevant here. The third group
consists only of China during the 1960s and 1970s, Kampuchea between
1975 and 1978, and Mongolia after 1956; these three cases are so different
that no relevant generalizations can be drawn.

The countries following the São Tomé path ended up primarily with a
system of state farms; they include Cuba, Grenada, Guyana, São Tomé,
and Seychelles. Before the Marxist seizure of power in these countries,
land ownership was usually highly concentrated in large estates operated
as single farm units, quite often owned by foreigners. In Grenada, land
was not so highly concentrated, but plans for collectivization (never realized) focused solely on the estate sector. Governments in nations with

[1] The two paths correspond, of course, directly with Lenin's two routes to large capitalist
farming: a German (Junker) path where feudal latifundia are transformed into agrobusi-
nesses; and an American path where large farms are formed by the gradual consolidation of
smaller farms. Several nations also made false starts and then changed the strategy of collectivization. For instance, Cuba first tried to turn the sugar estates into cooperatives and
then, after four years, converted them into state farms; in Nicaragua, the reverse occurred.

large land holdings rented out to tenants, such as South Yemen and some East European nations, formed collective, not state, farms.

Countries following the North Korean path ended up primarily with a system of collective farms; they include most of the European and Asian Marxist regimes. In these countries plantation estates were not frequent, although estates where land was rented to smallholders may have been important. The major exceptions to this generalization are East Germany and Poland, where plantations existed but were broken up during the land reform in the months following the end of World War II. Land density also appeared to play a causal role in some cases and it is noteworthy that of the three countries whose first collectivization drives failed, two (Afghanistan and Mongolia) had low population densities and the remaining country (Laos) had a land density in the middle range.[2]

Problems of classifying countries into these three groups occur in those Marxist regimes experiencing civil war (Afghanistan, Angola, Mozambique, Ethiopia, and Nicaragua). In Angola, for instance, where the government quickly took over most of the large foreign-owned estates, conflicting information is available about what share of the land formally designated as state or collective farms actually functioned in the specified manner. For Afghanistan and Nicaragua, it is also difficult to know what share of the agricultural units designated as collective and state farms functioned, because these farms were inviting targets for rebel groups.

The initial path toward collectivization was not always followed. Some time after the initial drives the Soviet Union and, to a lesser extent, Albania, Mongolia, and Romania began converting or combining collective farms (or, in the case of Mongolia, communes) into state farms in order to strengthen them financially and technologically by putting more investment resources at their disposal.[3] In the early 1970s, Bulgaria also combined its collective and state farms into very large units (agro-industrial complexes), which in most respects appeared to be like state farms and are classified as such. In 1989 the government began to break these farms down into their constituent units again. By way of contrast, Nica-

[2] The first Mongolian collectivization drive, 1929–32, is particularly curious since the most dramatic changes in ownership included expropriation of the nobility and the clergy. The government, however, tried to break up these holdings to form small collective farms, rather than large state farms.

[3] Kim Il-Song made authoritative announcements in the mid-1970s that this was to be the route taken in North Korea, and in the mid-1980s his son Kim Jong-Il reiterated the call. Unfortunately, no recent data are available by which to determine if this policy was put in practice.

By 1980 most of the few collectivized farms still remaining in Yugoslavia in the 1960s had gradually changed into state farms, although the self-management system used in state enterprises meant that in many respects, the state farms were managed little differently from the cooperatives.

ragua (which was not greatly collectivized) and South Yemen converted a few state farms into collective farms, and Seychelles announced its intention of taking the same step. For the most part (Nicaragua may be an exception), the state farms designated for conversion had been quite unprofitable, and such a transformation shifted responsibility for these losses to the (new) collective farm members. For the same reason some Soviet reformers in the late 1980s advocated either the same policy or distribution of the lands of unprofitable state farms to private farmers. The Seychelles government had a different rationale for conversion, arguing that collective farms allow much more participation by the workers than state farms. It did not plan, however, actually to take any concrete steps in this direction until the state farms became profitable.

The policy of China fluctuated most widely since that nation has moved from collective farms to communes to decollectivization. In the late 1980s, Kampuchea, Laos, and Viet Nam also had significant decollectivization drives, and, in the mid-1980s, the Sandinista government in Nicaragua began to privatize some of the collective farms, reacting to strong political pressure by farmer organizations. Of course, such changes may increase in importance not only in Nicaragua but also in Czechoslovakia, East Germany, and Hungary, which also voted out Marxist governments.

Implications of the Choice

Although the choice between collective and state farms was generally a function of initial conditions, certain implications of this decision must be noted. Most important, state farms have generally required more governmental subsidies than collective farms, in which the effects of poor performance are more heavily borne by the members in the form of low incomes. The economic losses on state farms, on the other hand, must be covered either by funds from the state budget or by loans from the state bank that will never be repaid because the workers are only paid employees. I should add that subsidies to state farms are almost inevitable in cases where the exchange rate is overvalued and export crops are an important part of their production. This is also true when the government has decided for political reasons to maintain low food prices in urban areas, when the government has decided to maintain state farm wages at a level close to wages in industry, a decision sometimes forced by farm worker unions in some of the Third World Marxist nations, or when the governmental administrative apparatus is unable to control farm costs and is unwilling to let such state farms go bankrupt (a "soft budget," to use the felicitous coinage of János Kornai).

Three important exceptions to this generalization about state farms' requiring higher subsidies must, however, be noted. First, in recent years the governments of some nations, such as the Soviet Union, mandated that collective farms must pay a certain minimum wage to their members at regular intervals throughout the year; if overall financial losses occurred as a result of such payments, the government or state bank compensated the farms in some manner. Second, in the Soviet Union and other nations where collective farms could borrow freely from state banks and where they learned that nothing happens to them individually if they default, such implicit subsidies to collective farms could run very high. Last, in cases where collective farms were voluntary, initial subsidies to establish and maintain them until they were running smoothly could also be considerable. For instance, the collective farm I visited in Seychelles had been in existence for several years, but state subsidies still covered more than 80 percent of its expenses.

It could be argued that Marxist governments have also been able to exercise more control over the activities of state farms than collective farms. This does not take into account that the legal form of the cooperative as an organization run by its members was often violated, so that the farm was really a pseudocooperative and resembled a state farm. Such interventions occurred in many countries in the early years of collectivization when the farmers were resentful from losing their land. Even in later years, however, such violation of the cooperative principle also occurred in most industrialized Marxist regimes, either by direct interference of state or party officials or by governmental crop quotas drastically limiting the area of choice by leaders of the cooperative. Nevertheless, members of the cooperative sometimes had a certain sphere of individual choice, such as how many labor days to perform in the work of the collective over the required minimum.[4] Sometimes collective farms generally also had more leeway than state farms in disposing of farm surpluses after the quotas mandated by the government were reached. Officials in these Marxist regimes also claimed that it was more difficult to introduce new technological methods on the collective than on state farms. This may, however, have been more a matter of the availability of credit to finance such changes, rather than the allegedly greater ability to order state farm managers to use a particular technology.

THE PHASING OF COLLECTIVIZATION

The phasing of collectivization involves a strategy about the timing of agrarian reforms and collectivization, the order in which various steps are

[4] The East European nations, North Korea, China, and some other well-established Marxist regimes have certain quotas of work days that must be met for privileges such as the right to a private plot to be obtained. In some of the African Marxist regimes such as Mozambique, farmers were reluctant to join collectives with such regulations. As a result, collective fields were often short-handed during harvest when members of the collective were working on their own fields.

taken, and the speed of the process. Table 4.2 summarizes the relevant information.

For the countries following the São Tomé path where plantations predominate (in Marxist terms, where there was a concentration and centralization of ownership), the strategy of collectivization was not problematic. In most cases the governments nationalized the estates quickly and easily.[5] For instance, several months after independence São Tomé nationalized the small number of Portuguese plantations in that island nation, most of whose owners had fled; in a few days the government gained control of 95 percent of the farmland. In Angola the process was similar, although it extended over a longer period, involved only about 50 percent of the land, and led to conversion of some of the Portuguese settler farms, which were often small, into cooperatives.

The driving forces behind such nationalizations can also be readily specified. Where the plantations were foreign owned, they were felt to be a remnant of interference in the affairs of the nation and were thus an obvious target for nationalist fervor. Where domestically held, the owners were generally strongly opposed to the Marxist government. Moreover, such plantations promised to be a ready source of large profits for the governments to finance their ambitious investment programs, an aim seldom realized, as I have previously suggested. Such nationalizations also did not require any previous land reform nor any action taken with regard to the multitude of smallholders. Indeed, the reverse was generally true and, as discussed in greater detail in chapter 7, in some African nations such as the Congo, Ethiopia, and Mozambique, the creation of a small number of state farms producing goods primarily for export led to an almost complete governmental neglect of the remainder of the agricultural sector. Such nationalizations also did not require the creation of a centrally planned administration of the economy, especially since most of these estates were producing for export markets.

[5] Nationalizing the estates was not completely without difficulties. For instance, in Guyana, Pierce (1984) describes how the nationalization discussions started off quite smoothly. Problems emerged, however, in trying to retain the technical aid provided by the foreign owners, as well as other services they had previously supplied to the government. Other difficulties arose concerning the sugar estate workers, who belonged to a labor union affiliated with the opposing political party and who had a profit sharing arrangement with the company. Shortly before nationalization, the government had imposed an export tax on sugar, which reduced the profits distributed to the plantation workers. After the foreign company was nationalized, the profits were thus taxed away so there were few to share. This was the cause of a long and bitter strike in 1977, which was the precursor of many future strikes of union workers against the new state enterprises.

One country in which nationalization of the estates was particularly difficult was Madagascar, where, according to Pryor (1990c, chap. 12), about one-fourth to one-half of the estate land was "lost" in the process. Although some of the land was apparently taken over by peasants and subdivided, an unknown amount was appropriated by politicians.

TABLE 4.2
Approaches toward Collectivization

	Speed and Years of Major Drive	Strategy of Collectivization
Africa		
Angola	No major drive; process reversing	Nationalization of abandoned plantation and collectivization of abandoned settler farms in 1976–77. Since then, many of these abandoned or taken over by private farmers. Some formal decollectivization in mid and late 1980s.
Bénin	No major drive	Few state farms except for a few foreign estates nationalized. No known collectivization strategy beyond slow expansion of collective fields.
Cape Verde	No major drive	After considerable nationalization of foreign farms in 1975, most of these lands continued to be rented to smallholders. One parastatal (EMPA) bought farmland in Paraguay to create the first multinational state farm. Cooperatives voluntary.
Congo	No major drive	No known strategy and little collectivization except for foreign estates and construction of new state farms on allegedly empty land. Some privatization of state farms in late 1980s and early 1990s.
Ethiopia	No major drive	Initial nationalization of estates and conversion of some to state farms. Financial incentives and, after 1984, villagization used to encourage a slow collectivization. Process reversed in 1990–91.
Guinea-Bissau	No major drive	Some plantations converted to state farms, but relatively few such farms. Cooperatives have been voluntary; some financed by state but after 1984 relatively more attention paid to profitable cooperatives.
Madagascar	No major drive; reversals in early and mid-1980s.	Nationalization of French estates primarily between 1975–78 and conversion to cooperatives and state farms. Most cooperatives disbanded in early 1980s. Mid-1980s attempts to lure back former owners were unsuccessful; management contracts given to foreign firms to operate some farms.
Mozambique	No major drive; reversals in early and mid-1980s.	Conversion of most settler farms and plantations into cooperatives and state farms. Villagization drive because seen crucial to collectivization. Intended to extend successful state farms, combined with voluntary formation of cooperatives. Many cooperatives are only nominal and disinte-

TABLE 4.2 (cont.)

	Speed and Years of Major Drive	Strategy of Collectivization
		grating; from 1984–86, privatization of much state farms land.
São Tomé	Rapid, 1975; slight reversal in late 1980s	Portuguese plantations quickly nationalized, consolidated, and converted into state farms; no cooperatives formed. Small pieces leased to private individuals in late 1980s; and management contracts to foreign firms to operate some farms.
Seychelles	Medium, 1977–87	Purchase of existing estates at low prices, in part due to overvalued exchange rate and resulting low food prices. Voluntary cooperatives but encouraged by financial incentives. Process slowed in late 1980s.
Somalia	No major drive	Cooperatives voluntary and little encouragement to them by mid 1980s. Little nationalization of individual properties and no known plans for major increase in either state or cooperative farm sector.
Zimbabwe	No major drive	European farms purchased and redistributed, for the most part to private farmers but also to cooperatives. Government support low for cooperatives, and process slowed in late 1980s.
Americas		
Cuba	Rapid, 1959–63	Large state farm sector created from existing plantations. Collectivization of private farmers slow until 1977; new drive but also slowed down by mid-1980s.
Grenada	Minor drive planned; not realized	Planned drive to transform some estates (comprising 14 percent of farmland) in 1984 into state farms; no plans to collectivize small farmers. Process reversed after 1983.
Guyana	Rapid, 1975–76	Nationalization of large estates and conversion to state farms. Cooperatives voluntary and creation is slow and neglected by government. Process reversed in early 1990s.
Nicaragua	No major drive and process reversing in 1990	Land holdings of Somoza and allies immediately converted into state farm and some cooperatives; later land expropriation and either turnover to peasants or to cooperatives; by mid-1980s began to convert state farms to cooperatives and private farms and to decollectivize.
Asia		
Afghanistan	No major drive	No known strategy to collectivize; although some

TABLE 4.2 (*cont.*)

	Speed and Years of Major Drive	Strategy of Collectivization
		cooperatives and state farms established 1978–81, government denies plans to collectivize.
China	Rapid, 1955–56	Mutual aid teams, 1950–54; collectivization in 1955–56; formation of communes, 1958; decollectivization, 1980–83.
Kampuchea	Rapid, 1973–76; reversals in 1978;	Began collectivization while still fighting; after victory, communized totally with economic and political power combined: no private land, no money, no markets. Extreme violence. After Viet Nam invasion in 1978, system transformed into mutual aid teams and with considerable private farming; slow collectivization in mid-1980s and much decollectivization thereafter.
Korea, North	Rapid, 1954–57	Collectivization began in period of high rural devastation from war. Three coop levels and rapid transformation to highest level, followed by collective farm amalgamations and, in 1961 with the designation of the Kun (prefecture) as a key administrative unit, to a unit with many parallels with the Chinese communes.
Laos	No major drive; reversal in late 1980s	Collectivization attempt in 1978–79 abandoned. Slow collectivization thereafter until 1988 when introduction of contract system led to considerable decollectivization.
Mongolia	Rapid, 1956–59	Collectivization drive of 1929–32 was total failure and rescinded after sharp cattle loss and civil war. The 1957–59 drive led to the creation of a type of commune. Decollectivization on reform agenda in 1990s.
Viet Nam	Rapid in North, 1958–60; reversal in late 1980s	Collectivization drive fast, but many cooperatives were merely nominal; transformation from lower to higher level cooperatives took another six years and many collectives remained nominal. Collectivization in southern Annan, 1979–82 fast and successful; in former Cochin China, collectivization from 1979–85 difficult and often only nominal collectives formed. Reforms after 1986 led to extensive decollectivization.
Yemen, South	Rapid, 1970–72	Collectivization combined with land reform. Nomads not included in drive. Several stages of production cooperatives introduced so that would encourage voluntary joining; but most in the lower stages. After 1980 relaxed drive and con-

TABLE 4.2 (cont.)

	Speed and Years of Major Drive	Strategy of Collectivization
		verted some unprofitable state farms into cooperatives. Process reversed in early 1990s merger with North Yemen.
Europe		
Albania	Rapid, 1956–60	Collectivization carried out in part to immunize peasants against Yugoslav ideas. Parts of Gheg highlands collectivized only later. Collective farm stages not used during drive, but employed later to ease transition from collective to state farms. Some decollectivization in 1991.
Bulgaria	Rapid, 1950–52	Some voluntary cooperative farms before and during World War II. Rent paid for land brought into collectives until 1959; only one form of collective farm used. Some decollectivization on reform agenda in 1990s.
Czechoslovakia	Medium, 1951–59	Collectivization started slowly and with incorporation of previous network of service cooperations; drive interrupted in 1953–55 with changes in USSR, then accelerated thereafter. Decollectivization on reform agenda in 1990s.
Germany, East	Rapid, 1958–60	Although collective and state farms set up early and farmers encouraged to join by various economic incentives, major drive started much later than in rest of East Europe, due to special political situation. Decollectivization on reform agenda in 1990s.
Hungary	Rapid, 1958–60	Three drives: drive starting in 1949 interrupted in 1953 by changes in USSR; 1955–56 drive interrupted by Hungarian revolt in 1956; third drive carried out flexibly and effectively. Decollectivization on reform agenda in 1990s.
Poland	No major drive	Reversal of collectivization policy in 1956 when collective farms embraced 23 percent of land. Many farmers left collectives and their relative importance has remained low ever since, although state farms have grown somewhat in relative importance.
Romania	Medium, 1952–60	Forced collectivization began in 1949, but to a limited extent. Brief respite of drive during 1953–55. Some decollectivization on reform agenda in 1990s.
USSR	Rapid, 1929–31	Drive violent; brief breathing spell in 1930 but then continued. In late 1950s drive to consoli-

TABLE 4.2 (*cont.*)

Speed and Years of Major Drive		Strategy of Collectivization
		date collective farms and either convert them or attach them to state farms. Very limited decollectivization on reform agenda in early 1990s.
Yugoslavia	No major drive	Reversal of 1949 collectivization drive in 1952 when collective farms were roughly 19 percent of agricultural land. Most farmers left collective farms thereafter. Gradual increase of socialist agricultural sector until late 1980s.

Source: The data come from a wide number of sources covering the individual nations. For the East European nations except Albania and the USSR, the dates of the major drive were determined by selecting the shortest period in which 50 percent of the land changed from private to collective ownership. Data for East Europe estimates come from U.S. Department of Agriculture, Economic Research Service (1969, p. 25).

Notes: A major drive covers conversion of at least 50 percent of farmland to socialist sector; the speed is measured by the years required to achieve this goal: "rapid" indicates the process occurred within five years; "medium," within ten years.

The North Korean path toward a collective farm system can be painful, and, for countries without the luxury of nationalizing large land holdings, phasing the land reform and the collectivization drives raises many policy dilemmas.

Some strong arguments can be made for carrying out land reform and only sometime thereafter collectivizing the land. Any land reform that transfers ownership of land from owners to former tenants, if *carefully* carried out, can generate considerable political support for the government (the Afghan case, where the land reform was not carefully carried out, is discussed in chapter 3). In those cases where the government is politically too weak to collectivize immediately, land reform can also serve to help consolidate political power necessary for the later success of collectivization, especially if the land reform destroys the old rural elite. Initially, reliable and trained cadre to carry out the complex process of collectivization might also be lacking, but in many situations, as indicated in the previous chapter, they can carry out a simple type of land reform. Indeed, in certain circumstances the land reform can be arranged to strengthen rural party cells and to allow cadre to emerge (generally poor peasants) who later play leading roles in the collectivization, as in the land reforms of both China and Viet Nam. Finally, land reform reduces the economic and political power of large landowners so that later collectivization can be carried out with less violence.

Against these various arguments two strong counterarguments can be raised: First, equalization of land holdings through land reform means that the pain of collectivization is experienced by a larger share of the rural population. Second, the longer the delay between land reform—particularly redistribution of land—and collectivization, the stronger the attachment between peasants and their new land and the more difficult collectivization becomes. Insofar as the land redistribution during the reform allows farmers who have dreamed for decades of owning their own land to obtain it, attachments to the land can become strong in just a few months.

In a number of cases a long delay between land reform and collectivization could not be avoided. In the Soviet Union the government required a decade to recover economically and politically from the chaos of the civil war and War Communism (during which a peasant land grab had occurred) and for Stalin to be able to consolidate his political power sufficiently to allow him to carry out collectivization. In North Korea, the Korean War intervened between the land reform and collectivization. In East Europe in the years immediately following World War II, the Soviet Union felt constrained by its relationships with its former allies to moderate the degree to which it imposed its economic institutions on these economies and to focus primarily upon agrarian reform, rather than collectivization. It was not until the institutionalization of the cold war and the Yugoslav-Soviet split in 1948 that collectivization in most East European countries began in earnest, only to be slowed down or reversed for a few years after the death of Stalin (the "new Course"), and then accelerated in the late 1950s.[6] Finally, in some countries such as the Congo, Ethiopia, and Mozambique, where peasant homesteads were scattered throughout the countryside, collectivization was difficult without first villagizing, a process requiring time and resources.

In countries without concentrated land holdings it is also possible, of course, to collectivize without a land reform, but this is painful and often requires considerable violence. Nevertheless, such a situation allows a number of knotty issues to be sidestepped, especially in those areas where the land tenure contracts are complicated and involve counterpayments. It can also avoid the political problems occurring in collectivization with prior land redistributions when many of the farmers who recently received land must give it up to the cooperative or state farm.

[6] Bulgaria, which the World War II allies recognized as firmly in the Soviet sphere of influence, is a partial exception to this generalization, because some collective farms began to be formed slightly before full liberation from the Nazis, and the process continued slowly thereafter. Still, a major drive did not begin until 1950, in which year state and collective farms accounted for only about 10 percent of all farmland. In East Germany, serious collectivization did not begin until the 1950s, a delay due in part to the political competition between East and West Germany for support of different strata of Germans.

Without a strong administrative apparatus and the willingness to apply almost unlimited coercion, however, such an approach has little chance of succeeding.

Two countries in southeast Asia, Kampuchea and Laos, provide evidence on the results of such a one-step approach. In Kampuchea under Pol Pot, collectivization and creation of communes (which operated in many respects as collective farms) occurred within a few weeks of the seizure of power, but the price was the murder of about a million people, one-sixth of the population, in three years. As I will point out in greater detail, either the Laotian government lacked the political will to bear such appalling human costs or it was unable to apply such violence; in any case, its collectivization drive failed.

Three possible methods for phasing land reform and collectivization, while minimizing difficulties of the latter, can be specified:

1. Collectivization can be delayed until the agricultural sector is highly developed and land holdings are concentrated into the hands of a relatively few owners, a solution chosen in Poland and Yugoslavia. This solution has been contested by those arguing that agricultural collectivization is essentially irreversible, especially if the system is nurtured and subsidized for several decades (a proposition examined in detail in chapter 9) and that any delay of collectivization increases the possibility that it may never occur (for example, Poland and Yugoslavia).

2. Collectivization can be carried out within a few years of land reforms, while the new owners are still learning their land, their productivity is low, and, most importantly, the social bonds in the countryside under the new land reform regime are still fluid. Such a solution was followed in China and Viet Nam. In many cases the basic assumption underlying such an approach may be incorrect; that is, land ownership in general, rather than a specific piece of land, may be the primary desire for previously landless peasants. This means that they might strongly resist collectivization, even though the land reform occurred only a few years before.

3. Land reform and collectivization can be carried out simultaneously, a solution followed in Cuba, the unsuccessful Mongolian campaign from 1930–32 and South Yemen. In all three countries these joint government policies were designed to destroy an entrenched rural elite which had previously held political power. In Cuba nationalization of the estates was the major means of collectivizing and some private peasants were given land they had previously farmed as tenants. Unless the government is content with a mixed agricultural sector, this approach still raises the problem of how to complete the collectivization process. In the first Mongolian collectivization campaign, the expropriation of cattle from the nobles and clergy was usually either simultaneous or close in time to col-

lectivization and resulted in civil war that could only be suppressed by Soviet intervention. The South Yemen action was not only an attack against the rural elite, many of whom were supporters of the former colonial power, but also a strike by the left wing of the ruling Marxist party against its right wing.

THE ADMINISTRATIVE MEANS TO COLLECTIVIZE SMALL PROPERTIES

How can collectivization be carried out? To what extent do administrative means complement or substitute for each other? And what is the impact of the means employed on the resulting production?

One Prerequisite: Power

Coercion seems to be a necessary aspect of a large-scale collectivization drive. Of course, some landless farm workers, tenants, and owners of very small plots welcome collectivization because they believe that their incomes might rise, so that if the initial collectivization focuses on this group, massive resistance is not encountered. In a controversial paper Allcock (1981) argues, for example, that this was the case in Yugoslavia. It proved difficult to carry out collectivization in such a surgical fashion and in most countries farmers owning land seemed reluctant to turn over their property to the state and to work either as collective farm members or as employees on a state farm. They lost the value of their land (the probabilities of receiving full compensation were low), the security of their wealth, and their decision-making autonomy. Moreover, many believed that the present value of the stream of their future incomes would be lower because their future incomes would depend not only on the forces of nature (as before), but also upon the uncertain actions of other members of the collective and its leadership. Furthermore, many believed that the average farm income for the group would probably be lower, because other members of the collective farm would not work hard.

According to many Marxist theorists and politicians, the resistance of peasants to collectivization arises from "false consciousness." Although most holding this position concede the validity of some of the above considerations in the short run, they argue that in the long run, collectivized agriculture would be more productive so that average incomes would be higher and, moreover, individual farming risks would be lower because they could be spread over a large group of people. Whether this long-run argument is correct, that is, whether it is the Marxists or the peasants who are suffering from false consciousness, is a matter I must leave until the empirical investigation of the performance of socialist agriculture in chapter 8. What is important is that relatively few peasants seem impressed by long-run theoretical arguments and, as a result, collectivization was a process that had to be encouraged by a suitable mix of coercion and incentives.

Coercion, let me emphasize, does not necessarily imply violence. Although class warfare and the physical elimination of former landlords and rich peasants as a class accompanied collectivization in the USSR, such violence was certainly not a necessary feature of the process. Indeed, it was not even necessary to remove this segment of the rural population from the land or to exclude them from the collective farm, for within a collective farm such a person would have much less independence than on the outside.[7] Moreover, given an effective land reform preceding collectivization, economic differentiation within the countryside is generally lessened, which reduces the net benefits of such class warfare even more. Although coercion is administratively more difficult to apply than physical violence, it also has the advantage of preserving human lives and physical capital.

Some Social and Economic Factors Raising the Costs of Collectivization

Certain types of social and economic situations raise the costs of collectivization. These are useful to consider before turning to the costs and benefits of various administrative means.

An increase in the cost of collectivization occurs where the population density is low and the topography rugged, so that farming can be carried out only in isolated homesteads. Most Marxist regimes have implemented land reform and collectivization measures only very slowly in such situations. Another costly situation occurs with nomadic herding. The government has the choice either of sedentizing such groups, as in Soviet central Asia where, according to Robert Conquest (1987), about one million people died as a result; or of creating quite special types of collective farms, as in Mongolia, where nomadic herding has continued. In the latter country, it should be added, it took more than four decades before the government was successfully able to implement such a collectivization, and the decision still rankled. In the political demonstrations

---

[7] Some years ago when strolling in a small village near Prague, a farmer came by who, when he learned I was a foreigner, began in a loud voice fearlessly to complain about the incompetence of the government, the stupidity of its agricultural policies, and the ineptness of the collective farm's management. Members of the collective farm in the village stood around and smiled benignly without attempting to stop him. I learned later that he was the village kulak who had been excluded from the collective. Since he was the only person able to repair the farm machinery, however, he earned a much higher income than others and, moreover, was able to say anything he wanted. He was, in short, a Czechoslovak version of the "holy fool."

in Ulan Bator in late 1989 banners were carried with the message "Animals to the Herdsmen." South Yemen and Somalia, two other Marxist regimes with important nomadic populations, were unable to collectivize this segment of the population even after almost two decades of power.[8]

Certainly the costs of collectivization are much higher when farms are scattered over the countryside, rather than clustered in villages. This scattering occurred in a number of Marxist regimes such as Ethiopia, Mozambique, Cuba, and in certain parts of Albania, Hungary, and other nations. Villagization or resettlement is costly; moreover, the isolated homesteads engender a type of individualism that makes the farmers unreceptive to ideals of cooperation and community.[9]

The costs of collectivization are higher if the country is experiencing a shortage of agricultural products, rather than a surplus. For instance, Beresford (1988, p. 156) notes that in Viet Nam a surplus occurred before the collectivization in the north in the late 1950s; and a shortage (induced in large measure by low prices paid to farmers) occurred in the south. She argues that these circumstances were important in determining the relative success of collectivization in the north and the relative failure in the south.

Reliance on agricultural exports can also raise the total costs of collectivization, particularly in the short run. For instance, where relatively small private producers are an important source of export crops, collectivization can result in a drop in exports which in turn jeopardizes the entire investment program. Colburn (1986) has analyzed such a situation in Nicaragua, where the government had to deal with these producers in a careful manner. A similar situation arose in Cuba, which may account for the comparatively careful manner and the economic incentives used by the government in the 1980s to encourage collectivization among private producers.

Costs of collectivization also increase where the country has an open border with another nation that also has a large number of people of the same ethnic group. In such a case a farmer about to be collectivized can simply cross the border and begin life anew in a familiar social environment. Such a situation arose during the collectivization campaigns in Albania among the mountain Ghegs, who went to Yugoslavia, and in North Korea, where the farmers fled to South Korea before and during the Korean War in anticipation of collectivization. In Laos, according to Brown

---

[8] Somalia did have "herding cooperatives," but these consisted of several hundred hectares of range land assigned to the herders with their private flocks if they agreed to follow certain herding practices recommended by the government. According to the sources available to me, the cooperative element in this arrangement was of secondary importance.

[9] A first-rate case study of this problem in Hungary is a village study by the anthropologist C. M. Hann (1980).

and Zasloff (1986, p. 197) roughly 10 percent of the population went to join the Lao population in Thailand between 1975 and 1983; most were farmers fleeing from the collectivization campaign. Another instructive example occurred in East Germany. The major collectivization campaign began in 1958–59, when the only part of the border open with West Germany was in Berlin. The flight of the farmers through this city after collectivization was an important contributing factor in the decision to construct the Berlin wall in August 1961.

The costs of collectivization are also higher where land is relatively equally distributed among independent peasants. I suspect that an important reason underlying a much more rapid migration from rural to urban areas in Bulgaria than in most other East European nations was the fact that land was more equally distributed there before collectivization than in other nations in the region, so that the total social costs occasioned by the loss of land was greater.[10]

Finally, interethnic problems can either increase or decrease the costs of collectivization. An important aspect of Marxist ideology is that it is a system of belief transcending tribalism or particularistic interests of individual ethnic groups. A special problem arises, however, if the government and party are led primarily by members of one ethnic group, so that the decisions of the Marxist regime are perceived by members of other ethnic groups merely as evidence of ethnic domination.[11] In such cases, resistance to collectivization may take on the characteristics of an interethnic struggle and, as a result, raise the level of necessary violence and cost to implement the program. For instance, in Albania the Gheg highlands were not collectivized until almost a decade after the rest of the country, in part because of the stark resistance against the Tosks who dominated the party and government. On the other hand, in situations where ethnic groups have been evicted from the land, as Germans were expelled from Czechoslovakia, Poland, and Yugoslavia after World War II, collectivization costs were much lower because the land was, in essence, empty.

[10] Other reasons for this rapid migration can also be given: (1) roughly 30 percent of the land was in mountainous areas and unsuitable for collectivization; (2) bureaucratization of the farm was greater as a result of the formation of agro-industrial complexes; (3) many of the farms were quite far from urban areas so that it was difficult to live in rural areas and work in the cities; and (4) Bulgarian authorities were willing to accommodate the influx into the cities by constructing housing. Unfortunately, Bulgarian sociologists do not appear to have carried out the type of empirical research from which it would be possible to determine the relative strength of these factors.

[11] Other political lines of fracture include struggles among clans (which, in Somalia or South Yemen have been as fierce as inter-ethnic struggles in other nations) or even among regions. For the point I am making, the ethnicity problem is the most illustrative.

A Digression on Inter-Ethnic Problems in Marxist Regimes

Complications raised by ethnicity are worth a brief digression because they raise the problem of the political legitimacy of the party and government. As I show in Table 4.3, roughly half of the Marxist regimes governed in multiethnic societies. In many of these nations, the communist movement was dominated by members of a particular ethnic group. In some countries such as Bénin or Guinea-Bissau, the Marxist regime appeared to be genuinely panethnic and acted to moderate interethnic disputes. In other countries such as Czechoslovakia and perhaps Albania, a situation of ethnic domination evolved into a panethnic party and government. In still other nations such as Mozambique, the party was dominated by certain groups but this state of affairs did not appear to have led to ethnic tension.[12]

The ethnic problem has not been so benign, however, in another group of Marxist regimes. In countries such as Ethiopia where the party was dominated by the Amhara, extremely severe tensions arose, and in the late 1980s the Ethiopian government was engaged in armed struggles against four different resistance armies representing different ethnic groups. In the Soviet Union, the Russians succeeded in dominating other ethnic groups for seventy years, but the political relaxation occurring under Gorbachev, combined with the embarrassing pullout from Afghanistan that destroyed the myth of Russian invincibility among the minority groups in the Soviet Union, led in the late 1980s to severe ethnic frictions and open fighting.

Ethnic domination can also increase the problems of making agricultural reforms. For instance, in Guyana, as I discuss in greater detail in chapter 10, the ethnic domination of the Afro-Guyanese led to an impoverishment of the agricultural sector that was dominated by the Indo-Guyanese. Any economic reforms benefiting the agricultural sector were bound to strengthen the political power of the Indo-Guyanese, a dilemma that in the early 1990s put the government in the position of acting against its political interests in carrying out needed changes in agriculture. A different kind of problem arose in Czechoslovakia, where the decline of the panethnic Communist party in 1990 was followed by considerable frictions between the Czech and Slovak republics, which in turn delayed the economic reforms in agriculture and other sectors and increased their economic difficulties as well.

It would take us too far afield to examine the conditions that have led

---

[12] In the late 1980s FRELIMO, the ruling Marxist party, took some measures to broaden the ethnic base of the leadership. Until more information about the ethnic composition of RENAMO, an insurgent group fighting a civil war with the government, it is difficult to determine how important the ethnic issue has been in Mozambique.

TABLE 4.3
Multiethnic or Multinational Marxist Regimes

	Share of Major Ethnic Groups in Population	Special Notes
Africa		
Angola	1980: Ovimbundu group, 38%; Mbundu group 26%; Central Bantu group, 11%	Civil war between Marxist groups: MPLA (predominantly Mbundu); UNITA (predominantly Ovimbundu); FLNA (predominantly Bakongo, but rapidly defeated).
Bénin	1980: Fon group, 41%; Bargu group, 22%; Gun and Mina, 15%; Yoruba group, 14%	Before Kérékou government, ethnic rivalries led to great political instability. Since then, such rivalries considerably muted.
Congo	1980: Kongo group, 47%; Téné group, 30%; M'bochi group, 11%	Kongo group more urbanized and educated. Last two important presidents were military men from M'bochi group but Marxist movement is panethnic.
Ethiopia	1980: Galla (Oromo), 40%; Amhara-Tigre, 32%; Kafa-Sidamo, 9%	Amhara gradually dominated leadership; civil war arose with Eritrean, Tigrean, Oromo, and Somalian secession groups. Tigre secession by a Marxist party.
Guinea-Bissau	1980: Balante, 30%; other Senegambian groups, 20%; Peul, 20%; Manding (Malinké), 13%.	From 1974–80, government dominated by Cape Verdians. Although Papel subsequently have held highest offices, the Council of State was ethnically balanced. Some Balante unrest.
Madagascar	1980: Merina, 27%; Betsimisaraka, 15%; Plains group, 20%; Escarpment group, 14%; Betsilio, 12%; Antaisaka, 10%	Merina and Betsilio are more urbanized and more highly Marxist; other groups more rural and less Marxist. Marxist government has led to dominance of Merina in cabinet.
Mozambique	1980: Makua-Lomwe, 38%; Tsonga, 24%; Lower Zambezi group, 10%; Shona, 10%	FRELIMO is panethnic; formed from three ethnic independence groups. Leadership appears dominated by Tsonga and other groups from south; wider representation only occurred in fifth Congress in 1989.

TABLE 4.3 (*cont.*)

	Share of Major Ethnic Groups in Population	Special Notes
Zimbabwe	1980: Shona, 68%; Ndebele-Nguni, 15%; Nyanja, 5%	ZANU-PF was Shona-based and gained dominance in the 1980s over Ndeble-based ZAPU; the parties merged in 1988.
Americas		
Guyana	1977: East Indian, 51%; Black, 31%; Mixed, 12%.	Indo-Guyanese constitute a large majority in rural areas: Afro-Guyanese, a large majority in urban areas. Two Marxist parties represent respectively Indo-Guyanese and Afro-Guyanese; the latter is dominant.
Asia		
Afghanistan	1967: Pushtun, 42%; Tajik, 23%	Two wings of Marxist party: Parcham: right wing, more Tajik, somewhat more urban and upper middle class; Khalq: left wing, more Pushtun, somewhat more rural and lower middle class. Dominant faction was first Khalq, then Parcham.
Laos	1975: Lao Lum, 45%; Lao Theung, 27%; Lao Soung, 11%; Lao Tai, 8%.	Dominance of Lao Loum (lowland Lao), especially after 1977, in both party and state.
Mongolia	1979: Khalka, 78%; Buryat, 2%; other Mongol, 10%; Kazakh, 5%; other, 5%.	Buyrat dominance during 1920s; by 1930s, Khalka dominance. Current situation not known.
Europe		
Albania	1975: Ghegs, about 51%; Tosks, about 45%.	Tosk dominance in both party and state in early years has declined and ethnic frictions dampened; by late 1980s much more political power for Ghegs.
Czechoslovakia	1980: Czechs, 64%; Slovaks, 31%.	Czech dominance in early years has declined; Slovaks have held many important posts. Federation in 1968 reduced many ethnic tensions, but did not eliminate problem. Considerable ethnic friction in early 1990s.
USSR	1979: Russians, 52%; Ukrainians, 16%; Uzbeks, 5%; Belorussians, 4%; Kazakhs, 3%; Tatars, 2%.	Russians have dominated top government and party organs disproportionately to their share in population. In 1970s and 1980s, more non-Russians admitted to leadership. In late 1980s considerable ethnic frictions.

TABLE 4.3 (*cont.*)

	Share of Major Ethnic Groups in Population	Special Notes
Yugoslavia	1981: Serbs, 36%; Croats, 20%; Slovenes, 8%; other, 36%.	Federated government; ethnic balance in central government preserved. Considerable ethnic frictions during 1980s and interethnic warfare in 1991.

Source: See Statistical Note C.

Notes: Multiethnic Marxist regimes include all those with one minority group comprising at least 20 percent of the population and with distinct social or political differences. Many nations with ethnic groups under this cutoff limit still have considerable ethnic problems, e.g., the Turkish minority in Bulgaria. Moreover, in other countries such as Somalia or Yemen, the populations are ethnically homogeneous although the clan structure acts in as divisive a fashion as ethnicity in other countries. Finally, some countries such as Romania do not have any single minority groups comprising more than 20 percent, although the combined share of minority groups (in this case, Hungarians and Gypsies) is over this cutoff point.

The identification of ethnic groups raises many difficulties. Some countries have different groups of people but they do not have sufficiently distinct social or political differences to constitute distinct ethnic groups: for instance, in 1981, 66 percent of the Cuban population was classified as "white," 12 percent as Negros, and 22 percent as mestizos, but they all participated in the same general Cuban culture and cannot be considered as separate ethnic groups. In Czechoslovakia, the classification of Czechs and Slovaks as different ethnic groups is controversial, but the frictions between them is undeniable. In some of the Third World nations, ethnicity is based partly on how one chooses to behave, rather than on parentage alone.

For Africa, special classification problems arise in grouping the many different ethnic subgroups. For this continent, I have followed the ethnic/linguistic groupings provided by Morrison and others (1989). FLNA = National Front for the Liberation of Angola; FRELIMO = Front for the Liberation of Mozambique; MPLA = Popular Movement for the Liberation of Angola; UNITA = National Union for the Total Independence of Angola; ZANU-PF = Zimbabwe African National Union-Patriotic Front; and ZAPU = Zimbabwe African People's Union.

to such different outcomes in the various multiethnic Marxist regimes. Clearly such simple "solutions" as federative, rather than unitary states, may be necessary but not sufficient conditions for interethnic harmony, as Yugoslavia has demonstrated. The theme of interethnic relations is of vital importance in understanding the operations and economic policies of the different Marxist regimes and, unfortunately, has yet to be analyzed in a satisfactory manner.

Social and Economic Incentives to Join Collective Farms

As the first nation to collectivize, the Soviet Union introduced no special social and economic incentives to encourage farmers to join the collective farms; peasants were simply forced onto the collective farms and the process was accompanied by considerable violence.[13] Most Marxist regimes attempting to collectivize smallholder properties since then have learned from these mistakes. As a result, they set up various types of incentives, both positive and negative, to encourage or coerce farmers to join the collective farms.

Since resistance to collectivization was supposed to be a function of the peasant's false consciousness, several techniques of teaching the benefits of cooperative activity and easing the transition were used. For the most part these consisted of the introduction of several intermediate organizational forms, and four such devices are of particular note. First, in some countries such as Bénin, Guinea-Bissau, and Mozambique (not to mention some non-Marxist regimes such as Tanzania), the government encouraged the cultivation of a few communal fields in each area. Second, in some countries such as Ethiopia, Poland, Somalia, and Yugoslavia, the government encouraged the formation of service cooperatives as a way not just to develop a mentality favorable to collectivization but also to provide tractor and other mechanized farming services to farmers so as to slowly incorporate them in collective farming.[14] Indeed, such an approach was advocated by Lenin in his 1923 articles on cooperatives (discussed briefly in chapter 2). Third, still other countries such as China, the Congo, Laos, and Viet Nam encouraged the formation of precooperatives among farmers such as mutual-aid teams, which consisted of various types of cooperation at particular stages of the production cycle. Such an approach often merely institutionalized traditional peasant practices. Fourth, most nations set up different levels of collective farms, where the levels varied according to the extent that means of production (land, equipment and tools, and draft power) were shared and income was divided according to the amount of land and labor contributed. Some countries, aside from the Soviet Union, have not employed such intermediate steps; these included nations moving directly to state farms or countries such as Grenada or Zimbabwe, which established collective farms on expropriated or purchased land, rather than by encouraging private farmers to combine their properties.[15]

[13] Mongolia actually began a major collectivization drive several months before that of the Soviet Union, but the Soviets were the first nation to establish a functioning collective farm system.

[14] Kovacić (1980) and Loncarević (1974) describe in detail the various ways in which the service cooperatives in Yugoslavia have provided such services to the private sector. Hegenbarth (1977) presents the same kind of discussion for Poland.

[15] With regard to Zimbabwe I refer to "Model B." "Model C" farms combine several of the above elements: they consist of a "core farm," owned cooperatively, which provides services and inputs to a group of associated individual farms. By 1989, however, the government had established only one such farm. The different models of farms are discussed in detail in Stoneman and Cliffe (1989); see also footnote 17.

It is not certain that any of these preliminary stages made farmers more willing to be collectivized, but if such measures were to have their intended effect, the process had to be slow. Unfortunately, many Marxist leaders became impatient. For instance, in the early 1950s Mao spoke eloquently about the importance of the slow introduction of intermediate steps so that the peasant would gradually understand the advantages of socialist over private agriculture; the Chinese originally planned a collectivization drive taking fifteen years to complete. At the end of 1954, 58 percent of the peasant households were participating in mutual-aid teams, when the collectivization drive began. No longer was there talk of the educative function with a slow progression from stage to stage; by the end of the next year, lower-stage agricultural producer cooperatives comprised 63 percent of peasant households. By the end of 1956, 88 percent of peasant households were in the higher-stage producer cooperatives. After a one-year hiatus, the system was overturned once more with the formation of communes, which included 99 percent of the rural population by the end of 1958. During these tumultuous three years Mao stopped speaking of the peasant as an active participant in the development of his own political consciousness, and, instead, argued that the peasant was "poor and blank," ready for change directed from above. "On a blank sheet of paper free from any mark . . . the freshest and most beautiful pictures can be painted."[16]

Marxist regimes intent on collectivizing set up a wide variety of incentives to encourage peasants to join the collective farm. For instance, in almost all countries direct taxes on private farmers were much higher than those on members of collective farms. In a number of East European nations production quotas were higher (or official prices paid for required crop deliveries were lower) for private farmers than collective farmers. In many countries collective and state farms also had a priority claim on scarce agricultural inputs and credit. Hungary offered considerable investment funds to the new collectives, and some countries such as Seychelles heavily subsidized the collective farms for a number of years. Bulgaria and Czechoslovakia forced private farmers to sell their equipment to government agencies and, as a result, the farmers were less able to carry out farming activities alone. In a number of countries farm inputs were also more readily available to those joining the collective farms.

In some cases collectivization had an important economic logic because the incentives were positive and unambiguous. For instance, in North Korea, collective farms began to be formed after the end of the Korean

<hr/>

[16] The data come from Eckstein (1977). The Mao quotation comes from, "Introducing a Cooperative" [4/15/58], Mao (1971), p. 500.

War because much farm capital had been destroyed, many farmers had fled south, and group efforts were often necessary to place the farms in working order. A parallel can be found in the experience of the Pilgrim fathers landing in America, who farmed collectively for the first few years for lack of capital. A similar situation arose with other types of deliberate resettlement programs. For instance, in its first decade Zimbabwe placed exclusive reliance on this method of collectivization, buying agricultural land from white settlers and distributing it, in part, to groups who agreed to farm the land together.[17] Unfortunately, this program was expensive and was plagued with financial, managerial, organizational, and other problems (Chitsike 1988; Bratton 1987), in considerable measure because the government failed to supply these farms with the promised finance and infrastructure, particularly irrigation (Stoneman and Cliffe 1989, p. 115). Other countries also employed the resettlement approach as one part of the collectivization drive that focused on special groups: for example, Nicaragua for war refugees; Somalia and Ethiopia for victims of the drought. In Ethiopia and Viet Nam, in contrast to other countries, resettlement was often forced, not voluntary, and the resulting farms had many problems.[18] The Somalia government resettled nomads from the 1974 drought on state farms, with the aim of gradually transforming the farms into cooperatives; such goals, however, were not realized.[19]

Marxist governments also offered services and social benefits for joining the collective farm. In Cuba, collective farm members were promised pension benefits. In Ethiopia, among the twelve incentives for joining the collective farms was exemption of the sons of collective farm members from the military draft.

Incentives and coercion can be focused on particular steps of the collectivization process. For instance, the process of obtaining land for the

[17] Most of the lands distributed in the 1980s in this way went, however, to private farmers (Model A); the cooperatives (Model B) received only about 5 percent of this land. In none of these cases did the resettled farmers receive title to the land, but only the permission to farm it. There was also a Model E for group ranching, but it is unclear whether any such farms were established.

[18] Clay and Holcomb (1986) and Giorgis (1989) discuss the case of Ethiopia; Crosnier and Lhomel (1987) and Desbarats (1987), Viet Nam.

In the latter country the resettlements had two phases. In an earlier period the resettlements in the mountainous areas were to relieve the pressure on the land in the Red River Delta. In a later phase, after 1975 and the incorporation of South Viet Nam, New Economic Zones (NEZs) were established to reduce urbanization in the South. Originally private peasants were to farm the NEZs, but later some of these were transformed into state farms. Conditions in the NEZs were hard: promised aid from the government did not arrive, the land was poorly chosen, and more than two-thirds of the farmers left.

[19] In four years the population in the resettlement farms decreased by 46 percent (Omar 1982, p. 195), and the resettled nomads still remained paid workers for the state rather than becoming collective farmers.

collective farms has been accompanied by the greatest direct or indirect coercion. Direct coercion occurred where the land was expropriated without compensation. For instance, in the Congo (ILO 1984, p. 36), the state farms got rid of the customary inhabitants "by bulldozer and barbed wire." Indirect coercion occurred in a number of East European nations where the promised monetary compensations for the farmers' land never materialized. By way of contrast, Seychelles has in most cases paid a market price for the nationalized land. It has, however, employed several unique policies to lower this price. It prohibited all foreign ownership of land in this vacation paradise, which considerably reduced demand and land prices. Moreover, by overvaluing its exchange rate and keeping the domestic price of foodstuffs low, it lowered the profits from agriculture and, thereby, the price of agricultural land. In other cases, I was told by former landholders that the negotiated price was lower than the farmer, who had no choice in the matter, believed the land was worth. Such a system worked because, in contrast to many other Third World Marxist regimes, the economy was relatively prosperous. The Seychellois government was able to maintain a rough balance in its foreign payments, and, until the late 1980s, the country was able to avoid excessive domestic inflation.

Quite often measures taken to encourage collectivization were not so benign. In North Korea, the government sometimes shut off the water supply of those not joining the collective and prevented them from getting fertilizer (Scalapino and Lee 1972, p. 1061). In other countries, Poland for one, private farmers were held to certain norms of "proper land utilization" and, if they were judged not to be farming according to such standards, their land was expropriated and placed in a state or collective farm.

To what extent did such incentives work? While a number of literary descriptions have appeared, unfortunately we have no systematic picture of the collectivization process from the peasants' point of view, except for Ethiopia, where a certain amount of survey work has been carried out on motives for joining or not joining collective farms, and Mozambique, where participant-observer methods have been used. These studies provide some interesting information.

In Ethiopia, according to a survey of Arsi Province (Dejene 1987, pp. 80), about 25 percent of the peasants said they wanted to join the collective farm eventually, but their primary reasons were economic, rather than any seeming inherent approval of such a form of agricultural production. More specifically, the greater government assistance, the greater access to draft power (oxen), the availability of more fertile land, and the promise of support for old age appeared the most important reasons for joining. Ghose (1985) provides evidence showing, as we might suspect, that it has been primarily the poorer peasants who joined the collective farms. Wondimu (1983) found little correlation between age and various social/political variables and the desire to join the collectives. According to the Dejene study, the main reasons given for not joining was that the respondents wanted their own farms (60 percent) or feared others would not work very hard (13 percent).

For Mozambique, Hanlon (1984) points out that obtaining scarce agricultural inputs was an important reason for forming (nominal) collective farms, especially for wealthier and more entrepreneurial peasants, and that they did not allow poor peasants to join their collective.[20] Additional evidence on this matter for Mozambique is provided by Dolny (1985).

Indeed, in other Marxist regimes such as Angola where the governmental administrative apparatus in the countryside was ineffective, we read of peasants subverting the state and collective farms for personal enrichment by obtaining government subsidies or agricultural inputs, rather than by any productive activities. In "soft states," the state or collective farms are less an instrument of production than of income redistribution, either for workers or for managers, especially when losses are subsidized either directly by the state or by the loans from the state bank that will never be paid back (Scott 1988). In many of these Third World Marxist nations collective farms have been primarily nominal; among other things this means that decollectivization is a much simpler process.

Any type of economic incentive promising inputs or special aid has one serious drawback. If the government is unable to fulfill its promises, the collective farms generally do not survive or their growth is slow, as in Ethiopia. In certain countries such as Guinea-Bissau, Mozambique, Somalia, and Zimbabwe, the fiscal crises and balance of payments problems led both to a virtual fiscal abandonment of most of the collectives and to a highly uncertain supply of agricultural inputs (the Mozambique case is examined by Binkert 1983). This state of affairs, in turn, led to the dissolution of many cooperatives and the abandonment of other governmental projects in rural areas (Hanlon 1984, p. 103; Rudebeck, 1988). Pressures to dissolve the collectives also came from the failure of the collective farms to raise peasant incomes. In some cases government assistance to cooperatives actually lowered production and profits. In Mo-

---

[20] Even in nations where the government had more control over collectivization than in Mozambique, similar phenomena have occurred. For instance, in the Soviet Union, one hears of cases where the wealthier farmers formed their own collective farm and excluded the poorer farmers, who had to form their own collective. In succeeding years the collective farms of the former prospered, because they had rich lands and considerable capital, while the collective farms of the latter fared poorly in comparison. It is, unfortunately, impossible from such stories to determine if this phenomenon was common, although in later years, equalization of average collective farm incomes was an excuse sometimes given for merging different farms.

zambique, for instance, planning the work of the collectives was often carried out arbitrarily from above, and the available inputs corresponded neither to the requirements of the plans or to other productive activities of the farm; for instance, rented tractors or promised seeds did not arrive on time. In such cases, private agricultural efforts resting on traditional methods yielded higher incomes. In Zimbabwe the fiscal crisis led to the cutting back of promised grants of one year's operating expenses—this was a contributing factor to the poor performance of many collective farms.

Administrative Problems and the Organization of Collectives

The formation of a collective farm is complex: not only must the cadre assigned to the task merge a considerable number of individual farms into a single functioning unit, but they must organize and manage a resentful labor force unaccustomed to working together. These collectivization cadres can belong to the rural apparatus of the state and party (as in China), or they can be a special unit of the central governmental apparatus (as in Viet Nam). They can consist primarily of people with rural backgrounds (as in China) or they can include a large number of urbanites as well (as in the Soviet Union).[21] The countryside can be flooded with cadre so that the process is carried out in a short time (as in China and North Korea), or fewer cadres can be used so that the process extends over a long period (as in East Europe). In this brief discussion I examine by means of minicase studies of the Soviet Union and China the administrative means employed by the cadre to establish the collective farms. For both facts and analysis I draw heavily upon Bernstein's (1970) brilliant study.

The Soviet Communist party was led primarily by urban intellectuals, and it came to power by a takeover of the major cities; before the revolution, it had only four village cells in the entire country. Even by late 1929, at the eve of collectivization, the party was not well organized in the countryside, in part because of party purges during the 1920s—only about one-third of the villages had party cells. Thus collectivization had

---

[21] It is also possible for a nation to rely on cadre from fraternal socialist nations to establish and manage collective farms, but the Vietnamese aid to Seychelles is the only case with which I am familiar. It is more usual for one socialist nation to aid the state farms of another. For instance, North Korea helped establish or run state farms in Ethiopia and Madagascar, Bulgaria and Romania aided Mozambique in a similar manner, and the Bulgarians, Cubans, and Soviets provided such assistance in Angola. Such aid sometimes generated intense animosity and bizarre stories were circulated about the activities of these foreign cadre. For instance, in Madagascar I heard rumors that North Korean experts in that country were stealing men's testicles and women's wombs and shipping them back to Pyongyang. Another Western scholar also reported such stories.

to be accompanied by wholesale recruitment of new leaders. Since the government found few local leaders who were responsive to the regime, and at the same time were respected by the peasants, it recruited about twenty-five thousand urban workers ("the best sons of the fatherland") to aid the collectivization drive (Viola 1987).

The Soviet government did not use any economic incentives to encourage the formation of collective farms. Although some mutual-aid teams (TOZ) and rural service cooperatives did exist before collectivization, the government did not generalize this experience and establish them all over the countryside. Nor did it establish any preliminary stages of collective farms. Indeed, the collectivization cadre had two tasks: to eliminate the economic and political power of the rich peasants and to establish the collective farms as soon as possible. Government cadre began to use the term *kulak* as a tool to force peasants into the collectives by redefining it to mean anyone resisting collectivization, a crime punishable by death or deportation. They also made few distinctions between real *kulaks* and middle peasants, treating both as potential enemies of collectivization.

The cadre were, in one sense, weak: they did not have time nor were they able to persuade the peasants, so they had to employ "command mobilization." They inherited the Tsarist administrative methods—coercion, exile, and the knout—and a major component of their activities was physical coercion and violence. According to Wädekin (1969), their work style was to "knock heads together, tighten the screws, and straighten things out." Higher levels of the administration sent down orders and received reports in the typical style of a strongly hierarchical bureaucracy. The leaders gave little advice or aid, which left the relatively untrained cadre to their own devices to produce results.

In the first part of the collectivization drives the farmers were not allowed to keep any land or farm animals for their personal use. Peasant resistance took many forms, including the killing of livestock and the destruction of property.

The Chinese Communists had come to power only after several decades of fighting, mostly in the countryside. The party had much more experience in dealing with the peasantry and was highly organized in the countryside—on the eve of collectivization, about 90 percent of the villages had party cells. The land reform carried out in the liberated areas in previous years was broadened and deepened to include the entire country. It had been formulated with care, its implementation was flexible, and in some measure it was carried out by village peasant associations (Shue 1980). Such a process in the first stage of the reform had also brought forward rural cadre who had the respect of the peasantry and could be relied upon by the government for aid in the redistributive stage and, later, collectivization.

The Chinese government had preceded collectivization with a massive propaganda campaign in 1953–54, combined with extensive training of rural cadre. Most members of the cadre participating in the collectivization drive were of rural background. In dealing with the peasantry they relied on a balance of persuasion, pressures, and coercion, rather than the more brutal methods employed in the Soviet Union, and in setting up the collective farms, they paid close attention to economic incentives. Farmers were allowed to keep small plots of land for their personal use as well as several farm animals. Collectivization stages were designated: lower stage collectives paid rent on both the land and tools donated by the individual peasants, and the transition to a full collective would not be made until the well-off middle peasants could earn as much from work points as they did when working on their own. As previously noted, the timetable for collectivization was accelerated, which may have been the cause for a certain amount of resistance. The most important point, however, is that the basic approach toward collectivization was much different than in the USSR.

The Chinese government imposed fewer ideas from the top and allowed an inductive learning process at the village level. The higher administrative levels also supplied more aid to the cadre and the bureaucracy was not as hierarchical. The fewer status differences gave the cadre in the field more confidence to use "participatory mobilization," rather than naked coercion, in order to form the collective farms. Force was, of course, employed, but violence was at a much lower level, and rich farmers and former landlords were allowed to stay in the village, albeit at reduced levels of wealth and status. As a result, the killing of farm animals and the physical destruction of property was not as extensive. Only one year after collectivization, however, the government instituted the Great Forward Leap and forced collective farms to combine into communes and starvation killed 30 million Chinese (Banister 1987, p. 85).

The conclusion of this brief discussion should be clear: to a certain extent economic and social incentives are substitutes for coercion and violence. The difference in administrative means to collectivize has, however, an important impact on agricultural production in the years immediately following the transformation. In most cases a high degree of coercion and violence has led to a fall in production, even if the marketable surplus increased. To the Marxist leaders, however, the latter seemed more important.

Some Unsuccessful and Successful Collectivizations

Consideration of several additional case studies allows us to tie together a number of strategic considerations. For purposes of this discussion an unsuccessful collectivization is one in which an intended major collectivization drive was rescinded. These include the 1978–79 drive in Laos, the 1928–31 drive in Mongolia, the drive in the early and mid-1950s in Poland, and the drive in the late 1940s and early 1950s in Yugoslavia. Indeed, one might add the drives in the early 1950s in Czechoslovakia and Hungary where a certain amount of decollectivization occurred in 1953–56 during the period of the thaw. The Mongolian drive was conducted under conditions of administrative chaos allowing little of general use to be learned and the East European experience has been well described by others (e.g., Wädekin 1982), but collectivization in Laos deserves consideration.

At the time of the Pathet Lao's seizure of power in 1975 Laos was a country with no real land shortage, little tenancy or landlessness, and very few large estates; therefore, no land reform was necessary. The government had considerable difficulty in imposing a tax on the rural population, especially since the tax was administered in a highly arbitrary fashion (Evans 1988; Stuart-Fox 1982b). With very little preparation of either the population or the cadre, therefore, the government attempted a full-scale collectivization, spurred on by fiscal difficulties and the need to overcome a flood crisis.

According to Stuart-Fox (1986) and Juhász (1986), several problems arose almost immediately. Cadre to aid in the formation of the collectives were insufficient in number and not well trained, so that considerable confusion arose. The government offered no financial support to the new cooperatives to help them get started; quite the reverse, it imposed a heavy tax on them as well as the requirement to deliver rice to the state at low prices. It set up collective farms on land in the plains and tried to resettle minority groups from the mountains in them. The collectivization drive also broke up traditional cycles of cultural activities since the people did not have sufficient food surplus to finance traditional rituals (Doré 1982). Finally, two natural disasters (a drought and a flood) occurred during the campaign (Evans 1990, pp. 50–51).

Except in areas devastated by war (Evans 1988, p. 38), peasants had no incentives to pool their resources and join the cooperatives. As a result, the cadre had to use considerable coercion to get them to join. In addition, the government was dominated by one ethnic group so that to many peasants collectivization was one more form of ethnic domination. Resistance to collectivization was immediate and took a number of forms including destruction of crops and property and flight. Many moved to the highlands, where collectives were not formed, while many others fled to Thailand, which had a large Lao minority. As an obvious result, agricultural production fell considerably. Following interventions by Soviet Prime Minister Aleksei Kosygin and Vietnamese advisors, the Laotian government rescinded the drive in 1979. The number of agricultural cooperatives fell by almost half (Evans 1988, p. 64), and then slowly increased until 1986, when the number was 50 percent more than in 1979. The introduction of a household contracting system in 1988 led to another decollectivization, although the existing information does not permit a definitive judgment on the extent to which producer cooperatives remained.

A successful collectivization drive is conducted with a minimum of violence and coercion and is accompanied by either steady or increasing agricultural production. Aside from those nations where the ownership of property was highly concentrated, the Hungarian drive of 1958–60, the Mongolian drive in 1959, and the North Korean drive of 1953–56 are cases in point. The Mongolian and North Korean collectivization drives provide few relevant lessons. In North Korea, for instance, most of the countryside had been severely damaged during the war, the rural power elite had fled either after the land reform or with the retreating United Nations armies, and the rural population was relatively docile, so that the government did not need to provide many special incentives but, with the aid of Soviet advisors and judicious use of coercion, collectivized rapidly and effectively. The Hungarian collectivization is more instructive.

The Hungarians, of course, had experience in collectivizing since the drive in 1958–60 was their third. The first drive occurred in the late 1940s and early 1950s and the second in 1955–56. Between each drive considerable decollectivization occurred. The presence of Soviet troops during the third drive added a note of hidden coercion that was not present during the first two.[22] Several incentives offered to the farmers are particularly noteworthy (Swain 1985). Rural class struggle was not the aim of the drive and, indeed, many wealthy peasants were not only admitted as full members of the collective farms but also served in leadership positions. Unlike most Marxist regimes, which attempted to carry out collectivization in an inexpensive manner, the Hungarian government changed its sectoral mix of investments and poured in considerable funds to provide for the necessary farm infrastructure and to modernize equipment. The government had a liberal policy toward private plots and it turned a blind eye to the sharecropping of some of the collective farm lands by its members. It paid for the livestock and certain equipment, as well as a rent on all land turned over to the collective; moreover, the rights to such rent were inheritable, so long as the heirs remained on the farm. The government did not impose compulsory crop deliveries and several years later in 1964–65, the farms gained considerable autonomy

---

[22] Open coercion was also, of course, employed. A literary reflection of the process is provided by György Konrád's (1980, p. 26) description of a man who received land after the postwar land reform, who signed it over (after a pencil was placed up his nose) to the collective farm in 1960, and who went insane, spending the rest of his life in a mental hospital trying to figure out why the government gave him land and then took it back during the collectivization drive.

in making their own input and output decisions, depending upon local conditions. Finally, the government provided the collective farmers with such social benefits as pensions. In sum, the Hungarians provided the means and the incentives to the collective farmers for the system to work. Although coercion played a certain role, it was only one of many incentives employed. As shown in chapter 8, the increase in total factor productivity of Hungarian agriculture was one of the highest in East Europe; part of this can be attributed to the relatively smooth third collectivization drive.

SUMMARY

As argued in chapter 2, major driving forces behind collectivization were ideological beliefs of political leaders who held them with such fervor that they were willing to bear the high costs of collectivization.

The ease of collectivization depended greatly upon the initial rural conditions facing the Marxist regimes. In nations with a high concentration of land ownership, collectivization provided few problems. In those countries where such farms were run as large plantations, most of the Marxist governments preferred to transform them into state, rather than collective, farms. Collectivization was much more difficult with smallholders or nomadic herders, or in mountainous areas, or in countries with open borders or tense interethnic relations.

Where Marxist regimes intended to transform smallholders into collective farms, the government had to choose an appropriate mix of violence, coercion, education, and economic and social incentives. The choice, in turn, depended upon the degree to which the party was willing to organize the countryside first and whether it also carried out a land reform. To a certain extent these administrative means were substitutes for each other, although coercion was also always necessary because of the general reluctance of peasants to join collective farms. In several cases, the degree of violence and coercion also had an important impact on later production.

In this chapter I have tried to outline the "what" and "how" of collectivization, and to infer the "why." Not until the governmental archives are opened or memoirs of the participants in the political leadership are published will we learn the process by which the decision to collectivize was made, the exact reasons for such a rural transformation, and the real costs of these policies. Collectivization has been a searing historical experience, and in chapter 9 I argue that in some cases it is probably irreversible. The extent to which collectivization can be reversed depends in a certain measure on how the sector is organized—the focus of analysis of the following two chapters of this book.

PART III

Structural Elements

Chapter 5

HORIZONTAL AND VERTICAL INTEGRATION
OF AGRICULTURE

STATE AND COLLECTIVE FARMS can be organized in many ways, depending upon the economic environment and a set of critical policy decisions by the government and the farm managers. This chapter focuses on two major macrostructural elements: the size of these farms, measured in terms of their land and labor (horizontal integration), and the degree to which individual farms produce their own inputs or process raw foodstuffs (vertical integration).[1] These macrostructural elements have important implications, not just on the functioning of the farm sector, but also on the ease of decollectivizing and moving to a market system. In chapter 6, I analyze microstructural elements such as the internal administration of the farms and the various ways in which they organize, motivate, and compensate their labor force.

Discussion of such issues is complicated because in each Marxist regime the farms operate in different economic environments. In most of the Third World nations the state and collective farms carried out their functions in market environments, but with considerable governmental intervention. In many cases the macrostructural elements differed little from the colonial period.[2] Exceptions to this generalization include such Third World nations as Cuba, China (until the early 1980s), Mongolia,

---

[1] This production of agricultural inputs or processing of outputs can be either for the farm itself or for other farms as well.

The agricultural literature often uses the terms *horizontal* and *vertical* in a somewhat different sense from that found in the literature on industrial organization, which I follow in this discussion. Except for fodder and seed, the farm sector does little selling of produce to itself. Moreover, the stages of production in agriculture (the cycle of crop growing or animal raising) are often less separated from each other than in manufacturing. As a result some agricultural economists speak of farms' purchases of services such as repairs or technology as "horizontal relationships" since they come from the rural sector, even though from the standpoint of production theory these should be considered as part of the vertical chain.

[2] For instance, the state farms in São Tomé, which cover 95 percent of the arable land, represent little more than a consolidation of the former Portuguese plantations; the "central planning" of agriculture, as I indicate in Research Note D, has little meaning. At one farm I visited, I commented to an official on the beauty of a large garden near the farm headquarters, remarking that the workers must enjoy walking in it after work. I was curtly informed that the garden was only for visitors and managers, which suggests that not only the economic but also the social relations of the colonial era have continued.

and Viet Nam, which attempted to introduce central administration of all major economic activities including agriculture. Except for Hungary and Yugoslavia, the state and collective farms in all nations in East Europe until the 1990s operated within the framework of a centrally administered economy and the decisions about macrostructural policy were made in this context.

Other difficulties in discussing these horizontal and vertical elements arise because insufficient information is available to determine the reasons underlying certain macro-organizational choices or the impact of these decisions. Structural elements also changed in some countries from year to year. Nevertheless, we can gain a sufficiently clear picture of the major parameters so that the range of variation can be determined.

HORIZONTAL INTEGRATION OF STATE AND COLLECTIVE FARMS

Horizontal integration is the combining of land, labor, and capital in a production unit to carry out farming operations on a large scale. In market economies, the size of the farm is primarily a function of market and technical considerations that have received considerable study. In many Marxist regimes the government has also played a major role in determining farm size by combining and transforming a large number of small farms, which means that the importance of economic and technical factors must be determined. By reviewing these key factors and their relevance to socialist agriculture, we can gain some necessary perspective for examining data on average farm size.

Some Relevant Theoretical Considerations

The economic justifications for the creation of large collective and state farms include economies of scale and size, as well as the other reasons reviewed in chapter 2 in the discussion of Stalin's arguments for collectivization. Here, however, it is useful to consider briefly some additional reasons bearing on the advantages and disadvantages of large-scale farming in either capitalist or socialist systems.

Certain economic factors render large farms more viable. For instance, a lack of active interfarm markets for inputs often leads to increased size and decreased specialization on the farms because they must produce these inputs themselves, even at levels below optimal scale. A related problem arises because of the indivisibility of inputs. In their discussion of agricultural organization, Binswanger and Rosenzweig (1986) point out that in market economies, markets for certain inputs such as draft animals and machines often do not exist, either because of their fragility and need for constant maintenance or because transaction and supervision costs are too high to permit markets for bundled services (machines plus an owner-operator). Although the need for such indivisible inputs places lower bounds on the efficient size of farm operations, in normal cases these lower bounds are far below the usual size of plantations or collective farms. A more important indivisible input is management; it is common to distinguish between managers and entrepreneurs. Managers administer farm operations and supervise workers, skills that are important, for instance, where highly technical operations must be carefully coordinated or where strict quality controls must be maintained.[3] Entrepreneurs make allocational decisions under uncertainty, where the returns may rise with the scale of operations, skills that are important in both market and nonmarket environments. These administrative and entrepreneurial skills may be scarce, especially in countries with relatively low average levels of education. Since these skills are indivisible, large farms are a method of utilizing them most efficiently.

Of course, large-scale farming occurs for political or social reasons as well. For instance, plantations have arisen in colonial situations where land or labor cannot be easily exchanged or sold.[4] In Marxist regimes, another factor appears important, namely that a system of smallholders might subvert other economic goals of the government. For instance, the farmers might be much more risk averse than the government and, if they received control over the land, they might convert much of it to the production of foodstuffs so that production of export crops would fall, thereby jeopardizing the government's investment program. In other words, although small-scale agriculture might ultimately be much more profitable than large-scale farming for all concerned, the short-run costs

[3] High-quality tea is sometimes categorized as a plantation crop, because maintenance of quality by individual farmers working with extension agents is allegedly too expensive. The existence of successful smallholder tea farms in Kenya and elsewhere raises some questions about this claim.

[4] In some of these nations that had slavery, plantations were a common productive unit because the enslaved workers earned much less than their marginal product, even though their marginal product might have been considerably lower than free workers. In other of these societies, land was not easily or willingly sold, often because large landholdings were associated with great political power.

Binswanger and Rosenzweig also raise the case of plantations arising where credit markets are imperfect, where certain tree crops with long gestation periods and high maintenance intensity are grown, and where land has a high scarcity value. The high-maintenance intensity makes short-term tenancy costly (since the trees can be destroyed through lack of maintenance), and the long gestation period implies high capital requirements so that the ability to obtain credit cheaply (i.e., plantations over smallholders) is a distinct advantage. At the same time, smallholders have labor cost advantages, so that there is likely to be a wide size range in holdings; for example, in cocoa, which is a plantation crop in some nations and a smallholders crop in others.

Although I argue in Research Note B that credit availability influences the size distribution of farms, I do not find this particular argument compelling. For instance, even smallholders without credit can transform their farm into cocoa farms, merely by planting a few trees at a time and interplanting the land with cash crops until the cocoa trees mature.

of providing the necessary financial and technological aid might be much higher than the short-run costs of setting up collective farms and trying to force the peasants to produce a particular quantity of export crops.

Compelling as the arguments for large-scale agriculture may seem at first glance, it is important to gain perspective by considering some reasons why large-scale farming may lead to lower production or productivity. In an extended discussion, Binswanger and Rosenzweig isolate the following important factors, all of which relate to various problems of supervising large labor forces. Some concrete aspects of these problems, especially with regard to the compensation of labor, are discussed in greater detail in the next chapter.

ASYMMETRIC INFORMATION

Information has value and is costly to acquire; self-interested individuals will not part with it unless it is to their advantage. Because of the specificity of agricultural work, the workers actually carrying out such operations have considerably better information than the supervisors about the state of the land and crop, the amount of his labor input applied, and other vital aspects of the farm operations. It is costly in terms of time and effort to transmit this information. Without it, the manager may not have the right information for making the proper technical decisions to direct the work of the labor force or to determine the most appropriate investments for increasing farm output.

INCENTIVE PROBLEMS

When information is costly and asymmetrically distributed, worker input cannot be easily supervised. It is often difficult to set up indirect incentives to encourage hard work, a matter discussed in detail in the next chapter. A different incentive problem arises when labor is employed to grow food crops and the expense of guarding the fields is too high for the farm to afford. In these cases, of course, workers have an incentive to steal the crop (praedial larceny), which suggests that large-scale agriculture, at least in capitalist nations, is more appropriate for industrial crops (for example, cotton, sunflower seeds or sugarcane).[5] It is possible that incentive problems become more serious with the use of more complex

---

[5] One state farm manager in São Tomé told me that praedial larceny of food crops amounted to 50 percent. In Cape Verde and Seychelles, farm managers told me such larceny was about 10 percent. In Guyana the top management of the state farms publicly complained of the severity of praedial larceny with regard to food grains and coconuts (Guyana Sugar Corporation 1990, pp. 7, 9), although managers with whom I tried to discuss the problem refused to give me a quantitative estimate. An American student working on a state farm in Cuba told me of special mounted police to prevent the stealing of food crops at harvest time.

agricultural technologies, because it is more difficult to establish work norms.

Except where it is possible to carry out gang labor at a single point, supervision costs are high when production is scattered over a large area. This requires extensive travel time of the overseers, extensive knowledge of the peculiarities of each plot of ground, and information about the random events occurring over the production cycle. Monitoring work efforts by looking at "results" also raises difficulties because animals and plants often require careful and sensitive care. Often the lack of such care cannot be detected until well after the workers have been paid. Moreover, if a number of people have participated in the production cycle at some time on a given piece of land, responsibility for success or failure of the crop is difficult to assign to any single individual, especially because the contribution of many of the activities in the agricultural production depend upon the quality of the work performed, which is not immediately visible. Supervision costs may also increase with more complex agricultural technologies because oversight of more repair work and maintenance costs is required.

Hiring of short-term labor can be costly, especially at seasons of peak demand. Where there are no off-peak jobs, there will be seasonal underemployment for laborers with long term contracts, and this raises labor costs. Furthermore, the system of hiring workers and paying them a fixed wage places *all* of the agricultural risks arising from weather, market, disease (of plants or cattle), and theft on the shoulders of the management.

Although these kinds of economic and technical factors are paramount in determining the optimal size of farms in the West, where response to market forces is crucial in determining the economic success of a farm, additional criteria are important for those making decisions about farm size in Marxist regimes, which are discussed below. Nevertheless, if policymakers in Marxist regimes did not pay close attention to these factors, farm performance, as measured by strictly economic criteria, might well be worse.

Forms of Horizontal Integration

On the production level raising the horizontal integration of a farm merely involves increasing its size. On the suprafarm level, however, several features deserve brief comment.

In most Marxist regimes state and collective farms are administered by a single ministry. Exceptions occurred in countries such as Ethiopia and Seychelles, where several ministries administered state farms, depending upon the type of farm, their location, their major product, or some other special feature.

Between the ministries and the farm, intermediate administrative units can also be formed. In most Third World Marxist regimes in Africa, such intermediate units either do not exist or else have relatively little power. In countries more able to administer a planned economy, these intermediate units often achieved a certain degree of autarky.[6] Those countries consciously pursuing regional self-sufficiency in agricultural products—in the 1970s and 1980s these included Bulgaria, China, North Korea, and Romania—set up such intermediate organizations on a regional level and gave them considerable decision-making powers, at the expense of power exercised by the ministry. For instance, in Bulgaria in the 1970s many powers of the ministry devolved to Okrug (regional) Agro-Industrial Unions, including control over some foreign exchange, administrative powers over input supply, food processing, and research. In 1977 political authorities also divided the country into 252 administrative subunits, each of which was supposed to be relatively self-sufficient in basic foods (supplied by the agro-industrial complexes in the region). This extreme form of horizontal integration, however, did not prove successful (Wyzan 1990a, 1990b).

It is difficult to generalize about the role of these intermediate units, since this role has differed from country to country and from time to time within the same country. Moreover, for an outsider it is often challenging to determine exactly what these units did or, indeed, the actual degree of autonomy of the individual farms overseen by such intermediate agencies. In some instances, however, it appears that these intermediate units made most of the key farming decisions, so that the intermediate unit really functioned as a regional farm, with the individual farms serving as subordinate units.

Horizontal integration has also occurred through the merger of collective farms with each other or with state farms. In some East European countries the government also encouraged collective and state farms to form interfarm production units in order to focus on one particular product. Such a unit might be an independent economic enterprise with its own policy board composed of representatives of the founding units or it might simply be an informal partnership or contractual agreement be-

[6] A peculiar case is provided in the Soviet Union in 1962 when Khrushchev set up Territorial Production Administrations (TPAs) to bring collective and state farms in a particular area under a single administrative roof in an *Oblast'* (a territorial unit). Laird (1967) argues that the TPAs were meant as a substitute for the political control formerly exercised by the machine tractor stations. This scheme was abandoned shortly after Khrushchev's downfall.

tween the founding units. I have been unable to locate information to determine the extent to which such interfarm organizations represent a totally new activity, or merely the combination of similar subunits within each farm so as to achieve economies of scale.

Size of Farm Units in Marxist Regimes

Although data are readily available on the average size of farm units in Marxist regimes, they must be used cautiously. Land as a measure is misleading because many American family farms are just as big, but farmed by only a fraction of the labor force. Further comparability problems arise because it is often unclear whether the data refer to total farm area, arable area, or area actually farmed, three variables standing in quite different relationship to each other in each country. Furthermore, in some Third World Marxist regimes, the collective farms are nominal since only a small portion of the total crop land is farmed collectively. As a result, any data on average acreage of the farm as a whole would overstate the size of the socialist sector.

Labor as a measure of farm size is also misleading because a large share of the labor force on the farm is not engaged directly in agricultural activities. For instance, for East Germany Schmidt and his colleagues (1990) report that in 1988, only 61 percent of the labor force on the collective and state farms were actually engaged directly in crop or animal production. The others were administrators, supervisors, or employed in the repair shops, cafeterias, kindergartens, or on building crews, and so forth.[7] In market economies many of these functions are performed either by separate enterprises (repairs, for example) or by the state (kindergartens and training). Thus the numbers of workers reflect in good measure the greater degree of vertical integration on these farms. For those countries interested in moving back to a market economy, a difficult resorting and reorganization of the rural labor force must be carried out.

A number of comparability problems regarding the labor force measurements also arise: (1) the measurement of female participation in the farm labor force is difficult, especially since many women carry out farm work only on a part-time basis; (2) many nations report only collective farm members, not actual farm labor force, so that we must make some

---

[7] The original source reported data for the entire agricultural sector; I have tried to remove the labor force from the interfarm enterprises and other nonfarm units so that only farms are included. In these production units, 12 percent of the labor force worked in the farm administration, and another 5 percent were brigade leaders (supervisors), 16 percent worked in the workshops and building crews, and 6 percent in education and cultural activities.

crude estimates; (3) the handling of permanent and temporary labor force varies from country to country; and (4) workers on farms in market economies usually work many more hours. For example, in West Germany farmers work roughly 3,000 hours a year, in comparison to roughly 2,500 hours or less in East Germany.

Table 5.1 reports data on the size of farm as measured by land area and labor force. Despite the problems of measurement listed here, the data reported permit a broad overview and can be compared for rough orders of magnitudes with similar data for average acreage of farms in capitalist nations presented in Research Note B, tables RB.1 and RB.2. As expected, the data show clearly that the average state and collective farms are much larger than average size farms in advanced capitalist market economies. If suitable comparisons could be made for the labor force, the differences would be even more marked since a majority of farms in the West are operated by a single family, sometimes with the help of a few hired hands.

Unfortunately, there is less to these data from Marxist regimes than meets the eye. In one sense the farm sizes designated in the table may be too small because the "farm" might be the political unit making the key decisions for the subunits that are called farms. For instance, one economist visiting the North Korean countryside told me his impression that in the 1980s the Cooperative Farm Management Council, which operates at the county level, became the key decision-making unit. Without a systematic investigation into what decisions are made at particular levels of the hierarchy, it is difficult to verify this judgement. In another sense the designated farm sizes may be too large because the individual subunits within the farms have had a certain autonomy. For instance, in both the early and late years of the agroproduction complexes in Bulgaria the individual units (which were previously independent) had considerable decision-making autonomy; it was only in the middle years of this period that such farms operated as a single unit.

In some Third World nations the large collective or state farms are merely a continuation of colonial plantations, but under state ownership. In most other cases the large farm size has been a deliberate organizational goal of the government. The most extreme horizontal integration occurred in Bulgaria in 1977 where the average agro-industrial complex (the label for a mechanized farm) was 32,834 hectares or 127 square miles; and the average industrial-agricultural complex (the label for a vertically integrated unit) was 54,714 hectares or 211 square miles (Cochrane 1989, p. 21). By the late 1980s the average farm had declined to less than one-third this size. At the end of 1989 the agro-industrial complexes dissolved into their earlier collective and state farm units.

One striking aspect of the data in the table is the difference in farm size from country to country; several factors underlying these variations can be identified. Clearly the population density in the rural sector is crucial. The relatively low density in Mongolia or the Soviet Union has led to an extensive agriculture and large average-size farms (in area). The high density in China and Viet Nam has led to an intensive agriculture and small average-size farms (in area). The kind of crop grown or animals raised also influences average farm size. For instance, wheat farms are generally large in area since this crop can be sown and harvested by giant machines. For other crops, such as vegetables, economies of scale or size can be achieved with a relatively small plot of land and few workers.

Population density also interacts with climatic conditions and the relative level of mechanization to influence the type of agriculture practiced, another determinant of farm size. For instance, in East Germany animal raising is carried out in stalls and feedlots, an intensive form of agriculture requiring little land. In Mongolia climatic conditions force the practice of transhumance in animal production, an extensive form of agriculture requiring an enormous amount of land. Similarly, population density and climate encourage intensive rice production in East Asia and extensive wheat production in the Soviet Union and East Europe. In past centuries these factors have, in turn, influenced population growth and density.

The administrative convenience of central planning and administration also appears to affect farm size. For instance, it is easier for central economic administrators to deal with a few large farms, rather than a large number of small farms, so up to a certain point centrally planned economies will strive to reduce this number by increasing the average size.[8]

The scarcity of trained farm administrators influences farm size as well, but opposing causal forces are present. It is possible that the fewer the trained farm administrators, the larger the size of the average farm because of the problem of indivisibility of skills. But it is also possible that in such a situation, the average farm size would be small because fewer skills are required for managing a smaller farm.[9] This question cannot be resolved with the data at hand, although the qualitative evidence suggests that the latter effect is more important.

The data in table 5.1 also show the area of state farms is usually larger

[8] Many decades ago Walter Eucken hypothesized that centrally administered economies generally have larger units of production than market economies. This proposition was tested and validated in the industrial sector using a sample of East and West European nations by Pryor (1973, chaps. 3 and 4).

[9] One of the reasons the voluntary collective farms in some African nations have had such difficulties is because the farms have been too large to administer, given the lack of management skills and experience of the members. The case studies of such collective farms in Zimbabwe discussed by Chitsike (1988), a sympathetic observer, provide some examples.

TABLE 5.1
Size of Collective and State Farm Units

	Date	Average Collective Farm			Average State Farm		
		Workers or Members	Area (hectares)	Hectares per Worker	Workers	Area (hectares)	Hectares per Worker
Africa							
Angola	1979	172	135	0.8	389	n.a.	n.a.
Bénin	1980–81	18	22	1.2	100	225	2.2
Cape Verde	1988	12	7	0.6	400	85	0.2
Congo	1973	n.a.	12	n.a.	160	636	4.0
Ethiopia	1982	n.a.	n.a.	n.a.	406	5,797	14.3
	1983–84	100	192	1.9	n.a.	n.a.	n.a.
Guinea-Bissau	n.a.	n.a.	n.a.	n.a.	n.a.	n.a.	n.a.
Madagascar	1984–85	n.a.	316	n.a.	n.a.	570	n.a.
Mozambique	1985–86	100	75	0.8	1,000	1,000	1.0
São Tomé	1987	None	None	None	630	5,556	8.8
Seychelles	1988	17	n.a.	n.a.	40	25	0.6
Somalia	1978	63	141	2.2	n.a.	n.a.	n.a.
	1984	n.a.	n.a.	n.a.	n.a.	2,681	n.a.
Zimbabwe	1984	147	2,710	18.4	278	27,722	99.8
Americas							
Cuba	1966	n.a.	n.a.	n.a.	n.a.	7,629	n.a.
	1980	29	206	7.1	1,430	14,161	9.9
	1987	49	689	14.1	1,448	14,084	9.7
Grenada	1981	n.a.	11	n.a.	n.a.	62	n.a.
Guyana	1986	n.a.	n.a.	n.a.	2,028	6,923	3.4
Nicaragua	1984	n.a.	n.a.	n.a.	598	12,196	20.4
	1986	21	577	28.0	n.a.	n.a.	n.a.
Asia							
Afghanistan	1982	158	126	0.8	457	1,622	3.6
China	1981	(only communes)					
		6,009	1,905	0.3	2,353	2,310	1.0
Kampuchea	1977	(communes)					
		1,500	n.a.	n.a.	n.a.	n.a.	n.a.
Korea, North	1963	(individual farms, not county)					
		520	488	0.9	n.a.	832	n.a.
Laos	1986	157	59	0.4	n.a.	n.a.	n.a.
		(only communes)					
Mongolia	1970	n.a.	48,050	n.a.	n.a.	233,000	n.a.
	1986	n.a.	43,262	n.a.	n.a.	165,192	n.a.
Viet Nam	1975	314	115	0.4	894	n.a.	n.a.
	1988	319	79	0.2	n.a.	1,532	n.a.
Yemen, South	1987	n.a.	1,939	n.a.	n.a.	222	n.a.
Europe							
Albania	1970	739	737	1.0	n.a.	3,100	n.a.
	1983	1,531	1,322	0.8	n.a.	n.a.	n.a.
Bulgaria	1970	1,237	6,323	5.1	978	5,999	6.1
	1987	—	—	—	n.a.	9,692	n.a.
Czechoslovakia	1970	113	669	5.4	590	4,265	7.2
	1985	410	2,605	6.4	736	6,204	8.4

TABLE 5.1 (cont.)

		Average Collective Farm			Average State Farm		
	Date	Workers or Members	Area (hectares)	Hectares per Worker	Workers	Area (hectares)	Hectares per Worker
Germany,	1970	99	574	5.8	364	866	2.4
East	1987	153	1,247	8.2	464	965	2.1
Hungary	1970	350	2,201	6.3	927	5,552	6.0
	1987	494	4,356	8.8	1,230	7,398	6.0
Poland	1970	33	215	3.8	126	906	7.2
	1987	83	314	6.6	393	2,706	6.9
Romania	1970	729	1,953	2.7	790	5,646	7.1
	1985	546	2,439	4.5	636	4,895	7.7
USSR	1970	506	10,821	21.4	594	45,872	77.2
	1986	479	9,323	19.5	523	34,650	66.3
Yugoslavia	1981	15	167	11.0	52	722	14.0

Source: See Statistical Note D.

Notes: The state farms exclude "institutional farms," *podkhozy*, experimental farms, municipal farms, and farm associations. Such a definition is less inclusive than that used in CMEA (annual) which, for instance, includes fishing cooperatives and associations of cooperatives.

The size of the state and collective farms covers total land areas including the private plots of the members on the farm. Whenever possible, I use total farm area rather than agricultural area, so that these data can be compared with similar data from Western nations.

The definition of workers on cooperative farms is not standardized, either across nations or often from one year to the next, with data for "total workers," "full-time workers," and "members" being given. I have tried to include only full-time workers and make other attempts at standardization, but the paucity of data excludes any but the most crude adjustments to the available data. Alternative series for average farm area using different definitions are found for the CMEA nations in Cochrane (1989) and CMEA (annual).

than that of cooperative farms, but that the number of workers are more similar, which indicates that the state farms are more mechanized. The state farms can also draw upon a greater pool of trained managers. In certain Marxist regimes, collective farm managers have often been politically loyal ex-urbanites with little knowledge of farm management; hence their skills are only suitable for smaller farms. Since communes combine both political and economic units, they generally have the largest number of workers.

Changes in Average Farm Size

Data on the changes in the average size of state and collective farms are readily available only for the CMEA nations. The data presented in table 5.1 show that in most countries the farms increased in average size. In the Soviet Union from the 1930s through the mid-1960s, the average size of both collective and state farms increased dramatically (data are provided by Rochlin and Hagemann, 1971). Since then the merger of collective farms and their transformation into state farms has resulted in a decrease in the average size of both, but a rise in the average size of all socialist farms combined. In China, the drive during the Cultural Revolution decade (1966–76) to move from the team (the smallest subunit) to the brigade as the accounting unit bore some resemblances to farm consolidation in the other nations. This was part of the "learning from Dazhai" campaign, which represented a last gasp of Maoist influence on agriculture.

This increase in the size of farm has had not only economic but also social and political implications. The farms began to embrace a number of villages, which led to a decline in importance of local power structures. Many of the leaders of the original collective farms, who were often of peasant stock, were replaced by technocrats who were trained in managing the large units. In Hungary this process has been called the "rural class struggle" because of the difference in class background of the two groups (Swain 1985; Szelenyi 1988).

Although changing farm size has been influenced in both Marxist and non-Marxist economies by such factors as the increased mechanization or migration to the city, the most important causal forces have been quite different. In particular, four additional factors operating in Marxist regimes are important to note: (1) farm consolidation in some countries, the Soviet Union and Albania, for example, was a method of providing state financing for investments in agriculture. Most of these governments preferred to give relatively large investment grants to a few units under their direct control, rather than small grants to many farms that could not be so strictly overseen; (2) consolidation of rich and poor collective farms also provided an easy means of reducing rural income inequalities, especially in situations (discussed in chapter 4) where farmers with fertile lands and considerable infrastructure excluded poorer farmers from their collective; (3) over time, the shortage of managers trained to administer large farms diminished with the rising level of managerial education; and (4) these farm mergers, according to a brilliant anthropological study of several Soviet collective farms by Humphrey (1983), provided an easy method of transferring production factors. She noted that in some countries including the Soviet Union, few mechanisms existed to transfer factors of production among farms; for instance, a farm with excess land could not, under the existing administrative rules, sell or give some of this land to a farm with too many cattle.

Of all of the Marxist regimes, East Germany engaged in the most extensive experiments to determine the optimal size and structure of farms. During the 1970s, the government began forming interfarm organizations (first the Cooperative Communities [KOG], later the Cooperation Departments for Plant Production [KAP], as well as similar organizations for vegetable and fruit farms), which would combine the crop growing parts of various collective and state farms into one specialized unit. By the 1980s, the organizational structure of agriculture had so evolved that collective and state farms emerged as highly specialized farm units, each producing only a few agricultural products. In 1987, for instance, one could find the following average sizes for five different types of specialized farms: Garden Cooperatives (GPG), 73 hectares; Agricultural Cooperatives for Crop Production (LPG[P]), 4562 hectares; Agricultural Cooperative for Animal Production (LPG[T]), 29 hectares; People's Own Farm for Crop Production (VEG[P]), 5024 hectares; and People's Own Farm for Animal Production [VEG(T)], 165 hectares; as well as several minor forms of Between-Enterprise Units (ZBEs).[10] Such a high degree of specialization gave rise to labor shortages since a single farm could not easily switch its labor from one crop to another as the situation demanded. This shortage, in turn, led to various types of "campaigns" with special work units composed of labor and equipment from various farms (e.g., the Central Harvesting Brigades, or ZET), going from farm to farm as needed. For farms using inputs produced on other farms, for instance, animal-raising farms using the fodder from crop-growing farms, coordination problems arose which were supposed to be solved by still another unit, the Cooperation Councils (KR). The system was sufficiently clumsy so that by the mid-1980s, mergers between different farm organizations began to occur to lessen the high degree of production specialization on a single farm. In the spring of 1990 the whole complex organizational system for agricultural production collapsed as the farms dissolved their bonds with certain organizations, broke up into smaller farms or spun off parts of the farms. Many animal-producing farms also merged with the farms supplying their fodder.

Horizontal Integration and Performance: An Hypothesis

The data reviewed in Research Note B suggest that the long-run average cost curves of farms fall rapidly and then reach a plateau. Such evidence, however, has been collected for farms that vary considerably in area, but have relatively few workers. In many of the Marxist regimes listed in table 5.1, the state and collective farms have a considerable number of workers—far exceeding the size of farms on which such generalizations about scale economies are based.

Although many policymakers in Marxist regimes have preferred large farms to small family farms, they have worried about how large the farms

[10] These data come from: German Democratic Republic, Staatliche Zentralverwaltung für Statistik, annual, 1987, p. 181.

should become. Several Hungarian studies purported to show, for instance, that during the 1970s, the collective farms reached their optimal size. It is difficult to evaluate these studies—or, for that matter, similar studies from other Marxist regimes—since in most cases only the results, and not the techniques of analysis, were reported. It seems likely, however, that many of these studies were made on the basis of technological, rather than economic considerations, especially since these results are difficult to square with data (at least from Hungary) showing that average profitability, capital productivity, and land productivity decreased as farm size increased, and that subsidies were proportionately greater for the larger farms (Hare 1981; Kornai 1986, p. 94).

If suitable data on a farm-level basis were available, we could test whether the large size of farm unit in the Marxist regimes has had ill effects. But when this book was written, such data were not available to me and I was left only with indirect evidence that far from proved the case; for instance, those Third World Marxist regimes attempting to set up *voluntary* agricultural production cooperatives found that small cooperatives were generally more successful in terms of productivity than large ones.

Since the available aggregative data also do not permit detailed exploration of the effects of average farm size without requiring us to make some heroic assumptions, all I can make is a relatively weak statement: According to the line of analysis pursued above and associated with the work of Binswanger and Rosenzweig, the large sizes of farms in Marxist regimes appear a major cause for poor agricultural performance, at least with regard to those indicators that reflect some aspect of efficiency. In the empirical analysis in chapter 8, the only indicator of this property is total factor productivity, and according to this criterion, the Marxist regimes have had a poorer performance than comparable non-Marxist nations. The exact role of farm size in determining this result could not, unfortunately, be disentangled.

VERTICAL INTEGRATION OF STATE AND COLLECTIVE FARMS

Vertical integration is the combining of two or more stages of the agricultural chain, such as the production of major farm inputs, farming, or the processing of farm products, into a single unit of management or contractual agreement. It is important to examine these vertical linkages for two reasons:

Disproportions. A number of specialists on the Soviet economy have argued that an important factor underlying the high costs of Soviet agriculture is not farm production per se, but rather the performance of the vertical linkages of the farm sector. On the upstream side (suppliers of major inputs and services), farm equipment has been unsuitable for many growing conditions, repair parts have been scarce, fertilizers have not been provided in the right proportions, and pesticides or fungicides have often not been available when needed. On the downstream side (processing of agricultural goods), drying, storage, and refrigeration capacities have been inadequate, transportation links have been poor, large amounts of many crops have not reached the consumer (according to Nazarenko 1991, up to one-third of total farm output), and the nutrient values of foodstuffs have often deteriorated before being sold. Although the 40 percent spoilage of perishable foods (fresh fruits, vegetables, and potatoes) can be readily understood, it must be added that losses of wheat were estimated at 20 percent of the crop, in contrast to roughly 2 percent in the United States (International Monetary Fund et al. 1990, p. 39). An effective investment program must proceed on a broad front; unfortunately, investment funds have been wasted because only certain of these bottlenecks in the agricultural chain were attacked. Similar problems of vertical linkages have also appeared in many other Marxist nations as well.

Creation of Competitive Conditions. As argued in detail in chapter 10, the structure of these vertical linkages considerably influences the ability of the government to create a competitive agricultural sector. In particular, the existence of decentralized vertical linkages, such as inter-farm enterprises supplying certain agricultural inputs or processing some farm output, allow the introduction of competition more easily than when these functions were handled by the central government.

Forms and Motives of Vertical Integration

Vertical integration can either occur at the farm level or at levels in the administrative hierarchy above the production units. At the farm level, following the analysis of Knutson, Penn, and Boehm (1983, 1990), it is useful to distinguish two types of vertical integration of the farm sector according to the tightness of the managerial linkage: *Contract integration* occurs when a farm signs a legal contract binding it to certain production or marketing practices. The partner can be either a cooperative, a state, or a private agrobusiness firm either supplying the farm with inputs or purchasing its outputs. This is really a very preliminary form of vertical integration since the farm in the contractual agreement still maintains its autonomy of decision-making and legal identity. *Ownership integration* occurs when a single owner has enterprises at two or more levels of the agricultural production and marketing system. For instance, a fruit-processing firm can own its own orchards.

These vertical linkages at the farm level, particularly on the input side, become increasingly important in agriculture as the level of technology rises. For instance, in the United States (all data are calculated from U.S. Department of Commerce, 1990) only 38 percent of the value of gross agricultural production comes from the farm directly, while 62 percent comes from purchased inputs. Although 30 percent of these inputs are supplied by the farm sector to itself (e.g., seeds or fodder), nine industries also supply 55 percent of the inputs, and many more industries supply the remaining 15 percent.

Perry (1989) distinguishes three broad determinants of vertical integration in market economies: technological economies, transactional economies, and market imperfections. For agriculture, technological economies occur for those crops or animals where careful breeding and control of genetic factors play a highly important role for either quality control or for productivity, and where the requisite knowledge for controlling such factors is available at only one stage of a multistage production process. Clearly these conditions are relevant in a centrally planned economy. Transactional economies occur in the produce markets where vertical integration can save certain crucial market transactions costs, especially where timing is important. For instance, certain highly perishable fruits and vegetables must be sold quickly to avoid spoiling or cane sugar must be harvested and processed within a short period of time, as the sugar content is rapidly lost (Roca 1976; Binswanger and Rosenzweig 1986).[11]

---

[11] Ownership integration is not absolutely necessary because, of course, contracts can be arranged so that it is unnecessary to combine growing and processing. Nevertheless, these may require specification of many contingencies so that negotiation of the contract is time consuming and expensive.

Export banana production, which occurs in a number of Third World Marxist regimes such as Cape Verde, provides another example of coordination problems being minimized by vertical integration since bananas must be placed in a cold boat within twenty-four hours of harvest to arrest further ripening. Moreover, harvesting must be coordinated so that a large section of a single refrigerated boat can be filled at one time. Although transportation and farming enterprises are sometimes separate, vertical integration is important (an example is provided by the U.S. Fruit Company).

More questionable kinds of economies of vertical integration are also discussed in the literature on plantations. For instance, Paige (1975) shows that plantation agriculture is most likely found for the following crops: bananas, coffee, cotton, grapes, palm oil, rubber, sisal, sugar, and tea. His approach is open to criticism (Pryor, 1982) and his theoretical explanation that these crops have considerable loss of bulk or weight in the primary stage of processing so that vertical integration is necessary begs the question as to why a private or cooperative company could not carry out such a task. The coordination costs approach of Binswanger and Rosenzweig (1986) appears to be more satisfactory, especially for a crop like sugar where processing and harvesting must be closely coordinated or the nutrient

Again, planned economies must take these considerations into account. Market imperfections also lead to vertical integration, but these are irrelevant to this discussion. Although a number of other theoretical factors influencing vertical relations can be discussed, neither these nor the considerations mentioned above allow us to predict accurately a general pattern of vertical relations in different subsectors of agriculture in the various market economies. As I argue in Research Note C, the available data on vertical integration suggest that these relations depend a great deal on institutions and historical circumstances that differ considerably from country to country.

During the Stalin era in the Soviet Union, such economic considerations played a secondary role; other criteria were more important. The organizational ideal was to minimize both upstream and downstream integration and the farms were supposed to be simply a productive unit carrying out agricultural activities under the supervision of the Ministry of Agriculture. Thus the Soviet government even discouraged side industries during the dead winter period or production of small-scale items such as handicraft products, since these activities might have distracted the attention of either farmworkers or managers from their main purpose of agricultural production. The supply of inputs and the processing of farm produce would be carried out by other production units, which would be under the authority of other ministries. Transfer prices among units on the production chain would not be a "problem" since prices for most goods and services would be set by the state, a condition lasting in East Europe up to 1990.

This approach to agricultural organization was most typified by the Machine Tractor Station (MTS), an institution renting equipment and equipment services (e.g., harvesting) to collective farms in most Marxist regimes. MTSs represented a type of vertical disintegration at the farm level because collective farms (but not state farms) were forbidden to own and operate large farm equipment. This arrangement was claimed to have two major economic advantages: MTSs would capture the alleged economies of scale existing in sharing this equipment among many farms, and they would save capital funds by avoiding duplicate investments on different collective farms. Any such economic benefits were outweighed by two major disadvantages: Scheduling problems arose so that it was difficult for collective farms to obtain such machine services when they were needed. Moreover, incentives between the farm and the MTS were often inconsistent. More specifically, MTS personnel were awarded bonuses, not according to indicators important to the success of the collec-

---

content falls rapidly. They also note that numerous crops feature economies of scale in processing and shipping and yet are unlikely to be grown in plantations.

tive farms such as overall production, but according to other criteria that might lead to a reduction of farm production. For instance, MTS tractor drivers were paid according to hectares plowed, which led them to plow less deeply than required for maximum farm production.

To digress for a moment, aside from their economic functions, MTSs also had two important political roles, namely overseeing production on the collective farms so that the farms could not subvert government policies, and serving as the party center exercising political control in the specific area. In the eyes of the government, the political roles were undoubtedly more important than the economic, at least in the early years of the system. In most other Marxist regimes this political role of MTSs did not seem so important.

All of the East European nations as well as most of the Third World Marxist regimes followed the Soviet Union's lead in creating MTSs. Five years after Stalin's death when Khrushchev dissolved the Soviet MTSs and sold their equipment to the collectives, most of these nations followed suit; Albania and Romania were exceptions. Strangely enough, many Soviet economists (including the writings of such émigrés as Medvedev 1987) are still disputing the wisdom of this step. Some of the Third World Marxist regimes such as Mongolia, Nicaragua, and Somalia still had MTSs in the late 1980s, but with an essential difference: collective farms could also own their own farm equipment if they wished, so the MTSs did not have a *de jure* monopoly on mechanical services. However, such a monopoly sometimes existed *de facto* since the MTSs generally received first priority to buy equipment.

In the 1980s Stalin's ideal of minimizing vertical integration in agriculture was followed by only a few countries such as Albania and Cuba. In the latter country after the "rectification" campaign of 1986, the government even shut down the handicraft industries of the wives of the male state farmers, so that these women had to work either on the farm or in different production units in urban areas. The opposite extreme was pursued by the Pol Pot government in Kampuchea (1975–78), which tried to arrange the economic system so that each commune was almost completely self sufficient in everything (Twining 1989).

Most industrialized Marxist regimes fall between these two extremes, abandoning Stalin's organizational ideal in various degrees shortly after his death. The pace of institutional change differed—up to the end of the 1980s the Soviet Union moved relatively slowly, while in other countries change was much more rapid. In those countries, two related developments occurred. First, nonfarm agricultural activities located on the farms increased. For instance, over the years Yugoslavia encouraged the development of large agro-industrial farms, which were generally located near urban centers and combined both agricultural production and processing of agricultural products (Almeyra 1983). In Hungary, farms began to sell inputs to each other, and in China, factories producing fertilizers and farm equipment were set up on the farms. Second, farms began to produce goods and services for urban use. For instance, in addition to its farming activities, which did not appear very profitable, the Slušovice Cooperative Farm in Czechoslovakia produced not only farm equipment such as hay-bailers but also a wide range of other goods and services far removed from agriculture.[12] The extent of these activities and their importance varied. In Czechoslovakia these non-agricultural activities served as a major source of farm profits for about one-fifth of the farms (Záhlava 1989). In Hungary in 1987, nonagricultural industries located on farms accounted for about one-third of total farm output and two-fifths of their profits (Economist Intelligence Unit 1987b).[13] By the same year in China, nonagricultural production in the rural areas exceeded the value of agricultural production.

In contrast, in most Third World Marxist regimes, vertical integration or production of goods and services not related to agriculture has not been great. In some cases the nonagricultural production on the farms followed along the lines inherited from the colonial economy, with only the most basic agricultural processing activities carried on. For instance, in São Tomé the major nonfarming activities on state farms were the processing of cocoa beans, exactly as in the time of the Portuguese.

Solving Coordination Problem by Organizational Means

How should the farm sector be organized in order to provide the smoothest coordination between the industries supplying agricultural inputs,

[12] Examples of this nonfarm production of goods and services on the Slušovice Cooperative Farm include personal computers, a travel agency, a hotel, a group carrying out contract research on alternative energy sources, the sale of ice cream in Prague, and the operation of a successful race track. I was told that the farm even owned several small farms abroad, so that it must be considered as a multinational collective farm. Slušovice has received a good deal of favorable attention both by outsiders (Myant 1989, p. 200; *New York Times*, 19 December 1988) and by Czechoslovak observers (Čuba and Divila, 1989). Recently, however, the farm has also received criticism that much of its success was due to political connections and massive subsidies (Hénard 1990b). As an outsider without first-hand information, it is impossible to evaluate these arguments for this specific farm, but its diversification into other areas is undeniable. A Czechoslovak farm that I actually visited invented and produced a machine for testing metallic impurities in oil, manufactured parts for computers and fax machines, produced pastries for Prague bakeries with the eggs from its poultry house that were too small to sell, and provided services for hire, including painting lines on rural highways and constructing homes and small buildings in urban areas.

[13] For 1979 in Hungary Csizmadia and Szíkely (1986, p. 145) show that only 57 percent of the output of cooperative farms arises from their basic activities, 32 percent from subsidiary activities, and 11 percent from totally unrelated activities. These numbers may not be comparable with those in the text.

the farms, and the food processing industries? If the system is not coordinated by a price mechanism, then the political authorities must design an administrative system which somehow balances all of the inputs to produce the proper mix of output, while providing the proper incentives for a large number of very different types of units of production. Three basic administrative models can be specified.

THE STANDARD "MINISTERIAL/PRODUCTION MODEL"

In this arrangement, sellers of agricultural inputs are subordinate to different ministries (e.g., fertilizer sellers to the Ministry of the Chemical Industry, tractor sellers to the Ministry of Agricultural Equipment) and the buyers of agricultural outputs are also subordinate to different ministries (e.g., buyers of cotton to the Ministry of Textile Production, buyers of meat to the Ministry of Food Products). These ministries can be either at the federal or the regional level. The farms sector must, therefore, deal with many different organizations that are connected to the central economic administration of the government by many different organizational channels.

This organizational arrangement existed in almost all European Marxist regimes at one time or another and, in the late 1980s, was also found in some Third World Marxist nations with centrally planned economies. Although it appears quite straightforward and simple, the arrangement gives rise to many difficulties in countries where prices do not have an important allocative function in balancing all inputs and outputs. The major reason for this is that the various units in this exchange network have different and conflicting interests. For instance, fertilizer producers may wish to produce one type of fertilizer which, given the specific costs and prices, allows them the highest bonus, while such a fertilizer may not necessarily be the most suitable for the farmers. And the farmers may wish to produce the foodstuffs that provide them with the highest bonus, but that the consumers do not want to buy. Without a price system to resolve such conflicts of interest, administrators must adjudicate matters by issuing new orders and changing the incentive system, a never-ending task as new problems arise.

THE SUPRAFARM VERTICAL INTEGRATION MODEL

This arrangement provides for a single organization to produce all farm inputs or to purchase and process all farm outputs. Such a monopoly organization of the entire agro-industrial system can occur either at the national or the regional level.[14]

[14] A terminological confusion arises because some in the Soviet literature designate this type of organizational pattern as horizontal because all communication occurs within the

This administrative structure, designed to overcome the clashes between organizations with different superior organs, raises new coordination difficulties. Conflicts of interest arise at different levels, this time between the food complex as a whole and other sectors and, moreover, between different branches of the ministry of agriculture. The fact that the level at which such conflicts are resolved is at the level of the ministry, not the council of ministers, does not change the means for adjudicating such disputes, namely orders and incentive changes, nor the problems arising from such administrative mechanisms.

A notable example occurred in the Soviet Union in the early 1980s with the formation of Raion Agro-Production Organizations (RAPOs), which were supposed to supervise all aspects of the food production chain in a particular district. This led to a considerable increase of local bureaucracy. Moreover, difficulties arose since many of the local organs under the supervision of the RAPO reported to different ministries. Gorbachev tried to solve this problem in 1985 by combining five ministries, a state committee, and bits and pieces of other ministries into one super-ministry, Gosagroprom.[15] Since basic farm supply problems arose from a lack of knowledge about what individual farms needed at particular times, however, such a centralization of authority did not achieve a flexible, local supply system and the farmers continued to have little choice of what farm inputs they received. The latter approach also did not appear to reduce costs or increase agricultural productivity. By 1989 Gosagroprom was disbanded, most RAPOs had disappeared, and the Soviet Union began experimenting with several different kinds of decentralized vertically integrated agricultural organizations such as agro-kombinats, agro-firms, and agro-industrial associations (Butterfield 1990), which had taken over some of the functions fulfilled by the RAPOs.

Suprafarm vertical integration has no necessary correlation with ver-

---

ministry. From the viewpoint of the stages of production combined in a single production unit, which is a more standard approach in the study of industrial organization, I designate such an approach as vertical integration since farm input suppliers, farms, and processors of farm produce are combined into a single production unit.

[15] Some notion of how this suprafarm vertical integration actually functioned can be gained by a joke circulating in the Soviet Union in 1988: John, a retired CIA agent, meets Ivan, a retired KGB agent, in a bar in Vienna. They reminisce about the cold war and drink together for many hours. After considerable alcohol has flowed, Ivan experiences a sudden flush of sobriety and whispers a crucial question, "Was Chernobyl really a CIA operation?" John looks furtively around and whispers back, "No, but Gosagroprom was."

Litvin (1987) presents an interesting analysis of the development of the Soviet agro-industrial complex; Doolittle and Hughes (1987) present a full description of the creation of Gosagroprom. The basic belief that centralization can solve all economic questions lies deep in the Soviet psyche; even critical émigré writers such as Litvin (1987) and Medvedev (1987) hailed Gosagroprom. Nove (1988b) has an extremely useful analysis of many of the specific difficulties this bureaucratic integration engendered.

tical integration at lower levels. Suprafarm and farm-level vertical integration have occurred together, for instance, in East Germany between 1968 and 1990. A single ministry oversaw most of the agro-industrial complex; part of this sector, however, consisted of a series of decentralized vertical organizations (see below). Suprafarm vertical integration could exist without farm-level vertical integration, as in the Soviet Union.

A variant of the suprafarm vertical integration model has occurred in relatively small Marxist regimes with a low level of industrialization. In these cases the foreign trade sector is relatively large and the vertical structure in agriculture is simple, with a monopoly importing agency selling agricultural inputs, usually to some agency of the ministry of agriculture, and a monopsonistic purchasing board buying the farm outputs, which is either another agency of the ministry if an export crop is involved, or the ministry of internal trade if a domestic foodstuff is the product.

<h3 align="center">THE DECENTRALIZED VERTICAL INTEGRATION MODEL</h3>

This arrangement provides for individual farms or intrafarm organizations to produce the needed inputs or purchase and process the food produce. Although these organizations may buy from a single input producer or sell to a single purchaser, farms are shielded at one remove from such monopsonies or monopolies. As I argue in chapter 10, under certain conditions this vertical integration at the farm level allows an easier transformation into a competitive environment for agriculture than either the standard ministry/production model or the suprafarm vertical integration model.

A system of decentralized vertically integrated enterprises reduces coordination problems by lowering the level of adjudication of production problems by the administrative hierarchy to a relatively local level. It also reduces the costs of collecting, processing, and transmitting information to the center, and it reduces coordination problems arising from incentive distortions including opportunism and the monopoly power of suppliers. For the enterprise itself, such vertical integration also reduces risks arising from uncertainties of input supplies due to difficulties in other sectors.

Nevertheless, this model may not allow economies of scale to be achieved unless the individual farms or the joint farm organizations are very large. Moreover, information regarding technology and manufacturing of a particular product is no longer centralized in a single ministry so information costs increase. If farms are sufficiently large to obtain economies of scale in nonfarm production activities, they may have exceeded the optimal scale for their farming activities. Moreover, large interfarm organizations can acquire interests of their own that are quite different from those of the constituent members, and the problems of incentive compatibility arise once again.

A system of decentralized and vertically organized farms appears to have much in common with "enterprise autarky" in the manufacturing sector of centrally administered economies, about which much has been written (e.g., Pryor 1973; Kroll 1988). The agricultural sector, however, is somewhat different, not just because the farm sector lacks the monopoly elements found in manufacturing but because problems of asset specificity, asymmetric information, and other factors encouraging vertical integration are not so important. The East European literature on vertical integration has focused relatively little attention on such factors as minimization of risks or lowering of transactions costs, which are important in market economies. Instead, discussion has centered around certain alleged benefits of these linkages: greater possibilities for technological improvement, greater efficiency of investment, better utilization of existing buildings and equipment, greater scope for specialization, more possibilities for reducing overhead costs, to name a few. Much of this literature is quite vague, since few convincing data are supplied.

Skepticism about these economic advantages is warranted since, in the words of a working group of economists from East and West Europe, "in the majority of eastern European countries . . . the governmental authorities (regional and local) usually played a very important, and often decisive role in promoting both horizontal and vertical integration," so the impetus came from above, rather than from the farms themselves (FAO 1977, p. 4). Decentralized vertical integration could have arisen as another bureaucratic panacea for the agrarian problem rather than from economic forces. Certain other motives appear to have played some role in the formation of such vertically organized farm and intrafarm organizations:

Relieving Local Governments of Unwanted Responsibilities. Many of the local governments and ministries were responsible for providing particular services to the farms under their jurisdiction. In many cases they were either unable or unwilling to provide such services in a satisfactory fashion and could evade their responsibilities by forcing the farm units to provide such services for themselves in the form of an interfarm organization or some other type of vertical integration.

Utilizing Local Resources. Creation of subsidiary production units supplying farm inputs can often use resources (including labor or knowledge of local conditions) that otherwise would have been idle because of seasonal considerations. For instance, in China, farms produced small agricultural tools and equipment for sale to other farms in the area that were adapted to the particular soil and other farming conditions in a local area.

Achieving Technical and Transactions Economies.   The growing importance of vertical linkages in the West for commodities where breeding and control of genetic factors are important for increasing productivity or quality control find a parallel development in East Europe, particularly in animal production. The transactional economies that occur, for instance, in sugar production (important in Cuba and Guyana) also have parallel influences in East and West.[16]

Examples of Vertical Integration in General

Ownership integration has occurred in centrally administered economies, but on a modest scale. The Soviet Union and most East European nations encouraged vertical linkages among farms at all stages of animal-raising, from the breeding to slaughter and preparation of meat products, where considerable vertical integration has occurred in market economies as well (Knutson, Penn, and Boehm 1983). Some of these countries also attempted to create vertical linkages between crop growers and food processors. For instance, Hungary combined a highly mechanized tomato farm and canning factory as well as vineyards and wineries. In part, the Hungarian government's encouragement of farms to set up various kinds of food processing firms by themselves or in groups was designed to break the monopoly of the urban food processing enterprises.

Ownership integration was the major purpose for the creation in Bulgaria in the mid-1970s of ten Industrial-Agricultural Complexes (not to be confused with the Agro-Industrial Complexes in the same country, which were large horizontally integrated farms). They were set up in sugar-beet, fruit, and grape production, but most of them did not prove very successful and many were later disbanded.

Contract integration was much more common. Such contracts have ranged from rather loose mutual aid of upstream and downstream enterprises, to projects carried out jointly by two or more enterprises, but

[16] Curiously, for almost two decades after the Castro revolution, sugar growing and sugar processing were carried out under the aegis of two different ministries so that the transactions cost savings discussed in the text were difficult to realize. According to Llovio-Menéndez (1988 pp. 308), once a high official of the sugar ministry, this situation arose because Fidel Castro somehow believed that combining sugar growing and processing under one management was capitalistic. It was not until 1980 when he was finally dissuaded of this notion that Cuba combined sugar growing and processing under one administrative head (Ministerío de Azucos, or MINAZ), creating at lower levels a series of Complejos Agro-Industria, which bear a strong resemblance both in name and form to the vertically integrated Industrial-Agricultural Complexes in Bulgaria.

with no separate legal structure, to the establishment by several enterprises of separate productive entities with contractual relations to the partners. In some cases of contract integration, considerable difficulties arose when the partners of such agreements were administered by different ministries.

One of the most extensive systems of contract integration occurred in Yugoslavia, where service cooperatives supply agricultural inputs, productive services (e.g., plowing), marketing services, and processing of agricultural products. Their work was supplemented by agro-industrial combines that both produce and process their own products and those of private and state farms around them. The contract linkages were sometimes mandatory, and Cochrane (1990) presents data showing that, as a result, inter-republic trade declined. This is a good example of where regional autarky was encouraged, but not by conscious design, a situation arising in other Marxist regimes as well.

Poland, another Marxist regime with a dominant private sector in agriculture, had a different system of contract integration. It encouraged Agricultural Circles that acted as a cooperative to supply inputs and market outputs. Moreover, the government also introduced a contract system that served both to stabilize state purchasing and to reduce the risks facing the individual farmers, especially since the prices paid on these contracts were generally higher than state prices on the open market (Quaisser 1987, p. 32).

Contract linkages have occurred between two farms that cooperate to supply an input or to market an output. For instance, Hungary encouraged individual collective and state farms to develop a technological package (technically operated production systems, or TOPS) which it then supplied to a group of associated farms, along with the necessary inputs such as fertilizers and special seeds, as well as the necessary training of personnel on these other farms and the extension services. Often, marketing services for the crop were also provided. In some cases the farm supplying the package also owned the equipment and was a separate entity distributing its profits to the members (the farms using the system). In other cases the farm supplying the package served more as a broker, with the individual farm owning the equipment and the package provider receiving a fee plus, which might include a share of the additional profits accruing to the farms adopting the system.[17] A particular farm could belong to several different TOPS groups and the various systems competed

[17] This business arrangement, which Hungarians call the "production system" or Bábolna model, raises a problem of terminology. The farms supplying the package were vertically integrated; however, the farms receiving the package were not structurally changed, so that many Hungarian economists designate the arrangement as horizontal since one farm cooperated with another. Elek (1980) has an interesting study of these TOPS.

against each other for members and, it should be added, against the foreign trade enterprises and other suppliers of agricultural inputs (Fekete 1989). In the middle 1980s more than sixty different TOPS packages were operating in Hungary.

As might be expected, East Germany set up the most elaborate system of vertically integrated organizations in the farm sector. For the most part these were small and flexible and served to coordinate the activities of the highly specialized production units. Such units included the voluntary Cooperation Organizations (Kooperrationsverbände, or KOV) and some Agro-Industrial Organizations (AIV).[18] Various KOV had quite different functions, ranging from organizing the exchange of information to serving as middleman, sorter, and packer of crops for sale in urban areas, or as coordinators of procurement for the member farms from any part of the nation. The KOVs could exclude applicants and usually consisted of the largest and most successful farms in a particular branch of agriculture. In the early years KOVs generally did not have legal independence and were solely the instrument of their member organizations. In the late 1980s, however, this began changing. AIVs were more regionally oriented and were usually set up around an Agrochemical Center (ACZ), which supplied fertilizers, seeds, and other inputs. Other vertical organizations included: Inter-Enterprise-Units (ZBEs), which served as building, potato-storage, or humus-preparation enterprises; Kombinats for Animal Fattening (VE-KIM); and inter-enterprise service enterprises (usually under the form of ZBEs). On a more local level there were also Cooperation Councils (KR), in which managers of crop and livestock farms met to arrange transfers of fodder and other products among them. In the spring of 1990, most of these decentralized vertical organizations in East Germany were in the process of becoming independent cooperatives or joint stock companies. Interfarm organizations producing or marketing either farm inputs or outputs were found in some other East European nations such as Romania and, in 1990, were also in transition to a different legal form.

In some countries a vertical disintegration occurred on the farm, accompanied by vertical integration on a broader scale through the creation of interfarm enterprises. For instance, the Soviet government encouraged the creation of interfarm construction organizations. These organizations consolidated the construction brigades of neighboring farms, ostensibly to permit greater economies of scale to be achieved; the real

---

[18] The organization of East German agriculture was complex because the government established so many different kinds of organizations. I draw especially on the discussions by Bajaja (1978), Franz (1976), and Schinke (1990). Schinke's discussion is particularly useful for the KOV, which he compares to the Soviet RAPOs and the analogous organizations in Bulgaria.

motive was probably to gain greater control over the construction activities of individual farms.[19]

Although many more examples of vertical linkages can be readily supplied, from this mass of institutional detail one important conclusion can be drawn. The pattern of vertical linkages in East Europe was quite different from that found in the market economies in the West, in large degree due to the different motives for establishing such arrangements and the different economic environment. Of particular importance is the fact that the network of vertical relations between a farm and either the suppliers of its inputs or the buyers of its output was not "dense" since most of nonfarm partners had monopoly positions. As a result, if a centrally planned economy wishes to marketize its agriculture, considerable efforts must be made to create a competitive structure, a subject taken up in detail in chapter 10.

A Digression: The Extent of Decentralized Vertical Integration

As I argue in chapter 10, some decentralized vertical structures allow a smoother transition to a competitive environment. Therefore, it is useful to consider briefly their actual importance in the agricultural sector.

In most Third World Marxist regimes, governments maintained those vertical linkages that were tied to technological or transaction savings and dissolved many of those linkages arising from special circumstances of colonialism. For instance, ties of ownership integration were broken where companies were given special concessions and developed a vertically integrated food processing or where companies other than the plantations could not obtain the capital to carry out these productive operations.[20]

Data on contract integration of a simple sort are not available for most countries except Poland, where sales from these contractual arrangements rose between 1960 and 1975 from 45 to 71 percent of private agricultural sales (Hegenbarth 1977, p. 20). Where vertical integration took the form of interfarm and interenterprise linkages of a more durable nature, one gathers the impression that the resulting vertical linkages were not very significant in most countries.[21] Combining qualitative evidence

[19] Humphrey (1983) points out that farm managers could count construction activities as part of gross farm output for purposes of achieving plan goals, and that this led to certain kinds of obvious abuses.

[20] An exception appears to be Mongolia, which created a number of intercollective organizations for producing fodder, providing transport, and constructing homes (Jaehne 1990b).

[21] Some idea of the relative importance of this integration can be gained by examining the breakdown of activities of the interfarm enterprises. For the mid 1970s such data are

with the few numbers that are available, it appears that by the late 1980s vertical integration was more advanced in Hungary and East Germany than in Czechoslovakia and Romania and in the latter pair more than in the Soviet Union and Bulgaria.

CONCLUDING REMARKS

Canonical Marxist texts tell us little about how state and collective farms should be organized or what is the proper degree of vertical and horizontal integration. Much depends upon the kind of farming that is practiced and the degree of education of the workers. Thus, it should not be surprising that the structural elements of state and collective farms were quite different from country to country, especially after Stalinist orthodoxy ceased to be enforced.

This chapter provides quantitative evidence that in most economically advanced Marxist regimes, horizontal integration was relatively high. By the late 1980s, for instance, only two countries, Poland and Yugoslavia, had average collective farms with fewer than one hundred members. At the same time in the Third World, the size of collective and state farms varied considerably. At first glance, it would appear that the process of horizontal integration is irreversible. After all, it is easier to merge collective or state farms than to dissolve them, especially if the farms invest in capital designed only for large-scale production, for instance, dairy barns. The question of irreversibility has many other facets as well, the focus of my discussion in chapter 9.

For vertical integration only qualitative evidence is available. It suggests that although suprafarm vertical organization occurred primarily in the more industrialized Marxist regimes, decentralized vertical integration was relatively unimportant except in a few countries such as China, East Germany, and Hungary. Among Third World Marxist regimes the degree of decentralized vertical integration generally changed little after the end of colonialism.

---

available for the Soviet Union and Hungary in FAO (1977) and for Czechoslovakia in Bajaja (1975). In the next decade the situation did not greatly change in Czechoslovakia (Záhlava 1989), while in Hungary these vertical links appeared to strengthen so that by the early 1980s, about 13 percent of the gross value of output of the food industry was produced in enterprises largely owned by the farms (Hartford 1987).

Chapter 6

THE INTERNAL ORGANIZATION OF THE FARMS

AGRICULTURAL PERFORMANCE is not only a function of the macrostructural elements of the farm sector, as discussed in the previous chapter, but also of the internal organization (or microstructural elements) of the farms. In this chapter I examine those internal aspects of the collective and state farms that seem to have the most important economic impacts, in particular, their economic autonomy, the combination of political and economic authority of their managers, the anatomy of their sub-units, the personal plots of their workers, and the various compensation systems used to provide proper work incentives for their labor force.

The available literature on the internal organization of state and collective farms is relatively skimpy. In many cases we have formal descriptions of the internal governance, for instance, steering committees, management boards, and general assemblies. But relatively little attention has been paid to how the key decisions are actually made and what role, if any, these governance units actually had. In most cases we have descriptions of other formal organizational elements, but little discussion has focused on the relative importance of these elements on the various farms in the nation, why certain organizational decisions were made, or what economic impact these changes have had. To make matters worse, in many Marxist regimes important changes in the internal organization of the farms have occurred at frequent intervals.

As a result, it is not possible to present a set of systematic comparisons; we must be content with only a description of many of these structural elements. Since this is not a treatise on farm management or governance, it is fortunately not necessary to examine many of these structural elements in great detail. They do, however, have an important influence on farm performance as well as the process of decollectivization. Moreover, the problems of compensating and motivating farm labor also raise a number of analytic issues for which some relevant theoretical and empirical evidence is available.

THE AUTONOMY OF THE FARM UNIT

The Stalinist conception of the state farm sector featured an extreme degree of organizational centralization, in which the subordinate units had little decision-making autonomy and existed primarily to implement production orders determined from higher administrative agencies and incorporated in the plans sent down from the state planning commission to the ministry to the farms. In theory the collective farms had greater decision-making autonomy and also greater participatory management than state farms. Nevertheless, in most centrally planned Marxist regimes, all farm managers have had to follow a production plan in the same manner. Moreover, election of farm managers in the collective farms was pro forma in many Marxist regimes until the late 1980s because higher political authorities (either party or state) appointed them. In many countries party authorities also intervened in production decisions of the farm.

The Stalinist conception was generally followed in most of the "core" Marxist regimes (chapter 1). In most of the "peripheral" Marxist regimes in the Third World, the role of the party/government was much weaker than in East Europe; exceptions include Albania, China, Cuba, Kampuchea, and North Korea, where the party was strong in the countryside. This weakness was manifested by a relatively greater share of nominal collective farms and also by less detailed and binding central plans for the agricultural sector, a matter receiving further discussion in Research Note D. Nevertheless, even in these nations managerial decision-making was administratively more constrained than in most capitalist market economies.

This lack of decision-making autonomy for both the state and collective farms led to several kinds of principal-agent problems between the superior administrative agencies and the farm managers, reinforced in the case of state farms by the separation of ownership and control.

Loss of Soil Fertility. The treatment of soil was costly to monitor by central authorities. Farm workers, however, had little incentive to preserve the fertility of the soil. The farm managers did have such an incentive, but only for the duration they would remain in this position.

Soft-Budget Constraint and Cost Increases. In those Marxist regimes with central planning, the primary output goals were stated in physical terms and costs of production were secondary. In some cases the treasury subsidized the farms directly; in other cases the government raised producer prices and subsidized some economic agency downstream that processed the foodstuffs. In still other cases financial authorities, particularly banks, accommodated these production goals by granting farms credits. As the farms were large, the government was loath to allow them to fail since the adverse impact on the local economy would be great. As a result, many loans received by the farms were never paid back and were eventually canceled. All of these were manifestations of the soft-budget constraint that has been analyzed by Kornai (1986).

The problems of soft-budget constraints were particularly serious where farm workers were paid regular wages, for instance, on the state farms. On the collective farms in some periods and in some countries (for instance, the Soviet Union during the 1940s), the workers could not legally leave the farms and received only the residual income after expenses were met, so that farms did not need to be subsidized. But as these collective farm workers were permitted to leave the farm and granted a minimum wage (in part, to reduce any massive outflow of labor), these farms also had fewer incentives for cost-saving, the budget constraint became softer, and subsidies increased. Since farm procurement prices in most Marxist regimes were based on average costs for the sector as a whole, these cost increases were eventually translated into higher prices paid by the state purchasing organs, a practice discouraging cost-saving even more.

Serious problems of the soft-budget constraints also occurred in a different context in small Third World Marxist nations where agricultural exports were particularly important and where the exchange rates were overvalued. For farmers to have any incentives to produce for export, subsidies had to be given. Once the process started, it was difficult to determine to what degree the subsidies were necessary because of the overvalued exchange rate or because the production units had stopped paying much attention to their costs.

Clearly the soft-budget constraint increases the drain on the governmental budget, distorts relative costs and prices, and increases tolerance for production inefficiencies. Brooks (1991) also notes that in those cases where political authorities tried to make producers "responsible" for their financial performance but did not give them greater control over the choice of outputs and inputs, the producers always succeeded in changing this policy since financial responsibility without broad decision-making autonomy is usually impossible.

Although these considerations should be relatively noncontroversial, an embarrassing problem about testing these ideas in an empirical fashion arises. It is difficult to measure these static inefficiencies, both because the proper data are not readily at hand and because the statistical techniques that are available rely on some questionable assumptions. I discuss these matters in greater detail in chapter 8.

Low Dynamic Efficiency. For those Marxist regimes with a centrally planned economy, a peculiar dynamic was established between the farms and the central authorities. It was difficult for central administrators to have a clear conception of the production possibilities on each farm because of the heterogeneity of growing conditions and, as a result, they had to resort to crude administrative tools such as the ratchet—raising plan goals every time the plan was exceeded. The farm manager had an incentive to hide surplus capacity so as to ease plan fulfillment, an action having an adverse impact on dynamic efficiency. An easy way to hide capacity lies in the investment process by not fully utilizing the new capital, a process almost impossible to monitor. In Research Note D, I present a formal model of this dynamic both for situations where farm managers have considerable decision-making autonomy (and can safely ignore the plan sent to them by the ministry) and in a centrally planned economy where their autonomy is considerably more limited. Fortunately, some key aspects of this low dynamic efficiency can be measured with the available data and some relevant empirical evidence is provided in chapter 8.

The autonomy of economic decision-making of collective and state farms was further constrained by the fusion of political and economic power, which gave rise to special problems. Political and economic authority on a farm were, in some cases, completely combined in a formal fashion as in a commune, a type of farm that was usually quite large and embraced the area and population of a political subdivision. This fusion gave farm authorities considerable power over the lives of commune members and, in most cases, the importance of the political function meant that the top leadership of these farm units had political, but not economic, expertise. Leaders also had to divide their time between the two functions, to the detriment of exclusive attention to either, a problem indicated by the complaint of agricultural cadre in China of the "five too-manys": too many meetings, too many organizations demanding attention, too many concurrent posts, too many documents, and too many departments. These conditions meant that farm leaders had time to serve only as transmitters of orders, not investigators or problem-solvers, a situation not conducive for technical efficiency or cost saving (Zweig 1989, p. 83).

As noted in chapter 1, communes were established in only a few countries. In many Marxist regimes, however, a certain fusion of economic and political authority did occur. One form it took was intervention in farm decisions by local government and Communist party authorities (at least up to 1990). In Eastern Europe this party interference was greatest in the Soviet Union and Bulgaria, where party officials were judged in part on how well the farms in their region fulfilled their physical plan, an incentive system leading to considerable day-to-day interference in farm management by party officials and a neglect of attention to costs.[1] In most

---

[1] Hedlund (1984, chap. 5) shows some of the consequence of this interference. Gor-

of the other East European nations, party inference was less heavy-handed and focused primarily on decisions with a long-run impact.

In most Third World Marxist regimes, where the party was numerically weak, its presence in the countryside was also weak and outside interference from this source did not often arise. Some interference in farm decision-making did come, however, from local governmental authorities. In other instances, these authorities assigned certain governmental functions to the farms, especially those relating to health, education, or welfare.

In recent years some of these nations made deliberate attempts to reduce such intervention, to separate party and government, and to encourage market incentives. In the 1980s, nations in this latter group included China, Hungary, Laos, Poland, Viet Nam, and Yugoslavia. In the 1990s the group expanded and included nations such as Czechoslovakia, East Germany, and Nicaragua, which voted Communist governments out of office.

Internal Organization

I list here a series of organizational elements that can be found in state and collective farms in all Marxist regimes. These features are important, not just to gain some idea of how well the farms function, but also, as I argue in chapter 9, to gauge the ease by which the farms can be decollectivized and dismembered.

The Anatomy of the Sub-Units

Collective and state farms have a series of overlapping subunits, and it is useful to distinguish between the ownership unit, the accounting unit, and the work unit. These three subunits need not be coincident.

Ownership units have effective control over the means of production and are entitled to compensation if either land or machinery is transferred. In most countries, the ownership unit was the state or collective farm itself. After the formation of the commune in 1958 in China, however, the ownership unit devolved rapidly from the commune to the brigade to the team, which generally encompassed a single village, and which "owned" the land and most of the farm equipment. At certain

bachev, despite his reformist tendencies, is not averse to party intervention in agriculture. On his path to power, he made a name for himself as a local party official in the Stavropol region by fostering the Ipatov method of harvesting. This involved centralization of harvesting operations in the regional (raion) party headquarters, which directed the battles on the grain front around the clock during the critical period.

times in a few other Marxist regimes, the subunits also had ownership rights, for instance, in both the early and late years of the agro-industrial complexes in Bulgaria.

Let me emphasize that "ownership" does not necessarily mean that the subunit possesses a formal title. Rather, ownership is defined in terms of "customary" actions or legal rights applying to all farms. As a result, ownership is sometimes difficult to determine except by means of interviews. For instance, in talking with collective farm members in East Europe I asked whether the farm manager could transfer tractors or buildings from one brigade or team to another without paying compensation. Some would answer that theoretically the manager had those rights, but that he would never exercise them because of the resentment these transfers would generate. This suggests that such ownership rights did exist, at least in an informal sense. Unfortunately, answers varied from farm to farm so that it is difficult to generalize for the country as a whole. Although subunit ownership rights might be more widespread than the literature suggests, it also seems safe to say that in most of the East European nations in most periods, the key ownership unit was probably the farm itself, not the subordinate units.

A devolution of ownership rights to the subunits represents an important decentralization. As argued in chapter 10, subunit ownership rights also greatly ease the decollectivization process by reducing the problems of dividing the equipment, buildings, and land among the individual members. A good part of the process already has been accomplished and the rest can be carried out by subunit members themselves in a more flexible and fair manner than if the decisions were made by the collective farm manager.

Accounting units are the smallest unit for which separate accounts are kept. In large enterprises in the West they are called "profit centers"; in the Marxist literature these units are said to have "economic accounting" (*khozraschet* in Russian). Since the work bonuses or net income are based on the results recorded by accounting units, their size is important in understanding the operation of the incentive system.

The relationship between ownership and accounting units varied considerably. For instance, following collectivization in Cuba and also in some other countries, even the state farms were not a separate accounting unit, but were merely part of a pool of units included in the budget of the ministry. In China the teams formed both the accounting and ownership unit. In North Korea the farm was the ownership unit, while the brigade or team made up the accounting unit. In some East European nations, such as Bulgaria, Czechoslovakia, East Germany, and the Soviet Union, theoretically the farms could introduce profit centers. In actuality, however, few appear to have availed themselves of the opportunity, although appropriate data for a firm generalization are not at hand.[2]

In some countries, as in the USSR (Yanov 1984) and China (Zweig 1989), the size of the accounting (and work) unit was the focus of fierce ideological disputes. Lives were lost and careers ruined as a result of this debate. In looking at these matters across Marxist regimes, however, it is difficult to find much correlation between ideological orthodoxy and the size of the accounting unit. This can be seen from some regimes which, during the 1980s, were relatively orthodox: in Albania the sub-team (link) of 10 workers was the basic accounting and work unit (Mury 1970, p. 112); in North Korea the accounting and work unit was often congruent with the sub-team; and in East Germany these units were also quite small (Schinke 1990).

Two additional problems in defining the accounting unit also deserve mention:

A serious problem occurs when a subunit such as the brigade is the de jure accounting unit, but its bookkeeping is so poor that it does not fulfill this function properly; it is an "incomplete" accounting unit. The consequences can be serious: the lack of proper accounting procedures at the subfarm level was a major factor in the failure of the Soviet attempt in the mid-1980s to introduce the collective contract system. Only crude indicators of output at the group level could, therefore, be used for decision-making and they did not take costs into account (Brooks 1990b, 1990c). This meant, in turn, that the system encouraged an increase in gross, but not in net, output.

In some situations different types of information are assembled from various levels of subordinate units for different purposes, resulting in "partial" accounting units. For instance, in talking with farm managers in São Tomé, I was told that the accounting unit was usually the state farm as a whole, but where several brigades carried out the same type of work on separate pieces of land, bonuses were sometimes based on gross production registered by the brigade.

Smaller accounting units have two useful features: the incomes of workers are more closely tied to their labor, and the workers have a

---

[2] In 1990 during the dismantlement of the centrally administered economy in Czechoslovakia, a collective farm manager described to me how he was breaking up the farm into a dozen or so profit centers. This had been a dream of his for a quarter of a century but he had, up to that time, been thwarted by the Ministry of Agriculture. The next day officials at the ministry assured me that for the last eight years any collective farm manager who wished could organize his farm around such profit centers. When I told them of my conversation on the previous day, the officials demanded to know the farm manager's name. Clearly the gap between "theory" and "reality" was wide in Czechoslovakia, as I suspect it was in the other countries as well.

greater first hand familiarity with the financial aspects of farming. It seems likely that both of these features would make decollectivization more acceptable to the farm workers.

Work units are the groups that actually carry out the agricultural work. Generally speaking, "brigades" are large work units, "teams" are small ones, which may or may not be subunits of the brigade, and "links" are subunits of the team. Among the various Marxist regimes, I must emphasize, this terminology is not completely standardized. The work units can be highly specialized (for instance, a tractor unit or a group working in the greenhouse), or highly generalized (for instance, a unit switched from job to job as the occasion demands).

The optimal size of these units, especially the most basic work unit, was a source of fierce dispute for many decades in Marxist regimes. In the Soviet Union, for instance, an instructive insight into this debate can be gained by examining the fate of the link (*zveno*), which was either a subunit of the team or a very small team. The link originated in the 1930s when authorities realized that the team and brigade were too large to be managed as a single unit to carry out specific tasks. At the Eighteenth Party Congress in 1939, the link received official sponsorship. These small groups numbered roughly half a dozen workers, who were often members of the same family. The golden age of the links was in the years immediately following the end of World War II, when they were especially favored by the Politburo's agricultural specialist, A. A. Andreev, and were extended to large-scale grain farming. Political currents were not propitious, however, especially after Stalin and his supporters condemned them as a "throwback to private property instincts" so that by 1949 they were effectively outlawed and replaced by the brigade system. In the early 1960s the link received political support from some of the top leadership such as Khrushchev and it was advocated by many agricultural specialists. One of the specialists, Ivan N. Khudenko, ended his life in prison in 1974 for his efforts.[3] Success in the reintroduction of

---

[3] The discussion in this paragraph is based on Laird and Laird (1988) and Ellman (1988). Khudenko not only championed the link as a work unit, but as an accounting and ownership unit as well. Yanov (1984), a participant in Khudenko's movement, argues that this autonomous link and the normal productive unit (state farm or cooperative farm in their present forms in the USSR) are incompatible and that the latter must give way to the former. Yanov also points out in the strongest terms that such institutional reforms of the farming unit run against the interests not only of the rural managerial and party elites at the district and provincial levels but also the brigadiers, agronomists, field recordkeepers, accountants, timekeepers, clerks, and others working on the farm, who would lose much of their power and, perhaps, income. He estimates (p. 38) the personnel not directly working in production at 40 percent of the labor force (p. 38), of which some would experience economic losses from a change in the system. This 40 percent figure is similar to the East German data presented in chapter 5. To conclude that resistance to any systemic change would be

the link remained limited until the early 1980s when it was again officially sanctioned. Other Marxist regimes have had debates and policy shifts on these matters as well, although not over so long a period.

The smaller and less specialized the work units, the more is the general farming experience each worker has. This would certainly ease the process of returning to a system of private production if the government tried to implement a decollectivization program.

The Focus of Labor Activities

Four different principles of organization can be employed in organizing the brigades and the teams: (1) *land-centered*, where the units are responsible for a piece of land and carry out all agricultural tasks associated with it for all products; (2) *product-centered*, where the units are responsible for the production of a given product (animal products, wheat, vegetables) and work on whatever land these products require, carrying out all of the associated tasks; (3) *function-centered*, where the units carry out particular functions (plowing, cultivating, or harvesting) required by all the crops, or where the units focus their activities on the use of a particular type of machine (a tractor or a combine); and (4) *temporary-task-centered*, where the units carry out a variety of short-term tasks to which they are assigned, which may deal with particular crops, equipment, or functions.[4] Some Third World nations such as Mozambique feature a variant of temporary-task-centered units on their collective farms, where all brigades work on all tasks according to the season, but on different days of the week. This allows a regular time schedule for working on personal plots.

Each of these four organizational principles has advantages and disadvantages. A land-centered organization saves transportation costs, not only in production but also for the workers getting to their jobs, and it also fixes the responsibility for maintaining the fertility of the land. Land-centered or product-centered structures allow the setting of meaningful individual or group work-norms, or payment-by-result schemes more

---

great requires closer analysis, because a large percentage of these administrators would continue in white-collar jobs, no matter how the farm system would be changed. Of course, their new employers might be an independent service unit, rather than the farm itself.

[4] In the Marxist literature, a different type of classification system is used: *specialized*, where the units are responsible for particular tasks such as cane cutting (this corresponds to my temporary-task-centered unit); *complex*, where the units are responsible for a variety of tasks on a particular piece of land (this corresponds to my land-centered unit); and *autonomous*, where the unit carries out a specialized tasks such as equipment repair all over the farm (this corresponds to my function-centered units). This classification system does not really account for those units that raise livestock on various parts of the farm where crops may also be grown.

easily than temporary-task or function-centered groups. A product-centered organization allows the easier introduction of new technology and labor specialization. A temporary-task-centered group provides a great deal of flexibility, especially during periods of peak-labor demand. A function-centered group allows greater specialization of skills. Standard agricultural management textbooks outline the pros and cons of these types of organizational principles in much greater detail (for instance, Schwarzbach and Burzek 1986, chap. 9).

It is noteworthy that these types of subunits are generally quite different in size. For instance, a study of 170 brigades in East Germany (Bajaja 1978, p. 143) reported that the land-centered brigades were the largest, the product-centered brigades were the second largest, and the function-centered brigades, the smallest. The size of the product-oriented brigades also depended to a certain extent on the type of crop.

Most of the Marxist regimes organized their state and collective farms according to several of these principles, the mix differing either because the farms grew different products or because political/management conditions were different.[5] On most state and collective farms some of the brigades were functionally-centered; for instance, carrying out only tractor services, or work on the irrigation system. At the same time some brigades were product-centered; for instance, focusing only on livestock or on plant production. To provide flexibility during peak periods, still other brigades were temporary-task-centered, or existing brigades were temporarily assigned to particular tasks at particular times of the year. Finally, a brigade might be land-centered, but the teams within the brigade, product-centered or vice versa. Such complexities make generalizations about the organizational principles actually followed difficult.[6]

An instructive example is provided by Cuba. Up to 1981, the brigades were almost exclusively function-centered (Gey 1990). In the middle 1980s, the regular brigades were replaced by "new type brigades" or "permanent brigades" (*Brigadas permanentes de producción*). Working

[5] Fforde (1989) has some interesting comparisons in the internal structure of "nominal" and "model" collective farms. The former had more land-centered brigades; the latter, more product- and function-oriented brigades.

[6] For all these reasons it has proven difficult for these governments to carry out statistical investigations of the internal organization of farms. My own interviews with farm directors were also difficult since we did not have a common vocabulary to discuss these matters. I received the impression that in East Germany in the late 1980s the farms were land-centered at the "section" (*Abteilung*) level, but that at the brigade level the situation varied considerably from farm to farm. In the past the farms had a greater production-centered organization. In Bulgaria the brigades were often land-centered, while the work groups were production-centered. In Hungary and Czechoslovakia the situation appeared more mixed, especially in Hungary where the farm managers had greater decision-making autonomy. In China, as noted elsewhere in the text, the brigades and teams were land-centered.

on a joint project with me, Maritza López-Novella visited a number of
Cuban farms to obtain information about a variety of issues of internal
farm management and the new brigade system. One farm, for instance,
had eight land-centered brigades and eight function-oriented brigades
(industrial activities, hydraulic system, distribution, workshops, machinery servicing, personnel services, construction, and shops and transportation). Each of the function-oriented brigades served all of the land-
centered brigades. Within the land-oriented brigades the teams (*grupos*)
were also organized in a mixed fashion: some were function-oriented and
worked primarily with the tractors; some were product-oriented and, for
example, focused on vegetable growing; and some were task-oriented
and did whatever needed doing. In 1989 the government ordered a reorganization of the state farms in order to reduce the function-oriented
brigades and to distribute their personnel among the land-centered brigades, which formed special function-oriented teams. The trained agricultural specialists would no longer hold staff positions at the central office and be consulted by all brigades, but would focus their efforts on a
single brigade.

These blanket organizational changes, of course, took little account of
local circumstances. López-Novella found that the farm managers faith-
fully followed instructions in making such changes, but they were unable
to provide her with any convincing justification for them or to explain
how they would improve farm performance. Such organizational changes
were endemic in most Marxist regimes and are of little consequence for
this analysis. The degree to which they were centrally mandated or decided by the farm manager varies from year to year and from country to
country. Cuba provides an extreme case of centrally mandated changes.

One important hypothesis should be advanced: A land-centered organization of labor eases the process of decollectivization because the workers are more prepared for private farming. That is, they are carrying out
all phases of the production cycle on the same land that they would use
as private farmers.

The Autonomy of the Subunits

Under the Stalinist conception the various types of subunits were established merely for the administrative convenience of implementing orders
from above. If the farm as a whole has relatively little economic decision-
making autonomy, it is highly unlikely that the subunits have much autonomy either and farm administration is highly centralized.[7]

---

[7] Of course, it is possible for the farm manager to set up shadow prices and other arrangements in order to induce autonomous subunits to produce according to plan. I have found

In certain Marxist regimes where subunits became the ownership unit, they not only gained a certain degree of autonomy but the decision-making powers of farm manager was correspondingly constrained. At the extreme, the collective became "nominal" (to use the terminology introduced in chapter 1). In this case, central management functioned primarily as a service unit, either to the brigades or the individual farmers, selling them inputs and marketing their output wherever it could achieve greater economies of scale in such activities than the individual work units. This conception of the collective farm was originally advanced in 1919 in the Soviet Union by A. V. Chayanov (1966, pp. lviii–lv). As pointed out in chapter 2, it appeared to receive support from Lenin in his last words on the subject.

During the 1980s, the introduction of the "contract system" was a means employed to increase the autonomy of the farm subunits. This development occurred in a number of countries such as China, the USSR, Viet Nam and, to a limited extent, in Bulgaria and other nations. In these nations the farms nominally retained the ownership unit but the subunits, which could range in size from a brigade to a family, were supposed to receive or bargain for a contract with the management of the farm.

It is useful to distinguish two basic kinds of contracts. In "collective contracts" (the terminology has been somewhat different in various countries), the subunits agree to supply certain products at a particular price, receiving certain inputs, equipment, and other services in return. In many cases the subunit has little choice about what to produce and what inputs to receive. In essence, it is really a special type of group piecework system and can be considered the functional equivalent of a sharecropping rent, except the landlord determines the major conditions of production. Of course, such a collective contract can be structured in a number of different ways. For instance, if a minimum wage is also guaranteed, the group piece-rate incentive is weakened. If a higher price is paid for production in excess of the contracted amount, the piece-rate incentive is strengthened. If costs are not carefully specified in the contract, the financial benefits of additional production for the farm brought

no evidence that any such indirect price incentives were ever used on a large scale in the agricultural sector of any of the Marxist regimes.

The centralization within a collective farm is often a function of size: When the farm is small, it can act as a genuine cooperative with all of the members participating in decision-making. When the farm is large, political authorities and technocrats from afar can make the key farming decisions and the farmers are, essentially, reduced to the role of wage laborers so that the farm is really a pseudocooperative, using the terminology introduced in chapter I. But even between farms of a given size, the degree of centralization can vary, so that the center can serve either as the command center for the entire farm or as a service unit to aid the various subunits.

about by the piece-rate system may be offset by extra high costs of production, a situation that occurred in the Soviet Union in the late 1980s (Brooks 1990b, 1990c).

In the "lease contract" (again, the terminology is not standard), the subunit agrees to pay a certain amount for land and a fixed price for units of inputs, equipment, and services provided by the central farm management. This is the functional equivalent to a fixed-rent system: it places more economic risks on the subunit and, at the same time, it provides the subunit with greater incentive for production, since all revenues exceeding the expenses can be retained. This kind of contract does not function well where the lessor (either the farm manager or a local official) has a monopoly position or can exercise coercion over the leaseholders. These leasing contracts have had varying successes where tried, depending in some measure upon the availability of inputs to leaseholders and the possibilities of their marketing the output independently of the lessor. In Hungary such contracts proved more popular than in the Soviet Union, where the government tried to encourage them in the late 1980s.

Of course, the contracts between the farm and the subunits can combine a number of features of both the collective contract and the lease. Moreover, in theory (but not so often in practice), either party is able to refuse the offer of the other. Indeed, with the continuance of coercive elements the differences between the new contract system and the old systems of compensation are not so great.

Personal Plots

In most Marxist regimes at least a few farmers had small private plots of land. In a number of these countries city workers, state farmworkers, or even collective farm workers could lease "individual" plots of land, either for personal or market production. Collective farms in most Marxist regimes also assigned their members small "personal" plots at no cost for private or market production. In some countries state farmworkers also had the same privileges; for instance, Hungary, Nicaragua, and São Tomé.[8] In this discussion I combine all these types of land holdings under the rubric "personal plots," because this tenancy form usually predominated.

These personal plots played quite different roles in the various countries: In some of the Third World Marxist regimes such as Mozambique, they were a primary source of food for the collective farmers. In other countries such as Bulgaria and Hungary they were highly integrated into

---

[8] In Nicaragua the situation was complicated because workers on state farms were often transferred from one farm to another, so that they could not tend their private plots on any one of these farms (Weijland 1988).

the production of the farm. In still other countries, such as Cuba and East Germany, they were either not very important or were farmed by the collective itself, with the profits or the food going to the farm members. And in a final group of countries such as Grenada and Seychelles, neither state farm workers nor collective farm members received these plots.

In Eastern Europe these personal plots generally accounted, at least formally, for 3 to 8 percent of the total land of the country. They provided a considerably larger share of total food or agricultural production: more than one-third in the case of the Soviet Union during the 1950s or Hungary in the 1980s and more than one-fourth in Bulgaria in the 1980s.[9] In recent years these personal plots have received considerable attention by Western analysts, in good measure because many Marxist governments began to reconsider their policies toward this subsector of agriculture.

Why did the personal plot system arise? Certainly large-scale farms in many market economies (especially in the economically more developed nations) do not provide land for workers to grow food, except for small kitchen gardens around their homes on plantation land. Since it does not seem likely that all land on a plantation is suitable for the main plantation crop, this lack of personal land seems curious since these plots would provide a means for the capitalist plantation to maintain a labor force and yet pay its members lower monetary wages. Further, if the plantation itself grew foodstuffs for sale to its workers or townspeople on lands unsuitable for the plantation crop, it would be difficult to prevent praedial larceny. The probable explanation is that the existence of such personal plots on a plantation would increase the risk to the plantation that labor supply would not be available at periods of peak demand, since it might be more profitable at these moments for the workers and their family members to be harvesting their own crops for sale.[10] Of course, it is possible that a worker might earn more by working for the plantation, than on a personal plot, so that such plots might not be necessary.

Several major reasons can be offered for the existence of personal productive activities on collective and state farms in Marxist regimes:

[9] The data come from Vulchev and Pamukchiev (1988, p. 70). As Hedlund (1989) has pointed out, comparisons of land productivity are almost meaningless because labor and other inputs are not taken into account. Moreover, the actual amount farmed individually is often not accurately represented because data on individual plots do not include the free use of meadows for privately owned cattle and other individually used but collectively claimed land.

[10] Szelenyi (1988, p. 21) points out that in many feudal countries farmers were forbidden to own horses and their private plots were limited so they would not spend too much time on them. Some East European Marxist regimes followed the same policies in the collectivization drives of the late 1940s and early 1950s.

1. Rural retail markets generally functioned less efficiently in these economies and, for the farmworkers to obtain their food, it was necessary for them to grow it.

2. These plots allowed for certain types of labor-intensive production tasks to be carried out that were uneconomic for the collective to supervise directly. In most Marxist regimes, the crops grown on personal plots accounted for a large share of certain foodstuffs requiring close attention during the production process such as fruits and vegetables. As a result the share of this private activity in total agricultural production varied enormously by crop or animal type.

3. Complementarities existed between personal plots and the collective sector on both the input and the production side. With regard to factor usage, complementarities arose when the private plots used labor unavailable to the collective such as children, retired people, family members working in the cities, or other relatives and when the plots were located on marginal land that was not used by the collective. Complementary relations on fertilizer inputs occurred when the collective farm obtained manure from the privately kept animals of its members, a relationship of importance in China (Fung 1974). In the production sector, complementarities arose when individuals agreed to carry out certain tasks such as weeding or the raising of piglets, tasks which require considerable individual initiative or heavy supervision, while the large farm carried out tasks such as plowing or harvesting or the fattening of pigs, activities with certain economies of scale.

4. Since considerable coercion accompanied the formation of collective farms in most Marxist regimes (chapter 4), these plots represented political concession to the peasantry in order to give them a certain amount of economic security that was independent of what the government chose to provide.

Although this list seems impressive, certain conflicts between the private production activities and production on state and collective farms must also be noted:

1. The socialist and private sectors were competing for much of the same labor force, especially prime age and entrepreneurially minded men or women who preferred to work for themselves, rather than on the collective. In research note G I present a formal model exploring a number of propositions about the relative amount of labor expended in both types of production, given different types of constraints. Some of the propositions derived from the model may not seem obvious at first glance. For instance, if farming on the collective land becomes more productive so that hourly income from this work rises, then farmers will work less on their private plots although it is unclear—because of offsetting income and substitution effects—whether they will work more hours on the collective land. Or if the govern-

ment increases the land available for private plots, the farmers may work fewer hours on both the collective land and in their private plots. Assuming that the collective farm markets a higher share of its production than the peasant with his personal-plot production, it is also likely that total marketable output will decline with an increase in the size of the private plot.[11]

2. Competition also arose in the use of scarce inputs. It seems highly likely that in many Marxist regimes, considerable fertilizer, pesticides, fodder, and other inputs were diverted from collective to private use, given the high administrative costs of preventing such larceny.

Others have approached the problem of the complementarities and competitiveness of personal plot and collective farm activities from a different standpoint and have argued that they resulted in a conflict between maximization of surplus and of output (Fung 1974). However the matter is viewed, the considerations I have outlined have not had the same saliency in the Marxist regimes in different periods and, as a result, the governments have pursued at different times quite diverse policies toward the personal plots. It should be added that the size limits on personal plots and the importance of farmers' markets were generally correlated, with the underlying causal variable being the party's view toward "micro-capitalism." The range of policies can be seen in two examples.

At one extreme some Marxist regimes have made considerable efforts to discourage such personal plots. Pol Pot allowed no personal plots in Kampuchea from 1975–78. In such countries as Albania and North Korea in the late 1980s, the personal plots ranged from 0.01 to 0.03 hectares and served primarily as a source of supplementary food for the family.[12]

At the opposite extreme is Hungary, which during the 1980s had five different types of personal plots; Bulgaria had a similar system.[13] These

[11] Based on his studies of individual plots in Bulgaria (Vulchev and Pamukchiev 1988), Nikola Vulchev argued in our interview that in his country, where the individual and collective agricultural systems are highly integrated, doubling the size of the individual plots (which occurred in Bulgaria in early 1990) would result in relatively little change in either total or marketable production. Rather, the major change would be distributional: more income in the pocket of the collective farmer, and less in the account of the farm.

[12] In North Korea alone, the private plots ranged from 70 to 100 square meters, according to Wickman (1981). In Romania, the Ceaucescu government planned to destroy most of the farm villages and resettle farmers in larger settlements, where they would receive personal plots of only 200 to 250 square meters. In Viet Nam, the personal plots were about 200 square meters. In most East European nations the private plots were much larger (Wädekin, 1982).

[13] In Hungary during the 1980s one could find a few private farms, the private plots of members of collective farms, auxiliary farms of state farmers and urban workers, "specialized cooperatives" that permitted considerable private activity, and sharecropping arrangements. Useful descriptions of such private farming activities are found in Hann (1980), Swain (1985), and Szelenyi (1988) and, for sharecropping, Volgyes (1980). Szelenyi argues

two nations attempted to integrate the personal plots into the collective's entire production program by supplying seeds and other inputs for certain crops requiring close attention or by turning over young animals to the private farmer, supplying fodder and then purchasing such output at contracted prices at the end of the production cycle (a type of agricultural "putting-out system"). In a number of East European nations personal-plot activities served as an important source of peasant income; produce was sold on active peasant markets in the cities and the plots provided a major source for city dwellers for certain foodstuffs such as vegetables and potatoes.[14]

Financial policies toward these personal plots were also quite different. In some countries the government bought produce grown on these individual plots at different prices from those paid to collective or state farms—for instance, Poland in the 1970s—while in other countries, such as the African nations, peasants were left to sell produce from these plots at any price they could obtain. In some countries, for instance, in the 1950s the Soviet Union, the government taxed the produce from these plots and thereby discouraged such production. In other countries the crops from these plots were included as part of the overall production of collective farms and were thereby encouraged; Hungary and, in the late 1980s, the USSR. And in still other Marxist regimes, especially in most African nations, the governments paid these plots little financial attention.

In most countries collective farmworkers were required to work a minimum number of days for the collective in order to receive land for personal plots. Collective farm chairmen also had simple ways of coercing additional work out of members, since they controlled job and plot assignments. In some Marxist regimes in Africa such as Mozambique, personal plots occupied most of the time of the collective farm members, and the collective fields were often shorthanded since the chairman did not have such coercive powers. In most Marxist regimes these personal plots were personally farmed: in Cuba they were collectively farmed, but the produce was distributed to the members of the farm (so that the designation of "personal plot" is a misnomer). On collective farms in Czechoslovakia, East Germany, and Hungary the possessor of a personal

---

that the increasing farm size, combined with the technological approach of the new managers, acted to reduce the importance of sharecropping at the same time as the sharecropping idea was carried over into the urban sector quite successfully through the creation of special work collectives. The Bulgarian situation is analyzed by Vulchev and Pamukchiev (1988).

[14] In Hungary in the early 1980s, private production accounted for 25 to 30 percent of the income of collective farmers and 9 to 10 percent of that of state farmers, according to Oros (1984).

plot could lease the land to the collective, which farmed it and paid the owner either a fee in money or in farm produce. In East Germany farmers received lower prices at the farmers' markets for most produce from their personal plot than the subsidized price paid by the government for foodstuffs produced by the collective farm, so there was little incentive for individual production.

Production from personal plots could be sold either to the farm itself, to state purchasing agencies, or to customers at farmers' markets. Government attitudes toward farmers' markets varied considerably among the Marxist regimes. In Albania, Cuba, Kampuchea, and North Korea, farmers' markets were either completely banned or highly restricted in the late 1980s. For example, in North Korea the prices at these markets were fixed and they took place only every ten to thirty days. The impact of price controls on farmers' markets depends both on the degree to which they are actually enforced and the extent to which these prices differ from equilibrium market prices. In the Soviet Union during the 1980s controls did not seem to dampen greatly these market activities, except during short periods when they were strictly enforced. In Romania price controls caused these markets to atrophy (Montias, forthcoming). In most cases price or other regulations on these free markets proved difficult to enforce, especially when the foodstuffs were not available elsewhere. For instance, some countries such as Czechoslovakia, South Yemen, or Viet Nam tried at one time to close private markets, but found it necessary to reopen them later when urban needs for particular farm products were unmet by the official distribution system.

For those interested in pursuing the subject of personal plots and farmers' markets, considerable information concerning such plots can be found for most of the East European nations.[15] Only sketchy details are available for most Third World Marxist regimes.

PAYMENT AND MOTIVATION OF LABOR

As suggested in chapter 5, problems of controlling and motivating of the labor force may be the major reasons that large-scale farming can result in lower productivity and efficiency than small-scale farming in both Marxist and non-Marxist regimes. These problems arise from difficulties in overseeing a labor force spread over a wide area and of determining either the effort expended by the workers or the quality of their labor. Problems also arise in ascertaining the contribution of individual workers when, over the production cycle, many different people work on a given

---

[15] For the Soviet Union, studies of personal plots include those of Hedlund (1989) and Wädekin (1973); for China, Walker (1965); and for Eastern Europe, Cochran (1988a, 1988b), Schinke (1983), and Wädekin (1982).

piece of land. Gang labor, which can be used for certain crops requiring a low level of technology and care, is the most important exception to these generalizations.

State and collective farms can choose from a wide variety of methods to compensate and motivate labor. It is difficult to specify which countries used which payment and motivation systems, since a single farm often employed several compensation systems, depending upon the job. In some countries the accounting units also had some choice as to which compensation and motivation system they would employ. Nevertheless, insight into the problems can be gained by examining briefly examples of the compensation systems, when and where they were used, and the possible impact they had.

Moral versus Material Incentives

One major decision to be made by farm managers is the relative importance to be placed on material and moral stimuli for production. The latter include *negative incentives* such as coercion and punishment, *participatory incentives* arising from greater control in working conditions and taking part in decision-making of the enterprise, and *positive incentives* such as competitions between teams or individuals, the awarding of medals or banners for meritorious work, public notice in newspapers, designations as heros of work, and so forth. For the most part Marxist regimes have placed almost complete reliance on material, rather than moral, incentives; the few exceptions deserve mention.

Kampuchea during the reign of Pol Pot (1975–78) provides the only example of a Marxist regime basing its entire agricultural production system on negative moral incentives. All farmers were assigned a certain work quota and, in return, received only in-kind payment—for instance, food distributed at communal dining facilities or clothing rations—that had no necessary relationship to that individual's work.[16] If the work quota was fulfilled in a few hours, one could stop work, but no rewards were given for extra work. If, on the other hand, the task took twenty hours, then this amount of work had to be carried out. Eyewitness accounts (May 1986) report a variety of punishments for unfulfilled or unsatisfactory work ranging from food deprivation to death. Although the available data are sketchy, it does not appear that these incentives resulted in a great upswing of production (Twining 1989).

[16] The communes had three castes: the cadre, the "old people" (the original villagers), and the "new people" (primarily city people relocated in the village). Payments varied by caste, with the cadre doing the least work and receiving the most food, while the new people did the most work and received the least food. The work quota system is described by Twining (1989).

Participatory incentives were used most extensively in Yugoslavia, which, through its system of worker management, attempted to involve the workers directly in the decision-making of the productive enterprises (including farms) through worker councils. As the productive enterprises grew larger, participation was increased in subunits of the enterprise through the organization of "basic organizations of associated labor," which were small worker councils with certain powers of control over their subunits. Although the formal structure appears quite impressive, a survey of six thousand young people taken in the mid-1980s revealed that only 28 percent felt favorably toward the system of self-management, 17 percent felt unfavorably, and 55 percent were indifferent (Economist Intelligence Unit 1986c). These results suggest that participatory incentives were not important for this age group and might also not be so crucial in the working lives of other age groups as well. Although many Marxist regimes attempted less elaborate ways to involve workers in the decision-making process of their enterprises, the actual impact of this type of moral incentive probably was not very great.

During short periods several Marxist regimes placed considerable emphasis on positive moral incentives either for groups or individuals; for instance, China in the early years of the Great Leap Forward (especially 1958 and 1959), Cuba during the 1960s when the Sino-Guevara model had influence (Bernardo 1971), or North Korea, where the Ch'ollima (Flying Horse) movement was used to encourage extra-diligent work through competitions and other devices (Scalapino and Lee 1972, p. 1115). Other Marxist regimes have carried out brief campaigns or less extensive positive incentive schemes. Generally, intense use of such positive moral incentives are effective for only brief periods, since it is difficult to maintain a population at fever pitch for long intervals of time.

Little direct evidence is available on the economic impact of positive moral incentives. The only survey data I have been able to locate are for Ethiopia (Wondimu 1983), where more than 90 percent of the peasants indicated they preferred respect and affection over money. About 75 percent also said they worked harder when there was competition among team members. Nevertheless, about 95 percent said they worked harder when they got objects of value, rather than simple recognition, 72 percent said that they worked harder when pay was related to effort, rather than equally distributed, and 62 percent said they liked to work harder and get paid more than others in the collective. In some Marxist regimes informal evidence suggests that workers had considerable suspicion of reported high production performance of certain labor heros (the basis of the Stakhanovite movement in the Soviet Union), regarding these results either as the consequence of a setup (that is, unduly favorable circumstances) or as an excuse to raise work norms. Competitions among work teams was sometimes regarded in a similar light, as it is in many capitalist nations. In the only lengthy study I have seen of the use of moral incentives in agriculture, Bernardo (1971) provides compelling evidence that for Cuba such moral incentives were a blunt administrative tool, that the labor supplied was often of poor quality, and that high production in one area resulted in low production in other areas (see also Roca 1976).

Of course, such scattered evidence is not conclusive. Nevertheless, the greater emphasis most Marxist regimes place on material over moral incentives is in line with reasonable expectations.

Wage Systems

The use of material incentives, however, raises a number of knotty problems. As noted in chapter 1, in a formal sense state and collective farms differ because labor compensation in the former is based on some type of wage system, while in the latter it is based on some type of sharing of residual income after expenses have been paid, according to the labor points earned by each individual. As noted, this distinction began to break down in the early 1960s, especially in East Europe, where collective farmers in countries such as the USSR and Hungary received some type of minimum wage, plus an additional amount depending upon their share of the residual profits.

The payment of monetary wages on the state farms or the assignment of work points in the collective farms (on which the person's share of total farm income is based) can be carried out according to several different principles:

STRAIGHT SALARY

With the exception of management, technical personnel, and some specialists, none of the Marxist regimes for which I could obtain information has used a straight salary system, except during the initial period of collectivization when the system was quite disorganized. In these cases the results were as expected; for instance, unskilled employees receiving a straight salary on state farms in South Yemen worked less than four hours a day (Stookey 1982, p. 82). The guaranteed minimum wage that was offered to state and collective farmers in a number of East European nations has many of the same features of a straight salary. Before farmers received such guaranteed wages, Soviet farm workers said: "Why work? They won't pay us anyway." After introduction of the guaranteed minimum wage system they said: "Why work? They'll pay us anyway" (Gray 1990a, p. 16).

TIME-RATES

A time-rate system has been more common. In a number of the Marxist regimes in Africa, all collective farm members received the same work points per hour. This compensation system rewards neither effort nor skill, but it is straightforward to administer, a considerable advantage in situations where few members of the collective or state farm have record-keeping skills. A variant occurred in China, where some teams were awarded daily work points according to a person's potential production, as reflected in age, sex, physical strength, and skills. Eastern Europe and the Soviet Union employed a more sophisticated time-rate system, where the various farm jobs were rated according to the criteria of skill or unpleasantness, so that a person's cumulated work points depended not only upon hours worked, but also on the type of job. Of course, these systems provided no reward for effort and, moreover, gave considerable power to the farm manager in the assignment of people and work points to a particular job.

INDIVIDUAL PAYMENT-BY-RESULTS

Result-oriented compensation systems tie compensation to both skill and effort. On a short-term basis this could be a simple piece-rate or task-rate system, for example, wages or labor points for a hectare of land weeded or one hundred kilograms of harvested potatoes.

Individual piece-rate systems are sometimes expensive to supervise, especially where the crops or the tasks are heterogeneous. In China, for instance, this type of compensation system was more frequently found during the period of peak labor demand whenever individual output (for instance, harvested crop) was easily measured, or in smaller teams where the performance of each member was easily monitored, or on farms that were shorthanded and wanted to encourage maximum effort (Parish and Whyte pp. 67–69).

Short-term payment-by-results in the form of individual piece-work systems were tried in several countries. For instance, in the early 1970s Romania required individual collective farm households to sign a type of share contract ("global accord") to be responsible for certain pieces of land with labor-intensive crops, whereby the farm plowed and fertilized the land, while the farmers delivered a certain base amount and kept an increasing fraction of crops above this base (Verdery 1976, 1983). The system broke down because the farm managers did not properly fulfill their responsibilities to supply particular services and, moreover, kept raising the required crop minimum (a ratchet effect), so that the share element became increasingly smaller. Furthermore, the plots were ran-domly assigned each year in order to avoid favoritism by the farm man-ager, but this meant, of course, that the individual farmers had no incen-tive to improve the land. In short, property rights were not stable (or "strong"), so that the incentives did not have their intended effect.

Other countries had a better experience with such individual piece-rate payments. For instance, Bulgaria introduced the "accord system" in the 1980s, but with greater care and fewer ratchet effects (Ganev and others 1990, chap. 2), starting first in tobacco and then extending it to other appropriate crops and adapting it for groups in some situations and individuals in other. According to public opinion surveys cited to me by Bulgarian economists, it proved popular.[17] The effectiveness of piece-work in raising agricultural output was, however, controversial. Although disaggregated data for particular villages showed greater productivity than under the old brigade system in particular villages, production data for the country as a whole reveal no acceleration since its introduction.

GROUP PAYMENT-BY-RESULTS

In 1989 the Soviets also started offering a team-share or individual-share contract, but they did not replace other types of contracts (Brooks 1990b, 1990c) and one wonders if the Romanian experience of share contracts would be repeated once again. Group payment-by-result systems also raise some additional problems.

Group Size.   The larger the group, the easier it is to specify the task and reduce suboptimizing (that is, concentrating on individual task fulfill-ment, regardless of whether total production is greatly raised or soil fer-tility is preserved). At the same time, however, individuals in the group have less influence on their own pay by working harder or by monitoring the degree of effort expended by others. It is noteworthy that in China, large teams were more likely than small teams to adopt the system of household contracts; the inability to manage the work effort of others in such large groups meant that they had more to gain by household farming (Lin 1987, 1988). The smaller the group, however, the more difficult it is to tie fulfillment of a given small task to a broader goal; moreover, the smaller the group, the more the system begins to encourage individual-istic behavior and other sprouts of capitalism.

Time Period.   The shorter the time horizon of the compensation system, the more suboptimization is encouraged. On the other hand, these task-specific piece systems also encourage great effort at particularly crucial times of the harvest cycle when every minute is precious. Generally, this short-run compensation system is employed only for a small number of

---

[17] A Bulgarian peasant woman I interviewed in 1990 claimed that under the piecework system, she was earning six thousand leva a year, about the same as a physician and three times her previous income. The farm director admitted that this was an extraordinary case. She allowed herself to be interviewed only for several minutes before quickly running back and beginning her work again.

tasks, although in some cases governments such as China during the 1950s (Crook 1970) encouraged a widespread use of this system.

Self-Monitoring. Group piece-rate systems are most effective where only a few products are grown and where the groups are sufficiently small so that members have some incentive to monitor themselves. If the group is large, the effort expended by person A in monitoring person B may be smaller than the benefit that individual A would receive by B's increased diligence. In such a case, the group might have to assign special personnel to the monitoring function, which is expensive. The benefit of close monitoring is also greater if the group bearing the cost of the process gets to keep the entire difference resulting from such efforts. If this is not the case, then even a specialized group monitor may not be worthwhile for the group as a whole.

Although these problems appear formidible, long-term group payment-by-result systems can be effective in certain situations, especially where thought is given to how the groups are organized and how suboptimization can be avoided. In North Korea, for example, the work groups were generally product-centered and composed of several links (subwork groups). The latter comprised five to twenty workers and was both the basic work and the accounting unit. The links were assigned equipment and special pieces of land, along with a harvest goal on which their compensation was based (Chung 1974, p. 17; Scalapino and Lee 1972, p. 1108). Although solid information is not available, it appears that the same links farmed the same land year after year. Performance was easily measured in production of major crops such as rice and, at first glance, it appears that the link had considerable incentive to carry out its own monitoring. As I will point out, however, certain aspects of the compensation system discouraged this monitoring process.

The "collective contract system" that was previously discussed occurred in the 1980s in China, Hungary, Laos, North Korea, the Soviet Union, and Viet Nam on a large scale and on a lesser scale in Bulgaria (Wyzan 1990b) and some other countries. For the most part it was merely a formalization of a long-term system of payment-by-results. It is compatible with management environments that are highly centralized (for instance, North Korea) or highly decentralized (for instance, China in the early 1980s) since the contents of these contracts can vary considerably. That is, they can be used either for individuals or groups of different sizes and can vary according to the autonomy accorded to the subordinates, the length of the contract and how the conditions of the contract can be changed, the degree and manner in which the subordinates are rewarded or punished according to contract over- or under-fulfillment, the degree to which the subordinate is responsible for obtaining needed inputs, the size of the group, and other agricultural policies complementing the contract system.

Despite the enormous attention focused on the contract system as a panacea for collectivized agriculture, it does not necessarily indicate a significant reform, but is often a mere administrative streamlining. For instance, in Viet Nam in the early 1980s, the contract focused on highly labor intensive chores for a single plot, but plowing, seeding, and irrigation were handled by specialized brigades of the collective (Beresford 1988, p. 139; Cima 1989a, 1989b; Crosnier and Lhomel 1987; Economic Intelligence Unit 1988; Hiebeck 1988). Originally the contracts were for the brigades, but by 1981 they were signed by households. Although contract deliveries were fixed for five years, and farmers were allowed to keep all crops above the contract limit, either to sell to the government or on the free market, the farmers had little autonomy. Moreover, there were no supporting institutions—for instance, credit or ready sources of inputs—to allow a flowering of farmer initiative. Many farmers either invested little in the land or actually returned the land given to them on the contract system. More changes in the system were made in 1986 that not only led to the breaking up of large farms but also raised producer prices and lowered the required share of the crop to be turned over to the state. In 1988 the collectives were released from oversight by the district level of government so that the contracts could not be overridden by higher political authorities. Although at the time this was written it was too early to make a firm judgement, it appeared that a significant increase in agricultural production occurred by the late 1980s when the contract system evolved into a genuine decollectivization.

SUBJECTIVE SYSTEMS

Other compensation systems depend upon subjective factors. For instance, in China during the 1970s the "Dazhai method" led to payments based on such factors as political participation, perceived ability, attitudes toward work, and so forth. In state farms this evaluation can be carried out by team or brigade leaders, since a hierarchical work situation is accepted. In collective farms, the social contract is different and, in order to avoid arbitrary appraisals by team leaders, the Chinese implemented the system through monthly mutual-appraisal meetings. Members would declare how long they worked and how many work points they believed they deserved; their teammates would then vote on the amount actually awarded, based on the various subjective evaluations. Although meant to encourage peer group pressures for harder work, the system actually led to wage egalitarianism since a worker perceived to be strong would receive the same as a weak worker if both contributed the same effort, and team members were loathe to designate their teammates as lazy. In the brigade in Chen Village (Chan and others 1984, p. 92) such a system had still another discriminatory effect, because the men insisted that no man should receive a lower work-point rating than any woman. Since women received from 6.5 to 7.5 work points per day, the range of men's work points was generally between 8.5 and 10.0 per day.[18]

Another subjective compensation system is payment according to need. This system is difficult, but not impossible, to administer for a large group.[19] A simple modification is merely giving everyone the same wage, independent of time worked, effort, or skill. For example, in 1958–59, in the early days of the Chinese communes, from 50 to 70 percent of a member's pay would be a straight subsistence payment on a per capita basis. In some of the East European nations, members received a small food allotment on a per capita basis as well, but this amounted to only a small fraction of total income.

MIXED SYSTEMS

In many Marxist regimes, mixed systems of compensation have been used. For instance, on a state farm the worker might receive a minimum time rate according the specific job performed, plus a bonus that can be structured in several ways: The bonus can be only a fixed amount. Or if the group overfulfills its plan (or its contract), it can either keep part of the overplan receipts or receive extra work points to be used in the division of the residual. The bonuses can also be based on several indicators. For instance, in the late 1950s Yugoslav state farms had a system whereby workers were given a plot of land, an output norm, and a total cost norm (Zmajic 1961). They received a certain fixed amount per unit of production (a piece rate) plus a bonus per unit of produce that rose if total production exceeded the norm and/or if costs fell below the norm. As a result, worker income rose or fell faster than production. In later years, the Yugoslavs began tying compensation of farm workers more closely to profit.

A different example of a mixed system with several bonus indicators is provided by Cuba where in the late 1980s state farms paid two types of bonuses:[20] a *prima*, which was paid from the wage fund on the basis of

[18] In a number of Marxist regimes where women and men carry out somewhat different tasks, women generally receive fewer work points than men, even though the tasks may demand the same strength or dexterity or involve the same discomfort.

[19] Some Kibbutzim in Israel, as well as some utopian socialist communities such as the Society of Brothers (formerly in Paraguay, now in the United States, England, and Germany) use such a system. From working with the Society of Brothers for a number of months, I can attest that the system can work successfully, as judged on almost any criteria. Nevertheless, this system requires a strong religious commitment and a shared system of values. Two fascinating studies that deal in part with the economics of these communities are by Wesson (1963) and Zablocki (1980).

[20] This description is based on the interview materials of Maritza López-Novella; it differs

overfulfillment of work norms at fairly short intervals so that the linkage between bonus and work was readily apparent; and a *premio*, which was paid from the farm's profit fund at the end of the year to an entire team or brigade as a result of their work. The *primas*, however, formally required a vote of the membership of the team, which often distributed them among many workers so as not to create jealousies. Furthermore, this bonus was seldom awarded according to the rules at frequent intervals, but rather at the end of the year. The *premio* also depended on political behavior of the recipients, such as participation in volunteer work.

Although many of these different payment-by-result schemes appear impressive, we should not be fooled by the formal aspects of the system into believing that they were effective; the administration of any bonus system is crucial to its success. As administered, neither type of bonus in Cuba appears to have had its desired effect of increasing work effort. Without specific information about administration, it is difficult to generalize about all of the nations in the sample. Even survey data may be suspect, particularly if carried out in a naive fashion or in a manner to make respondents believe that they might be punished for giving opinions that diverge from the official line.[21]

Ultimately, the income of a collective farmer depends upon production results since, no matter how the work points are distributed, the total to be shared depends upon the financial results of the farm. Although, as noted above, this principle was modified in a number of East European nations so that each member received a basic minimum wage at regular intervals and the division of funds according to work points only applied to the remaining amount at the end of the year, the revival of interest in the "collective contract system," represents a return to the original residual-principle of payment (Wädekin 1989).

A Note on Formal and Informal Share Contracts

As noted in chapter 2, Marx believed that sharecropping was a primitive form of contract that would gradually disappear with economic develop-

---

considerably from the description of Ghai, Kay, and Peek (1988), who seem to believe that the formal rules for distribution of the bonuses were actually followed. The workers whom López-Novella interviewed did not believe that either kind of bonus provided much incentive and, indeed, they paid little attention to them.

[21] For instance, in a sample survey of 321 farmers in thirty-five different collective farms in Ethiopia, Wondimu (1983) found that 90 percent of the sample claimed they worked harder on the collective lands than their own plot. It is difficult to know whether to believe this answer, especially given the fact that land productivity of the collective farms is roughly the same as private farms. An official East German survey revealed the same phenomenon (Gampe 1985, p. 27). For other types of questions, especially those relating to personal incentives, the answers reported are more believable because there is no official line.

ment, a prediction that has not been realized. Of course, piece-rate wage systems are a type of share contract, but without the autonomy provided by such a contract since supervision of the worker is much greater. Share-cropping contracts of the form found in market economies have not often occurred in Marxist regimes and these exceptional cases warrant brief examination.

As I discuss in chapter 10, Hungary introduced in the 1960s a type of socialist sharecropping, whereby farm households would take over plots of land or the animals raising and receive a share of either the produce or the profit, depending on how the contract was written. These were mostly for labor-intensive tasks. As farming became more mechanized, as the collective farms became larger and more dominated by profession-ally trained managers, such contracts became less common.

Informal share contracts can also arise in many situations where it has proven impossible to enforce minimal deliveries. If an obligatory delivery is at issue and if this delivery quota is changed according to conditions, then we have a de facto share contract. Of course, this share element can be modified by threats of contract revocation in the following period if deliveries fall below the minimum (Brooks 1990b, 1990c).

As noted above, a bonus system tied to output acts as a type of share system. Often, however, the share aspects of the compensation system are so layered that the incentive aspects are obscured. For instance, in North Korea in the 1960s the link (subteam) received a plan goal with a certain number of normed workpoints, which were tied to the produc-tivity norms of the work day for the particular tasks involved in raising the crop or livestock. Over- or under-fulfillment of the plan led to higher or lower work points than normed, depending on the share formula op-erative on the farm. Generally the work points added or subtracted were less than 10 percent of the total so that the share element was quite small (Wickman 1981; Chung 1974, p. 27). Moreover, the actual amount re-ceived for each work point depended on production of the entire team (after deductions were made for required deliveries, inputs, and so forth). Thus superhuman effort on the part a given link might have re-sulted in relatively meager results if other links of the same team did not work equally hard. Since one link could not monitor performance of an-other, a given individual's work efforts were still not closely tied to the income received. Furthermore, since all equipment and land were as-signed, the links had little incentive to invest.

CONCLUDING REMARKS

This chapter focuses on a variety of problems concerning the internal organization of state and collective farms. The range of solutions is wide and, to a considerable extent, few of the solutions are closely tied with classical Marxist ideology, although Marxoid elements (chapter 2) were sometimes introduced. This means that ideological prescriptions were less important and that changes in the systems were endemic as policy-makers searched for new incentives and new combinations of structural elements to increase production in the socialist agricultural sector. Any detailed description of the internal structure of state and collective farms in any country and year probably would have to be considerably modified if another time period several years later were selected. Further, there were many differences between the way in which the systems were set up to work, and their actual functioning. In trying to live with the mistakes of national-level decision-makers, individual farm managers often "modified" official regulations; often these changes were overlooked by the agencies of control so long as the farm was able to meet its plan goals.

Whatever decisions were made about the structural elements of the state and collective farms, it is also difficult to evaluate them. We look upon these problems from the outside, and only the farm managers have the detailed information of time and place necessary to make such judgments. Further, many of the production results obtained depend less on internal farm structure than on the effect of national policy. Indeed, separation of the effects of policy and structure on the final agricultural outcomes is a task to which I turn in the next two chapters.

PART IV

Policies and Performance

Chapter 7

SELECTED AGRICULTURAL POLICIES

ARE PROBLEMS in the performance of agriculture in Marxist regimes due primarily to the organizational structure of the sector or to the more general governmental policies toward agriculture? In previous chapters I argue that many of the difficulties have arisen from organizational aspects of the system, especially as a result of problems resulting from the excess size of the farms, the vertical links with processing and supplying industries, the administration of the farms, the procedures of labor compensation, the incentive structure for the managers, and the supply of auxiliary services.

It seems reasonable that many governmental policies are tied to the organizational structure. These can occur either as a result of the same ideological affinities toward agriculture that created the structure, or as a result of the exigencies of a planned economy reacting on and though the organization of the agricultural sector. Such a view is reflected in a statement by D. Gale Johnson, a highly regarded agricultural economist: "I believe that the socialized nature [ownership] of Soviet agriculture is not the major source of difficulties. Many other aspects of Soviet planning, management systems, and pricing are far more important in limiting agriculture's performance" (1983, p. 3).

A quite different approach is followed by those who claim that the agricultural difficulties in Marxist regimes are primarily due to general governmental policies toward agriculture that are completely independent of the structure of the sector. For instance, Marc Blecher, a U.S. political scientist, has argued with regard to China: "But none of these problems [of waste and inefficiency] was inherent to collectivism itself. There is every reason to believe that collectivism could have achieved much better economic results under a different set of state policies on commerce, planning and investment. Since the post-Mao leadership has made changes on all fronts at once . . . it is difficult to say for certain whether the impressive economic results that have been achieved in recent years are due to the new, less collectivist organization in the countryside or to other factors" (1988, p. 95).

If these latter arguments are correct, then why have the leaders in many Marxist regimes attempted to make drastic changes in the structure of the farm sector in the 1980s and the early 1990s? Most right-wing analysts reject the premise of the question. Left-wing analysts generally attack the question head-on, but see sinister plots, rather than economics, at work. For instance, Blecher asserts: "It can certainly be said that any claim collectivism had to be eliminated for economic reasons alone rests on very spurious logic. To the extent that the reform leadership was aware of this, its reasons for dismantling rural collectivism would lie elsewhere—perhaps, we can hypothesize, in its desire to create a politically conservative smallholding peasantry" (1988, p. 95).

This chapter tries to disentangle the relative importance of structural and policy factors on the performance of agriculture in preparation for the empirical analysis in the next chapter. Many snares, however, await those trying to analyze agricultural policies in Marxist regimes. For instance, those policies that are tied to the structure must be distinguished from those that are more general. The focus must be on policies that are actually implemented, not those that are merely announced. This latter distinction is particularly important for examination of a number of Third World Marxist regimes.[1] Moreover, only the most important agricultural policies can be examined, especially since it is clearly impossible to discuss all important agricultural policies in all thirty-three Marxist regimes. This means that many of the agricultural policies that are neither tied to the economic system as a whole nor to the ideology cannot be investigated in detail; for instance, specific policies concerning crop choice, rural economic, and social infrastructure, technology, research, credit, rural education and agricultural extension work, or conservation, to name a few.

Although it should be clear that this policy-versus-structure problem raises many analytic difficulties, it also provides a useful framework for understanding not only why agricultural performance of Marxist regimes has been different from that of non-Marxist nations, but also why agricultural performance has differed among Marxist regimes. I start by examining briefly some policy problems facing Marxist governments newly arrived in power, because many of the decisions made during this early period, both with regard to the structure and the general treatment of

---

[1] Of the countries in the sample, the Congo provides an interesting and extreme case study of this difference. Samuel Decalo, a well-known Africanist, has noted (1985): "Nowhere in Africa has international risk capital been more roundly and consistently vilified at home, and at the same time so assiduously courted abroad. Nowhere have the country's fundamental socioeconomic problems and their optimal solution been more clearly defined, with subsequent correction policies so utterly ineffectual. Certainly in no other Marxist regime in the continent is the level of dialectical sophistication and ideological rhetoric so high as in the Congo, and the self-criticism of its leaders so sincere, without either of these having the slightest effect on matters related to the real world. Indeed, few African states have projected an image of militancy and power, while exhibiting utter impotence to effectuate virtually anything in any domain."

the agricultural sector, place constraints on policy choices at a later time. I then turn to four major dilemmas of agricultural policy: bimodal versus unimodal development, rural versus urban interests, political versus economic leadership, and market versus administrative allocation. My major argument is that in many cases the organizational structure biases governmental policies regarding these dilemmas in a particular direction, even though these policy biases are not absolute. Indeed, for some of these policies I note some exceptions and try to understand why these countries are different from the others. Nevertheless, if I am correct that the structure biases policy, then organizational change may be the only way in which certain seemingly general policies can be reversed.

TRANSITION PROBLEMS

Marxist regimes coming into power face some acute problems of economic transition. A particularly acute dilemma arises from the necessity to restore and to increase agricultural production while, at the same time, accommodating demands of those groups responsible for the victory of the Marxist party. The manner in which these structural and general problems of transition are resolved often sets the guidelines for agricultural policies for many years in the future.

The more militant the revolution, the more likely it is to be caught in a dilemma between increased investment versus increased consumption. As Colburn (1986) and others have pointed out, the nature of the post-revolutionary crisis is inherently inflationary: the new government increases government expenditure in order to reward its supporters and to gain support from others. Without financial support from other nations, however, these government expenditures usually lead to balance of payments problems. At this point the Marxist governments usually attack the difficulties by imposition of a series of price controls, quotas, and food rationing.[2] Problems are compounded because such controls are often administered by a politically reliable but inexperienced bureaucracy. In addition, the government usually tries to set up a certain number of state and collective farms as models for future structural changes. These farms, however, require considerable subsidies and other assistance to become as modern as possible, which puts more demands on the government

[2] An interesting case is provided by Nicaragua. The Sandinistas raised minimum wages in the agricultural sector, lowered rents, and, as inflation began to pick up, kept official food prices from rising as quickly so that real food prices fell. Food in the official markets became scarcer, the parallel markets in food increased in importance, and almost every year the government passed new resolutions against these markets. Because the Nicaraguan people were adamantly set against rationing, the government introduced "guarantee cards," but even these could not serve their purpose if not enough food was available.

budget already strained by increased welfare expenditures. What begins as a commitment to improve consumption of the poor, particularly in urban areas, can lead to a generalized bias against agricultural producers, especially if the government attempts to keep food prices low and does not have sufficient tax revenues to finance a program of food subsidies to the producers.

An important countervailing factor must be noted, at least for small Marxist regimes with a high dependence both on imports and, to pay for them, on agricultural exports. In these cases producers of agricultural exports have a strong bargaining position with the government, especially if much of this production is carried out not by a few large estates but by numerous middle-sized farms. In Nicaragua, for instance, this led the Sandinista government to a set of differentiated agricultural policies that left these export producers in relative peace, but squeezed other farm subsectors. The latter policies included, for example, lowering rents for lands leased to tenants in order to gain or maintain their political support and, at the same time, to reduce the economic and political power of the landlords. Other agricultural policies favored by Marxist governments to achieve the same ends, for instance, raising minimum wages in the countryside, affected all rural producers employing labor and often led to a stagnation or fall in agricultural exports, a rise in the parallel market price for food in urban areas, and a further boost to the inflationary spiral mentioned above.

A concurrent transition problem is a decline in labor discipline. When estate owners are removed, constraints on labor discipline also fall. After the revolution in Cuba, productivity on the newly created state farms fell to roughly one-half that of private farms (Mesa-Lago 1981, p. 17), only part of which could be explained by overstaffing. In Nicaragua, labor norms also fell considerably (Utting 1987). On state farms in Grenada, workers paid by the day began to work many fewer hours (Pryor 1986), as did those in South Yemen, as noted in chapter 6. Such problems can be solved, but their solutions take time; and Marxist governments have a strong temptation to use administrative, rather than economic methods, to solve them quickly.

Several other transition problems also deserve mention. In some cases decapitalization of the farms occurs as land owners attempt to place the funds abroad that were previously earmarked for repairs, replanting, and reinvestment. The nationalization of export and import firms in order to prevent this capital flight can lead to an interruption of the linkages with foreign agricultural input suppliers with a corresponding shortage of these commodities necessary for production. Even if these channels of capital flight are closed, other channels are possible; for example, smuggling or, in the case of Nicaragua, the driving of large herds of cattle over the border, which allegedly reduced the nation's cattle stock by about one third. Finally, transition problems arising from any massive political change and the difficulties of inexperienced governments to gain control over the economy causes production problems.

In the past an important interaction between general agricultural policies and structural policies often developed. If the transitional policies led to a stagnation or decline of agricultural production, then Marxist governments were tempted to advance the date of land reforms or collectivization. If the government decided first to carry out agrarian reform, the expected positive impacts of these measures were seldom obtained in the short run because of the economic disruptions inherent in the process. If this short-run decline was not quickly reversed, the collectivization process was accelerated. But this, in turn, usually led to greater brutality, a greater disruption of agricultural production, and a further divergence of agricultural production from its potential. This phenomenon has been documented extensively in the case of the Soviet Union (Hunter 1988); for Third World Marxist regimes some supporting evidence is presented in the next chapter.

In short, the first few years of a Marxist regime are perilous. The impatience of the government to transform the economy leads to reliance on administrative methods for solving agricultural problems and these habits are often difficult to break, no matter how adverse an influence they have on agricultural production. The complete extent of these administrative regulations to meet transition problems are difficult for those on the outside to determine and require painstaking studies on a case-by-case base to understand. These policies are also quite independent of the policy dilemmas discussed below.

BIMODAL VERSUS UNIMODAL DEVELOPMENT

In a unimodal development pattern, the government spreads its resources to agriculture across the entire sector, so that all subsectors benefit. In a bimodal development pattern, the government focuses its resources either on a particular subsector such as the plantation, rather than the smallholder economy, or on a particular group of farmers. It is a variant of a "wager-on-the-strong" policy, an approach toward agriculture favored under Czar Nicholas II in Russia shortly after the turn of the twentieth century. In Marxist regimes, governmental agricultural resources are generally focused on "socialist agriculture" and, within this subsector, on state rather than collective farms. The bimodal strategy has been an important Marxoid element of the official ideology (chapter 2).

Bimodal strategies for agriculture have received considerable criticism among Western development economists (e.g., Johnston and Kilby

1975), who have shown through case studies that even if the modern sub-sector receiving such funds is run efficiently, rapid growth of the agricultural sector as a whole is not ensured. Moreover, they argue, subsidies to the farms in the modern subsector act often to benefit the urban population which obtains food more cheaply. Because average incomes are higher in urban than rural areas, these policies are inequitable to the population as a whole.

In some cases a bimodal strategy is inevitable because the government, either Marxist or non-Marxist, may simply not have the administrative capability to manage a widespread agricultural development program. A depressing case in point is the non-Marxist government of Malaŵi, as argued by Pryor (1990). Moreover, although a wager-on-the-strong (either to individuals or groups) widens rural income differentials, it is a defensible development strategy for any government if three conditions are met: when resources channeled to the strong are more productive than if expended on the rest of the agricultural sector, when there is some trickle-down of the benefits from the wealthier part of the agricultural sector to the poorer, and when the poorer part of the agricultural sector is not disadvantaged by other government policies, by natural conditions, or by its interactions with the wealthier part of the agricultural sector. In few Marxist regimes are these three conditions met.

Marxist governments often create a state or collective farm sector deliberately to channel resources to a small group of modern farms in order to create "growth poles" for the rest of the sector. In other cases, particularly in the Third World, such an investment pattern is more inadvertent. For instance, Joaquim Russo, the Angolan Vice Minister of Agriculture, once noted that the creation of state and cooperative farms from former Portuguese farms "appeared a simple solution. Unfortunately, agriculture is a science to be sure, but its technology is an extremely local matter. It appeared simple to arrange technicians, agronomists, seeds and fertilizer in order to start production up again. But in reality, everything was much more complicated" (Becker 1988, p. 124). Another easy justification for a lopsided investment policy is that investment destined for agriculture must be channeled into these socialist farms so that they will survive. But often such startup subsidies last for years while the private agricultural sector is starved for resources and inputs. The result is that the modern socialist sector is highly capital intensive, the traditional sector is highly labor intensive, and capital is inefficiently allocated because it has a very low marginal productivity in the former subsector and a very high marginal productivity in the latter subsector. Moreover, development of technology is skewed to the modern subsector so that the private subsector remains backward.

At this point two questions arise: To what extent have Marxist regimes followed bimodal strategies? And what are the problems of coexistence among state, cooperative, and private agricultural sectors that lead to bimodal strategies?

The Choice of a Bimodal Pattern

Governments find it both easier and politically more expedient to funnel its aid to a few large farms, rather than to a large number of small farms, as Robert Bates (1981) has pointed out. In contrast to the unorganized smallholders, estate workers are also in a better position to use strike threats and other tactics to realize their demands for higher incomes. Moreover, by directing its resources to such projects, rather than following a generalized price policy benefitting the entire agricultural sector, government leaders can obtain useful powers of patronage and, in addition, more focused political support. Of course, some of these political considerations for a bimodal strategy are valid in both non-Marxist and Marxist regimes and do not reveal the special circumstances of the latter group of nations.

The political reasons underlying the support for large farm units have some adverse consequences. In some cases this focus on large state farms has led to considerable political discontent by farm workers wishing to become smallholders. In the mid-1980s in Nicaragua, for instance, in the face of considerable peasant agitation, the government broke up about a fifth of the state farms into cooperative and private farms. In other countries these collective and state farms attracted those farmers who were least resourceful and least able to function as independent farmers. Empirical sociological studies supporting this proposition for Poland are summarized by Szwengrub (1968). If this is true, then these new state-sponsored farms would require considerably more governmental financial support than others types of farms.

In some Third World Marxist regimes, the choice of a bimodal strategy was not so much deliberate but as an outgrowth of short-term considerations. For instance, in Angola and Mozambique, Portuguese estate owners and managers fled after independence, destroying a good share of their farm capital. Moreover, many of the workers on these estates also left, either because they could now obtain land for their own farms or because they no longer were compelled by political or economic circumstances to work on these estates. Since these estates provided a considerable share of the export receipts, the government tried to reactivate them, and on the same capital intensive basis as before. Of course, this required considerable investment in equipment, mostly imported from abroad. Nevertheless, because the political leaders understood little about farming, they paid scant attention to problems of equipment repairs and the training of mechanics, so that most of the newly purchased equipment was soon out of operation and more had to be imported. In Mozambique in the late 1970s and early 1980s, 90 percent or more of the investment in the agricultural sector went to state farms. It took the governments of Angola and Mozambique almost a decade to realize that such a bimodal investment strategy led to very little increase in total production; meanwhile, the rest of the agricultural sector was starved for investment and inputs.

In contrast, in Ethiopia where such transition problems did not occur because there was no large plantation sector, the channeling of funds to the state and collective farm sector at the expense of smallholders was a deliberate policy choice. For instance, between 1980 and 1985, state farms received 76 percent of fertilizer, 95 percent of improved seed, and 80 percent of credit supplied to the agricultural sector, but these farms generated only 4 to 5 percent of total agricultural output on about 4 percent of the land (Economist Intelligence Unit 1989a, p. 15). Collective farms also received support in a variety of ways: they could demand the most fertile land for their farm activities and they paid lower taxes, obtained interest free credit, sold their produce to the monopsonist state marketing agency for higher prices, and enjoyed priority access to agricultural inputs and consumer goods (Cohen and Isaksson 1988). Such overwhelming support to the state and cooperative sectors at the expense of smallholders continued for more than a decade. For instance, in 1977–78 smallholders received only 16 percent of total government funds going to agriculture (investment and credit), and by 1982–83 this fell to 8.5 percent. In these two years state farms received respectively 39 and 60 percent (Teka and Nichola 1983), the remainder going to cooperative farms and other enterprises.

Some Third World Marxist regimes took longer than others to recognize the problems inherent in a bimodal strategy. An interesting example is provided by the People's Republic of the Congo, which became Marxist in the mid-1960s. The government's original economic strategy placed little importance on agriculture, and within agriculture, almost all subsidies and investments went to the 25 state farms and ranches.[3] Most of these farms ran deficits in almost every year (Hung 1987, pp. 37, 202; Parti congolais du travail 1984, p. 256). The smallholder sector, where one-third to one-half of the labor force in the country worked, was budgeted for a minuscule amount of governmental funds, most of which did not seem well spent. For instance, in the early 1970s, 38 percent of the agricultural agents, 71 percent of the principal agricultural agents, and 82 percent of the agricultural engineers lived in the two major cities

---

[3] Doulos (1983) says that until 1979 state farms got all state investment in agriculture.

rather than in the rural areas or small towns. Moreover, the combined salaries of these agricultural agents totaled more than the combined market sales of agricultural products by the smallholders. Not unexpectedly, private agricultural production showed no signs of increasing (Bertrand 1975, pp. 188, 256).[4]

For the 1982–86 period, the government attempted to change its ways and adopted a new investment strategy focusing on agriculture so that this sector could fulfill a number of ambitious tasks including the satisfaction of domestic food demands. The instrument for this transformation was, however, to be the state sector, and private agriculture was to become "an instrument for its self-destruction" (Parti congolais du travail 1984, p. 166), even though the party recognized that up to that point "technological and financial results of the state farms were weak."[5] Despite declining productivity on the state farms, the government planned for the first step along this new path to be a doubling of the size of the state farm sector (Association de la Maison de l'Afrique 1986, p. 36). Although the peasant sector was to receive about one-third of total agricultural investment, most of these funds went to design bureaus or were blocked so that after three years into the plan, less than 1 percent of total state investment actually reached the peasants (ILO 1984). At the end of the plan period, the final plan report revealed an enormous gap between planned and actual agricultural production, especially since the absorptive capacity of the state farms for new investment was limited. After almost two decades of difficulties with state farms, the government began to have some second thoughts. In 1987 it closed three state farms when no buyers could be found, and it began to try to sell off 10 others to private investors.

Although other examples of Third World Marxist regimes with a fatal fascination for state farms to the detriment of the rest of the rural economy can be provided (for instance, Cuba, Guyana, São Tomé), the phenomenon can also be found among the industrialized Marxist regimes. In Poland around 1980, for instance, the private sector accounted for more than three-fourths of the total land, but received only about one-third of the state investment funds in agriculture, not to mention the lowest pri-

[4] This problem appeared to persist. For instance, in 1981 46 percent of all agricultural technicians working for the Ministry of Agriculture were living in the capital city (Congo, Ministère de l'agriculture et de l'élevage 1983, p. 166). The problem is not, of course, unique to the Congo. In Mongolia around 1960, the party secretary and Prime Minister Yumjaagiyn Tsendenbal complained that most of trained agricultural specialists never left the capital city (Rupen 1979, p. 113).

[5] Other observers (such as the ILO 1984, p. 38) have used stronger language, noting that central guidance of the state farms was "rigid," "bureaucratic," and "inconsistent," that the management of the state farms was "disastrous," and that supplies of agricultural inputs were "irregular" so that the declining state farm productivity was quite understandable.

ority for agricultural inputs and credit (Cochran 1988b). In other East European nations where agriculture was almost completely collectivized, state farms received a disproportionate share of agricultural investment and inputs, at the expense of the collective and private farms. For instance, during the 1960s in Romania, half of the total investment in agriculture and half the fertilizer deliveries went to the state farms, which held less than 15 percent of the arable land (Montias 1967, p. 130). In Yugoslavia the government deliberately focused its fiscal efforts primarily on the socialist sector of agriculture and, until the systemic reforms of 1965, private farmers found it very difficult to buy farm machinery, purchase inputs such as fertilizer, or obtain bank credit. Even after 1965 private farmers found credit to buy farm equipment difficult to obtain. As a result, in almost all of these countries the capital-to-labor ratio was progressively lower as the view turned from state farms to collective farms to private farms. Holding the fertility of land constant, it also appears that in most Marxist regimes, subsidies per farm worker (either direct or indirect subsidies through capital grants, loans that were never paid back, and cheap inputs) were greatest for state farms and least for private farmers.

The bimodal strategy was even followed in agricultural price policy. Producer prices paid to state farms were often higher than those paid to collective farms, which in turn were higher than those paid to private farmers. In Yugoslavia, for instance, private farmers received prices 5 percent lower than state farms (World Bank 1975, p. 10; 1983b, p. 163). In the Soviet Union in 1987 collective farms received 90 percent or less of the state farm price for sugar beets, potatoes, milk, beef, eggs, and other products (Cook 1989). They did, however, receive a higher price for grain and vegetables. In Hungary, according to the calculations by Alton and others (1989), prices paid to private farmers for their crops increased more slowly from 1970 through 1987 than to state farms but, curiously, faster than to collective farms.

The existence of state and collective farms does not, of course, automatically dictate a bimodal strategy. Nevertheless, discrimination against the private sector was often an important means of creating or maintaining a state or collective farm sector (chapter 4). Agricultural policymakers did not want to eliminate such a bias until the sector was "secured and profitable," a point not yet reached after many decades.

It is certainly conceivable for a Marxist agricultural sector to function without a bimodal strategy. Gorbachev, for instance, seems to have a vision for Soviet agriculture in which state, collective, and privately leased farms would be competing against one another without governmental discrimination for or against any sector: each would allegedly receive the same prices and each would have the same access to agricultural inputs and credits. The Polish government took an important step along this path in 1982 by agreeing to a policy of nondiscrimination, so that within a few years the private sector's share of purchased farm equipment had risen to 51 percent. For other inputs such as fertilizer, the nondiscrimination agreement claimed less success. In the late 1980s governmental promises that future agricultural policies would be nondiscriminatory were greeted skeptically: It would require inconceivable self-control for a Marxist government to allow a large-scale collective or state farm to go bankrupt and cause a depression on the local labor market. The bimodal strategy is a prime example of organizational structure and ideology strongly influencing general agricultural policies.

Coexistence Problems

Nondiscrimination requires peaceful coexistence among the state, cooperative, and private sectors. Certain political difficulties in the early years of a Marxist regime have been often discussed; for instance, too large a private sector would mean too much power in the hands of potential opponents of the party, while too small a private sector might mean an erosion of popular support from peasants. The economic problems of "subsectoral coexistence" have received much less analysis, and yet these results of structural policies often led economic policymakers back toward bimodal general policies.

THE IMPACT OF UNCERTAINTY

Unless the government can convince the private farmers that their lands will no longer be touched by the structural policies, the specter of further collectivization can lead to a fall in investment or actual disinvestment in the private sector because it is difficult for any general policies to pacify these fears. These problems of private-sector fears were dramatically illustrated in a 1983 survey in Nicaragua, which revealed that 100 percent of its private cotton producers feared expropriation (Colburn 1986, p. 56). As I point out in greater detail in chapter 9, such problems also arise in the process of decollectivization since many farmers fear that if they invest heavily of their time and money in a private farm, the government will recollectivize.

Sometimes the decapitalization resulting from such fears was dramatic—for example, the reduction in the cattle stock through slaughter and consumption or "cattle flight" that took place during the Soviet collectivization, as well as in other countries such as Cuba and Nicaragua. In China (Donnithorne 1967, p. 41) and a few other Marxist regimes this slaughter took place even after collectivization. Sometimes the results of such decapitalization were much less noticeable; for instance, a slow deterioration of farm buildings and equipment, the nonreplanting of certain aging perennials, the refusal to adopt new methods requiring any significant investment in either time or money, or the education of children in non-agricultural skills so that the human capital stock in agriculture was not restored. In some cases, one segment of the private agricultural sector took defensive measures inflicting considerable damage on other sectors, for example, in Cuba where large cattle farms stopped buying half-grown cattle from smallholders because they feared such cattle inventories would be confiscated in the nationalization process (MacEwan 1981, pp. 39–41).

As a result of these uncertainties, most Marxist governments face an excruciating dilemma: if they delay collectivization until they have an administrative apparatus capable of reorganizing the agricultural sector in a competent fashion, the physical and human capital stock might be considerably depleted and total agricultural production would be depressed, no matter what other policies they follow.

CONFLICTS OVER SCARCE INPUTS

For many types of agricultural inputs, especially those imported during a period of shortage of foreign exchange, the struggle among the subsectors for inputs represents a zero-sum game. For instance, if spare parts are difficult to obtain, governmental administrators have a natural tendency to allocate them either to state farms or to government-owned MTSs so that their use may be more widely shared. The result is that private farmers receive a negligible part of such inputs and, if the MTS is in a monopsony position vis-à-vis the private or collective farmers, corruption is inevitable.[6]

Another more widely discussed input problem concerns competition for labor. In Third World nations with large plantation sectors, seasonal labor shortages often arose on the state and collective farms. This was either because the previous seasonal workers were engaged on their own land, since they were not forced to work for the estate, or because the managers of these farms lacked the informal networks used to obtain labor. Indeed, competition for labor between the private plot and the collective fields also existed within collective farms in almost all Marxist regimes with such farms, as noted in chapter 6. In Nicaragua the state farms experienced a severe labor shortage, not only because of withdrawal of peasants to their own (new) fields, but also because of considerable migration to the city, the withdrawal of farmworkers for the army, and the lessening number of teenagers available because of the increase

---

[6] Boguslawski (1986, pp. 36–37) has some interesting comments on this problem for Somalia.

in school attendance. State farms experiencing such labor shortages had often to resort to "volunteer" labor of urban workers and students, who were generally not very productive farm workers. For the harvest in 1990 in the Soviet Union, the urban population could no longer be so easily coerced to participate in the harvest and, as a result, much of the crop rotted in the fields. In other Marxist regimes such as Cuba, however, the governments retained sufficient strength to exercise such coercion.

DYSFUNCTIONAL ARBITRAGE

If the existence of state, cooperative, and private sectors is accompanied by multiple price systems (a phenomenon occurring in most Marxist regimes), the private farmers can often take advantage of the situation to the detriment of the system as a whole. A well-known example on the input side occurred in the Soviet Union, where farmers purchased subsidized bread for their private livestock from state stores as a substitute for much more expensive animal fodder, which they would have had to purchase at state outlets. Several different kinds of arbitrage are possible on the output side. In Cuba, private farmers received a ration book entitling them to subsidized foodstuffs at the state stores. They then bought food for their own consumption at low prices, while selling the food they raised at the farmers markets for high prices. Another type of arbitrage occurs in the Soviet Union, where farmers sold not only their own produce for the high prices at the farmers markets but also made arrangements with the collective or state farm management to sell some of their surplus as well, so that the latter received cash which they could hide from higher administrative authorities.

The arbitrage problem is further compounded by theft. In many Marxist countries, farmers on socialist sector farms steal inputs from the collective for their own private farming activities. This can take the form of illegally grazing cattle on collective or state farm fields; or carting off fertilizers, animal feed, seeds, and other inputs from the farm for their private use; or illegally using farm equipment. Such theft is extremely difficult to prevent.[7]

Some Consequences of a Bimodal Strategy

If resources are channeled primarily to one part of the agricultural sector, rather than another, several obvious ill-effects can occur:

INEFFICIENCY AND WASTE

Static allocational inefficiencies arise from bimodal policies because of differences in the marginal return to each kind of input between the three

[7] I briefly discuss another type of theft, praedial larceny, in chapter 5, footnote 5.

sectors. This can be clearly seen in a quantitative fashion from production function studies, where the calculated marginal productivities of various inputs and factors of production are quite different in the two sectors (for example, for Poland, a study by Boyd 1988; other studies are discussed in the next chapter). Thus we have a waste of these inputs in the favored sectors and the use of costly substitutes by the unfavored sectors.

SLOW TECHNICAL CHANGE

A bimodal strategy is likely to lead to a slower spread of technology across the agricultural sector for two main reasons: the unfavored sectors are unable to purchase the inputs embodying this technology, and they are unlikely to have equal access to agricultural extension services. For instance, in Yugoslavia the government did not provide the private farm sector with any extension services; in other countries such as Grenada, Guyana, Madagascar, and Nicaragua, the extension service to private farmers functioned extremely poorly, in good measure because of lack of serious governmental interest in the program (for Grenada and Madagascar, see Pryor 1986, 1990c). As a result of these factors, the new technologies used in the favored subsectors of agriculture seldom trickled down very fast to the other subsectors.

INCOME INEQUALITIES

A bimodal strategy is also likely to lead to large differences in farm incomes of workers in the state farms and those on the collective farm. The former receive a regular wage, even though the farm may require subsidies to continue operations. The latter may receive only their share of the residual income after all expenses have been met unless some type of minimum wage policy has been introduced, as in East Europe and the Soviet Union after the late 1950s.

Although such problems were generally recognized by clear-sighted agricultural officials in these nations, as well as by more hostile outside observers, the difficulties engendered by coexistence combined with the ideological fervor in favor of collective agriculture (chapter 2) led to a bimodal policy in most Marxist regimes.

RURAL VERSUS URBAN INTERESTS

Most Marxist movements are led by urban intellectuals and their regimes have their strongest power base in the cities or in ethnic groups that are more urbanized than others (table 4.3). Furthermore, Marxist governments rule in the name of the proletariat, and such workers are found primarily in urban areas. As a result, many Marxist regimes are said to have a policy bias against the rural sector; often the coercion employed in the collectivization drive is used as the major piece of evidence. The analytic problem is that bias can occur along many dimensions, and the results of such investigations depend, in part, upon the phenomena and the time period under investigation. Before turning to the empirical evidence, however, a certain amount of brush must be cleared.

Numerous observers have argued that although the European Marxist governments have shown a bias against agriculture because of the urban background of the party leaders, the situation was different for China and other countries, where the Communist party spent long years of fighting against the non-Marxist government in the countryside. This experience allegedly gave party leaders not just insight and empathy into the plight of the peasant but, more important, time to test various rural policies to determine their effectiveness and support by the peasantry.

Even with regard to China, the argument is not strong: if Mao and his colleagues were so sensitive to rural interests and so knowledgeable about rural conditions, why did they institute the catastrophic Great Leap Forward and the highly centralized commune system which led to about thirty million deaths, mostly in the countryside? If we broaden our scope of enquiry and look at other Marxist parties achieving governmental power after long years of fighting in the countryside (in particular, Albania, Cuba, Guinea-Bissau, Kampuchea, Laos, Mozambique, Nicaragua, South Yemen, Viet Nam, Yugoslavia, Zimbabwe and, to a much lesser extent, Angola), the conjecture becomes even less credible. In some cases, rural support was not strong because of difficulties in mobilizing peasants for political support (for instance, Mozambique and Zimbabwe). In other cases, the governments moved quickly to collectivize, which was not a popular organizational policy (Laos, as discussed in chapter 4, Kampuchea, and South Yemen). In still other countries the policies definitely did not favor the rural sector because of the emphasis of massive investment in urban areas (for instance, Guinea-Bissau). Zimbabwe may be the only example of a young Marxist regime whose general nonstructural agricultural policies appeared to favor rural interests. Like many other Third World nations the political support they received from the urban sector was crucial. It was unlikely, therefore, that decisions pitting rural and urban interests against each other, for instance, when setting prices of agricultural products, would be decided in favor of the rural sector.

Generalizations are, however, difficult to make since the outcomes of such sectoral clashes varied considerably from one Marxist regime to another, as well as from one period to another. Three aspects of bias are the setting of agricultural prices, intersectoral flows, and investment policies. Later in this chapter I also discuss bias in the context of the distribution of agricultural inputs.

Price Policy

Evgeny Preobrazhensky (1965), an influential Soviet economist in the 1920s, enunciated two important propositions: the government can increase investment by moving the internal terms-of-trade against the rural sector. Moreover, this policy can be carried out in a manner so that the real incomes of industrial workers will not decline. The first proposition is correct, but the second is wrong, at least under normal conditions.[8] A number of Marxist and non-Marxist economists have also argued that economic development of poor countries is only possible through financing of urban investment from resources transferred from the agricultural sector, a proposition that has been challenged on empirical grounds using data from a number of East Asian nations by Ishikawa (1967a). A more detailed examination of these issues in the context of agriculture in the Marxist regimes illustrates some of the key policy dilemmas of collectivized agriculture.

A shifting of the internal terms-of-trade against the farmer allows fewer industrial goods to be exchanged for a given amount of food. For a closed market economy a key problem arising from such a shift is to maintain a balance between domestic demand and supply for foodstuffs and industrial goods. Farmers will usually grow less and place fewer foodstuffs on the market to obtain cash to buy industrial goods if they receive a lower real price. If worker incomes are not reduced, they will demand the same amount of foodstuffs and either foodstuffs will have to be rationed (a nonmarket measure) or they will bid up the price of food through black-market purchases. If exports and imports are permitted, industrial workers may attempt to purchase more imported foodstuffs, which may give rise to balance of payments problems.

A shift in the internal terms of trade against agriculture can be deliberate and implemented through several measures. It can also be inadvertent; for example, the result of longer lags in setting agricultural prices than in other sectors in an inflationary situation or the consequence of an overvalued exchange rate that is not offset by special subsidies to agricultural producers. These inadvertent policies have occurred in a number of Third World Marxist regimes. For example, in Guyana the estates producing sugar for export became so impoverished that the real incomes of the state farm workers fell, agricultural infrastructure decayed, and the

---

[8] Sah and Stiglitz (1984) examine Preobrazhensky's two theorems with sophisticated mathematical methods for a general case, showing that the first is correct but the second is wrong. In Research Note E, I examine the propositions using a diagram for a closed economy and obtain the same results. Although my discussion is less general and rigorous than that of Sah and Stiglitz, it provides an intuitive understanding of the key economic forces in a much simpler fashion.

necessary quinquennial replanting of the cane was not carried out. In São Tomé it led to a similar decapitalization of agriculture, and in Nicaragua it led to a considerable shift in the mix of crops, away from exports and toward provision of the domestic market where prices were determined in large measure by market forces.

Several deliberate "market solutions" are open to the government to turn the internal terms of trade against agriculture and to withdraw sufficient purchasing power so as to keep supply-demand relations balanced and, at the same time, to allow command over resources to be transferred to the government. One means is a sales tax, which essentially sets up a dual price system, with producers receiving less than the amount consumers pay. Another means is a system of state monopsonistic purchasers paying lower prices for agricultural produce or state monopolistic sellers of agricultural inputs charging high prices. In both cases the amount of resources available to the government for investment increases, but at the cost of a fall in real income of both farmers and urban workers, a proposition that can be demonstrated rigorously in a simple fashion (Sah and Stiglitz 1984; Research Note E).

Few Marxist regimes possessing effective means of coercion have ever felt themselves constrained by "market solutions" to such a problem. Conceptually, the simplest nonmarket solution is to force the farmers to produce more than they would normally do at a given price, either by setting a production quota that must be met to avoid severe punishment, or collectivizing and seeing that the prerequisites of meeting the quota are met at all stages of the production cycle. This is, of course, the "tribute" from agriculture about which Stalin spoke. It is based on an assumption that a sufficient amount of production can be squeezed out of the agricultural sector to feed the workers without starving the farmers, an assumption proven tragically wrong in the Soviet Union in the early 1930s (Conquest 1987). As I will indicate, once the counterflows of industrial inputs from industry to agriculture are taken into consideration, the situation becomes more complicated.

Another nonmarket solution is rationing foodstuffs that are in short supply as a result of the impact of lower real producer prices received by the farmers. If industrial workers unable to obtain foodstuffs attempt to use such purchasing power to buy industrial commodities, then the supply/demand balance for these products may be upset, which will require rationing of these products as well. If workers have purchasing power that they cannot completely spend for what they want and if the government cannot eliminate it through taxes or a maximum wage level, then the country faces a situation of suppressed inflation leading either to flourishing black markets or to a decline of work incentives, or both. If the government allows prices to increase, then the shortfalls in agricul-

tural production induced by lower real prices can set off a cycle of inflation, a case in point being Nicaragua in the middle and late 1980s.

Up to this point, my discussion follows the standard line of Western
analysis of these questions. It rests on the implicit assumption that Marxist governments have turned the terms-of-trade against agriculture. In
recent years, however, this assumption has become questionable; empirical investigation is needed. To calculate the internal terms-of-trade, ideally we need an index of prices received by agricultural producers and
another index of prices which they pay for inputs and also for consumer
goods. Unfortunately, such indexes are available only for East Europe.
For Third World Marxist regimes it is possible, however, to calculate a
proxy internal terms-of-trade from national account statistics, where we
can compare the implicit price deflator of value added in the agriculture
sector (usually combined with forestry and fishing) with the implicit price
deflator of the entire factor price GDP excluding this sector.

For a number of East European nations relatively good terms-of-trade
data are available and the trends are mixed (Alton et al. 1989, tables 12–
17). Between 1970 and 1987, the terms-of-trade increased considerably
in favor of agriculture in Yugoslavia and slightly in Bulgaria, Poland, and
Romania, while turning against agriculture somewhat in Hungary and
Czechoslovakia. If price policies generally were biased against the agricultural sector, the shift in the terms-of-trade must have occurred before
1970; these price data series for a later period reveal no apparent bias
against agriculture.

For most Third World Marxist regimes I used the approximation of the
terms-of-trade from the national income statistics, and even these series
were not available for many countries. Other problems arose because
many of these countries had multiple agricultural prices (see below) and
it is unclear how they were handled in calculating the current and constant price indexes, from which the implicit price deflators were derived.
As a result of these and the other problems listed, my calculations must
be very cautiously interpreted.

For the ten countries for which GDP data are readily available (World
Bank 1988), this calculation of the terms-of-trade for the period from 1970
through 1986 shows agricultural prices either rising faster or roughly at
the same rate as prices for the rest of the economy in eight countries
(Bénin, China, Congo, Ethiopia, Guinea-Bissau, Guyana, Madagascar,
and Yugoslavia). Only in Nicaragua and Zimbabwe did agricultural prices
rise at a significantly slower rate than prices in other sectors. Since the
data series covered a period before the Marxist regimes took power, I
was not able to isolate any bias against the agricultural sector with respect
to price policies.

If the terms-of-trade were to turn in favor of agricultural producers, in normal cases farmers would market more products, and in most cases total agricultural production would also increase. I tested this latter proposition with data on total production and found little support. Three interpretations of these negative results can be adduced: prices paid to the rural sector were so low in the initial time period that the increase in prices was not sufficient to serve as an incentive; the farmers were unwilling to increase production because of shortages of consumer goods to the rural sector; or they were unable or unwilling to increase production very much either because of shortages of agricultural inputs or because of cost increases due to the disintegration of rural infrastructure. For some of those countries for which I used national income statistics to make this calculation of the internal terms-of-trade, it is also possible that the farmers did not actually receive the stated prices when they sold their produce; that is, the national income accountants included the marketing boards in the agricultural sector so that the index reflects the prices that they, not the farmers, obtained. Without detailed analysis of each country, we cannot determine which interpretation explained the situation.

The Problem of Intersectoral Flows

Discussion of intersectoral flows of finance between the agricultural and non-agricultural sectors has often been treated in a misleading fashion, especially by noneconomists. The fact that agricultural prices have fallen in comparison to industrial prices (the internal terms-of-trade) and that real incomes of farmers has fallen does not *necessarily* mean that the government has squeezed resources out of agriculture for investment in industry or that "farmers are financing industrialization." For instance, at the same time the resource flow of industrial inputs for agriculture might have greatly increased, especially if such inputs were being used less effectively or if special rural investment programs were undertaken or if the rural sector was receiving some type of direct fiscal subsidy. Thus a net flow of resources into agriculture can occur, even as the internal terms of trade are shifting against it.

To investigate the problem it is necessary to calculate directly the change in resource flows in ("imports") and out ("exports") of the agricultural system. Exports include the value of the goods flowing out plus other payments such as taxes; imports include the value of agricultural inputs, consumer goods, and governmental current and capital expenditures in the agricultural sector. Needless to say, this is not an easy task, especially for the Marxist regimes where data problems are severe; and such an exercise has been attempted only for the Soviet Union and China. A cruder way of approaching the phenomenon is to look at taxes from and subsidies to the agricultural sector. The results of these two kinds of studies can be quickly summarized.

For the first decade after collectivization in the Soviet Union, the agricultural sector had an import surplus from other sectors (Millar 1970, 1971, 1984; Ellman 1975), even though the terms-of-trade turned against agriculture. This occurred even while peasant living standards were falling for three reasons. First, many of these resources from other sectors were used to replace resources destroyed during the collectivization process; for instance, tractors for the horses that were killed. Second, the agricultural sector functioned less efficiently so that less was produced or marketed for a given unit of input of capital, fertilizer, and so forth (some estimates are provided by Hunter, 1988). Third, less effort appeared to be expended by the peasants, especially since they were no longer working for themselves.

Although no detailed calculations of such intersectoral resource flows for the Soviet Union have been made for the recent era, two subperiods can be distinguished. From the end of World War II to about 1960, according to Jerzy F. Karcz (1979, p. 328), the agricultural sector contributed considerably to domestic capital formation in the urban sector. Since that time, however, the agricultural sector began to be subsidized by the urban sector and the flow of resources appears to have turned toward agriculture. Of course, given the various nonmarket interventions of the Soviet government into the economy, subsidies to any sector do not necessarily indicate a corresponding net flow of resources. Nevertheless, such evidence provides a presumptive case for such a proposition.[9]

For China conflicting estimates are available. Early calculations by S. Ishikawa (1967a, 1967b) for the early and mid-1950s show a net import surplus in both absolute and relative (to total production) terms if the

---

[9] The key question is what prices farms would receive if there were free markets in all foodstuffs, in comparison to the weighted average of prices they now receive from the government and the farmers market. Wädekin (1982) concludes that the net flow of resources appeared to be toward agriculture in the Soviet Union and East Europe in the 1960s and 1970s for two reasons. First, the relative income of agricultural workers to nonagricultural workers is much higher than the ratio of the relative productivities of the two sectors (measured in market prices). Second, the share of gross capital investment flowing to the agricultural sector is higher (and rising) than agriculture's share in the net material product. Although I do not find these indicators completely convincing, they certainly provide presumptive evidence.

With regard to the price on farmers' markets, Lardy (1983, p. 120) argues that this does not necessarily indicate a resource flow out of agriculture; it depends on whether the urban rich or poor buy on these markets, their price elasticities of demand, both separately and in comparison to the price elasticity of supply.

calculations are made with 1952 prices. If they are made with prices of the mid-1930s, the reverse is the case although the export surplus is small. Lardy (1983, chap. 3) questions these results, pointing out a number of flaws in the price index for farm inputs that Ishikawa used for making these calculations. He makes a series of comparisons between various prices paid by the farmers and the prices they received, concluding that the apparent favorable increase to agriculture of its terms-of-trade with industry did not occur. From his data he generalizes that "the state transferred significant resources out of the agricultural sector over a sustained period." Still later calculations support Lardy's conclusions, and a recent estimate by the World Bank (1990, p. 38) suggests that between 1955 and 1985, 600 to 800 billion Yuan were transferred from the rural to the urban sector.

From these few conflicting empirical studies my conclusions must be inconclusive. Although the Marxist governments may have wanted to finance industrial investment by extraction of resources from agriculture, in some cases they were not able to carry out such a program and, instead, relied on some combination of foreign aid and loans, the lowering of real wages of urban dwellers—in the Soviet Union real wages fell in the late 1920s and did not reach their former level again until the mid-1950s—and profits from government monopolies, especially by maintaining an increase of real wages lower than that of labor productivity.

Many of the African nations had a relatively low share of collectivized agriculture (Table 5.1) and tried to extract resources from the agricultural sector by use of the same tool available to non-Marxist governments, namely, lowering agricultural prices and using the profits gained from exports of foodstuffs and other rural products for investment. Nevertheless, some special problems of this strategy arose, which, it might be added, occurred also in capitalist African nations. First, agricultural exports often fell, which brought about a balance of payments crisis, a decline in agricultural inputs, a further fall in exports, and a downward spiral. Madagascar provides a particularly tragic case study of this unfortunate state of affairs (Pryor 1990). Second, the state farms served as a bottomless barrel for receiving government subsidies, offsetting in many cases the financial gains from the profits of governmental monopsonistic marketing boards. Third, the fall in rural incomes occurring as a result of price and other policies led to a sizable migration from rural to urban areas in some nations. For instance, in 1960 in the Congo, 25 percent of the population lived in urban areas; by 1982 this had risen to 65 percent (ILO 1984, p. 7). This migration required social overhead investment in urban areas for housing and other facilities.

In sum, collectivization is certainly not necessary to "extract the agricultural surplus" and more traditional methods are available to accomplish the same task. And neither a Marxist government nor a collectivized agriculture necessarily insures that such a surplus will be extracted; the constraints on policy-makers are often too great.

SUBSIDIES

As noted, agricultural subsidies by themselves do not indicate a net flow of resources into agriculture, for they can be offset either by taxes flowing out or by maintenance of artificially low producer prices. The common distinction made in East Europe that subsidies to food-processing enterprises represent a consumer subsidy, while direct subsidies to the farms represent a producer subsidy, also does not hold. Until we can make comparisons with world market prices and determine the shadow exchange rate, we cannot determine the ultimate incidence of the subsidy. Nevertheless, changes in subsidies often provide important clues to resource flows.

In the Soviet Union, agricultural procurement subsidies soared from 3.2 billion rubles in 1965, roughly 1 percent of the GDP, to a planned 87.9 billion rubles (plus another 20.9 for other parts of the agro-industrial complex including suppliers of inputs) in 1989, which represented over 5 percent of the GDP (Markish 1989a, 1989b). An additional subsidy has been the periodic canceling of agricultural debt. It is unlikely that a significant share of the soaring debt of the farm sector will ever be paid off. This suggests, but does not prove, that for the last quarter-century, the Soviet agricultural sector has been a drain, not a source, of investable resources.

Readily available subsidy data for some other Marxist regimes are presented in table 7.1. Although the data are crude and not completely comparable, it is noteworthy that the relative importance of subsidies appeared to increase as the relative per capita income rose, a situation that

TABLE 7.1

Agricultural Subsidies in Selected Marxist Regimes in the Late 1980s

	Subsidy ratio		Subsidy ratio		Subsidy ratio
Bulgaria	25%	East Germany	53%	Poland	29%
China	20	Hungary	34	USSR	34
Czechoslovakia	62				

Source: See Statistical Note G.

Notes: The subsidy ratio is the ratio of monetary subsidies for agriculture and food processing industries to the net material product in agriculture plus subsidies. Since all of these data are rough estimates and are subject to many incomparabilities, only their orders of magnitude are important.

occurred in industrial capitalist nations as well. The subsidy ratios were, in general, large and because the subsidy rates varied according to the foodstuff, relative agricultural prices were highly distorted. These calculations do not include subsidies to agricultural inputs, which would raise the subsidy ratios in most countries even more. Roughly similar data for the West, taken from Ford and Suyker (1990) and OECD national accounts data, show subsidy ratios ranging roughly from 10 to 30 percent.

A different and more complete approach toward measuring subsidies requires producer and consumer prices of particular foodstuffs to be measured against a reference price of importing that foodstuff, a calculation requiring the estimate of a shadow exchange rate for most Marxist regimes. Such calculations take subsidies on producer inputs into account, as well as some, but not all, taxes. These estimates are extremely difficult to make, however, and are available on a comparable basis in a study by Cook, Liefert, and Koopman (1990) for only four Marxist regimes. Their data show that total net subsidies for foodstuffs for both consumers and producers, measured as a percentage of the reference price for a sample of products for China, Poland, the Soviet Union and Yugoslavia in 1986 were respectively 16, 57, 62 and 3 percent. Total net subsidies to producers alone for the same four countries were respectively −43, 7, 26, and 47 percent. Even these calculations, the best that are available, do not take into account other types of taxes on the rural population.

To what degree are these subsidies flowing into agriculture offset by taxes flowing out? The data on this issue are not very complete. As far as I could determine, taxes flowing out of agriculture, as a percentage of total agricultural subsidies, amounted, in East Germany, to about 40 percent; in Czechoslovakia, about 50 percent; and in Hungary, about 100 percent.[10] At least for the first two countries, the flow of net fiscal resources was to agriculture, and the same was true of the Soviet Union as well. In most of the Third World Marxist regimes, I suspect that the net flow of fiscal resources was away from agriculture, but generally the data are not of sufficient quality to be very reliable.

Government Investment Policies and Current Expenditures in Agriculture

The relative share of investment going to agriculture varied considerably from one Marxist regime to another. For the CMEA nations this ratio was higher than in West Europe (Pryor 1985a). For this continent the problem was not in the volume of investment, but rather its allocation.

[10] The data on taxes came from the same sources as the subsidies, which are described in statistical note F.

Investment efficiency suffered in East Europe and the Soviet Union for many reasons, including the variety of practices of spreading investment funds relatively equally among farms in the favored sectors in order to "level" production in the various units, rather than directing such funds where the marginal returns were highest, and the failure to address all production bottlenecks at the same time so that proportions were preserved.

For many Third World Marxist regimes the share of investment to agriculture was low, especially when one takes into account that more than 50 percent of the economically active population was in agriculture in most countries (table 1.1). In many non-Marxist Third World regimes, the same held true so that the macroinvestment policies did not appear to be a particular feature of the economic system.

Policy declarations also prove of little help in understanding the problem in these Third World nations. Political leaders in such Marxist regimes as Angola, Congo, Guinea-Bissau, Madagascar, and Mozambique have proclaimed that agriculture is the base and/or that industry is the motor of economic development. Whenever we meet some variant of this motto, we can suspect that investment in agriculture is neglected. For instance, after the Ratsiraka government in Madagascar coined this slogan, the relative share of investment in agriculture declined (Pryor 1990). In the Congo where this motto was proclaimed for the 1981–86 plan, only 6.6 percent of total state investment was planned for agriculture, in contrast to 21.1 percent destined for manufacturing and mining, and the actual investment in agriculture fell considerably short of the plan (Hung 1987, p. 16; ILO 1984). I must add that some countries without this motto have also neglected agriculture. For instance, the 10-year plan of Ethiopia for the 1980s allocated only 11 percent of total state investment to agriculture, mostly to the state farms (Dejene 1987, p. 7).

In many Third World Marxist nations where reliable data on governmental expenditures (current and capital) in agriculture do not exist, a neglect of agriculture can be seen in other ways, for example, the nonreplacement of rural capital and the gradual withdrawal of government financed services ("influence withdrawal"). For instance, from observations based on repeated visits to a particular village in Guinea-Bissau, Rudebeck (1988) chronicles the deterioration in economic overhead and the gradual disappearance of health, education, extension, and other governmental services. Although such neglect of the agricultural sector was often quite obvious in countries such as Mozambique, where the communal villages gradually disintegrated, other symptoms are also worthy of note. In the Congo and Madagascar, for instance, agricultural research essentially stopped for a decade (Hung 1987, 57; Pryor 1990). Madagascar was one of the few major rice producers in the world that had been untouched by the mid-1980s by the green revolution in rice production.

Although some of this neglect reflects an obvious bias against agriculture in certain countries, the decline of governmental investment and current expenditures in agriculture in other countries represented one aspect of the government's fiscal crisis. The inability to continue such governmental services to agriculture, which may have been originally financed by foreign aid, was a function of the failure to create a rural-based strategy of development, to sustain popular participation, to insure that the government represents the rural workers, and to create an adequate system of taxation.

In some Marxist regimes, especially China, rural investment and governmental services to agriculture were not neglected (at least until the 1980s), even though some important investments in agriculture were also financed by the sector itself. Indeed, a major reason for creating the communes in China was to obtain a labor force to carry out rural public works without requiring compensation by the government (Perkins and Yusef 1984).

Some Generalizations

In the Congo we find this peasant lament: "When our children come to power, they forget that they are the sons of peasants, they forget our difficulties . . . we are no longer of the same world" (Doulos 1983). It does not seem, however, that an urban bias of development policy was tied exclusively to a Marxist ideology. Although collectivization facilitates the favoring of urban over rural interests, it is certainly neither a necessary nor sufficient condition because a number of convincing reasons can also be offered for urban bias in development policies by non-Marxist regimes (Lipton 1976).

In particular, three important political reasons for the urban bias of development policies seem crucial to me, of which the first two apply equally well to Marxist and non-Marxist regimes. First, the ruling parties of many of these nations relied on urban groups to keep them in power, especially since the rural population found it difficult to organize itself politically to provide countervailing pressures. Second, the long-run consequences of turning the terms-of-trade against agriculture, extracting resources from agriculture to finance investment in industry, or starving the agricultural sector of government investment and current expenditures were not immediately apparent; many of these governments were focused almost exclusively on short-run problems. Third, in the Marxist regimes, the governments were influenced by an ideology focusing most of its attention on the industrial sector and viewing agriculture as merely a backward branch of industry.

Since thirty-three Marxist regimes are under review, these propositions cannot be explored for each case. One Marxist regime where the urban bias has been weakest is Zimbabwe, which deserves brief attention.[11] During the 1980s the government of Robert Mugabe raised relative agricultural prices, although not to their level in the early 1970s, increased the supply of governmental services to agriculture, and maintained roughly the same percentage of government investment in agriculture as the previous government. Some observers have attributed this to special political circumstances: these measures would appease the rural party chapters for redistribution of lands, a policy which was difficult to implement under the conditions of the Lancaster House Agreement establishing that nation. Others have attributed these policies to the wisdom and pragmatism of the prime minister, who wished to avoid the organizational chaos and decline in agricultural production that he had witnessed at first hand in Mozambique where economic policies with a strong urban bias were applied. In 1990 the Lancaster House Agreement expired. Mugabe's future policy actions will determine which of these explanations is more valid.

POLITICAL VERSUS ECONOMIC LEADERSHIP IN AGRICULTURAL TECHNOLOGY

A major justification for a Marxist regime is that the economic sphere is no longer autonomous, but subordinated to the political sphere. Two particular economic dilemmas arise requiring brief examination: the red-versus-expert problem and the problem of micromanagement.

Red-versus-Expert

To what extent should farm managers be chosen for their political or their technical capabilities? Marxist regimes at various times have answered this question quite differently.

Certain countries favored the red farm leader. For instance, Fidel Castro stated his approach in an uncharacteristically short statement: "Who should manage a farm? A revolutionary. What are his prerequisites? That he be a revolutionary" (Austin and Ickis 1986). In China, as noted in chapter 6, political rather than technical specialists were generally chosen to head communes.

[11] I draw particularly upon the work of Herbst (1989), Skålner (1989) and particularly Brattan (1989).

Given that agricultural management is relatively complex, particularly where machinery and advanced techniques are required, the disadvantages of such technically untrained red managers should be readily apparent. Even where agricultural technology is known to all, however, such practices have been attacked because the skills of a political leader are not necessarily those needed to lead a production enterprise. In his study of Viet Nam, Fforde (1989, p. 29) notes that the Vietnamese authorities attacked this practice, not only because it led to mismanagement but also because it was associated with "technological conservatism."

Other Marxist regimes chose technical experts rather than revolutionaries to head their state and collective farms. This was, for example, the approach in Nicaragua (Austin and Ickis 1985). The decision probably was made not for any reasons of principle, but because the Sandinistas had relatively few party members and soldiers who had fought with them a long time; Spalding (1987, p. 15) speaks of only one thousand Sandinista troops at time of victory. In Bénin, Ethiopia, and Madagascar, where no party existed before the nation became a Marxist regime, the red solution simply was not available.

Micromanagement by the Top Leadership

To someone sitting in a comfortable office in the city and making occasional visits to the countryside, farming looks easy. Top political leaders in Marxist regimes as varied as the Soviet Union, Cuba, and Ethiopia have usually found the urge irresistible to meddle in the details of farming, especially where matters of farm technology were concerned. Such meddling was, of course, not limited to top echelons of power since lower level officials and party leaders were similarly inclined. It lies at the heart of the analysis of "weak property" in the next chapters.

A typical example of such meddling in farm technology occurred in East Germany, where the minister of agriculture, Gerhard Grüneberg, was seized with the brilliant idea of building barns to house two thousand or more cattle. This investment scheme raised average farm costs (since fodder had to be transported longer distances), greatly increased problems of disease control, and created much ecological damage.[12] Before this time and shortly after collectivization a previous agricultural minister in the same country borrowed a Swedish idea and ordered the massive construction of roofless barns for cattle. Unfortunately he did not note that the Swedes employed these stalls only for calves and used special feedstuffs that did not freeze in wintertime, in contrast to East German

---

[12] The material in this paragraph was gathered from interviews in East Germany in the spring of 1990.

silage. As a result of such lack of attention to details, many cattle either died or used up the food energy in keeping warm, rather than producing meat or milk. Both of these schemes, I should note, were fought by agricultural specialists and farm managers, but resistance often led to reprisals such as loss of funds, or unemployment, or worse.

In the Soviet Union, to choose another example, inappropriate decisions about agricultural technology arising from meddling at the highest political levels abound.[13] Stalin was infatuated with the Williams' rotation scheme, which was quite unsuitable for many areas of the Soviet Union, and with technologies based on the Trofim Lysenko's crackpot ideas about genetics. Khrushchev's corn mania led to the planting of maize where it was not suited. Taboos on planting of perennial grasses in regions where they had long been important and negative official views toward summer fallow, considered essential in dry areas, were still other examples of unfortunate technological micromanagement. Sometimes officials were able to restrain themselves: in the spring of 1954 the minister of agriculture of the Russian Republic boasted that for the first time in more than thirty years no outside authorities were trying to impose cropping schemes and methods on farm managers and agronomists. But the rate of recidivism was high—this good behavior lasted only briefly, and then top political leaders were meddling again.

Many more examples can be supplied for other countries, especially Cuba (Dumont 1974), but the point should be clear. In any society where political leaders do not personally need to face the economic consequences of such meddling, such advice is easy to give. And where they do not face the results of the ballot box, the recipients of this "advice" find it hard to resist. In non-Marxist nations such technological meddling at the microlevel is not unknown. Nevertheless, in few market economies is power as concentrated as in these Marxist regimes so that such intrusive micromanagement is not feasible.

MARKET VERSUS ADMINISTRATIVE ALLOCATION

The dilemmas arising from conflicts between political and economic policies occur not only in problems of technology, but also in current production. Where the agricultural sector is an integral part of the centrally administered economy, the production units were subject to plans and quotas, and, according to plan directives, the state trading agencies purchased and transferred rural products to the city and urban products to the countryside. In the other Marxist regimes, the rural sector has op-

---

[13] For Cuba and Ethiopia, many examples of top-level meddling are provided by Dumont (1974) and Giorgis (1989). For the Soviet Union the examples in this paragraph are drawn from the discussion of Karcz (1964) and Joravsky (1967).

erated according to some mixture of plan and market. In all Marxist regimes, whether or not they were centrally planned, problems of price-setting for goods and land arise that deserve attention.

Pan-National Prices

In a fully functioning market economy producer prices for a particular agricultural commodity are the same throughout the country, once differences in transportation costs are taken into account. In most Marxist regimes, the government usually does not take into account transportation costs and it sets a single producer price in all locations.

Such a pan-national price system has several implications, depending upon the accompanying policies. If combined with a policy to buy a product at all points of production, it places a strain on the transportation system since it encourages production of particular agricultural commodities far from their markets since farmers no longer need to absorb the freight costs. If combined with a policy of regional self-sufficiency so as to avoid the strain on the transportation system, such policies may push production into crops that are quite unprofitable for the farmer.

Multiple Price Systems

A complicating factor in the price system of many Marxist regimes was the existence of several different producer price systems: the prices paid for products delivered according to the quota assigned by the agricultural authorities, one or more sets of above-quota prices paid for additional deliveries, a negotiated price sometimes paid for special products or for new products from the farm, an official price in state stores, and a market price when the product was sold at farmers markets. Moreover, the official price lists were sometimes differentiated according to whether the prices were paid to state farms, collective farms, or private farms. If such multiple price systems existed, the state farms usually received the highest price from the official crop purchasing enterprise; and the private farms, the lowest price. An interesting exception occurred in Romania, where authorities tried to base such purchase prices on costs, which meant that the cooperatives received higher prices than the state farms in the 1970s because their costs were higher (Tsantis and Pepper 1979, p. 235).

The existence of multiple price systems had several implications. It meant that official prices lost their function as signals of relative scarcity and calculation of farm profits became less meaningful. For this analysis, it means not only that calculations of intersectoral terms-of-trade are somewhat questionable, but that estimations of price elasticities of supply are even more difficult to make.

Rigid Prices

Generally official prices were set for a long period and their changes were an important political decision made after months of debate. Thus the producer prices often did not vary between years with adverse and favorable climatic conditions. Not only did this increase the rigidity of the system as a whole, but it meant, among other things, that in many cases aggregate farm incomes fluctuated more than if prices had been allowed to move since price and quantity movements often offset each other. In recent years in the Soviet Union, farms received bonus prices when production exceeded a certain level, which meant that in years of a bumper crop, average prices paid to the producer rose, rather than declined (Brooks 1990c).

In many countries most food prices were also constant over the year. Hence there was greater seasonality of quantity supplied than in market economies where there are seasonal fluctuations in price. For the Soviet Union, Gray (1990b) establishes this proposition empirically in a set of comparisons with the United States.

Problems of Taking Account of Differential Rents

A peculiar problem arises from differences in land fertility. Unless special measures are taken, state farms and those working on cooperative farms possessing very rich land will have much higher profits than state farms and those working on cooperative farms with poor soil. Marxist regimes have adopted one of three solutions.

1. In some Marxist regimes, Czechoslovakia and Hungary for example, the government charged each farm a different land rent according to the fertility of its soil. Because fertility had several dimensions, this system was often difficult to administer. Nevertheless, such a solution replicated in an administrative fashion the way in which the problem is handled in market economies. In other countries a pseudorent was charged in terms of higher profit taxes for those farms with high-quality soil (Brooks 1990c).

2. In some Marxist regimes, farms paid different producer prices according to the overall fertility of the land in the zone in which they were located. At one time in the Soviet Union, for instance, there were more than a hundred different zones for wheat, with grain prices in the north twice as high as in the south. Cattle prices were divided into seventy-four zones, and other products had still a different number of zones. The

different number of zones for different commodities reflected the multi-dimensional aspects of fertility and the fact that land in a particular area could be highly suitable for one crop, but not for another. Since soil fertility and other factors differ considerably from one farm to another in a single small area, such a system led to considerable income differentials among collectives.[14] Albania took this logic one step further: it charged differential input prices according to some measure of economic conditions; for instance, charges for MTS services were lower in mountainous areas than in the plains.

3. In some other Marxist regimes, particularly those in Africa, the government gave no heed to the problem and simply paid a pan-national price to the farms, regardless of the differences in fertility of the land in particular areas. China also disregarded this problem, which meant that on the same farm, one team could have an average income four times higher than another, mostly due to differences in agricultural conditions (Parish and Whyte 1978, p. 54).

Regional Self-Sufficiency: A Special Market-Negating Intervention

A number of Marxist regimes adopted policies that acted to increase regional self-sufficiency of foodstuffs. I will argue that there is a bizarre Marxoid element to these measures, but before making generalizations, it is useful to examine some examples.

In China the ostensible reason for such policies was to economize on resources used in the internal transportation of foodstuffs. Since most such transportation was by train, such measures could be easily enforced and, as a result, interprovincial trade in grain declined from 3.4 percent of production in 1953–56 to 0.1 percent in 1978 (Lardy 1983, p. 51). It should be added that the relaxation of agricultural controls in China in the early 1980s led to considerable shifts in the composition of agricultural output in the various provinces and a rise in interprovincial food trade which, in turn, contributed in an important fashion to the dramatic increase in agricultural production.

In most other Marxist regimes, however, such inter-regional transportation costs were hardly at issue. Nevertheless, Bulgaria and Romania wholeheartedly followed policies of regional self-sufficiency and others such as East Germany tended in that direction. In most cases, regional

[14] Timofeev (1985, pp. 58) describes two Soviet villages close to each other, one desperately poor and the other quite wealthy, which he attributes to differences in soil fertility and closeness to transportation. The first village was obviously enjoying the differential rent.

Considerable information is available on the Soviet system of zonal rents. Brooks (1990c) describes changes in this zonal system of prices in recent years.

agricultural organs of the government administered each of the self-sufficient units (in chapter 5 this is labeled "suprafarm integration"). Soviet policymakers also spoke of their attempts to achieve a certain degree of regional self-sufficiency of food supply, but the extent to which this was realized is not known. It might be added that at one time policy makers in tiny Nicaragua also tried, but without success, to reduce inter-regional trade in food.

In some cases subnational governmental units have taken the lead in reducing inter-regional trade in foodstuffs. For instance, in the late 1980s and early 1990s, the various republic governments in the USSR tried to ensure the food supply for their populations and took measures increasing the degree of regional self-sufficiency. The economic justification of such policies was dubious. Moreover, in large countries, especially China or the Soviet Union, agricultural conditions are quite varied in different provinces and these policies can lead to the planting of crops in localities for which the local conditions are highly unsuited.

Some Marxist regimes have inadvertently arrived at relative regional self-sufficiency of food, often without being aware either of the process or of the costs. In Madagascar, for instance, the government nationalized the purchasing of key crops and, moreover, many of the outlets providing consumer goods to farmers. The system of crop purchasing did not function very well and, as a result, fewer foodstuffs were transferred from food-surplus to food-deficit areas. Calculations (Pryor 1990) show that differences in the price of foodstuffs (more specifically, the coefficient of variation of prices for different foodstuffs) more than tripled in the decade following this nationalization.[15] After the national government allowed private crop purchasers to carry out their operations again, the provincial governments erected barriers so as to prevent foodstuffs from leaving their areas of administration; and it took considerable efforts on the part of the national government to begin to alleviate the problem.

As noted in chapter 5, Yugoslavia also appears to have inadvertently followed a similar policy of regional self-sufficiency. The republic governments set up regional monopolies for buying and selling of foodstuffs and these, in order to maximize profits, managed to impede the inter-regional flow of foods (Cochran 1990).

The common thread running through all these examples is a suspicion of "trade," an inability of state agencies to carry out this function in a satisfactory fashion, and the fear that reliance on foodstuffs imported from

---

[15] The data set underlying these calculations is quite unique. Similar data on the price of various foodstuffs for particular areas are available for Ethiopia so that similar calculations can be made. Unfortunately, the data refer only to the interval between 1981 and 1986, which is six to ten years after the reorganization of agriculture. In this period, the coefficient of variation of food prices shows no significant change.

other regions is dangerous, either to the consumers or to the competing domestic producers. Although these are not ideas that are directly stated in Marx, they are attitudes that can be inferred from the canonical texts and are shared by many Marxists.

Market and Administrative Elements

Even in the most rigid centrally planned economy, certain market incentives exist. During the 1980s, for instance, many East European governments attempted to increase the autonomy of decision-making by farm managers by reducing the number of plan indicators and other types of intervention. Moreover, some governments attempted to tighten the budget constraint by organizing these state and cooperative farms on a "self-financing basis," although such attempts to reduce subsidies were seldom successful because the political authorities were unwilling to see large collective or state farms fail. In some countries, for example in the Soviet Union in January 1988, the government also set up agricultural banks to supply more rural credit and farms were allowed to exchange labor with one another (the Vaktov system), a type of limping factor market. For my purpose, however, the cornerstone of the system remained: plan directives and compulsory purchases continued in most of these countries and official prices of foodstuffs still were not closely related to their market values.

In those Marxist countries without a central planning apparatus, food markets functioned imperfectly, in part because the government intervened not only in the operations of the state farms but also in the exchange arrangements for agricultural inputs and outputs. The most obvious sign was a thriving parallel market or farmer market in foodstuffs, where prices ranged from 50 to 100 percent higher than official prices (Madagascar), from two to three times the official prices (São Tomé), or from ten to fifty times (Angola).[16]

Examining more closely the markets for agricultural inputs and outputs, some severe problems in separating systemic and policy elements are encountered. Nevertheless, the exercise is useful, especially in light of endemic complaints in the press of these nations on the malfunctioning of these systems.

The state supply of consumer goods to the rural areas provides a simple starting point. J. C. Berthélemy and others (1988) have some interesting econometric studies of Madagascar and Mozambique, showing that the amount of crops offered to the market was significantly related to the

[16] The information for Madagascar comes from Pryor (1990); for São Tomé, from data I collected in that country; for Angola, from informal data gathered by visitors to that country.

amount of consumer goods available to the rural population. When these nations had balance of payment difficulties, urban areas usually had first priority not just for imported consumer goods, but also for the domestic consumer goods serving as substitutes. As a result, rural consumers suffered, marketed agricultural production fell, and the balance of payments problem was exacerbated because agricultural exports declined. The same appeared true for a number of other Marxist regimes, not just in the Third World. Although policy failures were clearly involved in these problems, the inability to replace the functioning of a rural market for consumer goods by administrative methods was a clear structural failure.

The supply of inputs for production and investment raised many problems for the farm sector. All Marxist economies, whether guided by a central plan or not, were, to one degree or another, shortage economies. That is, at any given price, important inputs were not available to producers who might have the money to buy them. These shortages arose from a number of causes ranging from planning errors, consequences of soft budget constraints, suppressed inflation, overvaluation of the exchange rate, and a misallocation of investment so that industrial bottlenecks were not widened at the requisite speed. Although structural problems gave rise to many of these causes, their consequences were exacerbated by policy failures. These shortages had several adverse consequences for agriculture.

First, agricultural production was reduced. A dramatic example occurred in Romania in the second half of the 1980s, where about one-fourth of the agricultural land requiring irrigation was unfarmed because of lack of electricity to operate the pumps (Montias, forthcoming). Misallocation occurred, of course, in less visible ways. For instance, according to crop experts with whom I spoke in Nicaragua, because of the overvalued exchange rate and low price of inputs, the state farms used far more insecticides and pesticides than were necessary, at the same time that private farmers could not obtain them and had lower production as a result. In Eastern Europe, my visits to farms in 1990 revealed an enormous amount of unused equipment, to a certain degree because spare parts were not available. If the Marxist regime was small and had a relatively low level of economic development, the shortages caused by balance of payments problems were particularly serious since agricultural inputs such as fertilizers, pesticides, and machine parts generally were imported.

Second, the shortages reinforced the bimodal approach toward agriculture. Unorganized rural producers generally stood at the end of the queue in receiving scarce inputs, particularly if they were imported. The state farms, which had the ministry of agriculture to serve as their lobby for these inputs, were in a better position to obtain them.

Third, inventory costs were much higher since producers with foresight would hoard inputs to avoid production losses because of shortages. And finally, farm costs were higher because of the deterioration of rural infrastructure that was caused, to a certain extent, by these shortages. In this respect transportation was particularly crucial, and a number of Marxist regimes ranging from Madagascar to the Soviet Union had very poor rural roads systems. I must add that other causes of this neglect of rural infrastructure can also be adduced; for instance, many Marxist regimes preferred to spend their investment funds on more visible projects such as factories.

As in the case of rural consumer goods, these shortages sprang primarily from structural causes, although they were reinforced by policy failures. The major result was that both static and dynamic efficiency of the agricultural sector suffered since inputs for both production and investment were not used where they had the highest return.

With regard to crop purchases, Marxist regimes usually replaced the private traders (table 3.1) because, it was alleged, these traders offered prices and credit that exploited the smallholders.[17] One of the immediate consequences of nationalization of the crop-purchasing function in a number of Third World Marxist regimes was a rural credit shortage. Furthermore, these private traders generally had operated in a very flexible manner, adapting themselves quickly to new circumstances. State enterprises supplying credit found it difficult to duplicate this flexibility by structuring the appropriate incentives for its staff.

It is difficult to gain sufficient oversight on the crop purchasing programs in the countries under review to separate structural and policy elements. Certain shards of evidence are available, for instance, the spoilage of foodstuffs between farm and consumer that is mentioned in chapter 5, the existence of black markets and multiple prices for the same foodstuff discussed here, and the endemic shortages of certain foodstuffs found in most Marxist regimes. For a few of the more industrialized Marxist regimes, detailed case materials of some crop purchasing programs are publicly available in Western languages (for instance, for meat and dairy processing in the Soviet Union, Gray 1990b). But they do not cover a sufficient number of countries or sectors in sufficient depth to allow easy generalizations about their impact on the farm sector per se. The publicly available materials on state crop-purchasing systems in Third World Marxist regimes are similarly skimpy.

It should be evident that the mix of crops that was produced did not

[17] In Madagascar, private traders charged interest rates ranging up to 20 percent for credit; several years after the government took over the credit function, it charged even higher interest rates, and, it might be added, loan payments were probably lower. Some details on this are found in Pryor (1970).

necessarily correspond to consumer demands, that the distribution system lacks the incentives for effectively performing its role, and that some serious policy problems were involved. But these are commonplaces that can be found in the newspapers of most Marxist regimes, as well as other places in the world where governmental intervention into the consumer goods market is significant.[18] Nevertheless, the endemic nature of these complaints, however, suggests that these policy problems were closely tied to a basic structural problem, namely the imperfect substitution of an administrative system for a market mechanism in a situation where speed of response and flexibility to consumer desires is of utmost importance.

Concluding Remarks

Mistakes in agricultural policy are not tied to economic systems. Many developing non-Marxist nations are as likely as Marxist regimes to favor urban over rural interests. Similarly most non-Marxist nations seemed likely to intervene in the setting of agricultural prices and, to a certain extent, to allocate credit and inputs.

In most Marxist regimes the structure of agriculture was significantly different because these interventions in the agricultural sector were more extensive. Where a government had almost complete control of credit, the neglect or misallocation of agricultural investment could be more severe. And where government agencies set almost all prices and distributed almost all agricultural inputs, prices could diverge more widely from values that would equate supply and demand and resources used in current production could be misallocated as well. The subsidy and tax policies followed by many Marxist regimes exacerbated these problems.

Some agricultural policies seem endemic to Marxist regimes, especially where agriculture is collectivized: the choice of a bimodal over a unimodal investment policy, political interventions into technological decisions, or the pursuit of regional self-sufficiency in food production. In these cases, it is the organization of agriculture that significantly raises the probability that these policy mistakes will be made, so it is not surprising that agricultural performance is significantly worse in Marxist regimes.

[18] For sub-Saharan Africa, Vengroff and Farah (1985) have an interesting cross-national study showing that gross agricultural production and other measures of agricultural performance are inversely and significantly related to the degree of state intervention in the supply of farm inputs and the purchasing of crops. Although objections can be made to their measurement of state intervention, these results certainly accord with our expectations. Unfortunately, I could not replicate this result with the sample discussed in chapter 8, primarily because of the crudeness of the variable measuring intervention.

The original question posed in this chapter—the relative importance of organization and policy variables in agricultural performance—cannot be easily answered because organization and policy are so closely tied. The examples and cases reviewed in this chapter, however, are meant to provide insight into this crucial linkage. At this point it seems likely that only in quite special circumstances is it possible to separate these elements. In the next chapter I review some of these cases.

One lesson from this discussion should be clear. Those who attribute any weaker performance in the agricultural sector of Marxist regimes almost completely to general economic policies pursued have completely disregarded the close links of policy and structure. Of course, it is easy to advise a Marxist regime to maintain collectivization but to change any inappropriate policies, just as it is always easy to tell alcoholics to mend their ways. If alcoholics have very strong wills, they can follow such advice and resist drinking, even though bottles of alcoholic beverages are set before them, because the bottles per se are not the ultimate cause of the drinking problem. Nevertheless, a removal of the bottles from view is useful, because in many cases the sight of the bottles acts as a proximate cause of drinking. Similarly, although the organization of agriculture may not be the ultimate cause of bad agricultural policies, it is often the proximate cause since it increases the probability for certain inappropriate agricultural policies. In order to reduce the temptations to adopt such harmful policies, a structural change such as decollectivization may be necessary.

Chapter 8

AGRICULTURAL PERFORMANCE

To WHAT EXTENT has the performance of agriculture in Marxist regimes been different from non-Marxist regimes? And, if there are differences, to what can they be attributed?

In chapters 5 and 6 I argue that a number of structural features of agriculture in Marxist regimes can have an adverse impact on their performance. These include the large size of the farms, their imperfect vertical linkages with other parts of the agro-industrial complex, and the peculiar incentive structures established not only by higher administrative authorities for the managers of state and collective farms, but also by the managers of these farms for the workers. In the previous chapter I also show how a number of governmental economic policies, often tied to the organization of agriculture, might also have a negative impact on production: the transition problems, the bimodal development pattern, the political interference in farm operations, and the administrative allocation system. It is now time to see if these propositions are empirically correct or if there are offsetting factors that I have not properly taken into account.

It might seem to many that these questions are old-fashioned and that history has given the answer—witness the enormous difficulties the farm sector has experienced in Marxist regimes in the early 1990s, especially in those countries experiencing decollectivization. But many of these problems clearly arise from transition difficulties such as overvalued exchange rates, transformation of the systems for supplying agricultural inputs and buying farm outputs, and restructuring farms and their production.

It is really necessary to view these performance questions from a longer perspective. For this purpose, I examine in this chapter some important macroeconomic indicators of the long-run performance of the agricultural sector in a group of comparable countries with different economic systems, testing them against a series of explanatory variables. More briefly and informally I also explore various indicators of short-run performance "crises" that might have contributed to the dramatic political changes in Eastern Europe in the late 1980s and the economic difficulties in the early 1990s.

The argumentation is straightforward. The first step is to identify some key issues in the empirical analysis, especially the nature of the performance criteria and the explanatory variables to be used. This continues the analysis in the previous chapter. Then I briefly review the results of other studies to provide perspective for my own empirical investigation. Finally I evaluate empirically the agricultural performance of thirty-four Marxist and non-Marxist nations from 1970 through 1987.

The most important difference revealed by the empirical analysis is that the Marxist regimes exhibit a slower growth of total factor productivity than comparable non-Marxist nations. In the third world, the growth of agricultural production is also slower among those nations which have a large collective or state farm system than among other nations. Although a number of Marxist regimes in East Europe exhibit indications of short-run agricultural crises, so do comparable Western nations. Their decelerating growth of agricultural production is, however, the only one of the five "crisis indicators" examined that shows much difference from comparable economies in the West.

KEY VARIABLES IN THE EMPIRICAL ANALYSIS

With so many countries to consider, I must rely on aggregative data with which to analyze the performance of the farm sector. The data available to me allowed exploration of four criteria of economic success: growth of agricultural production, growth of total factor productivity in agriculture, and fluctuations of production. I had hoped to examine static efficiency of agricultural production as well, but measurement problems proved insurmountable.

Although I tested a number of explanatory variables in preliminary experiments, only two appear very important: a variable representing the economic system and per capita gross domestic product (GDP). As suggested in the previous chapter, the causal linkage between system and performance is not completely clear. Three possible candidates for the crucial systems variable can be selected.

Marxist Regime

The Marxist designation of the systems variable is the most inclusive of the three definitions, since it embraces ideology, policy, and some structural features of these economies. With regard to ideology, Marx's contempt for farmers is briefly discussed in chapter 2, for instance, his remarks about the "idiocy of rural life" and the farmer as "barbarian." As elaborated in the previous chapter, this attitude was reflected in many agricultural policies that placed the rural sector at a disadvantage vis-à-vis the urban sector, the relatively little attention many political leaders in these nations gave to actual conditions in agriculture, and the policies they pursued that led to misallocations of labor, capital, and land. The aspiration in most of these countries to create a centrally planned economy with a collectivized agriculture was a defining feature of these Marxist regimes. One could conjecture that this definition of the systems variable would be correlated with a lower growth of total factor productivity and a lower degree of static efficiency than a capitalist economy. It would, however, not necessarily be related to the growth of agriculture per se or to the variability of agricultural production, except in those Third World nations experiencing problems of transition from capitalism to socialism in the agricultural sector.

Central Planning

Defining the systems variable in terms of the presence of central planning provides a somewhat narrower definition than the previous systems concept. Generally, it is difficult to have central planning without collectivized agriculture. The major exception was Poland, where central planning applied to industry, but not agriculture because it was still private. Given the incentive systems for managers that were established in centrally planned economies (discussed in detail in Research Note D), growth of total factor productivity with this system was likely to be lower than in market economies. Given the exogenous shocks to agriculture resulting from uncontrollable factors such as the weather, one would also expect that central administration of the sector would not have the flexibility to respond appropriately and, for this reason, fluctuations of agricultural production would be greater than in a market economy. No causal linkage can be made from theoretical evidence between central planning and the growth of agricultural production.

Collectivized Agriculture

Defining the systems variable in terms of the presence of an extensive collectivized agriculture is the narrowest concept because it omits consideration of the ideology and policies of the political leaders or the presence of central economic planning. The analysis of structural features in chapters 5 and 6 shows in a theoretical fashion why such a system might have a lower productivity growth and a lower degree of static efficiency than a system of predominantly private agriculture. Again, no special linkages can be discerned between this definition of the systems variable and either the growth of total agriculture production or the variability of this production.

A Survey of Previous Studies

My empirical study uses cross-sectional, macroeconomic evidence covering an eighteen-year period and explores all three systems variables. In order to place my results in perspective, it is useful to survey other empirical studies briefly, most of which use a systems variable defined in terms of a Marxist regime or, if they deal with subsectors of agriculture within a single country, with the separate performance of private, collective, and state farm sectors.

The survey reveals that various economic evaluations of the performance of collectivized agriculture yield quite different results, in good measure due to the kinds of data used in the analysis. I organize this brief review, therefore, according to whether the studies employ detailed microeconomic evidence at the farm level or whether they use various types of macroeconomic series, either on a cross-section or time-series basis.

Microeconomic Evidence

Although the best microeconomic evidence for systemic comparisons would be a large sample of farms in the private and socialist sectors of different countries, such data are not available. A number of studies of the operations of state or collective farms have been based on site visits and, in general, suggest that private farming is more efficient or productive than farming in the socialist sector.

One must, however, be careful in using these results since such studies are often quite impressionistic. It is also difficult to know whether the farms visited are typical or how the authors arrived at their interpretations. This does not necessarily mean that the conclusions are wrong; indeed, expert opinion is often the most solid evidence that we have for certain nations.

Examples of this case study approach can be found for Zimbabwe in the reports of two observers who are sympathetic to the formation of producer cooperatives in agriculture. Cliffe (1986, p. 51) notes that "there is not great disagreement about the very limited success [of cooperatives]." As reasons, he emphasizes their lack of capital, limited management, insecurity of tenure, and lack of technical backup. Chitsike (1988, p. 93) reports: "With the exception of a few agricultural cooperatives . . . the economic and financial performance has been very poor. Many collectives are in danger of total collapse unless a radical re-scheduling of their . . . loans is effective and there are changes in management." He argues (p. 145) that "the main reason for poor performance is poor management." He discusses the problems of the ineffective internal organization of work, difficulties in dealing with personnel (on one collective farm a group of members organized a strike), poorly structured incentives, and difficulties in dealing with local political authorities (in a number of cases neighboring chiefs claimed resources given to the collectives for their own subjects). These collective farms also lacked necessary capital, especially farm equipment, and could not discipline lazy workers (he notes that on some farms the members of some cooperatives work less than the local labor they hire). Chitsike also presents a series of financial, technological, and production indexes for a set of cooperative and private farms. His evidence provides many insights into the early stages of voluntary collective farming in nations where such farms received relatively little active support from the government. Unfortunately, he does not say how such farms worked after startup problems were overcome, nor does he allow easy separation of systemic and policy factors underlying the various difficulties.

For Ethiopia, Griffin and Hay (1985) present an interesting summary of the relative economic performance of different types of farms, which is presented in Table 8.1. Although they do not specify how they made these judgments, one can infer that the evidence included site visits as well as unpublished government data on a farm level. The authors argue that the state farms lost considerable money, not because of excess labor or high pay, but because of mismanagement, particularly by the state authorities overseeing the state farms. Much of the farm equipment was in disrepair and highly underutilized. Moreover, the plans were set in physical terms so that little attention was paid to costs, and individual farm managers had little discretion.[1] From survey data for the same coun-

TABLE 8.1
Relative Performance of Farms in Ethiopia in the Early 1980s

| | Rankings | | |
| | (1 = best; 3 = worst) | | |
Criteria	Peasant Farms	Collective Farms	State Farms
Capacity to absorb labor	1	2	3
Rate of profit on capital	1	2	3
Crop yield	1 or 2	3	1 or 2
Potential for accumulation	2	1	3
Marketable surplus	3	2	1

Source: Griffin and Hay (1985).
Note: Unfortunately, Griffin and Hay do not present their underlying data, which were collected for an ILO mission.

[1] Abegaz (1982) discusses other management problems on the state farms. He also

try, Rahmato (1984, p. 64) notes that the land reforms and collectivization did not make peasants more aware of technical innovations, which still had to be introduced from the outside.

While such farm-level evidence from particular nations provides useful insights into the operation of state and collective farms, it must be emphasized that applying the conclusions for one country to others raises many problems. It is also difficult to know whether the causal factors that are isolated are the most important sources of the differences among the performance of the various forms of farming since few of the studies are ever very explicit about why one explanation was chosen over another. Moreover, problems arise in determining whether the specific causes of differences among different forms of farming are due to country-specific causes, rather than reasons inherent in collective farming per se.

Sometimes the farm-level evidence is even more casual and more difficult to interpret. In Mozambique, for instance, it is believed that many cooperatives had considerably lower yields than family farms because they seemed to be able to survive only with subsidies from the state (Binkert 1983). It turns out, however, that these performance differences had little to do with either system or state policy, but rather occurred because local officials forced the cooperatives to sign contracts for tractor services that never arrived, thus delaying planting. In Cape Verde the manager of a collective farm told me that land productivity was also higher on the private than on the collective fields, but it was never clear whether this was due to the fact that more labor inputs were lavished on the private fields.

A final group of microeconomic studies focuses on specific practices, rather than the system as a whole, and use aggregative data. For example, Raup (1988) provides evidence that in comparison with West European nations the Soviet Union had unusually high seeding rates for grain, that the ratio of straw to grain was higher, that the fodder per cattle ratio was higher, that milk yields per cow were lower, and that the Soviets had excessive waste of harvested grain arising from poor storage and transport. Of course, the use of only the Soviet Union in such comparisons may mean that the results depend upon specific Soviet practices, rather than systemic factors or general Marxist policies *per se*. Dovring (1990), however, presents evidence that input costs in agriculture were much higher in East Europe than in West Europe; and some country studies have shown that the same was true for the energy consumption of agriculture as well (for instance, Hohmann 1988). Of course, the narrower the indicator of performance, the greater the possibility of compensating factors in other parts of the agricultural sector.

---

stresses the high costs arising from overmechanization. Giorgis (1989) provides some information on their operations from an insider's point of view.

Macroeconomic Evidence

Three different kinds of studies employing macroeconomic evidence can be distinguished, depending on the kind of evidence employed.

Cross-national studies permit overall performance differences between socialist and private farming to be distinguished. The major analytic problem is to hold constant all other types of causal variables such as climatic conditions, level of economic development, or different mix of farming types within a single country. In general, these studies suggest that farming in Marxist regimes was less technically efficient than in comparable non-Marxist nations and also that they had greater fluctuations of production. As I will point out, however, such conclusions can be disputed. Although these studies do not allow a direct determination of the causes for such differences between Marxist and non-Marxist nations, the larger the sample of nations included, the more likely that the source of the difficulties was the structure of the agricultural sector, rather than general agricultural policies of the government.

In an important study Karen McConnell Brooks (1983) estimates an agricultural production function for a sample including fifteen Soviet republics and Finland, ten U.S. states, and four Canadian provinces. She chose the comparison group to minimize the impact of different climatic factors. The production function included five inputs and a climate variable and the data covered the period between 1960 and 1979. She concludes (p. 146) that for the northern areas in the sample, private agriculture was 17 to 103 percent more efficient than socialized agriculture (depending on whether Finland is included or excluded from the sample), and for the southern areas, about 141 percent more efficient. For the Soviet Union as a whole, total factor productivity in agriculture increased at an average annual rate of 0.2 percent (falling in the northern, but rising in the southern republics), in contrast to the average annual rise of total factor productivity in agriculture in the comparison areas of 0.5 percent (p. 147).

This comparison of static efficiency raises some problems of interpretation. Although the results suggest that efficiency differences in the agricultural sectors of the Soviet Union and North America are enormous, it is unclear whether this was due to the agricultural policies pursued by the respective governments, to differences in the organization of agriculture, or to special characteristics of the four countries included in the sample. More vexing, the pooling of the samples from different countries is also based on the assumption that all face the same range of technological possibilities (that is, they are operating on the same production function). Koopman (1989) challenges this assumption, arguing that Brooks's results conflate productivity and efficiency. Using her data set he calculates a frontier production function for the subsamples from East and West and then shows that in each sample the average distance from the respective frontier production function was roughly the same, that is, the static efficiency measured in relative terms was similar. Of course, Koopman's interpretation can also be disputed: Why should the Soviet Union have a different production function when it had the same access to world agricultural technology as Western nations? And would the results be different if disaggregative data were used?[2] He does, however, agree with Brooks that the differences found in the growth of total factor productivity over time reveal much more telling differences between the performance of agriculture in the two systems.

Wädekin and his colleagues (1985) approach the problem in a much different manner by making seven paired comparisons of subnational regions within countries with different economic systems, where the regional pairs lie geographically close to each other so as to be similar not

[2] Several studies suggest that the results are not much different if disaggregative data are used. For instance, Skold (1990) calculates frontier production functions and shows with a sample of seventy-one state and collective farms in the Stavropol region in the USSR that the average level of technical efficiency (measured in terms of the frontier) ranges from 50.2 percent (vegetables) to 75.2 percent (grain). Using a roughly similar technique Aly and others (1987) show that average efficiency among grain farms in Illinois (USA) ranged from 47 percent (farms with gross revenues less than $100,000) to 64 percent (farms with gross revenues of $300,000 or more). In a different frontier production function study, Nehring (1990) shows that all sugar beet farms in the United States have an average technical efficiency of 65 percent, with variations ranging from 47.5 percent to 70.2 percent, depending upon the size and area.

Although, as I point out below, calculations of production functions of socialist and private agricultural sectors reveal different marginal productivities of the different inputs in the two sectors, which means that allocational inefficiencies exist, this lack of conclusive evidence that technical inefficiencies also exist seems peculiar. Four explanations can be offered: (1) the data on certain inputs, including fertility of the land, are simply not good enough to allow technical inefficiencies in the Marxist regimes to be found; (2) technological knowledge about agriculture is roughly similar from country to country, so that calculation of frontier production functions for the individual countries does not allow the gap between productivity of the best performing farms and the potential productivity of these farms to be measured; (3) there is an inverse correlation between static technical and allocative efficiency on the one hand and technological change and intensive economic development on the other hand (an argument made with considerable force by Whitesell, 1990); and (4) although farming in Marxist regimes is inefficient for one set of reasons, farming in non-Marxist regimes is inefficient for other reasons.

The debate about relative static efficiency of collective and private farming may last long after most such farms have been abandoned by practitioners for other reasons. Koopman and Brooks do agree on one major point, namely that the differences found in the growth of TFP over time reveal much more telling differences between the performance of agriculture in the two systems. I would wholeheartedly agree.

only in natural endowments and level of economic development, but also historically and culturally. These pairs include Estonia and Southern Finland, Byelorussia in the Soviet Union and Bialystok in Poland, and the Kyustendil and Blagoevgrad districts in Bulgaria and Yugoslavia (both have Macedonian populations). In each pair, both populations should have roughly the same knowledge of agricultural technology so that the confusion between productivity and efficiency should be minimized. Wädekin draws three conclusions from the individual studies. First, that agricultural performance among Marxist regimes varied considerably according to government policies. Furthermore, in the various Marxist regimes a number of circumstances determined whether or not the performance of agriculture in the socialist sector was superior to that of the private sector. Finally, according to various efficiency criteria, agricultural performance in non-Marxist regimes was generally superior to that of Marxist regimes. This was true not only for the regions as a whole, but also when comparing peasant agriculture in the different nations.

Two major objections can be raised to Wädekin's conclusions. First, the performance comparisons are made without formal statistical methods (for instance, estimation of production functions) under the assumption that the areas chosen are sufficiently similar that such techniques were not needed. Second, the ways in which the authors of each paired comparison separate the effects of policy and system in trying to explain the differences in performance are also informal. Although the studies are carried out carefully and the results are highly suggestive, they are also not definitive. Moreover, the systems versus policy problem could not be resolved except by the verbal acknowledgement that both factors probably played a role in explaining the results.

Two large-scale, cross-country studies analyzing growth and fluctuations also deserve mention. Using data on the aggregate value added in agriculture in twenty-three East and West European nations for the period from 1950 through 1979 and holding the level of economic development constant, Pryor (1985a) shows that growth rates of agricultural production were not significantly different in the two sets of countries. Since the share of total investment going to agriculture was much higher in the East than in the West, while the growth of labor inputs was roughly similar, these results suggest that growth of total factor productivity in agriculture was lower in the East than in the West. Without more formal analysis of factor inputs, however, this conclusion is not certain. With the same data set, Pryor also shows that the East European nations had significantly higher production fluctuations in agriculture than the West European nations. In another cross-country comparison focusing on just the fluctuations of hog stocks and pork production, Pryor and Solomon (1982) show, however, that there were no significant differences between East and West European nations. This result is surprising because the conventional wisdom suggests that hog cycles can only occur in a market economy where the fluctuation of prices creates a cobweb mechanism. Their explanation of these similarities is, unfortunately, conjectural and not based on further statistical investigation.

BETWEEN SECTORS WITHIN A SINGLE COUNTRY AT THE SAME TIME

Performance comparisons between the socialist and private agricultural sectors of a single country allow certain factors both exogenous (for example, weather) and endogenous (for example, general governmental policies toward agriculture) to be held constant. Such analyses seem most meaningful for countries where both sectors produce roughly the same types of crops, which means that for East Europe only Poland and Yugoslavia can be studied for this purpose.

This approach yields mixed results because of a severe methodological difficulty. More specifically, if the government followed a bimodal policy and treated the private and socialist sectors in a sufficiently different manner so that the two sectors employed different technologies and had different access to agricultural inputs, then statistical comparisons become difficult to interpret because not all endogenous factors can be held constant. In other words, the problem of conflating productivity and efficiency arises in yet another guise. More technically, when using a formal production function approach, the following problem occurs: If the data from the different sectors are pooled and dummy variables are used to determine differences in the performance of the socialist and private sectors, then the implicit assumption is made that the different sectors actually faced the same technological possibilities, which may not be correct.[3] If, on the other hand, separate production functions are calculated for the different sectors, then efficiency comparisons may be impossible to make if, at different factor ratios, the production functions cross, a circumstance actually occurring in several studies.

The simplest types of comparisons among sectors are for a single factor of production. For a number of Marxist regimes scattered data are available on the relative land productivity of private plots and collective or state farms. For example, in China private plots comprised about 5 percent of arable land, but accounted for 20 percent of farm income (Rawski

---

[3] In some cases statistical tests are made to determine whether the production functions for the different sectors are statistically similar so that they can be pooled. Although this is certainly the proper procedure to follow, if such tests show that the production functions are different, the results may be due less to actual differences in the technological possibilities faced by the two sectors than to differences in access to nonmeasurable inputs such as transportation or milling services at crucial periods, which force the private farmers to adopt less efficient techniques to circumvent the problems.

1982). In the Soviet Union such private plots comprised less than 5 percent of the land, but produced from one-fifth to one-third of total agricultural production, depending upon the year (Hedlund 1989).

This evidence is less meaningful than it appears at first sight for several reasons. In most cases the higher land productivity of private plots was due to the application of much greater labor per unit of land. Often the share of land accounted for by the private plots is understated since it does not include the pasturage that is allowed private plot farmers (this matter is discussed in detail for the Soviet Union by Hedlund 1989). In some countries such as the Soviet Union, private plot production was also valued in the prices received on the peasant markets, while collective and state farm production was valued in the lower official producer prices.

The most extensive formal comparisons of farm efficiency are for Yugoslavia where Boyd (1984, 1987) uses republic-level data over time to calculate separate Cobb-Douglas production functions for the private and socialist sectors, employing dummy variables to take regional differences in soil and climate into account. Although his static efficiency comparisons yield ambiguous results, he does show that total factor productivities of both the socialist sector (state and collective farms) and the private sector were not significantly different until the important economic reforms of 1965. From 1965 through 1979 total factor productivity grew significantly faster in the socialist sector, which he attributes in part to differential access to machinery and fertilizer in which technical change is embodied. As pointed out in chapter 7, during these years the private sector also had little access to agricultural extension, so that the socialist sector acted as the main bearer of technical progress.[4]

Using data aggregated by county, Boyd (1988) employs the same techniques in studying private and socialist farm performance in Poland. Although his results also do not allow an unambiguous comparison of technical efficiency, he shows that, in the period from 1960 through 1982, total factor productivity for agriculture as a whole decreased, but at a faster rate in the socialist than in the private sector. His technique does not allow us to determine if this was due to declining technical efficiency or to an actual technological regression.

Brada and King (1989) challenge these results. Using the same data set they make two important changes in the statistical analysis. First, they assume that the two types of farms faced the same technological possibil-

---

[4] Boyd (1984, p. 24) also points out that for the first few years after the 1965 reforms, which greatly increased the role of market forces, the socialist sector actually reduced its inputs of machinery and fertilizer. This suggests that such farms had received more such inputs than were economically justified, an interpretation also made by most Yugoslav observers.

ities and, therefore, they pool the data. Second, instead of a Cobb-Douglas production function, they calculate a deterministic frontier translog production function, employing a linear programming method and using slack variables to take into account differences between the two sectors. They conclude that there were no significant differences in technical efficiency (relation between inputs and outputs) between the two sectors, but that allocative efficiency differed, with the state farms overutilizing capital, land, and fertilizer inputs in comparison to the private farms, a state of affairs brought about by differential access to these inputs. In contrast to Boyd, they find no change in technological progress that, combined with their results about technical efficiency, suggests that total factor productivity growth was roughly the same in the two sectors.

Some studies have dealt with only the state and collective farm sectors. For the Soviet Union, for instance, Wyzan (1983) calculates production functions from a data set aggregated by republics for a seventeen-year period and finds only minor differences between the collective and state farm sectors, although the former had slightly greater returns to scale and somewhat greater technical progress.[5] Along the same lines Brada, Hey, and King (1988) compare economic efficiency of state and collective farms for crop production in the Czech and Slovak regions of Czechoslovakia. They find that collective farms had greater technological efficiency than state farms and, moreover, that regional effects were important, particularly in the earlier years.

Lin (1987, 1988) applies the sectoral comparisons in a quite different fashion. Using annual provincial data for China for several years, with a variable indicating the relative number of teams in each that had converted to the new system while the agricultural system was in transition, he analyzes the impact of the decollectivization on agricultural production. This allows him to separate the impacts of policy and system in a systematic fashion, since at any point in time all of the farms emerged from the same initial conditions and faced the same set of prices and other general policies. His results indicate that a major share of the increase in output can be attributed to institutional reforms, rather than changes in policy.

Some commentators have preferred the subsidy approach in analyzing relative efficiency of private and socialist agriculture, stressing that in most Marxist regimes, the state farms must be subsidized in order to

[5] In a pioneering study of Soviet agriculture Clayton (1971) uses time-series data for ten years to calculate production functions for state farms, collective farms, and personal plots. From her data it can be determined that total factor productivity grew considerably faster in the state and collective farm sectors than the private sector, but because she has series for only two types of inputs (land and labor), such results are more suggestive than convincing.

survive, while private farms do not receive such subventions. These subsidies, however, may not represent economic inefficiencies. For instance, in the case of export crops the exchange rate might be overvalued so that if the producer price is based on the export price in dollars multiplied by the exchange rate, the price these farms receive may be too low to meet their labor and other costs. Many subsidies are also due to the desire for low food prices for urban consumers, which means only that the private farms which do not receive such subsidies end up with lower labor incomes, not that they are more efficient.

These explanations do not, of course, hold in cases of dramatic losses that can only be attributed to inefficiencies of the state farms. For instance, although Soviet and Bulgarian specialists provided technical and financial support to several hundred state farms in Angola, the foreign exchange value of their output was lower than the foreign exchange expended for their inputs because of enormous wastes (Bhagavan 1986, p. 39). In most cases, however, the subsidy approach yields ambiguous results.

WITHIN A SINGLE COUNTRY AT DIFFERENT TIME PERIODS

Comparing agricultural performance in a single country in different periods can either be carried out directly or by methods allowing a judgment of the effects of reforms by comparing what would have occurred under the old system to what actually happened in the new system. If precautions are taken, it is also possible to separate the impact of changes in institutions and policies.

McMillan, Whalley, and Zhu (1989) analyze in an ingenious fashion the aggregate performance of Chinese agriculture over time for the period following the reforms in order to distinguish the impact of the systemic from policy changes. More specifically, from a production function estimation, they separate the impact on production in the postreform period of increased inputs on agricultural outputs. From data on supply and prices in a previous period with few policy changes plus a model of farmer decision-making under the old arrangements, they are able to separate the effects of price on increased supply. All remaining differences in production they attribute to changes in the institutional arrangements. They conclude that the relative price increases accounted for about one-fifth of the increase in total factor productivity, and the systemic changes, about four-fifths.

This approach has been criticized in regard to data, techniques, model, and interpretation. For my purpose it is important to note that taking account of the impact of certain factors such as price increases and then attributing all residual changes to systemic changes is risky. For China, it is likely that "residual changes" due to the relaxation of the priority of grain production and of regional self-sufficiency also played important roles in the increase of aggregate production. More specifically, as noted in chapter 7, interprovincial trade in grains declined greatly between 1953 and 1978. After 1978, such interprovincial exchange picked up considerably, and farms began to specialize more in crops for which their land was most suited. Although I make an argument in the previous chapter that such self-sufficiency policies during the period of collectivization were really a structural, rather than a policy feature of the system, such an interpretation is controversial. If the impact of these changes is factored out of the residual, the impact of the institutional changes would probably be much less.

Lin (1989) approaches the problem from a somewhat different angle with a rich data set from twenty-eight provinces for the period 1970 to 1987. Using a stochastic frontier production function, which includes a weather variable, he shows that from 1978 through 1984, 94 percent of the growth of total factor productivity could be attributed to the change in organization, and only 6 percent to changes in multiple cropping, in the product mix, and the market price. From 1985 through 1987, after the organization changes were completed, 16 percent of the growth of productivity was accounted for by a change in the share of land devoted to non-grain crops, 23 percent to a change in multiple cropping of land, and 61 percent to a change in the market price. It is noteworthy that in this period a worsening of weather offset the increase in output due to an increase in inputs (land, labor, capital, and fertilizer).

Two other studies arrive at quite different interpretations of the Chinese agricultural reforms. Using aggregative data for thirty-five years, Wen (1989) calculates a supply function and concludes that institutional changes were responsible for only 56 percent of the increase in farm output in the early 1980s. Using data at the team level from Dahe Township in Hebei Province and employing a production function approach, Kim (1989) finds the impact of these institutional reforms to account for only 5 to 11 percent of the productivity increases. He provides evidence that the major effects were caused by an increase in the decision-making autonomy of farmers in cropping and marketing (which led to a change in the composition of output) and the increased prices, both from the government and the development of free agricultural markets. He claims that these measures were independent of decollectivization, although one could make a good case that politically they could not have been implemented without the institutional changes.

Clearly the definitive econometric study separating the various factors accounting for the rapid increase of output resulting from the Chinese reforms has not yet been made. It is, therefore, useful to turn to a different type of comparison using data from contrasting time periods.

Brada (1986) compares the variability of crop output and crop yields of prewar (generally from 1920 through 1939) capitalist farming and postwar (generally 1945 through 1981) socialist farming in five East European nations. He finds the curious result that, although output variability had increased, the major cause was greater variability in acreage, rather than yield. For Poland, from 1960 through 1982, he shows that state and collective farms exhibited greater variability of acreage than private farms and that state farms also revealed greater variability in yield than did private or collective farms. For Hungary and Bulgaria, which have a much smaller private agricultural sector than Poland, generally the same results obtained, while in Czechoslovakia and Romania, the results were more mixed. He concludes that the greater output variability of socialized agriculture is "a self-inflicted wound" and largely the consequence of governmental policies.

Desai (1990) examines the variability of grain yields in fourteen *oblast'i* in the Soviet Union in two subperiods, 1958 to 1967 and 1968 to 1982, taking into account temperature and rainfall variables in each *oblast'*. She shows that holding the weather constant, grain yield variability increased during this period, that production became increasingly mechanized, and that fertilizer inputs per hectare increased. She conjectures, like Brada, that this greater variability was due in part to increasing interruptions of fertilizer deliveries and breakdown of agricultural machinery during the Brezhnev years.

An Empirical Study

For this comparative study of agricultural performance in a group of Marxist and non-Marxist regimes, as noted above, I have chosen three economic criteria of evaluation: growth of production, fluctuations of output, and the growth of total factor productivity (TFP), the part of the growth of agricultural production that is not accounted for by the growth of all inputs taken together. The third criterion embodies three phenomena which, with the statistical technique I am employing, cannot be separated, namely technical change, dynamic efficiency (placing investment in those sectors and locations with the highest return), and changes in static (technical) efficiency.[6]

[6] Separation of the causes of a slow TFP growth can be most easily understood using a simple production possibility frontier diagram. If the frontier is expanding very slowly, the low growth of TFP is clearly due to dynamic inefficiencies, which may be attributed either to slow technological change (or adoption of new technologies) or inappropriate investments. If the frontier is expanding at an appropriate rate, but production is increasing more slowly, then the low TFP is caused by a falling static efficiency (that is, the economy is moving relatively further from the production possibility frontier). Interpretative problems

Selection of Sample

Although I have identified thirty-three Marxist regimes, for purposes of this empirical study, the list had to be culled in order to remove five groups of nations that would make the results ambiguous: those that were Marxist regimes for not more than a few years (Grenada, Zimbabwe); those where a civil war raged with sufficient force in the rural areas to affect agricultural production in a critical fashion for a number of years (Afghanistan, Angola, Ethiopia, Kampuchea, Laos, Mozambique, Nicaragua, Viet Nam and Zimbabwe); those for which comparable output data were not available (Seychelles); those that carried out a significant decollectivization during the period under consideration so that the meaning of the systems variable raises problems of interpretation (China); and those that have admitted to falsification of the basic agricultural data during the period (Romania).

For each of the twenty Marxist regimes remaining, I attempted to select a non-Marxist nation that had roughly the same kind of agriculture, climate, level of development and population (ranked in descending order of importance). In most cases, not all of these criteria could be met, and I had to pick countries that fulfilled only some of them. I also had to eliminate additional nations, both Marxist and non-Marxist, in which the basic output series varied widely from source to source, which eliminated two more Marxist nations (Bénin and Guinea-Bissau) as well as several non-Marxist nations.

After a test for the quality of the data, the final sample consists of thirty-four nations and is presented in Table 8.2. Using all of the countries in a pooled regression obliterates some interesting differences in the causal roles of explanatory variables between the industrial and developing nations. For this reason I report the results separately for each subsample. The data are, in addition, considerably more reliable for the former than for the latter group of nations.

Data and Estimations

I have relied primarily on data from the files of the U.N. Food and Agricultural Organization (FAO) for my sample. Several of the input series, discussed in statistical note F, come from other sources.

Since data for the various countries in the sample are of quite different quality, questions arise as to the accuracy of my estimates. To approach this problem in a systematic fashion, I compared the FAO output series

---

arise in examining the available empirical evidence because it is difficult to know how fast the production possibility frontier is expanding.

TABLE 8.2
Characteristics of the Sample

	Marxist Regime	Significant Agricultural Collectivization	Centrally Planned Agricultural Production	1980 Per Capita GDP
Sample of Industrial or Semi-Industrialized Nations				
Albania	Yes	Yes	Yes	$2,366
Austria	No	No	No	8,230
Bulgaria	Yes	Yes	Yes	4,904
Czechoslovakia	Yes	Yes	Yes	7,002
Germany, East	Yes	Yes	Yes	7,891
Germany, West	No	No	No	9,795
Greece	No	No	No	4,383
Hungary	Yes	Yes	No	5,508
Ireland	No	No	No	4,929
Italy	No	No	No	7,164
Poland	Yes	No	No	5,006
Spain	No	No	No	6,131
USSR	Yes	Yes	Yes	5,626
United States	No	No	No	11,404
Yugoslavia	Yes	No	No	4,733
Sample of Developing Nations				
Africa				
Cape Verde	Yes	No	No	947
Congo	Yes	No	No	5,981
Gabon	No	No	No	2,973
Madagascar	Yes	No	No	589
Malawi	No	No	No	417
Mauitania	No	No	No	576
São Tomé	Yes	Yes	No?	684
Senegal	No	No	No	744
Somalia	Yes	No	No	415
Swaziland	No	No	No	1,079
Americas				
Costa Rica	No	No	No	3,031
Cuba	Yes	Yes	Yes	3,523
Guyana	No	Yes	No?	1,623
Panama	No	No	No	2,810
Asia				
Korea, North	Yes	Yes	Yes	1,184
Korea, South	No	No	No	2,369
Mongolia	Yes	Yes	Yes	614
Nepal	No	No	No	490
Yemen, South	Yes	Yes	No	541

Source: Collectivization data come from table 4.1. For GDP data, see table 1.2.
Notes: Collectivization is "significant" if the area of socialist agriculture exceeded 30 percent of the total farmed area.

with those of U.S. Department of Agriculture (USDA, 1988) and of the World Bank (WB, 1988). The coverage of the FAO and USDA estimates are roughly the same; the FAO, however, uses a modification of U.S. price weights, while the USDA estimates use a domestic price for weighing the different products in the index. If for any of the countries in the sample, Marxist or non-Marxist, the estimates from these two agencies differed by more than 1.1 percentage points, I eliminated the country.[7] The FAO and World Bank series have quite different coverage, since the FAO series is a semigross output series for agriculture alone, and the World Bank series is value added in agriculture, forestry, and fishing. If for any of the sample countries the estimates by these two organizations differed by more than 1.5 percentage points, I also eliminated that country from the sample. Unfortunately, similar tests could not be made with the input series.

The data set covers the period from 1970 through 1987; the latter date was the last year for which data were available when I made the calculations. For East Europe I wanted to start the series after the collectivization drives had been ended and the economies had assimilated these changes. Otherwise the results might have been contaminated by the transition difficulties discussed in chapters 4 and 7. For most of the Third World countries, the choice of 1970 means that the years both before and after the collectivization drives are included; thus the impact of the transition difficulties are present. For this subsample I would, therefore, expect that the growth of agricultural production would be lower than in the sample of comparable non-Marxist nations.

The only estimations that I needed to make myself were for total factor productivity (TFP). These were obtained by combining five different inputs (labor, land, capital stock, fertilizer inputs, and animal stock) into a Cobb-Douglas type index, and dividing this series into the output series. The exact sources and methods are described in statistical note G. Contrary to a recent study, my estimates show that TFP was positive in the East European nations. Since I used the same methods for estimating TFP in all nations, any possible upward bias in my calculations should appear in all nations and the systemic comparisons should not be greatly affected. The most important data series used in the regression experiments are presented in Table 8.3.

---

[7] Although the differences in the two series could arise from disparities in domestic and world market prices used in the weighing of the various physical output series, it seems most likely that discrepancies in the basic physical output series are the source of the difficulties. If the disparities in price are at fault, then those countries with the most distorted price systems are likely to underestimate gross agricultural output, due to concealment of output and smuggling. The 1.1 and 1.5 percentage point limits are, of course, arbitrary.

TABLE 8.3
Performance and Crisis Indicators

	Gross agricultural production: 1970–87				Total Factor Productivity		Farm Labor Outflow Problem
	Average Annual Growth	Declining per Capita Production	Deceleration of Growth	Annual Variability	Average Annual Growth	Deceleration	
Sample of Industrial or Semi-Industrialized Nations							
Albania	2.96%	No	Yes	1.04%	0.55%	No	No
Austria	1.62	No	No	0.69	3.14	No	Serious
Bulgaria	1.41	No	Yes	1.14	1.39	No	Serious
Czechoslovakia	2.32	No	No	0.73	1.93	No	No
Germany, East	2.09	No	No	1.11	1.72	No	No
Germany, West	1.46	No	No	0.64	2.55	No	Serious
Greece	2.11	No	Yes	1.19	1.71	No	No
Hungary	2.24	No	Yes	1.10	1.76	No	Medium
Ireland	2.38	No	No	1.64	2.61	No	Serious
Italy	1.38	No	No	0.80	1.44	No	Serious
Poland	1.02	No	No	1.08	0.02	No	No
Spain	2.71	No	No	1.06	3.21	Yes	Serious
USSR	1.16	No	No	0.93	0.25	No	No
United States	1.62	No	Yes	1.25	1.76	No	No
Yugoslavia	1.94	No	Yes	1.08	2.77	Yes	Serious
Sample of Developing Nations							
Africa							
Cape Verde	2.42	No	No	3.14	1.13	No	No
Congo	2.04	Yes	No	0.49	0.11	No	No
Gabon	2.61	Yes	Yes	1.01	-0.70	No	No
Madagascar	1.63	Yes	No	0.69	0.34	No	No

The Choice of Explanatory Variables and the Statistical Tests

Some difficulties arise in distinguishing the impact of the three systems variables because the two samples contain relatively few nations and because the three systems variables are highly correlated with each other. More specifically, among the industrialized and semi-industrialized nations the samples of Marxist regimes and of nations with collectivized agricultural systems differ by only two nations, Poland and Yugoslavia. And the samples of nations with collectivized agriculture and with central planning differ by only two nations, Poland and Hungary. Thus the differential behavior of the systems variable may reflect what is happening in these few nations, rather than the more general phenomenon examined here. Among the Third World Marxist regimes, this situation is even worse. Although a lower percentage of them are collectivized so that the correlation between the Marxist regime variable and the collectivization variable is not so great, almost all those nations with a high degree of collectivized agriculture have central planning. In the sample two exceptions are Guyana and São Tomé, where the agricultural sectors are organized into a small number of very large state farms, a situation inviting considerable intervention by the ministry of agriculture and a pseudo-central planning arrangement to arise.

Two approaches can be employed. We can include all three systems variables in the same regression in order to see which is strongest. Given the problems of collinearity between the system variables that is discussed above, it should not be surprising that the levels of significance of these systemic variables are low and that the regressions are difficult to interpret. We can also calculate separate regressions using each of these systems variables and then compare the results, declaring as the winner the regression providing the greatest explanatory power. Although I follow this latter procedure because the calculated regression equations are easier to understand, such an approach also does not provide completely unambiguous results. For the developing countries, I also choose to omit the central planning variable from the regression experiments since its meaning is even more ambiguous, so that only two systems variables are tested: the Marxist regime and the collectivization variables.[8]

Problems arise in the choice of other explanatory variables as well. At an early stage of the research, I experimented with a series of plausible causal variables that might have influenced the behavior of the three dependent variables; for instance, land density, weather variables, years under a Marxist regime, membership in the European Economic Com-

---

[8] I might also add that none of the regressions calculated for the Third World sample with the central planning variable yielded significant or interesting results.

munity, and so forth, as well as interaction variables calculated by multiplying the different independent variables with each other. Except for per capita income, the systems variables, and interaction variables between per capita income and system, none seemed to play a significant causal role. As a result, they are not included in the final estimations.

For the final calculations I started with the system variable and then added other explanatory variables. The criterion for keeping or eliminating such additional variables was whether the increase in the coefficient of determination (that is, explanatory power) was important. In order to keep the hypothesis testing as honest as possible, I made only a limited number of these statistical experiments and tried to restrain myself from fishing for higher degrees of statistical significance. I used only the most simple and plausible specifications of the regressions. Moreover, I have also employed only ordinary least squares regression techniques, given the relatively small samples and the low likelihood that problems of two way causation are sufficiently important to be taken into account.

The Results of the Regression Experiments

The results of these statistical experiments are reported in Table 8.4. Before analyzing them in detail, their major biases deserve brief consideration. Given the uncertainties in many of the estimations, particularly TFP, the statistical significance of the various calculated coefficients are understated and, moreover, certain subtle causal relations influencing the results might not be picked up in the calculations. It does not seem likely, however, that the errors in the variables are sufficiently different in the samples of Marxist and non-Marxist regimes so as to bias the calculated coefficient of the systems variable. Nevertheless, given these uncertainties of the data, it is not productive to be too dogmatic in the interpretation of the results.

The major conclusions from these calculations can be quickly summarized.

OUTPUT GROWTH

No statistically significant difference can be found in the growth of semigross agricultural output in the sample of industrialized nations between the countries with different economic systems, no matter how the systems variable is defined. For the developing nations, those countries with a significant degree of collectivized agriculture had significantly lower growth because of the transition difficulties and other problems discussed in the last chapter. The addition of other explanatory variables such as per capita income does not add much explanatory power or in-

TABLE 8.4

Results of the Statistical Experiments

Dependent variable	Constant	Systems variable (SV)			Per capita GDP (YCap)	YCap²	YCap × SV	N	R²
		Marxist regime	Collectivized agriculture	Central planning					
Sample of Industrial Nations									
Agricultural output	1.900* (8.485)	-0.006 (0.019)						15	.0000
Agricultural output	1.808* (9.342)		-0.223 (0.728)					15	.0391
Agricultural output	1.851* (9.953)			+0.137 (0.322)				15	.0137
Total factor productivity	2.343* (7.056)	-1.045* (2.384)						15	.3042
Total factor productivity	2.133* (7.056)		-0.866 (1.812)					15	.2017
Total factor productivity	2.095* (7.360)			-0.926 (1.879)				15	.2135
Variability	3.175* (3.764)	-1.266 (2.106)			-0.541* (2.375)	0.031 (2.149)	0.197 (0.098)	15	.4254
Variability	3.008* (3.647)		-1.187 (1.999)		-0.521* (2.281)	0.031 (2.088)	0.187 (1.892)	15	.4074
Variability	3.161* (3.961)			-1.319* (2.252)	-0.564* (2.517)	-0.033* (2.322)	0.203 (2.102)	15	.4541

Sample of Developing Nations

				N	R²
Agricultural output	2.408* (4.619)	-1.139 (1.585)		19	.1287
Agricultural output	2.299* (5.554)		-1.551* (2.106)	19	.2070
Total factor productivity	0.726 (1.843)	-1.035 (1.904)		19	.1757
Total factor productivity	0.590 (1.869)		-1.292* (2.300)	19	.2373
Variability	1.530* (4.814)	-0.090 (0.204)		19	.0024
Variability	1.455* (5.503)		+0.086 (0.183)	19	.0020

Source: See tables 8.2 and 8.3; however, per capita GDP is defined in thousands of dollars.

Notes: R² = coefficient of determination; N = number in sample. The T statistics are placed under the calculated regression coefficients, and an asterisk denotes statistical significance at the 0.05 level.

crease the statistical significance of the calculated regression coefficient for the economic systems variable for either of the two subsamples.

For the industrial countries the total factor productivity growth was lower in the Marxist regimes to a statistically significant degree. This systems variable is somewhat better at explaining the results than an agricultural collectivization or central planning variable, which suggests that it is the ideology and the resultant agricultural policies pursued by Marxist regimes, rather than collectivization per se that have had a more important influence in TFP growth. Nevertheless, given the relative similarity of the samples in the two sets of regression, one cannot place a great deal of weight on this interpretation. Addition of other independent variables does little to raise the explanatory power of the regression.

Given the considerable importance of controls of agricultural production in the European Community (EC), I thought that inclusion of a variable designating those non-Marxist nations belonging to the EC would strengthen the impact of the systems variable. This conjecture, however, is not validated by these data, probably because of the crudeness of the approach.

For the developing countries, the total factor productivity growth was lower in those nations with collectivized agriculture than in nations without these features. This systems variable is somewhat better at explaining the results than a variable indicating whether the nation has a Marxist regime, which is the reverse of the case of the industrial nations.

Given the uncertain nature of the TFP data, one cannot lay too much importance on slightly different degrees of statistical significance of the various system variables. What is important is that the regression results are consistent with the general belief that dynamic efficiency of agricultural production is lower in Marxist than in other regimes, and that in the former group of nations agriculture serves as a "black hole" for investment (Hedlund 1989).

For the industrial nations all three systems variables appear promising, although only the central planning variable is statistically significant. This appears to confirm the conjecture that the rigidity of central planning, when faced with exogenous shock in the agricultural sector, acts to amplify production fluctuations. Nevertheless, things are not so simple because per capita GDP and an interaction between the systems variable and per capita GDP also play a role. More specifically, the regressions suggest that below a middle range of economic development (defined as a per capita GDP in a band between $6,300 and $6,500), variability of output is less, but that above this level, variability is greater in the East than the West.

Such results have two possible interpretations. Either Marxist agricultural policies, central planning, and collectivization might be dysfunctional above the middle level of economic development. Or the particular policies associated with Marxist agriculture are always dysfunctional, but only those nations above the middle level of economic development actually carry them out.

For the sample of developing nations, the differences in production fluctuations were not great. Moreover, none of the different explanatory variables with which I experimented seemed to have played a causal role.

A DIGRESSION ON AGRICULTURAL "CRISES"

Since considerable public attention has focused on the "general agricultural crisis" in Marxist regimes, in contrast to the long run problems discussed above, it is useful to get this issue out of the way because such a short-term approach tells us little about the special nature of Marxist agriculture. My definition of "general crisis" focuses on phenomena that appear year after year. In any country agricultural crises appear from time to time because of droughts or other adverse climatic conditions. The approach I follow allows us to isolate several countries in both systems whose agricultural sectors are in serious trouble.

Discussions of such issues have mentioned five kinds of "crises of agriculture" in Marxist regimes. With the data from Table 8.3, we can examine these briefly in a systematic fashion.

A Declining Level of Per Capita Agricultural Production. According to the data such a crisis did not occur in any of the industrial nations, Marxist or non-Marxist. Much of the so-called food shortage in Eastern Europe was the result either of food prices set lower than the equilibrium level (or food subsidies set too large), or increasing difficulties in getting the food to the cities and distributing it. In contrast, a declining level of per capita gross agricultural production occurred in most African nations, regardless of system. For the other developing countries, the situation was mixed and appears unrelated to system.

Deceleration of Growth of Agricultural Production. For the developing nations in the sample such deceleration occurred in slightly more than one third of the countries; it does not, however, seem related to system. Among the industrial nations, however, the situation was quite different. In four of the eight Marxist regimes (Albania, Bulgaria, Hungary, and Yugoslavia), deceleration occurred, while this phenomenon is found in only two (Spain and the United States) of the six non-Marxist nations. Although the share of nations with decelerating production was higher among the Marxist nations, I do not believe that this systemic difference says much and may be traced to such factors as a slowdown in investment in the agricultural sector that had little to do with the economic system.

A Low Level of Growth of Total Factor Productivity. Defining a low level of growth of TFP as an average annual growth of less than 0.5 percent a year (0.0 percent a year might normally be used, but my TFP data may have an upward bias), then no systemic crisis appears to be occurring. Among the developing nations, five of the nine Marxist countries and three of the ten non-Marxist nations exhibited this problem. Of the fifteen industrial nations, such low TFP could be found in only Poland and the USSR. This cutoff point is, of course, arbitrary so that the approach is not very convincing. The real problem was the lower growth of TFP in the long-run, which has already been discussed.

Deceleration of Growth of Total Factor Productivity. This phenomenon occurred in only six nations in the two sub-samples and appears unrelated to whether the nation is Marxist or not. Clearly agriculture was in desperate straits in Guyana and South Yemen, since both had a negative total factor productivity and a decelerating total factor productivity. Although both of these were Marxist regimes, these problems do not seem a general condition of Marxist agriculture.

A Rapid Outflow of Agricultural Labor. Since migration out of the agricultural sector is primarily by younger workers, a very rapid outflow of such labor leads to a rising average age of the agricultural labor force. In Bulgaria, a number of rural villages became either depopulated or "retirement communities," a situation sufficiently alarming to the government to provide a major motive for agricultural reform even before the fall of Zhivkov. This problem occurred in three of the eight industrial Marxist nations in the sample (Bulgaria, Hungary, and Yugoslavia), but in five of the seven industrial non-Marxist nations (Austria, West Germany, Ireland, Italy, and Spain). In short, this seemed a problem more likely to be found in the West than in the East.

Concluding Remarks

A major purpose for comparing agricultural performance in Marxist and non-Marxist regimes was to distinguish between the effects of agricultural policy and of the organizational structure of the agricultural sector. The results are by no means conclusive. For total factor productivity in the industrialized or semi-industrialized nations, they suggest that economic policies associated with Marxist ideology, rather than collectivization per se might be more important in explaining the poorer performance in comparison to a set of non-Marxist nations. For the developing nations, on the other hand, the organizational variable appears more important. Since structural and other policies are so intertwined, as I argued in chapter 7, this is as far as the empirical evidence can take us. For individual countries such as China, where comparable data series are available for different regions, most—but not all—studies discussed provide evidence that the organization of agriculture, rather than the changes in governmental policies related to agriculture such as price and market policies was more important in explaining the spurt in agricultural production during the first half of the 1980s.

The most important empirical finding of this chapter is the lower TFP growth in Marxist nations or nations with collectivized agriculture, even though we cannot isolate the exact cause. To some, this result might suggest that their static efficiency in the agricultural sector was lower as well; that is, with their current land, labor, and capital, the agricultural sector could produce significantly more, as in the case of China in the early 1980s. Since I am unable to resolve very satisfactorily the structure versus policy issue, I cannot determine whether this would be true for the entire sample and we must wait a few years to see if a spurt in total factor productivity is occurring in the nations that have decollectivized. For the developing countries, I also find that output growth is lower in the nations with collectivized agriculture than in comparable nations with predominantly private agriculture; this is not true for the sample of industrialized nations. For other performance criteria the results are ambiguous.

Few important differences are found between East and West in the indicators of a short-term agricultural crisis. Such an exercise does, however, allow the isolation of certain Marxist regimes, such as Guyana and South Yemen, where the agriculture sector was in serious trouble.

Finally, in trying to evaluate the success of collectivized agriculture, none of the empirical investigations discussed or carried out in this chapter covers more than a few of many possible economic performance criteria. A set of broader criteria, not necessarily economic, come readily to mind.

For instance, I wanted to make comparisons of income inequality among farmers, but unfortunately, for the few countries for which relatively solid evidence is available, the data are incomparable and, it might be added, the results appear to have quite different causes. For instance, in China rural income inequality declined in the late 1940s and early 1950s, primarily as a result of the land reforms; such inequalities remained roughly the same thereafter, even after collectivization had taken place (Perkins and Yusef 1984, p. 106). Although rural income inequalities increased somewhat since the decollectivization (Zhu Ling 1991, p. 152), it appears that the major cause was a widening of interregional, rather than intraregional income differentials. In several individual counties for which data are available, income inequality generally decreased (Zhu Ling 1991, p. 73). Until the empirical studies now underway are completed, a definitive answer cannot be given. Rural income distribution data are available for only a few of the Marxist regimes and their interpretation raises many problems.[9]

I would have liked to compare the ecological damage created by different farming systems. Ecological studies of this nature, however, are available for only a few Marxist regimes, for instance, Bulgaria (Oschties 1985), Czechoslovakia (Oschties 1989), and East Germany (Spindler 1989). Unfortunately, the information is not comparable with data collected for non-Marxist nations.

I also wished to compare the degree of consumer satisfaction with agricultural production, particularly with regard to the composition of agricultural production and also to other aspects, such as processing and packaging. An example of the latter phenomenon is found in East Germany around the time of the currency union with West Germany, when consumers were purchasing West German foodstuffs, for instance, yogurt, that were double or triple the price of the East German products, allegedly because of quality differences in the foodstuffs. In most Marxist regimes the managers of collective and state farms, as well as food-processing enterprises, appeared to place more importance on meeting quantity goals than on producing a quality product that the consumers would want to buy, in large measure because consumers had few alternative outlets where they could purchase processed foods. Unfortunately, information on the composition and quality of agricultural production is primarily anecdotal so that at this time no systematic empirical comparisons can be made.

In addition, I also wanted to examine social criteria, but these raised even more measurement difficulties. The most important, of course, is whether such farming systems turned out better people, but this seems impossible to resolve. On a less cosmic level, some Marxist analysts have argued that collectivization of agriculture reduced social inequalities and gave the farmers greater control over their destinies, especially since they were no longer at the mercy of market forces. These claims are dif-

[9] One Marxist regime where such data have been analyzed is Madagascar. In this country rural income inequality increased between 1960 and 1980 (Pryor 1990c), not because of any structural changes (since collectivization was unimportant), but as a result of misguided government policies.

ficult to evaluate without detailed anthropological evidence and such studies are, unfortunately, few in number. Some of those which are available, it should be added, provide a different picture. For instance, from village studies in Hungary, Bell (1984) argues that the major positive changes in the social structure came with the land reforms and that collectivization brought a reduction in independence, as witnessed by negative attitudes toward farming, and the growing social gulf between farm officials and farm workers. Supporting evidence is provided in various other village studies in Hungary (Hann 1980; Swain 1985; Vasary 1987).[10] Still others have tried to evaluate collective farming with criteria which seem perverse. For instance, J. G. Patel, governor of the Indian Central Bank, has argued that the major attractiveness of some form of collectivized agriculture is that it offers a "better chance of disguising unemployment in a socially respectable form" (Anon. 1981, p. 47).

In sum, much remains to be done before a final evaluation of the performance of collectivized agriculture can be made. These preliminary results suggest, however, that this grand experiment in the organization of agriculture cannot be considered an economic success, particularly with regard to the long-term growth of total factor productivity.

[10] For Hungary, Hegedüs (1977) has some interesting evidence showing that farmworkers did not feel they were consulted often enough on important decisions by farm managers, a function of the increasing size of the collective farms.

PART V

Reforms and the Future

Chapter 9

WHEN IS COLLECTIVIZATION REVERSIBLE?

BY THE REVERSIBILITY of collectivization or by decollectivization I mean the conversion of state and collective farms into either private (corporate or individual) farms, or tenant farms with long-term leases, or genuine producer cooperatives.[1] The breaking up of these large farms is, of course, a more difficult process than conversion of these farms into corporations, in which the workers or others hold stock but the essential farming operations remain roughly the same. But in many countries farmers feel secure only if they have a land title or long-term leases in hand, rather than shares of some abstract legal entity. This means that creation of a large farm corporation is often not a politically viable option and a breaking up of the farm is required.

In certain situations agricultural collectivization is readily reversible, with relatively low short-run costs and considerable long-run benefits. Yugoslavia and Poland reversed their partial collectivization drives of the late 1940s and early 1950s in the early and mid-1950s. Although these decollectivizations had certain costs, both countries benefited more by avoiding the still higher costs of transition to a fully collectivized system. During the early 1980s, China decollectivized, albeit without privatization, and the same process occurred in Kampuchea, Laos, and Viet Nam in the latter part of the decade. Decollectivization in the form of a collapse of much of collectivized agriculture and reversion to private agriculture also occurred in some African nations in the late 1980s; for example, in Angola and Mozambique.

---

[1] Included in my definition of decollectivization are cases where private farming includes some group activities, for instance, when a rice field is irrigated by a single system maintained by a group, while the fields are subdivided into a number of strips, each farmed by a different household. Decollectivization can also occur without full marketization—for instance, creation of capital markets. It can also take place without a developed system of contract enforcement (as in China), although this would have to evolve quickly for the system to function effectively.

In the discussion in this and the following chapters I focus primarily on decollectivization in those Marxist regimes that have a relatively large socialist agricultural sector and where the problems are greatest. Although the small literature in decollectivization in non-Marxist regimes has some interest (e.g., Romm and Levy 1990), the external environments of these nations is so different that the lessons that can be drawn are of relevance only for those Marxist regimes with a relatively small collectivized sector of genuine producer cooperatives that function in a market economy, e.g., Zimbabwe.

Nevertheless, one major failure of decollectivization must be noted. In the late 1980s the Soviet Union took some tentative steps toward a partial decollectivization but, by the beginning of the 1990s, was unable to achieve any notable success. Although the outcome can be blamed in large measure on policy failures, it is also possible that in certain historical situations, collectivization is not reversible, so that *any* large-scale measures taken to return to individual farming are doomed to failure, as the designers of the collectivized system had intended.

As some Soviet observers have noted, it is easy to make fish stew out of an aquarium, but impossible to make an aquarium out of fish stew. This raises the prospect that the decollectivization efforts of some East European nations in the early 1990s might also be unsuccessful, at least in the foreseeable future. What I argue is that decollectivization depends less on whether a Marxist party is in power, than on a series of economic, social, and political factors.

To place this possibility in a broader context, consider for a moment why various economies are locked into inefficient technologies or standards. Why, for instance, do many industrial nations use the QWERTY keyboard on typewriters, when other keyboard arrangements, for instance, the Dvorak system, allow much faster typing? Why do most industrialized nations use relatively narrow gauges in their railroads when wider gauges are better and safer? The answers that have been given to these questions (for instance, David 1985, 1988; Puffert 1987) emphasize network externalities and embeddedness. These terms encompass the benefits gained by a given user when others use the same technology or standards, the interrelatedness and interdependencies of production technologies, the high short-run costs of breaking webs of interaction in comparison to the benefits, and the imperfect information of the individual economic agents with regard to the intentions of others. That is, no individual would want to bear the costs of being out-of-step with others, although all would benefit if they decided together to take a particular action.

Evidence cited in chapter 8 suggests that agriculture in Marxist regimes is inefficient in a dynamic sense and, quite likely, in a static sense as well, and that the inefficiency arises not just from the farm sector alone, but also from the complementary institutions. Now if nations can be locked into inefficient technologies and standards, then surely they can also be locked into inefficient institutions. Few economic historians, for instance, are willing to defend the economic efficiency of such aspects of feudal agriculture as the lack of factor movement or the system of labor dues. And yet these aspects of feudalism lasted many centuries after the initial causes underlying them had waned. The same may be said for slave agriculture, although the inefficiency of this institution is open to more dispute.

In many cases, the long-term benefits of change to the system as a whole far outweigh the overall short-run costs. To individual farmers or local officials overseeing the farms who are making such calculations to guide their own decisions, however, the costs to those individuals outweigh the benefits for several possible reasons. First, farmers may lack certainty that others will take similar actions (so that, for instance, the power of the collective farm chairmen will be reduced) or complementary actions (so that, for instance, alternative sources of agricultural inputs will be available to them). This means that their expected private net benefits of change will be less than the social benefits of changing the entire system. It is difficult to be an oasis of capitalism in a desert of central planning with scarce inputs. Second, even if they are certain that others will take similar steps, it may be impossible for them to take into account in their calculations the benefits accruing to them when others take similar and complementary actions. Third, the benefits to society may outweigh the costs, but the local officials who must implement any partial decollectivization program may end up worse off economically or politically. These officials have good reason to sabotage the program by assigning infertile land to those that request individual farms, charging high rents, and withholding agricultural inputs.

In this chapter I consider more specifically the most important economic, sociological, and political factors that make decollectivization difficult. The point of view I take is primarily that of the farmer and I examine the process of decollectivization by looking at it from the ground up. In the next two chapters I examine a number of policy problems and look at the decollectivization process from the top down. In this chapter my major thesis is that collectivized agriculture is more likely to be irreversible in three situations: where the level of agricultural technology in the country is relatively high, where collectivized agriculture has been the dominant form of production for many decades, and where state farms predominate. The examples of successful decollectivization previously noted did not have these characteristics.

ECONOMIC FACTORS

Decollectivization is most appealing to hard-working farmers whose incomes are not commensurate with the efforts they would be willing to expend in agricultural pursuits. From this simple postulate one could predict that farmers would be most attracted to decollectivization or some type of "responsibility system" in farming situations where it is difficult to monitor performance, so that shirking is not punished and hard work is not rewarded. This would arise, for instance, where the accounting and work units are large, an hypothesis confirmed in some interesting statistical analyses of data by Lin (1987, 1988, 1989) for China. Since the issues involved are clear, other propositions of a similar nature can be developed.

Decollectivization also implies, however, the creation of an entirely new institutional structure in agriculture to support individualized farming. This problem, which is the focus of the discussion below, is untidy to analyze because so many factors are involved. It requires us to distinguish those aspects of the existing market systems that are most essential for the system to function. It also forces us to consider what features of the market system allow the household farm to earn an acceptable economic return at a suitable level of risk. And it compels us to explore the consistency of decollectivization with other economic goals of the government, so that any program of individual farming has some likelihood of permanence.

Institutional Prerequisites of Successful Individual Farming

What exactly do individual farmers need that cannot be provided by the existing institutions in centrally administered economies? Most of these problems are clearly of a short-run nature and can be solved over time. Nevertheless, the short-run costs and time constraints may be too high to permit a leader facing considerable internal opposition to implement a successful decollectivization program.

ESTABLISHING A RELIABLE AND ACCESSIBLE SOURCE OF INPUTS

A chronic problem for collective farms within centrally planned economies has been obtaining the proper equipment, inputs and farm services (e.g., repairs, storage, or transportation) at the right time and in the proper amount. Collective and state farms have devoted considerable resources to developing elaborate networks for solving these supply problems, especially since the Stalinist agricultural model featured the sales of these intermediate goods and services by large units, usually urban based, that were far from the farms. For individual farmers these input supply problems are compounded for three reasons.

Since smallholders cannot afford the labor to maintain these supply networks, either institutions such as special retail outlets would have to be developed or the administrative remnants of the original collective farms would have to be maintained to fulfill this supply function. If the latter alternative is followed, then the leader of the remnant would have to be elected by the members since the incumbent farm directors have strong incentives for discouraging the system of individualized farming.

In other words, the network externality problems are compounded by active opposition of those gaining power from control over the existing network. In the Soviet press one finds many instances of collective farm managers reneging on their commitments to provide farmers using the various land-leasing systems with the proper inputs and the farmers being unable to obtain needed inputs on their own. As Zhores A. Medvedev has noted of the Soviet Union, "Small operators can't easily separate from the network a parent farm provides. A hundred difficult problems would come up daily. There are no sacks of fertilizer, only railroad cars full. The smallest normal tractor is 150 horsepower" (Kramer, 1989).

Even within the framework of a centrally administered economy, many measures are possible to relieve the agricultural input problem. In China, Mao encouraged the formation of rural industries producing many of the necessary farm inputs as well as consumer goods used by the rural population (American Rural Small-Scale Industry Delegation 1977; Travers 1986). Although many of these local industries failed and many had high costs, enough lasted so that, around 1980, virtually all hand tools and farm machinery with less than 20 horsepower, 80 to 90 percent of phosphorus fertilizer, and 54 percent of nitrogen fertilizers came from such rural enterprises (Wong forthcoming). Perkins and Yusef (1984, p. 61) declare: "One of the unique features of China's efforts to increase agricultural production has been the degree to which required inputs have been supplied by small-scale enterprises located in the countryside near those who use their products." Although the successes of Chinese rural industry often have been overdrawn, this effort created a capacity for manufacturing in the countryside and the potential for responsiveness to local needs. From 1978 through 1986 industrial production of these rural industries grew at an average annual rate of 23 percent (Bryd and Quingson 1990, p. 12) and by 1986 the gross value of output from rural enterprises exceeded the gross value of agricultural output for the first time (Wong 1988). These rural nonfarm industries were one of the great successes of the Chinese reforms during the 1980s—it is especially noteworthy that much of their production went to urban rather than rural producers and consumers.

Such local industries not only simplify the supply system but help to keep the system responsive to local demands, especially for small-scale equipment and tools.[2] By the end of the 1980s, however, such a rural-

---

[2] Hedlund (1989 pp. 91–96) chronicles an interesting Soviet schizophrenia: the economic authorities recognized the importance of small-scale equipment, but they seemed unable to produce it for the farmers in any volume commensurate with the need. Another example is found in Poland, where the government paid a high dollar price to purchase a license for producing giant Massey-Ferguson tractors suitable only for the large fields of the state

based input-supply system had appeared in only a few other Marxist re-gimes. In Europe, Hungary and Czechoslovakia were the leading exam-ples. In Asia, the North Korean government in the late 1950s encouraged the county-level (*kun*) management committees to develop rural indus-tries that would aid the collective farms under their supervision; by the mid-1960s allegedly half of total consumer goods came from these facto-ries (Chung 1974, p. 70). In the mid-1980s, Viet Nam also started to move in this direction by creating "agro-industrial districts," but whether this policy was effective remains to be determined.

These supply problems are also examples of the conditions of "strong complementarity" and of interrelatedness, which explain why inefficient institutions or standards may be locked in (David 1985, 1988). The more input-intensive the agricultural technology, the more serious is the sup-ply problem. Thus decollectivization in the Third World Marxist regimes is easier than in Marxist nations with more advanced agriculture.

DIVIDING THE EQUIPMENT

Large-scale mechanical equipment of a collective or state farm cannot be easily divided among newly independent farmers. The Chinese solution of leasing the equipment to competing groups, which sell mechanical ser-vices to the individual farmers, is quite possible for a highly labor inten-sive type of agriculture using relatively little large-scale equipment. The difficulties involved, however, must not be underestimated and it is note-worthy that the more mechanized farms were the last to adopt the system of household farming in China (Lin 1987, 1988). Although a Bulgarian system of distributing livestock through a lottery has some interesting features (Anon 1990), it seems practicable only in special circumstances. Creating equipment cooperatives or competing machine tractor stations is another option. Nevertheless, for the farms in Eastern Europe, which are much more highly mechanized, the newly private farmers would need to buy services to prepare the land, seed, weed, fertilize, and har-vest the crop.[3] The negotiations to coordinate these services might be

---

farms. Of course, most of the land in Poland was farmed in smallholdings for which these tractors were quite unsuitable.

[3] If the farm was "mechanized," it is also important to take into account whether the farm equipment was actually used. In some countries, as in Romania, much of the equipment existing on paper was inoperable because of lack of spare parts so that the division of equip-ment would not be a big problem.

The formation of equipment cooperatives raises some interesting economic issues. In a quite different context David (1971 pp. 212–14; 1975, p. 208) considers why farmers in the nineteenth century were willing to form cooperatives for the joint use of plowing equip-ment or equipment for post-harvest tasks such as corn shellers or threshers, but were un-willing to form such cooperatives for reaping, mowing, or harvesting machinery. He con-jectures that harvesting has a much greater time constraint and the problems of deciding who would have priority for the use of the equipment would have required the users to

time-consuming and difficult, especially since these services must be carried out in a particular time sequence and within a relatively short time period to be effective.

Whether or not this division of equipment is a problem depends not only upon the general level of mechanization, but also upon the major crop grown. Clearly the grape-growing collectives in Georgia SSR would be easier to decollectivize than the large wheat farms in Kazakh SSR. Similarly certain types of animal-raising farms, especially of small animals such as pigs or sheep, would be easier to decollectivize than highly mechanized dairy operations. Decollectivization would also be easier where the newly private farmers could substitute their own labor for these farm services as well as for some input supplies—for instance, substituting hand weeding for weeding using equipment and herbicides. This change in factor proportions represents, of course, a technological regression, and farm production in such situations might fall unless offset by much greater individual effort.[4]

It is also possible to undertake the production of farm equipment more appropriate to small-scale individual agriculture, as some Marxist regimes including Czechoslovakia and Zimbabwe have been doing.[5] Again, this solution takes time and resources.

CREATING THE NECESSARY INFRASTRUCTURE

The problems of creating the necessary infrastructure for individual farming are also very difficult, especially because much of the infrastructure

form complicated compensation arrangements that would have been difficult to negotiate. Given the relatively short growing season in most of the Soviet Union, these problems would be even more severe. This conjecture is controversial, and Olmstead (1975) has pointed out that in the United States in the mid-nineteenth century in the newly settled areas (but not in the long settled areas), the sharing of reaping equipment was common. Problems of risk-sharing were solved by moving the reaper around so that in poor weather, all of the co-owners suffered roughly the same percentage of loss. This solution to the problem might not hold for equipment where considerable economies of scale could be gained by using it fully on one farm at a time.

[4] Wierzbicki (1968) has some interesting examples of technological regression following the breakup of Polish collective farms, where the farmers began to use hand methods because machinery was not available. Production increased and, as one farmer noted to the author, "If we had worked as hard on the collective farm as we do now, we would have been millionaires." In China, farm machinery sales declined after the reforms, and sales of small tractors did not recover until 1983–84 (Wong forthcoming). Some foreign observers of the Chinese countryside reported a decline in farm mechanization during the 1980s, but these reports must be accepted cautiously.

[5] Goodman, Hughes, and Schroeder (1987) point out that in the USSR, both the eleventh Five-Year Plan (1981–85) and the 1982 Food Program stressed the importance of increasing production of small-scale agricultural equipment. The major emphasis still lay, however, on the production of large-scale equipment. Timofeev (1985 p. 80) notes that even such farm tools as shovels and rakes are poorly designed and too heavy for easy use by the children and older people who generally work the personal plots.

on the socialist farms was constructed for large-scale production. Barns were built for large herds of dairy cattle (in East Germany, for instance, barns housing more than two thousand cows are common), the material handling equipment was designed for massive amounts of supplies, and the silos hold a large volume of crops. Again, sharing or leasing arrangements can be made, but they take time and effort, and the intervening period can be disastrous for the newly established private farmers. Certain kinds of infrastructure, particularly a rural road network, would have to be improved, since each individual farmer has special transportation requirements.

Before turning to other institutional prerequisites for successful private farming, several aspects of the administrative context in the division of land, equipment, and capital deserve mention. Clearly in situations where the collectives are merely nominal, as in a number of Third World nations, decollectivization can be carried out without much difficulty since it merely formalizes what farm households were already doing, albeit surreptitiously. Decollectivization is also easier to carry out where the ownership unit on the farm is the team, rather than the farm itself,[6] and where the internal organization of labor on the farm is land-centered (a group of workers carry out all farm tasks on a given piece of land). In this case (exemplified by China), a small group can divide the land which all know well in a manner perceived as fair.[7] The opposite case is exemplified by the Soviet Union, where the ownership unit is the entire farm and where the internal organization is not land-centered, but rather structured around products and functions. Here the group is too large to make the apportionment decisions, the individual farm members are not well acquainted with specific pieces of land, and the farm manager must make the key decisions about the division of land. This state of affairs increases both the possibility that decollectivization measures promulgated from the top can be resisted by the local cadre and also the likeli-

[6] By the term *ownership unit*, I mean the group that has effective control over the land, equipment, and tools. In China, the farm manager could not transfer equipment from one team to another; in the Soviet Union, it could.

[7] This does not mean that division of the land was without problems in China, because the teams still had twenty to forty households. In Laos and Vietnam, the apparent ownership unit was also the team, while in Nicaragua it was the small farm (a subunit of a larger state farm, which had about the same number of workers as a Chinese team). In all these countries there was generally a land-centered labor organization that eased the processes of decollectivization occurring later.

The division of land among farm members is often constrained by certain guidelines to equality of division that are set and enforced by the central government. Otherwise, the process might be stymied by conflict between those households who brought (or whose forefathers brought) land into the collective and others who brought none.

hood of serious inequities, either inadvertent or deliberate. Both possibilities also raise the risk to individual farmers.

MAKING CREDIT AVAILABLE

Other institutional measures on the input side must also be taken into account. The creation of credit facilities and financial instruments allowing individual farmers to buy, sell, or rent farm assets are of particular importance. Without these financial institutions and the availability of credit, risk faced by farmers increases, especially where orderly bankruptcy procedures have not been established. The Soviet Union did not take many of these steps (Kramer 1989) and many that were taken were implemented in a purely formal manner, for instance, creating an agricultural bank without many local branches. In 1979 the Chinese government resuscitated the former Agricultural Bank, an institution supplying credit at a local level, and encouraged rural credit cooperatives. Although little is known of the activities of these institutions, they did supply some credit to farmers, although their major credit targets seemed to be rural industry. Viet Nam attempted to encourage credit cooperatives, but by 1990 they had run into considerable difficulties.

Although these experiences show the difficulties of resuscitating the supply of credit to farming households, two possibilities are open in the future. In some countries such as Viet Nam, the administrative part of the former collective farms that took over the role of a service cooperative to the household farms could also begin to serve as credit unions. Or private givers of credit, particularly those connected with crop purchasing, could again be allowed to operate.

SUPPLYING CONSUMER GOODS

The ready availability of consumer goods is an important incentive for individual farming. In the Soviet Union, instances have been reported in the press where hard-working, high productivity contract groups have dissolved because the local stores had nothing on which the members could spend their money and, without available goods, they preferred more leisure (Laird and Laird 1988; Kramer 1989; Vorob'ev 1989). As mentioned in chapter 8, Madagascar, Mozambique, and other Third World Marxist regimes have experienced declines in marketed agricultural output because of the unavailability of consumer goods in the rural sector.

Of course, in a rural sector with a low population density, it is difficult to maintain a varied consumer goods market that is easily reachable by a sizable number of people. By way of contrast, the Chinese government has encouraged the rise of rural traders and retail outlets. Moreover, the older marketing centers were never completely suppressed and, with a high population density, it is easier to resuscitate a varied consumer goods market accessible to a large number of rural workers. The development of a retail network servicing the rural population is not conceptually difficult, especially where the population density is high or where these markets exist in embryo, But it is a task requiring both time and commercial talents. The latter is in rare supply in a long-term bureaucratized economy, where the population has negative attitudes toward commerce and trade, or where a monetary overhang results in the channeling of consumer goods primarily to the urban areas where higher gains by diversion of goods to the black market can be made.

ESTABLISHING CONDITIONS FOR THE PROFITABLE SALE OF FARM OUTPUTS

Profitability is not only a function of the "official" prices of agricultural produce, whether determined by the market or by the central government, but also of the structure of agricultural procurement. Unless the government either breaks up the monopsonistic marketing boards purchasing farm output or raises the official prices paid to the farmers, the farmers may have no incentive to grow crops for the market. For instance, in the summer of 1988, the government of São Tomé attempted to assign some of its state farmlands to individual farmers. Since the state farms processed the cocoa produced by these farmers and paid very low prices, the incentive structure was not favorable for the aims of the reform, and the decollectivization failed.

Problems of Risk Facing the Individual Farmers

The decollectivization reforms must be carried out in a manner so that the return/risk facing individual farmers is sufficient to induce farmers to participate in individual agriculture. The risk problem affects in many different ways the willingness of collective farmers to take up household farming.

The first step toward decollectivization is usually the development of a contract system for agricultural outputs and inputs, but many farmers are reluctant to accept such contracts. For instance, a 1987 poll of Soviet farm specialists reported by Vorob'ev (1989) indicated that only 10 percent would wish unconditionally to farm under an individual contract system. A later poll of collective farm managers from the same source revealed that only 30 percent would be willing to take up such contracts. These polls reported considerable resistance to the proposed systems of private agriculture, with many voicing the fear that, after expending considerable energy and resources on their new farm, "in one beautiful moment government policies could turn 180 degrees and the [individual] farmer could lose everything."[8]

It is difficult, however, to interpret these polls. One Soviet poll in early 1990 (*Izvestiya* 1 March 1990, morning edition) showed roughly 40 percent of the rural population interested in taking up private farming, but only 10 to 14 percent actually ready to do so, in part because of the lack of laws providing legal protection for such activities. Another poll taken around the same time showed the same 40 percent interest, but suggested that a larger fraction was also ready to start (*Voprosi ekonomiki* 5 1990, p. 75). Aside from problems about representativeness of the sample and the manner in which the questions were posed, additional difficulties arise. One knotty problem lies in the importance of the influence of immediate political factors, a phenomenon reflected in a poll of Moscow residents in May 1990 revealing that 60 percent thought it "possible" or "quite likely" that in the next few years the government would nationalize most private businesses (Shiller and others 1990). By the fall of 1990 even Gorbachev (1990) was complaining that economic contracts were becoming difficult to enforce and was worried that property rights were neither "strong" nor stable.

Even some years after the effective decollectivization in China, people were concerned about policy reversals. According to Bernstein (forthcoming), a 1987 survey of 100 households showed that 80 percent still worried about whether "the party's policy that enables people to become rich will change," and rumors periodically swept the countryside that recollectivization was about to occur. The evidence about such uncertainty is mixed, however, and much depended on local circumstances. For instance, a much larger 1988 survey covering four counties by Feder and others (1990) showed that only 17 to 24 percent of the farmers in three of the counties believed that they would lose the contract on their land before the expiration date of their lease. In the fourth county, however, 75 percent of the farmers had such a belief because at that time there had been several well-publicized incidents of forced consolidation of small farms. More important, perhaps, in three of these counties between 76 and 86 percent believed that they had a low likelihood of being reassigned the same farms after their lease contract had expired; that is, they were pessimistic in the long run.[9] In a more informal study at about the

---

[8] The situation also existed in China in the early years of the reform. Nee (1989) cites one farmer saying: "My family has made considerable investment on contracted land. . . . But we always fear that some day the policy will be changed, and the land will be taken away from us, and our efforts will be wasted." Prosterman and Hanstad (1990) present survey data revealing the same fears.

[9] In a regression analysis, Feder and his associates explore, but do not find, a statistically significant relationship between feelings of short-term and long-term insecurity of the in-

same time that was based on interviews with eighty-one farm families, Prosterman and Hanstad (1990) argue that farmers were not undertaking the investments needed to increase production because of general uncertainties of tenure. The current leases lacked credibility because the collective still owned the land and had the power to take it back or violate the contractual conditions without much judicial recourse by the farmers. Productive investment by individual farmers was also not encouraged in the late 1980s because some level of government nullified lease contracts in some areas under the guise of enlarging operational size to exploit returns to scale (Lin and others 1991). In 1990 another unpropitious omen occurred when the government eliminated the responsibility system on the state farm and returned to traditional (Marxist) management practices, even though such state farms produced only a small share of total agricultural output.

It should be clear that the risks facing the newly private farmers in this transition period are considerably greater than the risks they had as collective farmers or would have after the market system has operated for some years. Farm incomes are more uncertain because markets operate more erratically. In dealing with the new farm markets during the transition period, the farmers are facing a situation in which they have few historical experiences on which to analyze the situation in order to make decisions. Because of lack of common expectations of the various participants in agricultural and food processing sectors, prices may also be more variable than in non-Marxist nations where individual agricultural markets have existed for many years.

Moreover, every inconsistency of government policy during this transition period, every conflicting statement by different government leaders about the future of agriculture, and every broken promise to the farmers by the government increases the risks farmers face in investing their resources in any individual farming arrangement. In addition, any general political or economic difficulties facing the government that raise the possibility it could be replaced—for instance, ethnic unrest, inflation, shortages, or political dissention—would aggravate such fears.

On a deeper level, the problem of confidence can be solved only by the creation of "strong" property rights, that is, rights that can be readily enforced against others and that cannot be suddenly taken away by the

---

dividual farmers and the capital stock of their farms. This counterintuitive result could arise, however, from two aspects of their specification of the regression: (1) their choice of the capital stock, rather than investment, as the dependent variable; and (2) their use of the short- and long-term uncertainty variables separately, rather than in some type of joint index. Since they also do not present a correlation matrix, it is impossible to know whether other types of multicolinearity between the independent variables may be influencing the results.

government (the concept of "strong" and "weak" property is developed by Karl Wittfogel 1957).

Weak property rights can arise from two opposite circumstances. In some countries such as Nicaragua during 1990, the government had too little power to enforce property claims. Thus owners of land expropriated by the Sandinista government and returned by the Chamorro government, as well as some large private landowners who had not had their land expropriated by the Sandinistas, suddenly found their lands occupied, either by ex-resistance fighters or by members of the Sandinista-dominated agricultural labor union. Since the security forces were still headed by Sandinistas, these private owners could not get the land occupiers removed through legal procedures. Given the precarious fiscal situation, the government also did not have the funds to compensate them.

Weak property rights have also arisen in other countries in which the government has too much power, so that individuals' rights are not enforced through an independent judiciary. In past centuries neither China nor the Soviet Union nor a number of other Marxist regimes had a legal system supporting strong property. Rather, property rights were arbitrarily determined by the current policies of the government or ruler. Even though Marxist governments nationalized property, the managers of this property had weak property rights since they were subject to orders emanating from above that affected these rights in arbitrary ways. For the Soviet Union, for instance, Nove (1967) emphasizes that the constant raising of goals ("upward pressure") of agricultural cadre led to the "repeated dishonoring of pledges about the size of the delivery quota, or promises to return 'borrowed grain' or the removal even of seed grain . . . and grain for livestock." This administrative style, of course, would create considerable risks for any farm household with a lease contract for a piece of land because some government agency might use such excuses as "state interests" (or "overriding farm interest") to annul a particular clause in the contract, intervene in the operations of the contract unit, or raise the rent.

The seriousness of the problem depends in part on local conditions. In the late 1980s, for instance, it was much more formidable in the Soviet Union, where the collective farm chairman made the decisions about the terms of the leases to the households, than in China, where local governmental officials whose careers were no longer tied to increases of agricultural production played an important role in these matters. Other factors more directly related to the legal system also play an important role. For instance, the Soviet Union and East Germany downgraded the legal profession considerably more than in Czechoslovakia and Hungary, so that by the late 1980s there were relatively few practicing lawyers; this increased the problems of creating a functioning legal system.[10]

The creation of strong and stable property rights also requires the system of justice and of government laws to have credibility. For instance, in 1983 the Polish government tried to strengthen property rights by introducing into the constitution a paragraph proclaiming and guaranteeing the permanency of individual landholding. As Kolankiewicz and Lewis (1988, p. 34) point out, however, it was "individual," rather than "private" landownership that was mentioned—individual property rights include the right to land by collective farmers—so that the uses to which such land could be put were still limited and credibility was not achieved. Of course, the strengthening of property rights becomes more credible if a strong non-Marxist party takes over leadership of the government and does not burden the property laws with such escape valves.

It is sometimes argued that without a cadastral survey after decollectivization has taken place, the property rights of the farmer for a particular piece of land would be too uncertain to induce the farmer to invest in the land. These surveys are difficult and often are accompanied by considerable violence. China, however, appears to have decollectivized without such a survey. Apparently the households in the team had a strong understanding about which land "belonged" to which household. This experience of decollectivization without a cadastral survey has relevance to other Third World Marxist regimes.

A different kind of risk problem arises from the form of contract signed by the farmer in order to lease land. In most Marxist regimes, contracts usually have specified fixed, rather than share rents, which increases the risk for the farmer. The most notable exception to the generalization about fixed rents was Hungary in the 1960s, which used share contracts on a large scale. Share elements were also important in several of the many transitional contracts in China during the period 1979–83. In some forms of lease contracts in the Soviet Union there is also a share element (Brooks 1990a), although this type of contract has not been widely adopted. Several countries also experimented with contracts combining fixed and share elements, as the Romanian or Soviet compensation systems reviewed in chapter 6.

In the decollectivization process share rents mean that the government or the collective farm signing the lease assumes some of their risks of late

[10] In some East European nations, there is a limited knowledge about creating a system of strong and enforceable property rights. A Bulgarian professor of law and economics whom I interviewed expressed amazement at my statement that a market economy would have a greater demand for legal services than a planned economy, because contracts are more detailed and must be adjudicated more quickly. By adopting most aspects of the West German land law, East Germany could draw upon West German expertise to overcome the difficulties in setting up a legal structure to enforce strong property.

inputs, climatic conditions, and timely collection of outputs. Marx's belief that share rents represent a less advanced form of rental agreement plus the unwillingness of collective farm managers and the cadre of state supply and purchasing organizations to bear the responsibility of their errors appears to have guided policy in most Marxist regimes toward fixed rents.

Decollectivization can include not only a division of farm assets but also of farm liabilities, which also influences the risks that farmers bear. If the collective farms are deeply in debt, many individuals may be unwilling to engage in individual farming while burdened with their share of this farm debt and the government may have to write off this debt to provide sufficient incentives to make the system work. In recent decades in the Soviet Union and a number of East European nations in the 1980s, collective and state farm indebtedness soared, especially after collective farms began paying minimum wages. In the Soviet Union, for instance, between 1970 and 1980, short- and long-term farm indebtedness increased five times, and, between 1980 and 1984 such debt more than doubled, even while the government began to write off much of this debt (Laird and Laird 1988; Medvedev 1987, p. 349). To place the magnitudes in perspective, this farm indebtedness was roughly equal to the total annual agricultural output.[11] In desperation the Soviets announced in 1990 that all long-term debts (60 billion rubles) and some short term debts (23 billion rubles) would be forgiven (Collender and Cook 1990). In Bulgaria and Romania in 1990, all farm debts were written off, and in March 1990, a partial debt write-off occurred in East Germany. In contrast, the Czechoslovaks and the Hungarians see the debt write-off process as initiating a dangerous precedent and have not followed suit. In the Marxist Third World, the budget constraint for collective farms (but not state farms) was much harder, primarily because of the greater fragility of the fiscal system. As a result, these farm debts were less important and, moreover, in some of these countries, such as Nicaragua, inflation has also almost wiped out most debts that were incurred. Furthermore, in China during the 1980s, much of the small amount of collective farm debt was written off when the land was transferred to individual households.

Three more personal types of risk must also be mentioned. In some

---

[11] To encourage household leasing, the Soviet Union in December 1989 offered farms contracting out a portion of their assets to households the opportunity to write off their debts in the same proportion (Brooks 1990c).

The partial write-off of East German farm debts that is mentioned in the next sentence was complicated. The law stated that all farm debts arising from "uneconomic tasks assigned to the farm by the central authorities" would be canceled. Of course, every farm will try to make this claim and enforcement will be difficult. A second kind of write-off occurred with the currency union, when all debts over a specified amount were written down 50 percent.

Central and East European nations, a residual memory of the price risks and economic hardships in market agriculture during the 1930s, particularly among those with little land, remains. In the early 1990s these market risks were also compounded because few of the Marxist regimes had an adequate social safety net in the rural areas. Furthermore, on some of the smaller collective farms in Third World Marxist regimes, certain pieces of land were too small to divide among several owners and were suitable for only one type of crop. In this case, belonging to a cooperative allowed such a farmer to share production risks, an argument I encountered in talking with farmers on a cooperative in Nicaragua. Finally, in a number of the economically more advanced Marxist regimes, collective farmers belong to the social insurance system. If leasehold farming implies the loss of social security, then many older farmers may be unwilling to accept the risks of providing for their more advanced years through farming. In countries including China, where a certain type of social insurance was offered by the commune or collective farm, decollectivization resulted in a reduction in the scope of these social benefits.

Consistency Problems Arising from Government Actions

In carrying out a decollectivization program, the government must take into account not only the problems of supplying the nation with sufficient food in the short run and of obtaining agricultural products for export, but also of integrating such a program into its macroeconomic policies.

Suppose, for a moment, that the government wishes to decollectivize agriculture only after certain reforms have been carried out in other sectors. If the microeconomic disequilibria that exist in most Marxist regimes, whereby a basic minimum of food is sold inexpensively in state stores while the remainder is sold at much higher prices on farmers' markets, is continued, then any shortfalls in the production plans of urban industries leading to suppressed inflation is usually reflected in a rising gap between official and farmers' market prices. As the gap rises, farmers have an increasingly greater incentive to withdraw their labor from collective or state farm work and to work on their individual plots instead to produce goods for the farmers' market. This dynamic was important in a number of Marxist regimes such as Viet Nam (Fforde 1989, chap. 10) and can be countered effectively only by force and coercion by collective farm authorities, which discourages private initiative. This process, of course, can also lead to an informal decollectivization if the government is unwilling to take these measures, as the farmers focus increasingly more energy on their individual plots. Nevertheless, this approach toward decollectivization leaves the agricultural sector as a whole enfeebled because the suppressed inflation and production difficulties in the urban areas make it more difficult for farmers to obtain either consumer goods or intermediate goods for agricultural production.

If the government attempts to decollectivize and yet, at the same time, continues to subsidize producers so that some foodstuffs can be sold at low prices in the city, then producer prices paid to the farmers must be higher than free-market prices. Otherwise, the government will find it troublesome to obtain agricultural products from the farmer. Given the fiscal crisis facing most formerly centrally planned economies in moving to a market economy, such extra-high agricultural subsidies could lead to higher budget deficits, increased inflation, and a greater gap between official food prices and prices on the farmers' market.

Generally decollectivization will lead to higher food prices for the consumer unless the government is willing to use its precious foreign exchange to import foodstuffs in order to moderate these price increases. This means that decollectivization must be accompanied by a series of measures in the urban sector to modify some of the worst social impacts of these higher prices. Moreover, steps must be taken to prevent the supplies of inputs from exercising their monopolistic powers to squeeze the farmers, which under usual conditions would lead to even higher food prices.

SOCIAL FACTORS

Sociological evidence about problems of decollectivization must be used in a delicate fashion, because explanations resting on social factors such as norms and values often have no verifiable meaning. It is said that economists explain why individuals make certain choices, while sociologists explain why society leaves individuals with no choices to make. The methodological pitfalls should be readily apparent.

Peasant Entrepreneurship

A common explanation of the success of the Chinese agricultural reforms and the failure of the Soviet changes is that Chinese farmers are more entrepreneurial than Soviet farmers. The Chinese have been fiercely individualistic for millennia, cooperating only with fellow clan members or in projects such as irrigation in which individual benefits were manifest. In contrast, since the feudalization of Russia in the sixteenth century, the Russian village has had strong communal elements. These elements were reinforced after the emancipation of the serfs in the 1860s by the designation of the rural community, not the individual peasant, as the primary subject of Tsarist law. Although the shoots of individualistic farming began to sprout in the early part of the twentieth century, they were crushed by collectivization.

Although evocative, this conjecture is difficult to demonstrate with convincing evidence, especially for countries as large and heterogeneous as China and the Soviet Union.[12] Although such macrosociological factors may well be valid, they are also difficult to apply to the other thirty-one Marxist regimes, except superficially. It seems more useful to focus attention on the specific social impact of the system of collectivized farming.

Farmers' markets were widespread in certain East European nations with centrally planned agricultural sectors such as Bulgaria, Hungary, and the Soviet Union, as well as in most Third World Marxist regimes. It can be argued that such legal and semilegal activities provided good entrepreneurial training for farmers. Of course, the management and investment decisions were small-scale, and, according to Hedlund (1989) the required skills were often geared to semilegal manipulation of state bureaucracies. Full-scale, commercial farming, according to his approach, requires a different mentality. Szelenyi (1988) provides some empirical evidence on this matter for Hungary, pointing out that the emerging socialist entrepreneurs in the countryside represented only a small sub-set of the occasional sellers of produce on farmers markets, and that certain aspects of their social background provided a better explanation of their entrepreneurial activities.

Time Factor

According to the conventional wisdom, a system of collectivized agriculture becomes increasingly irreversible with the passage of time as farmers forget how to function in a full-scale market economy. The hyperindustrialization of agriculture gradually transforms active peasants and farmers into passive proletarians, that is, rural workers who have little love of the land, who lack initiative and a sense of individual responsibility, and who do not want to work more than a standard eight-hour day.

This kind of argument certainly has merit and provides insight into the different experiences of agricultural reform in China and the Soviet Union in the 1980s. In China, the system of collectivized farming existed only for roughly twenty-five years before the 1979 reforms began; according to this explanation, the older generation still remembered the former system and was imbued with the attitudes necessary for success. In the Soviet Union, collectivized farming lasted more than fifty years before

---

[12] An interesting attempt is made by Goldman and Goldman, 1988.

Gorbachev began his reforms, hence few farm workers remembered or embodied the old attitudes and ways.

But this approach can also be overdone. For instance, a well-known Soviet writer interested in village life, Fyodor Abramov has observed (*Pravda* 17 November 1979, cited by Nove 1988, p. 13):

> When was it known that able-bodied peasants go away [to market] at the time of the harvest rush? . . . The old pride in a well-ploughed field, in a well-sown crop, in well-looked-after livestock is vanishing. Love for the land, for work, even self-respect is disappearing. Is all this not the curse of absenteeism, lateness, drunkenness?

More directly related to concerns about decollectivization, Tatiana Zaslavskaya, a leading sociologist has noted (Hedlund, 1990):

> I do not know . . . of any people who are interested in this [breaking up of the collective farm]. I have been to. many kolkhozy and talked to many people and those who would give me that chance, who dream of working individually, they just do not exist.

I find these easy generalizations difficult to take at face value, in part because the questions framing the investigation are unclear and, as a result, the conclusions are ambiguous. More specifically, the alleged peasant laziness may simply reflect a lack of proper incentives in the current system. Thus the apparent lack of interest in individual farming may reflect merely a rational evaluation of its costs and benefits under present conditions.

Rural sloth might also be a phenomenon only in the USSR, while the situation could be quite different in other Marxist regimes. For instance, in Bulgaria, Czechoslovakia, East Germany, and Hungary during the spring of 1990, I was struck by the amount of entrepreneurial activity underway by young managers of the farms I visited. For instance, to overcome underemployment in its repair facilities, one East German collective farm I visited planned to buy used cars in Hamburg, to have its tractor repairers fix them up, and to sell them to East Germans. And one Czechoslovak collective farm was taking steps to raise chickens according to special ecologically sound rules in order to tap a special niche market in West Germany for "eco-chickens." I found that under the leadership of young managers who had never experienced a market system, farms in all four countries were reorganizing themselves and changing their methods of worker compensation in order to lower costs (Pryor 1990a). In those Third World nations where collective farms were more important than state farms, it also seems unlikely that such rural proletarianization occurred on a massive scale. In China, Viet Nam, or several other Third World nations for which I have found shards of evidence on the matter, there was no strong resistance to the reintroduction to household farming.

Recently a joint team of Soviet and American scholars attempted to investigate this question more systematically by carrying out a sample survey on attitudes toward free markets in the two countries (Shiller and others 1990). Preliminary results showed few important differences between the two countries with regard to their opinions about income inequality or the impact of price increases, their beliefs in the importance of providing material incentives for hard work, or even in their understanding of the workings of markets. The authors conclude that the problems of transition to a market economy in the Soviet Union were political and institutional in nature rather than the result of basic attitudes of the population. Although the sample consisted of residents of Moscow and New York, it does not seem likely to me that rural attitudes toward markets would have been much different.

Another alleged impact of time or custom is that the centralization of political and economic power has acted to discourage independent thinking of any kind, which is reinforced by certain types of bureaucratic behavior. One Soviet author, Yu. Chernichenko, comments: "Crude shouting and directives [from government officials to farm managers] engendered a reluctance to think. Reluctance to think engendered stereotyped methods. Stereotyped methods make the harvest the helpless victim of weather conditions, weeds, and pests. The official who deprives himself of the right to act according to circumstances deprives himself of the right to make demands upon others. There arises a vicious circle of irresponsibility."[13] This appears an artifact of the present system, rather than a long-term problem under a system of individual farming.

The proposition that the longer collectivized agriculture has lasted, the more difficult it is to decollectivize does makes a good deal of sense. But it should not be interpreted in the absolutist sense revealed in the quotations I have cited. This approach also suggests that in the Third World, where the state farms represented simply a nationalization of the former capitalist plantations, decollectivization in the form of breaking up the farm should also be difficult in those countries where the farms had hired workers for several generations (for example, Cuba and Guyana) and considerably easier where the capitalist plantations originated relatively recently (for example, Nicaragua). In chapter 4 some evidence supporting this proposition is presented, which concerns the contrasting views toward breakup and ownership of the state farms (former capitalist plantations) by state farm workers in these three countries.

[13] Cited by Nove (1967), from *Novyi mir* 11 (1965): 182.

Composition of the Rural Labor Force

Much more convincing sociological evidence can be found in the composition of the rural labor force. If the rural population is aged, decollectivization is unlikely to succeed because few farmers would be willing or able to invest the time and energy to make the system work. This is because they could not reap the returns of such investment in the relatively short remaining span of life.

During the 1960s and 1970s, the Soviet rural population was rapidly aging and was composed predominantly of women, a consequence of the flight to the urban areas of many of the young people in the rural areas and the demographic impact of World War II (Goodman, Hughes, and Schroeder, 1987).[14] As I document in chapter 8, such migration was also found in other East European nations and was especially serious in Bulgaria and Yugoslavia.

In China there is little evidence of the aging of the farm sector, primarily because political authorities were able to enforce regulations preventing massive migrations to the cities. As a result, most of the youth and also most of the entrepreneurially minded men and women remained in the rural areas, but not necessarily as farmers. They were open to opportunities to increase production of their traditional crops, to plant new crops, and to engage in new economic activities on the side in order to improve their income.

The aging of the rural population was also not a serious problem in most other Third World Marxist regimes for still another reason. Because the relative share of the population in the rural areas was larger, the possibilities of absorption of any given rural age cohort into the cities was smaller than in the more industrialized nations.

If emigration to the cities was an important causal factor in the aging of the rural population, what, in turn, were its causes? For East Europe and the Soviet Union the most common explanation can be found in the considerable income and housing differentials between urban and rural areas (Nechemias 1990). Indeed, the narrowing of these differentials reduced migration in Czechoslovakia, Hungary, and East Germany. In

---

[14] Unfortunately, the Soviet government has not released census data to provide detailed evidence on this point. According to data from Danilov (1988, p. 42) and USSR, Goskomstat (1988, pp. 50–51), the average age of adults (those twenty or over) in the rural sector as a whole (including nonagricultural jobs) increased from 40.6 in 1926 to 43.3 in 1959 to 47.4 in 1987. In 1987 women constituted 56 percent of the rural population. The aging of the farm population occurring in other East European nations has also received comment and Salzmann (1983) and Argyres (1988) have some interesting comments about the implications of this process for Czechoslovakia and Romania respectively. The rural aging in Hungary is also a topic of comment and concern.

some of these Marxist regimes where the urban bias or the bias against individual farming by planners was most evident, as in Yugoslavia, this migration occurred up to the end of the 1980s because farm youth saw no future for private farming (Horvat 1976, pp. 78–79).[15]

In some Marxist regimes where collective farmers received social benefits from the state and had incomes roughly equal to urban workers, still other reasons must be adduced to explain the emigration of rural young people, despite attempts to stem the population movement, often ineffectual unless the government was willing to use considerable coercion. Peter Bell (1984), an anthropologist who carried out field work in Hungary, has argued that in the individual farming system, peasants were aware of differences in status between them and urban workers, but they had their independence, their farms, and their much more varied and interesting work. After collectivization the urban-rural status differences remained, but the peasants lost both their independence and farms, and their work became more specialized and monotonous. Moreover, as farm consolidation proceeded, status differences within the farm widened between farm officials and workers (Hollos and Maday 1983, p. 18; Szelenyi 1988). The rural population increasingly lost control over its destiny and became employees, but with lower prestige and more arduous work, than urban blue-collar workers.

Free education provided by the state was the avenue off the farm and into city jobs for young people, especially the more capable children of the former rural middle class that provided the major source of rural entrepreneurs (Szelenyi 1988). According to a controversial thesis of Gábor Havas (interview 1990), such "counter-selection" left behind a farm population primarily made up of former landless workers and their children, who have only specialized knowledge of particular aspects of farming and who, as a result, have little desire or ability to become independent farmers. Similar mechanism seemed to operate in some other socialist countries, as in Czechoslovakia (Salzmann and Scheufler 1974). For the Soviet Union, shards of evidence point to the same phenomenon; for instance, the difficulty in keeping specialists on the farm suggests that many of the most entrepreneurial farmers emigrated to the cities.[16]

[15] Until the late 1980s, private farmers found it difficult to obtain credit. In previous decades they were not able to obtain modern equipment, they could farm only a maximum of 10 hectares, and they received lower prices from monopsonistic crop purchasers than did collective farms.

[16] Bill Keller (1990) quotes a Soviet collective farm chairman as saying: "Here we have lost the tradition [of farming]. It's gotten so bad that in school they warn children: 'If you don't study hard, you will stay on the collective farm to work.' "

In Poland, the aging of the private farm population was probably due to the bleak future of the sector that was attributable to the government's discriminatory policies against it. In the early 1980s, however, jobs in the cities became more difficult to obtain and much of the

It is possible that a government could take measures to increase rural incomes sufficiently over urban incomes so as to encourage a migration back to the rural sector. Special incentives could be targeted to the entrepreneurially-minded former peasants to take over the newly created individual farms or, if they had been commuting to the city, to take up farming activities again.[17] Several problems would, however, occur.

This migration to the rural area would represent a moving down the social scale, so that the income differential might have to be very high to attract back ex-farmers in sufficient number. It is certainly easier to stem this rural out-migration, rather than to reverse it. Moreover, the higher urban food prices or the higher urban taxes to finance the program of reversing rural migration might be strongly resisted for social reasons. More specifically, since rural workers generally have a lower social status than industrial workers, the latter might find it politically unpalatable for the rural workers to receive considerably higher incomes. Of course, economists are not worried about such "compensating differentials," but in real life the phenomenon is often difficult for those concerned to accept.

Aside from the age structure of the rural population, one other crucially important social factor deserves consideration, namely the distribution of skills necessary for private farming. Some rural sociologists, Ivan Szelenyi (1988) among them, have argued that the industrialization of farm work on collective and state farms has made the average farm worker incapable of running an independent farm. That is, on these farms—especially state farms—a given individual may carry out only a few tasks so that the rural labor force has become, in an important sense, deskilled.

I tried out this argument on a number of collective farm managers in interviews in East Europe and found both heated agreement and disagreement with it. In any case, the problem appears much less severe in the relatively backward agricultural sectors of Third World Marxist regimes, or at least in their collective farms that have a much lower capital/labor ratio. It also appears more important in the state farms and in the more productive agricultural sub-sectors of the Marxist regimes in Europe, where running a modern farm takes a considerable number of different skills.[18]

---

discrimination against the private sector was reduced; at the same time, migration from the farm appeared to have been markedly reduced.

[17] Political means, for instance, discrimination in schools and housing, can also be used either to keep people in the farming sector or to encourage them to leave the urban areas where they have moved.

[18] The account of a year in the life of an American farmer by Rhodes (1989) provides a superb account of the number of different skills that a given farmer must master. Of course,

Finally, I must emphasize that although most Marxist regimes provide vocational farm education for the rural youth, this education has not provided the skills necessary for running an independent farm. As far as can be determined, no Marxist regime has any training programs like those for farm youth in the United States run by the 4-H or the Future Farmers of America clubs, which award money and prestige to youngsters for successful efforts in stockraising and other skills necessary for independent farming.[19]

Social Inertia

Social inertia occurs in all systems that have been in operation for some time. It is illustrated in the remark of a Byelorussian peasant, who is quoted as saying: "They drove us into collectivization. Let them drive us into perestroika." (Gellner 1990, p. 282). This social inertia is, to a considerable extent, tied to the calculation of individual returns and risks involved in changing the system.

In recent years anthropologists and sociologists have carried out village studies of collective farms, particularly in Hungary but also in China, Czechoslovakia, Laos, Nicaragua, Romania, the Soviet Union and Viet Nam.[20] Some of these studies suggest that the members of the collective farms exhibit considerable social inertia, as illustrated in claims that not even the older members of the Hungarian collective farms want to return to traditional farming (Vasary 1987, p. 129). According to this approach, decollectivization would disturb a functioning system of production to the extent that many would prefer a continuation of the old system, rather than undertake a total revision of farming practices that have become habitual.

Some public opinion data are available supporting this conjecture. For instance, during the Czechoslovak spring of 1968, about two-thirds of all farmers polled saw more advantages to collective than individual farming

---

in some countries the family farms are so autarkic that many of the skills acquired by the farmers would be unnecessary if they took greater advantage of the opportunities for specialization offered by the market.

[19] Of course, as Timofeev (1985) points out, rural youth in the Soviet Union carry out a good deal of farm work, but this is work for others, not themselves. He also reports (p. 112) an instance where preschool children were playing at stealing milk from the collective farm, which is a useful skill to learn for socialist, but not private, farming.

[20] Many of these have appeared in English. For Hungary recent studies include: Bell (1984), Hann (1980), a collection edited by Hollos and Maday (1983), Swain (1985), and Vasary (1987); for Czechoslovakia, Salzmann and Scheufler (1974); for the Soviet Union, Dragadze (1988) and Humphrey (1983); for Romania, Argyris (1988) and Verdery (1976, 1983); for China, Chan and others (1984), Huang (1989), and Mosher (1983); for Laos, Evans (1990); and for Vietnam, Houtart (1984).

(Piekalkiewicz 1972, p. 310) and roughly the same percentage believed that collectivization increased the cultural level and standard of living of the countryside.[21] In Hungary, one anthropologist provided evidence that a positive disposition toward the collective farm system was closely tied to the success of the collective to which the person belonged (Hollos 1983). The issue has become more current with recent legislation in most of the East European nations allowing farmers to take their land out of the collectives and to begin private farming. In 1990 public opinion pollsters began surveying the rural population about their intentions. In East Germany, fewer than 5 percent of current farmers intended to undertake such a step; in Czechoslovakia, fewer than 10 percent; in Bulgaria and Hungary, which have a less mechanized farming system, fewer than 30 percent.[22] In Bulgaria, where the communist party opposed a full-scale decollectivization, they received a higher percentage of votes than in the urban areas (Anon. 1990), and in the Soviet Union, the March 1991 referendum gave Gorbachev, who was in a conservative phase at that time, his largest majority. Of course, any poll or election results must be interpreted cautiously, because it is unclear exactly what the respondents were assuming about the future economic environment so that the support these give to the conjecture is limited.[23]

As noted, some of this social inertia can be traced to evaluations of the ratio of effort and risk versus economic return of the two systems of agriculture. In Slovakia, about three-quarters of the farmers polled agreed that the work of collective farmers was easier than that of individual farmers. In East Germany, more than half of the 453 farmers polled noted that collective farmers had more free time than individual farmers (McCardle and Boenau 1984) and, moreover, between 55 and 65 percent stressed that in comparison to capitalist farmers, they had no market worries, material or social insecurity, or anxieties over their own economic

---

[21] The sample includes 165 farmers in Slovakia. Piekalkiewicz (1972) also includes data on the answers of 886 nonfarmers in Slovakia to the same questions and, with the exception of a question about the rural areas subsidizing the urban areas, the two samples were in rough agreement.

[22] These results were cited to me in interviews with economists in the four countries. I was, unfortunately, unable to see the actual poll results.

It would be aesthetically pleasing if there were some symmetry between the processes of collectivization and decollectivization; for instance, the more coercion used in collectivization, the greater the degree of voluntary decollectivization. The public opinion data cited above suggest, however, that the degree of decollectivization might be roughly related to the capital intensiveness of agriculture.

[23] These comparisons are made with regard to the entire agricultural population. If, however, the denominator were the number of farm families with a household head between the ages of twenty and fifty-five who would be capable of taking over a family farm, then the relative number of applicants for such farms would appear more impressive, and the data would be more useful in predicting future developments.

existence. In Hungary, this sentiment was stated more bluntly in my individual conversations with several specialists who asserted that farmers on collective and state farms had too easy a life ever to want to return to individual farming.[24] Of course, if subsidies to collective or state farms were removed, these preferences might change.

Sociability

In talking with farmers on collective farms in Nicaragua, I received the impression that a number of them enjoyed working in a group and that they found household farming too isolating. In a Third World country where households are scattered and transportation is poor, this is an understandable concern. In certain cases, however, such sociability was forced insofar as a member could not leave the cooperative without forfeiting all claims on land of the cooperative. Decollectivization might be accelerated if laws were passed requiring each cooperative to give departing members their share of the land.

POLITICAL FACTORS

Political factors also add to the difficulties of decollectivization, especially for those nations where a Marxist party still retains power. In particular, the governments must recognize a serious crisis in agricultural production, readjust their "practical ideology" toward agriculture, exhibit the political will to enforce a decollectivization, overcome cadre resistance, and deal effectively with the economic problems of individual agriculture. In countries that had voted Marxist governments out of power, most of these factors were no longer important and their major difficulties were usually in the economic and sociological realm. It is, nevertheless, worthwhile to survey these political problems of decollectivization for Marxist regimes.

The Problem of Recognition

For decollectivization to occur, political leaders must recognize a serious long-term crisis in agricultural production. In China, as in other of the Third World Marxist regimes, the low level of economic development (and the high labor/land ratio) meant that the constraints on the growth of the entire economy arising from the agricultural sector were taken

[24] Regarding the problem of individual effort, Bill Keller (1990) cites a Soviet joke: "Which is better, individual sex or group sex? Group sex, of course, because it leaves you time to goof off."

much more seriously than in the Soviet Union. Some observers have argued that in the 1960s and 1970s, unfulfilled demand for agricultural products increased more than in the Soviet Union; Wädekin (1988) provides estimates of this phenomenon. In the Soviet Union, the per capita level of agricultural production was higher and, at least in terms of aggregate growth, per capita agricultural production was acceptable during the 1960s and 1970s, even if that growth was accompanied by very high investment costs. As a result, the recognition of a crisis was less generalized, and political leaders were less likely to take radical steps.

The extent to which an agricultural crisis is recognized has varied in the different Marxist regimes. In some of these nations such as Albania, Cuba, and North Korea, agricultural growth was quite respectable so that political leaders have not recognized a crisis, despite "secondary problems" such as shortages of particular foods or low quality foodstuffs or farms producing far below their potential. In Viet Nam, where agricultural growth had been relatively rapid, it is this recognition, combined with the realization that reforms in other sectors could not occur unless changes in the organization of the agricultural also occurred, that seemed to lead to decollectivization (Pryor 1991).

Political leaders must also recognize that the agricultural problems have arisen not from exogenous forces (weather or foreign machination), simple mismanagement by administrators and sloth of the workers, or imperfect plan indicators and misplaced incentives, but rather from the system of agriculture itself. Understanding of this last causal element, in turn, requires accepting several conditions: that the agricultural sector must have greater autonomy from the political sector, that agricultural institutions and policies need serious restructuring, and that a different environment for decision-making in agricultural production must be created. This is a long intellectual road to travel and it would be immeasurably aided by frank and public discussion of the problems, characteristics of debate that have been in short supply in many Marxist regimes.[25]

The Problem of Ideology

The ideals of socialism are noble and to many political leaders in the Marxist regimes, as I point out in chapter 2, agricultural collectivization is not only an end of socialism, but a means of achieving socialism as well.[26] A decollectivization program requires either a crisis of faith in the

[25] Judy Batt (1988) provides a fascinating account of this kind of intellectual evolution for the 1968 reforms in Czechoslovakia and Hungary. Although she focuses primarily on reforms in the industrial sector, her general conclusions are equally valid for agriculture.

[26] The strength of the idea that land cannot be sold and must be used only by those whom the government determines are the most capable farmers dies slowly. Bill Keller (1990)

entire socialist program or else a reordering of beliefs so that the institutional change is rationalized in terms of tactical manoeuver that will be reversed sometime in the future when the advantages of large-scale mechanized agriculture can be realized more easily, a belief still holding to the Marxist approach outlined in chapter 2. Indeed, the more advanced the economy, the sooner such recollectivization may occur. If this justification becomes public or if the party continues to stress certain ideological themes associated with collectivized agriculture (as in China, according to Bernstein, forthcoming), farmers will be reluctant to invest their time and resources in individual farming, and the decollectivization program will not achieve its goals. The ideology of the party also manifests itself in decollectivization programs based on land leases (e.g., China and Viet Nam), rather than individual ownership. In the USSR Gorbachev, for instance, has declared his unwillingness to see a system of general private ownership of agricultural land.

The Problem of Political Will

At several points I have mentioned measures that could be taken by a government to offset particular difficulties in decollectivization. Most of these are either economically costly, politically painful, or both, which raises some problems for the top political leadership.

Political will also implies the willingness to establish a court system with autonomy and to take other means to enforce property rights—measures that are lacking in a system of weak property (Wittfogel 1957). As emphasized, the relative strength of the rule of law over administrative orders from governmental organs at different levels is a crucial determinant of the risk of private farming.

If the top leadership is not fully unified so that its members are able to pay the high price of economic reform, follow a set of consistent policies leading toward decollectivization, and strengthen property, the risks facing any would-be individual farmer rise. If political leaders have other goals that conflict with decollectivization or if decollectivization is relatively low among their priorities, the risks to private farming also increase.

The Problem of Cadre Resistance

Decollectivization reduces the number of positions, the income, and the direct power of many party and state cadre in the agricultural sector. At

quotes a Soviet local party official contending, "From the point of view of morality and ethics, selling land is blasphemy. The land should not be treated as some prostitute who goes with the guy who pays the highest price."

the very top, Fidel Castro (Meso-Lago 1988, p. 86) summed up the problem at the most general level: "If [economic] mechanisms [in agriculture] were to solve everything, what would be then left for the Party to do? . . . These ideas involve a negation of the party." The resistance of local (and higher) state and party cadre to these measures can be expected; in order to enforce its political will, top-level political leaders face several options.

The government can, of course, crack heads and purge the recalcitrant local officials, but this raises the possibility that its entire authority in the rural sector may crumble. It can redefine criteria for the evaluation of the cadre so that its members are no longer judged by production in their district. It can also buy off cadre resistance by direct bribes or by placing its members in positions to enrich themselves in the decollectivized system, which happened in China (Oi 1986, 1989a, 1989b). Direct bribes occurred most spectacularly in Nicaragua at the "piñata Sandinista" during the period after the election before the government of Violeta Barrios de Chamorro took over: the Sandinista government gave titles of land, houses, stores, vehicles of various government agencies, and other assets to many of its loyal followers to the extent that the new government upon taking office found only a few million U.S. dollars in the Central Bank. Further discussion on the overcoming of cadre resistance in China, Hungary, the Soviet Union, and Guyana is presented in chapter 11.

The Problem of Recollectivization

Decollectivization is not necessarily the answer to all agricultural problems, and certain difficulties can arise that encourage more governmental intervention in the countryside. If such problems are important and cannot be resolved, even a recollectivization is conceivable. During the 1980s in China, for instance, decollectivization had some adverse economic effects: communal facilities such as irrigation began to be neglected, massive deforestation occurred (Ross 1987), agricultural productivity growth began to level off again, grain production did not significantly increase after the middle years of the decade (although other products did), the reintroduction of the market brought about a type of "hog cycle" (Wiens 1987), population growth in the countryside began to rise (White 1987), income differentiation proceeded to the point that many rural families allegedly had falling incomes and standards of living far below the socially acceptable norm, and rural violence began to rise again, at least up to the middle 1980s (Perry 1985). Although I believe that all of these problems can be resolved in a market environment, other problems may arise that are not so tractable. If collectivization is reversible, the same might be true of decollectivization.

REFLECTIONS ON DECOLLECTIVIZATION

Collectivization of agriculture has been the most radical institutional change in the economy undertaken by Marxist regimes. It has required considerable coercion and violence, great administrative efforts, and enormous personal dedication on the part of the political leaders, all in the name of a formal doctrine that did not offer much support for introducing such changes, particularly at low levels of economic development.

It is, however, not simple to reverse collectivization. It appears that it is easier where farming is not highly input-intensive or mechanized, where the agricultural labor force is not highly specialized, where the rural labor force is relatively young, where collectivization has not lasted a long time, where collective, rather than state farms, predominate, and where the government is strong enough to overcome a number of serious political problems, including cadre resistance.

Most of the economic difficulties arising from decollectivization—the creation of a reliable and accessible source of inputs, the provision for the profitable sale of outputs, the establishment of outlets for credit and consumer goods—fall into the category of network externalities and thus have parallels with the factors locking nations into inefficient technologies or standards, in particular costs external to the farm itself (pecuniary externalities), rather than classic production externalities. Most of the sociological difficulties are rather different and reflect the long-term consequences of self-reinforcing demographic and social-structural factors of the system of collectivized agriculture. Most of the political factors are the outcome of particular power configurations that differ considerably from nation to nation, so that few generalizations can be made.

In the long run collectivized agriculture faces a major problem: as more private farms become established and increase their production, agricultural prices may eventually fall below the average costs of the collectivized sector. The government can, of course, let such farms go bankrupt so that the most successful farms, either private or collective, can pick up the pieces. But over the last half-century few governments anywhere have shown such hard-headedness over this type of rural collapse and are quite willing to sacrifice all sorts of sacred oaths to the free market, GATT, and other doctrines and institutions to save the farmers. These political factors are, however, difficult to predict, in part because the fiscal health of the government budget is a key ingredient.

The impediments to decollectivization are less important in the Third World Marxist regimes and it seems likely that in most of these countries, the collective farms will be converted into individual farms, even though the state may still own the land in a technical sense. This proposition is also merely the reverse side of the approach toward collectivization of Nicolai Bukharin (of the Soviet Union) in the 1920s or Edvard Kardelj (of

Yugoslavia) in the early 1950s that successful collectivization can occur only when the labor force in agriculture is relatively small and production is relatively mechanized.

Two types of exceptions must be noted to these generalizations. In several countries such as Cuba and North Korea, a political leadership firmly committed to the maintenance of state and collective farms appears firmly entrenched and, moreover, growth of agriculture in these countries has been satisfactory, albeit at a high cost. Decollectivization does not seem likely unless some unexpectedly dramatic political changes occur. In other Third World nations, moreover, the breaking up of state farms will be difficult, especially where the state farms were formerly operated as private plantations for generations before they were nationalized. Given the administrative difficulties that many of these farms were experiencing in recent years and the increasing inability of the governments to subsidize their operations, it seems likely that in the 1990s most of these Third World Marxist regimes will follow the examples provided by Guyana, Madagascar and São Tomé and decollectivize by selling or leasing some of these money-losing state farms to private interests.

In Eastern Europe, after the political upheavals of 1989 and 1990, we might expect a partial decollectivization. For the bulk of the agricultural sector, however, marketization reforms or changes in the incentives facing farmers or conversion of the farms into joint stock companies appear considerably more likely than breaking them up. Indeed, even though communist parties have been dethroned in many of these countries, the calls for decollectivization were not sufficiently strong to receive attention in the Western press. Indeed, the only country in 1989 where reporters noted these demands was Mongolia ("Animals to the herdsmen"). As noted, the immediate response of the farmers to an increased opportunity to begin private farming was limited.

Underlying this study of decollectivization are several simple messages: Some major institutional changes may occur in the short run only with difficulty, if at all, even if the institutions to be changed are dysfunctional or highly inefficient. The costs of decollectivization are high, particularly in the short run. The system of collectivized agriculture introduced by Stalin in the Soviet Union in the late 1920s and implanted by Marxist parties in other nations is difficult to reverse where the system has been in existence for several decades and where the level of agricultural technology used on the farms has become relatively high. In considering the rise and fall of collectivized agriculture, I am sorely tempted to add a question mark after the word *fall*. This system of capital-intensive, estate farming with a large labor force may remain in many countries, albeit not so extensive as in the 1980s. Indeed, it may prove to be one of Stalin's lasting legacies.

Chapter 10

REFORMS OF AGRICULTURE: SECTORAL ISSUES

THIS CHAPTER focuses on three policy issues: a restructuring of property relations in agriculture, a marketization of foodstuffs, and the sequencing of these changes. Other types of agricultural policy changes, which are endemic in most Marxist regimes, receive attention only insofar as they are directly related to the reforms.

I examine the agricultural reforms from the top down, review the range of options facing would-be reformers, and draw upon the experience of a number of nations in order to provide perspective on the benefits and costs of particular choices. Because the discussion deals with problems on an issue-by-issue basis, the interrelations between particular parts of the agricultural reforms for a given country may not be clear. In Research Note F I present a brief survey of several quite different types of agricultural reforms, namely those of China, Guyana, Hungary, and the Soviet Union, so that for these four cases, the reforms can be viewed as a whole.

An important difference between economic reforms in general and agriculture in particular deserves emphasis. In a reform of the entire economy, an appropriate sequencing of reform measures is first macroeconomic stabilization, then marketization measures, and finally privatization (see, for instance, McKinnon forthcoming). Macroeconomic stabilization is the first essential step because otherwise prices would not rise in a one-step change but would spiral upwards without limit, which would make governmental interventions almost irresistible. Many have objected to marketizing before privatizing, arguing that it is impossible to have "capitalism without capitalists." But such property reforms take a long time to prepare and implement, so that it may be necessary to pass through a period of market socialism before the large industries can be sold off.

In agriculture, property reforms have somewhat different characteristics because three different elements of these reforms can be more easily separated and integrated with market reforms. One element is a reorganization of the productive units and a transformation of the state and collective farms to corporate and individual farms, often of a much different size than the former farms. This was, for instance, the type of reforms instituted by China during the early 1980s. A second element is a change in ownership and is independent of the first element. It can occur in one step or can be carried out by a gradual widening of the private sector. A third element is the "strengthening" of property relations, which makes the collective and private farms more autonomous decision-making units and reduces the authority of the governmental planning and administrative authorities. This latter element does not need to be accompanied by the first two elements and was underway by the end of 1990 in all East European nations except Albania.

The three elements of property reform can be carried out more quickly than in manufacturing. Because economies of scale are not significant in most cases, the production units can be quite small, and because the technical and commercial aspects of production are generally less complex in these smaller units, the managerial problems are not as severe.

Marketization has two major elements. The first is the creation of a competitive environment among the institutions selling agricultural inputs and purchasing agricultural outputs. This requires a restructuring of the industrial and commercial enterprises dealing with agriculture and, in some countries such as Hungary, began to occur in the 1970s and 1980s. The second element is the introduction of a price system for agricultural inputs and outputs that reflects the forces of supply and demand.

Economic reform is a process, not a single act, but the exact sequencing of marketization and property reforms appears at first glance to be less important in agriculture than in industry. For instance, the Hungarian reforms between 1968 and 1990 and the Chinese reforms after 1978 have shown that quite different sequences of property and marketization reforms can lead to substantial increases in production. A more careful examination of these problems is necessary, however, to determine if a minimum sequencing of property reform and marketization reform elements is necessary for success. For any type of agricultural reform to succeed, however, macroeconomic stabilization is crucial. This matter must be briefly discussed before turning to agricultural issues.

MACROECONOMIC POLICIES

My argument is very simple: For a successful agricultural reform, especially in those nations with important agricultural exports, macroeconomic stability should have the highest priority. If it does not, then agriculture usually is less able than most other sectors of the economy to obtain the resources necessary for its survival and to adapt to the new economic conditions; as a result, the agricultural reforms are imperiled.

The critical economic problem is inflation. During the transition from a centrally planned to a market economy, an important source of government revenues is lost when taxes on businesses are restructured in order

to encourage their investments and growth. At the same time rising unemployment during the transition places additional demands on government expenditures. In many countries in transition the government has
had to finance its expenditures by recourse of the printing press, either
directly or through the central bank, so that inflation has been inevitable.
The budget deficit leading to inflation feeds upon itself when taxes for
the previous year are paid in this year's depreciated currency units while
government expenditures rise apace with the inflation.

Urban interests are more easily able to mobilize political support of
large masses of people to prevent cuts in particular governmental programs affecting them. As a result, expenditures for such purposes as agricultural extension work or rural infrastructure are more likely to be cut
back or eliminated. For instance, during the deterioration of the economic situation in Guyana, the share of total government investment directed to agriculture fell from an average of 25 to 30 percent from 1955
through 1980 (Thomas 1984) to roughly 10 percent by the end of the
1980s (Guyana Government, annual). In many other Marxist regimes the
fall in agricultural investment, while not so dramatic, was also significant.

Although it might seem that the rural sector would profit from inflation—after all, everyone in the nation must eat, so foodstuffs should fetch
relatively high prices—a number of offsetting factors must be noted. If
the government officially sets prices for agricultural produce and has a
fixed exchange rate, these prices inevitably lag the inflation rate so that
real prices paid to farmers decline both for agricultural exports and for
those products purchased by a monopsonistic state purchasing agency.
This was again dramatically seen in Guyana, where the prices of foodstuffs sold on the free market outpaced inflation (Bank of Guyana 1990).
At the same time, for many years producer prices paid for agricultural
exports lagged inflation as the exchange rate became increasingly overvalued, so that overall real incomes of export farmers fell. A similar phenomena occurred in other countries as well.

Although the lagging exchange rate changes lead to inexpensive (in domestic currency) imported agricultural inputs such as fertilizers, pesticides, machinery, and spare parts, such imports are in greater competition with inexpensive imports demanded by other sectors. Since the
agricultural sector seldom is given the highest priority for scarce foreign
exchange, the volume of these imported agricultural inputs either falls or
is allocated to those rural groups with the greatest political influence,
namely the state farms. In this scramble for scarce imported agricultural
inputs, it should not be surprising that the private farmers usually are at
the end of the queue, either because they are unorganized or their interest groups are weak.

Although the overvalued exchange rate leads to cheap agricultural inputs, the low prices received for agricultural outputs have an even greater influence on production unless special export subsidies are granted. In periods where fiscal stringency is required to stop inflation, such subsidies are often reduced so that during the agricultural reform period, the agricultural sector bears an additional burden.

In the government's fight against inflation, credit controls are an important weapon. Given the longer production lags in agriculture than in most other sectors, these controls also hit the agricultural sector relatively harder than other sectors. Since credit scarcity also encourages private investments with very high yields and rapid payoffs, the share of agriculture in total investment usually declines at a time when the farms require additional investments for reorganization of production. Furthermore, in any situation where some agricultural prices are controlled, while others are not, the resulting price distortions also lead to inefficient investment allocations.

In many of the countries undergoing the transition to a market economy, macroeconomic equilibrium can be achieved only by raising taxes, cutting government expenditures, limiting credit, and raising real interest rates. These are difficult and politically painful tasks, particularly for governments in the Third World that do not have effective tax collection agencies.

PROPERTY REFORMS

The first element of property reforms, the reorganization of the productive units, and a transformation of the state and collective farms to corporate and individual farms, has received considerable attention in the previous chapter. In the discussion below I focus on the two other elements, namely change in the ownership of the land, and the strengthening of property rights in general so that the farms have greater decision-making autonomy. I analyze these problems primarily from the top down, that is, from the standpoint of the policy makers.

Land Ownership in General

If private farms are created, what is the appropriate size distribution and structure of tenancy? Although creation of a few large private farms hiring a large number of workers might solve the problem of managerial incentives, problems of structuring the proper incentives for workers still are not resolved. Although strong political arguments can be raised against creating a system of farm tenancies that might resolve incentive problems for those actually working the land, some important economic objections must be added. Sharecropping tenancies attenuate farmer incentives unless carefully structured, since the share given to the owner represents an equivalent tax. Fixed rent tenancies place all the risk on the renter, which, in the absence of a developed credit system, might be sufficiently high to discourage private farming. Just from simple economic considerations it can be argued (for instance, Stiglitz 1991) that the more egalitarian the distribution of land ownership, the better the incentive structure of the agricultural sector as a whole to achieve greater production. In most of the former or current Marxist regimes attempting significant land reforms, however, most discussion has focused on how to deal with different classes of claims on land, rather than on how land ownership could be distributed in an equal fashion to reduce tenancy.

In East Europe except for the Soviet Union, the land was never nationalized. Technically, most of it belonged to the original members of the collective farms or their heirs, even though this land was merged with other land and managed by the collective farm. Although land nationalization occurred more often in the Third World, in many cases this change in ownership was merely nominal because, if collectivization did not occur, the original owners continued to farm the land in the same manner as before. Decollectivization could also be quite simple: in the second half of the 1980s the Lao government simply permitted the farm families to use their former land as they saw fit, although asserting at the same time that the state had final legal title. Indeed, the former owners could rent the land to the cooperative farms, which would farm it (Evans 1990, p. 91). In certain countries where nationalization of land was more thorough, however, the lack of land registries made it impracticable to reconstitute the old property distribution.

Where nominal ownership still existed, changes in the rights associated with ownership could be easily restructured. For instance, in 1990 the governments of Bulgaria, Czechoslovakia, East Germany, and Hungary announced their intention of allowing owners or their heirs who remained on the collective farm to withdraw either their old land from the collective or, if this land lay in the middle of a field or had buildings constructed upon it, to take an equivalent amount of land in order to start up as private farmers. The governments of these four nations also announced their intention of assigning ownership to every parcel of land so that responsibility for the use and maintenance of the land could be established. Since Poland and Yugoslavia had relatively little collectivized land, such a measure was not necessary. China paid no attention to such legal niceties and maintained public ownership of the land, even as it decentralized control and leased individual plots to families, as did some other countries pursuing decollectivization where Marxist parties remained in control of the government. In still other countries, particularly in the Third World, where the socialist sector in agriculture was either small or dominated by state farms, few of these steps were taken by the end of 1990.

The decision to reassign some of the land back to its original owners can mean, of course, that land ownership might be quite unevenly distributed. Other policy problems, moreover, begin to multiply, because five distinct sets of interests must be taken into account in resolving the many conflicts: those of the previous owners of the land, those of the workers of that land, those of the citizens of the country, those of the farm itself as a unit, and those of the government. Governments must also devise measures to assign ownership in a quick and unambiguous fashion to reduce uncertainty so that investment can be encouraged. The last issue is crucial: although collectivization of agriculture in Yugoslavia lasted only about five years in the early 1950s and entailed about one-quarter of the land, lawsuits over ownership lasted for fifteen years after decollectivization.[1]

HOW AND WHEN ARE LAND CLAIMS TO BE RECOGNIZED?

A process of returning land to its previous owners can function only if the country had some type of formal land registration before collectivization, if the previous land titles were retained, or if the turn-back process occurs while previous land claims can still be remembered. Otherwise it is only feasible to divide the land either on a per capita basis (as in China) or a per worker basis (as in Viet Nam).

Although turning back land to the previous owners appears simple, problems arise when several land reforms took place before collectivization so that ownership is linked with a date. In this case, selecting a particular date for land claims to be recognized has proven to be a highly divisive political issue.[2]

[1] This information was supplied in an interview with a prominent Yugoslav agricultural economist in 1990. Part of the problem in Yugoslavia was that the extended family system in the country was breaking up, so that many of these ownership disputes were intrafamily quarrels brought about by decollectivization. The decollectivization in Poland in 1956 occurred more smoothly. In both cases, however, former property boundaries were still clear and relatively little large-scale investment on the farm had occurred.

[2] Some examples to illustrate the point can be drawn from events in four central European nations in 1990.

In East Germany, both East and West German officials during most of the negotiation over ownership issues appeared ready to accept the land reform of 1945 and to draw the line for recognizing land claims at 1949, when the East German government was first established. At the last moment before signing the first interstate agreement establishing an economic union between the two Germanies, this consensus was overturned by negotiators from the Free Democratic Party of West Germany, who managed to slip in a clause recognizing land claims between 1945 and 1949 for property not nationalized under orders of the Soviet military government (*Frankfurter Allgemeine Zeitung* 18 June 1990). As a result, legal problems in reassigning ownership multiplied. The second interstate agreement, how-

Other difficult problems arise when the land titles are held by those who are not members of the collective farms. The reassertion of their claims might lead to a system of extensive absentee ownership, which would be politically unacceptable in some nations. If the Marxist government had carried out a land reform before collectivization that had dispossessed the large landowners but not the owners of middle size properties, this can be a useful starting point, although some non-Marxist governments are loath to recognize communist land reforms. Devising a theory to predict the outcomes of these conflicts is beyond the scope of this study; it is worthwhile, however, to review the solutions to this problem in several nations and their consequences.

The claims of both members and nonmembers of the collective farms can be treated equally, a solution adopted in 1990 in East Germany upon insistence by the West German government during the negotiations of the interstate agreement. For Hungary, an empirical study by Szelenyi (1991) shows that such a solution with a 1947 land pattern would benefit urban households the most, while almost half of the rural household heads would become landless. It should not be surprising that this solution was rejected.

The claims of both can be recognized, but those not farming the land they own would have to pay a high annual absentee-ownership tax that would induce many to forfeit their claims. This would result in those farming the land either owning their land, leasing it from the government, or obtaining ownership through some type of compensation mechanism. At the end of 1990 Czechoslovakia seemed on the way of adopting

---

ever, appeared to approach the original concept. Groups of landowners expropriated before 1949 protested and in early 1991 the problem was in the courts.

In Bulgaria, the Nikola Petkov Agrarian Union and the Social Democrats argued that the crucial date for recognizing land claims should be 31 December 1944, so that the 1945–46 land reforms would not be recognized. This point, I should note, was not in their party platforms but was quite striking in conversations with various party members. Given the election victory of the Bulgarian Socialist Party in 1990 and the subsequent political stalemate, prediction of the outlines of the final outcome of the debate was impossible in early 1991.

In Hungary, the Agrarian Party, which was a member of the ruling coalition elected in 1990, demanded that the line be drawn at January 1947, that is, after the major "bourgeois" land reforms, but before the "communist" land reforms. Some factions of this party also insisted that no landholder could own more than fifty to one hundred hectares. They justified this position because most Hungarians now believe the land to have been too unequally distributed before the 1945–46 reform; this cutoff date would also prevent Jews, whose lands were expropriated by the Germans during the war, from advancing their land claims.

In Czechoslovakia, political groups formed around recognition of land claims after several different dates: 1939, 1945 (the reform directed against the Germans), 1947 (the reform directed against large landholders), and 1948 (the "communist reforms" directed against kulaks).

this solution. Some political parties in other East European countries have advocated a similar solution as well.

The claims of both can be recognized, but the users of the land can receive formal ownership and the former owners, who are not farming their land, can receive bonds gradually redeemed by special taxes on the new owners. This solution provides compensation for the former owners while creating a new rural bourgeoisie. It resembles the method Czar Alexander II adopted for the emancipation of the Russian serfs in the 1860s and is particularly favorable to the farmers if inflation is occurring. At the end of 1990 this solution seemed in the process of being adopted in Hungary and also in Nicaragua. In the latter country in October 1990, the government signed a "concertación agreement" with all major political forces in the country (except the representatives of the private entrepreneurs) to recognize the titles to the land granted by the Sandinista government, while promising compensation if an owner does not receive his confiscated land back.

The claims of both can be recognized, but nonusers of the land must sell it to anyone willing to farm it. This solution, urged by certain agrarian parties such as the Nikola Petkov Agrarian Union in Bulgaria, would greatly benefit the farmers since the land prices would undoubtedly be low.

Although other solutions can be imagined, they have received relatively little political attention. The worst possible situation occurred in Nicaragua before the concertación agreement when, as noted in the previous chapter, the new government could not enforce any property claims, neither those that were new nor those existing for many years; physical force became the key to ownership.

HOW IS LAND FOR PRIVATIZATION TO BE VALUED?

If compensation for land is to be paid to previous owners who do not wish to farm it, how can it be valued? In a fully functioning market economy the value of an asset is the discounted value of its stream of future earnings. Where market prices, including a discount rate and a price of land, have yet to be established by the market, rather arbitrary valuation methods must be employed that can lead to windfall gains or losses for the purchasers. Although various rough indicators of land fertility can and are being used, such indicators do not take into account other crucial factors such as quality and location of the transportation infrastructure; accessibility of labor, credit, and other inputs, and similar factors that influence the profitability of a farm.

Some have argued that for the proper incentives to be established, the land must be sold back to the farmers. There are historical precedents showing that giving away the land does not necessarily have adverse incentive effects; for instance, in the homesteading acts of the nineteenth century the U.S. government gave away half a continent.

HOW IS OWNERSHIP OF OTHER COLLECTIVE FARM ASSETS TO BE DISTRIBUTED?

In some East European countries, considerable discussion has centered on the problem of how the collective farms could be turned into corporations, with shares issued according to the amount of land brought into the collective and also to the number of years worked on the collective farm, in order to recognize an ownership interest created by labor. In Third World Marxist regimes, where agricultural work is highly labor-intensive, these collective assets were not very great, and the joint-stock approach did not receive much attention.

The joint-stock approach combining original land claims and claims arising from labor has many variants. In Czechoslovakia, one farm director told me that in the distribution of shares based on labor on his farm, he would weight the labor claims by the farm profit for the particular years worked so that, for instance, no shares would be assigned for labor claims in those years when the farm suffered a financial loss. He also argued that the level of responsibility at which a person worked should be taken into account in assigning the labor-based shares, a criterion which would, of course, give him more stock!

A closely related, but less frequently discussed, issue is the degree to which these shares in the farm could be sold, especially to those outside the farm. Since an active capital market did not exist in any of these nations in the early 1990s, transfer of shares could not easily occur. This lack of transferability means that the workers would have an incentive to inflate current wages at the expense of investment, a practice occurring in self-managed firms in Yugoslavia.

HOW ARE FARM DEBTS TO BE HANDLED?

As noted in the previous chapter, the various countries have handled farm debt in quite different ways, ranging from full cancellation in Bulgaria and Romania to partial cancellation in the Soviet Union and East Germany, to none in Czechoslovakia and Hungary. The approach adopted does not seem directly related to the amount of this debt; for instance, collective farm debts were not large in Czechoslovakia, but they were important in Hungary. Since many farm debts arose from a manipulated price structure or irrational demands placed upon the farms by central authorities during the period of central planning, the criteria on which these decisions about the debt cancellation were made are not clear. Further, much of the farm debt is uncollectible so that it makes little real difference whether such debts are cancelled or not. Indeed, a bankruptcy merely removes the debt more quickly from the books of the state banks without changing much else, since the production problems of the farm persist.

HOW ARE LAND AND ASSETS OWNED BY THE STATE TO BE TREATED?

In East Europe many of the collective farms used land or assets belonging to the state. This situation was not frequently found in the Marxist Third World, except where all land was nationalized. In most industrial Marxist regimes these state lands were not extensive and they could easily remain under state ownership for the while. Or, according to one Hungarian proposal, much of this state land could be transferred to local governmental agencies for disposal. Whether privatization is carried out by central or local governments, several schemes have been proposed to facilitate the process.

The government could sell the assets to the highest bidder in order to increase its revenues. Those actually farming the land might have the opportunity to purchase it at a reduced price. Given the fact that few citizens had bank accounts large enough to purchase the land and that credit was scarce, only those with close connections to the government, those obtaining money from illegal activities, or foreigners could actually buy it.

At first glance foreign purchasing does not seem a politically acceptable solution, but the exact circumstances must be known to make a judgment. For instance, Guyana is trying to sell the estates back to the previous British owner and, to this end, hired this firm in 1990 on a two-year management contract as a preliminary step. Those acquainted with the fiery literature against the foreign estates that preceded their nationalization in the mid-1970s might be astonished at the equanimity of the Guyanese to the return of the British raj. The government appeared to view this projected sale as an opportunity to obtain managerial expertise and funds for rehabilitation of an industry that could serve as a useful source of tax revenues in the future. In a peculiar fashion, some members of the government also viewed this possible sale as a means to achieve a more effective voice of agricultural interests in the political process than that of the previous company controlling the state-owned farms. Unlike Nicaragua, the workers did not seem interested in gaining immediate ownership of the (money losing) estates, although they did discuss some type of partial-ownership arrangements. The major agricultural labor union, dominated by the Marxist oriented People's Progressive Party, appeared to believe that in the long run this proposed privatization would be the only way the wages of sugar workers could be raised. Given the policies followed by the government after nationalization that acted against the agricultural sector, especially the overvalued exchange rate that eliminated profits of the estates and impoverished the workers, the union saw the potential new owners as a defender of worker interests. In short, "dependencia theory" has been turned inside out by the socialist factions in Guyana.

Another way of distributing state-owned assets is through a voucher system, where the government gives each citizen a wealth voucher, the face value of which would amount to a certain share of the total assets owned by the state. It would allow the citizens to use these vouchers to bid for land, cattle and farm equipment, their houses, the stores in which they work, or shares in corporations. This scheme, which appears to go back to a proposal by the Hungarian economist Tibor Liska, was strongly backed by Václav Klaus, the finance minister of Czechoslovakia. By the end of 1990 the plan was still under active consideration and preliminary steps for implementation were taken in Czechoslovakia, Mongolia, Poland, and Romania.[3] In the agricultural sector, this seems a better idea of distributing cattle and equipment than state farms as a whole.

The government could, of course, give the land it owns to any family showing an ability and willingness to farm it. This system was proposed in the summer of 1990 by the Yeltsin government in the Russian Republic of the Soviet Union (*New York Times* 25 July 1990), but it was apparently dropped sometime afterwards.

[3] Opponents have raised four major objections to this idea: Problems of arbitrary valuation of state property would be severe and could lead to unfair windfall gains or losses. Citizens have little experience in holding stock and might sell these vouchers for low prices to obtain foreign currency to purchase consumer goods abroad—in many electronic stores in Vienna in 1990, I saw enticing signs advertising articles in both Czech and Hungarian languages. This distribution would be unfair since children would receive the same share as adults who have worked in the system all their lives. The enterprises would not receive any new infusion of capital for their renewal.

None of these four objections is, I believe, fatal to the plan and all can be countered by suitable structuring of the program. For instance, the problem of valuation is resolved by a bidding system for state property proposed by Thomas Gale Moore (1990). Children need not be given the same number of vouchers as adults. Sale of vouchers can be forbidden to foreigners and usable only to obtain title to other property or capital assets.

The plan received some attention in East Germany, but the West Germans vetoed the idea for the interstate contract, fearing that West Germany would receive all the debts of the state farms and firms, while East Germany would receive all the assets. It also appears to have attracted little interest in Bulgaria and Hungary; I find it curious that some eminent Hungarian economists, for instance, János Kornai (1990), have dismissed the idea without serious discussion, apparently believing that the lack of tradition of holding company shares and of other forms of indirect ownership in East Europe makes the plan impractical.

According to a recent visitor to Mongolia, many Mongolian reformers were quite taken with the idea and prepared plans for using these vouchers, which would be bought and sold in special stockmarkets, to allow people to purchase cattle on the collective farms or share of state companies. By January 1991, however, none of this had been implemented. In Poland at the same time, preparations were underway for using the vouchers to purchase participation in mutual funds that, in turn, would hold the shares of individual companies owned by the state in 1990.

These problems of redistributing state-owned agricultural assets have been the subject of extensive public debate in the nations of East Europe. Up to early 1991 they received much less systematic attention in most Third World nations. Some of these latter nations, for instance South Yemen, appear to have opted for closed-door negotiations processes between claimants because, I suspect, few place much faith on reaching an equitable solution through a judicial process.

WHAT RIGHTS ON THE LAND SHOULD THE COLLECTIVE FARM RETAIN?

Many collective farms were highly integrated enterprises that achieved economies of scale in some of their activities. In order to protect these activities from dismemberment, many East Europeans have argued that certain powers must be given to the farm as a unit. In the late 1980s in the Soviet Union, for instance, it was the farm director who decided what land would be distributed to those requesting a leasehold and who also signed the contract governing rent and other conditions of the lease. Since farm directors had little interest in losing their power, many potential leaseholders complained of the obstacles placed in their way in obtaining such land.

Many of the collective and state farms were in need of new capital, which raises an additional problem. If shares in the state or collective farm are sold by the government, the firm or farm receives no funds for investment. If, as in Hungary and Poland, the state firm or farm can sell a certain fraction of itself to obtain such outside capital, problems of asset stripping arise. That is, farm directors can sell assets or land to themselves or their friends at low prices. Or they can make sweetheart deals with an outside buyer and offer a low price in return for a lucrative "management contract," thereby converting their status in the *nomenklatura* into property rights. Or if the buyer purchases 50 percent of the stock of the farm from the farm, then farm assets are worth 150 percent of the original, since the additional funds are added to the balance sheet, and the buyer gets an instant capital gain by obtaining 50 percent of the assets for only 33 percent of their value.[4] The problem of maintaining accountability of managers without significantly reducing the decision-making autonomy of their enterprises is a dilemma discussed often in the context

---

[4] The first two problems can be discouraged by having a state trustee approve all land sales, although this is not as simple as it seems. The last problem can be also circumvented in a simple fashion. One solution, which is being pursued in Yugoslavia, is for the group selected to "own" the farm or enterprise to issue bonds to the government equal in value to its assets at the time of purchase; the interest plus the principle must be repaid in full over a certain length of time. This would allow an infusion of new capital, yet assure that the state would receive full value for the enterprise. The danger of such an approach is that the group obtaining use of the assets could plunder the firm to enrich themselves and then declare bankruptcy so as not to have to repay the securities.

of industry (e.g., Lipton and Sachs 1990), but it occurs in agriculture as well, particularly on the state farms where the workers have no former claims on the land.

In some Marxist regimes such as China, Laos and Viet Nam, the cooperatives retained few rights in the land per se. Nevertheless, they continued to exist as service cooperatives providing certain functions for their members, for instance, purchasing inputs in bulk for distribution, buying certain crops to sell in bulk, or providing technical aid and mechanical services.

WHAT RIGHTS IN THE LAND SHOULD THE STATE RETAIN?

These include the right to tax and to set certain parameters of farm activity that, for instance, force the farm to take into account the ecological impact of their activities. In China these rights were not well thought out in the reforms beginning in the early 1980s. As a result, the irrigation infrastructure deteriorated, forests were cut down, and certain communal responsibilities in the field of health and education were neglected.

Expansion of the Smallholder Sector

Changes in either the ownership or control of land can occur, not only in quantum leaps at a single point in time for the country as a whole, but also as a process involving the gradual expansion of the smallholder sector. Two features of this approach deserve attention. First, the process does not necessarily involve privatization, but rather can represent the expansion of a leasing system. The two elements of property reform are quite distinct. Second, although the hesitancy on the part of many workers on the collective farms to become private farmers (chapter 9) may make infeasible a total decollectivization, a partial decollectivization is quite another matter. During 1990 East European economists and administrators discussed various ways in which this gradual expansion of the smallholders sector could occur. Several possibilities are open.

The government could merely expand the size of the private plots on all state and collective farms. If carried out rapidly, however, this approach has a number of disadvantages, especially if the farmers do not have the equipment to farm their plots alone and believe it too risky to contract plowing and all other services. Or the government could change the organization of farms, either breaking the collective and state farms into increasingly smaller units or, more simply, changing the unit of ownership and accounting from the farm to the brigade to the team to the link (subteam). The smaller ownership and accounting units must, however, be given decision-making autonomy and have the right to turn down tasks offered to them if they believe them unprofitable. Otherwise, this organizational change represents merely the introduction of a payment-by-result compensation system. Or the government could change the nature of the agreements between the farm and the households so as to reduce the scope of group responsibilities. China carried out a combination of all three measures over a four-year period, increasing the private plots in 1979, encouraging the reduction of the decision-making unit from the team to the link (called the "group") during the period from 1980 through 1982, and changing the nature of the agreements between the farm and the households, especially from 1981 on (Riskin 1987, pp. 286–90). These steps can be implemented separately or together.

Partial decollectivization was on the reform agendas of many Marxist regimes. One type occurred in both Bulgaria and Romania, which in 1990 increased the size of the individual plots of the collective farmers, even though land claims of previous owners had not yet been resolved. In Romania, for instance, personal, private, and individual plots increased from 13 percent of total arable land to about thirty percent. In countries as different as Bulgaria and Viet Nam, the government simply doubled the size of these household plots. These steps did not increase the size of individual holdings to the point that they could not be farmed primarily by hand methods. When I raised the possibility of a progressive widening of these individual plots over a period of years in order to give workers the opportunity to learn to be private farmers, a Hungarian collective farm manager argued that this approach would probably imply a part-time work arrangement on the collective farm, which would be difficult to monitor. Moreover, the final result might be a considerable reduction of total work effort from the farmers (a formal demonstration of this proposition is presented in research note G). Clearly a major source of opposition to this path toward expansion of the smallholding sector would be the collective farm managers, so that the initiative for an increase in personal land would have to come from, and be enforced by, the central government. In the Soviet Union, Prosterman (1991) also found very mixed attitudes toward this approach among the hundred peasants he interviewed in 1990.

Other types of partial, but politically more palatable, expansion paths of the smallholding sector can also be implemented. The government could breakup or privatize only those state or collective farms where a majority of members vote for the change, allowing these farms to reorganize in a manner the members see as most suitable. Or, as in the Soviet Union, the government could give any household working on a collective or state farm a piece of its land sufficient to farm individually if application is made. If that path is taken, then a critical factor is whether the collective farm managers or independent government officials assign the land. If it is the farm managers, they can sabotage the entire program by

For a market to function effectively, property must be relatively strong and individual property rights and governmental regulations of productive activities must be sufficiently stable to allow individual producers to make plans without facing undue risks and high transaction costs. This means a drastic reduction in required plan tasks for the farm to fulfill. Moreover, it means that the central or local governments cannot drown the individual producers in a sea of changing regulations (a problem occurring in the Soviet Union). Finally, it means that the rules governing the behavior of public agencies dealing with agriculture must be structured so that their own successes are not measured by a particular volume or assortment of agricultural products, which would induce them to intervene in farm operations.

The strengthening of property rights requires the government, in addition, actively to develop objective mechanisms for dispute resolution and contract regulation. It must also provide a clearly defined social framework, for instance, laws on product quality, payment of labor, usages of particular technologies or chemicals, plus an objective mechanism of enforcement, so that farms need not rely on political authorities interpreting vague directives from the central government—a problem arising in China according to Nee (1989).

REDUCING GOVERNMENTAL INTERVENTION

In a classical Soviet-type economy the managers of cooperative farms have only weak property rights over the assets of the farm, even though they are formally owned by members of the farm. Since managers must use those assets to fulfill a plan from the state, their decisions are subject to constant review and revision by state and party authorities, and the rules to be followed are constantly changing. Clearly the strengthening of property of the farm implies a reduction of required plan indicators and increasing the decision-making power of the farmers.

Reduction of governmental intervention in agriculture is, of course, closely tied to the manner in which agricultural production is coordinated. Between a strict planned economy (hierarchy) and a market, a number of other coordination systems can exist, including various types of "dual dependencies" (Kornai 1989), that is, coordination by horizontal

---

tions of a government agent; (3) he was forced to renegotiate the contract for the greenhouse when the collective farm leader decided that the contract, which followed government regulations, was "unfair"; (4) the farm delivered inputs different from those specified in the contract; and (5) the farm director nullified the contract after deciding that the engineer leasing the greenhouse still (!) made too much money. The article suggested that the engineer had no legal recourse to redress these contract violations, in part because those legal authorities in a position to aid him were beholden to the same governmental officials who were violating his contract and, therefore, they feared reprisals.

relations without flexible prices. This means that farms produce and sell what they want at fixed prices and differences between supply and demand are met by imports and by "occasional" direct orders from the government. Or the farms can be relieved of formal production goals and be burdened with "informal" goals. As Hungarian agriculture demonstrated in the 1970s and 1980s, even without a production plan, political authorities had a hundred different ways of intervening in farm decision-making. Another example is the Soviet Union, where the 1988 Law on Cooperatives abolished planned targets for collective farms. As many Soviet commentators have noted (e.g., Aganbegyan 1989, p. 115; Shmelev and Popov 1989, p. 255), the "administrative tyranny" of the various local party and government (for example, RAPO) authorities over the state and collective farms was not abolished. As a result, the farms still had little decision-making autonomy. Thus strengthening of property rights is clearly associated with the introduction of the market mechanism.

The strengthening of property rights can be easily reversed. Although by 1990 most East European nations abolished most of the production goals set by the government for collective farms, this situation was far from permanent. If production in succeeding years would not increase or if an assortment of agricultural products deemed "incorrect" by the government was produced, governmental intervention and a weakening of property rights could be a possible response. For instance, China, which abolished the central agricultural plan in 1985, began to reimpose production goals on a number of agricultural products in the late 1980s as grain production stagnated.

In a number of the Third World nations such as Nicaragua or Madagascar, the government did not directly intervene in decision-making on the farm. Rather, farm managers were supposed to maximize profits, constrained by various regulations about wages, retaining of foreign exchange, buyers of inputs and outputs, and so forth. In these situations, strengthening of property rights involves a loosening of these kinds of indirect constraints upon the farm managers.

CREATION OF A LEGAL FRAMEWORK

In 1990, the governments of the East European nations were creating a new legal structure to sustain a market economy and to strengthen property rights. Bankruptcy laws, laws for the formation of joint stock companies, laws on contract enforcement, and a wide range of other measures were all on the agenda. Whether these measures would take hold and would be enforced, whether the legal mechanisms for farms to defend their newly gained property rights would be effective, and whether the governments could be restrained from their decade-long habit of interfering in decision-making of the farms cannot, at this early date, be determined.

The strengthening of property is, I believe, considerably more important than privatization per se, because it lies at the heart of problems of individual risk and responsibility. Property property rights can be strengthened without creating private ownership, as the Chinese have shown in the leasing arrangements. Nevertheless, if government or party officials are judged for promotion on the economic performance of the units in their territory, this creates irresistible desires on the part of such officials to intervene if production problems arise. With the creation of private ownership and effective mechanisms for enforcing these rights, the chances of such direct intervention are reduced. In other words, strong property rights and private ownership appear mutually reinforcing, even though they can be implemented separately. And strong property rights are fortified by reliance on a market mechanism. There is, as Kornai (1990) has argued, an "affinity" between these three measures.

MARKETIZATION

As noted, marketization has two elements: the creation of a competitive economic environment for selling inputs to the farms and buying farm outputs, and the introduction of a price system for agricultural inputs and outputs reflecting the forces of supply and demand.

A Competitive Economic Environment

The major structural problem in moving to a competitive infrastructure in agriculture was noted in chapter 5: namely, in the late 1980s in almost all East European nations, vertical relations in agriculture were relatively few and, as a result, the farms had few options as to suppliers of their inputs or purchasers of their outputs. A price reform unaccompanied by changes in these vertical relations would, in most cases, leave the farms facing monopsonist purchasers of their products and monopolistic sellers of inputs. Although the economic environment for agriculture in many market economies is far from competitive, particularly in the European Community, a farmer faces many more options on both sides of the market, and the diversity of marketing channels is considerable.

The policy problems implicit in creating a more competitive economic environment depend on how vertical relations in agriculture were previously structured. In chapter 5 I discuss three types of possible arrangements: (1) the decentralized vertical structures model, where many of the

suppliers of agricultural inputs or purchasers and processors of farm outputs are inter-farm organizations; (2) the standard ministry/production
model, where the various suppliers of inputs and purchasers of outputs
are organizations reporting to different industrial ministries; and (3) the
suprafarm vertical integration model, where one ministry oversees the
suppliers of inputs, the farms, and the purchasers and processors of farm
outputs. The problems in moving toward a competitive infrastructure are
quite different for these three institutional arrangements.

DECENTRALIZED VERTICAL STRUCTURES

As noted in chapter 5, decentralized vertical structures occur primarily
in the economically more developed Marxist regimes. The problems arising in creating a competitive infrastructure depend very much on
whether the decentralized vertical structures are interfarm enterprises or
the farm itself.

If the interfarm enterprise is the vertical unit, then the agricultural
sector can move more rapidly toward a market economy than in other
cases. In this regard, the East German example is instructive.

In the early months of 1990 in East Germany these interfarm enterprises, most of which were relatively small, began to become independent economic enterprises ready to carry out business with any farm.
These newly-independent enterprises were formed either as joint-stock
companies with some shares held by the member farms and other shares
sold to raise additional capital, or else as cooperatives associated with the
West German Raiffeisen Association, an umbrella organization for cooperatives that provides them with market research, legal service, advice
on accounting, and other services.

Because the newly-independent enterprises could deal in bulk, they
could develop contacts with different suppliers of farm inputs, particularly from abroad, or with different purchasers of farm outputs more easily than the farms; thus they provided a vital service. Because they were
relatively small, they also provided the potential for considerable competition. This potential was enhanced because of East Germany's location
and special political ties since West German, Dutch, and Danish companies supplying agricultural inputs and buying farm outputs also easily
entered the market, a special advantage East Germany had over other
Central and East European nations.

Although these developments aided the farm sector, special problems
arose in the marketing of farm outputs. East German collective and state
farms found it difficult to sell their produce either in East or West Germany. This was true in part because their produce did not meet Western
standards, in part because they were producing the wrong crops—in
1990, many farm directors made their decisions on the basis of East Ger-

man prices and, in the summer, were stuck with mounds of produce, cucumbers for example, which sold for a fraction of the former East German price—and in part because the many processors of agricultural produce had plenty of sources in West Europe and the newly-independent East German enterprises serving a marketing function were inexperienced in competing against them.

Nevertheless, the embryo of a competitive structure was growing. Given the relatively short time of fifteen weeks between the election in March 1990 and the currency, economic, and social union at the beginning of July, a wide variety of national-level institutions began to spring up to supply credit, technical aid, market research, training and other special services to farmers. Development was rapid because in many cases these new institutions were simply replicas of West German institutions of a similar nature. In other cases, they represented a resuscitation of institutions that had existed before World War II. And in a few cases they were quite new institutions that were founded to meet a perceived need. Of course, given the fact that their economic survival was at stake, the speed is quite understandable; whether these new institutions will survive through the 1990s remains to be seen.

If the farm enterprise itself is the vertical unit, the situation is more problematical and depends in good measure on whether the nonfarm production units on a given farm serviced only that farm or whether such services were sold to other farms as well. These two situations were exemplified by Bulgaria and Hungary.

In Bulgaria, the former industrial-agricultural complexes, as well as the agro-industrial complexes supplied many of their own services and carried out a certain amount of production of inputs or processing of agricultural outputs. The orientation of these activities was toward the farm itself, and they did little contracting with other farms. When these large complexes were broken up in late 1989, the nonagricultural production units were often spun off as semi-independent enterprises selling services (for instance, transportation, storage, foreign trade marketing) to the individual farm units into which the agro-industrial complexes were divided. Theoretically, the individual farm units could purchase these services from any enterprise, but it did not work out this way in practice, especially since certain inputs were scarce and still selling at officially set prices. The newly constituted farms were a captive market for these semi-independent enterprises which, however, distributed their profits to individual farms that were their stockholders.

Clearly the breakup of the large agricultural complexes, while a necessary step to increase production efficiency, did nothing to create a competitive environment since the key players, the government enterprises producing the farm inputs and purchasing the farm produce were unchanged. Because of the political stalemate during 1990, the Bulgarians did little to resolve the problem.

In Hungary, farm units also served as sellers of inputs or buyers of outputs, but in a quite different manner. The TOPS systems (technical operating production systems, discussed in chapter 5) and the encouragement of farm processing units developed over several decades so that interfarm commercial bonds were extensive. The TOPS also competed against large governmental sellers of agricultural inputs and buyers of farm outputs, although not on a price basis since prices were fixed, but rather on such matters as auxiliary services supplied or quality determination, which influenced the price.

The transition to a functioning market economy in Hungarian agriculture should be relatively straightforward, especially if the government enterprises are broken into smaller units. One problem was that this "semicommercial" environment was not fully developed and, according to one Hungarian evaluation in the late 1980s, the markets for inputs were still "rudimentary" (Sipos and Halmai 1988). Moreover, it was oriented primarily toward large farms, so that individual farmers had almost no choice concerning from whom they purchased their inputs. Moreover, the processing plants were not greatly interested in buying products in small lots and, as a result, the marketing decisions of small farmers generally revolved around selling their outputs in farmers markets, or to large state-owned enterprises, or to a large farm nearby. The attempts by private groups in 1990 to reestablish the *Hangya* (ant), a system of service cooperatives that would sell inputs such as fertilizers and small machines to smallholders and that would also purchase their crops for selling in bulk, should help to alleviate this problem.

THE STANDARD MINISTRY/PRODUCTION MODEL

The problems arising from this kind of structure were exemplified by Czechoslovakia, where the sellers of agricultural inputs and buyers of farm outputs were primarily monopolistic state-owned commercial units operating under various ministries. Interfarm enterprises were much less frequent than in East Germany. This organizational arrangement was also found in many Third World Marxist regimes.

The approach of the new Czechoslovak government in 1990 was to separate these units from direct state supervision, divide them into their constituent factories or stores, turn each into a corporation, and have them operate as competitive units. In some cases the government forcibly separated the units, and in other cases establishments operating under one of these monopolistic enterprises could petition the appropriate ministry to become an independent unit. Such an approach had two major difficulties: The industrial establishments had little incentive to separate from the larger enterprises, especially if their participation in the enterprise allowed them to obtain their share of the monopoly profits by maintaining high prices for selling inputs or low prices for buying agricultural outputs. The mechanical breakup of certain state monopolistic enterprises did not automatically guarantee competition, especially if the newly established enterprises limited the major part of their activities to the district in which they were located, since this merely replaced a state-wide monopoly with a district-wide one. Although officials of the Ministry assured me that farms in one district could deal with enterprises in other districts, they seemed uninterested in my suggestion of publishing the prices offered by each of these enterprises in the newspaper to simplify interdistrict transactions for the farms and to create an embryonic commodity exchange. Although the Union of Cooperatives began to distribute price information to its members (a phenomenon also occurring in East Germany and Hungary, where the "official" cooperative associations were scrambling to take on new functions in order to retain their membership), the information was still quite primitive. Further, the newly emerging free press showed little interest in publishing it.

Officials in the Czechoslovak Ministry of Agriculture and Nutrition, as well as specialists at the Institute of Agricultural Economics and the Institute of Economics with whom I discussed the problem, were not greatly worried about the structure of markets supplying agricultural inputs and purchasing outputs. In contrast, every one of the collective farm managers with whom I spoke expressed extreme anxiety about the matter. Most were making plans to integrate forward, either by themselves, for instance, setting up stores in various cities to sell their products directly to the consumer, or starting up export operations,[6] or by combining with other farms, for instance, to establish a cooperative grain mill. At first glance such downstream diversification appears a reasonable response, but it would be economically viable only if the minimum efficient plant sizes in these processing industries were relatively small. Unfortunately, world trends of moving food processing from rural to urban areas in order to take advantage of economies of scale from new technologies suggest that this assumption does not hold (UNIDO 1981). Moreover, such downstream integration takes some time to function as a competitive force. Although prices of foodstuffs in Czechoslovakia had been raised in 1990 to approximate equilibrium prices, the floating of prices

[6] In chapter 10 I mentioned the attempts of a Czech farm director to tap the West German market for "eco-chickens" (ecologically raised chickens), which sell for more than normal chickens. He seemed unaware, however, that eco-chickens require a biodegradable wrapping (an eco-wrapping) if Western consumers in this interesting niche market are going to buy them. The effects of previous barriers to direct contact with foreign markets will take some time to overcome.

on 1 January 1991 resulted initially in a sharp increase in prices of beef, milk, cheese, bread, and other products, because many state food-processing enterprises were taking advantage of their monopoly position (*New York Times* 30 January 1991). Some Czechoslovak farms also were attempting to integrate upstream, for instance, pelletizing fertilizers or providing breeding services.

THE SUPRA-FARM VERTICAL INTEGRATION MODEL

From the viewpoint of the farm, the suprafarm vertical integration model provides few problems in the transition to a competitive environment in agriculture different from those arising from the standard ministerial/production model. The farms must still sell to large monopsonies and buy from large monopolies, albeit both are organized differently.

The Soviet Union provides a depressing example of this organizational model, because its response in 1988–89 to the deficiencies of the suprafarm vertical organization represented by Gosagroprom and the RAPOs was merely a reshuffling of organizations without any essential change of the system. More specifically, the government did not follow Gorbachev's guidelines for a more competitive agricultural sector, but backed away from the market in two important respects (Butterfield 1990). First, in restructuring vertical relations the Soviets appeared in good measure to have moved back to the standard ministerial/production model, albeit giving the production enterprises somewhat more freedom of manoeuver. Second, they focused considerable attention on restructuring of production units by encouraging new forms of large vertically organized enterprises (agrokombinat and agrofirms) and large horizontally integrated farms (agro-industrial associations). The government did not expend much energy in creating markets, either for agricultural inputs or farm outputs, and did not seriously address the problem of a competitive environment.

A NOTE ON THE THIRD WORLD

Most Third World Marxist regimes are much smaller than Marxist regimes in East Europe, and the role of foreign trade in agriculture, both inputs and outputs, is much more important. Marketization, therefore, is less a problem of rearranging the domestic supply system than reestablishing a competitive foreign trade sector. This, in turn, means determining a realistic exchange rate and encouraging the operation of competing exporters of agricultural produce and importers of agricultural inputs with whom the farms can deal. In the larger Third World nations, such as Viet Nam or China, the problems of creating a market-oriented agriculture are more similar to those encountered in East Europe.

Price Changes

Up to 1990 the distrust of markets led to extensive governmental controls of important agricultural prices, both on the consumer and producer sides, in almost all Marxist regimes. As a result, the official relative prices often had little economic meaning. In some countries the general level of prices was also below what it might have been if goods had not been rationed and people could have spent their money freely; that is, there was forced savings. A crucial step toward a market system is the freeing of prices to respond to the market forces and the simultaneous reforms in the systems of subsidies and taxes. The crucial question is how this can be achieved without high social costs and chaos.

To the extent that a price reform involves higher prices for foodstuffs which were previously subsidized, is the populace ready for such changes? Certainly doubts arise. Riots touched off by higher food prices to reduce food subsidies resulted in the fall of the governments of Władysław Gomułka in 1970 and Edward Gierek in 1980 in Poland. And Gorbachev's personal economic advisor, Nikolai Y. Petrakov, discussed public opinion polls showing that people preferred low prices of goods, rationing, and queues (especially during work time) to high prices and full stores.[7]

These shards of evidence, however, are not convincing. Certainly the Polish riots had other causes as well, not the least of which was a general distrust of the government. And it is difficult to judge the accuracy of the polls underlying Petrakov's interpretations, especially since other polls suggest quite the opposite, for instance, that of Shiller and others (1990). Furthermore, most Marxist regimes permitted farmers' markets and so the urban residents were already paying higher food prices. Most importantly, history marches on: the new Polish government floated prices in January 1990 without riots and the Soviet government finally raised food prices to a significant extent in April 1991 with little increment to the chaos that existed already at that time. Clearly, the political configuration is important for the success or failure of such policies, a topic that is discussed in the next chapter. Several important economic issues about price reforms are, however, quite relevant to the issues considered here.

MULTIPLE PRICES AS A TRANSITIONAL MEASURE

In 1985 the Chinese government abandoned the system of government production goals and substituted a contract system, by which farms could either sell their produce in markets or sign long term contracts to sell

---

[7] The report of Petrakov's remarks (Keller 1990) does not indicate the source of this survey, but it is quite likely S. I. Rukavishnikov (1989).

their produce to the government at a prespecified price. This led to four different price systems for farm produce—quota prices, above-quota prices, negotiated prices, and free-market prices. This system was cumbersome and, moreover, the government continued to impose some "sales obligations" or mandatory contracts on grain (Wiens 1987; Sicular 1988b). The mixed system was unstable and in late 1988, the government formally reintroduced grain quotas. Multiple prices do not seem the shortest route to the market.

THE PROBLEM OF SUBSIDIES

In the industrialized Marxist regimes a contentious question is how long farm subsidies should be continued. Some proponents of a price shock or "big bang" approach have proposed quick elimination of all major subsidies including those to farmers. Those fearing such consequences as massive bankruptcies and political unrest have proposed various schemes for a phased reduction and have noted that all Western industrial nations grant large subsidies to the farm sector as well. In this discussion, many economists in East Europe make a distinction between subsidies to the food-processing industry and direct subsidies to the farms, proposing to eliminate the former but not the latter. Both, of course, constitute parts of a wedge between the price paid by consumers and that received by farmers. Both ultimately act as subsidies to agriculture and differ primarily in their distributional impact. Of particular importance, producer subsidies aid especially two groups of farms: those with poor growing conditions or with poor management.

The data presented in Table 7.1 show that subsidies to agriculture in some Marxist regimes, particularly in East Europe, were high. This means that if massive and immediate bankruptcies within the farm sector were to be avoided when subsidies are removed, either the terms of trade between agriculture and other sectors would have to turn markedly in favor of agriculture or else subsidies would have to be eliminated only over a long period, so that farmer would have time to find alternative employment opportunities.

The changing terms of trade could occur in the context of a devaluation, which would allow the country to export its farm products and, more importantly, would lead to an increase in domestic prices of agricultural products as the prices adjusted to the foreign prices multiplied by the new exchange rate. This devaluation would also help to deal with domestic price distortions of agricultural produce arising from the fact that the differential turnover tax rates and subsidies were quite different for various foodstuffs. The subsidy data for East Europe and China suggest that these distortions were great and, from my casual observations, similar price distortions appeared in most Third World Marxist regimes as well.

The case of East Germany in 1990 provides an interesting example of how agricultural subsidies should *not* be eliminated. After the currency, economic, and social union with West Germany on 1 July, prices of agricultural goods began to approximate those of the West. Since the one-to-one exchange rate of the currency overvalued the East German mark, and since East German farmers could not easily market their products in the West while West German agricultural sales in East Germany expanded considerably, the results were catastrophic. East German economists whom I interviewed estimated that without income subsidies, farm incomes in that region would fall rapidly and about one-third of all farms would go bankrupt within a year without massive West German financial assistance.

If all prices in a Marxist regime were allowed to float and if proper exchange rate policies were followed, it is difficult to determine what would happen to relative agricultural prices (the terms of trade between agriculture and other sectors). Under a normal market situation, if subsidies to agriculture are removed, the retail price of food will rise and the producer price will fall, so that the future difference between them will represent only the retail margins and the costs of processing. Such "normal" conditions do not seem to hold in most Marxist regimes, so that determining even the direction of the impact of an elimination of price controls for food might be different. Indeed, it is even possible for producer prices to rise as well. Some examples of the uncertainties of these calculations from East Europe in 1990 are in order.

In some of these nations, Bulgaria for one, there was a disequilibrium in the retail markets for food, as manifested by shortages and by much higher free-market prices, so that floating food prices might have resulted in both higher retail and producer prices. In Hungary, producer prices had been held artificially low, so that the elimination of price controls resulted in a rise in both producer and retail prices. In Czechoslovakia in 1990, it seemed likely that producer prices would fall at the same time as consumer prices rose *unless* the currency was considerably devalued, which it finally was. Whether or not this measure was sufficient to increase the export of foodstuffs and to raise both producer and retail prices of food could not, when this study was closed, be determined. Let me add that in 1989, the Czechoslovak farms made only a slight profit in their food production, even taking into account the enormous subsidies they received. On those farms I visited, the greatest profits came from nonagricultural activities. Clearly, the problem of relative agricultural prices was of primary importance to the economic health of these farms.

To estimate relative agricultural prices a general equilibrium approach is necessary, which is impossible without more information and a clear picture of both the current and future tax and subsidy system. This problem is particularly difficult to solve for some of these countries, Bulgaria and Poland for example, where retail prices of almost all commodities, industrial or agricultural, were subsidized. A general release of price controls might result in higher or lower relative prices for agriculture, depending upon the relevant price and income elasticities, which are also not known. A very rough first approximation can, however, be made by taking advantage of Engels law; that is, real expenditures on food rise more slowly than total real consumption expenditures. If, in a given Marxist regime, the two variables have increased at roughly the same rate in the past when a general system of rationing, subsidies, and differential taxes were in force, consumers would probably switch expenditures from food to other goods when they become available so that relative food prices would fall. If, on the other hand, total consumption increased considerably faster than food consumption, then the reverse would occur. For East Europe such a calculation (assuming the "normal" income elasticity of food consumption to be 0.75) shows that relative agricultural prices were likely to rise in the 1990s in Bulgaria, Poland, and the Soviet Union, fall in Czechoslovakia, East Germany, and perhaps Hungary, and remain roughly the same in Yugoslavia.[8] This rough approximation is hardly infallible and could lead to erroneous results if other factors are not taken into account, especially the degree of monopoly in the selling of farm inputs and the purchasing of farm outputs. From the vantage point of late 1991, it appears that the short-run terms of trade turned against agriculture in almost all East and Central European nations.

THE PRINCIPLES OF PRICE SETTING

In the 1980s a number of Marxist regimes adopted a system of setting producer and consumer prices of agricultural goods so that certain prices were fixed, others had a price ceiling, and the remainder were floating. In East Europe, the share of foodstuffs with floating prices was relatively small.

[8] A discussion of these calculations is presented in Pryor (1990a). The data come from Alton and others (1989a, 1989b) and, for the Soviet Union, from the U.S. Congress, Joint Economic Committee (1982) and also various issues of U.S. Congress, Joint Economic Committee (annual). Such calculations also assume that the relative degree of agricultural subsidization is roughly the same as in the other sectors.

In the summer of 1990, Polish farmers were organizing mass demonstrations because of a fall in relative producer prices in agriculture. A number of explanations have been offered for this state of affairs, which could not be predicted by the simple Engels law approach: the demand for food fell as urban incomes fell at the same time that agricultural production declined relatively less, the agricultural terms of trade were higher domestically than internationally (to which prices were tending), profits of intermediaries rose, and the retail price increases of food were not passed on to the farmers.

An example of such a mixed system combined with subsidies and taxes is provided by Hungary, where roughly 10 percent of foodstuffs had floating prices in 1968, a percentage that was roughly the same in the mid-1980s (Csikós-Nagy 1969; Richet 1985, p. 240). Although such a system was also supposed to reduce price distortions and to move producer and consumer prices of foodstuffs closer together, these goals were not achieved (Sipos and Halmai 1988; Kornai 1989). Further evidence on the point is provided in chapter 7. Only in January 1990 did a significant price reform occur when most retail and producer prices of agricultural goods were allowed to float. It is important to realize that more orthodox Marxist governments have also made such changes (e.g., Laos in 1987) so that ideological barriers to such changes can be surmounted.

This type of change in the pricing of foodstuffs has three major implications: First, it unifies the various methods by which prices have been previously set, doing away with cross-subsidies, multiple prices depending upon the distribution channel, and different rules in setting administered prices in different areas. Second, it does not necessarily increase farm profit margins, especially if the prices of agricultural inputs supplied by state monopolies are changed at the same time. In Hungary, I was told that farm profits remained roughly the same, while in Poland in 1990, it appeared that these farm profits declined, at least in the short run. Third, this type of change does not mean that all agricultural subsidies are eliminated; for instance, in 1990 the Hungarian government continued to give income subsidies to unprofitable farms in areas not considered favorable for agriculture. These changes, however, do make it easier for both farmers and the government to determine what crops should be grown and what are the real costs of agriculture.

Complementary Policies

Some of the legal changes necessary for successful marketization have been discussed and others could be mentioned: property registration, development of a suitable contract law, mechanisms for quick resolution of contract disputes, and implementation of bankruptcy laws. I have neglected a wide variety of other important policies, institutions, and procedures. For example, combining a new property rights regime with a system allowing large price fluctuations generates high risks for the farmers. If credit were not readily available to provide a cushion against these risks, the rural sector might sabotage the reforms (Brooks 1991).

Other complementary policies include creating a suitable physical infrastructure for agriculture (for instance, roads and communications, which in some of the Third World Marxist regimes have been sadly neglected) and establishing new economic institutions including special exchange markets for staples, publication of price information, product quality standards, packaging regulations, labor laws and regulations for stable labor markets, creation of a social safety network, and the like. Other complementary policies include the setting of national policies to prevent local governments from dampening competition. In Yugoslavia in 1990, for instance, different republic governments introduced various kinds of measures protecting their farmers from competition in other republics.

Some of these complementary problems are of a short-run nature and can be remedied over time. For instance, even where the government had no central agricultural plan, commercial channels have generally atrophied because of the presence of monopsonistic state purchasing agents and monopolistic state sellers of agricultural inputs and commercial information about prices and markets for various domestic and foreign agricultural markets is scarce. Other problems are of a long-run nature and are difficult to resolve. For instance, the development of a network of farm credit has proven formidable in many countries, no matter what the system (Braverman and Guasch 1991). Other problems must be resolved in a wider context since they are linked more closely to the economic system. For example, in most centrally planned Marxist regimes the quality of foodstuffs declined because of long years of neglecting consumer wants. This was shown in a stark manner in East Germany after the currency union with West Germany. No matter how low their prices, many East German processed foods could not easily compete against higher-priced Western foodstuffs.

SEQUENCING PROBLEMS REVISITED

Assuming that macroeconomic equilibrium has been achieved and that a realistic exchange rate has been adopted, we can now reexamine with greater perspective the timing of property and price reforms in agriculture. Although the strengthening of property rights through the creation of an appropriate legal framework is a crucial step for economic reform and is independent of privatization or the breakup of the farms, it must be roughly simultaneous with a general price reform. Consider, for a moment, what happens when these reforms are not closely tied.

If property is strengthened without increasing the scope of market prices, several problems immediately arise because there are no mechanisms to balance supply and demand. The success or failure of the farms depends on arbitrary pricing decisions by the government and the farmers may have few incentives to increase production, a situation that appears to have arisen in the first half of the 1980s in Viet Nam, which tried to allow individual agriculture greater scope without significantly increasing the role of market forces. Instead, the governments may find it difficult to set market-clearing agricultural prices centrally to avoid shortages and surpluses so that it must step in again to guide production. Or public agencies, both government and party, may find it difficult to restrain from their old behavior and from intervening in farm operations so as to "improve" their own success. For instance, in 1982 Czechoslovakia attempted to increase decision-making powers of the farms by reducing the number of centrally issued indicators to only two—grain output and meat output—regulating the remaining production by contracts between the suppliers and consumers (Hajda 1990). Because prices were not liberated and the rules of behavior of government agencies were not greatly changed, the reduction in plan indicators did not last. To avoid this problem, at the beginning of their reforms the Chinese communist party deliberately forbade intervention into decision-making by the team (Riskin 1987, p. 285).

If, on the other hand, the price reform is carried out before property rights are strengthened (and, of course, before privatization), then other problems arise. The price reform is almost meaningless if production is still guided by the government, or if the rules of behavior of government agencies are not changed, and if they continue to intervene so as to further their own goals. If the farm managers are unable to respond to market signals and if they are also not held accountable for their actions, which cannot be properly done without strong property, the attempted socialist market economy will remain in a limbo and the managers would always have good reasons for appealing for subsidies. The system will end up in some peculiar hybrid, neither plan nor market, with few of the advantages of either.

The phasing of marketization and either privatization or the breaking up of the collective and state farms is less important. These reforms can, of course, occur simultaneously. Marketization can also occur first, as in Hungary in early 1990 when the provisional government announced a full floating of agricultural prices, while taking only very preliminary steps toward either privatization or farm break up. In certain situations the breaking up of the farms could even precede a marketization reform, but extreme care would have to be taken.[9] These reforms can also be phased and intertwined, as they were in China in the late 1970s and early 1980s when a certain degree of marketization occurred simultaneously with the breaking up of the farms and creation of the lease system, while more

[9] The problem, of course, is that the smaller farm units might not be able to survive if agricultural prices were low and if they, in contrast to the previous collective farms, were unable to obtain subsidies. In the summer of 1988, São Tomé also began a very preliminary type of decollectivization by leasing particular parts of the state farms to private individuals, before a significant marketization had occurred. Such an attempt raised so many problems that, under World Bank pressure, the attempt was quickly abandoned.

important marketization measures occurred immediately after the new productive units had been consolidated.

In 1990 the necessity of linking property and price reforms closely together seemed to be understood in most Marxist regimes with a large collective farm sector. In the Soviet Union, the situation was different, as Gorbachev ruefully noted in analyzing the political resistance to governmental plans to raise prices.[10]

This entire discussion, however, is predicated on the hidden assumption that the government is relatively strong and that policies set forth from above will be implemented. In some of the Third World Marxist countries this is not the case and, as a result, sequencing problems are somewhat different. More specifically, if the government is too weak to prevent state and collective farms or, for that matter, officials of the supervising ministry, from plundering the treasury, then decollectivization, privatization, and marketization might precede the strengthening of property rights. The first two measures would put an end to the fiscal drain from the subsidies to the socialist agricultural sector, and the marketization would merely legalize the extensive second economy. The government could then take its time in carrying out the politically sensitive task of firing the planners and agricultural cadre, who would have nothing to do as a result of this wholesale reduction in the functions of the public sector.

FARM MANAGEMENT CHANGES

Farm management changes do not represent an institutional change of the magnitude of reforms of property and marketization. Nevertheless, complementary measures to create viable farms that are able to compete in a market economy are important and require many changes in their organization, policies, and management.

Up to 1990 in most East European nations formal and informal governmental regulation and party resolutions played an important role in determining the organization and the management of the state and collec-

---

[10] In his initial speech at the twenty-eighth Party Congress in July 1990, Gorbachev proclaimed: "I would like to stress, however, that revision of retail prices cannot begin without thoroughly considered mechanisms of social protection and, to be sure, the transition to a market economy cannot start with price hikes. This is absurd. . . . When going over to a market economy we must single out the measures that come first. Even today nothing prevents us from beginning to turn state enterprises into joint stock companies, for granting real freedom of enterprise, from leasing small enterprises and shops, and putting up housing, stocks, shares and other equities, as well as part of the means of production, for purchase and sale" (*New York Times*, 3 July 1990, p. A6). By "freedom of enterprise" he meant, I believe, the strengthening of property rights. At the time this was written, the linkage between the price increases of April 1991 and property reforms was unclear.

tive farms, This also seemed true in most Third World Marxist regimes as well. Moreover, in some of the East European countries such as the Soviet Union and Bulgaria, the communist party also played a major role in day-to-day farm management so that technically trained farm directors were often overruled. In other nations such as Czechoslovakia, East Germany and Hungary, this daily party guidance was less important or minor. It was this central direction, for instance, that resulted in the hasty amalgamation of collective farms into unmanageably large units in the late 1960s and early 1970s in most of the East European nations.

With the strengthening of property rights, farms have much greater decision-making autonomy and can organize themselves and their management procedures more appropriately. And, indeed, these state and collective farms began to respond to the emerging market in five quite different ways: by changing top personnel, changing the size of the farm, changing their management techniques, diversifying the farm's economic activities, and rearranging production. In this discussion I use as examples the adjustments undertaken in Bulgaria, Czechoslovakia, East Germany, and Hungary, drawing upon observations from a visit in 1990.

Changing Top Personnel

In contrast to factories, farms can more easily change their top leadership through elections, because the farm members are more familiar with the operations of the enterprise as a whole. In 1990, elections took place for the top manager's position on many of the collective farms I visited in East Europe, and they seemed hotly contested with the candidates presenting alternative visions of how the particular farms should be run.

A number of entrepreneurial directors I spoke with in Czechoslovakia and East Germany had been newly elected to their post, replacing older and more bureaucratically-oriented or politically-connected directors. Several entrepreneurial middle managers I spoke with were also campaigning hard in order to unseat the current conservative farm directors. These minirevolutions on the farm were, of course, necessary for the emergence of a new entrepreneurial class. The process was often brutal because it had to occur quickly if the particular farms were to survive, and resentments building up over several decades came quickly to light. If my limited sample of respondents is representative, which is difficult to determine, I would say that the new entrepreneurial class in the countryside consists primarily of men between the ages of thirty-five and fifty-five who are technically trained and who are rapidly developing commercial skills. I met few older or female managers who were responding in a manner appropriate to a market economy.

Changes in the Size of Farms

The empirical investigation in chapter 5 of horizontal integration of the
agricultural sector suggests that most East European farms exceeded the
optimal size for a market economy. Although these farms had large-scale
facilities and employed technologies designed for large-scale farming,
considerable leeway in the choice of farm size was still possible. For instance, a strong argument can be made that if a decollectivization policy
is not chosen, the collective farms should at least be broken up into much
smaller units, each centering around a single village. Such a policy would
strengthen the village community as a social and political unit, transfer
power from the technicians managing the huge farms to the village, and
reduce any diseconomies of scale resulting from too large a farm for a
manager to retain an overview. The major losers under this policy would
be the current farm directors, who would have less power and resources
at their disposal. The government, therefore, would have to guide and
enforce this policy.

In East Europe farm dismemberment, however, seemed to be occurring on a significant scale only in Bulgaria and East Germany, and in
Bulgaria, the resulting farms were still very large (four thousand hectors
or so). By 1990 in the Third World, large-scale farm dismemberment took
place only in China, the Marxist regimes in Southeast Asia, and Nicaragua.

In Bulgaria, as noted above, a breakup of the very large agro-industrial
complexes into smaller units in 1988–89 was not a spontaneous movement but one ordered from above and encouraged by a series of contradictory decrees, policy declarations, and model statutes, all of which
probably had the effect of allowing the farm managers to do almost anything they pleased.[11] Along with a reduction in plan goals and the granting of more decision-making autonomy, it was part of a package assembled by the Zhivkov government to introduce more market elements into
agriculture, to raise farm incomes, and to reverse the flight from the land
that had left many villages depopulated and the agricultural labor force
aged. Although the farm units were still quite large, they embraced only
one to three villages. From what I was able to determine, the farm dismemberment was carried out in an intelligent manner to take into account local conditions, so that within a single agro-industrial complex, the
stronger farms were given more auxiliary services to handle by themselves (for example, transportation), while the weaker farms rented such

---

[11] The contradictory nature of these reforms are analyzed in an extremely useful survey
by Davidova (1990).

services from a central administration unit and focused their attention primarily on farming activities.

In East Germany a more spontaneous and complex reorganization was underway. For the last two decades individual farms specialized either on plant or animal production. In 1990 these farms began to merge and then, in many cases, also to divide so that one collective farm included only the lands around one village. This reorganization was often being forced from below and resisted by the farm chairmen, who were loath to give up their power over a large farm. It had the advantage of encouraging a revival of the village into a functioning economic and political unit.

In Czechoslovakia and Hungary, I saw much less evidence of changes in farm size. In this regard it must be noted that the development of a competitive economic environment in the agricultural sector had an important implication for farm size. This can best be seen by looking at an historical parallel in Germany beginning in the fifteenth and sixteenth centuries and lasting into the twentieth century, where the large agricultural estate (*Gutsherrschaft*) in the eastern part of the country was administered as a single unit, while the large estate (*Grundherrschaft*) in the western part of the nation was divided into individual farms and rented out.[12] In the west there were many towns and the farmers renting such land could easily obtain both farm inputs and markets for their outputs. In the east there were few towns and farmers had to face monopsonistic purchasers of their produce for long distance trade. Only the large farms had the countervailing economic power to counter such forces of monopoly.

Turning to the situation in the early 1990s, if East European farms are forced to integrate vertically both forward and backward in order to offset the monopoly power of upstream and downstream enterprises, they are destined to remain large. Another aspect of the same problem is the fear on the part of many farm managers that they might be unable to obtain inputs and, therefore, have to remain large in order to centralize purchasing and selling. I found this justification for not reducing farm size strong in Bulgaria and Czechoslovakia and, indeed, several of the farms I visited were planning on absorbing neighboring farms and becoming bigger for this reason. In East Germany, however, where a competitive economic infrastructure in agriculture was emerging, the reduction of farm size made considerable economic sense.

In the Third World, the situation was quite different. In some countries where the socialist sector consisted primarily of nationalized private estates growing plantation crops, little change was occurring. In Guyana, for instance, I was told that the state-owned company taking over the

[12] I would like to thank Karl-Eugen Wädekin for drawing my attention to this parallel.

private sugar estates in the mid-1970s ran them in a similar manner as
before (albeit reinvesting much less and handling labor relations in a different manner). In the 1990s it is unlikely that major changes in administration or size of the estates will occur when they are sold back to their
previous owners and other private investors. Exceptions are those parts
of the estates that the state-owned company used for nonsugar crops,
which will be sold off since the management company plans to focus primarily on sugar, a classical type of large-estate crop. In Nicaragua, the
Sandinistas divided up some of the state farms growing smallholder
crops, but in 1990 the new government did not follow this lead since it
was trying, to a considerable extent unsuccessfully, to return the estates
to their previous owners.

Changes in Farm Management Techniques

Farm directors were trying to change their management techniques so as
to respond more appropriately to market signals. Major changes in farm
management included decentralization of particular activities and tying
the income of farm workers much more closely to farm profits.

In Czechoslovakia, this meant the introduction or the strengthening of
a system of profit centers within the farms and basing wages on the economic results of each profit center. Transfer prices between profit centers
were not originally a problem when the government maintained price
controls; of course, the situation became more complicated as these controls were lifted in 1991. One collective farm manager explained to me
that the restructuring was an attempt to strengthen individual initiative
and to raise productivity without having to dismember the farm. Since
he also indicated that he saw considerable merit in the one-farm, one-
village arrangement as a means to resuscitate village life, he apparently
did not want to reduce the importance of his own job. For certain activities such as transportation, the farm leased trucks to individual drivers
who had to find a certain amount of work outside the farm if they were
to have satisfactory incomes. The farm director added that this reorganization of the farm into profit centers had been his dream for a quarter of
a century but that it had been prevented in past years by the ministry.

In Hungary, many farms were responding to the new conditions by
accelerating their drive to lease particular facilities such as pigsties,
chicken coops, and storage barns to individuals or groups. They were also
strengthening the system of contracting out particularly labor-intensive
activities to individuals (for instance, raising piglets up to a certain
weight, when they would be sold back to the farm). And they were concentrating managerial efforts on capital-intensive activities where economies of scale could be achieved. Such an approach unwittingly follows

the theoretical blueprint laid out by A. V. Chayanov in the early 1920s in the discussions in the Soviet Union about the future of Soviet agriculture (Solomon 1977; Cox 1986). In Hungary this process was called "privatizing without decollectivizing," a misleading description devised to make the process socially acceptable without actually privatizing.

Systems for compensating standard farm labor were also being changed, but in rather different ways in the four countries. Bulgaria was developing its own system of piecework, which had been introduced during the Zhivkov era and which was considerably more successful than a similar system in Romania discussed in chapter 6. Hungary was experimenting with certain types of sharecropping arrangements; this type of compensation scheme was even used in some greenhouses, an experimental practice that is practically unknown in the nursery business in the capitalist world.

What is unusual about these attempts at decentralization is that they had little in common with the Soviet approach in the late 1980s of leasing land to farmers who wished to take up a contract (discussed in Research Note F) or of setting up "collective contracts," which essentially were group piecework contracts (Brooks 1990b, 1990c; Van Atta 1990b). The new arrangements in East Europe were designed by the managers themselves, rather than imposed from above. The Hungarians did have some land leasing, but primarily where highly labor intensive crops were produced. The Bulgarians, who tried in the 1980s to implement a simple land leasing scheme, reported little interest in such arrangements by farm workers.

Given the varied conditions for producing different crops or for using different technologies, it is not possible to specify a standard method of paying agricultural labor to maintain the proper incentives. Until the recent political changes, however, these incentive problems did not receive the attention they deserved. In the future it is likely that individual farm managers will engage in considerable experimentation in this direction.

Diversification and Spinoff of Farm Activities

Diversification took several forms. As already mentioned, one form occurring in 1990 in Hungary and in Czechoslovakia was vertical integration in both forward and backward directions. Another form of diversification was directed into activities totally unrelated to agriculture, an approach most advanced before 1990 in the same two nations where the profits from such activities often supported the farming activities.[13] For

---

[13] In footnote 12 of chapter 6 I discuss Czechoslovakia's most famous example of nonfarm production on farms. One farm I visited invented and produced a machine for testing me-

East Germany I report some examples in chapter 8 in the discussion of entrepreneurship. In China, after the agricultural reforms in the early 1980s, industrial activity increased dramatically in the countryside, mostly steered by the local governmental authorities or by the rump of the remaining collective farm. By 1987 the value of nonfood production in rural areas actually exceeded the value of foodstuffs production.

Spinoffs of unprofitable activities also occurred. One East German farm manager told me of his joy in selling off the collective farm's cafeteria, which he claimed had taken more of his time than some major farming activities since he could not find anyone who could manage it according to the desires of the farm members. More significant spinoffs will undoubtedly occur when the managers determine what activities are profitable under the newly emerging prices.

Restructuring Production

Until 1990 in Bulgaria, Czechoslovakia, and East Germany, the farms had relatively little choice about what they produced and the land they used. Because of foreign exchange restrictions they were also limited in the countries from which they could import agricultural equipment and technologies. Only in Hungary did the farm managers have greater decision-making autonomy; for two decades state and cooperative farms in Hungary did not need to fulfill detailed state production plans.

At the time of this writing, many of the farm managers in these four countries were reconsidering their production mix, the lands they used in production, and the technologies they would employ. Most of the farm managers with whom I spoke in East Germany told me of their intentions to import West German technologies and to reduce the farm labor force by 50 percent in the next five years.

The major difficulty in carrying out a restructuring of production was a lack of knowledge about input and output prices. Although East German farms began to base their production plans on West German prices after the economic union, this easy option was not available for farms in the other nations, where farm managers expressed their frustrations at being unable to determine what would be most profitable and having to make production plans in the face of enormous price uncertainties.

In the Third World nations, the most severe restructuring problems arose in those countries where the exchange rate was highly overvalued

---

tallic impurities in oil, manufactured parts for computers and fax machines, produced pastries for Prague bakeries with the eggs from its poultry house that were too small to sell, and provided diverse services for hire, including painting lines on rural highways and constructing houses and small buildings in urban areas. Some pessimism is warranted about how many of these niche enterprises will survive if a complete market economy is achieved.

and the major crops were import intensive. In this case restructuring meant adopting less input-intensive technologies.

CONCLUDING REMARKS

Reforming the agricultural sector requires not only organizational and institutional changes, which have been the focus of this chapter, but also a series of changes in other policies toward agriculture. These include repairing the crumbling farm infrastructure in many of these countries, attacking the serious ecological problems, and equipping private farmers with small-scale agricultural equipment.

Predictions about the implementation and impact of agricultural reforms, especially at the beginning of 1991 were also hazardous, especially in those Marxist regimes with new governments. These governments are often fragile, their new leaders, inexperienced, and the politics, volatile. Moreover, in those countries with relatively free elections, the "politics of anger" were very important as long time resentments have led to political demonstrations making any type of reforms difficult. The governmental paralysis in Bulgaria in 1990 and the difficulties of the Czechoslovak, Nicaraguan, and Soviet governments in implementing significant reforms in the same year attest to the political difficulties of the economic reform process.

One ominous political factor also deserves mention. In a number of the Central and East European nations in the period before the two world wars, the rural sector provided a major support for authoritarian governments that, it must be added, were not interested in pursuing a liberal economic order. Although it is possible for such a political force to coalesce in the future to block further marketization and property reforms of the farm sector, these forces were still weak, at least at the end of 1990.

Of course, what is really needed to implement successfully both property and marketization reforms in the farm sector is a government that is strong enough to withstand populist pressures arising from the economic pain from the changes and that is also willing to withstand the temptation to intervene when the enterprises are not responding according to the government's expectations or desires. Unfortunately, this combination is unlikely to emerge in the chaotic transition from socialist agriculture.

The economic processes under examination, which had the aim of creating a market economy in several years, have few parallels with the birth of the market in West Europe, which took place over centuries. Nevertheless, the key building blocks should be clear: the strengthening of property, the creation of a competitive environment, the liberalization of prices, and the reorganization of management toward profit maximization.

By early 1991 much remained to be done. In cases where sequencing problems had not been carefully considered, inconsistencies among different parts of the system were appearing that were leading to production or distribution difficulties, not to mention social and political unrest. These, in turn, might weaken governmental resolve in later months and years for introducing a market economy. Other problems in implementing the agricultural reforms arose because the agricultural sector was only a small part of the entire economy. It is these larger issues of economic reform that are the subject of the next chapter.

Chapter 11

SOME BROAD ISSUES OF AGRICULTURAL REFORM

IN THE PRECEDING two chapters I analyze two types of economic connections between agriculture and the rest of the economy. The first linkage is the impact of inflation on the flow of resources into the agricultural sector. In Marxist regimes, inflation usually led to an attenuation of flows of government investment, credit, imported inputs, and consumer goods to the agricultural sector. Furthermore, real prices to producers of foodstuffs fell when the government-mandated prices lagged the general increases in prices of goods and services from other sectors. The second linkage is the role of agricultural inputs on the agricultural reforms. In Marxist regimes, agricultural reforms proved easier to implement when these inputs comprised a relatively small share of the value of total agricultural production. If agriculture was input intensive, then the general economic reforms of the economy could not "start" with agriculture, but had to proceed on a broad front.

Agricultural reforms are also linked to the rest of the economy through a series of much broader ties. In particular, I speak of issues related to the changing values in the economy and society as a whole, to political factors facilitating the reforms in both agriculture and other sectors, and to the attitudes of the population in general toward economic reforms. These three issues are the focus of this chapter, which ends with a set of final reflections on the rise and possible fall of collective agriculture.

ECONOMIC VALUES

To what extent did economic values change in the various Marxist regimes over the last four decades? To what extent did any change in values have to be taken into account in carrying out economic reforms, particularly in the agricultural sector?

Extreme opinions can be found regarding the extent of fundamental shifts in values that occurred under Marxist governments. In East Germany, for instance, a high official in the secretariat of the Central Committee of the communist party (now called the Party of Democratic Socialism) told me in 1990 that the party had erred in believing it had made a revolution. "The people think exactly the same now as they did forty years ago." He based this conclusion on the election results of March

1990 and the attitudes of the people toward the West German economic system. On the other hand, in Bulgaria in that same year, a sociologist explained to me that value shifts have been enormous. He cited as evidence a public opinion survey revealing, for instance, that 64 percent of the respondents agreed with the statement that maximum incomes should be no more than three times the minimum income, an attitude toward egalitarianism that did not exist before establishment of the Marxist regime. Although this particular belief is hardly congruent with a free-enterprise economy, it hardly tells the whole story.[1]

Most of the evidence on values is highly ambiguous. For instance, various public opinion polls and political manifestations in the Soviet Union revealed popular discontent with the urban "cooperatives" (actually small private enterprises). But this might have reflected unhappiness with the fact that many of these enterprises took advantage of the prevalent scarcities to charge extremely high prices or that many of them earned high profits by selling products obtained through illegal channels, rather than any fundamental views toward private enterprise per se.

It seems unlikely that forty years or more of intensive Marxist indoctrination did not have some permanent impact on the values held by the population.[2] But isolating this impact is difficult. For instance, in East Europe in 1990, most political parties generally agreed about the ends—the shift to a market economy with private enterprises—but they differed considerably about the means to achieve this goal. Did the conflicts about the means represent differences in values, in objective interests, or in understanding about how the economy functions? In the Soviet Union, the situation was different in that disputes about the final ends of the reform were also quite fierce, so that the value differences appeared much clearer.

From my visits to Marxist countries in various parts of the world I have received several general—perhaps superficial—impressions. In most of the Third World Marxist regimes, specifically "Marxist values" played little role except in the political games of the educated elite, in good measure because of the lack of resources to fund serious indoctrination programs.[3] In Eastern Europe, any such value shifts occurring under a

---

[1] The public opinion poll was directed by Andrei Reichev, the head of a public opinion research group operated by the Bulgarian State Council. I saw the unpublished tabulation of these data, and I do not know whether they have yet been published.

[2] Whether this impact increases over time is another controversial issue. In some countries, Czechoslovakia, for instance, it can be argued that "Marxist values" actually declined in importance in the last few decades. Certainly public demand for a "third way" between capitalism and communism or for "socialism with a human face" was much weaker in 1989–90 than in 1968.

[3] One example among many underlying this generalization is detailed in chapter 5, footnote 2 about colonial attitudes toward social stratification that have persisted until the pres-

Marxist regime were probably much less marked in the rural than in the urban sector. With regard to attitudes toward the market, the commercial values inherent in the long tradition of small-scale selling of agricultural products in rural markets continued and will serve rural populations well in the future. As indicated in chapter 9, the apparent lack of enthusiasm of many farmers to leave the collective farms appeared to have more to do with practical calculations of risk, costs, and economic returns than with ideological changes or shifts in values.

The impact of any alleged value shift on entrepreneurship is also problematic because entrepreneurs represent only a small portion of the population. In 1990 in visiting collective farms in Bulgaria, Czechoslovakia, East Germany, and Hungary, I met some extremely entrepreneurial top or middle farm managers who seemed both ready and willing to meet the challenges of the market economy. Indeed, it could be argued that in the past the constraints on their decision-making were so great that they had to develop a high degree of ingenuity and entrepreneurship in order to be able to survive in the system. But I also met farm managers who spent most of their time wringing their hands, paralyzed by the enormous economic uncertainties and incapable of thinking in market terms to maximize profits.

Difficult as it is to reach firm conclusions about changes in economic values that might influence the impact of economic reforms, I doubt whether these changes were a major factor explaining the slowness in implementing agricultural reforms. Any reforms are painful, particularly in the short run, and resistance is to be expected.

ECONOMICS AND POLITICS

The relations between ideology and agricultural reforms are not as strong as commonly believed. Significant agricultural reforms occurred or are occurring, of course, in those countries where the Marxist party lost power (for example, Hungary, Czechoslovakia). But the same reform processes were, or are, taking place in certain Marxist regimes where the government/party lost its ideological fervor (for example, Guyana, Madagascar, Mongolia, Mozambique), or even, in a somewhat different form, where the communist party maintained much of the original faith and power (China, Kampuchea, Laos, Viet Nam).[4] By the beginning of 1991

---

ent time. Cuba, which I have not visited, might represent a significant exception to the generalization that fundamental shifts in value have not occurred; but in the prevailing political climate of that nation it would be difficult to conduct research on these matters.

[4] I tried various statistical experiments to test whether decollectivization was related to path by which the Marxist party achieved power, but little of interest could be found. Part of the problem is that some of the nations under review have only talked about decollectiv-

agricultural reforms did not take place in certain Marxist regimes where the five political conditions for reform discussed in chapter 9 were missing (for example, Cuba and North Korea) or where the political leaders were unable to carry through the implementation of a set of consistent reforms (for example, the Soviet Union and, perhaps, Nicaragua).

Several political factors influencing agricultural reforms deserve particular attention: the phasing of the political and economic reforms, the political strength of the beneficiaries of agricultural reform, and political forces underlying the consistency of the reform. Since the range of possibilities regarding these three factors is too great to be covered in a single chapter, I choose instead to examine them in the context of four countries: Hungary, Guyana, China, and the Soviet Union. These countries represented quite different types of collectivized agriculture, featured quite different political and ideological currents, and exemplified quite different processes of agricultural reforms. A more systematic picture of the agricultural reforms in these four nations can be found in Research Note F.

The Phasing of Economic and Political Reforms

The problems arising from the phasing of economic and political reforms are most quickly revealed by a chronological survey of some major aspects of the reform process. Until 1990 significant economic changes in Hungary occurred either simultaneously or before political reforms; agricultural reforms also generally preceded reforms in other parts of the economy, but only by a few years. In China (as well as other Asian Marxist nations such as Laos and Viet Nam) the government has placed much greater emphasis on economic than on political reforms; and reforms were implemented successfully only in agriculture.[5] In Guyana economic reforms followed or occurred at the same time as some important political reforms, with human and civil rights increasing considerably in the second half of the 1980s (Guyana Human Rights Association 1988), and with the announcement of elections monitored by outside groups including the Carter Center for "sometime" in 1991. Through 1990 the Soviets placed more emphasis on political than on economic reforms.

Different kinds of problems arise, depending on whether economic re-

---

ization, and most others only decollectivized in a partial manner at the time these experiments were made. It may be a few years before a general theory of decollectivization can be tested. Let me add that in no country did the state of the agricultural sector per se play a significant role in the electoral defeat of communist parties.

[5] Laos and Viet Nam have also placed much greater emphasis on economic than political reforms, although a small measure of *glasnost'* has appeared in Viet Nam.

forms proceed, follow, or are simultaneous with the political reforms. For this reason it is useful to focus more attention on each of these four cases.

HUNGARY

The stream of systemic changes of the Hungarian economy from the mid-1960s up to 1990 can be dealt with quickly. Clearly these changes were closely tied to the political problems of the government in keeping the nation together after the revolt of 1956 and to the economic problems of maintaining agricultural exports, which at that time were a significant share of total exports. The Kádár government relaxed both political and economic restrictions slowly and simultaneously. The presence of the Soviet army constrained any political difficulties, either from the population or from the demoralized party and government apparatus.

The most important economic reforms came between 1965 and 1968, when the yearly production plan in both industry and agriculture was abolished, and in January 1990, when agricultural prices were dramatically liberalized. In the 1960s economic reforms preceded political reforms—indeed, they were probably acceptable to the Soviet authorities exactly for this reason. In preparing for these reforms the country was too small to try them out first on any particular geographical area. Instead, in 1965 the entire agricultural sector served as the experimental field for the more widespread reforms of 1968. The price reforms in 1990, which essentially allowed most agricultural prices to float, were made several months before the 1991 elections and represent an act of political courage and statesmanship by the Marxist party in power. These price changes were part of a slow but steady price liberalization that occurred for the entire economy between 1989 and the beginning of 1991. The reforms in agricultural prices were, however, more abrupt and radical than similar changes in other sectors, in good measure because of the fiscal crisis and the necessity of reducing governmental subsidies, than by any carefully premeditated phasing of economic and political reforms. In 1990 after the elections in March and April, other types of economic reforms became bogged down. Many aspects of agricultural reforms awaited resolution of the question of land ownership, which was an extremely divisive political issue. The recent Hungarian sequencing of political and economic reforms in a slow and simultaneous fashion runs the danger that the agricultural reforms may never be completed.

CHINA

Because of the size of the country, Chinese provincial economic authorities had more authority to institute experiments than their counterparts in the Soviet Union. The 1979 Chinese reforms began, as it were, on the periphery of the economy several years before in the poor and hilly province of Anhui (and, to a lesser extent, Sichuan).[6] The extensive experimentation and the successes enjoyed in these remote areas provided some dramatic reasons for their adoption throughout the country in the early 1980s during Deng's first years in power (Chevrier 1988).

Some political reforms following the death of Mao in 1976 preceded these economic changes. The most spectacular was the quick arrest and trial of the "Gang of Four," which had attempted to carry on the leftist legacy of Mao. In the next two years, the battle "to seek truth from facts" and to fight against the "two whatevers" (to believe whatever Mao had proclaimed and to follow whatever he said) were slogans indicative of an important expansion of intellectual freedom, and simultaneously a greater tolerance for intellectual and social diversity, a declining emphasis on the class struggle, and a rethinking of many basic issues (Halpern 1989). This was a Chinese version of *glasnost'*, but it was more controlled and focused, less noisy and dangerous. The struggle was also accompanied by changes in the political structure during the late 1970s. These included an increase in citizen rights, an introduction of due-process guarantees in the legal sphere, a strengthening of popular representation in the political arena by allowing competitive elections at a provincial level, the rewriting of legal codes, and the reduction of party interference in social life (Clarke 1987; Baum 1986; Womack 1984). In 1977–78 the government also carried out some minor economic changes in the countryside, for instance, reducing the number of nonproductive cadre.

In late 1978, Deng and his group began to gain key party and governmental positions to enable them to carry out the agricultural reforms. They consolidated their hold on the party not just with the removal of Hua Guofeng from the premiership in 1981 and his chairmanship of the party in 1982 but also through renewal of the party leadership, bringing a new generation of officials into positions of power (Clarke 1987). Although the degree to which Deng had formulated an exact blueprint of changes is unclear, his general ideas appeared well known to party members during his manoeuvering for power. Indeed, party support for his program played an important role in his political ascendancy; and this support meant that an entrenched old guard was less able to block important changes.

----

[6] Bernstein (1984) tells how the household contracting system had been quietly introduced in a number of districts in the 1960s. Aubert (1988) notes how Deng Xiaoping sent trusted allies such as Wan Li and Zhao Ziyang to Anhui and Sichuan in 1977, in part to carry out a set of agricultural programs exactly opposite to those being organized at the national level by Hua Guofeng. Chevrier (1988) argues that in the Soviet Union, this would have been akin to experimentation by Trotsky or Bukharin with anti-Stalinist economic policies in some remote republic in the Soviet far east. Wan returned to Peking in 1980 to become deputy premier in charge of agriculture and to extend the family contract system to the whole nation; Zhao returned to become premier.

The first step toward decollectivization was the reorganization of the internal management system of the communes through the introduction of the contract system. Although this did not appear a very radical step to Western eyes, it was a direct repudiation of the "learning from Dazhai" approach upon which the Maoists laid so much emphasis (Zweig 1989). What was crucial in the decollectivization process was that the property rights reforms were undertaken in small steps, each "unworthy of a major fight" (Zweig 1987).[7] Deng and his colleagues appeared to have a consistent vision of the broad outlines of what they sought, but they were quite flexible as to the manner by which the various policy measures were implemented. The successes achieved at each step, however, allowed a further more radical step to be taken quickly until the cumulative effect of the changes totally changed the system. The agricultural reforms had an administrative momentum that could not be achieved in the industrial sector.

From 1981 until 1989 few significant political changes occurred. Deng appeared to envision a more flexible and liberal economy, gradually spreading out from agriculture to the other sectors, combined with relatively tight political controls, albeit looser than during the reign of Mao. The strategy ran into three major difficulties during the second half of the 1980s: stagnation of grain production, although total agricultural production continued to grow; inflation as the result of fiscal deficits combined with inadequate controls on bank credit; and a growing discontent with the slowness of liberalization in the political realm, which culminated in the Tiananmen Square massacre in 1989. The Chinese sequencing of political and economic reforms ran the danger that the agricultural reforms might be reversed in the 1990s as political centralization increased.

GUYANA

After the death of President Forbes Burnham in 1985, the civil rights situation improved and, by early 1991, political thuggery has declined, the opposition press was lively, and arbitrary political measures were reduced. Over the 1970s and 1980s, per capita GDP had declined to such an extent that the need for economic reform was apparent to all. Nevertheless, the political situation was complicated because of racial/political factors that are found in a number of other Third World Nations (Table 4.3).

More specifically, most of the entrepreneurs in the city, as well as most of the sugar and rice farmers, were descendants of emigrants from the

---

[7] An interesting account of the ways in which the small steps took place in a single village is provided by Huang (1989, chap. 9). This account also illustrates how a brigade functionary, who opposed the contract system, stalled in implementing it but was finally forced to comply.

Indian subcontinent. These Indo-Guyanese constituted a bare majority of the entire population and were the power base of the People's Progressive Party (PPP), a relatively orthodox Marxist-Leninist party. For over three decades, however, national political power has been held by the People's National Congress (PNC) by means of a series of elections most observers believe were fraudulent (Singh 1988). This heterodox Marxist party had a power base among the Afro-Guyanese in the urban areas and in the bauxite mines. Amer-Indians constituted less than five percent of the population and had little political or economic significance.

The neglect of agriculture in favor of the urban consumer and the bloated government sector (in 1980 about one-fifth of the labor force worked directly in the government apparatus) were only a few of the techniques employed by the PNC to maintain its dominance and to keep its power base together (Pryor 1991). Its brand of Marxism meant ethnic domination, a feature appearing, as indicated in chapter 4, in other Marxist regimes as well.

Many of the key reform measures, for instance, the privatization of agricultural processing industries, improvement of the economic status of the agricultural sector through greater investment in key infrastructure, floating agricultural prices, reduction of the size of government, encouragement of entrepreneurship, and devaluation to stimulate exports would all act directly to benefit the Indo-Guyanese at the expense of Afro-Guyanese. A completely fair election would undoubtedly give the Indo-Guyanese community greater political power and, most likely, control of the government if the opposition parties could unite behind one presidential candidate. It is no wonder that the Guyanese government was running months behind its agreed schedule of reforms with the International Monetary Fund (IMF), or that it postponed elections from 1990, when they were constitutionally mandated.

Additional pressures were placed on the Guyanese government because the linking of political and economic reforms may be the only way to attract domestic or foreign capital. In a traditional state-oriented economy with a Marxist party in power, the lack of political liberalization means that no matter what contracts are signed or agreements made with the government, private investment projects are still subject to arbitrary constraints and interventions by the government, because the investor seldom has the possibility of restitution in the domestic courts. A liberal economy with a liberal trade regime reduces these political risks, at least if the government is sufficiently strong to prevent chaos. Thus if the Guyanese government wishes to attract capital, reverse the fall in total income and agricultural production (Table 8.3), and stem the labor migration, which had reached an annual rate of 3 percent of the labor force by the end of the 1980s (Commonwealth Advisory Group 1989), it would

have to undertake political and economic measures that might well lead
to its defeat in the next election.[8]

This dilemma, albeit in a less acute form, is found in other multiethnic
Third World Marxist regimes. History provides few examples of a political party willing to sacrifice itself for the economic good of the nation. In
early 1991, when this manuscript was closed, it took considerably opti-
mism about the power of the IMF to influence economic events in this
destitute nation, as well as the luck of continued disunity of the various
opposition parties, to believe that political and economic reforms in Guyana would continue to march forward together.

SOVIET UNION

The constellations of political and economic factors in the Soviet Union
were much different from those in China. When Gorbachev came to
power in March 1985, he appeared to have a much less specific and more
conservative program of economic change than Deng had in December
1978. Gorbachev had made his reputation in agriculture, where his name
was associated with two contradictory organizational innovations. The
first was the Ipatov system of harvesting, a centralizing measure by which
harvesting in a given region is coordinated by a single party office directing the allocation of the work force and the machinery for around-the-
clock operations. The second was a contract system, a potentially decen-
tralizing measure whereby teams of workers or even individual families
receive contracts and resources (including land and machinery) for a particular amount of work, with their income based on contract fulfillment.

Gorbachev faced a political elite still composed of many supporters of
the Brezhnev approach (Åslund 1989). Thus considerable political manoeuvering was necessary before dramatic changes in agriculture could be
introduced. His early conception of economic reform appeared, at least
on the surface, to be relatively traditional: tightening labor discipline,
streamlining administrative organs, creating super ministries to coordinate the complex interrelations between industries (including agriculture) more effectively, and raising goals for the 1986–90 plan period. In
his first few years, most of his statements on agriculture followed the
lines of the 1982 Food Program. The government bureaucracy interpreted the contract system in agriculture in a conservative fashion; that
is, as primarily a payment-by-results compensation system, rather than
as a first step toward decollectivization.

Gorbachev's reticence about radical reform in agriculture can be attrib-

---

[8] Sometimes an authoritarian right-wing government can convince investors that property is "strong" and their investments are safe from arbitrary intervention. Augusto Pin-
ochet of Chile was quite successful at this. But property is always safer in a liberal regime
with constraints on governmental actions.

uted either to his desire to minimize the economic and political costs of reform, to an initial belief that only minor policy tinkering was required, or to placing his priorities for economic reform on other productive sectors. At no point did he seem to encourage a general decollectivization. Rather, he appeared to envision an institutional pluralism with state farms, collective farms, and individual farms, which, to a certain extent, would specialize in different crops appropriate to their size.

The competing goals that he pursued led to a program with many inconsistencies. These raised the risks for farmers participating in the decollectivization opportunities by raising the specter that the socialist agricultural sector would always receive priority of inputs and resources over the individual agricultural sector. One example among many occurred in 1986 in the effort to enforce the decrees against "unearned income." Party and state officials in various areas closed down farmers' markets, reduced the availability of transportation of privately produced goods to these markets, and conducted a "pogrom" against private greenhouses (Åslund 1989, p. 158, citing Soviet sources). These measures, of course, increased the risks of individual farming and, although halted, left a bitter memory. This policy ambivalence continued through 1990, with Boris Yeltsin announcing a plan that would permit massive privatization of agriculture, Premier Nikolai Ryzhkov resisting, and Gorbachev appearing to temporize by announcing a referendum to approve privatization of agricultural land, a policy already approved in principle by the Soviet legislature in March 1990.[9] The drama proceeded in early December 1990 when Gorbachev finally declared himself against private land ownership, at the same time that the Russian Republic parliament was approving Boris Yeltsin's plan for private ownership, but with the significant constraint that owners of this property could not resell it to private individuals, but only to the government (Clines 1990). Of course, this regulation could significantly reduce incentives for long-run investment in the land because of uncertainty about whether the government would pay a fair price. Thus Russian policymakers repeated the same errors of the Chinese land lease system by making the farmers uncertain about their long-run prospects, a problem discussed in previous chapters.

The Soviet Union, like China, had numerous agricultural experiments, but their scale was smaller and their successes were less convincing before the government implemented them in a frontal assault on the rest of

---

[9] Curiously, this March law never used the term "private," and "private property" appeared to be the "institution that dares not say its name." In a few months, however, this terminological reticence changed. Nevertheless, in discussions about the Russian law, opposition to the private sale of land was often phrased in the rhetoric of "the land is our mother, and we can not buy or sell our mother." Other opposition arose because the buying and selling of land might lead to "speculation."

the country. It is noteworthy that the lease contracts in the Soviet Union, upon which Gorbachev has placed so much political capital, originated in the sparsely populated northern areas, far from the economic and political center of the nation.[10] Despite these attempted changes, top policymakers did not seem to view the agricultural sector as the forerunner of economic reform in other sectors.

These early tepid attempts at economic reform produced little change in economic performance. A major stumbling block in their implementation lay in the conservative bureaucracy, which had little to gain by carrying out such changes. By 1987, Gorbachev began to talk about more radical economic reforms and, moreover, tried to obtain more grassroots support through his program of *glasnost'*, a major political reform that was aimed at overcoming bureaucratic and political resistance to the proposed economic reforms by increasing their accountability to the public.[11] If political reforms precede economic reforms and if a large segment of the farm population fears decollectivization or other radical reforms in agriculture, such economic reforms may never occur. The Soviet sequencing of political and economic reforms runs the danger that the agricultural reforms may never really get started.

Beneficiaries of Reform

Government cadre supervising agriculture were, of course, a major beneficiary of the system. As noted in previous chapters the rural party apparatus played a major role in agricultural decision making in certain countries so that they must be considered beneficiaries as well.[12] Both

---

[10] Yanov (1984, p. 60) notes that the "link reform" in the early 1960s "roared from east to west like a forest fire" from the obscure Amur Region to the Omsk Province to the Altai Territory to Kazakhistan until finally reaching the north Caucasus and the Ukraine, the main breadbaskets of the nation.

[11] Since 1986 Gorbachev's statements about agricultural reform have been considerably in advance of the measures actually taken, and two interpretations can be offered. Although between 1987 and 1990 he had the political power to ram through a series of radical agricultural reforms, he preferred a Fabian approach in order to preserve his political capital for reforms in the urban sector. This meant that for agricultural policy he was trying to build a consensus around his proposals, quietly removing opponents to such ideas, and slowly but systematically preparing the groundwork for some dramatic change. An opposite interpretation is that Gorbachev had not yet consolidated his power to the extent that he could significantly change the structure of the agricultural sector and that his agricultural initiatives were continually sabotaged by an entrenched bureaucracy. By 1990 his ability to effect any significant reforms in agriculture appeared to be rapidly declining.

[12] The differences between party and governmental cadre should not be exaggerated. For instance, in 1990 East German government officials were quick to tell me that it was the party, not the government, that was responsible for the amalgamation of collective farms, the separation of crop growing and animal raising activities, the construction of open-air

groups of cadre have considerable incentive to prevent a marketization and decollectivization of agriculture that would leave them with less power and income. Reformers have chosen different ways to approach this problem in the four countries under review.

In Hungary the rural party apparatus played a much smaller role in economic decision-making than in the Soviet Union or China. This occurred because the party was relatively centralized and led by urban-oriented politicians. As a result, the rural party groups could not convince urban party leaders to move slowly on the agricultural reforms (Comisso and Marer 1986). During the late 1950s and early 1960s the local government apparatus subverted the central government's intention to eliminate most mandatory crop deliveries by instituting their own delivery quotas. But before the 1968 reforms the central government managed to change the parameters of local governmental authority so that their resistance to economic decentralization was significantly reduced. Since the overwhelming majority of farmers had recently been coerced into joining the collective farms, they had little desire for heavy-handed government intervention into their sphere of decision-making, so they did not resist this easing of regulations either. There was, in short, a tacit alliance between the farmers and the central party apparatus.

In the 1990 national and communal elections, the communist party (now called the Hungarian Socialist Party) was decisively defeated and the change in government also weakened the power of governmental cadre in intervening in farm decision-making. The collective farm directors still remained a major antagonist to certain agricultural reforms such as the dismemberment of the farms. To the extent that the directors could be removed from office by farm members, their power of resistance also diminished.

The Chinese reforms of the early 1980s also had a large rural constituency, but they encountered considerable local resistance among agricultural cadre (Bernstein 1984; Burns 1985–86; Unger 1985–86; Zweig 1983, 1987). Most cadre greeted the reforms "with less than enthusiasm," not only because these reforms would result in the reduction of their ranks but also because their relative incomes would (and did) suffer (Latham

stalls for cattle and then barns housing two thousand or more cows, and other policy disasters. There was, however, a considerable overlap of top government and party officials, most governmental officials were members of the party, and the government apparatus, of course, implemented these policies.

1985). The government took several political measures, however, that overcame this resistance.

Most important, the agricultural reformers of the central government took steps to separate local party and governmental officials from economic management. For instance, the amount of grain sold to the state no longer served as the major measure of cadre performance, and village officials did not suffer a shortage of funds if a harvest of a certain size was not produced (Oi 1989a).[13] The consolidation of power at the top ranks of the party of the agricultural reformers, combined with the rapid rise in peasant incomes and their push for further reforms, also placed pressures on both sides of the cadre to implement even those reforms that ran against their interests (Zweig 1987). Furthermore, many local agricultural cadre, who appeared to have a great deal of political power to lose by the reforms, could be "bought off" with increased economic power, since the reforms allowed them to increase their income in the following four ways.

1. In the process of distributing farm land and other assets among peasant households, they were in a position to obtain a favorable allotment (a case study for Chen village is found in Chan, Madsen, and Unger 1984).

2. Those farm families in the best position to gain wealth after the initial distribution of land and assets were the so-called specialized households. They engaged in certain economic activities allowing them priority access to credit and inputs. Of such families, 45 percent were said to be former agricultural officials (see research note F for more details).

3. The rural cadre had a broader network of contacts outside the farm and, for this reason, its members were in a better position than the average peasant to engage in trade, not just of farm inputs but also of consumer goods.

4. Marketization of the countryside was not complete and clientelist politics remained important. As Oi (1989a) has noted, "The reforms did not take power away from the cadre so much as they merely redistributed power among cadre and modified the list of resources they control. . . . The peasants are more vulnerable to the market and, most importantly, to *the local agents* of the state—both within the village and in the larger market environment—who are charged with implementing the directives of the state."

This buying-off of the cadre has occurred in other Marxist regimes as well. For instance, in Hungary, some of the most fervent advocates of marketization were party cadre who also had high managerial positions

---

[13] Hartford (1985) argues that top Chinese party leaders instructed local party cadre not to interfere with economic management in agriculture. Nevertheless, these party leaders, rather than the government, proclaimed the major lines of agricultural policy and held the local party cadre responsible for its implementation. Still, local party cadre were not responsible for production goals.

in industrial enterprises and who could solidify their position in the latter (not to mention increase their income) in a fully marketized economy by various types of manipulations during the privatization process. (These managerial cadre in the urban areas were called "red barons"; in the rural areas, "green barons.")

It should be emphasized that although the Chinese reforms were imposed from above, a major part of the reorganization of agriculture was implemented from below by the farmworkers themselves following general guidelines issued by the highest party organs. For instance, the teams divided a major share of the commune's assets among their members following general rules, but they also took close account of local circumstances and desires. This procedure represented an alliance, as it were, between the farm households and the reformers over the heads of the local farm bureaucracy and party apparatus (Unger 1985–86; Zweig 1987).

With each step and the success that followed, the scope of the changes and the pressures against the cadre intensified. Certain key economic measures encouraged the separation of the government and the party on the local level. These included changing the unit of production in agriculture from the commune to the farm household, increasing economic incentives for agricultural production, and introducing market elements into the sales of agricultural produce through elimination of the previous production quotas and dissolution of the monopoly purchasing agency.

GUYANA

Except for the small group managing the state farm company, government and party cadre did not play a major role in agriculture and resistance to the agricultural reforms per se appeared minimal. As previously indicated, there was resistance to the entire package of economic and political reforms because of its impact on the political fortunes of the party in power and of the Afro-Guyanese. What did not seem to occur in a major scale up to 1991 was asset-stripping or other measures to serve as bribes for the current governmental functionaries to yield power. Any assets stripped in the state-owned sugar estates would mean that the potential buyer would offer a lower price for these farms. Furthermore, because it had a management contract before purchasing these farms, the private company kept a sharp eye to prevent such thievery. For the rest of the economy it was impossible to determine whether corruption had increased during the first steps toward liberalization.

SOVIET UNION

Gorbachev's greater stress on political rather than on economic reforms reflected, in part, the fact that the Soviet Union had an educated and

urban population, which might have been less resigned to political op-
pression than the much less educated and rural Chinese population. Nevertheless, the Soviet organizational reforms were in large part imposed
from above and implemented by the agricultural hierarchy, especially by
the farm managers and the party representatives at local governmental
levels, rather than by the rural population. These cadre had a long history of resisting or subverting agricultural reforms;[14] it should not be surprising that the reforms met many roadblocks. For instance, even though
contracts for particular targets were signed that gave the small group considerable autonomy, farm managers still tried to assign farm workers to
particular jobs. The managers set up payment systems within the con-
tract-groups that were too complex for members to understand. And the
managers created difficulties when they felt that farmers in contract-
groups earned too much (Laird and Laird 1988). Furthermore, Gorbachev seemed of two minds about increasing farmer decision-making
autonomy. For instance, in a June 1987 speech he stressed increasing
individual initiative of family farmers and, at the same time, noted the
importance of increasing party influence in all aspects of economic work.
In a March 1989 address, he noted the serious food supply problems and
asked rhetorically how the party organization was to resolve them (Laird
1990).

The Soviet agricultural bureaucracy was formidable in size, particularly on a local level. Many regional agro-industrial committees had several times more bureaucrats than the number of farms in their region
(Shmelov and Popov 1989, p. 273). Even more important, the Soviet government did not restructure incentives of these cadre. For instance, despite official denials, it appeared that government and party cadre were
still judged by grain and other production in the farms under their jurisdiction. The Soviet government also appeared unwilling to buy the support of these cadre by placing them in positions to increase their incomes
through the reforms.

The deterioration of the Soviet economy in the late 1980s did nothing
to reinforce popular or party support for the tepid agricultural reforms.
Although the economic downturn introduced a sense of crisis that encouraged more radical reforms, it also encouraged greater bureaucratic
resistance. In sum, Gorbachev was unable to undercut the beneficiaries
of the old agricultural system or to institute Deng's virtuous circle of eco-

[14] Yanov (1984) provides details on the vital support these provincial and district elites
provided for the ouster of Khrushchev in October 1964. Brezhnev reverted from Khrushchev's strategy of organizational changes in agriculture to large investments in this sector
instead, pouring unprecedented resources into agricultural investment. This approach had
little success and capital productivity fell.

nomic successes, which reinforced and encouraged further economic reform.

Once Again, Consistency of Reform

Inconsistencies within the reform lead to ever-changing governmental
rules and regulations, which, in turn, imply weak property rights, a topic
discussed in the previous chapter. These inconsistencies can arise either
from the basic conception underlying the reform, from lack of agreement
among the various political groups formulating and implementing the reform program, or from difficulties in administering and implementing the
complex reform plans.

Clearly it is impossible to change an entire economic system at once.
The higher the level of economic development and the more complex
the economy, the more difficult it is to achieve consistency when far-
reaching changes are made. The key is to put a critical mass of reforms
in place at one time and then adjust the rest of the economy in the succeeding years to bring it into alignment with the basic vision. If the initial
reform conception is flawed, or if factions holding different views about
the nature of the reform gain temporary victories, or if the top leadership
is unable to enforce its vision, then the reform program faces serious dangers. Inconsistent measures will be issued, then more adjustments will
have to be made to correct for the flaws, and more uncertainty will result.
Again, the Soviet Union, Hungary, China, and Guyana provide instructive examples.

SOVIET UNION

For the Soviet Union, the problems of consistency were particularly severe. Despite the encouragement of private agricultural production provided by the 1982 Food Program, local officials continued to stop peasants from selling their produce in regions other than their own. It was
also difficult to give much independent decision-making authority to the
work units when the farm managers with power over them received a
rigid plan or when agricultural inputs and other supplies were difficult to
obtain. It was difficult to give flexibility to an agricultural supply system
when it continued to be centrally run so that local conditions could not
be taken into account carefully. It was difficult to produce the food consumers wanted when the farms had to produce according to a rigid plan
or state orders. Finally, it was difficult to generate much confidence in
the reforms or to taking up opportunities offered by legislation when, in
1988, Yegor Ligachev was appointed Central Committee Secretary for
Agriculture, a post that he occupied for two years before resigning. He
was an experienced politician with little taste for the market mechanism,

for breaking up the collective and state farms, or for implementing family leaseholds.

Some quantitative dimensions of the difficulty in achieving a consistent reform also are available (Litwack 1990). For instance, the 1987 Law on State Enterprises that affected state farms made defunct more than 1,200 previous all-union (national) plans, many of which appeared after 1985, as well as 7,500 republic-level decrees, not to mention 31,000 all-union and 800,000 republican ministerial rules and regulations. In 1989 this law was also altered and amended. The 1987 financial norms, which were supposed to have remained stable for five years, were overhauled in 1989 and 1990. In the two years following enactment of the 1987 Law on Co-operatives, which provided for stable tax rates and regulations for these organizations, the law was amended in December 1988, February 1989, August 1989, and October 1989. These amendments restricted cooperative activities, changed tax rates, and limited price-setting possibilities. Many of Gorbachev's own actions in agricultural policy-making gave rise to inconsistencies, for instance, he ordered lease contracting before laws were passed making it legal. Furthermore, once leasing was legalized, it was discovered that the laws conflicted with both governmental regulations and constitutional guarantees of free use of land by collective farms (Mustard 1989). Indeed, it was not until March 1990 that laws regulating leaseholding were finally passed.

HUNGARY

In Hungary after several years of preparation, the major pieces of the 1968 economic reforms were introduced at one time. The reforms had been carefully prepared and "sold" to the major groups in the party so that there was general agreement as to what was wrong with the economy and how the reforms would address those flaws (Comisso and Marer 1986). As a result, the changes had sufficient coherence so that the stream of corrections over the succeeding five years to resolve contradictions and inconsistencies that cropped up did not change the basic thrust of the reform program. It was only in 1972–73 that significant reversals took place, under the false assumption that the disequilibria appearing in the economy were of a temporary nature that could be handled by administrative restraints. By 1980, however, most important political figures had made a more realistic appraisal of the current economic problems and the role of the reforms so that the reform program, limited as it was, appeared on track again. In 1990, however, when the possibility of a systemic change appeared, the diversity of views within the parliament and government raised the saliency of the consistency problem once again.

In China, the problem of consistency was less severe. Measures changing the farm and changing the degree of marketization were in much greater synchrony. In the six-year period of reform, of course, complete consistency in a static sense was not achieved at any point. Nevertheless, the broad and rapid reforms on a number of fronts mutually reinforced each other, and this dynamic consistency provided a key element of the success of the entire package. For this reason it is also impossible to specify which of the many changes was most responsible for the remarkable increase in production since 1978.

GUYANA

The reforms in Guyana were primarily of a macroeconomic nature and the micro-economic ties were primarily to the three key exporting industries: sugar, rice, and bauxite. The entire reform was run quite centrally through the Planning Commission, the Ministry of Finance, and the Central Bank so that consistency problems were minimized. As far as I could tell, the Ministry of Agriculture had little say about the reform measures taken in agriculture.

GENERAL ATTITUDES TOWARD ECONOMIC REFORMS

By the end of the 1980s many of the Marxist regimes had serious economic problems. In several, especially in the Third World, unemployment was high; in others, prices were increasing steeply; and in still others, particularly in East Europe, shortages were becoming endemic as money held by the public was increasing at a considerably faster rate than production of consumption goods and services. Long-run problems were also becoming more apparent: in many countries technology was falling increasingly behind world levels and investment efficiency was declining. In the agricultural sector, this was manifested by relatively low total factor productivities.

In many cases it was difficult to grasp the magnitude of these problems. For example, an estimation of the monetary overhang is essential for formulating policies that would deal successfully with problems of suppressed inflation. In 1990 in Czechoslovakia the economists I interviewed estimated this magnitude anywhere in the range between 15 to 600 billion crowns.

In general, solutions to these short- and long-run economic problems usually require a decrease in real income for certain segments of the population; the more drastic the solution, the more incomes fall, at least in the short run. In the past, governmental efforts in Marxist regimes to solve these and similar economic problems with fundamental changes were often met with strikes and violence. For example, as noted in the previous chapter, two Polish governments fell in their efforts to reduce food subsidies by raising food prices and, at the same time, compensating those hardest hit by such measures. But in the "big bang" in Poland in January 1990, where almost all prices rose dramatically and real incomes fell, most of the population accepted these changes without turmoil. What factors underlay these quite different attitudes toward economic reform and the willingness of the population to put up with hardships in some cases, but not in others?

In Poland, the situation seems readily explainable. In 1990, in contrast to the other periods, most Poles were fully aware that their economy was in desperate shape. They also remembered that the previous reform drives aimed at improving the administered economy in an incremental fashion had failed. Furthermore, the new noncommunist government had a great deal of popular support. The Polish nation was also relatively homogeneous so that ethnic tensions were not important; and the Roman Catholic church supplied an additional unifying element. To a certain degree the government could also blame the necessity of this economic pain of the reform on the Soviet Union.

In other countries other factors have played a role in the acceptance of radical reforms. In East Germany the economic shock that occurred with the economic union in the middle of 1990 was politically acceptable because the population agreed to the implicit offer made by the West German Christian Democratic Union during the election: German unity as quickly as possible and, although it would be economically painful, aid by West Germany to provide a social net to ease the transition. In Czechoslovakia, after the installation of a non-Marxist government in 1990, public opinion data showed that the general public expected and was willing to accept lower real incomes and price increases in the future, if the long-run economic situation improved and the country "returned to Europe."[15]

If unacceptable, fundamental changes in the structure of agriculture can also be met by political countermeasures. Although a rural population is more difficult to mobilize for mob protests against government-mandated economic reforms, farmers have other ways of manifesting

[15] According to a public opinion poll of 2,700 Czechoslovak citizens that was reported in the *Frankfurter Allegemeine Zeitung*, 29 June 1990, 70 percent expected a noticeable reduction in their income, 80 percent believed that an increase in unemployment would occur, and 44 percent declared themselves ready to work harder. About half expected price increases of roughly 50 percent for necessary goods and, moreover, were willing to accept such price increases as long as they felt that these measures would lead to an improvement of the economy and a "return to Europe."

their discontent, for instance, slaughter of cattle, barn burning, sabotage of equipment so that crops cannot be planted or harvested, road blocks, and tractor caravans.

Of course, reforms in the agricultural sector are easiest to carry out if previous unpopular measures are revoked and, as previously noted, a large segment of the Chinese rural population welcomed decollectivization. Painful reforms are also more acceptable if the population supports its government and has confidence in its ability to implement the reforms in an impartial and efficient manner. This appears to describe the situation in Czechoslovakia, Hungary, and Poland after the fall from power of communist parties. But such confidence will surely not last if the new governments prove incapable of mastering the difficult economic situations within a reasonable time. In some cases, the desperate economic situation became sufficiently obvious to the people that they were willing to accept any change that had some hope, however remote, of succeeding, even if their own incomes are hurt. Such a factor seems to account for the change in attitude of the Soviet population from a resistance to general price increases that were proposed in the summer of 1990 to a relatively passive acceptance of dramatic price increases in April 1991.

Among Third World Marxist regimes the same mechanism was at work. The manifest failure of the Guyanese government to operate the state farms underlay the change of Guyanese public opinion from violent objections to the foreign ownership of these sugar estates in the middle 1970s to the acceptance of their sale to the former owners in the early 1990s. Similarly, the defeat of the Sandinistas in elections in early 1990 was probably due more to the average annual inflation of more than four thousand percent a year for the three years preceding the election than to a repudiation of their politics. In any case, the Sandinista election slogan, "Things will get better," rang hollow.

The optimal period of time for carrying out radical economic reforms, both in agriculture and in other sectors of the economy, may be short. In East Europe it was unfortunate that in some countries such as Czechoslovakia, Yugoslavia, and the Soviet Union, precious time was squandered in 1990 in trying to resolve long-standing interethnic disputes, and that in other countries such as Bulgaria, the new governments did not appear to have sufficient parliamentary and political strength to get an economic reform program approved by the legislature and implemented.

Among the Third World Marxist regimes at the beginning of 1991, the situation appeared even less promising for the economic reforms. Many had weak governments, either because of lack of suitable skills to implement the necessary reforms or, as in case of Nicaragua, because the governing coalition was splintered. Many had serious racial/political problems, as in Guyana. Some had collectivized without a land reform, which meant that decollectivization of cooperative by returning the land to the previous owners was sometimes difficult and that some type of new land redistribution is necessary. Although the Guyana case suggests that in some cases the state farms can be more easily returned to former owners, the former owners may not want these estates (which happened in Madagascar), because they would cost too much to rehabilitate; and furthermore, the governments may not be able to enforce their property claims of the new owners, as in Nicaragua. In sum, difficulties in implementing agricultural reforms, especially by inexperienced governments, may mean that the basic economic problems underlying the reforms will not be solved. Economic development depends not only upon the organization of the economy, but on the economic policies pursued by the government. For this reason it may turn out that in some Third World nations, no economic system will bring about prosperity and development.

THE FALL (?) OF COLLECTIVE AGRICULTURE

I do not believe that collective farming is a closed chapter in the book of the evolving economic history of the world.

The problems of transition to a market economy are too great to be easily overcome, and some Marxist regimes now undergoing economic reforms such as Bulgaria, Romania, and the Soviet Union, may fall back and return to a modified centrally planned economy with collectivized agriculture, albeit with a somewhat larger share of private agricultural production. In 1990, Chinese authorities were seriously discussing recollectivization as a means to overcoming production stagnation in agriculture and the neglect of the common irrigation facilities. In countries where a Marxist party was voted out, the party may be voted back into power if the new non-Marxist government proves unable to master the economic chaos, which was often exacerbated by the departing Marxist government. An extreme case occurred in Nicaragua where, in the interregnum before the anti-Sandinista coalition (UNO) took power in April 1990, the Sandinista government increased government expenditures, raised wages, issued considerably more credit, enacted legislation making it difficult to fire government employees, gave away considerable state-owned assets to party supporters, looted the state treasury, and took other measures that made it more difficult for the UNO government to tame inflation and stabilize the economy.[16] Moreover, after they left office, the Sandinistas undertook various political actions such as encour-

---

[16] Such cynical politics are not preordained: the transition government in Hungary took a series of unpopular economic measures that eased the difficulties of the coalition government headed by the Democratic Forum in mastering the economic situation.

aging land takeovers and strikes. This had the effect of discouraging badly needed private investment to aid the economy and of depriving the UNO government of some economic successes.

In some of the most radical Marxist regimes, for example, Cuba and North Korea, the governments may not attempt to decollectivize or to reduce the scope of central planning in agriculture, at least in the next few decades. Furthermore, as indicated in chapter 9, many current collective farmers may not want to decollectivize, so that the most that can be done is to transform the collective farms into either joint-stock companies or true producer cooperatives.

Indeed, situations actually encouraging agricultural collectivization in the future can be imagined. If rich corporate farms and plantations in the Third World account for a large share of total agricultural production, they will always provide tempting targets for politicians wishing to obtain new governmental revenues without raising taxes. For instance, in Guyana, the Marxist-oriented People's Progressive Party may well come to power some day, not because of its ideology but because of its political basis in the ethnic majority. If, at that time the private owners have put sugar estates on a firm financial footing, the estates may again be nationalized. Or in another country, some would-be political dictator might believe that although collectivized agriculture had many economic costs, it is an effective means of subjugating the peasantry. Or as capitalist agriculture inevitably fails in some countries, particularly in the Third World, some political elites might come to believe that many of the economic problems discussed in the previous pages did not arise as a result of structural but of policy problems and that many could be overcome if these collective and state farms were "properly organized" so as to avoid the "previous mistakes."

Marxist parties operating in some countries that decollectivized or are undergoing this process seem to believe if the nation ever recollectivizes again, it is scarcely believable that it will be able to reprivatize agriculture for some decades after that. According to this line of argument, the perceived risks facing farmers in the future would simply be too great to induce them to become full-time private farmers still another time. This thesis, I believe, has certain merit.

Collectivized agriculture represents one of the largest social experiments in history. The system can be described in highly idealistic terms, even though millions died and other millions suffered greatly in its creation and implementation. As I try to show, collectivized agriculture also took quite different forms in various Marxist regimes and cannot be considered a phenomenon whose essence can be grasped by looking only at a few countries.

In this study I try to make the different forces underlying the creation, management, and reform of collective and state farms understandable. I endeavor to separate out those causal forces related to the national traditions, the level of economic development, and other local conditions on one side, and more general ideological forces on the other in order to gain perspective on this complicated and fascinating set of institutions. I attempt to evaluate the system and to show, in contrast to reports in the popular press, that it did not fail because aggregate growth was too low, but that this growth occurred at a high cost, as manifested by the low growth of total factor productivity.

Much still remains to be learned about the creation, development, and impact of collectivized agriculture. Perhaps the greatest gap in our knowledge occurs in the social realm: What kinds of people did such a farming system produce? How did they structure their lives and were they any happier than farmers in other countries, who faced much greater economic uncertainties? The materials presented in this book do not reflect all there is to know about collectivized agriculture. Many issues—economic, political, and social—are left untouched. Nevertheless, if the comparative approach that I employ provides the outlines of collectivized agriculture as a whole, the reader has reaped the harvest of this book.

APPENDIXES

Research Note A

CLASSIFICATION OF MARXIST REGIMES

WESTERN SCHOLARS have approached the identification of Marxist regimes in very different ways. Two examples among many are Alvin Z. Rubinstein, an American political scientist and specialist on Soviet politics, and Bogden Szajkowski, an Anglo-Polish sociologist and editor of a multivolume series on Marxist regimes. Their lists of Marxist regimes appear in the third and fourth columns of Table RA.1. As a first step, both start with the way in which the particular government identifies itself. Rubinstein, however, appears to give more weight to another factor: whether or not the Marxist party in power is of a Leninist type. If it is not, he then asks whether the government is sufficiently centralized to serve this role. This would occur, for instance, when the army plays the role of the "vanguard" party; such a praetorian government Marx derisively called "barracks socialism." Szajkowski appears to rely exclusively on the rhetorical commitments by the governing elite to Marxist ideas without paying much attention to whether or not such governments have the power, ability, or interest to put their ideas into practice.

Still others feel it useful to define Marxist regime in terms of leadership by an "elite party." For this reason the penultimate column in Table RA.1 includes data on party membership as a share of the adult population. If we arbitrarily draw the boundary between "elite" and "mass" political parties at 7.5 percent of the adult population, then we must exclude from our list of Marxist regimes all the European nations (except Albania), China, Cuba, Mongolia, and North Korea (and perhaps also Seychelles, although party membership data are too uncertain to be included).

In East Europe in 1989 and 1990, many party members resigned. This suggests that they were members either for opportunistic reasons or because they had been forced in some manner to join. In either case, total party membership means little. For those Third World nations for which relatively reliable data are available, party membership has been quite small, so that by this strict numerical definition of elite, they would be included. Whether or not the party is an elite or not has little bearing on most of the questions I ask in this book. The data are, however, useful for explaining certain political forces discussed throughout this book.

Another political criterion for defining Marxist regimes concerns the degree of agreement of the country's foreign policy with that of the Soviet Union. The last column in Table RA.1 includes an index showing the concordance of United Nation votes from 1979 through 1987 on the Afghanistan and Kampuchean issues for each individual nation in comparison with the votes of the Soviet Union. Although a number of nations in the table have a voting pattern similar to the Soviets with regard to these "Third World issues," others such as Albania, Romania, and Yugoslavia and most of the Third World nations voted differently, except when they were important Soviet foreign aid recipients (Mozambique is an exception to this generalization).

Soviet social scientists approach the problem of classification in still a different manner: They distinguish countries ruled according to socialist principles as constituting the *world socialist system*. They subdivide those countries ruled by a communist party of a Leninist type into the *socialist commonwealth* (SC) nations, which follow Soviet leadership, and *other socialist* (OS) nations.[1] They also designate a second group of countries as countries of a *socialist orientation* (SO); these have not yet left the "world capitalist system" but are heading toward socialism.[2] Such nations are led either by *vanguard parties* or *revolutionary democratic parties*; the former have stricter class and ideological standards and have openly opted for "scientific socialism." Finally, they also distinguish *socialist oriented parties*, which are the ruling parties of nations tending toward a socialist orientation. This classification appears primarily to confer an honorary status on parties in Libya and similar countries without making concessions to ideological purity.

This Soviet approach is not completely unified since various scholars and politicians have offered lists somewhat more restricted than what is shown in the second column of Table RA.1. The Soviet list contains many anomalies and certain countries (Syria is one) are included probably for their backing of Soviet foreign policy goals (see U.N. voting index in the last column), rather than any real influence of Marxist ideas. Other anom-

[1] This discussion draws heavily upon the discussion of Wallace H. Spaulding (1983) and Richard Staar (1987).

[2] Lenin introduced the notion of noncapitalist (third path) development, most notably in his "Report of the Commission on the National and the Colonial Question" [1920] (LCW, vol. XXXI, pp. 240–45). After World War II when decolonization was occurring on a massive scale, Soviet officials began actively to advance the notion that under certain circumstances it was not necessary for the economy to pass through capitalism, that the postcolonial state could fulfill the "historic role" of the capitalist, and that by sufficient state investment, it could create the conditions for socialist transformation. This approach proved attractive to many Third World leaders, especially when the Soviet Union began to increase its economic aid to countries designated as having a "noncapitalist" or a "socialist" orientation. By 1989, however, some Soviet officials had begun to dismiss the importance of such concepts, which presaged an important shift in Soviet policy.

TABLE RA.1

Classification of Marxist Regimes in the mid-1980s

	Pryor	Soviet	Rubinstein	Szajkowski	Percentage of Adult Population in Party	U.N. Vote Index	Notes
Africa							
Algeria	No	SO, RD	No	No	—	+0.10	
Angola	Yes	SO, V	Yes	Yes	0.9 (1985)	+1.00	
Bénin	Yes	SO, V	Yes	Yes	<0.1 (1986)	+0.10	
Burkina Faso	No	SO, RD*	No	Yes	—	-0.15	2d Sankara government
Burundi	No	SO, RD*	No	No	—	-0.81	
Cape Verde	Yes	SO, RD*	No	Yes	5.5 (1986)	-0.05	
PDR Congo	Yes	SO, V	Yes	Yes	1.1 (1985)	+0.38	
Ethiopia	Yes	SO, V	Yes	Yes	0.3 (1985)	+1.00	
Ghana	No	SO, RD*	No	Yes	—	-0.86	2d Rawlings government
Guinea	No	SO, RD*	No	No	—	-0.67	
Guinea-Bissau	Yes	SO, RD	No	Yes	—	-0.14	
Libya	No	SOP*	No	No	—	+0.86	
Madagascar	Yes	SO, RD	Yes	Yes	—	+0.38	
Mali	No	SO, RD*	No	No	—	-0.29	
Mozambique	Yes	SO, V	Yes	Yes	1.9 (1983)	+0.52	
São Tomé	Yes	SO, RD*	No	Yes	6.2 (1985)	-0.05	
Seychelles	Yes	SO, RD*	No	Yes	—	+0.24	
Sierra Leone	No	SOP*	No	No	—	-0.81	
Somalia	Yes	*	No	No	0.8 (1977)	-1.00	
Tanzania	No	SO, RD*	No	No	—	-0.43	
Uganda	No	SOP*	No	No	—	-0.10	
Zambia	No	SO, RD*	No	No	—	-0.67	
Zimbabwe	Yes	SO, RD	No	Yes	—	-0.43	

TABLE RA.1 (cont.)

	Pryor	Soviet	Rubinstein	Szajkowski	Percentage of Adult Population in Party		U.N. Vote Index	Notes
Americas								
Cuba	Yes	SC	Yes	Yes	8.2	(1986)	+1.00	
Grenada	Yes	SO, RD*	Yes	Yes	0.2	(1982)	+0.80	Bishop government
Guyana	Yes	SOP	No	Yes	—		-0.33	
Nicaragua	Yes	SO, RD*	Yes	Yes	0.3	(1985)	+0.52	
Surinam	No	*	No	Yes	—		-0.81	
Asia								
Afghanistan	Yes	SO, V	Yes	Yes	0.5	(1987)	+1.00	
Burma	No	SO, RD?*	No	No	—		-0.86	
China	Yes	OS*	Yes	Yes	7.9	(1987)	-1.00	
Kampuchea	Yes	SC	Yes	Yes	0.2	(1985)	none	
Korea, North	Yes	OS	Yes	Yes	24.8	(1985)	none	
Laos	Yes	SC	Yes	Yes	5.0	(1985)	+1.00	
Mongolia	Yes	SC	Yes	Yes	8.4	(1985)	+1.00	
Syria	No	SO, RD	No	No	—	(1985)	+0.90	
Viet Nam	Yes	SC	Yes	Yes	5.8	(1985)	+1.00	
Yemen, South	Yes	SO, V	Yes	Yes	2.7	(1985)	+1.00	
Europe								
Albania	Yes	OS*	Yes	Yes	6.7	(1981)	-0.33	
Bulgaria	Yes	SC	Yes	Yes	14.1	(1985)	+1.00	
Czechoslovakia	Yes	SC	Yes	Yes	15.5	(1985)	+1.00	
Germany, East	Yes	SC	Yes	Yes	17.9	(1985)	+1.00	
Hungary	Yes	SC	Yes	Yes	11.4	(1985)	+1.00	
Poland	Yes	SC	Yes	Yes	8.4	(1985)	+1.00	
Romania	Yes	SC	Yes	Yes	23.1	(1985)	+0.14	
USSR	Yes	SC	Yes	Yes	10.1	(1984)	+1.00	
Yugoslavia	Yes	OS*	Yes	Yes	14.0	(1985)	-0.86	

Notes: Soviet classifications: SC = Socialist Commonwealth; OS = other socialist; SO = country with a socialist orientation; RD = revolutionary democratic party; V = vanguard party; SOP = socialist oriented party. An asterisk designates those parties that did *not* attend the April 1988 meeting in Prague of communist, vanguard, and revolutionary democratic parties (according to Anon 1988), which might indicate either that they have been downgraded or that they missed the meeting for some other reason. For Madagascar and Syria the Soviet-recognized parties attended.

The Soviet classifications are taken from Spaulding (1982), (1983), and Staar (1987). Burma is listed on Spaulding's earlier list, but not Staar's later list, so it may have been "demoted." Kampuchea began to be openly listed as a member of the Socialist Commonwealth in 1987. In Madagascar and Syria the Soviet-recognized communist parties cooperate or are members of the ruling coalition, but are not the dominant party. The exact status in the classification of Burkina Faso, Burma, Burundi, Comoro, Guinea, Grenada, Mali, and certain other countries where Marxist parties lost control of the government, is not entirely clear. The other classification ratings come from Rubinstein (1988, p. 58) and the list of planned books in the Marxist Regime series that is edited by Szajkowski (1990).

All political data refer, whenever possible to 1985 or the closest year for which data are available. Party members exclude, whenever the data permit, candidate members, as well as members of auxiliary organizations. Adults are defined as that part of the population twenty years of age and older. These data are very approximate since they are based on data published by the various parties, which often have an interest in inflating their membership count. In some cases these official numbers are modified by information from other sources; for some countries, for example, Seychelles, such modifications could not be made and, since the numbers are not credible, they are not presented.

For the most part the data members come from the estimates presented by Staar (annual), supplemented by Delury (1987), Foy (1988), Hodges and Newitt (1988), and Pryor (1986). Whenever possible, these data have also been checked against estimates presented in Hobday (1986), who has significantly lower estimates for party membership for Bénin and Kampuchea. In most cases population data come from U.N. (1988a); other sources include Rapawy and Baldwin (1982) and Pryor (1986). Adults were estimated by multiplying the population by the percentage of population over nineteen in the nearest year for which U.N. data were available; for Albania, Kampuchea, North Korea, Laos, Mongolia, Somalia, and Viet Nam, population structures from similar nations had to be used since age data were not available.

The U.N. voting data are taken from twenty-one votes on the Afghanistan and Cambodian votes in the U.N. from 1979–87; +1.00 = complete similarity with Soviet votes; -1.00 = complete dissimilarity from Soviet votes. The data come from UN (annual) and U.S. Department of State (annual).

alies of omission appear because the Soviet Union, for one political reason or another, has withdrawn recognition from some countries (for instance, Somalia).

A number of other scholars have provided still other political and social
criteria for distinguishing Marxist regimes. While such classification exercises have a certain bizarre fascination, it should be clear that they take
us far from the themes of this book. Although the Soviet Union may classify Burma or Syria as having a socialist orientation, I could find no evidence that Marxist ideas played any role in their organization of agriculture.

TESTS OF THE MARXIST THEORY OF
AGRICULTURAL DEVELOPMENT

IN THIS research note I test various Marxist propositions about the development of agriculture outlined in chapter 2, an exercise requiring us to examine a series of non-Marxist regimes over a long period of time. The empirical investigation shows that these propositions have a mixed record in predicting actual trends and, as a result, offer little support for collectivization.

As noted in chapter 2, Marx and Engels viewed the long-term evolution of the agricultural sector as similar to that of the industrial sector, and they considered events in England as prototypical of capitalist development in general. From their analysis they made five key predictions: (1) the average land area of productive units would become larger; (2) the farm sector would become increasingly differentiated and the inequality of the size distribution of farms would become greater, with the land being held by ever fewer people (a concentration and centralization of capital); (3) the smallholders would be unable to compete against the large farms and would lose their land ("become annihilated"); (4) these small farmers would be transformed into a proletariat, either staying on the land to work for others or emigrating to the city; the average number of workers per farm would increase; and (5) the form of payments to the landlord would change from a system of labor rents to sharecropping at fixed rents in money.

Although these propositions have general interest for those interested in economic development, they have received surprising little empirical analysis in a sustained and systematic fashion. Most discussions on the topic seem content to justify these "obvious truths" with a few numbers seized at random from some nearby source without paying serious attention either to differences among nations or to the different types of economic mechanisms underlying such organizational changes. To raise the level of discussion above mere statements of faith about which type of agricultural organization is "most advanced," it is important to test empirically these and several other common propositions about the long-term development of the organization of the agricultural sector in a more systematic fashion.

On a purely descriptive level I show that several of the long-term propositions of Marx and Engels were accurate for some countries such as the United States. For countries in Western Europe, on the other hand, their long-run predictions show even more negative results—although I am not holding up Western Europe as a model of agricultural efficiency. Of particular importance, I demonstrate that although farm size in terms of area has increased in most industrialized countries, farm size as measured by labor force per farm has not; thus, as argued in chapter 2, some traditional justifications for collectivization in terms of economy of scale require reexamination.

SOME PROBLEMS OF EMPIRICAL ANALYSIS

Certain data to test these five propositions are available, but this task, as simple as it appears, raises some serious difficulties. The most useful data for our purposes come from various censuses of agriculture. These are, unfortunately, available for long periods only for a limited number of industrialized nations. Moreover, analysis of these raw data raises some knotty problems since normal statistical methods bias in crucial ways the parameters describing the organizational evolution of the farm sector. Thus it is crucial to review briefly some of the most important problems in selecting and calculating these parameters.

Minimum Farm Size

Farm size distributions feature a very large number of "farms" on very small pieces of land, which dominate any calculations of average farm sizes. For instance, the nineteenth-century German agricultural censuses neatly classified farms into groups from 0 to 0.02 hectares, 0.02 to 0.05 hectares, 0.05 to 0.20 hectares, and so forth; it appears that they considered almost all pieces of rural land as "farms," even if they were primarily the property of men working in the city while their family cultivated a garden to improve the quality of their food consumption. This means that in 1882, the German "farms" under 2 hectares in size accounted for only 5.4 percent of the total farm land, but 58 percent of the "farmers." Some nations such as the United States try to avoid this problem by including small properties as farms only when they meet certain criteria, for instance, a certain minimum of sales or production. Since these criteria have been changed in different censuses, some comparability over time is lost.

I have tried to minimize this problem in the discussion below by eliminating from consideration all rural "farms" under 2 hectares (for some countries 1 hectare had to be chosen as the cutoff point). This limit is, of course, arbitrary and is chosen because of the way that the available data are presented. A more satisfactory limit would require determination of the minimum size of plot necessary to feed a given farm family, which is difficult to determine for most nations. This procedure also means that my data do not reflect what is happening to the proprietors of minifarms (farms under 2 hectares), who often provide the labor force for other farmers, work in the towns, or eventually move from the land.

Definition and Measurement of Farm Area

This analysis focuses on the unit of production (i.e., "holding"), not the unit of ownership, and includes all of the separate plots farmed by a single producer. The area of a holding can be defined in several different ways, of which the most unambiguous is the total area. A number of nations have followed this practice, which means that farms include ranches and plantations. For other types of analyses, some national censuses have measured land in terms of "usable areas" (that is, total land excluding the land covered by ponds, forests, gullies, buildings); while still others have focused on the actual area used for farming activities (crop land, permanent pastures, and sometimes temporary pastures), an approach raising some obvious measurement problems. The more exclusions, the more are the opportunities for subjective judgments on the part of the census takers, and, it should be added, the greater the difficulties in arriving at accurate measurements of the land.

In the interests of achieving a rough comparability between nations, I have used the most inclusive measure possible, the total area of the farm. This measure also allows comparisons with the data on collective and state farms that are presented in chapter 4. Further, I have either dropped those cases where the definition has changed, or flagged these results in the tables with NCC (not completely comparable). Often, but not always (for example, in the Scandinavian countries), the more inclusive measure generally yields a considerably more unequal distribution of farm size. A number of other problems arise in comparing the various censuses and, in some cases, estimates had to be made. These are flagged in the tables with an E (estimate) and the particular assumptions are specified in the notes.

Time Period Covered

Considerable discussion of the issues raised by Marx focuses on the German agricultural censuses of 1882 and 1895, but many authors miss two important points. First, between the two census years almost no important change occurred (some data are presented in Table RB.2). Second, since Marx and Engels were talking about the "really" long-run, it is necessary to examine longer periods. In the tables, I focus on fifty- and one hundred-year periods.

Definition of Agricultural Labor Force

Statistical organizations vary considerably in the definition of the farm labor force, especially with regard to the counting of farm wives, children, and other part-time workers. In some cases, the labor force is counted as those working on the day the census was taken; in other cases consideration is made of the part-time nature of this work. Farm proprietors who participate actively in farming are generally included as workers. There is no easy way to standardize these data so that they are left unadjusted. We encounter similar problems, it should be added, in examining the work force on state and collective farms in chapter 4.

Organizational versus Social Structure

The data on the size distribution of farms have sometimes been given social or political interpretations with which I do not agree. Rather than going into the matter in detail, let me simply state that such data do *not* reflect social class structure, which is determined in part by the ownership of land and equipment, the renting-out or renting-in of such land and equipment, the hiring-in or hiring-out of labor, the technology employed, and net receipts. I discuss some aspects of this problem in chapter 3.

THE DATA

For the United States we can draw on a considerable body of statistical information. I have chosen to start with data from U.S. agricultural censuses from 1880 (when the sector had 7.7 million workers and proprietors, or 44 percent of those economically active), and compare them with data from 1930 (when the sector had 10.5 million workers, or 21 percent of the labor force), and from 1982 (when the sector had 3.4 million workers, or 3 percent of the labor force).[1] It is useful to separate the trends in the various regions in order to factor out the impact of the changing regional concentration of agriculture. The relevant data are presented in Table RB.1.

For other economically developed nations, I have chosen to rely primarily on data presented in the 1930 and the 1980 world censuses of

---

[1] These data come from U.S. Bureau of the Census (1975, p. 127) and U.S. Bureau of the Census (annual, 1988). The labor force includes those age 16 and over. The 1982 data include Hawaii and Alaska, which are not included in table RB.1.

Parameters of the Farm Sector of the Continental USA, 1880–1982

Year	Number of Farms (1000s)	Average Farm Size, (hectares)	Gini Coefficient of Size Inequality	Percent of Farmland in Largest 5 Percent of Farms	Percent of Farms under 8.1 Hectares (20 acres)	Percent of Farmland in Farms under 8.1 Hectares
USA Total						
1880 E	4004.6	56.1	.483	28%	9.7%	0.8%
1930	6245.6	63.9	.633	42	14.0	1.0
1982	2166.0	183.2	.745	53	26.0	1.3
New England						
1880 E	206.9	42.2	.399	14	12.1	1.3
1930	122.9	47.0	.480	21	14.6	1.3
1982	24.1	76.2	.527	22	26.1	3.3
Middle Atlantic						
1880 E	488.2	38.2	.386	13	14.1	1.5
1930	353.4	40.1	.419	19	13.9	1.4
1982	103.5	61.6	.496	28	25.5	3.8
East North Central						
1880 E	984.6	42.7	.352	13	6.4	0.6
1930	962.7	46.6	.377	16	8.2	0.7
1982	394.1	91.0	.545	24	23.2	2.5
West North Central						
1880 E	712.3	62.6	.311	13	3.2	0.2
1930	1108.1	97.0	.481	30	5.5	0.2
1982	512.4	209.8	.611	35	13.1	0.6
South Atlantic						
1880 E	643.5	60.6	.549	35	13.3	1.0
1930	1054.0	33.2	.531	30	17.8	2.4
1982	266.8	86.8	.686	28	35.8	3.8
East South Central						
1880 E	568.8	51.5	.519	30	13.1	1.3
1930	1060.5	27.8	.513	27	21.5	3.8
1982	273.7	72.8	.631	43	33.4	4.3
West South Central						
1880 E	316.7	99.2	.725	62	13.2	0.7
1930	1098.8	67.7	.700	53	13.5	1.0
1982	332.0	228.3	.748	54	22.6	1.0
Mountain						
1880 E	25.0	82.4	.671	50	19.1	1.0
1930	234.0	271.3	.756	51	12.1	0.2
1982	115.9	859.3	.768	n.a.	26.1	0.2
Pacific						
1880 E	58.5	154.5	.569	45	5.2	0.1
1930	250.4	97.8	.811	60	30.2	1.1
1982	142.6	188.3	.863	75	55.2	2.1

Source: See Statistical Note G.
Notes: E = estimated.

agriculture. These have been supplemented in several cases by national data. All calculations are presented in Table RB.2.

ANALYSIS OF THE RESULTS

The results can be most easily summarized by examining separately the evidence for each of the individual propositions:

Average Land Area of Farms

Marx's proposition that the average land area of farms increases over time appears generally correct for both Western Europe and North America. We must not, however, confuse size with scale, since such measurements show nothing about the labor force per farm. Moreover, Marx's explanation of the mechanisms underlying such changes is faulty, since a number of other causal factors appear more important.

For the United States, as well as for the individual nine regions within the nation, average farm (and ranch) sizes measured in terms of area have increased dramatically over the entire period. With four exceptions, Austria (1930 to 1980), Belgium (1895 to 1929), Japan (1929 to 1980), and the Netherlands (1886 to 1930), the same trend occurred in the other countries listed in Table RB.2 as well. These changes occurred during a period when, in most nations, the number of farms was decreasing markedly. As a first approximation, the Marxist proposition appears correct but only if size is defined in terms of land per farm and not, as I show below, workers per farm. If data for the developing countries had been available for a similar period, however, many more examples of decreasing average farm size could be shown. For instance, the twenty-year series presented by Hayami and Ruttan (1985) show that twelve of the nineteen developing countries had declining average farm sizes.[2] In general, the data for any given country show an inverse relation over time between average farm size and number of farms.

Although the average land area of farms is increasing in most industrial countries, the plausibility of Marx's explanation for this phenomenon, namely that the larger farms have lower costs and gradually drive the smaller farms out of business, seems doubtful. Most production function and other empirical studies have not revealed at a single point in time

[2] The data for 1960 and 1980 come from table A.4, Hayami and Ruttan (1985). Of the twenty-four industrial or semi-industrial nations, twenty-one had increasing average farm sizes. Relevant to the discussion in the next paragraphs about the inverse relation between changes in average farm size and number of farms, the nineteen developing countries revealed only two exceptions to the rule; the twenty-four industrial countries had only three exceptions.

either important economies of scale or economies of size for most crops.[3] Indeed, even the case for economies of scale or size for traditional plantation crops is open to question.[4]

Hayami and Ruttan (1985, table 6.1) have produced the most important empirical study that shows economies of scale in agriculture. Using a cross-national sample and calculating a metaproduction function, they argue that economies of scale in agriculture occur in economically developed nations but not in developing nations. They tie these conclusions to the greater importance of mechanical to biological/chemical innovations in the industrial nations where labor costs are high, and the reverse in the developing nations where the population density is high and labor costs are low. This feature, in turn, can be traced to the different proportions of land, labor, and capital in the rural sector of each set of nations.

Before accepting their results, which are based on somewhat uncertain data, one must subscribe to their two basic assumptions: (1) farmers all

[3] Heady and Dillon (1961, chap. 17) survey fifty-five production function studies covering twelve countries; only eight revealed statistically significant economies of scale. In a more recent survey Harold R. Jenson (in Martin 1977, pp. 3–89) concludes: "Most economies to size studies have shown that important economies to size exist but that most of these are exhausted within the scope of a family farm operation." Studies of the United States by Madden (1967) and Miller, Rodewald, and McElroy (1981), U.S. Congress, Office of Technology Assessment (1986) provide additional evidence for this conclusion about economies of size. For instance, the latter study concludes that "small farms in many field crop regions are nearly as technically efficient as large farms." In a recent study of fifteen developing nations Cornia (1985) also finds no significant economies of scale.

In contrast to these studies, Kislev and Peterson (1982) report a number of articles showing significant economies of scale or size in agriculture. They argue, however, that such estimations have a number of flaws that bias the results. They do not mention one other bias of these studies, namely that few calculations of production functions include farms with fifty or more workers, primarily because such large farms are not very common in industrialized market economies, in large measure because these farms have not met the test of the market.

Several econometric studies show that for a number of farm products, the relatively flat segment of the cost curve extends over a considerable range of output, so that the lack of economies of scale or size does not necessarily imply that medium-scale farming has higher average costs than family farming.

[4] For instance, in cases of crops such as tea, plantations are claimed to be necessary in order to sustain a high quality of production; however, the success of smallholder tea farms (e.g., in Kenya) belie the assertion that the plantation is the *only* organization of agriculture where such standards can be maintained. In other cases the alleged economies of scale occur not in the production process itself, but in subsidiary activities. For instance, in the growing of cane sugar, large estates permit the coordination of the harvesting with the capacity of the sugar mills since cut sugar cane quickly loses its sugar content and the sugar mills can only process a limited amount of cane at one time. Although this is a serious problem, it does not mean that alternative arrangements for small scale sugar growers are uneconomic. A variety of these issues are explored in some of the new literature comparing plantation and smallholding farming.

TABLE RB.2
Parameters of the Farm Sector in Other Economically Developed Nations

Year	Number of Farms (1000s)	Average Farm Size (hectares)	Gini Coefficient of Size Inequality	Percentage of Farmland in Largest 5 Percent of Farms	Percentage of Farms under 10 Hectares	Percentage of Farmland in Farms under 10 Hectares
Austria						
1930	314.6	23.9	.690	54%	55.3%	11.6%
1980	256.4	21.5	.576	38	43.7	10.2
Belgium						
1846 E	274.0	9.5	.643	43	84.5	33.8
1895 E	255.3	9.7	.587	38	83.5	37.5
1929	292.6	6.4	.473	30	85.9	50.0
1979	93.9	15.5	.478	22	48.9	15.2
Canada					(under 8.1 hectares)	
1931	708.9	93.1	.482	22	6.2	0.4
1981	313.6	229.7	.593	30	5.9	0.1
Denmark						
1901 NCC	165.3	14.4	.537	32	43.7	9.9
1929 NCC, E	191.4	16.1	.486	22	50.1	16.5
1979 NCC	118.6	24.6	.447	22	55.8	22.6
England and Wales					(under 8.1 hectares)	
1875	470.0	23.1	.635	33	n.a.	n.a.
1930	395.8	25.7	.630	29	44.7	5.6
1966	312.2	31.5	.650	34	42.8	3.6
Finland						
1930	209.1	10.4	.482	25	67.6	31.2
1980	204.0	11.9	.400	18	57.8	27.5
France						
1882	3504.3	13.8	.656	47	75.2	23.4
1928	2951.6	15.1	.564	32	63.1	20.9
1978–79	1143.0	25.7	.494	24	35.3	6.1
Germany						
1882	2214.5	17.2	.610	40	69.3	22.7
1895	2322.0	17.6	.609	41	69.9	24.5
Italy						
1930	2705.2	9.5	.680	53	84.9	31.1
1981–82	2224.0	10.5	.698	53	82.5	26.5
Japan						
1929 E	3637.4	1.3	.290	20	Almost all	
1980	2723.7	1.2	.354	22	Almost all	

TABLE RB.2 (*cont.*)

Year	Number of farms (1000s)	Average Farm Size (hectares)	Gini Coefficient of Size Inequality	Percentage of Farmland in Largest 5 Percent of Farms	Percentage of Farms under 10 Hectares	Percentage of Farmland in Farms under 10 hectares
Netherlands						
1886 NCC, E	120.5	14.3	.465	20	54.6	20.2
1930	234.1	9.0	.500	21	71.0	31.3
1979	131.8	16.8	.448	20	44.7	14.0
New Zealand						
1930	85.2	206.1	.781	55	23.8	0.3
1980	71.5	297.0	.793	61	18.6	0.3
Norway						
1929	132.6	6.7	.369	20	84.2	57.4
1979	100.7	9.2	.404	18	69.7	38.0
Puerto Rico					(under 8.1 hectares)	
1930	50.8	15.7	.743	57	69.8	13.9
1978	31.8	13.4	.708	60	75.2	13.5
Sweden						
1932	307.4	11.6	.487	29	69.1	31.8
1981	73.7	21.2	.543	29	48.7	13.2
Switzerland						
1929	196.2	7.2	.418	24	80.6	49.1
1980	98.2	12.7	.399	14	46.6	17.5

Source: See Statistical Note G.

Notes: E = estimated; NCC = not completely comparable.

over the world face the same metaproduction function; and (2) such results from aggregative data would also be found on the level of individual farms. The first assumption requires information on agricultural technology to flow easily and for farming conditions to be "relatively" similar so that these technologies can be easily adapted. The problems arising from this assumption also bedevil the comparisons of static efficiency of agriculture in Marxist and non-Marxist nations discussed in chapter 8. The second assumption raises many problems of comparability of the aggregate data for each country. I would place more faith in production function calculations based on farm level data for a single country that do not show such economies of scale. The latter results also are more consistent with theoretical expectations arising from the argument that land is a much different type of production factor than capital: it is much more heterogeneous, its maintenance and preservation requires much greater attention, and its productivity is more tied to exogenous events (weather) which cannot be easily controlled. Hence production processes are less subject to routinization, individual initiative and responsibility for maintenance are much more important, and supervision costs are much higher than in factory work. Furthermore, various production tasks are carried out sequentially so that if different workers are employed on a given piece of land at different times, it is difficult to assign responsibility of the results to any single workers, a problem that raises difficulties in introducing many types of common incentive systems. Thus increasing economies of scale arising from greater mechanization can be offset by higher labor or supervision costs.

Of course, this kind of empirical evidence does not exclude the possibility that certain productive activities within the farm, such as land preparation, exhibit economies of scale, as many have argued. But if this is the case, then such services can be contracted from service cooperatives or private entrepreneurs, and the scale or size of the farm unit can remain small.

What are we to make of references to empirical studies in the East European economic literature that economies of scale or size do, indeed, exist in agriculture and that the optimal size farm is relatively large? For the most part these studies have been internal documents for policymakers and are not available for public examination. In discussing their methodology with economists from these countries, however, it seems likely that many of these studies are statistically biased for several reasons: (1) since the political abilities of farms to obtain current and capital inputs are roughly correlated with their size, the larger farms have lower average costs because they have less need to make do with inappropriate inputs such as the wrong mix of fertilizers, inadequate machines, or outdated technologies; (2) many of the studies omit smaller farms from consideration completely so that the whole range of farm size does not receive attention; and (3) some of these studies are based solely on engineering norms, e.g., a thresher of a particular size can service X hectares and a completely equipped repair shop that fully utilizes its machines can handle a fleet of Y threshers, so the optimal farm should be Z (X times Y) hectares. Of course, such an approach omits labor and other costs that may not always stand in a constant ratio to threshing machines, so that the results tell us nothing about actual economies of scale or size.[5]

What then are the reasons for the increase in average farm area over

---

[5] A good example of such a cost is found in a nonpublished Czechoslovak econometric study that I was shown revealing that transportation costs *within* a collective farm increase about 1.3 percent for every 1.0 percent increase in farm size.

time? Several mechanisms provide alternative explanations to those offered by Marx:

Factor Price Mechanism. Kislev and Peterson (1982) present a simple two-stage production function (labor and machinery combine to produce "mechans"; land and biological inputs such as fertilizer and pesticides combine to produce "terrans." "Mechans" and "terrans" combine to produce food. They show that a rise in the wage of urban labor (the opportunity cost of the farmers labor hours), a fall in the relative price of machinery, and technological change in agriculture (either neutral technological change or labor-saving "mechans") lead to fewer farmers, more machinery, and larger average farms remaining in the agricultural sector. A fall in the price of biological inputs or technological improvements in such inputs cannot be unambiguously tied to a particular type of change in average farm size until the relative magnitudes of the elasticity of demand for food and the elasticity of substitution between land and biological inputs are specified.

Biased Technological Change Mechanism. Hayami and Ruttan (1985) and contributors in Binswanger and Ruttan (1978) argue that technological change is biased toward saving the most scarce factor. For those countries with relatively scarce labor (high land to labor ratios), under specified circumstances the technological changes will occur more frequently in the mechanical devices that save labor. For those countries with relatively scarce land (low land to labor ratios), under specified circumstances technological change will occur more often in biological innovations (new seeds or new fertilizers) that save land. If the relative prices of land, labor, and capital remain the same, the former case will yield a faster growth of labor productivity than land productivity; in the latter case, the reverse is true.

Push/Pull Mechanisms. The most important pull mechanism is, of course, the ability of the urban sector to absorb the rural labor force at incomes higher than could be earned on the farm. In many countries, especially at low levels of industrialization, the urban labor market has not had this absorptive capacity and, as a result, the rural labor force has increased in absolute size and the average farm size has often decreased. It is irrelevant that urban wages are much higher than rural wages if this is the result of a disequilibrium so that there are no urban jobs to be had at such wages. In most of the countries in my sample, the absorptive capacity of the urban labor force was not a problem for the period under examination, although in many developing countries not included such as Bangladesh, Egypt, Pakistan, or Sri Lanka the situation was different.

A strong push of farmers off their farms arises from some inheritance in-stitutions, with some form of primogeniture more easily releasing farm workers than an equal division of the land among the children of the farmers. Although the English system of primogeniture is well docu-mented, such an inheritance system is relatively rare in other countries.

Land Availability.   An obvious but seldom mentioned factor influencing the average size of farms is the farmer's decision to expand production at the intensive or extensive margin. In Belgium from 1895 to 1929 and the Netherlands from 1886 to 1930, the number of farms increased and, since population density in both nations was quite high, it appears to have been more economic to increase the intensiveness of farming, rather than increase total farming area by pushing back the extensive margin (which, in the Netherlands, involved the construction of more dikes). The oppo-site situation occurred in the United States between 1882 and 1930 where the number of farms increased in a number of sparsely populated areas in the West, Center, and South; but sufficient fertile land was still available so that it proved more economic to expand on the extensive margin, rather than increasing farming intensiveness.

Government Policy.   Governmental policies toward agriculture have in-fluenced the average size of farms. In some cases, such as Austria from 1930 to 1980, nationalization of land after World War II played a role. Although the average size of private farms decreased, if state-owned farms are included in the calculations for 1980, then average farm size increased slightly (in 1930 state farms do not seem to have been very important). Government land policy can also encourage consolidation of farms or the removal of inferior land from farming. For instance, since World War II, the French government has had an active program and has provided many economic incentives for farm consolidation into larger units (*remembrement*). Tariff and other policies protecting small farms have also played an important role in some countries (Wade 1981).

Availability of Credit.   Owners of large farms are often better able than those of small farms to obtain more credit, both for productive or con-sumption purposes (Calomiris 1991), which can have a long-term impact on farm size. In the United States, for instance, the rapid growth in av-erage farm size is mainly attributable to the growth of the largest farms that could obtain the credit they needed.

Differential Transfer of New Technology.   The proposition that large farms are in a better position to adopt new agricultural technologies rests on the implicit assumption that such technological transfer has a lower hectare cost on larger farms because of some type of high fixed cost of information acquisition. Given the fact that much new agricultural technology is spread either by private firms supplying the new technology or government extension agents covering all farms within an area, this assumption is open to challenge. The slower growth of total factor productivity in the systems of large collectivized farms in East Europe than in the small family farms in West Europe (shown in chapter 8) also casts doubt on the proposition.

For the thirteen nations in Tables RB.1 and RB.2 for which we have data on production factors and output for the period from 1960 to 1980, the ratios of capital to labor, capital to land, and land to labor rose; in most of the countries, the rates of increase were greatest for the first ratio and least for the last.[6] Furthermore, in all countries the output to labor and also the output to land ratios rose as well, the former faster than the latter; and the output to capital ratio declined. The same trends can be observed for a longer period from 1880 through 1980 in the United States and Japan. Thus technological change in these nations has been labor saving. Furthermore, relative prices of machinery and biological inputs fell as the relative price of labor rose. Although these changes in factor proportions, output to factor ratios, and factor prices do not tell us anything directly about the nature of economies of scale in agriculture, they do provide insight into how the increase in farm size over time can be traced to factors other than economies of scale or size per se.

These considerations show in still another way that agricultural land is a quite different type of factor of production than capital: Except in a frontier situation, it is often much more expensive to expand. Furthermore, economies of scale and the changes in optimal farm size due to technological change are only one of several causal factors to be taken into account in analyzing changes in the average sizes of farms. I must leave for others, however, the determination of the degree of influence of the factors mentioned above on the farm size data presented in the above tables.

Inequality of the Size Distribution

Marx's proposition about the increasing size distribution of farms appears valid in North America, but not in Europe.

The inequality of land holdings is shown in Tables RB.1 and RB.2 by the Gini coefficient and by the percentage of farm lands in the largest 5

---

[6] These ratios are calculated from data presented in appendices A, B, and C by Hayami and Ruttan (1985).

percent of farms.[7] Two other measures of inequality were also calculated (Theil coefficients and log variances) but they tell roughly the same story as the Gini coefficients and are not presented.

In the United States the two measures of inequality *increased* for the nation as a whole, and, with a few exceptions, within the nine regions as well. One notable exception is the South Atlantic region, where the percentage of farmland occupied by the largest farms declined throughout the period. This appears related to the breakup of the large cotton plantations, particularly in the earlier period.

In the other countries changes in the inequality of land holdings, as measured by the Gini coefficients, present a much more mixed picture. Inequality *decreased* in more countries (Austria, Belgium, Denmark, Finland, Japan, France, Switzerland, and, after 1930, the Netherlands) than it *increased* (Italy, Norway, Sweden, and, before 1930, the Netherlands). With a few exceptions the statistics on the percentage of farmlands in the largest farms show the same pattern, although the changes are generally small.

Without highly detailed data that do not seem available on a comparable basis, it is difficult to determine exactly what happened in Europe. I would hypothesize, however, two key causal mechanisms: one is tied to crop specialization by farm size and the forces of international competition; the other, to the pattern of farm expansion as the agricultural population declined.

Crop Specialization.   The larger farms in Europe that produced different grain crops may have been unable to compete against imported grains from the Americas and Australia, while the smaller farms could still flourish, both because they produced vegetables and other crops with less important economies of scale and because such products had higher transoceanic unit transportation costs than grains. This type of market mechanism could, of course, be easily subverted by governmental price and trade policies for particular crops. In some countries where small farmers are politically mobilized, it would seem rational for a coalition government with a slim majority of votes to provide special protection for vegetables and other small-farm crops. For example, France had a two-tiered farm system up to the 1950s, with a certain number of large modern farms, primarily in the north, and a large number of small farms practicing "polyculture" (Wade 1981). Nevertheless, the impact of policy may have been somewhat different than intended. Although agricultural protection was high during this period and although

---

[7] The Gini coefficient designates the share of land that must be redistributed in order to achieve perfect equality; it ranges from .000 (perfect equality) to 1.000 (total inequality).

small farmers were politically mobilized, such protection did not prevent the gradual disappearance of the smallest farms at the gain of the middle-size farms. Average farm size increased, while the distribution of farm sizes became more equal.

Farm Expansion Pattern.   The size distribution of farms accompanying the decline in the farm population can be influenced by several quite different factors. First, in many countries the cost of farm land is some multiple of the discounted stream of farm earnings, because land is a desirable investment for providing a hedge against inflation. The higher the multiple, the more difficult it is for small farmers to obtain credit to purchase land; furthermore, the more they must reduce their consumption in order to pay interest payments on any credit received. Trends in size distribution appear highly dependent on this price multiple. Second, where the extensive margin is being pushed back, either in a frontier situation or in local areas, credit is needed not only to purchase the land but also to construct the necessary infrastructure to farm the land. Such land development appears in many situations to feature economies of scale. Again, this type of investment would be more attractive to large landholders, who have greater access to credit and who are in a better position to offer part of their land as a collateral for such a risky venture. In this case as well, the increase in average farm size is accompanied by an increasing inequality of farm size. Third, where farm size is increasing primarily through the absorption of existing farms by other farms, however, it is more likely that the small neighboring farms would be purchasing such land, since large farm holders would achieve few economies of scale by purchase of scattered plots. The absorbers would not be the smallest and poorest farms, but rather those of a middle size, which could obtain sufficient credit to purchase such small parcels. If this occurs, the increase in average farm size would be accompanied by a decreasing inequality of farm size.

Most of these arguments are not novel and were raised—albeit in a different form—in the discussion of the late nineteenth-century German agricultural census data. Both Kautsky and Lenin pointed out that the size distribution of farm sales would be a better measure of Marx's basic idea about increasing inequality than the size distribution of land. More specifically, the owners of the smaller farms spend a proportionately greater amount of their time working either in urban areas or for others, and even if the size distribution of farms has not changed, the smaller farms are supplying an increasingly smaller percentage of farm output. For the United States, considerable evidence shows that this argument has merit.[8] For Europe, some evidence suggests the same phenomenon has also occurred (Binswanger and Ruttan 1978).

Annihilation of the Small Farmer

Marx's proposition that the smallholders would become "annihilated" receives mixed support from the available evidence. It has also been disputed by some Marxists who have argued that smallholders have not responded to market signals in the "appropriate manner" but have preferred to remain on their farms and receive less than the opportunity cost of their labor, rather than face the unknown risks of urban life. There may be a grain of truth to this proposition in the nineteenth century, but I have been unable to locate any convincing evidence. In the twentieth century as transportation costs from the farm to the city decline through the improvement of roads, it has been possible for farmers to obtain urban income but continue farming their minifarms, at least on a part-time basis. This phenomenon would, of course, dampen any rise in the average size of farms and, at the same time, would preserve the small farmer from annihilation.

Tables RB.1 and RB.2 present two statistics of relevance to this proposition: the percentage of farms under 10 hectares in size and the percentage of farm land in these small farms. The data are not very reliable since problems arise in determining whether a particular small tract of rural land is, or is not, a farm; and various census agencies have handled the problem in different ways at different times. As noted, I have tried to remove the minifarms by using an arbitrary 2-hectare cutoff.

For what they are worth, the U.S. data show that the percentage of farms under 8.1 hectares (20 acres), as well as their share of land, is *increasing*. In Europe, where the relative importance of farms under 10 hectares is much greater than in the United States, the opposite phenomenon appears to be occurring: the percentage of farms under 10 hectares as well as their share of land is *decreasing* in Austria, Belgium (after 1929), Finland, France, Italy (slightly), Norway, Sweden, Switzerland, and the Netherlands (after 1929), and is *increasing* only in Denmark and the Netherlands (before 1930). In Japan the situation does not appear to have greatly changed over the last half-century—the number of farms larger than 10 hectares is sufficiently unimportant that the government statistics do not provide a separate classification.

The European results appear related to the process of transfer of work-

---

[8] For instance, the 1982 census of agriculture (U.S. Bureau of the Census 1985, table 48) shows an inverse correlation between farm size category and the share of farm operators whose principle occupation is farming. Data on farm and off-farm income per farm operator family show the same phenomenon (Hayami and Ruttan 1985, p. 229).

ers from agriculture to industry and suggest that where the agricultural labor force is still relatively high, the process proceeds more rapidly among those with relatively small farms that have not achieved an optimal scale (and hence have lower incomes).[9] If this explanation is valid, then Marx is correct and Kautsky's and Lenin's counterargument (that such small farmers would prefer to opt for "self exploitation" than to leave the farm) is put to rest. Another explanation is that the lowering of transportation costs between the farm and the city does not occur until the sector with the smallest farms has been considerably reduced.

The U.S. results have several explanations: the rising importance of small farms represents production of niche crops, such as endive farms in Massachusetts, where economies of scale are low and demand is rising, the high percentage of income earned from off-farm activities, and the fact that many of these appear to represent "hobby farms" and vacation homes where, for tax purposes, certain fields are farmed or rented out.

Marx was clearly right that the peasantry as a social class is being annihilated. This is not because small farms are necessarily an economic anachronism, but because modern communications and transportation have eliminated their isolation and have tied these agriculturalists into urban culture so that they are transmuted either into small-scale capitalist farmers or into part-time farmers relying for income primarily on wage work in an urban area.

Rise of a Rural Proletariat

Marx's proposition about the rise of a rural proletariat does not seem accurate for West Europe; for the United States the situation is more complicated. It is the rise of the rural proletariat, combined with the growth of the land area of farms, that provides the most simple way of examining economies of scale in agriculture.

Marxists have painted the plight of the rural proletariat in somber colors; and we can enjoy the irony that many rich American capitalists have taken the cowboy, a member of this group, as their role model. While it is true, as Marx argued, that the shift of the labor force represented a shift from independent farm work to wage work in the urban areas, the proletarianization of agriculture rests squarely on his assumption about

[9] It is sometimes argued that zoning regulations preventing the purchase of land around major cities for residential use can lead to small farms being sold at prices considerably higher than the capitalized value of the earnings for strict agricultural purpose. The preservation of these small "farms," which would normally be absorbed by larger farms, reduces the increase of inequality of land holdings. It is further claimed that this kind of mechanism appears more important in Europe than in the United States or Canada; the data under discussion appear to refute this proposition.

economies of scale, uninfluenced by any kind of changes in factor prices or factor-biased technical change.[10]

As noted above, economies of scale in agriculture have been difficult to find so that we should have little assurance of finding an increase in the proletarianization of the agricultural sector over time. Our search is also impeded by measurement problems, especially with regard to the counting of women workers, other family laborers, and temporary workers. Statistical practices have differed considerably over the last half-century so that for Europe roughly comparable series are available for only five countries.

The data for Austria, Belgium, France, Sweden, and Switzerland all reveal the same trend, namely, a decline in the share of hired labor.[11] For the thirteen countries in table RB.2, the ratio of the male labor force to the number of farms decreased in all countries except the Netherlands from 1960 through 1980, which suggests the same conclusion—that proletarianization has declined and the family farm has increased in relative importance.[12] The increase in labor-saving machinery has allowed individual farmers to carry out their work in much larger production units without hiring additional labor. For Europe Marx was wrong: it is not capitalism that has been a threat to family farming, but socialism.

Over the century from 1880 through 1980 Hayami and Ruttan (1985) show for the United States and Japan that technological change was sufficiently labor-saving so that the increase in average farm area was not associated with an increase in the labor force per farm. The situation in the United States, however, is somewhat more complicated; we can draw upon some recent data to examine some of the reasons why the future of the family farm in this country appears more precarious. From 1910 (when comparable data began to be collected) until 1970, hired workers

[10] Economies of size do not necessarily lead to an increase in the labor force as the land area of the farm increases. For this reason, the argument is phrased only in terms of economies of scale.

[11] The data come for the International Institute for Agriculture (1939) and FAO (1983–87). The data for the 1980 period generally include just permanent family and hired workers; the data for the 1930 period often include temporary family workers. Although the data are thus not comparable, the ratio of hired to total workers for the later period is biased upward. Even with this bias, the share of hired workers appeared to decline in all five countries.

[12] These data come from Hayami and Ruttan (1985), appendix A; the Netherlands is the only exception. For a number of developing countries, however, an increase in proletarianization can be observed with this measure. This type of partial measure leaves something to be desired since it does not pick up the increasing proletarianization in the USA. The FAO (1981, p. 297) present data for the entire rural labor force for 1970 and 1960. For the world as a whole the share of hired workers has declined; however, roughly the same number of countries show an increase as a decrease.

comprised about 25 percent of total employment in agriculture.[13] From 1970 through 1985, however, this rose to 40 percent. Furthermore, in 1985, farm workers employed more than 150 days a year constituted roughly 75 percent of this total, so that these data are not greatly inflated by inclusion of occasional labor. Other time series on farm labor, such as those of Oliveira and Cox (1989) or Oliveira (1989) show a much lower share of hired farm laborers working 150 days or more; however, they also show a rising share of steady farm work. The explanation of this phenomenon is complex since the number of hired farm workers has been declining over most of this period, but at a slower rate than family labor.

Four popular explanations of this surge in the relative importance of hired labor can be quickly dismissed. The phenomenon does not seem to be traceable to the increasing availability of low-wage Hispanic workers, since these workers account for less than 10 percent of the (recorded) farm laborers. It also does not seem to be due to special regional influences since the share of hired workers ranges between 25 and 35 percent in the ten major farm regions and, furthermore, the greatest changes in the share of the farm labor force accounted by hired labor occurred respectively in quite disparate areas—South Atlantic, Pacific, and East North Central regions.[14] In addition, the phenomenon does not appear related to the change in the composition of output.[15] Finally, although some have argued that the rising relative importance of hired workers in America can be traced to changes in American farm technologies and the

[13] These data come from U. S. Bureau of the Census (1975, p. 467) and U.S. Council of Economic Advisers (1986, p. 362). The data on length of employment are estimated from a different series on agricultural employment in U.S. Bureau of the Census (annual, 1988, p. 623).

[14] Data on Hispanic workers come from U.S. Census Bureau (1983, table 135), Oliveira and Cox (1989), and Oliveira (1989). Other data used in this discussion come from U.S. Department of Agriculture (annual, 1961, table 616) and (annual, 1981, table 649).

[15] The share of hired farm workers varies considerably by agricultural product, being highest for cotton, vegetables or melons, and horticulture and lowest for beef cattle, other livestock, and miscellaneous agriculture (in between are other field crops, tobacco, grains, and dairy). Given such differences in the relative importance of hired labor, rough experiments did not suggest that the changing composition of agricultural output would explain much of the overall rising share of hired farm workers.

These generalizations, based on data from Oliveira and Cox (1989), give rise to two measurement problems making a definitive analysis difficult. First, defining hired farm workers raises problems because some of those classified as hired farm workers operated a farm or did unpaid farm work as well; similarly those classified as farm operators worked as farm workers and did unpaid farm work. In calculating the ratios of farm workers to total farm labor force (paid farm workers, unpaid farm workers, and farm operators), I was unable to exclude the overlapping groups. Second, I have included all farm workers, whether they were casual, seasonal, or year-round. If only those farm workers working 150 days or more are included, the greatest share of farm workers occurred in cotton, horticulture, and dairy products and the lowest share occurred in tobacco, other field crops, and grains.

differences in this technology from that used in Europe, the supporting evidence is not very impressive for explaining trends in more than a few small subsectors of agriculture.[16]

Two conjectures explaining the rising relative importance of hired farm labor in the United States seem more convincing. Both, however, require further investigation.

First, the phenomenon may represent a substitution of different types of farm labor tied to the changing nature of the farm family. For instance, Oliveira and Cox (1989) claim that "the trend toward fewer but larger farms contributed to the substitution of hired workers for family workers" since there were fewer (unpaid) family workers to spread over more area. A contributing cause to this problem appears related to the rising share of female farm managers and the increasing importance of off-farm income for owners of relatively small farms. Such hired farm workers, who are roughly 80 percent male, may either perform those farm tasks which require particular physical strength or else carry out the seasonal work which the women cannot accomplish alone because their husbands are working in urban areas. Why such factors are more important in the United States than in Europe requires some difficult research.

Second, the phenomenon may reflect economies of scale of risk-bearing or management and seem related to the much more rapid increase in average farm size in the United States and Canada than in most other nations in table RB.2. Part of the problem of risk arises from the functioning of the credit market. In particular, American farms are not only highly capital intensive but such capital intensiveness has been increasing very fast. This, in turn, has driven the farmer's need for credit. Those able to obtain such credit and to accept the accompanying risks hire others who are more risk averse or who are unable to obtain financing. Closely related are the economies of scale of management that arise because of the risks occurring in situations of rapid technological change and price uncertainties.[17] If it is true that price and technological uncertainties are much greater in the United States than in Europe, then such economies of scale are less important in Europe. This type of argument also requires that in the United States, price and technological uncertainties in the last two decades were much greater than in decades previous

---

[16] Martin and Olmstead (1985) discuss some of the arguments that innovation in agricultural machinery in the U.S. has been skewed away from processes requiring a single farmer and toward processes requiring considerable complementary unskilled labor. This appears true, however, only for particular crops that do not constitute a very large fraction of total farm output.

[17] Such economies of scale include high fixed costs in obtaining sufficient information to make rational production decisions and the greater ease of obtaining credit when incorrect decisions are made.

to the increase in the relative share of hired labor, a conjecture needing to be proven.

A Shift in Tenancy Arrangements

Marx's proposition about the demise of sharecropping appears incorrect, although the empirical evidence on this matter is far from satisfactory.

In common with most other nineteenth-century thinkers (Sismondi, a major landholder, was an important exception), Marx considered share-cropping to be a backward form of land tenancy; the basis of this belief is analyzed by Cheung (1969).[18] Marx did not, however, integrate his ideas about sharecropping with the rest of his ideas about the evolution of the structure of the farm sector, and, as far as I can determine, these ideas were disassociated from the arguments they used in explaining the evolution of other structural elements.

The data on land tenancy are difficult to work with since many countries do not use standardized definitions or methods. For the countries in Europe, I was able to locate long-term series on tenancy only for the United Kingdom, which showed a considerable decline in the share of tenancy from the late 1800s to 1966 (United Kingdom, 1968). For a shorter period, roughly comparable data are available for six nations: between 1930 and 1980 three (Austria, Belgium, and Switzerland) show an increase in the share of land rented, while three (Italy, Netherlands, and Sweden) show a decrease. In the period between 1950 and 1970, the percentage of land rented by the farmer, increased in Austria, Belgium, Canada, Germany, Italy (10 years), and Sweden; and decreased in France (10 years), Japan, the Netherlands (10 years), and the United Kingdom (FAO, 1981, Table 15.13). In many of these countries, the change was very small. For the U.S., the share of land rented by tenant farms has decreased slowly from 1890 to the present; another type of measure focusing on total land renting shows a slight increase.[19]

[18] Neither Cheung nor other modern writers on the topic of rental contracts (a useful survey is provided by Binswanger and Rosenzweig 1984) have discussed in detail the implication of their ideas for changes in agricultural tenancy over time. Developing a suitable analytical framework for handling these temporal changes would take us too far from the major issues of this essay, especially since the Marxian ideas on the topic received no theoretical justification worthy of note.

[19] The former generalization comes from U.S. Department of Agriculture (annual, 1986), table 372; it classifies farms according to the main type of land tenure arrangement. The latter generalization comes from data from various censuses of agriculture and includes all rented land, regardless of whether the renter owns most of the land that is farmed. U.S. Bureau of the Census (1962), p. 1006 has a first-rate study of changes in tenancy from 1880 to 1959, taking full account of changes in definition of different types of tenancy. Although sharecropping appears to have increased, its specific form has changed. For a much shorter time period the FAO (1981, p. 290) has compared the percentage of land rented by the

Data on the type of tenancy are not available from the census of any country except the United States. From the late nineteenth century to 1959, share contracts in the U.S. were *increasing* as a share of total rental contracts, a phenomenon appearing in many U.S. regions as well. Such a trend is, of course, at complete variance with Marx's prediction.

In order to look at this phenomenon in a somewhat different way, I conducted a number of statistical experiments on a cross-section sample of nations presented in Table RB.3, testing a variety of hypotheses to explain the relative importance of both land rental in general and of the sharecropping contract in particular. Although it would take us too far from the main focus of this research note to report the results, one negative result must be mentioned: there seems to be no statistically significant relationship between the level of economic development (measured by the per capita GDP in a common currency) and either of these tenancy phenomena. Clearly, the causal roots of sharecropping are considerably more complex than those postulated by Marx and Engels; the results suggested that further investigation of the linkage between the major crop and the type of contract would be promising.

Marx's belief about the backwardness of sharecropping has had one peculiar reverberation in present-day Marxist regimes, namely a predisposition in the agricultural reforms to favor systems of fixed rent contracts, rather than share arrangements. Given the increased risks that some of the organizational changes of these reforms entail, these arrangements may discourage farmers from responding in the desired manner to the reform measures, a problem discussed at greater length in chapter 9.

SOME BROADER IMPLICATIONS

Although the study of industrial organization has been highly developed over the last decades, no such attention has been given to agricultural organization. As a result, for many of the topics discussed, only the most important issues could be touched upon. Nevertheless, the actual development trends in the organization of agriculture that are revealed in the empirical investigation provide a useful background for the analysis of structural aspects of agricultural organization in chapters 5 and 6.

Other Structural Features

The five Marxist propositions do not exhaust the important macrostructural elements of the agricultural sector, and two other elements deserve brief comment.

---

holder in 1950, 1960, and 1970. The picture is quite mixed, with about the same number of countries showing an increase as a decrease.

TABLE RB.3
The Relative Importance of Land Rental
and of Sharecropping

	Date	Rental ratio	Sharecropping ratio
Africa			
Egypt	1961	.397	.118
Asia			
Bangladesh	1960	.182	.894
Indonesia	1963	.098	.544
Iran	1960	.716	.881
Lebanon	1961	.164	.673
Pakistan	1960	.482	.916
Philippines	1961	.304	.923
Sri Lanka	1961	.106	.713
Thailand	1960	.043	.675
Europe			
Norway	1962	.107	.024
Spain	1963	.205	.371
Yugoslavia	1960	.038	.301
North America			
Costa Rica	1963	.017	.191
Dominican Republic	1960	.106	.483
Mexico	1960	.071	.128
Nicaragua	1963	.036	.203
Panama	1961	.080	.218
U.S.A.	1959	.349	.681
South America			
Argentina	1960	.223	.095
Columbia	1960	.106	.601
Paraguay	1961	.063	.018
Peru	1961	.172	.047
Venezuela	1961	.032	.218
Oceania			
New Zealand	1960	.493	.046

Source: See FAO (1966, 1967, 1970).

Notes: Rental ratio = the ratio of total area rented by cultivators to total area rented and owned by cultivators

Sharecropping ratio = the ratio of area farmed under a sharecropping arrangement to total area of rented land under all tenancy arrangements

The data on area rented or owned by cultivators excludes the area held under other types of tenancy arrangements such as service rents, mixed fixed and share rents, or miscellaneous tenancy schemes. The data on fixed rent arrangements include both cash and crop rents.

The sharecropping ratios for Egypt, Iran, Norway, Paraguay, and Spain required some estimating and, therefore, are not as reliable as the other data.

SPECIALIZATION

One oft-noted structural element is the degree of production specialization found on individual farms. In industrialized nations we might conjecture that such specialization has increased over time, especially as transportation costs have fallen so that farmers can purchase the products of other farms at relatively lower prices. After a certain size limit has been reached, it also seems likely that specialization increases as farms become larger. Data for the United States, however, suggest that the relationship between size and specialization is not as strong as such conjectures suggest; indeed, it is not at all certain if farm specialization has increased in the past few decades.[20] Unfortunately, the census data serving as the information source for most other countries in this discussion do not provide the information to test these hypotheses further.

For small family farms several offsetting forces influence the degree of specialization. On the one hand, minimal economies of scale for many crops dictate a certain crop specialization. On the other hand, specialization on a single crop increases labor demand during certain critical periods; low specialization means that the farmer can more evenly spread his work load over the year without recourse to outside labor. Moreover, if the farmers obtain a considerable share of their income from off-farm sources so that crop production is aimed primarily at feeding the farm family, low specialization is also desirable.

In many Marxist regimes political leaders have encouraged the formation of highly specialized state and collective farms as a means of achieving economies of scale. This trend was taken to the extreme in East Germany, which separated plant growing and animal raising on different state and collective farms. With such specialization the peak-labor demand problem becomes serious and, without either a well-functioning rural labor market or smooth mechanisms to move labor from one farm to another, such labor demands can only be met by political means such as impressing urban dwellers or undesirables such as students into rural work brigades.

VERTICAL INTEGRATION

In my discussion I have confined the analysis to the farm sector, but some important questions can be asked about some important structural elements of the food production sector as a whole. Of particular importance, to what extent is vertical integration between farming and processing of foodstuffs or between farming and the production of farm inputs changing? The data relevant for this question are, unfortunately, sparse and are reviewed in Research Note C. As I show in chapter 10, for Marxist

[20] An interesting study with support for these conclusions is by White and Irwin (Ball and Heady, 1972, pp. 190–213).

regimes the particular manner in which these vertical production relations are structured is an important factor in the ease of decollectivization.

Some Consequences of Developmental Trends

Turning to the major focus of this chapter, in various parts of the discussion I have examined a number of causal elements underlying the evolution of the macrostructure of the farm sector. Most obviously, government land policies such as the homesteading acts in the United States, the land nationalization program in Austria, the program of France and postwar Germany to consolidate scattered plots, and the land reforms that have taken place in a number of Western nations, can influence the average size and the size distribution of farms. Many other measures, however, must also be taken into account: inheritance practices; land transfer procedures; tax, tariff, price support, and subsidy policies; and agricultural extension, credit, and transportation policies. These and other governmental actions differentially influence the costs and returns of small and large farms and can, therefore, also have very important effect on the parameters of farm structure discussed above.

What all this means, of course, is that Marxist regimes do not need to remain passive in the face of adverse changes in farm size, increased differentiation in land holdings and rural wealth, or other alleged long-run trends. Since they have the same policy tools as governments of market economies to deal with these situations, collectivization is not necessary.

The analysis also reveals that projection of trends in agricultural organization of a particular nation depend less on broad economic forces operating in every country than upon less general economic factors operating at the national or local levels. The contrasts between the data for the United States and Europe make it painfully clear that a considerable number of causal factors have operated in the various countries, that a rather complex model would be necessary to construct in order to take them all into account, and that the policies adopted in one country may not be useful for another. Although collectivization appears an easy way of dealing with certain long run problems of agricultural organization without having to deal with these subtle issues, such a policy, as I show in the text of this book, has a certain cost.

In sum, dogmatism about the long-term development of agricultural organization does not seem warranted. Restructuring of the productive units of agriculture on the basis of the propositions advanced by Marx and Engels on historically necessary organizational developments in the farm sector rest on an uncertain scientific basis, and such decisions can have quite unfortunate consequences.

THE VERTICAL STRUCTURE OF AGRICULTURE IN
MARKET ECONOMIES

DESCRIPTIVE MATERIALS on vertical contracts and integration for various market economies can be located for a number of countries (e.g., Kirsch 1976; FAO 1977). Nevertheless, relatively complete data on both contract and ownership integration for various agricultural products seem readily available only for the United States; such data are presented in table RC.1.

These data reveal a surprisingly high degree and variability of vertical integration: 38 percent of total production is linked by some type of vertical relation, ranging from 100 percent for sales of vegetables, fruits, and nuts to 5 to 7 percent of sales for wheat and feed grains. Although ownership integration is important where technological or transactional economies occur, most vertical relations are due to contract integration, which appears a relatively recent development. Around 1970 the level of contract integration was minuscule in the few countries reporting such data and, moreover, appeared primarily in fruits, vegetables, and other perishables (FAO 1981, p. 258).

Although data on ownership integration could not be located for other countries, some relatively recent data on contract integration for marketing are available and are presented in table RC.2. They show considerable variation among countries and also among products. Some of these differences can be attributed to differences in technology. For instance, the fine-tuning of genetic properties in meat and meat products has not reached the same level in Spain as in the United States, and vertical integration is lower. In other cases, the existence of a high degree of industrial concentration among purchasers has forced producers to band together into selling cooperatives to offset this economic power (for instance, wool production in some countries). In still other cases, historical forces have played an important role; for instance, in countries such as Norway, where governmental legislation has given special advantages to cooperative marketing arrangements, or in Portugal and Spain, where cooperative marketing arrangements grew out of mutual credit and insurance arrangements (for cattle) and from various arrangements arising from the joint operation of irrigation systems. Many of the differences can also be attributable to interactions between technology and market

TABLE RC.1
Vertical Integration in the United States Farm Sector, 1987
(percentage of total production)

| Commodity | Contract Integration | | | | Ownership Integration | Total Integration |
| | Cooperative Contract | | Proprietary Contract | | | |
	Marketing	Production	Marketing	Production		
Milk	65	0	30	0	3	98
Eggs	0	2	0	50	37	89
Broilers	0	12	0	77	10	99
Turkeys	0	18	0	46	28	90
Hogs	0	0	0	8	8	16
Fed beef	0	0	0	30	6	36
Wheat	2	0	3	0	0	5
Rice	59	0	8	0	5	72
Feed grains	2	0	5	0	0	7
Soybeans	3	0	7	0	0	10
Cotton	13	0	7	0	10	30
Vegetables						
Fresh	7	0	0	24	35	66
Processed	0	20	0	65	15	100
Citrus	65	2	5	0	35	95
Other fruits and nuts						
Fresh fruit	40	0	5	0	10	60
Processed	65	0	30	0	5	100
Weighted average	13	0	6	12	6	38

Source: Knutson, Penn, and Boehm (1990), p. 278.

Notes: This table covers about 90 percent of all farm sales; it excludes production for seed and certain industrial crops, for instance, sugar. The marketing contracts include call, delayed, or deferred pricing contracts. For citrus, the row total is less than the sum of the parts because of an overlap: one major packer is a member of a cooperative.

The Knutson, Penn, and Boehm data are rearranged. Although they do not specify how they handled a situation when both a marketing and a production contract are signed, it appears that they classified it as a marketing contract. These data do not differ for similar estimates for 1981 from Knutson, Penn, and Boehm (1983), p. 245.

Marketing Contracts or Cooperative Marketing in the Farm Sector of Several
West European Nations (percentage of sales)

Commodity	France Production Arrangements	France Marketing Coops	France Processing Coops	Norway	Spain	United Kingdom
Milk		45		100	18	
Milk products			38			98
Eggs		25		61	11	22
Wool				80	3	100
Meat			35	72		
Poultry/meat	40				9	29
Cattle-calves/meat	14				5	2
Sheep-lambs/meat					3	2
Pigs/meat	50				3	57
Wheat		77				
Cereals						36
Fodder crops			95		2	
Potatoes				100		9
Cotton					34	
Sugar beet						100
Hops						100
Olives for oil					52	
Oil plants		70				
Flowers					51	
Fruit/vegetables				38		
Vegetables						11
Legumes	18	30			10	
Fruit	52	40	44			15
Fresh					18	
Dried					10	
Olives for table					48	
Grapes					49	
Other						2
Weighted average	n.a.	n.a.	n.a.	82	n.a.	40

Source: FAO (1977), pp. 92, 142, 313, and 334.

Notes: The data for France are for 1975. "Production arrangements" cover "production controlled by groups of producers," who cooperate at certain stages of production; it does not necessarily imply group farming. Marketing cooperatives also include cooperatives for harvesting. Fodder crops are only dehydrated luzerne. Processed fruits include legumes as well. The table uses the midpoint whenever the original source presents a range.

The data for Norway are for 1973–74. They include only sales of farmer cooperatives and refer to total marketed production. The weighted average is estimated on the base of sales values, excluding cereals. The data for Spain appear to refer to the early 1970s. Cereals and fodder crops are combined. The legumes are an unweighted average of different types of legumes. The data for the United Kingdom are for 1970–71; they include both marketing board schemes and cooperative contracts; however, with the exception of eggs and top fruit, this percentage is relatively small. Milk and milk products are combined.

conditions. For instance, vertical integration in the growing of wheat (a highly standardized commodity that does not easily spoil and is easily transportable) is very low in the United States, moderately high in Spain (FAO 1977, 285–86), and very high in France. In the United States wheat farmers have large plots and are operating in an environment with highly developed spot and futures markets; thus, the price of wheat paid to a producer by a grain elevator in the middle of Kansas is little different from the price of wheat in Chicago. In Spain, the plots are small and farmers must often combine their land to be able to use efficiently the large farm machinery that is available; such joint production leads easily to joint marketing arrangements as well. In France, it appears that wheat farmers have combined for certain political reasons and have issued controls on their members, so that noneconomic forces underlie the "production cooperation."[1]

The available data do not separate downstream and upstream vertical integration. The descriptive literature suggests, however, that although many market economies feature cooperative buying of farm inputs, for instance, fertilizer and pesticides, especially since production of these products is generally quite concentrated, there are few vertical linkages with providers of farm services such as construction, equipment rentals or repairs, or special types of spraying.

[1] Even the noneconomic motives for different types of vertical arrangements appear to differ from country to country. For instance, the FAO (1977, p. 357) reports some startling survey results for Portugal, where 67 percent of all members of marketing cooperatives mentioned as an advantage that the cooperative has brought them "peace of mind," in contrast to 34 percent mentioning an improvement in sales and prices, or 3 percent mentioning a better use of their time. In other countries, one receives the impression that quite different motives are important.

MANAGERIAL DECISION-MAKING ON STATE AND COLLECTIVE FARMS

IN THIS NOTE I explore in a more rigorous fashion a structural element of state and collective farms discussed briefly in the text: how the ministries of agriculture compensate the farm managers in order to guide their decisions and how, as a result, these managers act differently from private farmers. From such an investigation some hypotheses can be derived that guide the empirical analysis of agricultural performance in chapter 8.

A ministry of agriculture faces a variety of options in influencing managerial behavior. If the agricultural sector functions essentially as a market economy, the ministry can act as a capitalist holding company, paying the managers a base salary plus some bonus based on profits so that the farm sector operates as a plantation economic system. Few Marxist regimes have shown such forbearance and, as discussed in chapter 7, have intervened to set producer prices, directed production of collective and state farms, and, in other ways, acted to limit decision-making autonomy of farm managers. The most extreme cases have occurred in the Soviet-type economies of Eastern Europe (except Hungary and Yugoslavia), and in China (before 1979), Cuba, North Korea, and Mongolia, where the agricultural sector was integrated into a centrally directed economic system, with the managers receiving both a plan and a bonus schedule tied to plan fulfillment. In most of the Third World Marxist nations, the nature of governmental intervention is less pervasive.

For some Marxist regimes information about formal managerial compensation can be located; unfortunately, it is much more difficult to find information about the bonus system, especially informal kinds of rewards. In interviewing farm managers, I sometimes received answers indicating that in some years when the harvest was particularly good, they received a bonus, while in other years with the same plan and equal harvest, they did not. This means either the bonus system changed, or that they were not completely aware of the elements that enter into the calculation of their bonuses. Officials in the ministry were often similarly vague as well.

In lieu of such detailed information, it is necessary to rely on several simplified cases in order to explore what might be the most important elements. In this research note, I use a highly stylized model of managerial decision-making in a state farm in a Soviet-type economy and investigate two aspects of farm behavior: production efficiency of agriculture over time and the fluctuations of agricultural production from year to year. I then argue that the collective farm must be considered as a variant of the state farm since the bonus schedule for managers of both were relatively similar. The major difference arose from the greater uncertainties in obtaining the requisite labor force on the collective farms. This approach toward the collective farm avoids the fiction, accepted in most of the theoretical literature in the West, that the collective farm is really a cooperative where the managers are altruistically maximizing profits per worker, rather than their own bonus. From my model, I also draw some conclusions for market oriented farms in Marxist regimes in Third World nations.[1]

KEY ASSUMPTIONS AND APPROACH

The analysis on a verbal level is supplemented by several diagrams, so that the qualitative implications can be fully explored. All the major pieces of the models discussed below have received full mathematical exposition in the economic literature. Unfortunately, the mathematical apparatus of these studies has generated hypotheses that cannot be easily tested and, in other cases, has obscured some propositions about observable behavior making these kinds of farms distinctive from their capitalist counterparts that could be tested with the available data.

The model outlined below focuses on observable behavior. It also allows connections to be drawn between the socialist state farm and the capitalist "managerial firm or bureau," where the managers are not maximizing profits, but rather some variable tying their income to variables such as sales, output, or (in the case of a government bureaucrat) the size of their budget. These various managerial models often differ from each other only according to the constraints imposed upon the decision-maker.[2]

[1] I do not discuss many social issues of managing these collective and state farms. For instance, in Marxist regimes most farm managers are men. Some aspects of this phenomenon for the Soviet Union are explored by Bridger (1987).

[2] Examples of the analysis of manager-dominated firms or bureaus in capitalist countries include discussions by Baumol (1967), Marris (1964), Niskanen (1971, 1975), Penrose (1969), and Williamson (1966). A number of managerial models have also focused on Soviet-type firms, e.g., Ames (1965), Gindin (1970), or Portes (1969). Much of the analysis of the impact of different bonus schemes is cited below; Oxenstierna (1987) has a useful summary of several schemes. I omit mention of the vast literature on preference revealing bonus systems, which have not been important in any of the countries under discussion. There is also a vast literature on the behavior of communes (*kolkhozy*) and other institutions in which

My approach is neoclassical: I assume that the managers are trying to maximize their income and minimize the effort they expend in earning that income. With little loss of generality, I assume that the managers have a separable utility function so that the utility derived from income and the disutility derived from effort can be examined in isolation from each other. I further assume that the managers are sufficiently farsighted to take into account the consequences of their current actions on their future income and effort. The utility-maximization problem facing the managers is striking some balance between the discounted utility of the stream of future income and discounted disutility of the stream of future effort. Further, I assume that their marginal utility of income is declining, which means, among other things, that they would prefer a somewhat lower fixed income to an income that is slightly higher on average in monetary terms but that fluctuates considerably around this average.[3] The declining marginal utility of income is shown in the right-hand panel in diagram RD.1a, where Y is income and U is utility. Finally, I assume that the budget constraint is hard, that is, that the farm must at least break even. During the 1980s in East Europe, this condition was not met, so in this important respect the model is not completely realistic.

Although most centrally planned Marxist regimes changed the elements underlying the managerial compensation schedules considerably over time, in the 1970s and 1980s managerial income was generally based on gross farm output, subject to some special constraints depending on the economic environment; these constraints differed from one Marxist regime to another. In some of the Third World Marxist regimes where foreign trade in agricultural products was very important or where the influence of their recently (capitalist) past was still strong, profit considerations played a more central role.

Throughout the discussion, I assume that there is a single output, which is a function of the manager's effort and some random factor representing weather and supply difficulties. For simplicity I also assume that, in the short-run, labor and capital cannot vary greatly on individual farms, so that the level of managerial effort is crucially important for determining the level of production.[4] We can include variation in the labor

---

the objective function is profit (or total net earnings) per worker. As I will argue, most of these models are irrelevant to the actual operation of these farms.

[3] The assumption also implies that if actors in the model pick a particular combination of two risky activities creating utility and if the risk of one activity increases, they will focus their efforts more than previously on the other activity. If the two activities are production of income and leisure, increased risk in income production will lead to greater leisure. In this case I am assuming that the substitution effect outweighs the income effect because the increased risk lowers real income; this is a strong assumption about risk aversion.

[4] Farm managers are forbidden by law or custom to reduce their labor force, and the general immobility of labor makes it difficult to increase the labor force. Although students,

supply with relative ease, but this complicates the exposition without adding any important insights and assumes a factor mobility that is seldom found. The relationship between effort and production exhibits the usual type of diminishing returns and is shown in the left-hand panel in diagram RD.1a, where Q is production.

In the manufacturing sector of many Soviet-type economies, as observers have pointed out, plans are changed throughout the year as central administrators learn more about the objective constraints facing managers. I doubt if these changes occurred so often in the agricultural sector; indeed, given the much greater importance of weather and other random factors, these plan revisions would be endless if they were ever attempted. I am, therefore, assuming fixed yearly plans.

Throughout the analysis, I also emphasize the distinction between "formal" and "actual" variables. A formal bonus system, for instance, specifies a schedule linking monetary payments to the bonus indicator; the actual bonus system links the utility of the bonus payments to the bonus indicator and takes into account the future consequences of the bonus payments. Similarly, the formal plan outlines the various stated output goals of the policymakers, while the actual plan, generally unknown to most people, specifies what the planners really expect to achieve, given their evaluation of such objective factors as weather, incompetency of their subordinates, and other conditions and events. An important clue to the actual plan is the level of production below which managers begin to have their salary reduced.

Managerial Compensation

The formal compensation system is relatively simple. The actual compensation system I discuss takes into account both the ratchet and uncertainty and is much more complicated.

The Formal Compensation System

In the model the state farm managers' formal compensation is directly linked with both the level of production and the production plan goal. The managers receive a base salary plus possibly a fixed bonus (hereafter the "base bonus") if they meet the plan goal. Despite this seeming simplicity, their compensation schedule has three different segments: If

townspeople, and army personnel are available and are an important source of labor (see, for instance, the calculations of Hedlund [1989] for the USSR), they are only a short-term expedient. Similarly, in most of these countries the managers face limited possibilities in the short run for varying the amounts of fertilizer, pesticides, and other inputs or their use of capital equipment such as tractors because of the general scarcity of these products.

managers produce more than the plan goal, they receive their base salary plus the base bonus plus a bonus for each unit of production above the plan. If they produce below the plan goal but above the "punishment point," (which is a certain percentage less than the plan goal), they receive their base salary plus a possible bonus for each unit above the punishment point. This bonus, however, is much less than the bonus for above-plan production and, indeed, can be zero. If they produce less than punishment point, they receive their base salary plus some fine for every unit short of the punishment point. Nonmonetary fines such as dismissal can also be applied.

Diagram RD.1b shows the compensation schedule graphically, with managerial income on the vertical axis and farm production on the horizontal axis. The dotted line Y_f shows the managers' base salaries, which are independent of production as long as production is above a certain minimum, Q_f; below this point, they are punished by means of a reduction of income or fine (which may also mean dismissal and a lower-paying

RD.1. The Formal and Actual Compensation Schedules

RD.1a. Relationships between Effort and Production, Income and Utility

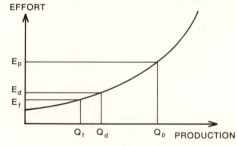

RD.1b. The Formal Compensation Schedule

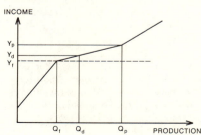

RD.1c. The Actual Compensation Curve, No Ratchet, No Uncertainty

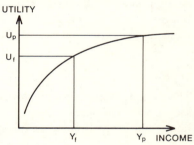

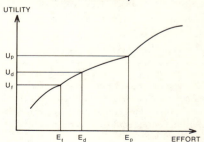

job). The solid line shows the manager's total income, that is, salary plus bonus. As drawn, the compensation schedule has two points of inflection: the punishment point Q_f and the plan fulfillment point Q_p.

The distance between the punishment point and the plan fulfillment point provides useful information about the nature of the economic environment in which the state farm managers are operating. In an environment where weather fluctuations are considerable, we would expect a greater distance between the two points, since production shortfalls would be beyond the managers' responsibilities. In an environment where qualified farm managers are scarce, we would also expect not only a greater distance between the two points but also a lower fine if production falls below the punishment point. A similar result would occur where the planners are quite inexperienced or where they have little information on which to base their plans. On the other hand, we would expect that where weather uncertainties are not great, where a pool of experienced people are available to manage the farms, and where the planners have considerable information about the potential for production of each farm, the punishment and the plan fulfillment points would not only lie close to each other, but also that the fines for production that is less than the punishment point would be greater.

Some informal evidence confirming these conjectures is available from interview materials. São Tomé is a country with few qualified farm managers and extremely inexperienced planners. In 1987, a year of average weather, production fell short of the agricultural plan by a considerable margin for some important crops: for instance, cocoa (the nation's chief export), 24 percent; coffee, 63 percent; copra, 38 percent.[5] A state farm manager whom I interviewed told me that he had received no fines or other sanctions and had been in no danger of losing his job. He also suggested that no one in the government took these plans very seriously because of lack of information on real production potentials of the farms. In Seychelles, where weather conditions are rather uncertain and the planning apparatus was in its infancy, a state farm manager told me that he received a straight salary (the Y_f schedule), no matter what he produced. Other examples can be cited where enormous discrepancies existed between actual and planned agricultural production and where the managers appeared to receive a straight salary.[6] In the Soviet Union

[5] These data were supplied to me by the Ministério da Agricultura e Pescas.

[6] In Mozambique in 1982, actual production of the state sector reached 15 percent of planned production for soybeans, 28 percent for wheat, and 29 percent for tobacco (Egerö 1987, p. 100). During a five-year period in Angola marketed production often reached less than one-tenth the plan goal and, although this covered the entire agricultural sector, it does not seem likely that the state farm production was much better (Bhagavan 1986, p. 61 has plan and actual data for twenty-five products). Although the situation is not entirely

where replacement managers for the state farms have been more readily available and the planning apparatus has had many years of certain experience, the situation has been different. In her anthropological study of two collective farms in Siberia, Humphrey (1983) describes how the careers of farm managers suffered sharp reverses because of relatively small plan shortfalls; the same is likely to have occurred for state farm managers as well.

If the planners raise the plan goals, the entire compensation schedule slides to the right. If state farm managers have more labor, capital, and farm inputs at their disposal, the compensation schedule in diagram RD.1b does not change, but the managers need to exert less effort to achieve a certain level of production. One major task of the planners is to adjust the compensation schedule so that it corresponds with the capacity of the various farms.

Diagram RD.1c shows a translation of the formal compensation schedule into a curve relating the managers' utility of the income received, and their disutility of effort expended in production. This is labeled the *actual compensation curve*, to distinguish it from the formal compensation schedule defined above. It is calculated by taking any level of production Q, determining the income Y obtained and, from the right-hand panel in Diagram RD.1a, the corresponding utility U. Then from the left-hand panel in Diagram RD.1a, the corresponding degree of effort E is determined and the pair of points U, E is plotted. Since both the production-effort and the income-utility curves are monotonic, this is a simple task. The punishment and plan fulfillment points—E_f, U_f and E_p, U_p—still define the three segments of the curve. The three line segments are, however, no longer linear but concave: their exact shape and slope depend on the slope of the compensation schedule, the rate of diminishing marginal utility of income, and the rate of diminishing marginal productivity of labor.

If the planners raise plan goals, the entire compensation curve shifts to the right; for any given effort, income (and the utility of income) is lower. If more labor, capital, and other farm inputs are available to the state farm managers, the compensation curve shifts to the left. That is, any specific income can be achieved with less managerial effort and, moreover, the production corresponding to the punishment and plan fulfillment points can be obtained with less effort as well. In short, increasing plan goals and increasing the factors and inputs of production act in exactly opposite ways, an important part of the argument below. If the planners believe that the state farm managers are expending an optimal

---

clear, it appears that state farm managers in these two countries received essentially a straight salary.

amount of effort, they would raise plan goals in a manner to offset exactly the impact of the increased production factors and inputs so that the managerial compensation curve (Diagram RD.1c) remains exactly in the same place.

The Actual Compensation Curve with the Ratchet and Uncertainty

The shape of the compensation curve changes both share and position when we take into account two additional phenomena: the ratchet effect and the uncertain relation between effort and production because of random factors.

The ratchet is a simple phenomenon. In the Soviet Union and other East European nations, planners generally start the planning efforts by examining the achieved level of production, since this is a simple (albeit misleading) indicator of capacity. If the state farm overfulfills the plan in this year, the ministry will undoubtedly raise the plan goals next year so that the managers will have to expend more effort merely to meet the plan. Similarly, an underfulfillment may result in a lowering of next year's plan goals and less managerial effort needed to meet the plan.

The ratchet is a common management tool used in both East and West whenever superiors do not have complete information about the production capacity available to subordinates and, at the same time, want to encourage their subordinates to work as hard as possible. As shown, it dominates the behavior of the state farm manager. Although its effects cannot be handled in a completely rigorous fashion without the use of mathematics, it is possible to adjust the diagram of the compensation curve so that its major effects can be taken into account in a qualitative fashion.

In deciding how much to produce, the state farm managers must thus take into account the impact of this year's decisions upon their next year's income and effort, which requires discounting the disutility arising in the necessity to expend greater energy in future years. This is a difficult gaming problem to solve, especially when uncertainty is involved. A formal solution for a very simplified version of the problem is provided by Keren, Miller, and Thornton (1981).

In this model the problem is handled in a more intuitive fashion. I frame the discounting problem in terms of net utility, that is, the utility of the income minus the disutility of the effort required to obtain it. Suppose, for a moment, that obtaining a higher monetary income today results in an increase of utility of income by three units and a disutility of effort by one unit so that total utility of income increases by two units. In the future, however, the ratchet would insure that income falls back to its original level but the additional disutility of effort of one unit would have to be expended for a given number of years in the future, say five years. If we assume no time rate of discount, this means that the net utility of increasing production is not two units, but rather negative three units (the two units of utility in the first year, and the negative unit of utility for each of the next five years). Moreover, this stream of disutilities is even greater at higher levels of current production because of the diminishing returns to effort so that utility of income begins rapidly to decrease after a given level of production (and effort).

This line of argument means that in a situation with complete certainty (assumed up to now), the compensation curve (CC′) does not increase forever, as the compensation schedule does in diagram RD.1b; rather, it hits a peak and then declines.[7] The corresponding utility and effort points and the punishment and plan fulfillment points are E_f, U_f' and E_p, U_p'. Although shaped like a hill, the actual compensation curve still maintains the inflection points marked by the punishment point where the managers are fined and the plan fulfillment point, as shown by the dashed line in diagram RD.2, where the first derivative to the schedule is discontinuous. The exact location of the peak depends upon the relation between utility of income at the plan fulfillment point and the effort required to achieve it. If, for instance, the plan is difficult to meet with normal ef-

RD.2. The Actual Compensation Curve with the
Ratchet and Uncertainty

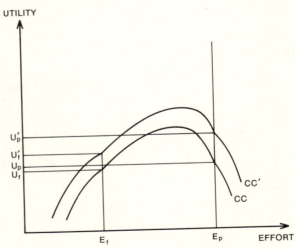

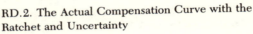

[7] If the punishment and plan fulfillment points are widely separated so that the former is easy and the latter is difficult to achieve with normal efforts, then it is possible that the compensation curve will be bimodal, with the larger hump between the two points and a smaller hump to the right of the plan fulfillment point. Although this bimodal case can be handled, I omit further consideration of such a case to simplify discussion.

forts, then the peak of the compensation curve will lie to the left of the plan fulfillment point. In this case the managers will underfulfill the plan for a sufficiently long period of time to lower the plan. If the peak is so "impossible" that it is to the left of the punishment point, the managers may expend almost no effort at all and either accept their fine and wait until some time in the future when the plan is lowered, resign if they can obtain another job where utility is higher, or, as was the case in Stalin's Russia, appear to make a credible effort, hope for superb weather, and await prison.

One last complication now deserves consideration, namely the fact that farm production involves considerable uncertainties arising from the impact of weather, plant and cattle diseases, and the lack of proper farm inputs at the required time. These are not known in advance to either the central planners or the state farm managers; nevertheless, their impact is important in the compensation received by the managers. Using diagram RD.2 we can, however, take into account qualitatively some of the major impacts of uncertainty; a rigorous mathematical treatment is provided by Keren (1972).

With the introduction of uncertainty, the actual compensation curve now reflects the expected utility of income for any given amount of managerial effort. Expected utility is the weighted sum of the probability of the utility of various outcomes that reflect the different random elements specified above. It is shown in diagram RD.2, with the pairs of utility and effort at the punishment and plan fulfillment points labeled as E_f, U_f and E_p, U_p. This compensation curve (CC) lies below the compensation curve with no uncertainty because of diminishing marginal utility; that is, the utility of the income gained by producing X more than expected is not so great as the utility of the income lost by producing X less than expected. With uncertainty the peak would lie somewhat to the left of the peak without uncertainty, since random events might push production over the plan and in a segment of the curve where utility is decreasing rapidly because of the ratchet effect.

Raising the plan goals shifts the actual compensation curve to the right and downward, because for a given amount of effort, income is lower (since a lower percentage of the plan goal is produced with such effort) and, of course, utility is lower as well. This is shown in diagram RD.3 in the curve labeled CC'. The curve also changes shape in an indeterminate way, which is the outcome of two opposite effects. On the one hand, the segment of the curve to the left of the peak (the key segment for this analysis) might be steeper, because at any point on this segment a given number of effort units from the peak, income is lower and the marginal utility of income is higher. This means that a given change in production, which leads to a given change in income, would lead to a correspondingly greater change in utility than before the plan goal was raised. On the other hand, the segment of the curve to the left of the peak might be less steep, because at any point on this segment a given number of effort units from the peak, more effort is required to raise production by one unit. This means that a given change in effort would lead to a smaller change in income and, possibly, a lower change in utility. To determine which effect is stronger, we need to have specific information on the marginal utility of income curve, the marginal product of effort curve (shown respectively in the left and right panels of diagram RD.1a), as well as the compensation schedule (shown in diagram RD.1b).

THE MANAGERS' PRODUCTION DECISION AND IMPLICATIONS

Two types of implications are considered: the propositions we can draw directly from the model about how the system works; and the propositions about the difference of such state farms and private plantations in a capitalist economy.

Operations of the Model

In diagram RD.3 curves I_1, I_2, and I_3 are the indifference curves indicating the various combinations of effort (which represents a disutility) and utility at which the managers are indifferent. The subscript indicates the level of utility; indifference curve I_1 indicates the level of utility below which managers will resign since they could obtain an equal utility at

RD.3. The Manager's Production Decision

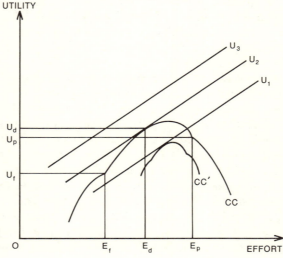

another available job. Indifference curve I_3 is infeasible and cannot be achieved. Since effort is a measure of disutility and the utility of income and disutility of effort functions are assumed to be separable, the indifference curves are straight lines; if the utility functions are not separable, the indifference curves would be convex.

Point d is where the indifference curve I_2 is tangent to the compensation curve. This point, corresponding to a utility of income U_d and an effort E_d, designates the highest utility that managers can achieve. From the relationship between managerial effort and production, the expected production and income can be determined (as shown in diagram RD.1).

It is noteworthy that this desired point falls somewhat short of the peak utility point or, for that matter, the plan fulfillment point so that a certain amount of farm capacity goes unused. If the plan goal is highly ambitious the point left of the peak might actually lie in the region where the managers are fined, so that they have the choice of resigning or suffering the fine until, in some future year, the ministry lowers the plan goal. In special cases the ministry can ensure plan fulfillment if the plan is not too ambitious and if it provides little or no bonus for production below plan and a one-step bonus when the plan is achieved. At this point the diagram would have a notch. Although such a bonus system was used during the time of Stalin, it did not seem to be in common use in the 1980s. In this Stalinist system, the managers are more likely to aim for the plan goal if they are able to hide over-plan production from the authorities in case of unexpectedly good weather so that their plan would not be unduly raised next year. That is, if the ministry uses a ratchet, it is in the short- and long-term interest of the higher authorities to allow the managers to cheat on them!

The officials of the ministry of agriculture do not sit passively by and watch as the state farm managers select their ideal point of production. Rather, the ministry tries to adjust the plan-fulfillment point in order to encourage the greatest production from the managers. If the plan increases, the compensation curve shifts (in the manner discussed above) so that the farm managers are at a lower level of utility. If the plan is at a level where it can be achieved with relatively little effort on the part of managers, the income effect of the bonus can be sufficiently strong that the managers are willing to work harder and reduce their leisure in order to compensate in part for reduced income, so that production increases. This process cannot last forever. If, by way of contrast, plan fulfillment already requires great effort, then the managers may choose to reduce their effort (because each unit of effort yields less income) and production falls, especially if they are willing to endure several years of lower income until the ministry lowers the plan again.

Diagrammatically, this differential response can be seen by considering the change in shape of the compensation curve occurring when the plan goal is raised. If the curve is steeper, as I have drawn the CC' curve in Diagram RD.3, managers will increase their effort. If the curve is less steep (which occurs when the marginal productivity of effort is not very great), it is possible that they will decrease their effort. A mathematical treatment of this differential response to an increase in the plan goal is provided by Keren (1972).

A complementary factor that cannot be included in these diagrams is discussed in a classic article on optimal tautness by Hunter (1961). He argues that as plan goals are raised, the level of tautness of the system rises and shortages begin to appear, which impede production. After tautness has passed a certain point, production is actually lower.

Two important conclusions can be drawn from this discussion: The optimal plan goal maximizes production, but it may lead to production that is less than the plan goal. Furthermore, this optimal plan goal depends on an objective factor (the formal compensation schedule) and two subjective factors (the relation of managerial effort to production and the relation of the managers' utility to their income). Other interesting conclusions about managerial behavior can be drawn from the model, particularly with regard to changing risk, but they cannot be easily tested and are not discussed further.

Thus the common criticism of centrally planned economies that plan goals are not achieved is beside the point, since the gap between the plan goal and actual production may maximize managerial effort; in my terminology, the actual plan is lower than the formal plan. Since the gap between plan goal and actual production may also arise because of random factors, or the planners may have temporarily overestimated the optimal level (Keren 1972), we cannot interpret any gap as directly signifying the difference between the actual and formal plans. The gap may also indicate that the punishment point and the output bonuses are so unimportant to the managers that the ministry does not really control their behavior, as shown in the cases of São Tomé and other countries that are discussed above.

From manipulation of the curves in the diagram it can be shown that the ministry can also increase production by moving the punishment point closer to the plan-fulfillment point. Since the slope of the compensation curve to the left of the peak increases, this would lead to an increase in effort. There is, however, a limit to this behavior by the ministry because of the unfairness resulting from punishment of farm managers for performance due to poor weather; this unfairness undoubtedly would reduce the pool of available farm managers.

Since it is very difficult for the ministry to have a completely clear idea about the production potential of a given farm, the managers have one extremely important weapon, namely, hiding surplus capacity from their superiors. Since the ministry generally knows the size of the labor force, this can be done either by using more land than is officially reported or hiding capital, that is, concealing information about the quality or quantity of capital. Soviet economists tell of satellite surveys revealing considerably more arable land used than the farms have officially reported to the ministry and of small-scale, focused livestock censuses indicating more animals than the ministry had previously counted. Spare capital capacity cannot be suddenly created; it can, however, be accumulated in a quiet fashion over time in the investment process, either by not reporting investment (e.g., to improve the quality of the soil) or by under-reporting the effective capacity of a given capital investment. More specifically, almost any type of productive investment can lead to higher production. It is, however, very difficult for central administrators to specify the exact increase, because this depends greatly on local circumstances. Thus, if managers invest so that actual productive capacity increases 10 percent but they only report an 8 percent increase in formal capacity, they can lead an easier life without much chance of being detected.

This kind of game on the part of managers has another implication that refers to special cheating when producing perishable crops. Suppose the managers choose a level of effort to produce 95 percent of the plan on the average: in good weather, they produce 105 percent of plan; in bad weather, 85 percent. Because of the ratchet, with good weather they may report only 102 percent of plan, using the unreported 3 percent either to distribute for consumption to farm workers or to exchange in some way for additional inputs in the second economy. With bad weather, they may report only 80 percent of production, using the unreported 5 percent for similar purposes. If the ministry inquires about the low production, the managers have the good excuse of bad weather ("the hail ruined one-tenth of our crop and the excess rain damaged another tenth"), and it is difficult for the ministry to check up on them, especially when it has no agency operating in the countryside like the MTSs, which have a good overview of total production and microclimatic conditions. Indeed, the managers gain considerable advantage by exaggerating the effects of weather fluctuations on the downside: as a result the ministry may widen the distance between the plan-fulfillment and the punishment points, and the managers will have more resources to create unreported capacity, which reduces their effort in obtaining a given amount of income.

Differences from a Capitalist Farm

An owner-managed farm or plantation in a market system and a state farm operating according to the model I have described behave differently in several important ways.

Capitalist farmers try to maximize profits. Since profits are a residual after fixed costs have been paid, the marginal return to effort is greater. Although capitalist farmers may elect to work only a sufficient amount to keep themselves out of bankruptcy (the capitalist punishment point), in most cases it is likely that they will work considerably harder and longer because they do not receive a base salary independent of effort. Because of the absence of a ratchet, the formal compensation schedule and the actual compensation curve have fewer differences in shape: the actual compensation curve turns down only when the disutility of additional effort outweighs the utility gained by higher income from more production.

Many have argued that because capitalist owners are likely to work more, other things being equal, production for a given amount of land, labor, and capital will be greater than on a state farm. Although, as pointed out in chapter 8, this proposition can be tested, it turns out to be exceedingly difficult because of problems in determining the production function. Two other propositions, however, are considerably easier to test.

First, private farmers have no incentive to hide capacity. As a result, the impact of investment on production and total factor productivity (productivity taking account of all inputs) will be greater in market than in centrally planned economic systems, other things being equal. Reinforcing this phenomenon is the practice in some centrally planned economies of giving equipment to state farms through investment grants. Although this equipment may not be suitable, the managers do not need to use it so that, without any penalty to the managers, the investment is wasted. An owner-manager would not act in this fashion.

Second, private farmers also have no incentive to overstate production losses in times of bad weather so as to gain a secret amount of surplus capacity. As a result, fluctuations of reported agricultural production would be greater in centrally planned systems than in market economies, other things being equal. These fluctuations in reported production in planned economies are reinforced by the supply system that generally works less smoothly because such inputs are allocated centrally, rather than sold on a market, so that farm managers in centrally planned economies often face shortages in farm inputs. More technically, the farm managers in centrally planned economies face more sources of independent random shocks than their confrères in market economies. As a result they might carry higher inventories, adopt production methods minimizing inputs, or produce such inputs on their own farms, thereby raising their costs.

These two propositions receive empirical testing in chapter 8, where data on production and productivity are assembled for a variety of Marxist and non-Marxist regimes. Some problems arise in making tests because in some non-Marxist nations, plantations are not managed by their owners but by hired managers so that principal-agent problems similar to those encountered in the state farms also arise.[8] The data on agricultural production cover all types of agriculture and, in the non-Marxist nations under examination, the production attributed to plantations run by hired managers does not predominate in total production. The proposition about total factor productivity differences receives strong empirical support; the proposition about fluctuations receives weaker support and counteracting influences appear at work.

Other differences between the farming environment in Marxist and non-Marxist regimes deserve mention, because they bear on the discussion in the text, even though they lead to no hypotheses that are easily testable. For instance, capitalist owner-managers bear all the risk if receipts are less than costs; in a state farm the managers bear none of this risk since the government makes up any difference between receipts and sales through various kinds of subsidies. Among other things, owners of capitalist plantations of an export crop find it in their interest to encourage the government to avoid an overvalued exchange rate (or to lobby for higher domestic producer prices for farm products), since any significant overvaluation lowers export receipts, raises the cost of imported farm inputs such as fertilizer, and brings them closer to bankruptcy. A state farm manager, of course, has no such incentives.

The rural labor market in most centrally planned economies is also more imperfect than in capitalist economies, because wages are relatively standardized and labor mobility is less since it is very difficult to fire a worker. Thus the state farm managers have less range of choice in adjusting levels of output by changing the variable factors; as a result, the cost curve is steeper in that portion of the curve significant for decision-making.

Relevance of the Analysis for Other Types of Farms

In a formal sense a collective farm is a cooperative so that the managers should be trying to maximize the per capita utility of the farm members. This type of maximand leads to quite different behavior from either total profits or gross output; a huge literature explores the matter.[9] Most of

---

[8] Some analysts of managerial capitalism such as Marris (1964) have suggested that capitalist managers have an incentive to expand production even more than an owner-manager, since the manager's bonus is based in part on gross sales, rather than profits, subject to the constraint of a minimum profit. Although this analysis of managerial firms in capitalism is simplistic because it omits consideration of risk, it seems safe to say that such a managerial firm would produce as much, if not more, than an owner-managed firm; the analysis assumes, however, the absence of a ratchet.

[9] Major articles include Bonin (1977), Bradley (1971, 1973), Domar (1966), and Oi and

this literature is quite irrelevant to the actual behavior of collective farms, not just because of the constraints placed on such maximizing behavior, but because in many Marxist regimes the managers alone make the major decisions, and their interests are quite different than those of the collective as a whole.

In essential respects collective farm managers have a formal compensation schedule quite similar to that of state farm managers. For instance, as Nove (1988a) has pointed out, these managers often force members to carry out various tasks that bring these workers very little net return (since the utility of their return may not be much greater than the disutility of the effort). However, such efforts may bring total farm production closer to the plan goal so that the managers will receive their bonus.

The collective and state farm manager's tasks, however, are different in several important ways. Most important, the labor supply is less certain, especially if the members have achieved their minimum hours necessary to retain their private plots. Nevertheless, in a number of East European nations collective farmers receive a minimum wage income and have as little control over their time as state farm workers; the major difference is in the bonuses paid to the workers at the end of the year.

In most East European countries collective farm managers must also meet forced delivery quotas and, moreover, face a more complicated price schedule since many governments pay one price for the quota deliveries and a higher price for above-plan deliveries. Such prices are not necessarily equal to the prices received by the state farms and, for the forced deliveries, are usually lower.

Nevertheless, collective farm managers have the same incentives as state farm managers to hide surplus capacity so that their total factor productivity will be lower than that of private farmers in a market economy. Because of the forced deliveries, however, managers will be less able to hide surplus capacity in years with bad weather (or lack of inputs) so that it is quite unclear whether fluctuations of reported production will be more or less than in market economies.

In the Marxist regimes that are not centrally planned, that is, most of the Third World Marxist regimes, it is difficult to generalize about the behavior of farm managers. In many of these nations agricultural exports are relatively more important (table 1.4) and, moreover, the trade sector is relatively larger in relation to the GDP. As a result, market elements play a much more important role in managerial decision-making. The governments intervene in the operations of the state farms (less so in the

Clayton (1969). An interesting book with models with quite different objective functions is by Fekete, Heady, and Holden (1976). Pryor (1983) surveys this literature and raises questions about its empirical relevance.

collective farms) to affect performance in different ways, but such intervention is often not systematic. It seems likely that performance would be worse than in comparable market economies, at least with regard to total factor productivity and production fluctuations, but complete certainty is not possible. As a result, we must approach the comparisons of relative performance in chapter 8 in a more inductive fashion.

Another analytic problem occurs when state farm managers receive a bonus tied to the profit of the farm, rather than gross output, a situation similar to that of many plantations operated by managers in capitalist nations. In such cases the state farm might function very similarly to the plantation and the hypotheses discussed above would not hold. As far as I could determine, however, in no country in the sample were state farm managers compensated in this fashion.

THE TERMS OF TRADE BETWEEN AGRICULTURE AND OTHER SECTORS

THE PURPOSE of this exercise is to explore how the government in a closed economy can finance an industrialization program by changing the terms of trade between agriculture and other sectors.

Let us imagine an economy with two goods: food and industrial goods, which are represented respectively on the vertical and horizontal axes of diagram RE.1a and the following diagrams. The industrial workers get paid in industrial goods and the original income of the farmers comes in food. The two groups then trade food and industrial goods. The curves in the diagram do not show how much total food is produced and retained by the farmer, nor do they show how many industrial goods are produced and retained by the worker. For simplicity, however, let us assume that OA industrial goods are produced, no matter what the industrial workers are paid, and that the workers receive OB in wages, so that AB is invested.

If OI' of industrial goods are traded by the workers for OF' of food, the relative price of the two products is represented by the slope of a line from the origin to the point represented by exchange. Curve OF represents the amount of foodstuffs farmers are willing to exchange at various prices. In economists' jargon this is called a "reciprocal demand curve" or an "offer curve," and it is a standard analytic tool in the study of international trade. It can be easily shown that utility (real income) increases for the group in question as one moves up the curve (that is, as the price becomes more favorable for foodstuffs). The curve has the particular curvature shown in the diagram because with each additional unit of industrial goods which is offered to them, they are willing to part with fewer units of foodstuffs. Curve OW is the same offer curve for the workers; it has the opposite curvature because the workers are paid in industrial goods and, with increasing amounts of food offered to them, are willing to exchange ever fewer units of industrial goods.

Point X represents a free-trade equilibrium, that is, where the amount of food offered by the farmers for a certain amount of industrial goods is exactly equal to the amount of industrial goods offered by workers for a certain amount of food; that is, the economy is in supply/demand bal-

RE.1. The Terms of Trade between Agriculture and Other Sectors

RE.1a. A Market Equilibrium

RE.1b. Governmental Coercion in Agricultural Production

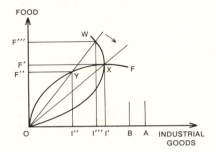

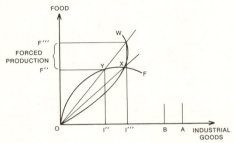

RE.1c. Governmental Tax on Wages

RE.1d. Government Imposition of a Dual Price System

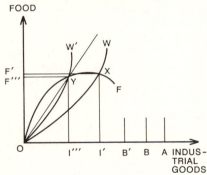

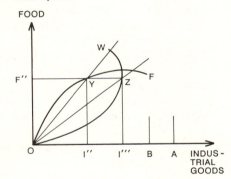

ance. If, instead, the price-line were OY (the relative price of food is lower since much more food is required to obtain the same amount of industrial goods), farmers would want to exchange F″ of food for I″ of industrial goods, while industrial workers would want to trade OI‴ of industrial goods for OF‴ of food. The quantity of food demanded is greater than that supplied; and quantity of industrial goods supplied would be greater than the quantity demanded. The relative price of food would, therefore, rise while the relative price of industrial goods would fall so that the price line would be driven back to OX.

Suppose that a government wishes to obtain more investment funds by lowering the relative price of food and "squeezing the peasants" so that the price line is shifted from OX to OY. In order to achieve a balance in supply and demand, and yet obtain more industrial goods for investment in this closed economy, the government can follow one or more of the following three policy alternatives.

1. The government steps in between the farmers and industrial workers and conducts all trade at price OY. It forces the farmers to produce F''' (diagram RE.1b), while only receiving OI'' of industrial goods (that is, the farmers are coerced into an exchange they would not voluntarily accept). The workers give the government I''' of industrial goods and receive F''' of food, so they remain on their offer curve, but at a higher level of utility. This also means that the government has made a profit of the difference between I'' and I''' in this trading arrangement, which it uses for investment purposes. Such a system, it must be emphasized, can only be maintained by extraeconomic coercion. If the government does not have means for exercising sufficient force in the rural areas to coerce the farmers into such extra production, supply and demand will no longer be in balance and the price will tend toward OX.

2. The government can pay the industrial workers less in a direct fashion or pay them the same monetary wages but impose an income tax. In either case, the net wages fall from OB to OB' (diagram RE.1c). With a lower income, the OW curve shifts toward the OF axis to OW'. In this case there is a supply/demand balance, albeit with less trade between urban and rural areas and lower total utility of both farmers and industrial workers (the former are at a lower point on their offer curve; the latter have received lower net wages). Nevertheless, the government ends up with additional resources B-B' for investment.

3. The government can institute a trading monopoly with a dual price system (diagram RE.1d). It sets the price of OY for the farmers, who offer OF'' of food and get OI'' of industrial goods. It sets the price of OZ for the workers, who offer I''' of industrial goods and get OF'' of food. The government retains the difference between I'' and I''' for additional investment. Such a trading monopoly can be literally in this form or, more usually, in the form of a sales tax on food and industrial goods so that producers receive a different amount than consumers pay for their products. Again, both workers and farmers have a lower utility because they are trading at lower points on their offer curves.

The notion that the farmers can bear all the costs of investment for industrialization works only if the government employs coercion. In the other two schemes, where such coercion is not applied, both groups bear some of the costs of this investment program.

Research Note F

FOUR SHORT CASE STUDIES OF AGRICULTURAL REFORM

AGRICULTURAL REFORMS consist of a series of interrelated measures and it is their totality, rather than individual steps, that is most crucial. The purpose of these four short case studies of Hungary, China, the Soviet Union and Guyana is to give concrete evidence of this rather banal assertion so as to understand better the interrelations and interactions among the different types of changes, and the quite different outcomes that can result.

HUNGARIAN REFORMS

The Hungarian reforms constituted a series of small steps over a period of twenty-five years. Before 1956 the agricultural sector was partially collectivized, but the marketing of most agricultural products was entirely in state hands. Following the 1956 revolution Hungary undertook a series of measures that cumulatively led the agricultural sector toward both full collectivization (1958–60) and a partial marketization in the years that followed, that is, toward a type of limping market socialism.

After collectivization, private production by collective farmers and the few remaining private producers nevertheless accounted for a significant share of agricultural production in the decades that followed. Decollectivization, either in a formal sense or in terms of an increasing share of private production did not appear on the political agenda, at least until 1990.[1] The same year also saw the introduction of measures that should significantly accelerate marketization.

[1] Some have argued that this was due to Soviet influences on Hungarian policy, so that a policy reversal in the 1990s should be expected. Public opinion data, however, did not support a forced decollectivization, as shown in separate public opinion polls in the summer of 1989 (Hankin 1990; the numbers are shown in parentheses) and May 1990 (Szelenyi 1990; the numbers are shown in brackets). In both polls the sample was one thousand people who were asked what should be done with the agricultural sector. The results are as follows: give land back to original owner (18%) [24%]; sell land to highest bidder (7%) [5%]; keep property in the agricultural cooperatives (28%) [23%]; keep as property of the cooperative, but allow the possibility of leasing or buying (33%); transfer land to the local community (10%); don't know (4%); members of cooperatives should decide what to do [41%]; some other solution [8%].

Property Right Changes

Until 1990 reforms of agriculture featured no significant changes in ownership: the system of state and collective farms remained intact, although very small private farms were permitted. After the parliamentary elections in 1990 the Democratic Forum formed a government with several smaller parties, including the Smallholders. The latter insisted that land be returned to the owners of 1947, a policy that would leave about 50 percent of the agricultural workers landless (Szelenyi 1991). This solution raised many fears, even among members of the Democratic Forum, and in late November 1990 a compromise appeared to be reached that resembled the manner in which Czar Alexander II freed the serfs. In essence, the 1947 owners would receive government bonds for their lands which would be paid off by special taxes on those who were actually farming the land. In early 1991, however, it was still unclear whether this compromise would be generally accepted and implemented.

Decision-Making Autonomy

In 1956 the short-lived Nagy government eliminated the mandatory deliveries of crops by farms and the Kádár government continued the policy. This did not eliminate government meddling in farm decision-making since government plans still specified acreage quotas. Moreover, lower level governmental and party cadre were still judged on various indicators of farm output, so that they had good reasons to intervene directly into farm decision-making. Nevertheless, such changes provided the seed of a change that sprouted in the next decade.[2]

The agricultural sector became the experimental field of the 1968 economic reforms for the entire economy (Robinson 1973), a reform marked by a consistent underlying theme and introduced in one piece from one day to the next. In 1965 the farms were relieved of many state orders and, except for bread grain (an exception eliminated in 1969), could decide what to grow, how much land to devote to particular crops, and which animals to raise. Further, they were not responsible for fulfilling

In the March 1990 elections, the Smallholders Party, which urged returning the land to the original owners as of 1947, received roughly 12 percent of the vote, about the same as the former communist party. Such a vote amounted to roughly one-third of the rural vote and reflected the obvious fact that most of the peasants joining the collectives brought relatively little land with them. In local elections later in the same year, the Smallholders Party also received relatively few votes. As noted in the text, if ownership relations returned to the 1947 pattern, the major winners would be the urban population and half of the current land workers would be landless.

[2] The amount of farm autonomy during the early 1960s should not be exaggerated. According to Vasary (1987, p. 81), forty to fifty state agencies could intervene in farm decisions.

any mandatory quotas issued by county and district government and party officials. After 1985, workers on the state farm selected their managers and, according to some, the government interfered less in the election of collective farm managers as well. Nevertheless, even in 1990, the Hungarian economic literature featured complaints that the farm cooperatives were not free of governmental interference, and that they needed "complete autonomy" (Csáki and Varga 1991).

Until the late 1980s other restrictions existed so that the size distribution of farms was skewed (Kornai 1989). More specifically, state and cooperative farms were generally quite large, while private farms had acreage restrictions so that they were quite small—the middle-sized farm was lacking.

Farm Prices, Taxes, and Subsidies

The collectivization drive in 1958–60 was accompanied by the establishment of a land rent system and higher agricultural prices. Several parts of a fully functioning market were not, however, in place. An important price reform occurred in 1968, where a system was established with 60 percent of farm output sold to state agencies at fixed prices, another 30 percent at prices fluctuating between upper and lower limits, and only 10 percent at fully floating prices (Csikós-Nagy 1969). Over the next two decades, these percentages changed, but by the 1980s, they were not greatly different from those of 1968 (Csikós-Nagy 1969; Richet 1985, p. 240). The fixed prices were tied to a system of long term contracts between producers and processors for certain key crops and animal products, which reduced farm risks at the price of flexibility.

Although the thrust of the 1980 price reforms was to bring industrial prices closer to world market levels, the government rejected such a concept for the agricultural sector and merely announced its intention to bring average producer prices closer to average costs so that subsidies could be reduced. In the following years, even this goal proved elusive and, moreover, producer and consumer agricultural prices also did not seem to come closer together (Antal 1983, 1985).

Some evidence exists that relative procurement prices in agriculture were moving toward the relevant relative opportunity costs (Marrese 1983). It should also be emphasized that the agricultural sector was far from operating on the principles of a genuine market socialism. Although many price distortions were eliminated, many still existed both on the input and output side (Kornai 1989). In the mid-1980s, the overall level of protection of Hungarian agriculture in comparison to world market prices was, according to a careful empirical investigation by Gyula Varga and his associates (1988), relatively small, especially in comparison to a number of West European nations. The same study showed that both the subsidies flowing into agriculture and the taxes flowing out were a relatively large percentage of total agricultural production (subsidy data are presented in Table 8.1), but that the two flows were roughly equal.

By the end of the decade, Hungarian economists were also decrying the fact that agricultural producer and consumer prices were still "disconnected" (Sipos and Halmai 1988). In 1989 in the light of a deteriorating economic condition, the government made a major attempt to raise agricultural producer prices in order to reduce subsidies and bring consumer and producer prices closer together so that in three years subsidies would be less than 40 percent of their previous level; these new subsidy levels were still considerable. Clearly the Marxist government was either unwilling or unable to depoliticize consumer prices of food in order to create a functioning market system. The price reforms in the next year were a giant step forward.

In the quarter-century following the original reforms, products on the farm input side became somewhat less monopolized because some competition was introduced through upstream vertical integration and TOPS farms selling inputs (chapter 4). According to one Hungarian evaluation, the markets for inputs were, however, still "rudimentary" (Sipos and Halmai 1988).

One of the consequences of the low producer prices and the soft budget constraint in Hungary was that only a small group of farms was able to earn significant profits, farm debts soared, and, as the government was unwilling to let too many farms go bankrupt, debts had to be canceled.[3] This price problem of the 1980s had two important systemic consequences as well: Any kind of decollectivization was impossible because the farmers would find it difficult to survive. Furthermore, by keeping consumer prices below equilibrium levels, assortment problems caused by inappropriate prices would be minimized because shortages in one type of food would be made up by other low-priced foodstuffs, which would serve as imperfect substitutes.

Markets

After 1968 farms could sell most products directly to the consumer, either at home or abroad; and, moreover, they could purchase inputs from any source they chose. While the collective and state farms focused on grains and fodder, the private sector grew more labor-intensive crops. The government also encouraged the farms to set up food-processing enterprises and permitted them to set up nonagricultural enterprises as well, which acted to prevent urban migration. Although private farmers

[3] According to Csizmadia (1983), in the early 1980s only 29 percent of collective farms had funds to invest and 56 percent were running losses. A few years later Csizmadia (1985) noted that 40 percent of collective farms required subsidies to survive.

could obtain some credit, land markets remained stunted because of restrictions on land leased or owned by private farmers.

Several important steps toward marketization occurred in the late 1980s when the government allowed the farms more freedom in dealing directly with foreign buyers of their products and sellers of farm inputs. After the decision to hold free elections, the caretaker government took an even more important step in January 1990 by adopting some sweeping changes that allowed consumer foodstuff prices for all but a few key foodstuffs to float. On the producer side most prices also floated, although guaranteed minimum prices for a few major products, for instance, maize, beef cattle and pigs, were also set.

Entrepreneurship

According to a fascinating sociological study by Szelenyi (1988), a group of entrepreneurs in agriculture began responding to the existing economic incentives, starting at first from various types of sharecropping or putting-out arrangements with the collective farms, or from small-scale second-economy farm sales, and then branching into elaborate investments of specialized buildings or equipment. In many cases they continued to hold jobs in the urban sector as well, which cushioned their income risks, but focused more of their efforts on farm production and less on their other work. In both 1970 and 1987, the share of agricultural production by all private producers was about 37 percent (Hungary, CSO annual 1987, p. 34); nevertheless, the share of private sector agriculture by those farmers devoting a significant share of their time to such activities increased considerably during the 1970s and 1980s (Kornai 1989, p. 51), which indicates the rise of a group of rural entrepreneurs.

After January 1990 rural entrepreneurs had a freer hand and by the beginning of 1991, it appeared they will be increasingly less constrained by acreage limitations. In order to reduce the risks facing would-be private farmers, the rural service cooperative Hangya ("ant"), which was active during the interwar period, was revived. In 1990, this organization planned to set up a network of outlets for agricultural supplies in the next few years and, in addition, wanted to serve as a middleman in marketing the products of its members.

Summary

Most industrial countries, no matter how marketized their industrial sector may be, feature considerable subsidies, planting restrictions, and other government interventions in the agricultural sector. Hungary was no exception, except that the magnitude of these direct and indirect governmental measures were considerable, although very much less than in

most other East European nations. Certainly decision-making autonomy
of farm managers was greater than under the centralized Stalinist agricultural system, since farm managers received no plan to follow. As a
result, the farms could specialize in those crops most suitable (given the
distorted price structure) for local conditions. Farm managers also had no
reason to hide capacity and total factor productivity during the 1970s and
1980s rose at a respectable rate (chapter 8). Local shortages of particular
foodstuffs were by no means eliminated and the assortment produced was
not the same that consumers would have purchased at market clearing
prices, but the system functioned and performed better than most other
East European nations.

CHINESE REFORMS

For a few years after the death of Mao in 1976, governmental agricultural
policies were contradictory, which was a reflection of the struggle for
power between Deng Xiaoping and Hua Guofeng. The radical marketization and decollectivization reforms in agriculture as well as the impressive reforms of the foreign trade system began only after Deng's political successes at the Third plenum of the Eleventh Central Committee
meeting in December 1978.

A few months after this crucial, but incomplete, victory, the Chinese
government promulgated the first few measures of the "responsibility
system linking remuneration to production" in agriculture. The reforms
moved rapidly ahead in the next few years, leading to the dismantling of
the communes, a return to household agriculture (although the peasants
did not receive formal ownership of the land), an elimination of the system of required sales to monopolistic state purchasing agents, and marketization of large subsectors of agriculture. The degree to which the reforms followed a single conception is unclear; but some have argued that
the agricultural reforms were inspired by the approach underlying
Deng's "60 Articles" of 1962.[4] The results of these reforms were spectacular: from 1978 through 1986 in China, per capita gross agricultural production increased at an average annual rate of 4.8 percent and per capita
rural incomes doubled.[5]

[4] Lin (1989, p. 100), Nee (1989, p. 179), Perkins (1988), and Shirk (1989, p. 352) claim
that the reform conception was "open-ended," and that there were no blueprints or coherent theoretical formulations when they began in 1979.

[5] These reforms were accompanied by relatively low investment in agriculture, so the
gains cannot be attributed to growth of capital inputs. More specifically, the share of total
state investment placed in agriculture during the 1981–85 period was 6 percent of total
investment, in contrast to 12 percent in the previous 29 years (Ash 1988; other data are
presented by Stone 1988). Investment at the local level appeared to fall as well. The sources
of growth were different: both official and Western reports suggest that following the re-

Property Right Changes

The first agricultural reform steps began with the introduction in 1979 of a system whereby the team leased particular pieces of land to subgroups and promised to supply machinery, fertilizer, and other inputs in return for a certain amount of production as a lease payment (*bao chan dao zu*). Essentially this was a compensation contract (payment-by-results, with the contract group supplying only the labor) and followed a system first introduced in the previous two years in the province of Anhui.[6] A number of other types of contract systems were also introduced in 1979–82 so that the government gained considerable experience on the advantages and disadvantages of different arrangements (Hartford 1985; Zweig 1987). The main line of evolution was the introduction in 1980 of contracts between the team and the individual household (*bao chan dao hu*), following the lines of the previous contracts between brigade and the team. In the next year a still more radical form of this contract (the "lease everything contract") gained in importance, whereby the team leased land, animals, and equipment to households, who agreed to certain (low) production quotas and tax obligations (*ban gan dao hu*). By 1983, about 95 percent of all agricultural contracts were of this latter form, and the two previous types of contracts were no longer in use (Ash 1988). The commune as an economic unit was dissolved.

With the introduction of the household contracts and the demise of the commune, it was necessary for the team to divide land among the various groups and households. Acting on directives from above, they carried out this task in a relatively egalitarian fashion: in about 70 percent of cases, they distributed the land according to household size; in 8 percent, according to number of workers per household; in 21 percent according to some combination of the above; and in less than 0.5 percent according to other criteria (Kojima 1988). The land was also highly splintered: on the average each household received 9.7 parcels (Nolan 1988, p. 87), so that each

---

forms resources began to be used more efficiently and, moreover, the rural population began to work much harder.

Nevertheless, the Chinese agricultural successes have not occurred on all dimensions; for example, the new system has given rise to more environmental degradation (e.g., deforestation), higher population growth, and some deterioration of the water control system (Bernstein 1984; Lampton 1987b).

[6] Experiments with group and household contracts began in Anhui, one of the poorest provinces, as early as 1959 with "field responsibility system," an innovation introduced at the height of the nationwide campaign to introduce communes. Because of the hilly topography, extension of irrigation and other water control measures were not very practical; thus the necessity of amassing large amounts for labor for such projects—a major economic advantage for the introduction of the commune—was not present. Although details about such innovations are not available, it is possible that they represented a response to the failures of the communes introduced during the Great Leap Forward in this area.

would receive (to use a Vietnamese slogan) some "near land, far land, good land, bad land." Forests, pastures, and fishing grounds were either broken up when possible or leased to specialized farmers. In succeeding years, a certain reconsolidation of household farms proceeded, either by trading of leases or by subleasing certain plots and renting others. Although the land still belonged to the government in a narrow legal sense, these leases had many of the features of private ownership. In 1984 the contracts were extended to a term of fifteen years, as long as the contract obligations were fulfilled; a few years later, the contract period was supposed to be lengthened to fifty years.[7] Some limitations on the amount of land that could be farmed by a single family seemed to remain in place.

The teams also divided the farm animals and equipment. Since such capital was often not enough to go around, the teams introduced various arrangements including public ownership (by different units of local government) with use-rights by individual farmers, public ownership with leasing to special groups who, in turn, contracted such services to the farmers, cooperative ownership and use, or private ownership through purchase from the team, often on the installment plan.

Decision-Making Autonomy

In 1979 the Chinese government also began to take a series of measures to increase the decision-making autonomy of both the communes and subordinate units (Ash 1988). Most important, grain purchase quotas were reduced and any grain left over after the fulfillment of the state purchase quotas for various crops could be sold on the free market. For other crops the degree of detail in the sales and production plans, as well as the level of procurement quotas, were reduced. In 1985 the government substituted a contract system for compulsory grain quotas. This meant that the farms would sign sales agreements with the government, which would promise to buy a specified amount of product; the first 30 percent would be bought at a list price, the remaining 70 percent at a higher price. Grain not covered by contract could be sold either at the free market price or, if this fell below the list price, would be purchased by the state at list price.

Farm Prices, Taxes, and Subsidies

Price changes at all levels played an integral role in the Chinese agricultural reforms (Field 1988; Sicular 1988a). In 1978 the government began

---

[7] Kojima (1988) discusses ownership changes in greater detail; Palmer (1988) analyzes the new inheritance law. In her work in rural China in the late 1980s West (1990) noted that fifteen-year contracts still seemed to be the norm. Rents were stable for periods of at least three years.

raising prices paid to the farmers, originally to allow the communes sufficient profits to invest in further mechanization, later as a spur for private
production. Between 1978 and 1986 average state procurement prices
paid to the farm sector increased at an average annual rate of 7.4 percent,
with individual prices for vegetable oils, grains, hogs, and other crops rising from 50 to 150 percent. In 1979 the government also began to raise the
retail prices of farm inputs (an average of 2.8 percent a year, according to
Kueh 1988a). In 1985 it undertook an important increase in prices of retail
food sold to urban consumers (Lin 1989) in order to reduce the ballooning
state subsidies to food consumption. Nevertheless, China had no economy-wide price reform either before or during the reforms in the 1980s.

As the reform movement gathered momentum, the price system
changed in two ways. First, a dual price system emerged, where an enterprise would sell a certain quota of goods to the government for a specified price and then sell above-quota goods for whatever price it could
obtain. Second, although rural market prices became increasingly governed by supply and demand forces, the price structure was still highly
distorted. For instance, grain prices were too low (Wiens 1987), and one
heard reports that a certain amount of group farming was reestablished
by local governments that were unable to collect this grain from household farmers and had to meet grain quotas imposed by various levels of
government. In 1988 the government reimposed price controls or unified
procurement prices over a variety of consumer, producer, and agricultural products such as tobacco and silk cocoons.

Land and other types of direct taxes were still very low (according to
Wiens 1987, about 3 percent of gross income). Until agricultural prices on
all products were allowed to reach an equilibrium level, payment of a land
rent reflecting the true scarcity of land would impoverish the farmers.

The initial reforms in the late 1970s had seen a rise in agricultural subsidies, as producer prices to farmers rose faster than consumer foodstuff
prices. Such subsidies rose considerably over the 1980s, creating a serious fiscal problem for the government. Consumers were further subsidized by an overvalued exchange rate so that by the end of the decade
the ratio of free market to border prices at a shadow exchange rate was
less than unity (Lin et al. 1991). By 1990 the government faced a dilemma: it believed that a rise in urban foodstuff prices was politically
unwise, and that it needed to increase grain production and to reduce
overall agricultural subsidies (which mainly went to food-processing industries).

Markets

Following the transformation of the households into full-fledged production units and the crucial systemic transformation of the system of farm

sales, farmers were encouraged to "swim in the billowing ocean of the commodity economy." Although the grain market was not free, production quotas for certain other products such as vegetables or pork were abolished and replaced by free exchange in the market. By no means was a full-scale market in operation throughout the rural sector, especially because monopsonistic procurement agencies still functioned and, in addition, markets were splintered. For instance, in the mid-1980s four different price systems for farm produce—quota prices, above-quota prices, negotiated prices, free market prices—operated in the rural sector.

With the introduction of the contract system in 1985, the government also abandoned the monopsonistic procurement system for agricultural products. Thereafter, the agricultural production plan was supposed to have only a guidance or reference function, although the government continued to impose some "sales obligations" or mandatory contracts on grain (Sicular 1988b; Wiens 1987). In late 1988, however, it formally reintroduced grain quotas since the low grain prices did not provide farmers sufficient incentive to grow the amount desired by the government. In early 1991 it was too early to tell whether such a policy reversal was merely a temporary backsliding before adjusting grain prices or whether this measure represented a reassessment of the previous changes and a recentralization.

In 1983 and 1984 the government opened up rural commerce and transportation services to private households and individuals. Although the government had monopolies in certain farm inputs (Prybala 1990), markets for some farm inputs (pesticides, plastic) began to appear for products manufactured by new factories sprouting in the countryside. An interesting example is provided by Shirk (1989, p. 332), who notes that by the mid-1980s, eighty factories had begun to produce and sell small farm equipment suitable for the new family leaseholds. The state created new market towns and created special credit institutions for individual farmers, although up to the late 1980s they did not carry out well their function as a source of credit for agricultural activities (Wiens 1987). Trade in certain products such as diesel fuel, however, remained in the hands of the state and, moreover, in the late 1980s certain reversals occurred for other products. For instance, in 1988 the government reasserted its trading monopoly for agricultural products such as grain and cotton, and agricultural inputs such as chemical fertilizers, pesticides, and plastic sheeting. Whether it can enforce these new monopolies remains to be seen.

Markets in production factors were more limited than agricultural inputs. By the mid-1980s leaseholders were permitted to hire labor. Although there was a migratory work force of roughly twenty million, regulations and other institutional barriers did not allow it to be channeled to where it would be most effective (Lin et al. 1991). Land markets were also restricted: although in April 1988 the government amended the constitution to legalize the transfer of land-use rights and to permit subleasing, only in May 1990 did it promulgate policies to implement this provision (Lin et al. 1991). By the fall of 1990 the scope and terms of such transactions as well as the enforceability of contracts appeared uncertain.

Entrepreneurship

The government set up a system of "specialized households," which were rural households focusing at least 60 percent of their time in producing nonagricultural products or particular farm products of which at least 60 to 80 percent was marketed (Nee 1989). Such households were more easily able to receive credit and inputs and earned roughly three times the average rural income. Although estimates of the number of such rural entrepreneurs run from 2.3 to 14 percent of rural households, in a recent survey Nee (1989) believes the latter figure is closer to the mark. The composition of this group is unclear: In a Shaanxi survey 43 percent of such specialized households consisted of former agricultural cadre; in a Fujian sample, the share of cadre was very much lower (Nee 1989). Of greatest importance, an entrepreneurial class was emerging.

Although rural investment increased, most of this was for house construction and consumer durables. One survey of a south China county showed savings amounted to 19 percent of household income (before taxes), but only two-fifths of this was for productive purposes, mostly for equipment yielding relatively high returns (West 1990). The relative unimportance of long-term investment suggests that such farmers had little confidence that liberal government policies toward individual farming would continue.

Considerable changes in the Chinese income distribution occurred with the rise in importance of rural markets and entrepreneurship, as well as the general increase in rural incomes. The relative increase of rural to urban incomes meant that the overall income distribution in China became more equal. The income distribution within the rural sector, however, appeared to have become somewhat more unequal, for instance, average interprovince income differences rose (Kueh 1988). Since rural income increased so fast, many of the adverse impacts of such increased inequalities were modified.[8] The new system also required the local governments to maintain a welfare fund, financed by taxes, to aid

[8] Zweig (1987) presents some data on rural income distribution showing that the gini coefficient of inequality actually decreased between 1978 and 1983.

the poor in particular localities. In addition, in 1985 the government announced plans for direct subsidies to the poorest farming areas ("blood
transfusions"). The extent of such transfers is not known, but I have seen
no evidence that it was great, especially since the government also announced its preference for investment grants to make agriculture more
productive in these areas ("blood making") (Ash 1988).

Summary

It must be stressed that it was not the contract system per se that led to
the success of the Chinese reforms, but a combination of policies, combined with considerable decision-making powers by the households and
with an expansion of rural private enterprises in nonagricultural activities. Of crucial importance in the first half of the 1980s, the Chinese were
also able to carry out the agricultural reforms in a phased manner, which
allowed momentum for further reform to continue, which did not create
the chaos or large losses that might have accompanied a shock-therapy
type of reform, and which appeared to destroy the rural bureaucracy tied
to the old agricultural system. In the industrial sector, unfortunately,
they were not so fortunate. Nor were they so skillful in building upon the
agricultural reforms, especially with regard to price policy, which would
have allowed a satisfactory growth of grain production during the second
half of the 1980s. The reform agenda was far from completed by the end
of 1990.

SOVIET REFORMS

In May 1982 in the waning months of the Brezhnev era, the Soviets began a series of important economy-wide changes, but not reforms, in the
agricultural sector with the Food Program. At that time, Mikhail Gorbachev was the Politburo specialist on agriculture, but most experts do
not attribute a dominant role in this program to him. After his ascension
to power in March 1985, Gorbachev first tried to build on and extend
these policies, while simultaneously attempting in the next few years to
reorient the contract system specified in the Food Program toward small
groups and households. The Soviet and Chinese reform drives in agriculture thus seemed to have a similar beginning, but thereafter actual
changes in Soviet agricultural policies reflected a more bureaucratic process of reshuffling the types of supply organs and ministries than reforms
with important economic significance.

Although the Soviet leaders did not appear to have the desire for either
full decollectivization or marketization, they certainly wanted to increase
the scope of family farming and to restructure incentives so that the en-

tire system would be more responsive. Despite efforts by top political leaders to initiate such institutional changes, by the end of 1990 the basic organization of agriculture at the lower levels remained essentially the same; and, moreover, market forces in agriculture had not greatly increased in importance. This lack of basic reforms was reflected in the unimpressive production results. For instance, from 1980 through 1987 in the Soviet Union, per capita gross agricultural output increased at an average annual rate of only 1.2 percent and average rural incomes changed little; other more qualitative indicators yield a similar picture.[9]

Property Right and Structural Changes

The Soviet government undertook two types of structural changes. The first, part of the May 1982 Food Program, was the introduction of a collective-contract (*kollectivnyi podryad*) system to encourage greater personal incentives and responsibility in agriculture; on a limited scale, these contracts had also been used in the 1960s and 1970s. They were supposed to incorporate agreements between the unit of production and various subgroups to carry out specific tasks (e.g., a certain amount of production of a particular crop) with a certain amount of inputs. The contract (*podryad*) might be better translated as an "assignment," since its content was determined by the collective farm management and the work unit had little power to refuse it. The types of collective contract varied considerably according to circumstances, as shown by the various labels used to describe these contracts or the parties signing the agreement: some concerned large work units such as the contract brigade (*podryadnaya brigada*), while other less common contracts referred to much smaller work units such as the normless link (*beznaryadnoye zveno*), which included from five to ten workers. Through these contracts the basic compensation system consisted of a minimum wage plus a bonus based on output results.

The collective-contract system was highly touted and rapidly introduced. By January 1984 about one-fifth of all brigades and teams oper-

[9] Production data come from Field (1988), Kingkade (1987), and U.S. CIA/DIA (1989, p. 70). For the Soviet Union, the gross agricultural production index is net of feed, seed, and waste; the population data are extrapolated to 1987 using the rate from 1980 through 1985.

In the Soviet Union the share of gross fixed capital investment directed toward agriculture for the 1980–87 period was 18.7 percent (CIA/DIA 1989, p. 66). Although the share in the 1970s was considerably higher, this investment was considerable.

Data on consumption come from Kueh (1988) and U.S. CIA/DIA (1989). In the Soviet Union, per capita consumption for the entire nation increased about 2.6 percent between 1980 and 1987; there is no indication that the rate of increase of per capita consumption in the rural sector increased much faster. In the Soviet Union work effort appeared low at both the beginning and the end of the 1980s (Kramer 1989).

ated by it, by the end of 1985, almost half, and by the end of 1988 the entire agricultural sector was supposed to operate under the system. In many cases the system was introduced in a traditional Soviet campaign style (Van Atta 1989b). Although the state and collective farms experienced a considerable change in form, the expected successes were not achieved. The manner in which the contracts were structured and introduced brought an increase in production costs from higher wages and greater purchased inputs, but production growth was slow (Brooks 1990a).

After March 1986 household lease contracts (*arendnyi podryad*) were also permitted, although they were only endorsed at the March 1989 Plenum, which led to a law a year later permitting a type of private ownership of land. Under this contract the leaseholders received the residual after their produce had been sold and their expenses met. Until 1990, however, neither the autonomous links nor the household lease contracts were very frequent (Brooks 1990a; Gray 1987, p. 18). Indeed, in farm situations characterized by considerable interdependence of work units, decision-making autonomy of these subunits is difficult to achieve unless such units are allowed to buy and sell services to each other.

The lease contract system had strong support from Gorbachev and, in 1988, official recognition. In 1988 he also began to speak of extending the contract terms up to fifty years, so that contract groups could carry out particular investments and develop quasiownership rights. This idea was incorporated in a resolution of the March 1989 Central Committee plenum.

In 1990 the central government passed three important laws affecting property relations on the land: the Law on Leasing, the Law on Property, and the Law on Land. These laws set a framework for more radical reform and the introduction of quasiprivate property by permitting individuals to lease land on a long-term basis, both within and outside the framework of the collective sector. They permitted a restricted type of individual proprietership in which rights to use the land are inheritable, but the rights cannot be bought, sold, or mortgaged. Local governments can also grant such rights if the collective farms are unwilling to do so. One of these land laws also specified that the possesors of these use rights to the land must use the land "efficiently" or presumably the rights can be taken away. In the same year the Russian Republic passed a law that does permit the buying and selling of land, but only to the government.

The establishment of new property regulations was far from completed. In December 1990, Gorbachev declared himself opposed to private property of agricultural land. In the next month he announced that three to five million hectares of underutilized land would be turned over to individuals wanting to farm it and, moreover, that unprofitable state and collective farms would be dissolved. But the conditions under which private individuals would hold this land were unclear. At the beginning of 1991 it was also uncertain whether Gorbachev's proposed national referendum approving private land ownership would ever take place or that the provisions of these land laws would ever be implemented.

A seemingly important structural change occurred earlier in 1985 when a major reorganization of agriculture occurred earlier at the top of the administrative pyramid with the formation of a single ministry overseeing most aspects of the agro-industrial complex. This centralizing institution was unworkable and it was disbanded four years later. In the late 1980s, the Soviet Union began to experiment with new vertical or horizontal units in agriculture (Butterfield 1990).

Decision-Making Authority

Some types of contracts such as the normless link and the lease contract offered the possibility of considerable decision-making autonomy by the work unit signing the contract. More specifically, they specified the renting of land and machinery to a group in return for a given amount of production. Once the contract or assignment was signed, the work unit could then decide by itself how the contracted task would be carried out, rather than receiving orders from above.

The form of contract, however, must not be confused with its content. The changes were often cosmetic and many of the contract brigades appeared quite similar to the old brigades, except for the addition of an unimportant output bonus (Ellman 1988).[10] In many cases autonomy could be limited: one recent eyewitness reported that on the farms he visited, the farm still planned, budgeted, and supplied the lease contractors, dictated planting dates, issued machines and seeds, and mandated marketing plans (Kramer 1989). Moreover, although such leases were supposed to extend for one to three years, in many cases either party had the right to abrogate the contract on thirty days' notice, which meant that the contract unit operated in a situation of considerable uncertainty.[11] In addition, the work groups had very little choice about accepting or rejecting the task or norm assigned to them by the farm director, in contrast to Hungary and other countries, where the contract had a more voluntary cast. Indeed, the work group also seemed to have little choice

[10] The top-down approach also led to schematism. For instance, the head of a trade union council in Orenburg province noted: "One has only, it is being said, to bring people together in the corresponding brigades and links, to fix formally in a document their task, assign them land and machinery, sign a contract, and then things work out by themselves. Practice tells a different story" (Wädekin 1988, p. 68).

[11] Don Van Atta (1989a), citing E. Manucharova in *Izvestiia*, 1 October 1988, p. 2.

about the composition of its membership, although it was possible for a self-selected group or household to approach the farm management and propose to sign a contract.

Although the 1988 Law on Cooperatives abolished planned targets for collective farms, many Soviet commentators have noted (e.g., Aganbeg-yan 1989, p. 115; Shmelev and Popov 1989, p. 255) that the "adminis-trative tyranny" of the various local party and government authorities over the state and collective farms was not abolished. As a result, the alleged "independent decision-making," either within the collective farms or the leaseholds was often violated.

An interesting example of the problem is provided by Bekker (1989), a Soviet journalist discussing a situation arising in Novosibirsk. A lease-holder there contracted to rent a newly constructed greenhouse at rates established by the government, but within a short period: (1) the collec-tive farm did not turn over the greenhouse when it promised; (2) the collective farm director forced the leaseholder to sign a new lease so that his profits would be lower; (3) the regional governmental agronomists in-sisted that the leaseholder (an agricultural engineer) follow the "ap-proved" methods of planting, rather than his own judgments on the mat-ter; (4) the farm director delivered earth and not the sand that the leaseholder had contracted; and (5) finally the collective farm director dissolved the lease when he decided that the venture was too "capitalis-tic." The leaseholder did not seem to have any recourse to legal action; indeed, it may not have been prudent for him to sue those officials on whom he was dependent. As the Romanian introduction of household contracts (discussed in chapter 6) showed in a different context, admin-istrative regulations can easily destroy any attempt to give the farmers more decision-making authority or to provide incentives for higher pro-duction through a household contract system.

Farm Prices, Taxes, and Subsidies

The price changes can be quickly summarized: during the decade of the 1980s no major changes in the method of determining the fixed govern-mental prices occurred. In 1982 the government raised producer prices in order to avoid a further increase in farm debts, and in 1990 similar steps were prepared. Farm debts were partially written off twice during the decade; according to a law in 1990, they would be totally written off.

The major price reform promised for the economy as a whole for 1990 was repeatedly postponed; agricultural producer prices, however, began to be raised. The government also introduced some price flexibility by allowing negotiated prices in cases where the purchaser did not have a state order. It is also reducing the number of price zones (the areas where the state set prices were the same), which was the first step toward introducing a roughly uniform national price that might possibly equal marginal costs, if Soviet policy makers could ever agree that this was desirable (Brooks 1990c).

The tax system for agriculture was not significantly changed—the subsidy system was expanded. Foodstuff prices paid by consumers remained highly subsidized and in the latter part of the 1980s, these subsidies amounted to roughly 6 to 8.5 percent of the factor cost GDP.[12] Although these subsidies benefited high-income much more than low-income Soviet consumers (Aganbegyan 1989, p. 26), political considerations at that time dictated against a general increase in food prices and allowing such prices in general to reflect market forces. For special categories of foodstuffs such as fruits and vegetables, however, more price flexibility was allowed. In April 1991 a major increase in retail food prices was finally announced.

Markets

After the 1987 Law on Cooperatives, collective farms no longer had to follow a state plan, although they were subject to "state orders," which often amounted to the same thing. In 1989, they were also allotted dollars and other hard currencies for producing much more than their historic average for certain products, an administrative change that was undercut by subsequent regulations.[13] Other economic incentives provided by formal increases in decision-making autonomy were limited in other ways; for instance, in the early years of the contract system, informal income caps were sometimes imposed on the contracting unit to prevent their incomes from diverging too much from other workers on the farm (Laird and Laird 1988). Although the importance of these caps is not known, the degree to which income differentiation in the countryside should be allowed to proceed was a matter of considerable controversy. Some commentators such as Medvedev (1987, pp. 357–59) feared the

[12] Soviet sources claim that these subsidies amounted to 40 billion rubles in 1983 (Nove 1986, p. 115) and that they increased considerably in succeeding years so that in 1989 food subsidies were planned to be 87.9 billion rubles, while subsidies to the rest of the agroindustrial complex (primarily subsidies to farms suffering losses) were to amount to another 20.9 billion rubles (Markish 1989a, 1989b). The national account estimates on which the ratio of subsidies to GDP is based comes from CIA/DIA (1989).

[13] Goldman (1989) notes that soon after regulation, the government prevented the peasants from spending more than one-third of these earnings on consumer goods and, moreover, limited the selection of available goods. They also raised the prices of these imported goods and imposed a service fee, while refusing to pay interest on any dollar deposits held in Soviet banks. As a result, although the 1989 harvest was 16 million tons more than 1988, sales to the state fell by 26 million tons.

emergence of a "new *kulak* class," a situation quite different from China where government officials proclaimed that "it is glorious to become rich."

Marketization of agricultural products was slow in the 1980s. In 1989 the introduction of a policy of agricultural self-sufficiency at a regional or republic level, combined with transportation bottlenecks and financial stress, led to a decline in sales to the all-union grain fund without any replacement by wholesale trade. Thus any increases in marketization which occurred were primarily at a local level (Brooks 1990a).

Up to the end of the 1980s, inputs were still distributed by administrative methods. As Soviet commentators have noted (e.g., Aganbegyan 1989, p. 36; Shmelev and Popov 1989, p. 256), if the distribution plan said that a particular state farm was to have ten tractors, then it received those tractors whether it wanted them or not, often financing them with a bank loan that would probably never be paid back. Aganbegyan also points out (p. 37) that in state and collective farms that broke themselves up into leaseholding collectives, roughly half of the existing machinery was not requested and was simply surplus stock.

Entrepreneurship

The government undertook several important measures to try to increase the role of market forces. In the middle 1980s it attempted to encourage private plot production by allowing larger plots and by allowing this production to be counted in the farm's production index. In 1986 it also passed two contradictory laws, the first opening up the scope for private economic activity and the second limiting "unearned income," which Åslund (1989, p. 61) has designated as Gorbachev's compromise with Ligachev. Local officials, who had decades of experience in harassing private plot producers (Hedlund 1989, chap. 5), focused on the latter law, sending teams to chop down private orchards (Hedlund 1989, p. 112) and to smash private greenhouses, an action Shmelov and Popov (1989, p. 265) have called, a "pogrom of greenhouses." These privately grown vegetables and fruits constituted an important share of total consumption and, after sales on farmers markets declined (Åslund 1989, p. 159), this attack on the private sector ended a year later. These kinds of actions by local governments had unfortunate effects. In the short run, sales on farmers' markets declined in 1988; in the longer run, such actions certainly did not encourage an increase in private agricultural entrepreneurship.

Further evidence that the development found in Hungary of a developing group of rural entrepreneurs is unlikely in the Soviet Union in the early 1990s is found in the popular distrust toward the government and the feeling that investment in such private production would not have long-term rewards. For instance, survey workers asked the following question: "If you work more or better, will your work compensation increase?[14] In 1986 and 1988, only 40 percent and 34 percent of industrial and collective farmworkers answered affirmatively. Most felt that if they earned more money in the short run, their norms would be raised so that in the future they would be working harder and receiving the same amount as before. Clearly it was possible for the government to carry out such a leveling process for legal private sector activity by raising taxes, setting price limits, and other such measures. As noted, leaseholds were canceled when too much income was earned, and "cooperatives" (actually family enterprises) were dissolved because they are too "capitalistic."

Summary

The Soviet changes led neither to marketization nor to decollectivization. In large measure this was because of policy failures: the changes were not implemented in a manner that would create a momentum toward a systemic change. At this time of writing it is difficult to determine the degree to which this was due to an inconsistent conception on the part of Gorbachev of what the final goals should be, or to inconsistencies arising from political compromises he was forced to make in order to implement even part of his program.

GUYANESE REFORMS

The reforms in Guyana formally began in 1988 with an agreement between the government and the International Monetary Fund and the drafting in June of a Policy Framework Paper by a team composed of Guyanese authorities and World Bank and IMF specialists.[15] In the next year, consistent with these guidelines, the government announced a three-year "Economic Recovery Programme" (Commonwealth Advisory Group 1989), the implementation of which would be monitored by the IMF. On the macroeconomic level this program focused on policies to reduce the deficit of the governmental budget, achieve sufficient financial stability to lower the rate of inflation, take measures to attain greater equilibrium in the balance of payments stability, and normalize relations with foreign creditors so as to become eligible for new loans from the World Bank and other international organizations. On the microeco-

[14] Boikov (1989). I would like to thank John Litwack for this citation. His fascinating article (1990) analyzes this and similar surveys.
[15] Materials for this discussion were gathered from interviews in Guyana in late January and early February 1991.

nomic level the program outlined an ambitious privatization and marketization drive, especially in agriculture.

The targets for reducing the government budget deficit and the rate of
inflation and of increasing the rate of economic growth were far from being met in 1989. Preliminary data for 1990 suggested similarly disappointing results for 1990. Progress was made, however, with the refi-
nancing of the foreign debts, and massive devaluation of the currency in
1989 and 1990, combined with the legalization of a free market of foreign
currencies, were positive measures. The first steps toward privatization
in agriculture were also taken. Unfortunately, the Guyanese government
fell behind its schedule for transfering the various categories of exports
and imports from the official to the free market exchange rates, so that
until March 1991 both rice and sugar exporters were still receiving domestic currency from their foreign exchange receipts converted at the
official exchange rate and were allowed to keep only 10 percent of their
foreign exchange earnings.

Property Rights and Structural Changes

The most important change in the agricultural sector was the plan to sell
off the state farms. The agricultural producer cooperatives had been
mostly nominal and had disappeared by the end of the 1980s, reportedly
reverting to private farms.

The state farms were administered by the Guyana Sugar Corporation
(Guysuco) and consisted of the sugar estates that had been nationalized
in the mid 1970s. In contrast to most Third World Marxist regimes, this
nationalization had not been confiscatory and the government paid a relatively fair compensation to previous estate owners. Among other things,
this meant that in the 1990s the government would have no worries about
the claims of former owners.

The first step toward this privatization occurred in the fall of 1990
when the government signed a two year management contract with the
English firm Booker Tate, which would begin the rehabilitation of these
sugar estates. A part of this firm, Booker McConnell, had owned most of
the Guyanese estates before nationalization and at that time accounted
for about 80 percent of sugar exports, as well as a considerable share of
trade, manufacturing, and other production in this former British colony
(Shahabuddeen 1983). In 1990 the government still owed the company
about 5 million pounds that were incurred during the nationalization;
presumably, this would finance a large share of the purchase.

The management contract gave Booker Tate a chance to evaluate the
seriousness of the government in pursuing its reform program, in actually
implementing a liberal exchange rate and tax regime that would not pe-

nalize the estate sector, and in attracting capital from governments and international organizations. All of these steps would reduce the company's investment risk.

The government appeared to view this projected sale as an opportunity to obtain managerial expertise, as well as funds for rehabilitation of an industry that could serve as a useful source of tax revenues in the future. In a peculiar fashion, it also viewed this privatization as a means for agricultural interests to have a more effective voice in the political process than the previous state-owned company controlling the state farms.

Unlike Third World nations such as Nicaragua, the workers did not seem interested in gaining immediate ownership of the estates. The major agricultural labor union, dominated by the Marxist-Leninist People's Progressive Party, appeared to believe that in the long run privatization would be the only way wages of sugar workers could be raised. The policies followed by the government in the past decade had acted against the agricultural sector, especially by means of an overvalued exchange rate that eliminated profits of the estates. The estate workers had been impoverished and saw Booker Tate as a defender of their interests. In short, "dependencia theory" was turned inside out by the various socialist factions in Guyana.

Private farmers produced most of the nonsugar agricultural products and in early 1991 it appeared that this private share would increase, because Booker Tate planned to sell off most of the nonsugar production of Guysuco. For most products this diversification program of Guysuco was a costly failure and a diversion of its managerial efforts and capital from sugar growing.

Decision-Making Autonomy

The state farms were run as a single corporate entity and, as the government planned to sell Guysuco to a single buyer, rather than selling off each estate separately, no change in corporate structure was anticipated. Although Booker Tate began to tighten previous management systems, they did not foresee making any drastic changes in this direction either. As far as I could determine from an interview with a high functionary of the central office who had experienced the changeover from private to state ownership, Guysuco had not greatly changed the management system from the successful private companies except to take into account the declining funds available for investment and the loss of skilled personnel. Direct governmental intervention into decision-making of Guysuco was limited and in this respect the state farms had decision-making autonomy; but through a series of governmental regulations about the exchange rate, the percentage of foreign exchange that could be retained,

the wage norms, and other such matters, Guysuco's autonomy of decision-making was constrained. If the plans for liberalizing exports and the
other aspects of the economy were implemented, these constraints would
be loosened.

Farm Prices, Taxes, and Subsidies

Since the early 1980s Guyana has moved a long way toward a competitive
domestic trade in agricultural products. By mid-1990 domestic price controls existed only for sugar, rice, powdered milk, margarine, and salt; in
1991 this list was even shorter. The government did not subsidize agricultural production and taxes on the sector were low for two reasons: For
sugar, Guysuco seldom had enough profits to tax and for the nonsugar
products sold in local markets, taxes were difficult to collect. The overvalued exchange rate served, however, as an implicit tax on agricultural
exports. If plans to set the exchange rate for a certain period according to
a weighted average of the free market exchange rate for the previous
months were implemented, this type of implicit tax on exports would be
reduced, at least in so far as export levies would not keep the domestic
producer price at the same level. Up to the beginning of 1991, however,
the government was slow to implement this part of its reform program.
Indeed, it required conversion of export receipts from rice and sugar at
the official exchange rate, which was still overvalued, although not to the
same degree as in previous years.

Markets

At the end of the 1980s the domestic markets on most raw food products
were free. Furthermore, the government's role in food processing and
crop purchasing was also declining. Although in early 1991 the sugar estates and mills remained state-owned monopolies, in other crops the situation was changing rapidly. For rice, a high official of the Guyana Rice
Marketing Board told me that in 1988 about 70 percent of the milling
capacity was state owned, while at the beginning of 1991 this percentage
had fallen to 20 percent. Some of the government mills were sold off,
primarily to different foreign consortia, while some of the small private
mills were expanded so as to reach the production level where average
costs level off. This approach increased competition and, moreover, expanded greatly the scope of private exporting of rice. For other agricultural crops and for livestock, private exporters were dominant and were
assisted in their private foreign trade efforts by a state agency, the Guyana Marketing Corporation, which was reorganized for this purpose.

    With the legalization of a free market in foreign exchange so that anyone possessing foreign exchange could import, the government attempted to liberalize the market for agricultural inputs. In early 1991 there were two ministers of agriculture, one of whose portfolio was centered exclusively on facilitating agricultural inputs.

Entrepreneurship

Other than importing foreign entrepreneurs to run the sugar estates, the government took no particular measures to encourage agricultural entrepreneurship or investment in the agricultural sector. Although the faster increase of domestic prices of agricultural products than the general price level certainly appeared to make agriculture a more profitable pursuit, production costs in agriculture were also increasing because of a disintegration of the infrastructure for agricultural trade, for instance, roads, sea walls (much of the farm land is below sea level), storage and collection points, and so forth.

Summary

In comparison with the other countries, the agricultural reforms in Guyana were quite simple and focused primarily on sugar and rice. The progress of the micro and macroeconomic reforms, as noted in chapter 10, was placed in doubt by a racial/political factor. A slight majority of the population were descendents from indentured workers from the Indian subcontinent, while most of the remainder were descendents from slaves brought from Africa. Most of the workers on the sugar estates and rice farms, as well as most of the country's entrepreneurs, were Indo-Guyanese, while governmental power was held by means of fradulent elections by the People's National Congress, whose power base was among the urban Afro-Guyanese and the workers in the bauxite mines. Most of the economic reforms would directly benefit the Indo-Guyanese at the expense of the Afro-Guyanese, at least in the short run.

With an election scheduled for 1991, which would be monitored by outside observers including the Carter Center, the economic reforms were undercutting the political base of the party in power. History provides few examples of a political party alienating its power base shortly before an election—the government faced the dilemma of postponing the election, which had been constitutionally mandated to take place in 1990, or slowing the economic reforms.

LABOR SUPPLY AND COMPENSATION ON
COLLECTIVE FARMS: A MODEL

THE WAGE SYSTEMS of the state farms result in compensation problems little different from those in estate agriculture in capitalist nations, other than the fact that it has generally been more difficult for managers to fire or lay-off workers on the state farms. The compensation systems in the collective farms, by way of contrast, have many aspects of a share contract and raise some novel issues because workers share the residual income according to their accumulated points. What generalizations can be made about the supply of labor on collective farms? In the discussion I discuss two approaches: The first is the standard model followed by many in the literature. The second is a simple model to illuminate some fundamental problems, especially those arising from a competitive relationship with the private plots for labor, that the standard model does not cover.[1]

THE STANDARD MODEL

Israelson (1980), Putterman (1981) and Sen (1967) have sophisticated theoretical models of the work-point situation leading to the counterintuitive conclusion that collective farm members work more than they would on their own private property. The basic argument is simple: for an extra hour worked, private farmers earn only the marginal productivity of their labor and for an extra hour worked on the collective they receive an hourly wage equal to the average productivity of all farm members (that is, their share of the total product). Under conditions of diminishing returns, the average productivity is higher than their marginal productivity so that it pays them to work longer hours.

This model does not predict, of course, that the total work *effort* per

---

[1] The literature on labor supply in cooperatives is vast and analyzes some intricate situations. For instance, what the properties of a system are in which team members have interdependent utility functions (e.g., Putterman 1981) or where marginal productivity is less than average productivity, so that a gaming situation arises because one person gains by persuading his teammates to work less so that his own work points (based on average productivity) are worth more (a situation analyzed by Chinn, 1980). In this discussion, however, I try to focus on more basic issues. Empirical materials to illustrate the propositions of the model are usually of an anecdotal nature. One systematic study of such labor competition is Fforde's (1989) study of North Vietnamese collective farms.

hour, in contrast to total hours worked, would be higher. It also assumes that all other factors remain equal and, moreover, that the farmer has no other source of income than that received from the collective farm, that the administration of the work-point system is perfect, that work points are commensurate with effort, and that collective farm members are able to vary the number of hours that they work. Moreover, this model does not take into account the constraints placed on individual farmers to farm what they believe is more appropriate than what the farm manager tells them; or the risks to them because they cannot easily control the intensity of work by other farm members. The latter means that their work hours may pay considerably less than they could obtain by working on their personal plots (Nove 1988a, 1988b). These are strong assumptions and, although the model is rigorous, it may have little application to real-life situations where such assumptions are not met (as Putterman [1985] has readily admitted).

From this formal model Blecher (1988), who seems willing to believe whatever Chairman Mao has said (one of the "two whatevers" against which China struggled at a later date), jumps to the conclusion that the compensation system used in the communes really led to harder work on the part of the Chinese peasantry. As empirical support, he uses his interview data from former collective farmers now living in Hong Kong, claiming that peasants worked hard for the collective and that their "only" problems arose from the fact that they did not reap gains commensurate with their efforts. Of course, village studies made within China suggest that reality was quite different. For instance, Mosher (1983, pp. 36–45) has described the slothful work habits of those working on the collective where he lived in 1979. In Chen Village (Chan et al. 1984, p. 171), peasants would attempt to conserve their energy working on the collective fields so as to be able to be more productive in their individual activities.

An Alternative Model

The intensity with which members of a collective farm work, of course, depends a great deal on the management of the farm and the degree to which the managers can harness social pressure to encourage work effort; and it is difficult to generalize much more than this. The question of work hours, however, is also a problem since collective members may wish to spend most of their time on private, rather than collective, activities. This problem can be handled with the aid of a model by Elizabeth Clayton (1976) that I have borrowed and simplified.

Suppose that there is only one kind of consumption good ("income") and that farmworkers have a choice between working on the collective or working on their personal plots. The diagrams have as their vertical axes income, and as their horizontal axes the number of leisure hours, with point C representing twenty-four hours of leisure a day.

In diagram RG.1a and succeeding diagrams, curve GFXBC is the compensation curve showing the relation between income earned and hours worked. It is composed of three segments: (1) Line segment BC represents the wages received from the collective; the steeper the curve, the higher the wages per hour. MC designates the number of *minimum* hours that farmers are required to work for the collective in order to obtain the land for their personal plots.[2] (2) Curve DFXB represents the returns to labor from the farmers' personal plots; it is, in other words, their production-possibilities curve. (3) At a particular point, however, the return on the farmers' plot becomes so small (because of diminishing returns) that they will prefer to work additional hours for the collective. This is the GF segment, which is parallel to the BC segment and tangential to the DFXD curve.

In a number of Marxist regimes in Africa such as Mozambique, the farmers were not obligated to spend any minimum time working on the collective. In this case, the line segment BC no longer exists and the compensation curve appears as in diagram RG.1b. In these countries, average productivity (and wages) on the collective farm were relatively low because of management problems, so that the segment GF was very flat.

Curves I_1, I_2, and I_3 in diagram RG.1a represent indifference curves between income and leisure, with the subscripts measuring the units of utility. The farmers will choose to work at point X, that is, to work NM hours on their personal plot and MC hours for the collective, because this is the highest level of utility that they can achieve—a level of utility of 3 is infeasible. The indifference curves can be drawn so that point X lies on the line segment GF, in which case the farmers work on the collective land more hours than the minimum. In those countries without a required minimum of hours on the collective and where the GF segment is very flat, the workers will spend little time on the collective (except during the slack season when such work is not needed) and the collective farms will be short of workers at the crucial peak periods. In diagram RG.1b, where farmers are not required to work any minimum number of hours on the collective, PC hours will be worked on the personal plot, and NP hours, on the collective.

With the aid of this simple model, we can see the impact of several types of changes, taking into account the conflict between the income

---

[2] Contrary to Clayton, I have drawn this curve as a straight line, because the number of work hours of single farmers seems unlikely to affect the hourly rate that all will receive.

RG. 1. Labor Supply on Collective Farms

RG. 1a. The Basic Relationships

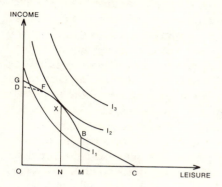

RG. 1b. Compensation Curve with No Minimum Work Requirement

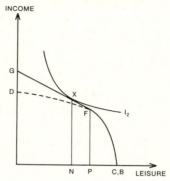

RG. 1c. Impact of a Higher Wage

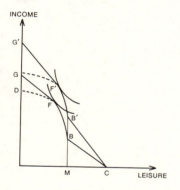

RG. 1d. Impact of Increasing Minimum Work Requirement

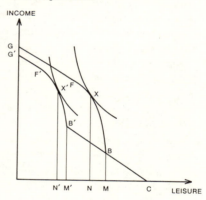

RG. 1e. Impact of Increasing Size of Personal Plot

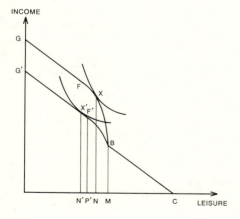

effect (if income per hour is higher, the farmers will choose to consume more leisure and will work less) and the substitution effect (if income per hour is higher, the farmers will choose to work more hours since an hour of leisure is worth now less in terms of consumption goods).

Suppose, for example, that the collective farm becomes more productive so that wages per hour rise; this can occur either because of an increase in nonlabor inputs, a rise in technology, or because the farm management is more effective in getting the other members of the collective farm to work harder. In diagram RG.1c, this is reflected by a steeper wage function, which affects the position of the other segments of the compensation curve as well (see diagram RG.1b), so that the segment of the new personal-plot production function is higher than the previous curve. If leisure is a normal good and if the optimal point X has previously been on the FB curve, then the collective farmers will work fewer hours on their personal plot (a pure income effect); if, however, the curves were drawn so that the optimal point X was on the GF segment, more information would be needed to determine whether the farmers would work more or fewer hours on the collective since the income and substitution effects work in opposite directions.

Since real income depends not only upon monetary compensation, but also upon risk, the diagram can also be used to examine this factor as well. The analysis is complicated, however, by the fact that the collective farm form both reduces and creates risks. On the one hand, if a given farmer's yields are much different than the neighbor's because of microclimatic differences, then the collective farm allows a type of risk sharing that can be achieved in a usual smallholder economy only by crop insurance or by farming plots in scattered places so as to minimize the impact of the microclimatic problems in a single area. On the other hand, the farm creates certain types of risk. The farm managers can break their word to the workers about compensation and, given the inadequate legal system and the lack of an independent judiciary in some of these countries, the workers have little recourse. Moreover, the worth of a labor point is not determined until the end of the year and depends not only upon normal uncertainties such as the weather, but also on uncertainties in the diligence of other members of the collective and the competence of the farm managers. By creating certain risks that did not exist before, the collective farm thereby lowers real income.

Clearly, the stronger the risk-creation effect is to the risk reduction effect, the lower the real wage from the collective (and the flatter the real wage segments). If the optimal point X lies between F and B, then the more time collective farmers would also spend on their personal plot. Again, if the optimal point X lies between G and F, we could not determine whether the farmers would work more or fewer hours on the collective plot unless information is supplied about the relative strength of the income and substitution effects.

The government has three tools with which to influence the amount of time spent on collective farm work. First, it can raise the hourly compensation (for instance, by increasing prices paid for agricultural goods from the collective), which is like the case previously discussed and shown in diagram RG.1c so that segments CB and GF approach each other and the farmers find it increasingly profitable to work extra hours on the collective farm (that is, on segment GF) rather than their own plot. Although it can be easily shown that the work on the collective would increase, we need additional information about the relative strength of the income and substitution effects to know whether or not this would raise total labor hours and production (collective plus personal-plot production). Second, the government can also increase the minimum time needed to work on the collective in order to obtain a personal plot (lengthen CM). As shown in diagram RG.1d, this pushes the FB segment of the compensation curve to the left; and both income and substitution effects occur. The way the curves are drawn, the income effect predominates, and the farmers work longer hours, albeit fewer on their personal plots (that is, N'C is greater than NC, although N'M' is less than NM). Third, the government can reduce the land available for personal plots, a situation shown in diagram RG.1e. This reduction makes the personal-plot production possibility curve smaller (FB is pivoted to F'B in the diagram) and the left side of the compensation curve is lowered. Again income and substitution effects come into consideration. The way the curves are drawn, the income effect predominates and the farmers not only work longer hours, but also work N'P' hours voluntarily on the collective (in addition to the required MC hours) because their personal plots are so small that their total yield is small, a state of affairs that is just what the government wanted.

Diagram RG.1e also shows why Marxist regimes have been loath to increase the size of personal plots, even though personal plots per hectare of land are much more productive than collective plots. Starting from curve G'X'F'BC, let us increase the size of the personal plots so that the compensation curve is GFXBC. If the income effect is stronger than the substitution effect, farmers would work fewer hours on the collective as well as fewer hours on their personal plots, so that total agricultural production would fall. If, on the other hand, the substitution effect is stronger than the income effect, total production would not fall. These are important to keep in mind when considering decollectivization proceeding by expanding the size of the personal plots, a topic discussed in chapter 10.

These exercises lead to several important conclusions. First, although collective and personal-plot production may compete for the scarce labor time of the collective farm member, we cannot say whether production of one will increase or decrease at the expense of total production until more information is available about the relative strength of the income and substitution effects, that is, the utility function of the farmers. Since these may differ from country to country, generalization over the entire range of Marxist regimes is impossible. Second, in any case where the hourly wage on the collective is less than the hourly return for work on a personal plot, the requirement of a certain minimum number of hours is resented. This coercive element is likely to have an adverse effect on work on the collective farm, especially regarding effort expended per work hour, which often cannot be easily monitored by farm authorities. Third, the exact mix of policies regarding agricultural prices (hourly returns to collective farm workers), the size of the personal plots, and the minimum number of hours of work on the collective depends on what the government is trying to maximize: total agricultural production, total collective production or total welfare of the farm population, and the minimal use of coercion. Changes in these goals are probably a major reason for the great variations in policies regarding the personal plot that are discussed above.

Statistical Note A

DATA SOURCES FOR TABLES IN CHAPTER 1

TABLE 1.1

The percentages represent the share of the economically active population working in enterprises owned either by some level of government or by collective farms. I have tried to exclude "precooperatives" and other preliminary forms of collectives in these totals. In cases of mixed ownership, the practices of the statistical agencies of each nation are followed, since sufficient data to adjust for complete comparability are not available. The percentages in the "non-specified" sector of the labor force are omitted from the individual sectors but are included in the totals.

Afghanistan. Central Statistical Office (1983, p. 61). The public sector is slightly overstated because in construction, the public sector is defined to include all those working on government projects, some of whom may be workers for private companies under contract.

Albania. The data come from Misya and Vejsiv (1979, p. 71) and apparently refer to families, rather than to the economically active. Unfortunately, these data do not add up to 100 percent; presumably the missing 2 percent are independent craftsmen and professionals.

Angola. Data on the economically active come from Bhagavan (1986, p. 52). Data on workers and employees in the public sector come from a confidential document of an international organization; the range reflects two sets of estimates.

Bénin. International Labour Office (1984a).

Bulgaria. Tsentralno statistichesko upravlenie (1968, pp. 269–74).

Cape Verde. Ministério do Plano e da Cooperaçao (1986, p. 38).

China. The workers employed in hamlet (subvillage) institutions are classified as private, which means that the data in the table for the socialist sector are somewhat understated. Further, it is possible that some of the labor classified as "state" at the township and village level should really be considered in the collective farm sector. The basic data come from State Statistical Bureau (1988, p. 93); they are supplemented by data from *China Agriculture Yearbook 1987* (pp. 247–48). Labor force in the rural sector in the "government" and the "finance" sectors are assigned to the state sector.

Congo. International Labour Office (1984b, p. 109) gives the total number of economically active in the state sector (including the army, state owned firms, and mixed enterprises) in 1982 as 106,000, or 79 percent of the modern sector. In 1974 the participation ratio was 54.4 percent, following the Congolese practice of counting the entire population over fifteen as part of the economically active (Congo, Centre national de la statistique 1978, p. 72), or 37.1 percent using a more restricted definition (p. 31). The latter procedure, however, appears to omit many women who spend some time in agriculture or other economic activities. Applying these two ratios to the 1982 population (Hung, 1987, p. 6), ratios of government employees to the economically active of 11.9 percent and 17.5 are derived. The number in the table is the mean of these two percentages.

Cuba. Comité Estatal de Estadísticas (annual, 1984, pp. 263–64, 281–82). The data on state, collective, and private sector are drawn from occupational data and then matched to the industrial data; the calculation required certain arbitrary assumptions so the results are not exact.

Czechoslovakia. Federální Statistický úrad (annual, 1986, pp. 184, 192). The original data omitted the collectives (JZDs), which were added into the labor force in the socialist sector.

Germany, East. German Democratic Republic, Staatliche Zentralverwaltung für Statistik (annual, 1987, p. 112). Apprentices were excluded in calculating the percentages.

Grenada. Pryor (1986, p. 337).

Guyana. Guyana (Caricom, n.d., vol. 2, p. 376). For Guyana one often finds the estimate that the government controls 80 to 90 percent of the economy. The original source of this estimate is never supplied, nor is information available as to what this datum refers or how it was calculated.

Guinea-Bissau. The census for 1989 (Ministerio da Coordençao Economica e Plano 1981) indicates about 15.8 percent of the economically active worked for wages (and 8.1 percent of the economically active were in public administration). To the degree that female workers in the agricultural sector were undercounted, these percentages have an upward bias. According to the Economist Intelligence Unit (1986a), in 1984 about 80 percent of the wage labor force worked for the public sector (public administration and public enterprises), and another 5 percent, for mixed companies. I have assumed that the 1979 percentage of wage workers was the same in 1984. Subsequently the number of workers in public administration has been reduced.

Hungary. Central Statistical Office (annual, 1987); the data refer to the end of the year.

Korea, North. The data come from Vreeland and Shinn (1976, p. 63) and classify the labor force according to occupation (collective farm worker, office worker, factory worker). These data apparently include all of the economically active; no more recent information could be located. In the agricultural sector I have assumed that the percentage of workers on state and collective farms was the same as the land in these respective forms of farming; these data come from table 4.1. I have also assumed that no more private farmers existed in agriculture.

Madagascar. Pryor (1988, p. 70).

Mongolia. SEV (annual, 1988, p. 21).

Mozambique. The estimates are quite rough. Data on the economically active by sector, as well as workers in collective farms, come from Mozambique, Conselho Coordenador de Recenseamento (1983). Data for workers on the state farms for 1981 came from Verschuur et al. (1986, p. 86); I have assumed this number did not change between 1980 and 1981. Wuyts (1989, p. 61) gives the percentage of production accounted for by state-owned enterprises in 1983 for various sectors; I have assumed that these percentages held for 1980. I have further assumed that all workers in education and health worked for the government, as well as 90 percent of the "other service workers" who were employed for a wage or salary.

Nicaragua. Instituto Nacional de Estadísticas y Censos (annual, 1982, p. 42). The estimate of 44,000 economically active in agriculture, forestry, and fishing is clearly too low, given the average of 332,000 economically active population (measured in man-years) in this sector between 1975 and 1978 (Peek 1982, p. 17). I have, therefore, assumed 360,000 economically active for 1982. According to Kaimowitz and Stanfield

(1985), state farmworkers (including non agricultural workers) numbered about 50,000 in the early 1980s. I assume that 40,000 of them were agricultural workers. According to Medal (1988, p. 36), in 1982 the collective farms had 7,895 members. The totals are adjusted according to these changes.

Poland. These census data come from Główny Urząd Statystyczny (1980, pp. 153–54, 161). The collective farms (producer cooperatives plus farms of Agricultural Circles) include only agricultural cooperatives; other cooperatives, which were relatively unimportant, are included for the state sector. More recent estimates, which do not come from census data, are presented in Główny Urząd Statystyczny (annual, 1987, pp. 59–60).

Romania. Direcţia Centrală de Statistiçă (1980). Collective farms include both the C.A.P. and other collectives. The mass organizations (the women's organization, the party, the youth organization, the labor unions) are considered as the private sector.

São Tomé. Ministério do Plano, Dirrecção de Estatística (1987).

Seychelles. These estimates were calculated from: Republic of Seychelles (1978) and various issues of Republic of Seychelles (annual). Mining is included in construction, rather than manufacturing.

Somalia. The estimates are presented by ILO, JASPA (1987, p. 55) and originally appeared in an Economic Community publication *The Socio-Economic Development of Somalia, 1981–82*, which was unavailable to me. The public sector data are somewhat different from data from a 1978 labor force survey (ILO, JASPA 1987, p. 50) and I have made one adjustment to achieve greater consistency, namely assigning 10,000 workers to the public sector. For the collective farm sector, which apparently included multi-purpose collective farms, I removed 14,000 workers; the resulting estimate still appears too high, and from data presented in Somalia, State Planning Commission (1979), the true percentage may be closer to 0.9 percent.

Viet Nam. The data for state farms come from Crosnier and Lhomel (1987), who drew the data from the statistical yearbook, which I could not obtain. These data, however, appear to conflict with those from the 1979 population census, which show a socialist sector (state and collectives) of 74.8 percent (or, for instance, in industry, of 76.7 percent). From the qualitative information about the relatively small degree of nationalization in the south, the census data seem high and I have chosen to use the data from a later date.

Beresford (1988, p. 73) reports that cooperatives included more than two thirds of the rural population, which consisted of 71.8 percent of the economically active. The estimate in the table is derived by assuming that collectives were exclusively in the country (there were some urban cooperatives, but apparently they did not include a very large share of the economically active) and that "more than two-thirds" means 70 percent. Obviously the estimate is very approximate; moreover, a large share of the cooperatives were really nominal (Fforde 1989), so the estimate in the table overestimates the importance of the collective farm sector.

USSR. Tsentral'noe statischeskoe upravlenie (1973, p. 194).

Yemen, South. The data are GDP, not labor force data; and they come from Cigar (1985). Mixed corporations are included in the data for collectives. To derive the data for non-agricultural sectors, national account data from Yemen, Central Statistical Organization (annual, 1986, p. 176) on the sectoral distribution of production are used.

Yugoslavia. The basic data on the economically active population, as well as workers and employees, own-account workers, and so forth come from International Labour Office (annual, 1988, pp. 126–27). Unemployed and not classified by industrial branch were eliminated; "not classified" within branches were assigned to the private sector. From the total workers and employees were subtracted workers in the private sector for the same year from Savezni zavod za statistiku (annual, 1988, p. 134).

Zimbabwe. The data come from Roussos (1988, p. 33) and represent contributions to the GDP of each sector, not labor force.

TABLE 1.3

Data on the economically active population in agriculture come from FAO (annual-b, 1986, table 3). The ratio of value added in agriculture, forestry, and fishing to the factor price GDP are calculated from data from World Bank (1988), supplemented by United Nations (1987).

For Cape Verde, the labor force data come from Cape Verde, Secretaria des Estado (1983); the GDP data, from Cape Verde, Dirrecção Geral de Estatística (n.d.). For Grenada the data come from Pryor (1986, pp. 298, 335). For São Tomé the labor force data come from São Tomé

(1987, vol. 2): the GDP are rough estimates by the author. For Seychelles, the labor force data are estimated from Seychelles (1978) and various issues of Seychelles (annual); the GDP data come from Seychelles (1987). For Bulgaria, Czechoslovakia, East Germany, Hungary, Poland, and Romania, the data on both economically active population and value added refer to 1982 and come from Lazarčik (1985, pp. 391–92). For the Soviet Union, the data come from Pitzer (1982, p. 54).

Data on agricultural exports and imports come from FAO (1985, table 6, pp. 132–93), supplemented by United Nations (1988b), which is also the source for the major agricultural exports. For São Tomé, the estimates are based in part upon unpublished data supplied by the government. The estimates, although rough, indicate relative magnitudes.

Statistical Note B

DATA SOURCES FOR TABLES IN CHAPTER 3

TABLE 3.1

Afghanistan. Land distribution data in the pre-Marxist period vary from source to source due to differences in the samples and the definitions employed. According to some sources (Smith and others, 1973, p. xxxvi; Chiliard 1982, p. 21; or Schröder 1980, p. 62), who draw from a 1967 survey covering about one half of the total area, ownership of land (apparently including non-agricultural land) had a distribution yielding a Gini coefficient of 0.66. In 1978 the Taraki government estimated a land ownership distribution which had a Gini coefficient of 0.47 (cited by Noorzog, 1983). Gupta (1986, p. 30) cites land ownership data yielding a Gini of 0.411 from still another source; and from a Soviet source that appears to adjust land for quality, Gupta provides Soviet data from which a Gini of 0.51 can be calculated. These various sources, plus qualitative statements by Dupree (1978) and other authorities indicate that holdings by very large landowners were not the source of ownership inequality; rather it was the number of landowners with only minuscule plots. These sources also indicate that the number of landless families numbered between 400,000 and 680,000 (omitting the nomads); Grötzbach (1982) places the number of landless farmers at 20 to 35 percent; Nyrop (1986, p. 180), at 33 percent. Most of the landless were renting land so that the distribution of land usage was much less unequal than these land ownership statistics.

Official sources (Afghanistan, Central Statistical Office, 1978/79, p. 66) cite a figure of 665,660 hectares redistributed to 295,988 families (roughly 23 percent of all rural families), but these data are questionable. The denominator of the ratio is total crop land, taken from official sources (Afghanistan, CSO, 1983, p. 90); since some of the redistributed land was probably not arable, the datum in the text represents an upper limit.

Albania. According to data reflecting the distribution of holdings before the land reform in 1945, the Gini coefficient was 0.56 (Drejtoria e Statistikës annual 1961, pp. 123–24). The renters consisted of about 13.9 percent of rural families; and according to Lange (1981, p. 31), about 5.4 percent of the families worked on the latifundia, so that the number of landless was roughly 19.3 percent. Nevertheless, since 23 percent of rural families farmed less than 0.5 hectares, it is likely that a certain number of family members worked for wages on the farms of others. For this reason I have rated the landless as "medium." The amount of violence has not been closely studied, but reports of resistance, cattle slaughter, and the like suggest that some violence was employed.

Angola. In 1970, about half of 8.8 million hectares of farm land was occupied by 700,799 peasant farms and about half, by 6,412 commercial farms and plantations (Hodges 1987, p. 85). Furthermore, less than 5 percent of available land was cultivated. Wage laborers constituted about 10 percent of the economically active in 1973 (Bhagavan 1986, p. 52); roughly half of these were migrant workers who farmed elsewhere and who worked to obtain cash to pay taxes, so that landlessness per se did not seem to be a problem. The extent of collectivization or decollectivization is unclear; in many places the peasants simply took the land, especially since the state could not supply agricultural inputs or management for the farms; in the mid-1980s, according to Bhagavan (1986, p. 19), only a "few hundred" of the six thousand former Portuguese plantations and farms were still functioning. In 1984–85 the government began a formal program to dissolve some of the state farms, and by 1988 the government still announced decollectivization measures as if little had taken place before (*Journal de Angola*, 9 February 1989, p. 16).

Bénin. In 1976–77, the Gini coefficient of land in the province of Atacora was 0.34 (International Labour Office 1982, p. 28), and there is no reason to believe that the land distribution was much different in the other provinces for which data could not be located. In 1979, only 5 percent of the labor force in agriculture was wage workers (Bénin, Ministère du Plan, de la Statistique et de l'Analyse Economique 1983, p. 367). Although data on the amount of rented land are not available, most sources believe that such land constituted only a very small fraction of total land.

Bulgaria. According to official land distribution data, in 1934 the Gini coefficient was 0.46 (Bulgaria, Direction Général de la Statistique 1941, p. 203). According to Zagoroff (1955, p. 50), hired agricultural workers constituted 5.1 percent of the total agricultural labor force. Various sources differ on the amount of rented land; the most complete source is Grigoroff (1956), who presents data showing about 7.6 percent of all farmers in 1934 rented 50 percent or more of their farmland. Estimates of the total amount of land distributed to individual farmers varies in different sources from 120,000 to 150,000 hectares; I use the high estimate from Rochlin (1957, p. 37).

Cape Verde. According to data presented by Portugal, Ministério do Ultramar (1965), the Gini coefficient of land holdings was 0.54 in the early 1960s. The same source reveals that 58 percent of all land was rented. Although data on hired labor in agriculture are not available, such labor was probably a relatively small share of the rural labor force since the large holdings were generally rented out, rather than farmed as a single unit. Although data on the number of renters and owners are also not available, the evidence on land rental suggests that a high proportion of the rural population was landless.

Reliable data are also not available on the number of farmers receiving expropriated land. According to FAO (1986a), 61 percent of the land was still rented in 1981, which suggests that only 3 percent of the land had changed from rental to ownership between 1961 and 1981. The 1985 data from *Estatísticas Agrícoles* (July 1986) for eight districts suggest little change from the 1981 situation.

China. The land reform began before the seizure of power was complete; indeed, in some areas, land reform began in the 1930s. According to 1929–33 survey data from Buck (1956, p. 217), the Gini coefficient of farm size was 0.38. These data have been criticized as oversampling northern provinces and also areas along main transportation routes. Moreover, Buck standardized them by size category according to region so that in absolute terms they are not comparable for the nation as a whole. According to the larger 1936 survey by the National Agricultural Research Bureau (NARB), the Gini was 0.57 (data cited by Myers, 1969); the evaluation in the table is based on the NARB data.

According to Buck's survey 54 percent of all peasant households were full owners of land, while 17 percent were full tenants. According to the NARB survey full tenants included 29 percent of all peasant households (Lippit 1974, p. 64). Buck (p. 297) placed the labor-day equivalents of hired workers as 15 percent of total labor; and other sources place hired labor in the 10 to 15 percent range.

Accurate data on the extent of the land reform are not available. The estimate in the table is based on official data cited by Wong (1973, p. 161); estimates by other official sources are somewhat higher or lower. Several percentage points of the redistributed land probably went to the state farms, not to the peasants.

Congo. According to data presented by FAO (1978), the Gini coefficient of cultivated land in the traditional sector was 0.29 in 1972–73. The estates constituted a small percentage of total land and their inclusion would not have greatly changed this statistic. According to Congo, Centre national de la statistique et des études economique (1978), salaried employees and wage workers constituted about 2 percent of the total economically active in agriculture. Although data on land tenure are not available, various sources suggest that a relatively low percentage of the land was rented. In the traditional sector, however, a fee was usually paid to the traditional authority who assigned the plot, which might be considered as a form of rent.

Czechoslovakia.   Size distribution data (International Institute of Agriculture 1939, vol. 1, p. 165) yield a Gini coefficient of 0.63 for agricultural land (and 0.75 for total land) for 1930. According to Czechoslovakia, Office de Statistique (1936, tables 6, 16), 20 percent of all Czechoslovak farmers rented at least half of their land, and 38 percent rented at least 10 percent of their land. Nonfamily employment on the farms amounted to 14 percent, so that the total landlessness ranged from 34 to 53 percent, depending on how it is defined. I have classified this as medium. Data on land redistribution to farmers comes from Salzmann (1983, p. 5); the denominator of the ratio includes both arable land and permanent meadows and comes from FAO (annual-b 1950, p. 3).

Cuba.   Data on the size distribution of land holdings in 1946 from Ministerio de Agricultura (1951, p. 84) yield a Gini coefficient of 0.7908.

Although official data indicate a landless population of about 70 percent, this is misleading since many had small plots. Pollitt (1982) places the number of rural proletariat at roughly 50 percent of agricultural workers shortly before the revolution. To this should be added another 14 percent of farmers who rented land, although they might have also owned some land. Given the rough nature of these data, 60 percent for "landless farmers" seems to be a conservative estimate.

Within ten years of the revolution, about 70 percent of the agricultural land was in the state sector. The first agrarian reform in 1959 immediately expropriated 60 percent of the land; only 8.8 percent of total agricultural land was transferred to small peasant (MacEwan 1981, p. 45). The extent of the second agrarian reform in 1963 is not so clear, but it appears that it resulted in the transfer of roughly 15 to 19 percent of total agricultural land to the state sector.

Ethiopia.   According to data presented by Teka and Nichola (1983, p. 31), the Gini coefficient of land holdings in 1974–75 was 0.47. Commercial farms amounted to less than 10 percent of the total cultivated area, and many were quite small. According to data for 12 provinces in the late 1960s, presented by Mengisteab (1984), 36.2 percent of all rural population (the data apparently include adult men and women) farmed completely on rented land, while another 9.5 percent rented some of their land. In a survey of four areas of the country, Rahmato (1984, p. 57) places rural workers at 4 to 6 percent of rural population. The combined number of tenants and rural workers amounted to roughly 50 percent of the rural population. Data on the amount of redistributed land are not available; in the table I have assumed that the plot of an average full tenant was 80 percent that of an owner, and that part-tenants rented half of their land.

Germany, East.   The data on land distribution and landlessness are for 1939 and apply to the current boundaries of East Germany. According to data from German Democratic Republic, Staatliche Zentralverwaltung für Statistik (annual, 1955, p. 194), the Gini coefficient for agricultural land was 0.68 (and for economic area, 0.74). According to data from Germany, Statistisches Reichsamt (1943b), 8.6 percent farmed only rented land, another 14.6 percent owned land comprising less than 50 percent of the entire farm, and another 33.2 percent rented land comprising less than 50 percent of their total farm land.

According to data from Statistisches Reichsamt (1943b), workers and employees amounted to 34.3 percent of the people engaged in farming. Depending on the cutoff point, landlessness ranged from 50 to 57 percent of the agricultural sector.

The data on redistributed land come from Piskol et al. (1984). The degree of violence of the reform is difficult to assess. Although groups such as the Arbeitsgemeinschaft deutscher Landwirte und Beamten (1955) have recorded many instances of violence, many of these were connected with the occupation of the land by the Soviet army, rather than with the land reform per se. Of course, the Soviet occupation force was also the guiding force underlying the reform.

Grenada.   According to data from Pryor (1986, p. 317), the Gini coefficient was 0.60 in 1981. The relative importance of land rentals was low and most of the workers on the plantations also cultivated some land of their own. The determination of landlessness is based on qualitative information and is uncertain.

Guinea-Bissau.   According to data presented by FAO (1966, vol. 1-C), the Gini coefficient of cultivated land of individual farms was 0.39 in 1960–61; however, much of this was due to great differences in household size and the counting of extended families as a single household. On a per capita basis the Gini coefficient was 0.25. Data on farm labor and land renting are not available; however, all qualitative statements about such matters found in the literature suggest that land renting was relatively low or nonexistent except among several of the small, stratified ethnic groups such as Manjaco. Plantations were also relatively unimportant.

Guyana. For 1977, one year after the land nationalization, data on the size distribution of farms can be found in materials published by the Guyana National Farm Registry (GNFR) (International Fund for Agricultural Development 1982, p. 42). Using this as my basic source I added the 13 estates existing in 1974, which had previously covered 120,000 acres (Singaravelou 1978, p. 108). Although the acreage data supplied by Singaravelou covers only planted land, I have estimated total potential crop land to make these data comparable with the GNFR data. The derived Gini coefficient was 0.74; if these estates are eliminated, the Gini was 0.67.

In 1960, according to Trinidad and Tobago, Central Statistical Office (1964), 60 percent of those working in agriculture in Guyana were employed workers, in contrast to 40 percent self-employed farmers and their families.

Hungary. According to data presented by Zagoroff (1955, p. 160), the Gini coefficient of the distribution of total area was 0.82 in 1935. As a percentage of the agricultural labor force (including dependents), the same source (p. 161) gives the share of farm hands and landless laborers as 35.5 percent and the share of tenants of holdings from 0.6 to 2.9 hectares as 18.6 percent.

The amount of land redistributed to the farmers varies from source to source. According to Donáth (1980, p. 133), it was 1.89 million hectares.

Kampuchea. According to the data presented by Hu (1982), in 1962 the Gini coefficient for farms (apparently total farm area) was 0.50; Delvert (1961) presents data for 1956, which have a Gini coefficient of 0.54. Hu also presents data showing that tenants amounted to 5.8 percent of household heads, with "perspective tenants or sharecroppers," amounting to another 8.0 percent. Through some type of unexplained statistical manipulation, Hu arrives at a figure of tenants and sharecroppers as higher than 25 percent. The 1962 population census (Cambodia, Institut national de la statistique et des recherches économiques. n.d.) shows that 1.4 percent of the economically active in agriculture were employees and, combined with Hu's data, the degree of landlessness is rated as "low." Although other sources based on older data suggest both higher tenancy and employment (e.g., tenancy up to 20 percent), the quality of the data leave something to be desired. My impression that total landlessness still appeared low in 1960s is supported by most authorities. Before seizure of power the Khmer Rouge carried out a land reform that consisted of rent and interest reduction and, apparently, debt reduction.

Korea, North. Data on the distribution of farms for North Korea could not be located, although such a document (in Japanese) does exist. For Korea as a whole in 1938, Grajdanzev (1942) presents a size distribution yielding a Gini coefficient of 0.28; I have assumed that in this regard there was little difference between the two parts of the nation.

According to Scalapino and Lee (1972, p. 1067) the *kulak* class was small. Chung (1974, pp. 4–5) points out that for Korea as a whole, 72 percent of all farms were smaller than 1 hectare, while only 4 percent were larger than 5 hectares. From these clues and after experimentation with different size distributions using these parameters, I have classified the farm-size distribution as medium.

According to Scalapino and Lee (1972, p. 1016) or Chung (1974, p. 5), who present slightly different data, tenants amounted to 41 to 43 percent of the rural population in 1943 and "primarily tenant but owning some land," another 14 percent; farm laborers amounted to another 0.8 percent.

Data on redistributed land come from Scalapino and Lee (1974, p. 1017).

Laos. Few data are available so that these evaluations are based on scattered or qualitative information. Brown and Zasloff (1986, p. 204), for instance, present data showing that except for Vientiane Province, tenancy in the five other provinces was less than 4 percent. Many others, for instance, Juhász (1986), assert that there were no big estates and almost all the land belonged to the tillers. Stuart-Fox (1986, p. 39) says that a few large holdings of exiled "feudalists" were confiscated after seizure of power.

Madagascar. According to Pryor (1988, p. 4), the Gini coefficient of total land holdings of smallholders was 0.445 in 1961–62. Since smallholders farmed about 95 percent of the land (Pryor 1990c), inclusion of rough estimates of the estate lands does not greatly change this statistic. In the same year, rented lands accounted for less than 10 percent of the total farmed area (Madagascar, Ministère des finances et du commerce and INSRE 1966). The relative unimportance of either plantations or land rental suggests that landlessness was low.

Mongolia. The key data refer to livestock, not land. According to Lattimore (1962, pp. 110–11), about one-quarter of the total livestock belonged to the nobility, while another quarter belonged to monasteries.

According to a Russian source used by Murphy (1966, pp. 41–42), the Khalka nobility included 5.7 percent of the male population and the lamas, another 44.5 percent. Of the latter, however, only 37.9 percent lived in the monasteries (i.e., 16.9 percent of the male population) so that their share of the livestock was not much greater than their share in the population. Using these two benchmarks, experiments with the distribution of cattle holdings of the remaining various 56.4 percent of the male population yielded Gini coefficients all falling between 0.20 and 0.50; for this reason the distribution is classified as "medium." A Mongolian source cited by Sanders (1987, p. 89) suggests that 50 percent of the livestock was owned by the nobility, which would make the distribution of livestock highly unequal; the Lattimore evaluation may be more reliable.

Qualitative descriptions of the prereform era suggest that almost all families had their herds, although they might also herd for others as part of their feudal dues, but not for a salary. Thus total herdlessness did not seem common.

The land reforms from 1921–22 to 1929–30 were less of a consistent package than a series of policies implemented along with various political measures to consolidate central power. The degree of violence entailed in the reforms is impossible to judge, because a great deal of violence was being employed for political purposes, rather than agricultural reasons.

Because the expropriation of cattle from the nobles and monasteries and the formation of collectives were either simultaneous or close in time, it is difficult to say how many cattle went to private farms. After the collective farms were disbanded in 1932, almost all of the expropriated cattle went into private hands.

Mozambique.   According to the data presented by Lott (1979), the Gini coefficient of holdings was 0.71. This is somewhat misleading, however, since it appears that only agricultural land was counted in the traditional sector while total land was included in the commercial sector. The two sectors contained about the same amount of land. According to census data from Portugal, Instituto Nacional de Estatística (1974), permanently employed and other wage labor amounted to 13 percent of the agricultural labor force. A considerable share of these workers had their own farms, however. Data on tenancy are not available; a considerable amount of unused agricultural land was available, and no source available to me indicated that tenancy was a problem.

Although some sources indicate that no land was redistributed (for instance, Wuyts 1989), the difference in size between land cultivated by settlers and plantations before independence suggests that some of the abandoned estates and farms probably went to private individuals as a result of informal land takeover. Further, the government did distribute some empty land to peasants (Hanlon 1984, p. 113). The official redistributions of such lands, mandated by the Land Act of 1979, only began in April 1988 with the transfer of titles to seventeen farmers (*Mozambique Update*, no. 16, 21 June 1988). Between 1984 and 1986 land from state farms had declined roughly 100,000 hectares (Miech-Chatenay 1986, p. 200, gives data for the two years), and this was distributed through some type of semipermanent lease to private individuals. This is the basis of the data in the table.

Nicaragua. According to the data on the size distribution of the total agricultural holdings in 1963 (Nicaragua, Dirección General de Estadísticas y Censos 1966, p. xiv), the Gini coefficient was 0.80. Less detailed data for later years show roughly the same degree of inequality. Data on the employed labor force in agriculture, forestry, and fishing for 1971 come from Nicaragua, Direccíon General de Estadísticas y Censos (1966) and amounted to 46 percent of the economically active in this sector. Extrapolating the number of renters from 1961 to 1971 yields about 7 percent of the agricultural labor force in the latter year; there is, however, some overlap between the two measures of the landless labor force, so that the data presented in the table represents a rough estimate. Deere et al. (1985) present different kinds of data: landless seasonal workers, 17 percent; permanent wage workers, 20 percent; and minifundists, 36.4 percent, which raises the number.

From October 1981 through December 1985, individuals received 194,939 manzanas of land from the redistribution, which amounts to about 2.4 percent of total farm land. For another 17.4 percent of the land they received legalization of their title (Reinhardt, 1987), but this does not seem to represent a true form of land redistribution since they had already been farming this land without rent. According to Medal (1988, p. 38), 372,000 manzanas of land were "abandoned" in 1986; this appears to represent the state farms that were turned over to peasants and represents 4.6 percent of total land. The data in the table represent this "abandoned" land plus the land previously transferred; the distribution of land titles to former squatters is not included, since this program did little to change the status quo except legally.

Poland. The most complete agricultural census for Poland was in 1921; according to the data presented by Mieszczankowski (1960, p. 19), the Gini was 0.717 for total farm land. According to the less complete data that he presents (pp. 329, 333, and 337; public land holdings are omitted) for 1939 (corresponding to a 1921 sample with a Gini of 0.648), the Gini

462   STATISTICAL NOTE B

was 0.609, so that the land reforms between the two sample dates had only a moderate effect. Philipp (1983) presents some estimates for 1939 for the prewar and postwar boundaries, from which Gini coefficients of 0.708 and 0.773 can be derived. Thus the land within the postwar boundaries was quite unequally distributed.

According to Institute of Agricultural Economics (1954, p. 9) in 1921 about 10 percent of farmers rented land, either wholly or partly. Nevertheless, 55 percent of these plots were less than 1 hectare, and another 37 percent, between 1 and 5 hectares. It seems likely that less than 2 percent of Polish farmers rented a significant portion of the land they farmed. The number of agricultural workers varies from source to source, ranging from 12 to 17 percent of the farm population. The former estimate by Lepinski (1955, p. 7) includes only agricultural workers on private farms; the latter (Institute of Agricultural Economics 1954, p. 7) includes some part-time workers. Since about 34 percent of all farms in 1921 had less than 2 hectares of land, which was not enough to support a farm family, it is likely that many of these farmers worked on a part-time basis so that the total of "landless" peasants was probably between 30 and 40 percent of the rural agricultural labor force.

Korbonski (1965, p. 93) indicates that the peasants mistrusted the communists, and had no revolutionary zeal to destroy the landlords. This suggests that violence was minimal. The amount of land redistributed varies slightly from source to source (Spulber 1957, p. 231; Korbonski 1965, p. 97), but was roughly 6 million hectares, which is expressed in the table as a fraction of total agricultural land (Neetz 1969, p. 17).

Romania.   Zagoroff (1955, p. 233) presents 1931 data on the size distribution of farms that yield a Gini coefficient of 0.57. According to the same source (p. 50), hired laborers amounted to 8.9 percent of the rural labor force (15.7 percent of land-poor farms smaller than 1 hectare are included). Although 0.4 percent of the farms were fully rented, another 27.8 percent rented some land (p. 50). The relative importance of rented land cannot be ascertained, however, by these data. Mitrany (1930, p. 248) presents data showing that only 6 percent of the land was rented, which suggests that tenancy was relatively unimportant. Using the 1941 agricultural census (which did not cover certain areas), Roberts (1951) presents data of the same order of magnitude.

Total land redistributed to peasants comes from Turnock (1986, p. 180); the denominator is total agricultural land from Neetz (1969, p. 16). In 1953 a very small additional amount of land was redistributed to private peasants; the amount, however, is never specified.

São Tomé.   According to data presented by Portugal, Ministério do Ultramar (1968), the Gini coefficient of land holdings was 0.96 in the early
1960s. The fact that only 5.5 percent of the land was held in farms fewer
than 50 hectares and that the larger farms were plantations owned by the
Portuguese means that landlessness among the São Toméans was extremely high.

Seychelles.   According to data presented by United Kingdom, Colony of
the Seychelles, A.W.T. Webb (n.d.), the Gini coefficient of land holdings
was 0.82 in 1960 if land under 2 acres is excluded; if included, the Gini
coefficient was 0.92. Data from the same source state that roughly 98
percent of those engaged in agricultural production were associated with
the plantations, either as laborers, managers, or owners. Although the
survey appears to undercount the smallholders sector, we can only conclude that landlessness was very great.

   For several years starting in 1979, the Seychelles government leased
some of the estate land (which was bought or expropriated) to smallholders (called "blockers"). According to Bulbeck (1984), they numbered 650
in 1982. Nevertheless, the program was phased out because most of the
blockers did not farm the land for commercial purposes and, according to
one agronomist, less than 3 percent were "adequate" farmers.

Somalia.   Data on the distribution of holdings for the nation as a whole
are not available. Massey (1987, p. 107) presents data for a sample of 667
farms in the Bay Region (an interriverain region in part of the area where
most crop farming was carried out) for the early 1980s; the Gini coefficient was 0.20. The Massey sample also shows that only 7.6 percent of
the rural families in his sample had no land. Moreover, since most land
was held under traditional tenancy arrangements, land renting was limited.

   For the country as a whole, plantations comprised only a small proportion of the total land. In the mid 1970s, workers on the banana estates
(ILO, JASPA 1977, p. 95) comprised less than 1.3 percent of total agricultural labor (calculated from data presented by ILO, JASPA 1987, p.
55).

   None of the sources available to me designated inequality of land holdings, land tenancy, or agricultural wage labor as a major problem.

Viet Nam.   According to the data for the 1929–31 period presented by
Henry (1932), the Gini coefficient of land holdings was 0.605 in the area
that became North Viet Nam and 0.811 in the area that became South
Viet Nam (the data for Annam were redistributed by province to the two

areas). According to data presented by Moise (1983, p. 150), the Gini coefficient of ownership (not holdings) inequality of land was 0.576 in North Viet Nam in 1945. These data exclude lands held communally or by churches, which amounted to 26 percent of the total. For unexplained reasons, only 94 percent of rural households are included; apparently nonagricultural households are omitted. The distribution of land holdings was more equal since most lands held by landlords were generally rented out, rather than farmed as a single unit. For this reason I have rated the inequality of land holdings as "high/medium."

In South Viet Nam (Annam and Cochinchina) the Gini coefficient of inequality of land holdings (Lott 1979) was 0.582 in 1960–61, but after the Land to the Tillers program of 1970, land holdings and ownership in the Mekong Delta (but not former Annam) were, according to Wiegersma (1988), sufficiently even that a full scale land reform was not necessary.

According to Moise (1983) and Vickerman (1986, p. 65), the households of landless peasants comprised 20.6 percent of the rural population (21.8 percent if the percentage is recalculated to exclude nonagricultural households). "Poor peasant" households amounted to 35.4 (37.5) percent. If two-thirds of the poor peasants were full tenants, then landlessness was 44.2 (45.6) percent. (Estimating differently, landlords held 22.5 percent of the land; and the French, about 0.01 percent). In South Viet Nam the extent of landlessness is not known. According to the data from Lott (1979), only 1.1 percent of the households had no land, and another 13.5 percent had holdings of fewer than 0.5 hectares.

A great deal of controversy exists about the amount of violence in the North Viet Nam land reforms. For instance, Moise (1983, p. 208) presents evidence that the accepted figure of fifty thousand deaths may be overstated tenfold. Nevertheless, other forms of coercion took place.

Land redistribution actually began in 1945 in North Viet Nam, but the total of land redistributed is not known. One Vietnamese source cited by Moise (1983, p. 266) claims that after the rectification of errors campaign, about 50 percent of the land had been redistributed. Data he presents on pages 151 and 162 (the data on p. 151 are roughly adjusted so that the area is the same) suggest, however, that 48.5 percent of the land was redistributed before the rectification. The distributed land also includes a small amount that was turned into state farms. Trang (1972, pp. 287, 289) and Vickerman (1986, p. 61) claim that 810,000 hectares were redistributed, which amounts to 38 percent of all agricultural land. I have used the latter figure in the table.

According to Crosnier and Lhomel (1987), about 400,000 hectares of agricultural land (about 16 percent) was redistributed in the South; it is unclear, however, how much of this went to individual peasants rather than to collective farms.

USSR.   The data presented by Volin (1970, p. 133) for a sample of peasant households in European Russia before the revolution (the table title is for all of Russia which, at that time, was mainly in Europe) yield a Gini coefficient of 0.44 for sown area. This apparently includes rented land but excludes land farmed directly by the estates. If the data were total farm area, so as to be more comparable with the other data he presents, the Gini would be higher. An upper limit is provided by Lenin's data for 1905 ("The Agrarian Programme of Social-Democracy," 1907, LCW vol. XIII, p. 293), which presents a table on allotment land and another on private land holdings. Although it is not quite correct to combine these tables to generate a size distribution of all land ownership, the resulting Gini coefficient is 0.62. Since many of the large estates included non-agricultural land, since many of the estates were divided into smaller holdings, and since much of the estate land was bought by peasants between 1905 and 1917, the Gini coefficient for land holdings would be much lower in 1917. For this reason, I have classified the distribution of holdings as medium/high.

Landlessness is also difficult to judge. In 1917 (Volin 1970, p. 135), 11.5 percent of the households had no sown land, but it is not clear they were landless; they might have rented out this land to others. Robinson (1949, p. 798) cites data for four Gubernia in 1910–12 with landlessness amounting to 6.7 percent of all households. In the same sample agricultural workers amounted to 3.8 percent of the number of households (or probably about 2 percent of the total workers in agriculture). Most estate land was rented out so that the number of workers directly employed on these lands could not have been great. For the early part of the century Jazny (1949, p. 145) says that rented land amounted to about 20 percent of the size of the allotment land. By 1917, however, peasants had bought much of this land and several of the sources consulted suggested that rented land (often just meadows) supplemented the peasants' allotment and purchased land; and did not provide the main source of subsistence for the household. Under the definitions employed in this table, landlessness appeared "low."

According to Carr (1952, p. 38), the peasant takeover of land went smoothly in those areas where agriculture was advanced, but disorderly and violently elsewhere. Other descriptions of the land takeover describe considerable looting and other acts of destruction, but little physical violence to the landowners, who were generally not present.

Volin (1970, p. 133) presents data for 1916 on total land held by large private estates (75 million desyatina), imperial estates (6.5 mil. des.), peasant allotment land (138.8 mil. des.), peasant private land (26.4 mil. des.), and public domain (18.0 mil. des.). Farmland is estimated by assuming that all land was suitable for agriculture except that of the public domain land (which was mostly forest) and one-third of the private estate land. Total land redistributed to the peasants is estimated by assuming that all of the private and imperial estates plus one third of the land privately purchased by peasants was involved in the land seizures. Although the assumptions are somewhat arbitrary, the resulting estimate provides some order of the magnitudes involved.

Yemen, South.   No information could be located that would give sufficient clues for even a guess as to the farm size distribution. Given the high degree of tenancy and the primitive farm technologies employed, one suspects that the distribution of holdings could not have been greatly unequal. With regard to landlessness, however, scattered information is available. According to the data for a single area presented by Alkhomov and Gusarov (1976, p. 37), tenants consisted of 47 percent and agricultural laborers another 26 percent of the household heads. Other sources such as Nyrop, ed. (1979, p. 121), speak of tenants comprising two-thirds of the agricultural population. In contrast, one source (Bujra 1971, p. 65) reported relatively little tenancy in his area.

In order to carry out land redistribution, the government encouraged the peasants to seize the land, particularly in 1972 in the Western provinces. The process has not been well described, and the degree of physical violence is unclear.

According to Deeb (1986), roughly 55,000 hectares of land was seized for redistribution to 30,000 families. At that time, according to him, this represented roughly 45 percent of total irrigated and non-irrigated crop land. Nevertheless, the government did not give full title to the land, and the recipients were required to join a production cooperative, so that almost no land ended up in private hands. Nonneman (1988) presents data showing that 51,000 hectares were redistributed to 31,000 peasants. He notes that this was 55 percent of arable land but had "small impact on equity."

Yugoslavia.   According to 1931 data presented by Zagoroff (1955, p. 296), the Gini coefficient was 0.53. According to the same source (p. 50), agricultural laborers amounted to 9.3 percent of the agricultural labor force (15.2 percent if land poor farms under 1 hectare are included) and (p. 52) tenancy was "almost non-existent."

Reports of implementation of land reform are extremely sketchy, but it does not appear as if much violence was used. Data on land redistributed to individual peasants come from Yugoslavia, Savezni zavod za statistiku (annual, 1955) and are presented as a percentage of total agricultural land.

In 1953 the government carried out another land redistribution after lowering the amount of land allowable to private owners from 15 to 10 hectares. Almost all of this was turned over to the Land Fund, and less than one half of one percent of total land was redistributed to private farmers.

Zimbabwe.   According to calculations by Whitsun Foundation (1976), *Report on Agriculture*, the Gini coefficient for large scale commercial farms (LSCF) was 0.71 in 1974. Using land density data from the 1969 census the report calculated a Gini coefficient of 0.43 for the tribal trust lands (now communal areas) and 0.50 for the African purchase area (now the small-scale commercial farms). Since the average farm sizes in the LSCF sector were very much larger than in the latter two areas, the Gini coefficient for the nation as a whole was undoubtedly much larger than 0.71; unfortunately comparable data for the various sectors are not available.

According to Gordon L. Chavunduka (1982, pp. 65, 87), in 1980 there were 327,000 hired farm employees, 1,040,000 full-time farmers, and 1,512,000 part-time farmers. There were, however, few tenants. Counting part-time farmers equal to one-half of the full-time farmers, hired farm laborers equaled 22 percent of the agricultural labor force. Real landlessness was, however, considerably less than this because many of these workers were migrant workers whose families operated their farms. For this reason, I have evaluated landlessness as medium/low.

By the end of 1984, about 1.836 million hectares had been redistributed to 32,973 families (Zimbabwe, Department of the Commissariat and Culture 1985). By 1988, about 40,000 families had been resettled (Economist Intelligence Unit 1989b), and I have assumed that the average amount of land per family was the same as at the end of 1984 so that 2.23 million hectares of land were involved. Accurate estimates of the number of land squatters is difficult because other estimates range considerably and, in addition, many squatters were evicted. At one time it appeared that the number of squatters was equal to the number of resettled families.

DATA SOURCES FOR TABLES IN CHAPTER 4

TABLE 4.1

Afghanistan.   Central Statistical Office (1983, pp. 61, 91, 97). The government sector also includes farms of local governments; and the data may include some arable but noncultivated land.

Albania.   Albania, Drejtoria e Statistikës (annual, 1984, pp. 78–79). In 1970 private agriculture amounted to 0.7 percent of cultivated land; the estimate of 0.5 percent in 1983 in the table is a guess. In 1970 the share of state farms in cultivated lands was 14.2 percent, indicating that the announced conversion of collective to state farms had proceeded only slowly.

Angola.   Due to the informal decollectivization and the disruption caused by the civil war, no data are available on the number or extent of functioning state farms and (after 1980) collectives; according to Hodges (1987), 90 percent of the countryside was considered "unsafe."

Bénin.   Data on collective farms come from Godin (1986, pp. 203, 228). The datum for collectives includes the *coopératives agricole de type socialiste* and the *coopératives d'aménagement rural*. The datum for state farms includes *fermes d'état, sociétés agro-industrielles*, and the units belonging to schools, local governments, and the like. The datum on total farm land comes from Table 1.3. The share of the socialist sector is somewhat understated because its area is defined in terms of cultivated hectares, while the denominator is defined in terms of land used in all of agriculture.

Bulgaria.   SEV (annual, 1988).

Cape Verde.   Interview material from Cape Verde.

China.   Xue (1982, p. 392).

Congo.   Ministère du plan (1980, pp. 196, 202). Citing data from the 1982–86 plan for the early 1980s, EDIAFRIC (1982, p. 34) shows that 29.0 percent of the land was owned by the government (17 percent was held by SUCO alone) and 0.8 percent of the land was held by collectives. This appears to refer to total land, whether or not it was cultivated at that moment. The datum for collective farm land appears to include precooperatives as well.

Cuba.   SEV (annual, 1988).

Czechoslovakia.   SEV (annual, 1988).

Ethiopia.   Economist Intelligence Unit (1989a, p. 15).

Germany, East.   SEV (annual, 1988).

Grenada.   Pryor (1986, p. 115). The plan for January 1984 foresaw the state farm sector embracing 26.0 percent of the agricultural land, but the government fell before the nationalization was carried out.

Guinea-Bissau.   Caballero and others (1987, pp. 24, 29). I have assumed that the twelve state farms averaged 1,200 hectares each (which is the case for several of the farms). The share of land held by collective farms is a guess based only on qualitative information and may be too high. By the mid-1980s some of the collectives were apparently disbanded.

Guyana.   International Fund for Agricultural Development (1982, p. 34). These data do not appear very accurate. The area covered by actual producer cooperatives was very small and probably amounted to no more than 2 percent.

Hungary.   SEV (annual, 1988).

Kampuchea.   All eyewitness accounts claim that land belonged either to the communes or to the state farms during the Pol Pot era.

Korea, North.   Chung (1974, p. 11).

Laos.   The data come from Evans (1988, p. 69), who also has some data for earlier years. His data are roughly the same as those presented by Juhász (1986) for 1984. Much lower estimates of the areas of cooperatives are presented by the State Planning Office (1985, p. 104), and it is impossible to determine the reasons for the data discrepancies. It is possible, however, that the estimates in the table include mutual aid teams. I have assumed that the forty-four state farms and other agricultural production centers averaged 100 hectares.

Mongolia.   SEV (annual, 1988).

Madagascar.   FAO (1986b).

Mozambique.   Azam and Faucher (1988, p. 103).

Nicaragua.   Medal (1988, p. 38). The private farm sector includes service cooperatives (CCS) where land was farmed individually. These data from MIDINRA differ somewhat from other data presented by Medal (1988, p. 36), which come from other ministries.

Poland.   SEV (annual, 1988).

Romania.   SEV (annual, 1988).

São Tomé.   Material obtained from the São Tomé government.

Seychelles.   Material obtained from interviews in Seychelles. These estimates are very approximate and serve only to indicate relative magnitudes.

Somalia.   The data are for cultivated land and are based on estimates presented by Boguslawski (1986, p. 34). The estimate for state farms of 21,600 hectares seems low since the irrigation projects had a total (not cultivated) area of 70,000 hectares, and the Crash Program and Resettlement Farms, 47,000 hectares (World Bank 1985). As a very rough adjustment, I have doubled Boguslawski's estimate of the area of the state farms, reducing the area of the private sector correspondingly. His data on cooperatives also raise problems. More specifically, data for collectives include both *multipurpose cooperatives*, which were really service cooperatives, and *group farming cooperatives*, which consisted of fields farmed in common plus private farms. Somalia had no full collective farms. In 1978, according to Somalia, State Planning Commission (1979, p. 91), the multipurpose and group farms were almost exactly the same in area; and I have assumed that this situation was the same in 1984 since the combined area of the two types of cooperatives did not greatly change. I have included only the *group farming arrangements* as cooperatives and have reassigned the rest to the individual farms, although some observers such as Samatar (1988, p. 92) suggest that even the group farming arrangements are cooperative only in name.

A different type of estimate can be made from data from the World Bank (1985), which are for total registered agricultural land (thereby excluding the half of the cultivated area that consists of unregistered private farms). After adjustments the data yield estimates of 67.8 percent for private land, 9.3 percent for cooperative land, and 22.8 percent for state lands. The original data for state farms include the irrigation projects, the farms of the Crash Program and the Resettlement Farms. Since most of the Crash Program Farms (5.1 percent of total land) and some of the Resettlement Farms (6.9 percent of total land) were distributed to individual farmers by 1984, I have reassigned 7.0 percent of the total land from the state to the individual sector. I have also reassigned half of the land from the cooperative sector to the private sector for the same reason as above.

A third set of data, much less systematic than the above, is presented by Rogers (1985, pp. 74, 77, 81).

Viet Nam.   The 1986 data come from Viet Nam State Planning Commission, FAO et al. (1990); the datum for state farms is the percentage of arable land and privately cultivated land is a residual. These data, however, are different from those reported in SEV (annual, 1988), which refer to total agricultural land; the SEV data assign 61.4 percent of the land to collective farms and 9 percent to state farms. The 1975 data come from Fforde and Paine (1987, p. 188). The data for collectives overestimate the degree of collectivization since up to three quarters of the collectives were nominal (Fforde, 1989, p. 8). Since 1986 Viet Nam engaged in an important decollectivization program, as described in Pryor (1991).

USSR.   SEV (annual, 1988).

Yemen, South.   Central Statistical Organization (annual, 1988, tables 1.7, 4.7, 5.7).

Yugoslavia.   FAO, 1986c. The state farms in Yugoslavia operated on the principles of worker management and would be considered cooperative farms in other nations.

Zimbabwe.   Zimbabwe, Ministry of Finance, Economic Planning and Development (1986, pp. 121).

TABLE 4.3

Afghanistan. Ethnicity data come from Dupree (1978, p. 59); party characterization data from Hammond (1984, p. 32) and Anwar (1988, p. 49). Arnold (1983) analyzes Khalq-Parcham rivalry.

Albania. From data from the 1930 population census, Busch-Zantner (1938) reports that among the native Albanians, Ghegs numbered 52.8 percent; Tosks, 47.2 percent. Further, non-Albanians amounted to 11.5 percent of the total population. In the 1970s, non-Albanians were reported to amount to less than 5 percent of the population (the exact amount differs by source; apparently many of the non-Albanians declared themselves Albanian). I have assumed 4 percent non-Albanian and have used the 1930 percentages.

Hoxha was a Tosk, and many sources report qualitative evidence of Tosk dominance in the early years. The Hoxha government attempted to dampen ethnic tensions, and Hoxha's successor as Party leader, Ramiz Alia, is a Gheg. In the West the state of ethnic tensions in Albania has not, however, been known.

Angola, Bénin, Congo, Ethiopia, Guinea-Bissau, Madagascar, Mozambique, Somalia, and Zimbabwe. Ethnicity data are estimates from Morrison and others (1989). In a few cases—especially Madagascar—I have separated their "types" or "groups."

Czechoslovakia. Ethnicity data come from Salzmann (1983, p. 105); although Czechs and Slovaks had quite different histories, it may be incorrect to label them separate ethnic groups. Czech dominance can be inferred from the biographies of leading officials in late 1940s and early 1950s from Busek and Spulber (1957, pp. 418); only two out of eighteen with identifiable birthplaces were Slovaks.

Guinea-Bissau. Characterization of ethnic balance is based on the evaluation of Forrest (1987).

Guyana. Ethnicity data come from Hope (1979, p. 62).

Laos. The data come from Gum (1982) and are only approximate. Other estimates place Lao Tai higher and both Lao Loum (valley Lao) and Lao Soung (mountaintop Lao) lower. Lao Theung (mountainside Lao) and Lao Soung were composed of several different ethnic groups. Gum (1982), Wekkin (1982), and Stuart-Fox (1986, p. 131) discuss ethnic domination.

Madagascar.   Data on the ethnic background of the cabinet for the entire independence period come from Pryor (1990c).

Mongolia.   Ethnicity data are from Sanders (1987, p. 44). Evidence on Buryat dominance in the 1920s come from Rupen (1964, pp. 201–2).

Mozambique.   Characterization of ethnic dominance in political leadership comes from Nelson (1984, p. 96). Torp (1989, p. 83), has some brief remarks about ethnic domination and frictions resulting therefrom.

USSR.   Nationality data come from USSR, Central Statistical Board (1983, p. 13).

Yugoslavia.   Ethnicity data are from Yugoslavia, Savezni zavad za statistika (annual, 1987, p. 123). Muslim members of the various Slavic ethnic groups are excluded and placed in a special ethnic class amounting to 9 percent of the population. (This is not the case for non-Slavic groups, for instance, the Turks and the Albanians, which are listed separately.)

DATA SOURCES FOR TABLES IN CHAPTER 5

TABLE 5.2

Afghanistan. Afghanistan, Central Statistical Office (annual, 1983, p. 97). For the state farms I use the total number of workers in the state sector in agriculture (13,710) (p. 61) and the 48,663 ha turned over to the state farms in the land reform (Afghanistan, CSO, annual, 1980, p. 66). Amstutz (1986, p. 465) reports 40,486 ha of land divided in November 1982 among 30 state farms and claims (no source given) that only about 4,860 ha were actually cultivated. I assume 30 state farms and use the official figure. Dupree (1980a, 1980b) says that state farms covered only 29,200 ha.

Albania. The data on collectives come from Albania, Drejtoria e Statistikës (1984, p. 78). To estimate the number of workers, I multiplied the number of families by 2.39, since data for the 1960s (Drejtoria e Statistikës, annual 1964, p. 187) showed this number "employed" in collective sector for every family. Many Albanian families included several generations, which is apparently why there are more than two adults per family. State farm data come from Russ (1979, p. 180). For both, I use cultivated land; for state farms the average arable land was 4,340 hectares.

Angola. These data come from Offermann (1988, p. 391), and include precooperatives. Fituni (1985, p. 164) has some similar data; quite different data are presented by Centre tricontinental (1981) for earlier years. The data for state farms are for 1978 and cover 450 farms, as reported by Ottaway and Ottaway (1986, p. 120). These exclude, however, four large agro-industrial enterprises, where the number of individual farms and workers on these farms are not specified.

Bénin. The data come from a complete sample of various types of farms (except family farms) carried out by the Ministère du Plan, de la Statistique et de l'Analyse Economique (1982). The land includes only the cultivated area. The collective farms include both the *Coopérativ agricole d'état de type socialiste* and the *Groupement révolutionnaire à vocation coopérative.* The state farms include both the state farms and the farms of the agro-industrial societies (the latter are much larger). These data are quite different from those presented by Godin (1986) and are roughly the same as those from ILO (1984, p. 363).

Bulgaria. Land data include just agricultural land. Data for 1985 come from Cochrane (1989, p. 21); the 1970 data are from Bulgaria (annual, 1971, pp. 197, 239, and 241).

Cape Verde. The data on cooperatives are very rough; they come from interview material from the Cape Verde, Instituto Nacional das Cooperativas. The land data include both irrigated and non-irrigated land. In 1988 there were several experimental farms, several parastatal farms for specialized purposes, one parastatal farm in Paraguay, and one major state farm in the country (Justino Lopez). The data in the table concern only this latter farm and come from materials obtained from interviews at this farm. The land includes both irrigated and nonirrigated land; the labor force includes temporary workers (comprising about half the labor force), who appear to work most of the year.

China. The basic data come from State Statistical Bureau (1981, pp. 134, 189). The sown land for communes is converted to cultivated land by eliminating double-cropped land (an estimate is made using data for 1983 from *China Agricultural Yearbook 1985*). To the cultivated land of the state farms I add land in rubber plantations and orchards from Gerhold (1987, p. 61). For both state and collective farms the labor force includes those working in nonagricultural activities.

Congo. The data on land and number of farms come from Congo, Ministère du Plan (1980, pp. 292, 207) and refer to cultivated land. No more recent data on size could be located; since then the number of state farms increased from twenty-three to twenty-five. The size of the labor force raises difficulties. According to Congo, Centre National (1974), there were 5,703 employers and salaried workers in agriculture, forestry, and fishing. We can estimate the workers in state farms by arbitrarily reducing this by 30 percent to account for forestry and fishing (although these sectors account for only about 10 percent of the economically active in agriculture, forestry, and fishing, a much higher share was in the "modern sector") and by assuming that the land/labor ratio of land in the state sector was the same as in the private modern agricultural sector (which means that the state farms had 3,676 workers).

Cuba. State farm data cover total farm area, exclude Servicios Agropecuarios, and include the agro-industrial complexes. The raw data come from Thielen (1985, p. 126); Cuba, CEE (annual, 1987, pp. 306–7; annual, 1981, pp. 85–96).

Czechoslovakia.   Land data include just agricultural land. The raw data come from Czechoslovakia (annual, 1986, pp. 305–7; and 1972, pp. 306, 308, and 314).

Ethiopia.   The data for the producer cooperatives come from Ethiopia, Ministry of Agriculture (1985) and include cooperatives at all stages. The total membership represents households and was multiplied by 1.5 to estimate the number of workers; the land includes the total land of the cooperative; arable land represents 56 percent of this. A number of different estimates for land and labor in the producer cooperatives are available for different years that yield somewhat different averages, but my source seemed the most authoritative estimate. The data for state farms come from Griffin and Hay (1985) and represent twenty-six farms that seem to cover about half the state farm sector. The workers include only permanent workers; and the land is total land area. The ratios are also somewhat misleading because state farms employed about three times as many seasonal as permanent workers (Abate and Kiros, 1980).

Germany, East.   Land is total agricultural land. The labor force on cooperatives includes just the "standing working members." The collectives also include not just the LPGs, but also the KAPs, ZBEs, GPGs, and other secondary forms. The number of workers on state farms is difficult to determine: the "total workers in agriculture" minus the "standing workers in cooperatives" gives a very small number (sometimes negative); the "workers and employees in agriculture and forestry excluding apprentices" gives too large a number. I took the latter data and arbitrarily reduced it by 20 percent to exclude forestry plus some workers in agricultural services who are counted as agricultural workers. The raw data come from: German Democratic Republic, Staatliche Zentralverwaltung für Statistik (annual, 1988, pp. 115, 181–83).

Grenada.   The data come from Pryor (1986, p. 115).

Guyana.   All data come from Thomas (1984). In 1976 (p. 134) there were ten estates and I assume that two years after the nationalization, there were the same number of state farms. In 1978 (p. 40), 126,141 acres of sugar cane were harvested on the estates; two years before (p. 37), the estates owned and rented a total of 171,000 acres (but harvested only 121,628 acres); I assume, therefore, that the total farm area in 1978 was also about 171,000 acres. In 1978 (p. 52), an average of 19,314 employees worked in the fields each week. I have adjusted this datum upwards by 5 percent to include nonfield employees of the state sugar farms.

Hungary. The land data are total farm area. The data on collectives include specialized cooperatives, but exclude cooperative associations, which are not independent. The raw data come from: Central Statistical Office (annual, 1987, pp. 183–85; annual, 1971, p. 211).

Kampuchea. On the basis of scattered evidence, Twining (1989, p. 127) makes an educated guess that a typical collective (commune) had a total population, including nonworkers, of about 2,000. Given the extreme labor mobilization, I estimate the number of workers on a commune to be 1,500 persons.

Korea, North. The farm data come from Chung (1974, pp. 15–17, 33). I assume that the number of workers on the collective in 1961 was the same as in 1963. If the *kun* (county) unit is considered as the basic unit, rather than the individual collective farms, then the average number of workers and amount of land would be (using Chung's estimate of 22 collective farms per kun) 11,440 workers and 10,736 hectares. Taking into account Kim Il-Song's strong statements (for instance, his 1974 speech reported in Kim 1981, p. 156) that the county should be the key decision-making unit and also the fact that the various farms receive large farm equipment from the county as grants, an argument can be made for defining the collective farms on a countywide basis.

Laos. The data for collective farms come from Evans (1988, p. 69) and allegedly include the cultivated area of just full-scale cooperatives. Juhász (1986) has certain similar data for 1984. For state farms I have used the data described in statistical note C, table 4.1, for Laos but must note that various sources of data for state farms are quite contradictory. The Economist Intelligence Unit (1986b) claims that there were forty-four state farms with a total area of 80,000 ha (about 20 percent of total agricultural land), which apparently includes large forest tracts since it is greatly different than other sources. For the early 1980s Stuart-Fox (1986) reports data on fewer state farms, each not much different in size than the cooperative farms; his data are more in line with those I use.

Madagascar. The data come from FAO (1986b). Other data on cooperatives for the late 1970s are presented by Camacho (1982).

Mongolia. The data come from SEV (annual, 1988) and include total agricultural land. Less than one percent of this land is cultivated; the rest is range land. The cultivated lands in these farms are much smaller: according to Mongolia, Central Statistical Board (1981, p. 236) in 1979 they averaged 500 hectares in the communes and 10,300 hectares in the state farms. The state farms also averaged 500 workers in this year.

Mozambique.   The data for collectives are for cultivated land and come from Miech-Chatenay (1986, p. 200); the basic data are relatively rough. For collectives, in 1982, state farms included 200,000 ha, of which 140,000 ha were cultivated; they employed about 140,000 permanent and seasonal workers (Azam and Faucher 1988, pp. 98, 104). Miech-Chatenay (1986, p. 200) claims that in 1986 there were 42 state farms with an average of 1,000 ha and with 150,000 employees, with the difference in size between 1984 and 1986 representing the impact of privatization. Either the figures for size or for employees are incorrect. I have assumed that the size/worker ratio remained the same between 1982 and 1986 and have adjusted her employment datum correspondingly.

Nicaragua.   The data for the collectives come from Medal (1988, p. 36); they refer only to the CAPS (*Cooperativas Agrícolas Sandinistas*) and cover total farm land. The state farm estimates give rise to many more difficulties. In 1984, Medal (1988, p. 38) presents data from which we can estimate these farms covered a total area of about 1,122,100 hectares, a datum I accept. According to Kaimowitz and Stanfield (1985), in the early 1980s, the state farms employed 50,000 workers, of which an unknown fraction was employed in the processing units and mills, rather than agriculture. In 1984 (Thomas and Kaimowitz 1985) this figure had risen to 64,855; I arbitrarily assume that 55,000 worked in agriculture in 1984. According to Kaimowitz and Stanfield, in the early 1980s the state farms were organized into 1,200 UPEs (*Unidad de Producción Estatal*), which were combined into 170 complexes (*complejos*), which in turn were grouped into 27 enterprises (*empresas*). In 1983, the UPEs were further consolidated into 800, each of which consisted of several farms; and by 1984 there were 92 *empresas* (Thomas and Kaimowitz), each of which had financial autonomy. All commentators are agreed that the UPEs were not the key decision-making unit and, for the most part, did not have financial autonomy. Collins (1986) suggests that the *complejo* was the key unit, while the two studies by Kaimowitz and his collaborators suggest that the *empresa* played this role. The latter examined these types of organization questions with much more care than Collins, and I am following their analysis, assuming that there were 92 state farms.

Poland.   The land data are total agricultural land. The number of collectives includes only regular producer cooperatives, and not the Agricultural Circles. I adjusted the state farm labor force data for 1987 to remove the farmers working in state nonagricultural organizations by assuming that such farms had the same labor density as the state farms. The data come from Poland (annual, 1988, pp. 268, 274–75, and 297; and annual, 1977, pp. 41, 214, and 219).

Romania. Of the collectives, just the CAPs are included; land is total farm area. The labor force measurement on collectives includes just full-time cooperators workers. The raw data come from: Direcţía centrală de statistiça (annual, 1986, p. 159; annual, 1984, p. 132).

São Tomé. Data on the fifteen state farms come from interview materials gathered in São Tomé. The land statistic is for total area, of which 44 percent is cultivated.

Seychelles. The data come from various interviews in the Seychelles and include total agricultural land in the farms. For state farms the data cover only the five farms operated by the Seychelles Development Corporation. They exclude the state farms operated by the Island Development Corporation and the one state farm (of 200 ha) operated by Union Estate.

Somalia. The data for cooperatives come from Somalia, State Planning Commission (1979, p. 91) and include only the group farming cooperatives. The land data appear to cover total farm area. The state farm data are an average of thirteen state farms (farms operated by state industrial enterprises and settlement farms are excluded) presented in Boguslawski (1986, pp. 48–49). The data are for total farm area; the total cropped area is roughly 1,357 ha.

Soviet Union. Land includes total farm land. The raw data come from USSR (annual, 1987, pp. 222, 287, 291; annual, 1970, p. 290).

Viet Nam. Land data for 1975 are for North Viet Nam and include only cultivated area. For the collectives the number of workers comes from table 72 (Fforde and Paine 1987, p. 189); the other data from table 71 of the same source. These data differ somewhat from data in other Western sources. For the state farms the data come from Fforde and Paine (1987, pp. 187–89). For 1988 the data come from Viet Nam Ministry of Planning, FAO, and others (1990) and cover cultivated land in both North and South Viet Nam. The data for collectives include both producer co-operatives (HTX) and "primary cooperatives" (TDSK), where the peasants farm individually but the cooperative farm supplies various services.

For producer cooperatives alone the average number of workers was 158 and the average cultivated hectares, 49.3. For state farms I have assumed that the number was unchanged from 1985 and that they comprised 13 percent of total cultivated (rather than arable) land.

Yemen, South.   Data are for cultivable area (actual cultivated area is somewhat smaller) and come from Yemen, Central Statistical Organization (annual, 1988).

Yugoslavia.   Data on the number and size of holdings of cooperative and state farms come from FAO (1986c). Data on the permanent labor force on these farms come from Yugoslavia, Savezni zavod za statistiku (annual, 1982, p. 242).

Zimbabwe.   Cooperative farm data come from Gustafsson (1987); these data vary somewhat from source to source. I am assuming two workers per family. State farm data come from Zimbabwe, Ministry of Finance, Economic Planning and Development (1986) and include only permanent workers, but each farm also employs on an average of 889 temporary workers. Only a small fraction of the land on the state farms is cultivated.

DATA SOURCES FOR TABLES IN CHAPTER 7

THE ESTIMATIONS of the subsidy ratios are rough and are presented so that some idea of orders of magnitude can be gained.

Bulgaria. The data on subsidies in 1988 come from interviews in Sofia.

China. The subsidy data come from China, Ministry of Finance (1989, pp. 88, 146) and the NMP data come from Chinese State Statistical Bureau (1989), p. 51. The subsidy data were reduced by 17.6 percent to remove industrial subsidies not related to agriculture; subsidies include those for grain, cotton, oil, and meat; the industrial subsidies include processing of grain and edible oil.

Czechoslovakia. The data for 1989 come from budget data given to me from interviews in Prague and from tax data supplied by the Ministry of Agriculture and Nutrition.

East Germany. The 1987 data come from German Democratic Republic, Zentralverwaltung für Statistik (1988, p. 264).

Hungary. The estimates are based on 1986 data on subsidies as a percentage of agriculture and food processing from Varga (1990). The ratios in terms of agricultural production alone are calculated from net material product data by sector from United Nations (annual-a, 1989).

Poland. The 1986 data come from World Bank (1989).

Soviet Union. The data for 1986 come from Markish (1989a, 1989b). Data on net material production in agriculture come from U.N. (annual-a, 1989), extrapolated from 1986 to later years by information from the national statistical yearbook.

Statistical Note F

DATA SOURCES FOR TABLES IN CHAPTER 8

Data Problems

THE MEASURE of agricultural output used in the calculations is an index of semigross output; it excludes fodder and certain other inputs provided by the farm sector for its own use. I obtained these series from the FAO data bank; preliminary data are also published for selected years in FAO (annual-b). The input data come from different sources:

For the agricultural *labor force* for all East European nations except Albania (but including Yugoslavia), I use data from Rapawy (1987) and Alton et al. (1988), supplemented by additional information supplied by Gregor Lazarčik. For OECD countries I use data on the economically active in agriculture, forestry, and fishing from OECD (1989b). For the remaining countries (the Third World sample), I use agricultural labor force data from FAO (1989), supplemented by additional information from the FAO data bank. These estimates were extrapolated from 1980 onward and, as a result, leave something to be desired.

Land is measured in terms of total arable land used for annual and permanent crops. In no country did land inputs greatly change over the period. The data come from the FAO data bank and appear in FAO (annual-b).

The *capital stock* is measured in terms of a proxy variable, namely the stock of tractors. Data come from the FAO data bank, which are also published yearly in FAO (annual-b). Certain obvious biases might arise from this approach, so it is useful to compare this series with constant price data on the net capital stock in agriculture for three Western countries for which such data are readily available (OECD 1989a). The results are mixed: the two series for West Germany are quite similar, but for both Greece and the United States, the net capital stock series grew considerably faster than the tractor stock series, which gives an upward bias to the estimation of joint factor productivity. For a number of East European nations, additional problems arise because of a deliberate investment program of substituting larger for smaller tractors; for this reason I use series of the horsepower of the tractor stock from SEV (annual), various years, instead of the stock as measured in numbers. Although the handling of the capital series is far from satisfactory, their relatively small weight in the total factor productivity index reduces the importance of any errors introduced by my estimation methods.

Fertilizer is measured in terms of the combined weight of phosphate, potash, and nitrate fertilizers. This measurement, of course, does not include organic fertilizer. For several of the Third World countries, fertilizer inputs increased tenfold over the period, dominating the entire input index and yielding nonsensical total factor-productivity estimates. In such cases, I took the logarithm of fertilizer inputs as my measurement of this input instead. The data came from the FAO data bank; they are also published in FAO (annual-a).

Livestock is measured by an index using U.S. price weights for ten animals. Since the output index omits fodder and animal feed, it is necessary to include this type of input, which is literally a capital stock indicator for the animal products sector. The data come from the FAO data bank, but are also published in FAO (annual-b).

METHODS OF CALCULATION

Ideally total factor productivity would be calculated from a production function of the five input measures and the measure of output. Because of problems of multicollinearity of some of the inputs, all are strongly related to time, the calculations do not make much sense. For this reason I calculated a Cobb-Douglas input index instead; Wong (1986) faced the same problem and also used this solution.

The choice of weights to combine the five different input indices raises serious problems. Since the prices of inputs in a number of the nations in the sample reflect only a political decision, these cannot be used. Various economists have, however, computed metaproduction functions of the agricultural sector for the entire world, and I have used these as my weights. It is reassuring that these various metaproduction functions, reviewed in Hayami and Ruttan (1985, pp. 144–49), show a rough constancy, so that such a procedure is less arbitrary than it appears at first.[1] More specifically, I have used the following weights for the exponents in the input series: land, 0.05; labor, 0.40; fertilizer, 0.25; machinery, 0.10; and livestock, 0.20.

[1] Wong (1986) calculates a metaproduction function for just nine Marxist regimes (eight in East Europe plus China) for the period from 1950 through 1980 and arrives at the following marginal productivities: land, 0.042; labor, 0.155; fertilizer, 0.239; machinery, 0.173; livestock, 0.391, which he uses in the calculations reported in table SF.1b. For other regression experiments reported in his table 3.1 (p. 37), he arrives at higher marginal productivities for labor and land; lower marginal productivities for fertilizer, machinery, and livestock. My choice of weights from the world metaproduction functions also differs from Wong's weights in these directions.

TABLE SF.1
Growth Rate Data from Other Sources

SF.1a: Comparisons of Average Annual Growth Rates from Different Sources

| | 1970–80 | | | | 1970–86 | | | |
| | SAO | | TFP | | SAO | | TFP | |
	Pryor	Wong	Wong	Lazarcik	Pryor	USDA	Pryor	Lazarcik
Bulgaria	1.8%	1.5%	-0.6%	1.1%	1.6%	1.8%	1.3	0.6%
Czechoslovakia	2.2	2.1	0.9	0.6	2.3	1.9	1.9	0.1
East Germany	2.2	2.1	1.8	0.5	2.0	1.7	1.7	0.3
Hungary	2.9	3.3	2.1	0.7	2.4	2.8	1.8	0.6
Poland	1.4	0.6	-2.3	-0.8	1.0	0.0	-0.1	-0.9
Yugoslavia	2.7	3.2	0.8	3.4	2.1	2.0	3.0	3.4
USSR	1.3	1.4	-1.3		1.1	1.0		
China	3.0	4.4	-3.2		4.1	5.0		

SF.1b: Coefficients of Determination between the Various Series

Variable	Comparison	1970–80	1970–86
SAO	Pryor-Wong	0.86	—
SAO	Pryor-USDA	—	0.94
TFP	Pryor-Wong	0.76	—
TFP	Pryor-Lazarcik	0.81	0.75
TFP	Wong-Lazarcik	0.15	—

Source: USDA data either supplied by this organization or presented in USDA (1988).

Notes: All growth rates are calculated by fitting an exponential curve to each series.

SAO = Semi-gross agricultural output, i.e., all agricultural products except those used in agricultural production (e.g., fodder).

TFP = Total factor productivity.

USDA = United States Department of Agriculture.

The Wong output data (1986, pp. 67, 130) are based on USDA data plus his own price weights. His input data come from a variety of sources. The Lazarcik data (1989, p. 272) are calculated from a Cobb-Douglas type production function with two independent variables and with net agricultural output as the dependent variable and with two independent variables, labor and a nonlabor input series, where all of these inputs are aggregated using an arithmetic index and adjusted factor prices as weights.

Comparisons with Other Estimations

Various other estimations yield somewhat different results, as shown in tables SF.1a and SF.1b. What is important, however, is the degree to which they are correlated, since the statistical tests reported in the text are for differences, not absolute levels.

For the output series, the results for the three sources are highly correlated, as revealed by the high coefficients of determination. For TFP, as expected, the various estimations are more divergent. What is curious is that my own estimates are relatively highly correlated with both the estimates of Lazarcik and Wong, although these two estimates are not very strongly correlated with each other. Insofar as any of the results reflect reality, such comparisons give some grounds of confidence in my estimates.

DATA SOURCES FOR TABLES IN RESEARCH NOTE B

TABLE RB.1, UNITED STATES

The definition of farm has varied from census to census; for comparability I have eliminated all "agricultural places" of less than 3 acres (1.2 hectares). For 1880 and 1930, all agricultural places larger than this area are included, irrespective of farm sales; for 1982 only agricultural places with sales of at least $1,000 of agricultural produce are included.

The census data for 1880 contain only the number of farms in each farm size; the averages for each size group for the region are taken from the 1900 census of agriculture (the first agricultural census to contain this information). For the share of land in the five percent of largest farms, an arithmetic interpolation of the cumulative size distribution was used; this procedure proved satisfactory except for the Mountain region for 1982, where the largest 16.6 percent of farms covered 86.2 percent of the land.

The data come from: Census Office (1883 and 1902), and U.S. Bureau of the Census (1932 and 1985).

TABLE RB.2, OTHER COUNTRIES

Unless otherwise specified, the data come from International Institute of Agriculture (1939) and FAO (1983–87).

Austria. For 1980 I have excluded lands owned by the government; if such lands are included, the data show a slight increase in average farm size between 1929 and 1980, but the other statistics yield roughly the same conclusions.

Belgium. The cutoff for farms is 1 hectare. The estimates for 1846 and 1895 are rough and average farm sizes are estimated from midpoints. The original data come from Commission centrale de statistique (n.d.) and Commission génerale de la Belgique (1914).

Canada. The cutoff for 1929 is 5 acres, and for 1981, 4 acres. Given the manner in which "farms" are defined, this makes little difference.

Denmark. Problems of comparability occur because the basic choice of measured unit appears somewhat different. The 1979 data refer to agricultural land, the 1929 data refer to cultivated land, and the exact reference for the 1901 data is not clear. The cutoff point for all three years is 1.7 hectares. The 1901 data come from Denmark, Statens Statistiske Bureau (1911).

England and Wales. The 1875 and 1966 data come from United Kingdom, Ministry of Agriculture, Fisheries and Food (1968); the lower limit of farm included was not clearly specified. The 1930 data come from International Institute of Agriculture (1939); the lower limit is 1 acre. The area included is crop and grassland.

Finland. The data are classified and measured in terms of arable land. The distribution of total land is considerably more equal.

France. The 1978/79 data are classified by agricultural area, the 1929 data refer to agricultural land, and the 1882 data refer to "exploitations agraires" and apparently measure total land. These differences should not greatly affect comparability. The cutoff point for all three years is 1 hectare. The 1882 data come from France, Ministère de l'agriculture (1887, pp. 280–81).

Germany. The data come from Germany, Kaiserliches statistisches Amt (1898, p. 11). Because the boundaries of the administrative areas in Germany changed considerably between the late nineteenth century and the present, it did not prove feasible to adjust these data to fit the current boundaries of West Germany.

Italy. Farm sizes have a 1 hectare cutoff.

Japan. In both years arable land (total land excluding land under permanent crops and land under permanent meadows and pastures) is used. The farm sizes have a 0.5 hectare cutoff.

Netherlands. Farm sizes have a 1 hectare cutoff. There was a change in the definition in farm size after 1970 and it is unclear how this affects comparability. The 1886 data may be incomplete since my estimate for total agricultural land appears low. Data for 1886 come from Netherlands, Commission centrale de statistique (1897).

New Zealand.   The 1980 world census of agriculture computer printout did not give the date for the "1980" New Zealand agricultural census. For 1930 the cutoff limit is 1 acre; for 1980 it is not specified.

Norway.   The 1929 data refer to arable lands plus meadows; the 1979 data, to agricultural lands. This difference should not greatly influence comparability.

Puerto Rico.   For 1930 the cutoff limit is under 3 acres; for 1978 the cutoff point covers holdings with sales over $1,200.

Sweden.   The data are classified and the farm size is measured by arable hectares.

Switzerland.   The cutoff point is 1 hectare. The data for 1929 are classified by productive area; the data for 1980, by cultivated area. Farm size for both years is measured in terms of productive (agricultural) area. The handling of common pasture land is unclear, although in many places such "common" pastures are held by a cooperative-corporation. The data for 1929 exclude "summer holdings," while the data for 1980 include such land. Such holdings are sufficiently small that the results should not be greatly influenced.

BIBLIOGRAPHY

Abate, Alula, and Fassil G. Kiros. 1980. *Land Reform, Structural Change and Rural Development in Ethiopia.* Discussion Paper 7, Institute of Development Economics. Addis Ababa.

Abegaz, Haile Yesus. 1982. *The Organization of State Farms in Ethiopia after the Land Reform of 1975.* Saarbrücken: Breitenbach, 1982.

Abramov, Fyodor. 1963. *One Day in the 'New Life'.* Translated by David Floyd. New York: Praeger.

Afghanistan. Central Statistical Office. 1980. *Statistical Yearbook 1357 (March 1978–March 1979).* Kabul.

———. 1983. *Statistical Yearbook 1360 (March 1981–March 1982).* Kabul.

Aganbegyan, Abel. 1989. *Inside Perestroika: The Future of the Soviet Economy.* New York: Harper and Row.

Albania. Drejtoria e Statistikës. Annual. *Vjetari Statistikor i R.P.Sh.* Tirana.

———. 1984. *40 Vjet Shqipëri Socialiste.* Tirana.

Allcock, John. 1981. "The Collectivization of Yugoslav Agriculture and the Myth of Peasant Resistance." Bradford, West Yorkshire: Postgraduate School of Yugoslav Studies, University of Bradford.

Algeria. Ministére de la Planification et de l'Aménagement du Territoire. 1981. *Annuaire statistique de la Algerie.* Algiers.

Alkhomov, P. G., and V. I. Gusarov. 1976. *Ekonomika narodnoi demokraticheskoi respublik Iemen.* Moscow: Nauka.

Allen, Chris, Joan Baxter, Michael S. Radu, and Keith Somerville. 1989. *Bénin, the Congo, and Burkina Faso: Politics, Economics and Society.* New York: Pinter Publisher.

Almeyra, Guillermo. 1983. "Agrokombinats at the Crossroads." *CERES* 16 (July–August): 27–33.

Alton, Thad P., et al. 1988. *Agricultural Output, Expenses and Depreciation, Gross Product and Net Product in Eastern Europe, 1976–1986.* Occasional Paper 96, Research Project on National Income in East Central Europe. New York: L.W. International Financial Research.

———. 1989a. *Agricultural Output, Expenses and Depreciation, Gross Product, and Net Product in Eastern Europe, 1975–1988.* Occasional Paper 106, Research Project on National Income in East Central Europe. New York: L.W. International Financial Research.

———. 1989b. *Money Income of the Population and Standard of Living in Eastern Europe, 1970–1988.* Occasional Paper 108, Research Project on National Income in East Central Europe. New York: L.W. International Financial Research.

Aly, Hassan, et al. "The Technical Efficiency of Illinois Grain Farms: An Application of a Ray-Homothetic Production Function." *Southern Journal of Agricultural Economics* 19 (July 1987): 69–78.

American Rural Small-Scale Industry Delegation. 1977. *Rural Small-Scale Industry in the People's Republic of China*. Berkeley: University of California Press.

Ames, Edward. 1965. *Soviet Economic Processes*. Homewood, Ill.: Irwin, 1965.

Amstutz, J. Bruce. 1986. *Afghanistan: The First Five Years of Soviet Occupation*.
Washington, D.C.: National Defense University.

Anon. 1981. "India Survey." *The Economist* 278, no. 7178 (March 28).

Anon. 1988. "Communique." *World Marxist Review* 31, no. 6 (June): 5–6.

Anon. 1990. "East European Farming: No Yeomen They." *The Economist* 316,
no. 7664 (July 21).

Antal, Endre. 1983. "Die Preisgestaltung in Nährungsgütersektor Ungarns." In
Armin Bohnet and Eberhard Schinke, eds. *Preise in Sozialismus: Kontinuität
im Wandel*. Vol. 1. Berlin: Duncker and Humblot.

———. 1985. "Das ungarische Agrarpreise." *Osteuropa Wirtschaft* 30, no. 1
(March): 1–25.

Anwar, Raja. 1988. *The Tragedy of Afghanistan: A First-Hand Account*. London:
Verso.

Arbeitsgemeinschaft deutscher Landwirte und Beamten. 1955. *Weissbuch über
die "Demokratische Bodenreform."* Hanover.

Argyres, Andreas. 1988. "Peasant Production, State Articulation and Competing
Rationalities: The Collective Economy of Rural Romania." Ph.D. diss., University of California, Davis.

Arnold, Anthony. 1983. *Two Party Communism*. Stanford: Stanford University
Press.

Ash, Robert F. 1988. "The Evolution of Agricultural Policy." *China Quarterly*
116 (December): 529–56.

Åslund, Anders. 1989. *Gorbachev's Struggle for Economic Reform*. Ithaca, N.Y.:
Cornell University Press.

Association de la maison de l'Afrique. 1986. *Rencôntres africains: Dossier Congo*.
Paris.

Aston, T. H., and C.H.E. Philpin. 1987. *The Brenner Debate: Agrarian Class
Structure and Economic Development in Pre-Industrial Europe*. Cambridge:
Cambridge University Press.

Aubert, Claude. 1988. "The New Economic Policy in the Chinese Countryside."
In Brada and Wädekin, eds. (1988), 271–97.

Austin, James, and Joch C. Ickis. 1986. "Management, Managers and Revolution." *World Development* 14, no. 7 (July): 775–90.

Azam, J. P., and J. J. Faucher. 1988. "The Case of Mozambique." In J. C. Berthélemy et al. (1988).

Bachman, Kenneth L., and Raymond P. Christensen. 1967. "The Economics of
Farm Size." In Herman M. Southworth and Bruce F. Johnston, *Agricultural
Development and Economic Growth*. Ithaca, N.Y.: Cornell University Press,
234–57.

Bajaja, Vladislav. 1975. *Theoretische Grundlagen und praktische Entwicklung
landwirtschaftlicher Betriebsgrössen in der Tschechoslowakei*. Berlin:
Duncker and Humblot.

————. 1978. *Organisation und Führung landwirtschaftlicher Grossunternehmen in der DDR*. Berlin: Duncker and Humblot.

Ball, A. Gordon, and Earl O. Heady, eds. 1972. *Size, Structure, and Future of Farms*. Ames: Iowa State University Press.

Banister, Judith. 1987. *China's Changing Population*. Stanford: Stanford University Press.

Bates, Robert. 1981. *Markets and States in Tropical Africa*. Berkeley: University of California Press.

Batt, Judy. 1988. *Economic Reform and Political Change in Eastern Europe*. London: Macmillan, 1988.

Baum, Philip. 1986. "Modernization and Legal Reform in Post-Mao China: The Rebirth of Socialist Legality." *Studies in Comparative Communism* 19, no. 2 (Summer 1986): 69–105.

Baumol, William. 1967. *Business Behavior, Value and Growth*. Rev. ed. New York: Harcourt, Brace and World.

Becker, Joachim. 1988. *Angola, Mosambik und Zimbabwe: Im Visier Südafrikas*. Cologne: Pahl Rugenstein.

Bekker, Alexander. 1989. "How They Stamped Out a Farmer's Coop." *Moscow News* 3380, no. 28 (July 16–23): 9.

Belgium. Commission centrale de statistique. N.d. *Exposé de la situation du Royaume, 1861–1875*. Brussels: Th. Lesigne.

Belgium. Commission génerale de la Belgique. 1914. *Exposé de la situation du Royaume de 1876 à 1900*. Brussels: George Piquart.

Bell, Peter D. 1984. *Peasants in Socialist Transition: Life in a Collectivized Hungarian Village*. Berkeley: University of California Press.

Benewick, Robert, and Paul Wingrove, eds. 1988. *Reforming the Revolution*. London: Macmillan.

Bénin. Ministère du Plan, de la Statistique et de l'Analyse Economique. 1982. *Enquête sur le machinisme agricole*. Cotonou.

————. 1983. *Recensement general de la population et de l'habitation*. Vol. 2, *Resultats definitifs*. Cotonou.

Beresford, Melanie. 1988. *Vietnam: Politics, Economics and Society*. London: Pinter.

————. 1989. *National Unification and Economic Development*. New York: St. Martin's Press.

Bernardo, Robert M. 1971. *The Theory of Moral Incentives in Cuba*. University, Alabama: University of Alabama Press, 1971.

Bernstein, Thomas Paul. 1970. "Leadership and Mobilization in the Collectivization of Agriculture in China and Russia: A Comparison." Ph.D. diss., Columbia University.

————. 1979. "The State and Collective Farming in the Soviet Union and China." In Raymond F. Hopkins and others, eds. *Food, Politics, and Agricultural Development: Case Studies in the Public Policy of Rural Modernization*. Boulder, Colo.: Westview, 73–107.

————. 1984. "Reforming China's Agriculture." Paper presented at conference, "To Reform the Chinese Political Order" (June).

Bernstein, Thomas Paul. Forthcoming. "Ideology and Rural Reform: The Paradox of Contingent Stability." In *China's Rural Reforms: Ideological and Political Constraints*. Armonk, N.Y.: M. E. Sharpe.

Berthélemy, J. C., J. P. Azam, and J. J. Faucher. 1988. *The Supply of Manufactured Goods and Agricultural Development*. Paris: OECD, 1988.

Bertrand, Hughes. 1975. *Le Congo: Formation sociale et mode de développement économique*. Paris: Maspero.

Bhagavan, M. R. 1986. *Angola's Political Economy 1975–1985*. Research Report No. 75. Uppsala: Scandinavian Institute of African Studies.

Binkert, Gregor H. 1983. "Agricultural Production and Economic Incentives: Food Policy in Mozambique." Discussion Paper 154, Harvard Institute for International Development. Cambridge, Mass.

Binswanger, Hans P., and John McIntire. 1987. "Behavioral and Material Determinants of Production Relations in Land-abundant Tropical Agriculture." *Economic Development and Cultural Change* 36, no. 1 (October): 73–101.

Binswanger, Hans P., and Mark Rosenzweig. 1984. "Contractual Arrangements, Employment, and Wages in Rural Labor Markets: A Critical Review." In Binswanger and Rosenzweig, eds., 1–41. *Contractual Arrangements, Employment, and Wages in Rural Labor Markets in Asia*. New Haven: Yale University Press.

———. 1986. "Behavioral and Material Determinants of Production Relations in Agriculture." *Journal of Development Studies* 22, no. 2 (April): 503–40.

Binswanger, Hans P., and Vernon W. Ruttan, eds. 1978. *Induced Innovation: Technology, Institutions, and Development*. Baltimore: Johns Hopkins University Press.

Birman, Igor. 1990. "The Budget Gap, Excess Money and Reform." *Communist Economies* 2, no. 1: 25–47.

Blecher, Marc. 1988. "The Reorganization of the Countryside." In Benewick and Wingrove (1988), 91–108.

Boguslawski, Michael von. 1987. "The Crop Production of Somalis." In Conje and Labahn (1986), 23–55.

Bohnet, Armin, and Günter Jaehne. 1990. "Chinas Weg am Amfang der 90er Jahre." *Berichte Nr. 6, Justus-Liebig Universität*. March.

Boikov, V. 1989. "Khoziaistvennaia reforma v plenu otchuzhdeniia." *Ekonomika i Organizatsiia Promyshlennogo Proizvodstva*, no. 3: 3–19.

Bonin, John. 1977. "Work Incentives and Uncertainty on a Collective Farm." *Journal of Comparative Economics* 1, no. 1 (March): 77–99.

Bonin, John P., and Waturu Fukuda. 1987. "Controlling a Risk-Averse, Effort-Selecting Manager in the Soviet Incentive Model," *Journal of Comparative Economics* 11, no. 2 (June): 221–33.

Booth, John A. 1987. *The End and the Beginning: The Nicaragua Revolution*. Boulder, Colo.: Westview.

Boyd, Michael L. 1984. "The Comparative Performance of Social and Private Agricultural Organization: The Case of Postwar Yugoslav Agriculture." Ph.D. diss., Stanford University.

———. 1987. "The Performance of Private and Cooperative Socialist Organization: Postwar Yugoslav Agriculture." *Review of Economics and Statistics* 69, no. 2 (May): 205–14.

———. 1988. "The Performance of Private and Socialist Agriculture in Poland: The Effects of Policy and Organization." *Journal of Comparative Economics* 12, no. 1 (March): 61–73.

Brada, Josef C. 1986. "The Variability of Crop Production in Private and Socialized Agriculture: Evidence from Eastern Europe." *Journal of Political Economy* 93, no. 3 (June): 543–63.

Brada, Josef C., Jeanne C. Hey, and Arthur E. King. 1988. "Inter-regional and Inter-organizational Differences in Agricultural Efficiency in Czechoslovakia." In Brada and Wädekin, eds. (1988), 334–43.

Brada, Josef C., and Arthur E. King. 1989. "Is Private Farming More Efficient than Socialized Agriculture?" Unpublished paper.

Brada, Josef C., and Karl-Eugen Wädekin, eds. 1988. *Socialist Agriculture in Transition: Organizational Response to Failing Performance.* Boulder, Colo.: Westview.

Bradley, Michael E. 1971. "Incentives and Labour Supply on Soviet Collective Farms." *Canadian Journal of Economics* 4, no. 3 (August): 342–52.

Bradley, Michael E. 1973. "Incentives and Labour Supply on Soviet Collective Farms: Reply." *Canadian Journal of Economics* 6, no. 3 (August 1973): 438–42.

Bratton, Michael. 1987. "The Comrades and the Countryside: The Politics of Agricultural Policy in Zimbabwe." *World Politics* 39, no. 2 (January): 174–203.

Braverman, Avishay, Karen Brooks, and Csaba Csáki, eds. Forthcoming 1991. *Agricultural Reform in Eastern Europe and the USSR: Dilemmas and Strategies.* Washington, D.C.: World Bank.

Braverman, Avishay, and J. Luis Guasch. 1991, forthcoming. "Agricultural Reform in Developing Countries: Reflections for Eastern Europe." *American Journal of Agricultural Economics.*

Bridger, Susan. 1987. *Women in the Soviet Countryside.* Cambridge: Cambridge University Press.

Brooks, Karen. 1983. "Productivity in Soviet Agriculture." In Johnson and Brooks (1983), 117–195.

———. 1990a. "Agriculture and Five Years of Perestroika." Staff Paper P90-12, Department of Agricultural and Applied Economics. University of Minnesota.

———. 1990b. "Lease Contracting in Soviet Agriculture in 1989." *Comparative Economic Studies* 32, no. 2 (Summer): 85–109.

———. 1990c. "Soviet Agricultural Policy and Pricing under Gorbachev." In Gray, ed. (1990), 116–30.

———. 1991. "Property Rights in Land and the Transition to Post-Collectivist Agriculture in Eastern Europe and the USSR." In Braverman, Brooks, and Czáki (1991).

Brown, Albert L. 1988. "An Overview of the Eastern Caribbean Agricultural Sector," Contract research for U.S. Agency for International Development. Washington, D.C.: Chemonics International Consulting.

Brown, MacAlister, and Joseph J. Zasloff. 1986. *Apprentice Revolutionaries*. Stanford: Hoover Institution Press.

Buck, John Lossing. 1956. *Land Utilization in China*. New York: Council on Economic and Cultural Affairs.

Bujra, Abdalla S. 1971. *The Politics of Stratification: A Study of Political Change in a South Arabian Town*. Oxford: Clarendon Press.

Bulbeck, C. 1984. "Socialism in the Seychelles." *Australian Outlook* 38, no. 1 (April): 40–44.

Bulgaria. Direction Général de la Statistique. 1941. *Annuaire Statistique du Royaume de Bulgarie*. Vol. 33. Sofia.

Bulgaria. Tsentralno statistichesko upravlenie. Annual. *Statischeski godishnik*. Sofia.

————. 1968. *Rezultati ot prebroyavane na naselenieto n 1.xii.1965 g*. Vol. 1, part 1. Sofia.

Bulmer-Thomas, Victor. 1987. *The Political Economy of Central America Since 1920*. Cambridge: Cambridge University Press.

Busek, Vratislav, and Nicolas Spulber, eds. 1957. *Czechoslovakia*. New York: Praeger.

Burns, John P. 1985/6. "Local Cadre Accommodation to the 'Responsibility System' in Rural China." *Pacific Affairs* 58, no. 4 (Winter): 607–25.

Busch-Zantner, Richard. 1939. *Albanien: Neues Land im Imperium*. Leipzig: Goldmann Verlag.

Butterfield, Jim. 1990. "Devolution in Decision-Making and Organizational Change in Soviet Agriculture." *Comparative Economic Studies* 32, no. 2 (Summer): 29–65.

Byrd, William A., and Lin Qingsong, eds. 1990. *China's Rural Industry: Structure, Development, and Reform*. Washington, D.C.: World Bank.

Caballero, Laurenzo, et al. 1987. *The Guinea-Bissau: A Study of the Land and Agricultural Sector*. Uppsala: International Rural Development Centre, Swedish University of Agricultural Science.

Cabral, Luís. 1979. *Strategy in Guinea-Bissau*. London: Mozambique, Angola and Guiné Information Center.

Calomiris, Charles W. 1991. "Government Policies to Improve Agricultural Capital Markets." In Braverman et al. (forthcoming 1991).

Camacho, Martin. 1982. "Bilan de la politique de coopérativisation de l'agriculture, 1976–1980." *Terre malgache/Tany malagasy* 21 (August): 155–81.

Cambodia. Institut national de la statistique et des recherches économiques. N.d. *Resultats finals du recensement géneral de la population 1962*. Phnom Penh.

Cape Verde. Dirrecção Geral de Estatística. N.d. *Boletin Anual de Estatística, 1987*. Praia.

Cape Verde. Ministério do Plano e da Cooperaçao. 1986. *Il Plano Nacional de Desenvolvimento, 1986–1990*. Praia.

Cape Verde. Secretaria des Estado da Cooperação e Planeamente. 1983. *Iº Recenseamento Geral da Populacão e Habitação–1980*. Praia.

Cardenal Chamorro, Roberto. 1988. *Lo que se quiso ocultar: ocho años de censura sandinista*. San José, Costa Rica: Asociacion Libro Libre.

Caricom. N.d. *Population Census of the Commonwealth Caribbean: Guyana*. Kingston, Jamaica: Printing Unit, Statistical Institute of Jamaica.

Carr, Edward Hallett. 1952. *The Bolshevik Revolution*. Vol. 2. New York: Macmillan.

Carr, E. H., and R. W. Davies. 1969. *Foundations of a Planned Economy, 1926–1929*, Vol. 1, part 2. New York: Macmillan.

Centre Tricontinental. 1981. *La reorganisation de l'agriculture en Angola comme phase de la transition*. Ottignies and Louvain-la-Neuve, Belgium.

Chabal, Patrick. 1983. *Amílcar Cabral: Revolutionary Leadership and People's War*. Cambridge: Cambridge University Press.

Chan, Anita, Richard Madsen, and Jonathan Unger. 1984. *Chen Village: The Recent History of a Peasant Community in Mao's China*. Berkeley: University of California Press.

Chavunduka, Gordon L. 1982. *Report of the Commission of Inquiry into the Agricultural Industry*. Harare, Zimbabwe.

Chayanov, A. V. 1966. *The Theory of Peasant Economy*. Edited by Daniel Thorner et al. Homewood, Ill.: Richard D. Irwin.

Cheng, Chu-Yuan. 1963. *Communist China's Economy, 1949–1962: Structural Changes and Crisis*. South Orange, N.J.: Seton Hall University Press.

Cheung, Steven N. S. 1969. *The Theory of Share Tenancy*. Chicago: University of Chicago Press.

Chevrier, Yves. 1988. "NEP and Beyond: The Transition to 'Modernization' in China (1978–85)." In Feuchtwang, Hussain, and Pairault (1988), 7–30.

Chiliard, Gérard. 1982. *Report from Afghanistan*. New York: Viking.

China. 1987. *China Agriculture Yearbook 1987*. Beijing: Agriculture Publishing House.

China. Ministry of Finance. 1989. *Chinese Financial Statistics, 1950–1988 (Zhongguo Caizheng Tongji, 1950–1988)*. Beijing: China Financial and Economic Publishing House.

China. State Statistical Bureau. 1981. *Statistical Yearbook of China*. Hong Kong: Economic Information and Agency.

———. 1988. *Statistical Yearbook of China*. London: Longman.

———. 1989. *Statistical Yearbook of China*. Beijing: Chinese Statistical Press.

Chinn, Dennis L. 1980. "Diligence and Laziness in Chinese Agricultural Production Teams." *Journal of Development Economics* 7, no. 3 (September): 331–45.

Chitsike, Langford T. 1988. *Agricultural Co-operative Development in Zimbabwe*. Harare: Zimbabwe Foundation for Education with Production.

Chung, Joseph Sang-hoon. 1974. *The North Korean Economy*. Stanford: Hoover Institution Press.

Churchill, Winston S. 1950. *The Hinge of Fate*. Boston: Houghton Mifflin.

Cigar, Norman. 1985. "State and Society in North Yemen." *Problems of Communism* 34 (May–June): 41–59.

Cima, Ronald J. 1989a. "Viet Nam in 1988: The Brink of Renewal." *Asian Survey* 29, no. 1 (January): 64–72.

Cima, Ronald J. 1989b. "Viet Nam's Economic Reforms: Approaching the 1990s." *Asian Survey* 29, no. 8 (August).

Clapham, Christopher. 1988. *Transformation and Continuity in Revolutionary Ethiopia*. Cambridge: Cambridge University Press.

Clarke, Christopher M. 1987. "Changing the Context for Policy Implementation: Organizational and Personnel Reform in Post-Mao China." In Lampton, ed. (1987), 25–47.

Clay, Jason W., and Bonnie K. Holcomb. 1986. *Politics and the Ethiopian Famine, 1984–1985*. Cambridge, Mass.: Cultural Survival.

Clayton, Elizabeth. 1971. "Productivity in Soviet Agriculture: A Sectoral Comparison." In Hans Raupach, ed., *Jahrbuch der Wirtschaft Osteuropas*. Vol. 2. Munich: Olzog Verlag: 315–29.

———. 1976. "Price, Appropriability and the Soviet Agricultural Incentives." In Thornton (1976), 255–66.

Cliffe, Lionel. 1986. *Policy Options for Agrarian Reform in Zimbabwe: A Technical Appraisal*. Harare: Paper submitted to FAP and Government of Zimbabwe.

Clines, Francis X. 1990. "Russian Republic Backs Private Farm Plan but Rejects Private Sale of Land." *New York Times*, 4 December.

CMEA. *See* Council of Mutual Economic Assistance.

Cochrane, Nancy J. 1988a. "East European Private Agriculture." *Problems of Communism* 37, no. 2 (March–April): 47–54.

———. 1988b. "Economic Reform and the Private Sector in Poland." *RSEEA, Newsletter for Research on Soviet and East European Agriculture* 10, no. 3 (September): 1–2.

———. 1989. *Agricultural Statistics of Eastern Europe and the Soviet Union, 1965–85*. Statistical Bulletin no. 778, U.S. Department of Agriculture, Economic Research Service. Washington, D.C.: Government Printing Office.

———. 1990. "Republic and Provincial Barriers in Yugoslav Agricultural Marketing." Forthcoming.

Cohen, John M. 1984. "Agrarian Reform in Ethiopia: The Situation on the Eve of the Revolution's 10th Anniversary." Discussion Paper 164. Cambridge, Mass.: Harvard Institute of International Development.

———. 1986. *Integrated Rural Development in Ethiopia: CADU after 1974*. Paper 228, April. Cambridge, Mass.: Harvard Institute for International Development.

Cohen, John M., and Nils-Ivar Isaksson. 1987a. "Food Production Strategy Debates in Revolutionary Ethiopia." Discussion Paper 255. Cambridge, Mass.: Harvard Institute of International Development.

———. 1987b. "Villagisation in Ethiopia's Arsi Region." *Journal of Modern African Studies* 25, no. 3 (September): 435–65.

Colburn, Forest D. 1986. *Post-Revolutionary Nicaragua: State, Class, and the Dilemmas of Agrarian Policies*. Berkeley: University of California Press.

Collender, Robert, and Edward Cook. 1990. "Agriculture is Thwarting Soviet Economic Reform," *Newsletter for RSEEA (Research on Soviet and East European Agriculture)* 12, no. 4 (December 1990): 8–9.

Collins, Joseph, et al. 1986. *What Difference Could a Revolution Make?* 2d ed. San Francisco: Institute for Food and Development Policy.

Comisso, Ellen, and Paul Marer. 1986. "The Economics and Politics of Reform in Hungary." *International Organization* 40, no. 2 (Spring): 421–54.

Commonwealth Advisory Group. 1989. *Guyana: Economic Recovery Programme and Beyond.* Alister McIntyre Report. Georgetown. Mimeo.

Congo. Centre national de la statistique et des études économique. 1978. *Recensement general du Congo 1974.* Vol. 4. Brazzaville.

Congo. Ministère de l'agriculture et de l'élevage. 1983. *Agriculture congolaise 1982: Faits et chiffres.* Brazzaville..

Congo. Ministère du plan. 1980. *Annuaire statistique 1980.* Brazzaville.

Conje, Peter, and Thomas Labahn, eds. 1986. *Somalia: Agriculture in the Winds of Change,* EPI Documentation no. 2. Saarbrücken.

Conquest, Robert. 1987. *Harvest of Sorrow.* New York: Oxford University Press.

Cook, Edward C. 1989. "Deriving Soviet Agricultural Producer Prices." *RSEEA, Newsletter for Research on Soviet and East European Agriculture* 11, no. 1 (March): 9–11.

Cook, Edward, William M. Liefert and Robert Koopman. 1990. "Government Intervention in Soviet Agriculture: Estimate of Consumer and Producer Subsidy Equivalents." Agriculture and Trade Analysis Division, Economic Research Service, U.S. Department of Agriculture. Unpublished paper.

Cornia, Giovanni Andrea. 1985. "Farm Size, Land Yield and the Agricultural Production Function: An Analysis for Fifteen Developing Countries." *World Development* 13, no. 4 (April): 513–34.

Council of Mutual Economic Assistance, Secretariat (CMEA). *Statistical Yearbook, 1979.* London: IPC Industrial Press, 1979.

Cox, Terry. 1986. *Peasant, Class and Capitalism: The Rural Research of L.N. Kritsman and His School.* Oxford: Clarendon Press.

Crook, Frederic W. 1970. "An Analysis of Work-Payment Systems Used in Chinese Mainland Agriculture, 1956–1970." Ph.D. diss., Fletcher School of Law and Diplomacy.

————. 1975. "The Commune System in the People's Republic of China, 1963–74." U.S. Congress, Joint Economic Committee. *China: A Reassessment of the Economy.* Washington, D.C.: Government Printing Office: 366–410.

Croll, Elizabeth. 1988. "The New Peasant Economy in China." In Feuchtwang, Hussain, and Pairault (1988), 77–100.

Crosnier, Marie-Agnès, and Edith Lhomel. 1987. "Viet Nam: Les mécomptes d'un socialisme asiatique." *Le courrier des pays de l'est* 320 (July–August): 3–45.

Csáki, Csaba, and Gyula Varga. 1991. "Problems and Reforms in Hungarian Agriculture." In Braverman, Brooks, and Csáki (forthcoming 1991).

Csikós-Nagy, Béla. 1969. "The New Hungarian Price System." In Friss, ed. (1969), 133–62.

Csizmadia, Ernö. 1983. "New Features of the Enterprise Structure in the Hungarian Agriculture and Food Industry." *Acta Oeconomica* 31, nos. 3–4: 225–240.

Csizmadia, Ernö. 1985. "Recent Experiences of Cooperative Farming in Hungary." *Acta Oeconomica* 34, nos. 1–2: 1–12.

Csizmadia, Ernö, and Magda Szíkely. 1986. *Food Economy in Hungary.* Budapest: Akademiai Kiadó.

Cuba. Comité Estatal de Estadísticas. Annual. *Anuario Estadístico.* Havana.

———. 1984. *Censo de Población y Viviendas, 1981.* Vol. 16. Havana.

Cuba. Ministerio de Agricultura. 1951. *Memoria del Censu Agrícola Nacional 1946.* Havana: Fernandez y Cia.

Čuba, František, and Emil Divila. 1989. *Cesty k prosperitě: JZD Agrokombinát Slušovice.* Prague: Nakladatelství Svoboda.

Czechoslovakia. Office de Statistique. 1936. *Recensement de exploitation agricoles: La Statistique Tchéchoslovaque.* Tome 3, partie 4. Prague.

Czechoslovakia. Federální Statistický úrad. Annual. *Statistiká Rocenka.* Prague: SNTL, ALPA.

Danilov, V. P. 1988. *Rural Russia Under the New Regime,* trans. Orlando Figes. Bloomington: Indiana University Press.

David, Eduard. 1903. *Socialismus und Landwirtschaft.* Berlin: Verlag der Socialistischen Monatshefte.

David, Paul A. 1971. "The Landscape and the Machine: Technological Interrelatedness, Land Tenure and the Mechanization of the Corn Harvest in Victorian Britain." In Donald N. McCloskey, ed. *Essays on a Mature Economy: Britain after 1840.* London: Methuen, 145–215.

———. 1975. *Technical Choice, Innovation, and Economic Growth.* New York: Cambridge University Press.

———. 1985. "Clio and the Economics of QWERTY." *American Economic Review* 75, no. 2 (May): 332–37.

———. 1988. "Path Dependence: Putting the Past in Economics." Technical Report 533, Institute for Mathematical Studies in the Social Sciences (November).

———. 1989. "A Paradigm for Historical Economics: Path Dependence and Predictability in Dynamic Systems with Local Network Externalities." Stanford University, Center for Economic Policy Research. Unpublished paper.

Davidova, Sofia. 1991. "Agricultural Policy in Bulgaria: A View from the Inside." In a forthcoming collection. Edited by Karl-Eugen Wädekin.

Davidson, Basil. 1981. *No Fist is Big Enough to Hide the Sky: The Liberation of Guinea-Bissau and Cape Verde.* London: Zed Books.

Davidson, Jean, ed. 1988a. *Agriculture, Women, and Land: The African Experience.* Boulder, Colo.: Westview.

Davidson, Jean. 1988b. "Land Redistribution in Mozambique and Its Effects on Women's Collective Production: Case Studies from Sofala Province." In Davidson (1988a), 228–50.

Decalo, Samuel. 1985. "Socio-Economic Constraints on Radical Action in the People's Republic of Congo." *The Journal of Communist Studies* 1, nos. 3–4 (1985): 39–57.

———. 1987. *Historical Dictionary of Benin.* 2d ed. Metuchen, N.J.: Scarecrow Press.

Deeb, Marius. 1986. "Radical Political Ideologies and Concepts of Property in Libya and South Yemen." *The Middle East Journal* 40, no. 3 (Summer): 445–82.

Deere, Carmen. 1986. "Agrarian Reform in Transition." In Richard R. Fagen et al. *Transition and Development*, 97–143. New York: Monthly Review Press.

Deere, Carmen, et al. 1985. "The Peasantry and the Development of Sandinista Agrarian Policy, 1979–1984." *Latin American Research Review* 20, no 3: 75–111.

Dejene, Alemneh. 1987. *Peasants, Agrarian Socialism, and Rural Development in Ethiopia*. Boulder, Colo: Westview.

Delury, George E. 1987. *World Encyclopedia of Political Systems and Parties*. 2d ed. New York: Facts on File Publication.

Delvert, Jean. 1961. *Le paysan Cambodgien*. The Hague: Mouton.

Denmark. Statens Statistiske Bureau. 1911. *Statistisk Aarbog 1911*. Copenhagen.

Desai, Padma. 1990. "Grain Yield Variability under Socialism Versus Capitalism." In Wädekin, ed. (1990).

Després, Laura, and Ksenya Khischuk. "The Hidden Sector in Soviet Agriculture: A Study of the Military Sovkhozy and Auxiliary Farms." *Soviet Studies* 42, no. 2 (April): 269–93.

Desbarats, Jacqueline. 1987. "Population Redistribution in the Socialist Republic of Vietnam." *Population and Development Review* 13 (March): 43–76.

Djurfeldt, Göran. 1981. "What Happened to the Agrarian Bourgeoisie and Rural Proletariat under Monopoly Capitalism?" *Acta Sociologica* 24, no. 3: 167–93.

Dolny, Helena. 1985. "The Challenge of Agriculture." In John S. Saul, ed. *A Difficult Road: The Transition to Socialism in Mozambique*. New York: Monthly Review Press.

Domar, Evsey D. 1966. "The Soviet Collective Farm as a Producer Cooperative." *American Economic Review* 56, no. 4 (September): 734–57.

Donáth, Ferenc. 1980. *Reform and Revolution*. Budapest: Corvina Kiadó.

Donnithorne, Audrey. 1967. *China's Economic System*. London: Allen and Unwin.

Doolittle, Penelope, and Margaret Hughes. 1987. "Gorbachev's Agricultural Policy: Building on the Brezhnev Food Program." In U.S. Congress, Joint Economic Committee (1987b), 26–45.

Doré, Amphay. 1982. "The Three Revolutions in Laos." In Stuart-Fox (1982a), 101–15.

Doulos, Victor. 1983. "Quel système de production agricole pour le Congo?" Brazzaville: Ministère de la culture, des Arts et de la Recherche Scientifique. Mimeo.

Dovring, Folke. 1990. "Costs of Agricultural Growth and Development." In Gray, ed. (1990a), 48–68.

Dragadze, Tamara. 1988. *Rural Families in Soviet Georgia*. London: Routledge.

Duggett, Michael. 1975. "Marx on Peasants." *The Journal of Peasant Studies* 2, no. 2 (January): 159–83.

Dumont, René. 1974. *Is Cuba Socialist?* New York: Viking.

Dupree, Louis. 1978. *Afghanistan*. Princeton: Princeton University Press.

Dupree, Louis. 1980a. *Afghanistan*. Princeton: Princeton University Press.

———. 1980b. "Red Flag over the Hindu Kush." Part III, "Rhetoric and Reforms, or Promises! Promises!" *Reports*, no. 23, Asia. Hanover, New Hampshire: American Universities Field Staff.

Eckstein, Alexander. 1977. *China's Economic Revolution*. New York: Cambridge University Press.

Economist Intelligence Unit (EIU). 1986a. *Country Profile: Senegal, The Gambia, Guinea-Bissau, Cape Verde, 1986–87*. London.

———. 1986b. *Country Report: Indochina, Vietnam, Laos, Cambodia, 1986–87*. London.

———. 1986c. *Country Report: Yugoslavia*. No. 4. London.

———. 1987a. *Country Report: Pakistan, Afghanistan*. No. 3. London.

———. 1987b. *Country Report: Hungary*. No 4. London.

———. 1988. *Country Report: Indochina, Vietnam, Laos, Cambodia*. No. 2. London.

———. 1989a. *Country Profile: Ethiopia, Somalia, Djebouti, 1989–90*. London.

———. 1989b. *Country Profile: Zimbabwe 1989–90*. London.

EDIAFRIC. La documentation africaine. 1982. *L'économie congolaise*. Paris.

Egerö, Bertil. 1987. *Mozambique: A Dream Undone*. Uppsala: Nordeska afrikainstitutet.

Elek, Peter. 1980. "The Hungarian Experiment in Search of Profitability." In Francisco et al. (1980), 165–85.

Ellman, Michael. 1975. "Did the Agricultural Surplus Provide the Resources for the Increase in Investment in the USSR, 1928–32." *Economic Journal* 85, no. 4 (December): 844–64.

———. 1984. *Collectivization, Convergence and Capitalism*. London: Academic Press.

———. 1988. "Contract Brigades and Normless Teams in the USSR." In Brada and Wädekin, eds. (1988), 23–32.

Ello, Paul Stephen. 1967. "The Commissar and the Peasant: A Comparative Analysis of Land Reform and Collectivization in North Korea and North Vietnam." Ph.D. diss., University of Iowa, Iowa City.

Ethiopia. Ministry of Agriculture. 1985. *General Agricultural Survey*, Vol. 4, *Producer Cooperatives, Preliminary Report, 1983–84*. Addis Ababa.

Evans, Grant. 1988. *Agrarian Change in Communist Laos*. Occasional Paper no. 85. Singapore: Institute of Southeast Asian Studies.

———. 1990. *Lao Peasants under Socialism*. New Haven: Yale University Press.

FAO. *See* Food and Agricultural Organization.

Feder, Gershon, Lawrence J. Lau, Justin Lin, and Xiaopeng Luo. 1990. "The Determinants of Farm Investment and Residential Construction in Post-Reform China." World Bank, Policy, Research and External Affairs, *Working Papers*. Washington, D.C.

Fekete, Ferenc. 1989. "Progress and Problems in Hungarian Agriculture." In Roger Clarke, ed., *Hungary: The Second Decade of Economic Reform*, 59–75. Chicago: Longman.

Fekete, Ferenc, Earl O. Heady, and Bob R. Holden. 1976. *Economics of Cooperative Farming: Objectives and Optima in Hungary*. Leyden: A.W. Sijhoff.

Feuchtwang, Steven, Athar Hussain, Thierry Pairault, eds. 1988. *Transforming China's Economy in the Eighties: The Rural Sector, Welfare and Employment*. Boulder, Colo.: Westview.

Fforde, Adam. 1989. *The Agrarian Question in North Vietnam, 1974–1979: A Study of Cooperative Resistence to State Policy*. Armonk, N.Y.: Sharpe.

Fforde, Adam, and Suzanne H. Paine. 1987. *The Limits of National Liberation*. London: Croom Helm.

Field, Robert Michael. 1988. "Trends in the Value of Agricultural Output, 1978–86." *China Quarterly* 116 (December): 556–91.

Fituni, L. L. 1985. *Angola: Natureza, População, Economia*. Moscow: Edição Progresso.

FitzGerald, E.V.K. 1985. "The Agrarian Reform as a Model of Accumulation: The Case of Nicaragua since 1979." *Journal of Development Studies* 22, no. 1 (October): 208–27.

Food and Agricultural Organization (FAO). Annual-a. *FAO Yearbook: Fertilizer*. Rome

———. Annual-b. *FAO Yearbook: Production*. Rome.

———. 1966, 1967, and 1970. *Report on the 1960 World Census of Agriculture*. Rome.

———. 1977. *Symposium on Forms of Horizontal and Vertical Integration in Agriculture*. ECE/AGRI/29 New York: United Nations.

———. 1978. *Report of the 1970 World Census of Agriculture. Census Bulletin No 21*. Rome.

———. 1981. *1970 World Census of Agriculture: Analysis and International Comparison of the Results*. Rome.

———. 1983–87. *Report on the 1980 World Census of Agriculture*. Rome (preliminary microfiche version).

———. 1985. *1984 Trade Yearbook*. Vol. 38. Rome.

———. 1986a. *Report on the 1980 World Census of Agriculture*. Report 23, *Cape Verde*. Rome.

———. 1986b. *Report on the 1980 World Census of Agriculture*. Report 25, *Madagascar*. Rome.

———. 1986c. *Report on the 1980 World Census of Agriculture*. Report 24. *Yugoslavia*. Rome.

———. 1987. *1986 Production Yearbook*. Vol. 40. Rome.

———. 1989. *Comprehensive Demographic Estimates and Projections, 1950–2025*. Rome.

Ford, Robert, and Wim Suyker. 1990. "Industrial Subsidies in the OECD Economies." In OECD, Department of Economics and Statistics, *Working Papers* no. 74 (January).

Forrest, Joshua B. 1987. "Guinea-Bissau since Independence: A Decade of Domestic Power Struggles." *Journal of Modern African Studies* 25, no. 1 (March): 95–117.

Foy, Colm. 1988. *Cape Verde: Politics, Economics and Society.* New York: Columbia University Press.

France. Ministère de l'agriculture. 1887. *Statistique agricole de la France.* Nancy: Imprimerie administrative Berger-Levraut.

Francisco, Ronald A. et al. eds. 1980. *Agricultural Policies in the USSR and Eastern Europe.* Boulder, Colo: Westview.

Franz, Marie-Luise. 1976. *Die zwischenbetriebliche Kooperation in der Landwirtschaft der DDR.* Cologne: Verlag Wissenschaft und Politik.

Friss, István, ed. 1969. *Reform of the Economic Mechanism in Hungary.* Budapest: Akadémiai Kiadó.

Fung, K. K. 1974. "Output versus 'Surplus' Maximization: The Conflict between the Socialized and the Private Sector in Chinese Collectivized Agriculture." *Developing Economies* 12, no. 1 (March): 41–51.

Gampe, W. 1985. *Leistungsbewertung und materielle Stimulierung in sozialistischen Landwirtschaftsbetriebe und Kooperation.* Band 2. Halle: Martin-Luther Universität.

Ganev, Atanas, et al. 1990. *Akordut v selskoto stopanstvo.* Sofia: Paratizdat, 1990.

Gellner, Ernest. 1990. "Ethnicity and Faith in Eastern Europe." *Daedalus* 119, no. 1 (Winter): 249–77.

Gerhold, Richard. 1987. *Staatsgüter in der Volksrepublik China,* Abhundlungen zur Agrar- und Wirtschaftsforschung des Europäischen Ostens. Band 149. Berlin: Duncker and Humblot.

German Democratic Republic. Staatliche Zentralverwaltung für Statistik. Annual. *Statistisches Jahrbuch.* East Berlin.

Germany. Kaiserliches statistisches Amt. 1898. *Statistik des deutschen Reiches.* N.F. Band 112. Berlin.

Germany. Statistisches Reichsamt. 1943a. "Die Berufstätigkeit der Bevölkerung." *Statistik des Deutschen Reichs.* Band 557. Berlin: Verlag für Sozialpolitik, Wirtschaft und Statistik.

————. 1943b. "Landwirtschaftliche Betriebszählung." *Statistik des Deutschen Reichs.* Band 560. Berlin: Verlag für Sozialpolitik, Wirtschaft und Statistik.

Gey, Peter. 1987. "The Cuban Economy under the New 'System of Management and Planning': Success or Failure." In Peter Gey and others, eds. *Crisis and Reform in Socialist Economy,* 71–99. Boulder, Colo: Westview.

————. 1990. "Cuba: A Unique Variant of Soviet-Type Agriculture." In Wädekin (1990), 90–107.

Ghai, Dharam, Cristobal Kay, and Peter Peek. 1988. *Labour and Development in Rural Cuba.* New York: St. Martin's Press.

Ghose, Ajit Kumar. 1985. "Transforming Feudal Agriculture: Agrarian Change in Ethiopia since 1974." *Journal of Development Studies* 22, no. 1 (October): 127–50.

Gindin, Sam. 1970. "A Model of the Soviet Firm." *Economics of Planning* 10, no. 3: 145–57.

Giorgis, Dawit Wolde. 1989. *Red Tears: War, Famine and Revolution in Ethiopia.* Trenton, N.J.: Red Sea Press.

Glen, Leslie. 1984. "The Parallel Economy and Economic Adjustment: A Preliminary Review of the Guyana Experience." Paper presented at the Twenty-first Meeting of Technicians of Central Banks of the American Continent. Montevideo.

Godin, Francine. 1986. *Bénin, 1972–1982: La logique de l'état africaine.* Paris: l'Harmattan.

Goldman, Marshall. 1989. "Piecemeal Reforms Make Many Soviets Long for Brezhnev." *Wall Street Journal,* 14 February.

Goldman, Marshall, and Merle Goldman. 1988. "Soviet and Chinese Economic Reforms." *Foreign Affairs* 66, no. 3: 551–74.

Gol'tsberg, I. A., ed. 1972. *Agroklimaticheskii Atlas Mira.* Moscow: Gidrometeoizdat.

Goodman, Ann, Margaret Hughes, and Gertrude Schroeder. 1987. "Raising the Efficiency of Soviet Farm Labor: Problems and Prospects." In Joint Economic Committee (1987b), 100–126.

Goodman, David, and Michael Redclift. 1982. *From Peasant to Proletarian: Capitalist Development and Agrarian Transitions.* New York: St. Martin's Press.

Gorbachev, Mikhail. 1990. "Excerpts from Gorbachev's Remarks on Economic Change." *New York Times,* 18 September, 6.

Göricke, Fred V. 1979. *Social and Political Factors Influencing the Application of Land Reform Measures in Ethiopia.* Saarbrücken: Breitenbach.

Gray, Kenneth R. 1987. "Reform and Resource Allocation in Soviet Agriculture." In Joint Economic Committee (1987b), 9–26.

————, ed. 1990a. *Contemporary Soviet Agriculture: Comparative Perspective.* Ames: Iowa University Press.

————. 1990b. "Soviet Utilization of Food: Focus on Meat and Dairy Processing." In Gray, ed. (1970a), 94–115.

Grajdanzev, Andrew. 1942. "Memorandum on Korea's Agriculture and Resources." In Institute of Pacific Relation, *Conference Papers,* Secretariat Paper no. 7. New York. Mimeo.

Griffin, Keith, and Roger Hay. 1985. "Problems of Agricultural Development in Socialist Ethiopia: An Overview and a Suggested Strategy." *Journal of Peasant Studies* 13, no. 1 (October): 37–67.

Grigoroff, G. 1956. *Réform agraire et collectivisation de l'agriculture en Bulgarie.* Paris: Fondation national des sciences publiques, Centre d'études des relations internationales, mimeographed.

Grötzbach, Erwin. 1982. "Die afghanische Landreform von 1979-Durchführung und Probleme in geographische Sicht." *Orient* 23, no. 2: 394–413.

Gruson, Lindsey. 1990. "Ex-Contras, Citing Broken Promises, Seize Land and Talk Again of War." *New York Times,* 29 October, A4.

Guinea-Bissau. Ministerio da Coordenação Economica e Plano. 1981. *Recenseamento Geral da População e da Habitação, Resultados Provisorios.* Bissau.

Gum, Geoffrey. 1982. "Theravadas and Commisars: The State and National Identity in Laos." In Stuart-Fox, ed. (1982a), 76–100.

Gupta, Bhabani Sen. 1986. *Afghanistan: Politics, Economics, and Society.* Boulder, Colo: Lynne Rienner.

Gustafsson, Allan B. 1987. "Economy-Wide Implications of Resettlement in Zimbabwe." Ph. D. diss., Stanford University.

Guyana. Bank of Guyana. 1990. *Statistical Bulletin*, June.

Guyana Government. Annual. *Estimates of Public Sector*. Georgetown.

Guyana Human Rights Association. Annual. *Guyana Human Rights Report*. Georgetown.

Guyana Sugar Corporation. 1990. *Annual Reports and Accounts, 1989*. Georgetown, Guyana: Guyana National Printing Ltd.

Hajda, Joseph. 1990. "Continuity and Change in Czechoslovakia's Food and Agricultural Policy." In Wädekin, ed. (1990).

Halliday, Fred, and Maxine Molyneux. 1981. *The Ethiopian Revolution*. London: NLB, 1981.

Halpern, Nina. 1989. "Economic Reform and Democratization in Communist Systems: The Case of China." *Studies in Comparative Communism* 12, nos. 2 and 3 (Summer/Autumn 1989): 139–55.

Hammond, Thomas T. 1984. *Red Flag over Afghanistan: The Communist Coup, the Communist Invasion, and the Consequences*. Boulder, Colo: Westview Press.

Hankin, Elemér. 1990. "In Search of a Paradigm." *Daedalus* 119, no. 1 (Winter): 118–215.

Hanlon, Joseph. 1984. *Mozambique: The Revolution under Fire*. London: Zed Books.

Hann, C. 1980. *Tázlár: A Village in Hungary*. Cambridge: Cambridge University Press.

Hare, P. G., et al. eds. 1981. *Hungary: A Decade of Economic Reform*. London: Allen and Unwin.

Hartford, Kathleen. 1985. "Socialist Agriculture is Dead; Long Live Socialist Agriculture! Organizational Transformation in Rural China." In Perry and Wong, eds. (1985), 31–63.

———. 1987. "Socialist Countries in the World Food System: The Soviet Union, Hungary, and China." *Food Research Institute Studies* 20, no. 3: 181–245.

Hayami, Yujiro, and Vernon W. Ruttan. 1985. *Agricultural Development: An International Perspective*. 2d ed. Baltimore: Johns Hopkins University Press.

Heady, Earl O., and John L. Dillon. 1961. *Agricultural Production Functions*. Ames: Iowa State University Press.

Hedlund, Stefan. 1984. *Crisis in Soviet Agriculture*. New York: St. Martin's Press.

———. 1989. *Private Agriculture in the Soviet Union*. New York: Routledge.

———. 1990. "Private Plot as a System Stabilizer." In Wädekin, ed. (1990).

Hegedüs, András. 1977. *The Structure of Socialist Society*. New York: St. Martin's Press.

Hegenbarth, Stanlislawa. 1977. *Kooperationsformen in der polnischen Landwirtschaft*. Berlin: Duncker and Humblot.

Helmberger, Peter, et al. 1981. "Organization and Performance of Agricultural Markets." In Martin, vol. 3 (1981), 503–653.

Hénard, Jacqueline. 1990a. "Für die neue Regierung in Prague ein wirtschaftliches Mammutprogram." *Frankfurter Allgemeine Zeitung*, 6 June.

————. 1990b. "Das Vorbild verliert seinen Glanz." *Frankfurter Allgemeine Zeitung*, 3 April.

Henry, Yves. 1932. *Economie Agricole de l'Indochine*. Hanoi.

Herbst, Jeffrey. 1989. "Political Impediments to Economic Rationality: Explaining Zimbabwe's Failure to Reform its Public Sector." *Journal of African Studies* 27, no. 1 (March): 67–84.

Hiebeck, Murray. 1988. "Less Cooperation in Store: Vietnam Downgrades the Importance of Collective Agriculture." *Far Eastern Economic Review* 140, no. 17 (April 28): 78.

Hobday, Charles. 1986. *Communist and Marxist Parties of the World*. Santa Barbara: ABC Clio.

Hodges, Tony, 1987. *Angola to the 1990s: The Potential for Recovery*. London: Economist Publications.

Hodges, Tony, and Malyn Newitt. 1988. *São Tomé and Príncipe: From Plantation Colony to Microstate*. Boulder, Colo.: Westview.

Hollos, Marida. 1983. "Ideology and Economics: Cooperative Organization and Attitudes toward Collectivization in Two Hungarian Communities." In Hollos and Maday, eds. (1983), 93–122.

Hollos, Marida, and Bela C. Maday, eds. 1983. *New Hungarian Peasants: An East Central European Experience with Collectivization*. New York: Columbia University Press.

Hohmann, Karl. 1988. "Energy Consumption in GDR's Agriculture." In Brada and Wädekin, eds. (1988), 209–22.

Hope, Kempe R. 1979. *Development Policy in Guyana*. Boulder, Colo: Westview.

Horvat, Branko. 1976. *The Yugoslav Economic System*. White Plains: International Arts and Sciences Press.

Hough, Jerry. 1986. *The Struggle for the Third World: Soviet Debates and American Options*. Washington, D.C.: Brookings Institution.

Houtart, François, and Geneviève Lemercinier. 1984. *Hai Van: Life on a Vietnamese Commune*. London: Zed.

Hu, Nguen. 1988. "Individuelle Leistungsverträge." *Internationale Zeitschrift der Landwirtschaft*, no. 4: 285–87.

Hu, Nim. 1982. "Land Tenure and Social Structure in Kampuchea." In Kiernan and Boua (1982), 69–86.

Huang, Shu-min. 1989. *The Spiral Road: Changes in a Chinese Village Through the Eyes of a Communist Party Leader*. Boulder, Colo: Westview.

Humphrey, Caroline. 1983. *Karl Marx Collective: Economy, Society and Religion in a Siberian Collective Farm*. Cambridge: Cambridge University Press.

Hung, G. Nyuyen Tien, and others. 1987. *Agriculture and Rural Development in the People's Republic of the Congo*. Boulder, Colo: Westview.

Hungary. Central Statistical Office. Annual. *Statistical Yearbook*. Budapest: Központi Statisztikai Hivatal.

Hunter, Holland. 1961. "Optimal Tautness In Developmental Planning." *Economic Development and Cultural Change* 9 (July): 561–72.

———. "Soviet Agriculture with and without Collectivization, 1928–1940." *Slavic Review* 47, no. 2 (Summer): 203–17.

Hunya, Gábor. 1989. "Village Systematisation in Romania: Historical, Economic and Ideological Background." *Communist Economies* 1, no. 3 (September): 327–43.

Hussain, Athar, and Keith Tribe. 1981a. *Marxism and the Agrarian Question.* Vol. 1, *German Social Democracy and the Peasantry, 1890–1907.* London: Macmillan.

———. 1981b. *Marxism and the Agrarian Question.* Vol. 2, *Russian Marxism and the Peasantry, 1861–1930.* London: Macmillan.

———. eds. 1984. *Paths of Development in Capitalist Agriculture: Readings from German Social Democracy.* London: Macmillan.

ILO. *See* International Labour Office.

Infield, Henrik F. 1945. *Cooperative Communities at Work.* New York: Dryden Press.

Institute of Agricultural Economics (Poland). 1954. *The Polish Countryside in Figures.* Warsaw: Polonia.

Instytut Filozofii i Socjologii, Polskiej Akademii Nauk. 1968: *The Annals of Rural Sociology.* Warsaw: Zakład Narodowy im Ossolińskich.

International Fund for Agricultural Development. 1982. *A Food Sector Strategy for Guyana.* Rome.

International Institute of Agriculture, 1939. *The First World Agricultural Census.* Rome.

International Labour Office (ILO). Annual. *Yearbook of Labour Statistics.* Geneva.

———. 1982. *Disperité de revenus entre les villes et les campagnes au Bénin.* Addis Ababa: Organisation International du Travail.

———. 1984a. *Emploi d'abord: Elements de strategies pour la priorité à l'emploi au Bénin.* Addis Ababa.

———. 1984b. *Migrations rurales et urbanisation en République Populaire du Congo.* Version provisoire. Addis Ababa.

International Labour Office. Jobs and Skills Program for Africa (JASPA). 1977. *Economic Transformation in a Socialist Framework.* Addis Ababa.

———. 1987. *Generating Employment and Incomes in Somalia.* Addis Ababa.

International Monetary Fund (IMF). Annual. *International Financial Statistics Yearbook.* Washington, D.C.

International Monetary Fund, et al. 1990. *The Economy of the USSR: Summary and Recommendations.* Washington, D.C.: 1990.

Isaacman, Allen, and Barbara Isaacman. 1983. *Mozambique: From Colonialism to Revolution, 1900–1982.* Boulder, Colo: Westview.

Ishikawa, Shigeru. 1967a. *Economic Development in Asian Perspective.* Tokyo: Kinokuniya Bookstore.

———. 1967b. "Resource Flow between Agriculture and Industry: The Chinese Experience." *Developing Economies* 5, no. 1 (March): 3–50.

Israelsen, L. Dwight. 1980. "Collectives, Communes and Incentives." *Journal of Comparative Economics* 4, no. 4 (December): 99–124.

Jackson, Karl D., ed. 1989. *Cambodia 1975–1978: Rendezvous with Death.* Princeton: Princeton University Press.

Jackson, Marvin R. 1989. *A Crucial Phase in Bulgaria's Economic Reform.* Bundesinstitut für ostwissenschaftliche und internationale Studien, No. 72. Cologne.

Jaehne, Günter, 1990a. "Privatisierung der LPGs in Rumänien." *Ernährungsdienst,* 7 April 1990, 12.

———. 1990b. "Socialist Agriculture Outside Europe: New Ways in Mongolian Agriculture." In Wädekin, ed. (1990).

JASPA. See International Labour Office, Jobs and Skills Program for Africa.

Jazny, Naum. 1949. *The Socialized Agriculture of the USSR.* Stanford: Stanford University Press.

Johnson, D. Gale. 1983. "Policies and Performance in Soviet Agriculture." In Johnson and Brooks (1983), 3–116.

Johnson, D. Gale, and Karen McConnell Brooks. 1983. *Prospects for Soviet Agriculture in the 1980s.* Bloomington: Indiana University Press.

Johnston, F. Bruce, and Peter Kilby. 1975. *Agriculture and Structural Transformation.* New York: Oxford University Press.

Joravsky, David. 1967, "Ideology and Progress in Crop Rotation." In Karcz (1967a), 156–74.

Juhász János. 1986. "The Reorganization of the Agricultural Sector of the Lao People's Democratic Republic Through Production Cooperatives." *Land Reform, Land Settlement and Cooperatives* no. 1–2: 61–72.

Kaimowitz, David, and David Stanfield. 1985. "The Organization of Productive Units in the Nicaraguan Agrarian Reform." *Inter-American Economic Affairs* 39, no. 1 (Summer): 51–70.

Karcz, Jerzy, ed. 1967a. *Soviet and East European Agriculture.* Berkeley: University of California Press.

———. 1967b. "Thoughts on the Grain Problem." *Soviet Studies* 18, no. 4 (April): 399–434.

———. 1970. "Back on the Grain Front." *Soviet Studies* 22, no. 2 (October): 262–94.

———. 1979. *The Economics of Communist Agriculture: Selected Papers.* Bloomington, Indiana: International Development Institute.

Katz, Zev. 1975. *Handbook of Major Soviet Nationalities.* New York: Free Press.

Kautsky, Karl. 1902. *Die Agrarfrage, Eine Uebersicht über die Tendenzen der modernen Landwirtschaft und die Agrarpolitik der Sozialdemokratie.* 2d ed. Stuttgart: Dietz.

Keefe, Eugene, and others. 1971. *Area Handbook for Albania.* Washington, D.C.: Government Printing Office.

Keller, Bill. 1990a. "Gorbachev Delays Economic Plans." *The New York Times,* 25 April.

———. 1990b. "Plight of Soviet Farming: A Collective Indifference." *New York Times,* 19 August.

Keller, Edmond. 1987. "Afro-Marxist Regimes." In Keller and Donald Rothchild, eds., 1–21. *Afro-Marxist Regimes*. Boulder, Colo: Lynne Rienner.

Keren, Michael. 1972. "On the Tautness of Plans." *Review of Economic Studies* 39, no. 4 (October): 469–86.

Keren, Michael, Jeffrey Miller, and James P. Thornton. 1981. "The Ratchet: A Dynamic Managerial Incentive Model of the Soviet Enterprise." Unpublished paper.

Kiernen, Ben, and Chanthou Boua, eds. 1982. *Peasants and Politics in Kampuchea, 1941–1981*. London: Zed Press.

Kim, Il-Sung. 1981. *For the Implementation of Rural Theses*. Pyongyang: Foreign Language Publishing House.

Kim, Si Joong. 1989. "Productivity Impact of Decollectivization in Rural China." Brown University. Providence, R.I. Unpublished paper.

Kingkade, W. Ward. (1987) "Demographic Trends in the Soviet Union." In U.S. Congress (1987a), 160–86.

Kirsch, Ottfried C. 1976. *Vertical Cooperation among Agricultural Producers in Western Europe and in Developing Countries*. Saarbrücken: Research Center for International Agrarian Development.

Kislev, Yoav, and Willis Peterson. 1982. "Prices, Technology and Farm Size." *Journal of Political Economy* 90, no. 3 (June): 578–95.

Knutson, Ronald D., J. B. Penn, and William T. Boehm. 1983. *Agricultural and Food Policy*. Englewood Cliffs, N.J.: Prentice-Hall.

————. 1990. *Agricultural and Food Policy*. 2d ed. Englewood Cliffs, N.J.: Prentice-Hall.

Kohler, Berthold. 1990. "Wir brauchen eine schnelle, radikale und umfassende Reform: Ein Gespräch mit dem bulgarischen Ministerpräsidenten Lukanov." *Frankfurter Allgemeine Zeitung*, 14 May.

Kojima, Reeitysu. 1988. "Agricultural Organization: New Forms, New Contradictions." *China Quarterly* 116 (December): 706–36.

Kolankiewicz, George, and Paul G. Lewis. 1988. *Poland: Politics, Economics and Society*. London: Pinter.

Konrád, George. 1980. *The Loser*. San Diego: Harcourt, Brace, Jovanovich.

Koopman, Robert B. 1989. "Efficiency and Growth in Agriculture: A Comparative Study of the Soviet Union, United States, Canada, and Finland." Agriculture and Trade Analysis Division, Economic Research Service, U.S. Department of Agriculture. Staff Report no. AGES 89–54.

Korbonski, Andrej. 1965. *Politics of Socialist Agriculture in Poland: 1945–1960*. New York: Columbia University Press.

Kornai, János. 1986. *Contradictions and Dilemmas*. Cambridge: MIT Press.

————. 1989. "The Hungarian Reform Process: Visions, Hopes, and Realities." In Nee and Stark, eds. (1989), 32–95.

————. 1990. *The Road to a Free Economy: Shifting from a Socialist System, the Example of Hungary*. New York: Norton, 1990.

Kovačić, Matija. 1980. *Sozialistiche landwirtschaftliche Kooperation in Slowenien*. Berlin: Duncker and Humblot.

Kramer, Mark. 1989. "Can Gorbachev Feed Russia." *New York Times Magazine*, 9 April.

Kroll, Heidi. 1988. "Transaction Cost Economics and Planning Failure: Vertical Integration and Steel Utilization in Soviet Machine Building." *Journal of Institutional and Theoretical Economics* 144, no. 5: 857–64.

Kueh, Y. Y. 1988. "Food Consumption and Peasant Incomes in the Post-Mao Era." *China Quarterly* 116 (December): 634–70.

Lackner, Helen. 1985. *P.D.R. Yemen: Outpost of Socialist Development in Arabia*. London: Ithaca Press.

Laird, Roy D. 1967. "Khrushchev's Administrative Reforms in Agriculture: An Appraisal." In Karcz (1967), 29–51.

———. 1990. "Gorbachev's Rural 'Revolution from Above.' "

Laird, Roy D., and Betty A. Laird. 1988. "The Zveno and Collective Contracts: The End of Soviet Collectivization?" In Brada and Wädekin, eds. (1988), 34–44.

Lampton, David M., ed. 1987a. *Policy Implementation in Post-Mao China*. Berkeley: University of California Press.

Lampton, David M. 1987b. "The Implementation Problem." In Lampton, ed. (1987a), 3–24.

Lange, Klaus. 1981. *Die Agrarfrage in der Politik der Partei der Arbeit Albaniens*. Munich: Trofenik.

Laos. State Planning Office. 1985. *10 Years of Socio-Economic Development in the Lao People's Democratic Republic*. Vientiane.

Lardy, Nicholas R. 1983. *Agriculture in China's Modern Economic Development*. Cambridge: Cambridge University Press.

Latham, Richard J. 1985. "The Implications of Rural Reforms for Grass-Roots Cadre." In Perry and Wong, eds. (1985), 157–73.

Lattimore, Owen. 1962. *Nomads and Commisars*. New York: Oxford University Press.

Lazarčik, Gregor. 1967. "The Performance of Czechoslovak Agriculture since World War II." In Karcz (1967a), 385–406.

———. 1985. "Comparative Growth of Agricultural Output, Inputs, and Productivity in Eastern Europe, 1965–82." In U.S. Congress, Joint Economic Committee (1985).

———. 1989. "Comparative Agricultural Performance and Reforms in Eastern Europe, 1975 to 1988." In Joint Economic Committee, U.S. Congress, *Pressures for Reform in the East European Economies*. Vol. 1, 255–79. Washington, D.C.: Government Printing Office.

LCW. *See* Lenin.

Lele, Uma. 1981. "Cooperatives and the Poor: A Comparative Perspective." *World Development* 9, no. 1 (January): 55–72.

Lenin, V. I. 1960–71. *Collected Works*. Moscow: Foreign Language Publishing House and Progress Press/London: Lawrence and Wishart, 1960–71. (Abbreviated in text as LCW.)

Lepinski, Edward. 1955. *Development of Agriculture and Industry*. Warsaw: Polonia.

Lewin, Moshe. 1968. *Lenin's Last Struggle*. New York: Monthly Review Press.

———. 1975. *Russian Peasants and Soviet Power: A Study of Collectivization*. New York: W.W. Norton.

Lin, Cyril Zhiren. 1989. "Open-Ended Economic Reform in China." In Nee and Stark, eds. (1989), 95–137.

Lin, Justin Yifu. 1987. "The Household Responsibility System Reform in China: A Peasant's Institutional Choice." *American Journal of Agricultural Economics* 69, no. 2 (May): 410–15.

———. 1988. "The Household Responsibility in China's Agricultural Reform: A Theoretical and Empirical Study." *Economic Development and Cultural Change* 36, no. 3 (April, supplement): 199–225.

———. 1989. "Rural Reforms and Agricultural Productivity Growth in China." UCLA Working Paper no. 576. Los Angeles.

Lin, Justin Yifu, Richard Burcroff, and Gerson Feder. 1991. "Reforming the Agricultural Sector in a Socialist Economy: The Experience of China." In Braverman et al. (forthcoming 1991).

Linz, Susan J., and Robert E. Martin. 1982. "Soviet Enterprise Behavior under Uncertainty." *Journal of Comparative Economics* 6, no. 1 (March): 24–37.

Lipton, David, and Jeffrey Sachs. 1990. "Privatization in Eastern Europe: The Case of Poland." *Brookings Papers on Economic Activity* no. 2: 293–343.

Lipton, Michael. 1976. *Why People Stay Poor: A Study of Urban Bias in World Development*. Cambridge: Harvard University Press, 1976.

Lippit, Victor. 1974. *Land Reform and Economic Development in China*. White Plains, N.Y.: International Arts and Science Press.

Lirenso, Alemayehu. 1986. *Food Aid and its Impact on Ethiopian Agriculture*. Research Report 26, Institute of Development Research. Addis Ababa.

Litvin, Valentine. 1987. *The Soviet Agro-Industrial Complex: Structure and Performance*. Boulder, Colo.: Westview.

Litwack, John M. 1990. "Discretionary Behavior and Soviet Economic Reform." Stanford, Ca. Unpublished paper.

Llovio-Menéndez, José Luis. 1988. *Insider: My Hidden Life as a Revolutionary in Cuba*. New York: Bantam.

Loncarević, Ivan. 1974. *Die Kooperation zwischen den privaten Landwirtschaftsbetrieben und den gesellschaftlichen Wirtschaftsorganization in der Landwirtschaft Jugoslawiens*. Berlin: Duncker and Humblot.

Lott, Charlotte E. 1979. *Land Concentration in the Third World: Statistics on Number and Area of Farms Classified by Size of Farm*. Land Tenure Center Paper no. 28 (April). University of Wisconsin.

McCardle, Arthur, and A. Bruce Boenau. 1984. *East Germany*. Landham, Md.: University Press of America.

MacEwan, Arthur. 1981. *Revolution and Economic Development in Cuba*. London: Macmillan.

McGowan, Pat, and Thomas H. Johnson. 1984. "African Military Coups d'Etat and Underdevelopment: A Quantitative Historical Analysis." *Journal of Modern African Studies* 22, no. 4 (December): 633–66.

McKinnon, Ronald I. 1990. "Stabilizing the Ruble: The Problem of Internal Currency Convertibility." Paper presented to the OECD Development Centre, Paris.

——. 1991, forthcoming. *The Order of Economic Liberalization: Financial Control in the Transition to a Market Economy.*

McMillan, John, John Walley, and Lijing Zhu. 1989. "The Impact of China's Economic Reforms on Agricultural Productivity Growth." *Journal of Political Economy* 97, no. 4 (August): 781–808.

Madagascar. Ministère des finances et du commerce and Institut national de la statistique et de la recherche économique. 1966. *Enquête agricole.* Antananarivo: Imprimerie nationale.

Madden, J. Patrick. 1967. *Economies of Size in Farming: Theory, Analytical Procedures, and a Review of Selected Studies.* U.S. Department of Agriculture, Economic Research Service, Agricultural Economic Report no. 107. Washington, D.C., February.

Mandaza, Ibbo, ed. 1986. *Zimbabwe: The Political Economy of Transition, 1980–1986.* Dakar: Council for the Development of Economic and Social Research in Africa.

Mao Tse-tung. 1971. *Selected Readings from the Works of Mao Tse-tung.* Peking: Foreign Languages Press.

——. 1975–77. *Selected Works of Mao Tse-tung,* Peking: Foreign Languages Press. (Abbreviated in text as SWMT.)

——. 1986. *The Writings of Mao Zedong, 1949–1976.* Vol. I, *September 1949–December 1955.* Edited by Michael Y. M. Kau and John K. Leung. Armonk, N.Y.: M.E. Sharpe.

Markish, Yuri. 1989a. "Agricultural Reforms in the USSR: Intensification Programmes of the 1980s." *Communist Economics* 1, no. 4: 421–45.

——. 1989b. "New Semenov Data on State Subsidies." *RSEEA Newsletter (Research on Soviet and East European Agriculture)* 11, no. 1 (March): 11–12.

Marleyn, Oscar, David Wield, and Richard Williams. 1982. "The Political and Organizational Offensive in Mozambique: Its Relation to State Agricultural Policy." Paper presented at the University of Leeds Conference on the transition to socialism in Africa (May).

Marrese, Michael. 1983. "Agricultural Policy and Performance in Hungary." *Journal of Comparative Economics* 7, no. 3 (September): 329–45.

Marris, Robin. 1964. *The Economic Theory of "Managerial" Capitalism.* New York: The Free Press of Glencoe, 1964.

Martin, Lee R., ed. 1977–81. *A Survey of the Agricultural Economics Literature.* 4 vols. Minneapolis: University of Minnesota Press.

Martin, Philip L., and Alan L. Olmstead. 1985. "The Agricultural Mechanization Controversy." *Science* 227 (8 February): 601–6.

Marx, Karl, and Friedrich Engels. 1961–67. *Marx-Engels Werke.* East Berlin: Dietz Verlag. (Abbreviated in text as MEW.)

Massey, Garth. 1987. *Subsistence and Change: Lessons of Agropastoralism in Somalia.* Boulder, Colo.: Westview.

May, Soreth. 1986. *Cambodian Witness.* New York: Random House.

Medal Mendieta, José Luis. 1988. *Nicaragua: Crisis, Cambio Social y Política Económica*. Managua: Editado por Dilesa.

Medvedev, Zhores A. 1987. *Soviet Agriculture*. New York: W. W. Norton.

Mengisteab, Kidane. 1984. "The Political Economy of Land Reform: An Exploratory Study of Structural Change in Ethiopia's Agriculture, 1975–1981." Ph.D. diss., University of Denver.

Mesa-Lago, Carmelo. 1981. *The Economics of Socialist Cuba*. Albuquerque: University of New Mexico Press.

———. 1988. "The Cuban Economy in the 1980s: The Return of Ideology." In Sergio G. Roca, ed. *Socialist Cuba: Past Interpretations and Future Challenges*. Boulder, Colo.: Westview, 59–101.

MEW. *See* Marx and Engels.

Miech-Chatenay, Michele. 1986. *Mozambique: The Key Sectors of the Economy*. Paris: Indian Ocean Newsletter, 1986.

Mieszczankowski, Mieczysław. 1960. *Struktura Agrarna Polski Międzywojennej*. Warsaw: Państwowe Wydawnictwo Naukowe.

Millar, James R. 1970. "Soviet Rapid Development and the Agricultural Surplus Hypothesis." *Soviet Studies* 22, no. 1 (July): 79–93.

———. 1974. "Mass Collectivization and the Contribution of Agriculture to the First Five Year Plan: A Review Article." *Slavic Review* 33, no. 4 (December): 750–66.

———. 1983. "Views on the Economics of Soviet Collectivization of Agriculture: The State of the Revisionist Debate." In Stuart (1983), 109–17.

Miller, Thomas A., Gordon E. Rodewald, and Robert G. McElroy. 1981. *Economies of Size in U.S. Field Crop Farming*. Report No. 472, U.S. Department of Agriculture, Economics and Statistics Service, Agricultural Economic. Washington, D.C. (July).

Misja, Vladimir, and Ylli Vejsiv. 1985. *Demographic Development in the People's Socialist Republic of Albania*. Tirana: The "8 Nëmtori" Publishing House.

Mitrany, David. 1930. *The Land and the Peasant in Rumania*. London: Oxford University Press.

———. 1961. *Marx Against the Peasant: A Study in Social Dogmatism*. New York: Crowell-Collier Publishing Company.

Moise, Edwin. 1978. "Radical, Moderate and Optimal Patterns of Land Reform." *Modern China* 4, no. 1 (January): 79–90.

———. 1983. *Land Reform in China and North Vietnam: Consolidating the Revolution at the Village Level*. Chapel Hill: University of North Carolina Press.

Mondjannagni, Alfred Comlan. 1977. *Campagnes et villes au sud de la République Populaire du Bénin*. Paris: Mouton.

Mongolia. Central Statistical Board. 1981. *National Economy of the MPR for 60 Years*. Ulam Bator.

Montias, John Michael. 1967. *Economic Development in Communist Romania*. Cambridge: MIT Press.

———. Forthcoming. "The Romanian Economy: A Survey of Current Problems."

Moore, Thomas Gale. 1990. "A Privatization Program for Gorbachev." *Wall Street Journal*, 30 May.

Morrison, Donald George, et al. 1989. *Black Africa: A Comparative Handbook.* 2d ed. New York: Macmillan.

Moskoff, William. 1984. *Labour and Leisure in the Soviet Union.* New York: St. Martin's Press.

Mosher, Steven W. 1983. *Broken Earth: The Rural Chinese.* New York: Free Press.

Mozambique. Conselho Coordenador de Recenseamento. 1983. *Iº Recenseamento Geral da Populaçao: Informação Pública.* Maputo.

Mumbengegwi, Clever. 1984. "Agricultural Producer Cooperatives and Agrarian Transformation in Zimbabwe: Policy, Strategy and Implementation." *Zimbabwe Journal of Economics* 1, no. 1 (July): 47–60.

Munslow, Barry. 1985. "Prospects for the Socialist Transition of Agriculture in Zimbabwe." *World Development* 13, no. 1 (January): 41–58.

————, ed. 1986. *Africa: Problems in the Transition to Socialism.* London: Zed Books.

Murphy, George G. S. 1966. *Soviet Mongolia: A Study of the Oldest Political Satellite.* Berkeley: University of California Press.

Murrell, Peter. 1989. *The Nature of Socialist Economics: Lessons from East European Foreign Trade.* Princeton: Princeton University Press.

Mury, Gilbert. 1970. *Albanie: Terre de l'homme nouveau.* Paris: Maspero.

Mustard, Allan. 1989. "Ruminations on Gorbachev's Agricultural Policy, or Two Years Observing Perestoryka." *RSEEA Newsletter (Research on Soviet and East European Agriculture)* 11, no. 1 (March 1989): 2–3.

Myant, Martin R. 1989. *The Czechoslovak Economy, 1948–1988.* Cambridge: Cambridge University Press.

Myers, Ramon. 1969. "Land Distribution in Revolutionary China: 1890–1937." *Chung Chi Journal* 8, no. 2 (May): 62–78.

Nazarenko, Viktor. 1991. "Reform in Socialist Agriculture: The USSR Experience." In Braverman et al. (forthcoming 1991).

Nechemias, Carol. 1990. "Recent Changes in Soviet Rural Housing Policy." In Gray, ed. (1990), 155–76.

Nee, Victor. 1989. "Peasant Entrepreneurship and the Politics of Regulation in China." In Nee and Stark, eds. (1989), 169–208.

Nee, Victor, and David Stark, eds. 1989. *Remaking the Economic Institutions of Socialism: China and Eastern Europe.* Stanford: Stanford University Press.

Neetz, Roger E. 1969. *Agricultural Statistics of Eastern Europe and the Soviet Union, 1950–1967,* Economic Research Service, U.S. Department of Agriculture no. 252. Washington, D.C.

Nehring, Richard F. 1990. "Measurement of Technical Efficiency by Region, Farm Size and Tenure Status on United States Sugar Beet Farms." Economic Research Service, Resource and Technology Division, U.S. Department of Agriculture. Unpublished paper (February).

Nelson, Harold P., ed. 1984. *Mozambique: A Country Study.* Washington, D.C.: Government Printing Office.

Netherlands. Commission centrale de statistique. 1897. *Annuaire statistique des Pays Bas.* s'Gravenhage: Van Weelden and Mingelen.

Nicaragua. Dirección General de Estadística y Censos. 1966. *Censos Nacionales 1963: Agropecuario.* Managua.

———. 1974. *Censos Nacionales 1971, 1971, Populación.* Vol. 3. Managua.

Nicaragua. Instituto Nacional de Estadísticas y Censos. Annual. *Anuario Estadístico.* Managua.

Niskanen, William A., Jr. 1971. *Bureaucracy and Representative Government.* Chicago: Aldine Atherton.

———. 1975. "Bureaucrats and Politicians." *Journal of Law and Economics* 18, no. 3 (December): 617–43.

Nolan, Peter. 1988. *The Political Economy of Collective Farms: An Analysis of China's Post-Mao Rural Reforms.* Boulder, Colo.: Westview.

Nonneman, Gerd. 1988. *Development Administration and Aid in the Middle East.* London: Routledge.

Noorzog, M. Siddieq. 1983. "Alternative Economic Systems for Afghanistan." *International Journal of Middle Eastern Studies* 15, no. 1 (February): 25–45.

Nove, Alec. 1967. "Peasants and Officials." In Karcz (1967a), pp. 57–73.

———. 1969. *An Economic History of the USSR.* London: Allen Lane.

———. 1971. "The Decision to Collectivize." In W. A. Douglas Jackson, ed., *Agrarian Politics and Problems in Communist and Non-Communist Nations,* 69–98. Seattle: University of Washington Press.

———. 1986. *The Soviet Economic System.* 3d ed. London.

———. 1988a. "Labor Incentives in Soviet Kolkhozy." In Brada and Wädekin, eds. (1988), 13–22.

———. 1988b. *Soviet Agriculture: The Brezhnev Legacy and Gorbachev's Cure.* Santa Monica, Cal.: RAND/UCLA Center for the Study of Soviet International Behavior, JRS-03.

Nyrop, Richard F., ed. 1979. *Area Handbooks for the Yemens.* Washington, D.C.: Government Printing Office.

———. 1986. *Afghanistan: A Country Study.* Washington, D.C.: Government Printing Office.

OECD. *See* Organization for Economic Cooperation and Development.

Offermann, Michael. 1988. *Angola zwischen den Fronten.* Pfaffenweiler: Centaurus Verlagsgesellschaft.

Oi, Jean C. 1986. "Peasant Grain Marketing and State Procurement." *China Quarterly,* no. 106 (June): 270–90.

———. 1989a. "Market Reforms and Corruption in Rural China." *Studies in Comparative Communism* 22, nos. 2-3 (Summer/Autumn): 221–33.

———. 1989b. *State and Peasant in Contemporary China.* Berkeley: University of California Press.

Oi, Walter Y., and Elizabeth M. Clayton. 1969. "A Peasant's View of a Soviet Collective Farm." *American Economic Review* 59, no. 1 (March): 37–59.

Oliveria, Victor J. 1989. *Trends in the Hired Farm Work Force, 1945–87.* Agriculture Information Bulletin no. 561. U.S. Department of Agriculture, Economic Research Service. Washington, D.C.

Oliveira, Victor J., and E. Jane Cox. 1989. *The Agricultural Work Force of 1987.* Agricultural Economics Report no. 609. U.S. Department of Agriculture, Economic Research Service. Washington, D.C.

Olmstead, Alan L. 1975. "The Mechanization of Reaping and Mowing in American Agriculture, 1833–1879." *Journal of Economic History* 35, no. 2 (June 1975): 327–53.

Omar, Osman Mohamed. 1982. "Probleme der ländliche Entwicklung in der Demokratischen Republik Somalia, 1974–1980." Ph.D. diss., Free University of Berlin.

Organization for Economic Cooperation and Development (OECD). Department of Economics and Statistics. 1989a, *Flows and Stocks of Fixed Capital.* Paris.

————. 1989b. *Labour Force Statistics, 1967–1987.* Paris.

Oros, I. 1984. "Small Scale Agricultural Production in Hungary." *Acta Oeconomica* 32, no. 1–2: 65–90.

Ortega, Marvin. 1985. "Worker Participation in the Management of the Agro-Enterprises of the APP." *Latin American Perspectives* 12, no. 2 (Spring): 69–83.

Oschties, Wolf. 1985. "Aus Sorge von 'Mutter Erde': Umweltschutz and Ökologiedicussion in Bulgarien." *Berichte des Bundesinstituts für ostwissenschaftliche und internationale Studien*, no. 8.

————. 1989. "Böhmens Fluren und Haine sterben: Zur Umweltkatastrophe in der Tsechekoslovakai." *Berichte des Bundesinstituts für ostwissenschaftliche und internationale Studien*, no. 29.

Ottaway, Merina, and David Ottaway. 1978. *Ethiopia: Empire in Revolution.* New York: Africana Publishing Company.

————. 1986. *Afrocommunism.* 2d ed. New York: Africana Publishing Company.

Oxenstierna, Susanne. 1987. "Bonuses, Factor Demand, and Technical Efficiency in the Soviet Enterprise." *Journal of Comparative Economics* 11, no. 2 (June): 234–44.

Paige, Jeffrey. 1975. *Agrarian Revolution: Social Movements and Export Agriculture in the Underdeveloped World.* New York: Free Press.

Palmer, Michael. 1988. "China's New Inheritance Law: Some Preliminary Observations." In Feuchtwang, Hussain, and Pairault, eds. (1988), 169–97.

Parish, William L., and Martin King Whyte. 1978. *Village and Family in Contemporary China.* Cambridge, Mass.: Harvard University Press.

Parti congolais du travail. 1984. *3'eme congrés ordinaire.* Brazzaville: 1984.

Peek, Peter. 1982. *Agrarian Reforms and Rural Development in Nicaragua (1979–81).* Geneva: International Labour Office, World Employment Programme Research.

Penrose, Edith. 1959. *The Theory of the Growth of the Firm.* Oxford: Blackwell.

Perkins, Dwight Heald. 1988. "Reforming China's Economic System." *Journal of Economic Literature* 26, no. 2 (June): 601–45.

Perkins, Dwight, and Shahid Yusef. 1984. *Rural Development in China.* Baltimore: Johns Hopkins University Press.

Perry, Elizabeth J. 1985. "Rural Collective Violence: The Fruits of Recent Reforms." In Perry and Wong, eds. (1985), 175–92.

Perry, Elizabeth J., and Christine Wong, eds. 1985. *The Political Economy of Reform in Post-Mao China*. Cambridge, Mass.: Council on East Asian Studies and Harvard University Press.

Perry, Martin K. 1989. "Vertical Integration: Determinants and Effects." In Richard Schmalensee and Robert D. Willig, eds. *Handbook of Industrial Organization*. Amsterdam: North Holland.

Philipp, Helene. 1983. *Landwirtschaft und Agrarproduktion in Polen*. Berne: Peter Lang.

Piekalkiewicz, Jaroslaw A. 1972. *Public Opinion Polling in Czechoslovakia, 1968–69*. New York: Praeger.

Pierce, Paulette. 1984. *Noncapitalist Development: The Struggle to Nationalize the Guyanese Sugar Industry*. Totowa, N.J.: Royman and Allanheld.

Piskol, Joachim, et al. 1984. *Antifaschistisch-demokratische Umwälzung auf dem Land*. Berlin: VEB Landwirtschaftsverlag.

Pitzer, John. 1982. "Gross National Product of the USSR." In U.S. Congress, Joint Economic Committee (1982).

Pollitt, Brian. 1982. "The Transition to Socialist Agriculture in Cuba: Some Salient Features." *IDS Bulletin* 13, no. 4 (September): 12–23.

Poland. Główny Urzad Statystyczny. 1980. *Narodowy spis powszechny z dnia 7 XII 1978 g*. Statystyka Polski Nr. 128. Warsaw.

———. Annual. *Statystyczny Rocznik Statystyczny*. Warsaw.

Portes, Richard D. 1969. "The Enterprise under Central Planning." *Review of Economic Studies* 36, no. 2 (April): 197–212.

Portugal, Instituto Nacional de Estatística. 1974. *IV Recenseamento Geral de População 1970 Resumo Geral*. Lourenço Marques.

Portugal. Ministério do Ultramar. 1965. *Recensémente Agrícola de Cabo Verde, 1961–63*. Lisbon.

———. 1968. *Recensémente Agrícola de São Tomé e Príncipe, 1961–64*. Lisbon.

Pouliquen, Alain. 1988. "The Contract Brigades: Toward a Neo-collectivism in Soviet Agriculture." In Brada and Wädekin, eds. (1988), 45–54.

Powelson, John P., and Richard Stock. 1987. *The Peasant Betrayed: Agriculture and Land Reform in the Third World*. Boston: Oelgeschlager, Gunn and Hain.

Preobrazhensky, Evgeny. 1965. *The New Economics*, trans. Brian Pearce. Oxford: Clarendon Press.

Prosterman, Roy L., and Timothy M. Hanstad. 1990. "China: A Fieldwork-Based Appraisal of the Household Responsibility System." In Roy L. Prosterman, Mary N. Temple, and Timothy M. Hanstad, *Agrarian Reform and Grassroots Development: Ten Case Studies*, 103–39. Boulder, Colo.: Lynne Rienner Publishers.

Prosterman, Roy L., et al. 1991. "The Prospects for Individual Farming in the Soviet Union." Washington, D.C.: The Curry Foundation.

Prybyla, Jan S. 1990. "Economic Reform of Socialism: The Dengist Course in China." *Annals of the American Academy of Political and Social Sciences* 507 (January): 113–23.

Pryor, Frederic L. 1973. *Property and Industrial Organization in Communist and Capitalist Nations*. Bloomington: Indiana University Press.

————. 1977. *The Origins of the Economy: A Comparative Study of Distribution in Primitive and Peasant Economies*. New York: Academic Press.

————. 1982. "The Plantation as an Economic System: A Review Article." *Journal of Comparative Economics* 6, no. 3 (September): 288–317.

————. 1983. "The Economics of Production Cooperatives: A Reader's Guide." *Annals of Public and Cooperative Economy* 54, no. 2 (June 1983): 133–73.

————. 1985a. "Growth and Fluctuations of Production in O.E.C.D. and East European Nations." *World Politics* 37, no. 2 (January): 204–38.

————. 1985b. "Some Economics of Utopia: Full Communism." *Survey: A Journal of East and West Studies* 29, no. 2 (Summer): 70–102.

————. 1986. *Revolutionary Grenada: A Study in Political Economy*. New York: Praeger.

————. 1988. *Income Distribution and Economic Development in Madagascar: Some Historical Statistics*. World Bank Discussion Paper 37. Washington, D.C.

————. 1990a. "East European Economic Reforms: The Rebirth of the Market." *Hoover Essays*. Stanford, Ca.

————. 1990b. "The Political Economy of Microcommunism." *Communist Economics* 2, no. 2 (1990): 223–51.

————. 1990c. *The Political Economy of Poverty, Equity, and Growth: Malaŵi and Madagascar*. New York: Oxford University Press for World Bank.

————. 1991. "Economic Reform in Third World Marxist Nations." *Hoover Essays*. Stanford, Ca.

Pryor, Frederic L., and Frederic Solomon. 1982. "Commodity Cycles as a Random Process." *European Journal of Agricultural Economics* 9, no. 3 (1982): 327–47.

Puffert, Douglas J. 1987. "Spatial Network Externalities: A Model with Application to the Standardization of Railway Gauge." Unpublished paper, Technology and Productivity Workshop, Department of Economics, Stanford University.

Putterman, Louis. 1981. "On Optimality in Collective Institutional Choice." *Journal of Comparative Economics* 5, no. 4 (December): 392–402.

————. 1983. "A Modified Collective Agriculture in Rural Growth-with-Equity." *World Development* 11, no. 2.

————. 1985. "Intrinsic versus Intrinsic Problems of Agricultural Cooperation: Anti-incentivism in Tanzania and China." *Journal of Development Studies* 21, no. 2 (January): 175–204.

Quaisser, Wolfgang. 1987. *Agrarpreispolitik und bauerliche Landwirtschaft in Polen*. Berlin: Duncker and Humblot.

Rahmato, Dessalegn. 1984. *Agrarian Reform in Ethiopia*. 1984. Uppsala: Scandinavian Institute of African Studies.

Rapawy, Stephen. 1987. "Labor Force and Employment in the U.S.S.R." In U.S. Congress, Joint Economic Committee, *Gorbachev's Economic Plans*. Vol. 2. Washington, D.C.

Rapawy, Stephen, and Godfrew Baldwin. 1983. "Demographic Trends in the Soviet Union: 1950–2000." In Joint Economic Committee, Congress of the

United States, *Soviet Economy in the 1980s: Problems and Prospects*. Part 2, 265–96. Washington, D.C.: Government Printing Office.

Raup, Philip. 1988. "The Soviet Market and U.S. Agricultural Exports." In Brada and Wädekin, eds. (1988), 408–21.

Rawski, Thomas. 1982. "Agricultural Employment and Technology." In Randolph Barker and Radha Sinha, eds., *The Chinese Agricultural Economy*, 121–36. Boulder, Colo.: Westview.

Reinhardt, Nola. 1987. "Agro-Exports and the Peasantry in the Agrarian Reforms of El Salvador and Nicaragua." *World Development* 15, no. 7 (July): 941–59.

René, France Albert. 1982. *Seychelles: The New Era*. Victoria: Ministry of Education and Information.

Rhodes, Richard. 1989. *Farm: A Year in the Life of an American Farmer*. New York: Simon and Schuster.

Richet, Xavier. 1985. *Le modèle hongrois*. Lyon: Presses Universitaires de Lyon.

Riddell, James C., and Carol Dickerman. 1986. *Country Profiles of Land Tenure: Africa 1986*. Land Tenure Center Paper 127. Madison, Wisconsin.

Riskin, Carl. 1987. *China's Political Economy: The Quest for Development since 1949*. Oxford: Oxford University Press.

Roberts, Henry L. 1951. *Rumania: Political Problems of an Agrarian State*. New Haven: Yale University Press.

Robinson, Geroid Tanquary. 1949. *Rural Russia under the Old Régime*. New York: Macmillan.

Robinson, William F. 1973. *The Pattern of Reform in Hungary*. New York: Praeger.

Roca, Sergio. 1976. *Cuban Economic Policy and Ideology: The Ten Million Ton Sugar Harvest*. Beverley Hills, Ca.: Sage Publication.

Rochlin, R. Peter. 1957. *Die Wirtschaft Bulgariens seit 1945*. Deutsches Institut für Wirtschaftsforschung Sonderheft N.F. 38, Reihe A. Berlin: Duncker and Humblot.

Rochlin, R. Peter, and Ernst Hagemann. 1971. *Die Kollectivierung der Landwirtschaft in der Sowjetunion und der Volksrepublik China*. Berlin: Duncker and Humblot.

Rogers, J. D. 1985. *Patterns of Rural Development and Impact on Employment and Incomes: The Case of Somalia*. Addis Ababa: International Labour Office.

Romania. Direcţia Centrală de Statistiçă. 1980. *Recensămîntul populaţiei si al locuintelor*. Vol. 2. Bucharest.

———. Annual. *Añuarul Statistic*. Bucharest.

Romm, Tsilia, and Amnon Levy. 1990. "Decollectivization and Collectivization: A Longitudinal Study of the Organizational Transformation of an Israeli Desert Agricultural Settlement," *Comparative Economic Studies* 32, no. 4 (Winter): 62–85.

Ross, Lester. 1987. "Obligatory Tree Planting: The Role of Campaigns in Policy Implementation in Post-Mao China." In Lampton, ed. (1987), 225–52.

Roussos, Peter. 1988. *Zimbabwe: An Introduction to the Economics of Transformation*. Harare: Beobab Books.

Roy, Oliver. 1986. *Islam and Resistance in Afghanistan.* Cambridge: University Press.

Rozman, Gilbert. 1988. *The Chinese Debate about Soviet Socialism, 1978–1985.* Princeton: Princeton University Press.

Ruchwanger, Gary. 1989. *Struggling for Survival: Workers, Women and Class in a Nicaraguan State Farm.* Boulder, Colo.: Westview Press.

Rubinstein, Alvin Z. 1988. *Moscow's Third World Stragegy.* Princeton: Princeton University Press,

Rudebeck, Lars. 1974. *Guinea-Bissau: A Study of Political Mobilization.* Uppsala: Scandinavian Institute of African Studies, Uppsala; and New York: Africana Publishing Co.

———. 1988. "Kandjadja, Guinea Bissau, 1976–1986." *Review of African Political Economy* 41 (September): 17–30.

Rukavishnikov, S. I. 1989. "Ochered'." *Sotsiologicheskieye Issledovaniya,* no. 4: 2–12.

Rupen, Robert A. 1964. *Mongols of the 20th Century.* Bloomington: Indiana University Uralic and Altaic Series. Vol. 37, part I.

———. 1979. *How Mongolia is Really Ruled: A Political History of Mongolian People's Republic, 1900–1978.* Stanford: Hoover Institution Press.

Russ, Wolfgang. 1979. *Der Entwicklungsweg Albaniens.* Meisenheim am Glan: Verlag Anton Hain.

Sah, Raaj Kumar, and Joseph E. Stiglitz. 1984. "The Economics of the Price Scissors." *American Economic Review* 74, no. 1 (March): 125–39.

Salzmann, Zdenek. 1983. *Three Contributions to the Study of Socialist Czechoslovakia.* Research Report 22, Department of Anthropology, University of Massachusetts. Amherst, Mass.

Salzmann, Zdenek, and Vladimir Scheufler. 1974. *Komárov: A Czech Farming Village.* New York: Holt, Rinehart and Winston.

Samatar, Abdi Ismail. 1989. *The State and Rural Transformation in Northern Somalia, 1884–1986.* Madison: University of Wisconsin Press.

Samatar, Ahmed I. 1988. *Socialist Somalia: Rhetoric and Reality.* London: Zed.

Sanders, Alan J. K. 1987. *Mongolia: Politics, Economics and Society.* London: Pinter.

Sanders, Irwin T. 1958. *Collectivization of Agriculture in Eastern Europe.* Lexington: University of Kentucky Press, 1958.

São Tomé. Ministério do Plano, Dirrecção de Estatística. 1987. *Iº Recenseamento Geral da População e da Habitação-1981.* São Tomé.

Scalapino, Robert A., and Chong-Sik Lee. 1972. *Communism in Korea.* Part 2. Berkeley: University of California Press.

Schinke, Eberhard. 1983. *Der Anteil der privaten Landwirtschaft an der Agrarproduktion in den RGW-Ländern.* Berlin: Duncker and Humblot.

———. 1990. "New Forms of Farm Organization in the GDR as Compared to the USSR and East European States." In Wädekin, ed. (1990), 251–62.

Schmidt, Klaus, et al. 1990. *DDR auf dem Weg in die Marktwirtschaft.* Berlin: Institut für Agrarökonomie der Akademie des Landwirtschaftswissenschaften der DDR (April). Mimeo.

Schröder, Günter, ed. 1980. *Afghanistan zwischen Marx und Mohammed*, Reihe Internationale Informationen, no. 6. Giessen: ISZ.

Schultz, Theodore W. 1953. *The Economic Organization of Agriculture*. New York: McGraw-Hill.

Schwarzbach, R., and A. Burzek. 1986. *Ökonomie und Organisation der Arbeit in sozialistischer Betriebe der Pflanzenproduktion und des Gartenbaus*. Berlin: Deutscher Landwirtschaftsverlag.

Scott, Catherine V. 1988. "Socialism and the 'Soft State' in Africa: An Analysis of Angola and Mozambique." *Journal of Modern African Studies* 26, no. 1: 23–36.

Sen, Amartya. 1967. "Labour Allocation in a Cooperative Enterprise." *Review of Economic Studies* 33: 361–71.

SEV. *See* Sovet Ekonomicheskoi Vzaimopomoshchi.

Seychelles. Government. 1978. *1977 Census Report*. Victoria.

———. Annual. *Statistical Abstract*. Victoria.

———. 1987. *Statistical Bulletin, National Accounts*. Victoria.

Shahabuddeen, M. 1983. *From Plantation to Nationalization: A Profile of Sugar in Guyana*. Georgetown: University of Guyana.

Shiller, Robert, Maxim Boycko, and Vladimiar Korobov. 1990. "Popular Attitudes toward Free Markets: The Soviet Union and the United States Compared." New Haven, Conn. Unpublished paper (August).

Shirk, Susan. 1989. "The Political Economy of Chinese Industrial Reforms." In Nee and Stark, eds. (1989), 328–65.

Shmelev, Nikolai, and Vladimir Popov. 1989. *The Turning Point: Revitalizing the Soviet Economy*. New York: Doubleday.

Shue, Vivienne. 1980. *Peasant China in Transition: The Dynamics of Development toward Socialism, 1949–1956*. Berkeley: University of California Press.

Sicular, Terry. 1988a. "Agricultural Planning and Pricing in the Post-Mao Era." *China Quarterly* no. 116, (December): 671–705.

———. 1988b. "Plan and Market in China's Agricultural Commerce." *Journal of Political Economy* 96, no. 2 (March): 283–307.

Singaravelou. 1978. "Culture commerciale et cultures vivrières den Guyana." In Jean-Pierre Chardon and others, eds. *De l'Orenoque a l'Amazone*, Centre d'études de geographie tropicale, Domaine universitaire de Bordeaux. Bordeaux.

Singh, Chaitram. 1988. *Guyana: Politics in a Plantation Society*. New York: Praeger.

Sipos, A., and P. Halmai. 1988. "Organizational System and Economic Mechanism in Hungarian Agriculture." *Acta Oeconomica* 39, no. 3–4: 199–230.

Skålner, Tor. 1989. "Group Interests and the State: An Explanation of Zimbabwe's Agricultural Policies." *Journal of Modern African Studies* 27, no. 1 (March): 85–107.

Skold, Karl. 1990. "The Relationship between Technical Efficiency and Farm Characteristics in the Stavrapol Region, USSR." *Working Paper*, Center for Agricultural and Rural Development, Iowa State University. Ames, Iowa.

Solinger, Dorothy J. 1987. "The 1980 Inflation and the Politics of Price Control in the PRC." In Lampton, ed. (1987a), 81–119.

Solomon, Susan Gross. 1977. *The Soviet Agrarian Debate: A Controversy in Social Science, 1923–1929*. Boulder, Colo.: Westview.

Somali Institute of Development Administration and Management. 1975. *Somalia in Transitions: Proceedings of the IDEP-SIDAM Seminar*. Mogadishu.

Somalia. Ministry of Planning and Coordination. 1971. *Development Programme, 1971–1973*. Mogadishu.

Somalia, State Planning Commission. 1979. *Three Year Plan, 1979–81*. Mogadishu.

Sovet Ekonomicheskoi Vzaimopomoshchi (SEV). Sekretariat. Annual. *Statisticheskii ezhegodnik stran chlenov Soveta Ekonomicheskoi Vzaimopomoschi*. Moscow: Finansy i statistika.

Spalding, Rose J., ed. 1987. *The Political Economy of Revolutionary Nicaragua*. Winchester, Mass.: Allen and Unwin.

Spaulding, Wallace H. 1982. "Checklist of the 'National Liberation Movement,' " *Problems of Communism* 31, no. 2 (March/April): 77–83.

——. 1983. "The Communist Movement and its Allies." In Ralph M. Goldman, *Transnational Parties: Organizing the World's Precincts*, 25–60. Lanham, Md.: University Press of America.

Spindler, Berndt. 1989. "Ökologische Probleme." In Forschungsstelle für gesamtdeutsche Wirtschaftliche und soziale Fragen, *Agrar-Forschung: Agrarwirtschaft und Agrarwissenschaften in der DDR an der Schwelle der 90er Jahre, FS Analyse* no. 5: 51–72.

Spulber, Nicolas. 1957. *The Economics of Communist Eastern Europe*. New York: MIT Press and John Wiley & Sons.

——. 1971. *Socialist Management and Planning: Topics in Comparative Socialist Economics*. Bloomington: Indiana University Press.

Smith, Harvey H., et al. 1973. *Area Handbook for Afghanistan*. Washington, D.C.

Srivastava, R. K., and I. Livingstone. 1983. "Growth and Distribution: The Case of Mozambique." In Dharam Gahi and Samir Radwan, eds. *Agrarian Policies and Rural Poverty in Africa*. Geneva: ILO, 249–80.

Staar, Richard. 1987. *USSR: Foreign Policy after Detente*. Rev. ed. Stanford: Hoover Institution Press.

Staar, Richard, ed. Annual. *Yearbook on International Communist Affairs*. Stanford: Hoover Institution Press.

Stalin, J. V. 1952–55. *Works* (Moscow: Foreign Language Publishing House/London: Lawrence and Wishart. (Abbreviated in text as SW.)

Standing, Guy, and Richard Szal. 1979. *Poverty and Basic Needs: Evidence from Guyana and the Philippines*. Geneva: International Labour Office, 1979.

Stiglitz, Joseph. 1991. "Incentives, Organizational Structures, and Contractual Choice in the Reform of Socialist Agriculture." In Braverman et al. (forthcoming 1991).

Stone, Bruce. 1988. "Developments in Agricultural Technology." *China Quarterly*, no. 116 (December): 767–822.

Stoneman, Colin, and Lionel Cliffe. 1989. *Zimbabwe: Politics, Economics and Society*. New York: Pinter.

Stookey, Richard W. 1982. *South Yemen: A Marxist Republic in Arabia*. Boulder, Colo.: Westview.

Stuart, Robert C. 1983. "Russian and Soviet Agriculture: The Western Perspective." *ACES Bulletin* 25, no. 3 (Fall): 43–52.

———, ed. 1983. *The Soviet Rural Economy*. Totowa, N.J.: Rowman and Allanheld.

Stuart-Fox, Martin, ed. 1982a. *Contemporary Laos: Studies in the Politics and Society of the Lao People's Democratic Republic*. New York: St. Martin's.

Stuart-Fox, Martin. 1982b. "Laos in the 1980s." *Internationales Asienforum* 13, nos. 3–4 (November): 251–67.

———. 1986. *Laos: Politics, Economics, and Society*. London: Pinter.

Summers, Robert, and Alan Heston. 1988. "A New Set of International Comparisons of Real Product and Price Levels: Estimates for 130 Countries." *Review of Income and Wealth* 34 (March): 1–25.

SW. *See* Stalin.

Swain, Nigel. 1981. "The Evolution of Hungary's Agricultural System since 1967." In P. G. Hare et al., eds., *Hungary: A Decade of Economic Reform*, 225–52. London: Allen and Unwin.

———. 1985. *Collective Farms Which Work?* Cambridge: Cambridge University Press.

Schwarzbach, R., and A. Burzek. 1986. *Ökonomie und Organisation der Arbeit sozialistischer Betriebe der Pflanzenproduktion und des Gartenbaus*. East Berlin: Deutscher Landwirtschaftsverlag.

Szajkowski, Bogdan. 1982. *The Establishment of Marxist Regimes*. London: Butterworth Scientific.

Szelenyi, Ivan. 1988. *Socialist Entrepreneurs: Embourgement in Rural Hungary*. Madison: University of Wisconsin Press.

———. 1991. "The Social Impact of Agrarian Reform: Social and Political Conflicts of the Post-Communist Transformation of Hungarian Agriculture." In Braverman, Brooks and Csáki, eds. (forthcoming 1991).

Szwengrub, Lili Maria. 1968. "Place of Cooperative Farmers in the Social Structure of the Village." In Instytut Filozofii i Socjologii (1968), 174–86.

Tabibi, Latif. 1981. "Die afghanische Landreform von 1979: Ihre Vorgeschichte und Konsequenzen." Ph.D. diss., Free University of Berlin.

Taylor, Jeffrey R. 1988. "Rural Employment Trends and the Legacy of Surplus Labour, 1978–86." *China Quarterly*, no. 116 (December): 736–66.

Teka, Tegigne, and Tennassie Nichola. 1983. *Rural Poverty Alleviation: The Case of Ethiopia*. Research Report 17, Institute of Development Economics. Addis Ababa: Addis Ababa University.

Thielen, Helmut. 1985. *Agrarreformen in Lateinamerika zwischen Ökonomie und Ökologie: Modellfall Nicaragua*. Frankfurt a.M.: Haag and Herchen.

Thomas, Clive Y. 1983. "State Capitalism in Guyana: An Assessment of Burnham's Cooperative Socialist Republic." In Fitzroy Ambersley and Robin Cohen, eds. *Crisis in the Caribbean*. New York: Monthly Review Press, 27–49.

————. 1984. *Plantations, Peasants, and State: A Study of the Mode of Sugar Production in Guyana.* Los Angeles: University of California, Center for Afro-American Studies.

Thomas, Joseph R., and David Kaimowitz. 1985. "Agrarian Reform." In Thomas W. Walker, ed. *Nicaragua: The First Five Years*, 299–315. New York: Praeger.

Thornton, Judith, ed. 1976. *Economic Analysis of the Soviet-Type System.* Cambridge: Cambridge University Press.

Timofeev, Lev. 1985. *Soviet Peasants.* New York: Telos Press.

Torp, Jens Erik, L. M. Denny, and Donald I. Ray. 1989. *Mozambique. São Tomé and Príncipe: Politics, Economics and Society.* New York: Pinter Publisher.

Trapeznikov, S. P. 1981. *Leninism and the Agrarian and Peasant Question.* 2 vols. Moscow: Progress Press.

Trang, Tran Nhu. 1972. "The Transformation of the Peasantry in North Viet Nam." Ph.D. diss., University of Pittsburgh.

Travers, Lee. 1986. "Peasant Non-Agricultural Production in the People's Republic of China." In U.S. Congress, Joint Economic Committee (1986), 376–87.

Trinidad and Tobago. Central Statistical Office. 1964. *British Guyana: Population Census 1960.* Vol. 2, part B. Port of Spain, Trinidad.

Trotsky, Leon. 1971. *The Revolution Betrayed.* New York: Pathfinder Press, 1971.

Tsantis, Andreas C., and Roy Pepper. 1979. *Romania: The Industrialization of an Agrarian Economy Under Socialist Planning.* Washington, D.C.: World Bank.

Tuma, Elias H. 1965. *Twenty-six Centuries of Agrarian Reform: A Comparative Analysis.* Berkeley: University of California Press.

Turgeon, Lynn. 1983. "A Quarter Century of Non-Soviet East European Agriculture." *ACES Bulletin* 25, no. 3 (Fall): 27–41.

Turnock, David. 1986. *The Romanian Economy in the Twentieth Century.* London: Croom Helm.

Twining, Charles H. 1989. "The Economy." In Jackson, ed. (1989), 109–51.

Unger, Jonathan. 1985. "Remuneration, Ideology and Personal Interest in a Chinese Village, 1960–1980." In William Parish, ed., *Chinese Rural Development: The Great Transformation.* 117–46. Armonk, NY: M.E. Sharpe.

————. 1985/6. "The Decollectivization of the Chinese Countryside: A Survey of Twenty-eight Villages." *Pacific Affairs* 58, no. 4 (Winter): 585–606.

USSR. Central Statistical Board. 1969. *Soviet Union: 50 Years, Statistical Returns.* Moscow: Progress Publishers.

————. 1983. *The USSR in Figures for 1982.* Moscow: Finansi i Statistika.

USSR. Goskomstat SSSR. 1988. *Nacelenie SSSR 1987: Statisticheskii Sbornik.* Moscow: Finansi i statistika.

USSR. Gosudarstvennyy Komitet SSSR po Statistike. Annual. *Narodnoye khozyaystvo.* Moscow.

USSR. Tsentral'noe statischeskoe upravlenie. 1973. *Itogi vsesoiuznoi perepisi naceleniia 1970 goda.* Vol. 5. Moscow: Statistika.

United Kingdom. Colony of the Seychelles. A.W.T. Webb. N.d. *Agricultural Census of the Seychelles Colony: Report and Tables for 1960*. Victoria. Mimeo.

United Kingdom. Ministry of Agriculture. Fisheries and Food; Department of Agriculture and Fisheries for Scotland. 1968. *A Century of Agricultural Statistics: Great Britain, 1988–1966*. London: HMSO.

United Nations. Annual-a. *Statistical Yearbook*. New York.

————. Annual-b. *Yearbook of the United Nations*. New York.

————. 1987. *National Account Statistics: Main Aggregates and Detailed Tables, 1985*. New York.

————. 1988a. *1986 Demographic Yearbook*. New York.

————. 1988b. *1986 International Trade Statistics Yearbook*. Vol. 1. New York.

United Nations Industrial Development Organization (UNIDO). 1981. *First Global Study of the Food Processing Industry*. N.p. Mimeo.

United States. Bureau of the Census. Annual. *Statistical Abstract of the United States*. Washington, D.C.: Government Printing Office.

————. 1932. *Fifteenth Census of the United States: 1930, Agriculture*. Vol. 5. Washington, D.C.: Government Printing Office.

————. 1962. *U.S. Census of Agriculture: 1959*. Vol. 2, *General Report*. Washington, D.C.: Government Printing Office.

————. 1975. *Historical Statistics of the United States*. Part 1. Washington, D.C.: Government Printing Office.

————. 1983. *1980 Census of Population: General Social and Economic Characteristics*. Washington, D.C.: Government Printing Office.

————. 1985. *1982 Census of Agriculture*. Vol. 1, part 51, *United States Summary and State Data*. Washington, D.C.: Government Printing Office.

United States. Census Office. 1883. *Report on the Productions of Agriculture, Tenth Census, Census Reports*. Vol. 3. Washington, D.C.: Government Printing Office.

————. 1902. *Census Reports*. Vol. 5, *Agriculture*. Part 1. Washington, D.C.: Government Printing Office.

United States. Central Intelligence Agency and U.S. Defense Intelligence Agency. 1989. "Gorbachev's Economic Program: Problems Emerge." In U.S. Congress, Joint Economic Committee (1989), 3–70.

United States. Congress. Joint Economic Committee. Annual. *Allocation of Resources in the Soviet Union and China*. Washington, D.C.: Government Printing Office.

————. 1975. *China: A Reassessment of the Economy*. Washington, D.C.: Government Printing Office.

————. 1982. *USSR: Measures of Economic Growth and Development, 1950–80*. Washington, D.C.: Government Printing Office.

————. 1985. *East European Economies: Slow Growth in the 1980s*. Vol. 1. Washington, D.C.: Government Printing Office.

————. 1986. *China's Economy Looks Toward the Year 2000*. Vol. 1, *The Four Modernizations*. Washington, D.C.: Government Printing Office.

————. 1987a. *Gorbachev's Economic Plans*. Vol. 1. Washington, D.C.: Government Printing Office.

————. 1987b. *Gorbachev's Economic Plans.* Vol. 2. Washington, D.C.: Government Printing Office.

————. 1989. *Allocation of Resources in the Soviet Union and China-1987.* Hearings before the Subcommittee on Natural Security Economics. Washington, D.C.: Government Printing Office.

United States. Congress. Office of Technology Assessment. 1986. *Technology, Public Policy, and the Changing Structure of American Agriculture.* OTA-F-285. Washington, D.C.: Government Printing Office (March).

United States. Council of Economic Advisors. 1986. *Economic Report of the President, 1986.* Washington, D.C.: Government Printing Office.

United States. Department of Agriculture. Annual. *Agricultural Statistics.* Washington, D.C.: Government Printing Office.

United States. Department of Agriculture. Economic Research Service. 1969. *Agricultural Statistics of Eastern Europe and the Soviet Union, 1950–66.* ERS-Foreign 252. Washington, D.C.

————. 1988. *World Indices of Agricultural and Food Production, 1977–86.* Statistical Bulletin no. 759. Washington, D.C.

United States. Department of Commerce. 1990. "Annual Input-Output Account of the U.S. Economy." *Survey of Current Business* 70, no. 1 (January): 41–56.

United States. Department of State. Annual. *Report to Congress on Voting Practices in the United Nations.* Washington, D.C.

Utting, Peter. 1987. "Domestic Supply and Food Shortages." In Spalding (1987), 127–48.

Valkenier, Elizabeth K. 1983. *The Soviet Union and the Third World: An Economic Bind.* New York: Praeger.

Van Atta, Don. 1989a. "The Political Economy of Agrarian Perestroika." Paper submitted to workshop on "Political Control of the Soviet Economy." Yale University (March).

————. 1989b. "The USSR as a 'Weak State' " Agrarian Origins of Resistance to Perestroika." *World Politics* 42, no. 1 (October): 129–49.

————. 1990a. "Full-Scale, Like Collectivization, but Without Collectivization's Excesses": The Campaign to Introduce the Family and Lease Contract in Soviet Agriculture." *Comparative Economic Studies* 32, no. 2 (Summer): 109–44.

————. 1990b. "Toward a Soviet 'Responsibility System'? Recent Developments in the Agricultural Collective Contract." In Gray, ed. (1990), 130–55.

Varga, Gyula, et al. 1988. *Prices, Taxes and Subsidies in the Food Producing Sector.* Budapest: Agrárgazdasági Kutató Intézet.

Vasary, Ildiko. 1987. *Beyond the Plan: Social Change in a Hungarian Village.* Boulder, Colo.: Westview.

Vengroff, Richard, and Ali Farah. 1985. "State Intervention and Agricultural Development in Africa: A Cross-National Study." *Journal of Modern African Studies* 23, no. 1: 75–85.

Verdery, Katherine Maureen. 1976. "Ethnic Stratefication in the European Periphery: The Historical Sociology of a Transylvanian Village." Ph.D. diss., Stanford University, December.

————. 1983. *Transylvanian Villagers.* Berkeley: University of California Press.

Verschuur, Christine, et al. 1986. *Mozambique, dix ans de solitude*. Paris: l'Har-mattan.

Vickerman, Andre. 1986. *The Fate of the Peasantry: Premature 'Transition to Socialism' in the Democratic Republic of Vietnam*. Yale University Southeast Asia Studies Monograph no. 28. New Haven, Conn.

Viet Nam, State Planning Commission, United Nations Food and Agricultural Organization, et al. 1990. *Viet Nam: Agricultural and Food Production Sector Review*. N.p.

Viola, Lynne. 1987. *The Best Sons of the Fatherland*. New York: Oxford University Press.

Vogeler, Ingold. 1981. *The Myth of the Family Farm: Agribusiness Dominance of U.S. Agriculture*. Boulder, Colo.: Westview.

Volgyes, Ivan. 1980. "Dynamic Change: Rural Transformation, 1945–1975." In Joseph Held, ed. *The Modernization of Agriculture: Rural Transformation in Hungary, 1848–1975*. New York: Columbia University Press.

Volin, Lazar. 1970. *A Century of Russian Agriculture: From Alexander II to Khrushchev*. Cambridge: Harvard University Press.

Vorob'ev, Iu. 1989. "Ob Arende-Otkrovenno." *Pravda*, 18 April, p. 2.

Vreeland, Nena, and Rinn-Sup Shinn, eds. 1976. *Area Handbook for North Korea*. 2d ed. Washington, D.C.: Government Printing Office.

Vulchev, Nikola, and Hristo Pamukchiev. 1988. *Strukturno i organizatsionno preustroistvo na lichnoto stopanstvo na nacelenieto*. Sofia: Iszdatelstvo na Bulgarskata Akademiya na Naukiate.

Wade, William Windsor. 1981. *Institutional Determinants of Technical Change and Agricultural Productivity Growth: Denmark, France, and Great Britain*. New York: Arno Press.

Wädekin, Karl-Eugen. 1969. *Führungskräfte im sowjetischen Dorf*. Berlin: Duncker und Humblot.

―――. 1973. *The Private Sector in Soviet Agriculture*. Berkeley: University of California Press.

―――. 1982. *Agrarian Policies in Communist Europe: A Critical Introduction*. Totowa, N.J.: Allanheld, Osmund.

―――. 1988. "Agrarian Structures and Policies in the USSR, China, and Hungary: A Comparative View." In Brada and Wädekin, eds. (1988), 55–74.

―――. 1989. "The Re-Emergence of the Kolkhoz Principle." *Soviet Studies* 41, no. 1 (January): 20–39.

―――, ed. 1985. *Agriculture in Inter-System Comparison: Communist and Non-Communist Cases*. Berlin: Duncker and Humblot.

―――. 1990. *Communist Agriculture: Farming in the Soviet Union and Eastern Europe*. London: Routledge.

Walker, Kenneth R. 1965. *Planning in Chinese Agriculture*. Chicago: Aldine.

Weijland, Hermine, et al. 1988. "Agrarian Transformation and the Rural Labour Force: The Case of Nicaragua." *Development and Change* 19, no. 1 (January): 115–39.

Wekkin, Gary D. 1982. "The Rewards of Revolution: Pathet Lao Policy toward the Hill Tribes since 1975." In Stuart–Fox (1982a), 181–98.

Wells, H. G. 1921. *Russia in the Shadows*. New York: George H. Doran Company.

Wen, Guanzhong James. 1989. "The Current Land Tenure and Its Impact on Long Term Performance of the Farming Sector: The Case of Modern China." Ph.D. diss., University of Chicago.

Wesson, Robert G. 1963. *Soviet Communes*. New Brunswick, N.J.: Rutgers University Press.

West, Lorraine. 1990. "Farm Household Savings Investment Behavior in Guangdong Province." Lecture, East Asia Center, Stanford University (March 1).

White, Blanche Tyrene. 1985. "Population Policy and Rural Reform in China, 1977–1984: Policy Implementation and Interdependency at the Local Level." Ph.D. diss., Ohio State University. Columbus.

————. 1987. "Implementing the 'One-Child-per-Couple' Population Program in Rural China: National Goals and Local Politics." In Lampton, ed. (1987), 284–317.

Whitsun Foundation. Ian Hume, ed. 1976. *Background Papers to the Whitsun Report*. Harare, Zimbabwe.

Wickman, Stephen B. 1981. "The Economy." In Frederica M. Bunge, ed. *North Korea: A Country Study*. 3d ed. Washington, D.C.: Government Printing Office.

Wiegersma, Nancy. 1988. *Vietnam: Peasant Land, Peasant Revolution*. London: Macmillan.

Wiens, Thomas B. 1987. "Issues in the Structural Reform of Chinese Agriculture." *Journal of Comparative Economics* 11, no. 3 (September): 372–84.

Wierzbicki, Zbigniew T. 1968. "The Collective Farm and Change in the Rural Community." In Instytut Filozofii i Socjologii (1968): 186–91.

Williamson, John. 1966. "Profit, Growth and Sales Maximization." *Economica* N.S. 33, no. 1 (February): 1–16.

Williamson, Oliver E. 1975. *Markets and Hierarchies: Analysis and Antitrust Implications*. New York: The Free Press.

Wittfogel, Karl. 1957. *Oriental Despotism*. New Haven: Yale University Press.

Womack, Brantley. 1984. "Modernization and Democratic Reform in China." *Journal of Asian Studies* 43, no. 3 (May): 417–39.

Wondimu, Habtamu. 1983. *Some Factors Which Affect Peasant Motivation to Work in the Ethiopian Agricultural Producer's Cooperatives*. Research Reports 21 and 40. Institute of Development Economics. Addis Ababa: Addis Ababa University.

Wong, Christine. 1988. "Interpreting Rural Industrial Growth in the Post-Mao Period." *Modern China* 14, no. 1 (January): 3–30.

————. 1991 forthcoming. *Maoism and Development: Rural Industrialization in the People's Republic of China*.

Wong, John. 1973. *Land Reform in the People's Republic of China*. New York: Praeger.

Wong, Lung-Fai. 1986. *Agricultural Productivity in the Socialist Countries*. Boulder, Colo.: Westview.

World Bank. Annual. *World Development Report*. Washington, D.C.

528 BIBLIOGRAPHY

World Bank. 1975. *Yugoslavia: Development with Decentralization*. Baltimore: Johns Hopkins University Press.

———. 1983a. *China: Socialist Economic Development*. Vol. 1, *The Economy, Statistical System, and Basic Data*. Washington, D.C.

———. 1983b. *Yugoslavia: Adjustment Policies and Development Perspectives*. Washington, D.C.

———. 1985. *Somalia: Agricultural Sector Survey Task Force Reports and Working Papers*. Vol. 1. Internal report. Washington, D.C. Mimeo.

———. 1988. *World Tables*. 4th ed. Washington, D.C.

———. 1989. *Poland: Subsidies and Income Distribution*, Internal Report 7776-Pol. Washington, D.C.

———. 1990. *China: Between Plan and Market*. Washington, D.C.

Wubneh, Mulatu, and Yohannes Abate. 1988. *Ethiopia: Transition and Development in the Horn of Africa*. Boulder, Colo.: Westview.

Wuyts, Marc Eric. 1989. *Money and Planning for Socialist Transition*. Aldershot, U.K.: Gower.

Wyzan, Michael L. 1981. "Empirical Analysis of Soviet Agriculture Production and Policy." *American Journal of Agricultural Economics* 63, no. 4 (August): 475–83.

———. 1983. "The Kolkhoz and the Sovkhoz: Relative Performance as Measured by Productive Technology." In Stuart, ed. (1983): 171–98.

———. 1990a. "Bulgarian Agriculture Since 1979: Sweeping Reform and Mediocre Performance (So Far)." In Wädekin, ed. (1990).

———. 1990b. "The Bulgarian Experience with Centrally Planned Agriculture: Lessons for Soviet Reformers?" In Gray, ed. (1990), 220–43.

Xue, Munqiao, ed. 1982. *Almanac of China's Economy: 1981*. New York: Ballinger.

Yanov, Alexander. 1984. *The Drama of the Soviet 1960s: A Lost Reform*. Research Series no. 56. Berkeley: Institute for International Studies.

Yemen. Central Statistical Organization. Annual. *Statistical Yearbook*. Aden.

Yugoslavia. Savezni zavod za statistiku. Annual. *Statistički godišnjak SFRJ*. Belgrade.

Zablocki, Benjamin. 1980. *Alienation and Charisma: A Study of Contemporary American Communes*. New York: Macmillan.

Zagoroff, S. D. 1955. *The Agricultural Economy of the Danubian Countries, 1935–45*. Stanford: Stanford University Press.

Záhlava, František. 1989. "The Nature and Role of Agricultural Cooperative Societies in Czechoslovakia." *International Review of Applied Economics* 3, no. 2: 214–32.

Zerom, Tewelde. 1984. "Agricultural Development Policy in Ethiopia: A Retrospective and Prospective Analysis." Ph.D. diss., University of Pittsburgh.

Zhu Ling. 1991. *Rural Reform and Peasant Income in China*. New York: St. Martin's Press.

Zimbabwe. Department of the Commissariat and Culture. 1985. *Zimbabwe: At Five Years of Independence*. Harare.

Zimbabwe. Ministry of Finance, Economic Planning and Development. 1986. *Socio-Economic Review of Zimbabwe, 1980-1985*. Harare.

Zmajic, Josip. 1961. "Systems of Wages Per Unit of Product on Agricultural Establishments." In Jordan Blazevski and others, eds. *Transformation of Yugoslav Agriculture*, 73–76. Belgrade.

Zweig, David. 1983. "Opposition to Change in Rural China: The System of Responsibility and People's Communes." *Asian Survey* 23, no. 7 (July): 879–900.

————. 1987. "Context and Content in Policy Implementation: Household Contracts and Decollectivization, 1977–1983." In Lampton, ed. (1987a), 255–83.

————. 1989. *Agrarian Radicalism in China, 1968–1989*. Cambridge, Massachusetts: Harvard University Press.

NAME INDEX

Abate, Alula, 476, 489
Abate, Yohannes, 90, 91, 528
Abegaz, Haile Yesus, 236, 489
Abramov, Fyodor, 283, 489
Aganbegyan, Abel, 312, 432–34, 489
Alexander II (czar), 303, 418
Alia, Ramiz, 472
Alkhomov, P. G., 466, 489
Allcock, John, 114, 489
Allen, Chris, 489
Allende, Salvadore, 21
Almeyra, Guillermo, 153, 489
Alton, Thad P., 204, 212, 322, 482, 489
Aly, Hassan, 239, 489
Ambersley, Fitzroy, 523
Ames, Edward, 397, 490
Amin, Hafizollah, 93, 95
Amstutz, J. Bruce, 474, 490
Andreev, A. A., 170
Antal, Endre, 419, 490
Anwar, Raja, 95, 472, 490
Argyres, Andreas, 285, 288, 490
Arnold, Anthony, 472, 490
Ash, Robert F., 422–24, 428, 490
Åslund, Anders, 343–44, 434, 490
Aston, T. H., 40, 490
Aubert, Claude, 340, 490
Austin, James, 220–21, 490
Azam, J. P., 470, 478, 490

Bachman, Kenneth L., 490
Bajaja, Vladislav, 160, 162, 172, 490
Baldwin, Godfrew, 365, 517
Ball, A. Gordon, 491
Banister, Judith, 3, 129, 491
Barker, Randolph, 518
Barrios de Chamorro, Violeta, 293
Bates, Robert, 291, 491
Batt, Judy, 291, 491
Baum, Philip, 340, 491
Baumol, William, 397, 491
Baxter, Joan, 484
Bebel, August, 43
Becker, Joachim, 200, 491
Bekker, Alexander, 310, 432, 491

Bell, Peter D., 261, 286, 288, 390, 491
Benewick, Robert, 491
Beresford, Melanie, 69, 116, 187, 451, 491
Bernardo, Robert M., 182–83, 491
Bernstein, Thomas Paul, 88–89, 127, 275,
    292, 340, 346, 423, 491
Berthélemy, J. C., 227, 492
Bertrand, Hughes, 203, 492
Bhagavan, M. R., 244, 401, 447, 454, 492
Binkert, Gregor H., 126, 237, 492
Binswanger, Hans P., 136–38, 148, 150,
    377, 387, 492
Birman, Igor, 492
Bishop, Maurice, 363
Blazevski, Jordon, 529
Blecher, Marc, 195–96, 441, 492
Boehm, William T., 149, 158, 393, 508
Boenau, A. Bruce, 289, 510
Boguslawski, Michael von, 206, 470, 479,
    492
Bohnet, Armin, 490, 492
Boikov, V., 435, 492
Bokassa, Jean-Bedel, 20
Bonin, John P., 411, 492
Booth, John A., 74, 492
Borge-Martínez, Tomás, 86
Boua, Chanthou, 8, 508
Bouterse, Desi, 21
Boycko, Maxim, 520
Boyd, Michael L., 208, 242, 492
Brada, Josef C., 242–43, 246, 493
Bradley, Michael E., 411, 493
Bratton, Michael, 124, 220, 493
Braverman, Avishay, 324, 493
Breznev, Leonid, 349, 425
Bridger, Susan, 397, 493
Brooks, Karen McConnell, 165, 169, 175,
    185, 190, 224–25, 238–39, 278–79, 323,
    331, 430, 433, 434, 493, 507
Brown, Albert L., 493
Brown, MacAlister, 116–17, 459, 494
Buck, John Lossing, 455, 494
Bujra, Abdalla S., 466, 494
Bukharin, Nicolai, 41–42, 47, 57, 294, 340
Bulbeck, C., 463, 494

Rosenzweig, Mark, 136–38, 148, 150, 387, 492
Ross, Lester, 293, 518
Rothchild, Donald, 508
Roussos, Peter, 451, 518
Roy, Oliver, 93, 519
Rozman, Gilbert, 519
Rubinstein, Alvin Z., 361, 363–65, 519
Ruchwanger, Gary, 519
Rudebeck, Lars, 56, 126, 218, 519
Rukavishnikov, S. I., 319, 519
Rupen, Robert A., 473, 519
Russ, Wolfgang, 474, 519
Ruttan, Vernon W., 372–73, 377, 379, 382, 384–85, 492, 504
Ryzhkov, Nikolai, 344

Sachs, Jeffrey, 308, 510
Sah, Raaj Kumar, 210, 519
Salzmann, Zdenek, 285, 286, 456, 472, 519
Samatar, Abdi Ismail, 519
Samatar, Ahmed I., 471, 519
Sanders, Alan J. K., 460, 473, 519
Sanders, Irwin T., 519
Sankara, T., 363
Sassulitsch, Vera. See Zasulich, Vera
Saul, John, 499
Scalapino, Robert A., 125, 182, 186, 459, 519
Scheufler, Vladimir, 286, 288, 519
Schinke, Eberhard, 160, 169, 180, 490, 519
Schmalensee, Richard, 516
Schmidt, Klaus, 141, 519
Schröder, Günter, 453, 520
Schroeder, Gertrude, 271, 285, 503
Schultz, Theodore W., 520
Schwarzbach, R., 172, 520, 522
Scott, Catherine V., 126, 520
Selassie, Haile, 89
Sen, Amartya, 440, 520
Senghor, Leopold, 9
Shahabuddeen, M., 436, 520
Shiller, Robert, 275, 284, 319, 520
Shinn, Rinn-Sup, 449, 526
Shirk, Susan, 422, 426, 520
Shmelev, Nikolai, 312, 349, 432, 434, 520
Shue, Vivienne, 53, 86, 89, 128, 520
Sicular, Terry, 320, 424, 426, 520
Singaravelou, 458, 520
Singh, Chaitram, 342, 520

Sinha, Radha, 518
Sipos, A., 316, 323, 420, 520
Sismondi, J.C.L. Simonde de, 387
Skålner, Tor, 220, 520
Skold, Karl, 239, 520
Smith, Harvey H., 453, 521
Soilih, Ali, 20
Sokolov, V. V., 62
Solinger, Dorothy J., 521
Solomon, Frederic, 240, 517
Solomon, Susan Gross, 44, 331, 521
Somerville, Keith, 489
Somoza, Anastasio, 35, 73, 98, 108
Southworth, Raymond P., 490
Spalding, Rose J., 521
Spaulding, Wallace H., 74, 362, 365, 521
Spindler, Berndt, 260, 521
Spulber, Nicolas, 88, 462, 472, 494, 521
Srivastava, R. K., 521
Staar, Richard, 362, 365, 521
Stalin, J. V., 15, 16, 33–34, 41, 44–58, 112, 136, 152, 170, 211, 222, 521
Standing, Guy, 12, 521
Stanfield, David, 449, 478, 507
Stark, David, 513
Stiglitz, Joseph, 210, 300, 519, 521
Stock, Richard, 86, 516
Stolypin, P., 65
Stone, Bruce, 422, 521
Stoneman, Colin, 122, 164, 522
Stookey, Richard W., 183, 522
Stuart, Robert C., 522
Stuart-Fox, Martin, 130, 459, 472, 477, 522
Summers, Robert, 27, 572
Suyker, Wim, 217, 501
Swain, Nigel, 131, 146, 178, 261, 522
Szajkowski, Bogdan, 361, 363–65, 522
Szal, Richard, 12, 521
Szelenyi, Ivan, 146, 176, 178, 282, 286–87, 302, 417–18, 421, 522
Székely, Magda, 153, 498
Szwengrub, Lili Maria, 201, 522

Tabibi, Latif, 93, 522
Taraki, Nur Mohammed, 93, 453
Taylor, Jeffrey R., 522
Teka, Tegigne, 91, 202, 456, 522
Temple, Mary N., 516
Thielen, Helmut, 476, 522
Thomas, Clive Y., 12, 298, 476, 522–23
Thomas, Joseph R., 478, 523

COUNTRY AND SUBJECT INDEX